Fiscal Fragmentation in Decentralized Countries

Fiscal Fragmentation in Decentralized Countries

Subsidiarity, Solidarity and Asymmetry

Edited by

Richard M. Bird, *Professor Emeritus of Economics, University of Toronto, Canada*

Robert D. Ebel, *Senior Fellow, Urban Institute/Brookings Institution Tax Policy Center, USA*

Edward Elgar

Cheltenham, UK • Northampton, MA, USA

Published by
Edward Elgar Publishing Limited
Glensanda House
Montpellier Parade
Cheltenham
Glos GL50 1UA
UK

Edward Elgar Publishing, Inc.
William Pratt House
9 Dewey Court
Northampton
Massachusetts 01060
USA

A catalogue record for this book
is available from the British Library

ISBN 978 1 84542 402 2

Printed and bound in Great Britain by MPG Books Ltd, Bodmin, Cornwall

Contents

Preface

Belgium, Bosnia and Herzegovina, Canada, China, Germany, India, Indonesia, the Philippines, Russia, Spain and Switzerland constitute a diverse set of countries with an important characteristic in common: each contains within its boundaries a significant, territorially-based group of people who are, or who consider themselves to be, distinct and different in ethnicity, in language, in religion, and/or in history (ancient or recent) from most of the population. Indeed, contrary to the common view that the most natural nation state is a unified and homogeneous entity, such 'fragmented' countries are found worldwide, thus heterogeneity, not homogeneity, is the general rule in most nation states.

These countries have another common feature: they have, to some extent, used the tools and strategies of an intergovernmental (decentralized) society to maintain both national cohesion and an effective state. To do so, to greater or lesser degrees, their intergovernmental systems, be they federal or unitary systems, exhibit some degree of asymmetry in the way in which they treat different regions.

Some potentially fragmented countries have—often through a prolonged historical process, sometimes including civil war—reached an equilibrium in which their political, fiscal and institutional structure balances the diverse forces and sustains an effective nation. The 'effectiveness' of a nation in this context relates not only to how efficiently and equitably public services are provided, but also to how a country's public finances are structured in order to hold a fragmented nation state together.

How asymmetry in intergovernmental and regional fiscal structure can become an important tool for national cohesion has risen to the forefront of public policy analysis in some countries torn by civil conflicts, for example, Bosnia and Herzegovina and, as this book goes to print, Iraq and Sudan (Darfur). However, the question resonates much more widely in a world in which even such well-established nations as the United Kingdom have been attempting to grapple with forces of fragmentation as globalization interacts with a renewed sense of regional pluralism by decentralizing as one way to accommodate ethnic, religious, cultural and income diversity.

The question of whether the right degree and kind of 'asymmetric fiscal fragmentation' can not only accommodate subsidiarity, but can also serve as a vehicle for national cohesion, is one of the great policy issues of our time. This book examines this question through a series of case studies. Even though only history can provide a definitive answer for any particular country, the cases studied here offer many lessons, and some warnings, to those who would follow this path. They also cast new light on some fundamental issues about the relationship between 'state' and 'nation' that deserve much closer attention by scholars of both fiscal federalism and political economy.

This book reflects multiple contributions by many people in addition to those who are listed as contributors. Recognizing that we will surely miss naming all who contributed, we wish to especially acknowledge our colleagues Ehtisham Ahmad, Junaid Ahmad, Giorgio Brosio, Amadou Cisse, Lual Deng, Wolf Linder, Jennie Litvack, Endre Stiansen, Victor Vergara, Dana Weist and Serdar Yilmaz. A special acknowledgement also goes both to our manuscript editor, Alice S. Faintich, and to her team of Cindy Stock (desktopping), Bernice Eisen (indexing) and Shirley Ratliff (proofreading), who together made the manuscript flow as a readable whole. We also wish to thank Alan Sturmer and the Edward Elgar staff. Finally, we would like to acknowledge the financial support from the Canadian International Development Agency trust fund that is administered by the World Bank Institute.

RICHARD M. BIRD
Toronto

ROBERT D. EBEL
Washington, DC

Contributors

Benoît Bayenet, Professor, Free University of Brussels, Faculty of Law, Brussels

Richard M. Bird, Professor Emeritus, University of Toronto, Toronto

Bambang Brodjonegoro, Professor of Economics, University of Indonesia, Jakarta

Philippe de Bruycker, Professor, Free University of Brussels, Faculty of Law, Brussels

Bernard Dafflon, Professor of Public Finance, University of Fribourg, Fribourg

Robert D. Ebel, Senior Fellow, Urban Institute, Washington, DC

J. Fitz G. Ford, Lead Economist, World Bank, Urban Division, Washington, DC

William Fox, Professor of Economics, University of Tennessee, Knoxville

Teresa Garcia-Milà, Professor of Economics, Universitat Pompeu Fabra, Barcelona

Sebastiana Gianci, Research Associate, World Bank, Washington, DC

Rosario Manasan, Research Fellow, Philippine Institute for Development Studies, Manila

Jorge Martinez-Vazquez, Director of International Programs, Andrew Young School of Public Policy, Georgia State University, Atlanta

Therese J. McGuire, Professor of Economics, Northwestern University, Evanston

M. Govinda Rao, Director, National Institute of Public Finance and Policy, New Delhi

Saloua Sehili, Senior Poverty Economist, World Bank, Poverty Reduction and Economic Management Network, Washington, DC

Nirvikar Singh, Professor of Business Economics, University of California, Santa Cruz

Paul Bernd Spahn, Professor of Economics, J. W. Goethe University, Frankfurt, and Chief Administrator, International Monetary Fund, Bosnia and Herzegovina

François Vaillancourt, Professor of Economics, University of Montreal, Montreal

Christine Wallich, Country Director for Bangladesh, World Bank, Dhaka

Jan Werner, University of Frankfurt, Frankfurt

Christine Wong, Professor of Economics, University of Washington, Seattle

PART I

Introduction

1. Subsidiarity, Solidarity and Asymmetry: Aspects of the Problem

Richard M. Bird and Robert D. Ebel

> *Some countries are born decentralized; some become decentralized; and some have decentralization thrust upon them.*[1]

What can the diverse set of countries included in this book—Belgium, Bosnia and Herzegovina, Canada, China, Germany, India, Indonesia, the Philippines, Russia, Spain and Switzerland—possibly have in common? One important answer is that each contains a significant, territorially-based group of people who are, or who consider themselves to be, distinct and different in ethnicity, in language, in religion or just in history (ancient or recent) from the majority of the population. Indeed, contrary to the common view that the most 'natural' nation state is a unified and homogeneous entity, such fragmented countries are found throughout the world (Bird and Stauffer 2001).[2] Homogeneous nations are more the exception than the rule. Of the countries studied here, China and Germany are by far the most ethnically homogeneous, but even in China, people who differ from the majority occupy significant areas of territory, and in Germany the recent re-joining of the former East Germany has greatly increased economic differences between regions and strained the fiscal federal system that had been developed in the former West Germany. Heterogeneity, whether ethnic or economic, is a more common feature of most countries than homogeneity.

A second important characteristic of many countries, including those discussed in this volume, is that to greater or lesser degrees they exhibit some asymmetry in the way in which their intergovernmental fiscal systems treat different regions. While such asymmetry is often most obvious in formally federal countries—seven of which are studied here—it comes up, sometimes in surprising ways, in almost every instance. Thus one aim of this book is to explore the manner in which intergovernmental fiscal relations demonstrate asymmetry in the 12 countries studied here and the extent to which they do so. In particular, the way in which such asymmetrical treatment helps or hinders the maintenance of an effective nation state is examined.

Effectiveness in this context may be understood in two distinct ways. The first relates to the normal focus of economic analysis of public sector activities, that is, how effectively, efficiently and equitably are public services provided throughout the national territory? The second meaning, however, lies well outside the normal field of economists' expertise, namely, what are the connections between how a country's public finances are structured and how a fragmented nation state holds together in the first place? This question has risen to the forefront of public policy analysis in relation to the creation of 'new' countries out of regions torn by civil conflicts, for example, Bosnia and Herzegovina, one of the countries studied here, but it is also much on the minds of those concerned with public policy in some long-established countries, such as Belgium, Canada and Spain, which are also discussed in this volume.

This introductory chapter elaborates on some of the basic terms used in the discussion and introduces some of the key questions raised in the case study chapters. Chapter 2 completes the introduction to the volume by providing a comparative overview of the countries studied and sketching the principal conclusions that emerge from the diverse set of experiences covered in this book. Because, as is common in policy analysis, 'the devil lies in the details', much more can be learned from the specifics laid out in the 12 case study chapters that constitute the remainder of the volume. While each chapter is different, reflecting the reality of the countries covered, the primary focus is on depicting the precise nature and extent of the asymmetry found in the intergovernmental fiscal structure. Also considered is the broader question of how the structure of public finances relates to both economic and, to a lesser extent given the authors' professional background, to political outcomes.

In many fragmented countries, including those discussed here, the majority group's political domination is not surprising. Sometimes a particular minority carries more political weight than its size warrants, perhaps because of its wealth and power, perhaps because of historical factors. Occasionally, as may be argued to be the case even in such large federal countries as Brazil and the United States, important overriding factors may suppress much or all of the potential political influence of ethnicity.[3] Nonetheless, even in countries such as Argentina, Brazil or Germany, in which most people are ethnically and linguistically homogeneous, the economic situation of different regions may be extremely varied, ranging from large, rich, metropolitan areas to remote, impoverished settlements or areas rich in petroleum or other highly valued natural resources. Regional problems may be most obvious when regions are dominated by people of a different ethnicity from the majority of the population, and such problems may be most bitterly contested when ethnic and economic factors combine, but even countries without this combination of characteristics usually have regional problems.

Some potentially fragmented countries have—often through a prolonged historical process, sometimes including civil war—reached an equilibrium in which their political, fiscal and institutional structure balances the diverse forces and sustains the maintenance of an effective nation state.[4] Others, however, remain in turmoil. Some nation states have fallen apart under such pressures: the former Yugoslavia, the former Soviet Union and the former Czechoslovakia are obvious recent examples. The integrity and effectiveness of other countries, even such long-established and prosperous countries as Belgium and Canada, sometimes seem, at least to those who live there, to remain under constant threat. In recent years such pressures have increased in many countries, in part because of globalization and the related, if not fully consistent, phenomenon of new regional economic unions, such as the European Union and the North American Free Trade Agreement. These have upset the established balance of wealth and power, and hence called into question, at least in the minds of some, the desirability and sustainability of some established nation states.

Partly in response to such factors, decentralization is clearly in the academic air. It is also very much on the policy ground. Whether in industrial countries, developing countries, transition countries, federal countries or unitary countries, some kind of decentralization seems to be taking place, or is at least being discussed. But what exactly is going on? And why is it going on? An incredible variety of rationales and institutional arrangements can be encompassed under the portmanteau label of decentralization.

WHAT IS DECENTRALIZATION?

Some of the confusion about decentralization that prevails in many circles arises simply because the term can mean quite different things to different people.[5] Political decentralization in the sense of devolving decisionmaking power to locally elected officials, for example, is not the same as, or necessarily associated with, administrative decentralization, and the reverse is also true. Administrative decentralization may, for instance, simply redistribute responsibilities among different levels of the central government, up to and including the creation of moderately autonomous field administrations. This process is sometimes referred to as deconcentration. Deconcentration does not place any political decisionmaking power in the hands of locally representative bodies, and hence is unlikely to give rise to serious intergovernmental conflicts. Similarly, if the administrative responsibility for particular functions has been fully devolved to local governments, such conflict should not arise in principle. In practice, however, conflict often arises even with apparently full devolution, because even the most decentralized regional and local governments tend to remain dependent to a large extent on central financing. Following the well-known principle that he who pays the piper, calls the tune, even allegedly independent subnational governments are often subject to a certain degree of central influence, monitoring and, in some instances, control. Thus distinguishing some forms of devolution from what is usually labeled delegation, in which the subnational government is in principle only an agent of the central government, and thus not an independent actor, can be difficult.[6]

To add to the prevailing confusion, in most countries decentralization, whatever form it takes, need not, and indeed usually does not, occur evenly across the board. For example, some activities or parts of some activities may be decentralized to some degree or another while others may not be; expenditures may be more decentralized than revenues, or the reverse may hold; some transfers may be much more heavily conditioned by the central government than others; and borrowing may or may not be tightly controlled. Understanding, measuring and analysing the extent and nature of decentralization in any country is far from simple (Ebel and Yilmaz 2003).

WHY IS DECENTRALIZATION OCCURRING?

However decentralization may be defined or understood, why is it occurring? A recent World Bank study (World Bank 2000) notes correctly that the evidence with respect to all the traditional rationales for decentralization found in the conventional economic literature on fiscal federalism is, to say the least, mixed.[7] The study looked at the following issues:

- Does decentralization increase the efficiency and responsiveness of government? According to the literature, it may, or it may not. It depends. We are not sure.
- What about equity? Does decentralization help or hurt poor regions? What about poor people? Again, it may or it may not. It depends. We are not sure.
- What about the third horseman of the conventional public finance trinity: stability? Again the answers appear to be the same. Decentralization may or may not imperil macroeconomic stability. It depends. We are not sure.

There is a certain degree of monotony in these answers, and some, no doubt, would dispute them, illustrating what another World Bank study (Litvack, Ahmad and Bird 1998, p. 3) called the 'curious combination of strong preconceived beliefs and limited empirical evidence' that characterizes much discussion of decentralization. Still, given how little we appear to know with any degree of certainty about these relationships, attributing much of the recent decentralization observed around the world to traditional economic concerns about efficiency, equity and stability seems implausible.

On the contrary, as the World Bank (2000) argues, in many countries the interest in decentralization appears to be motivated more by political factors than by economic efficiency, growth or the other factors on which economists are accustomed to ruminate. Chechnya, East Timor, Kashmir, Kosovo, Macedonia, Moldova, Sri Lanka and Sudan—the list of territorially-based ethnic minorities taking up arms against the nation state and/or each other is lengthening. Thus some countries' attempts to pre-empt such pressures by decentralizing some activities is not surprising (see Esman and Herring 2001 for detailed consideration of the role that development assistance may play in exacerbating, or alleviating such pressures). As the World Bank (2000, pp. 207–08) puts it, '[W]hen a country finds itself deeply divided, especially along geographic or ethnic lines, decentralization provides an institutional mechanism for bringing opposition groups into a formal, rule-bound bargaining process'. The same study goes on to offer the following five specific political rationales for decentralization:

- Decentralization may sometimes serve as a path to national unity. The examples cited are South Africa (see Ahmad 1998; Bahl and Smoke 2003; Simeon and Murray 2000) and Uganda (see Bahl 1997). In this book, Chapter 3 on Canada and Chapter 5 on Switzerland discuss two cases that might also fall under this heading.
- Decentralization may in some instances offer a potential political solution to a civil war. The example the report cites is Sri Lanka (see Welikala 2003 for a recent consideration of the fiscal aspects of decentralization in Sri Lanka). To some extent, as discussed in Chapter 13 on Bosnia and Herzegovina, these countries offer other instances of this approach.
- Decentralization may serve as an instrument for deflating secessionist tendencies, as has occurred to some extent, according to the report, in Bosnia and Herzegovina and in Ethiopia.[8] In addition to the discussion of the former case in Chapter 13, Canada and perhaps Spain (Chapter 7) might also fit this rationale to some extent.
- Decentralization may attempt to achieve a similar aim by conceding enough power to regional interests to forestall their departure from the republic. The example given is the Russian Federation (see also Martinez-Vazquez and Boex 2001; Treisman 1998). In addition to Russia (Chapter 8), perhaps Canada and Spain, as well as Belgium (Chapter 6), may also illustrate this thesis.

- Decentralization may be used to co-opt grassroots support for central policies, and the report asserts that Colombia provides a relevant example.[9] While it may be stretching matters a bit, perhaps China (Chapter 9) may also be said to be following this path to at least a limited extent.

THE TRADE-OFFS OF DECENTRALIZATION

Whatever one thinks of the various arguments, whether decentralization in any of its myriad forms helps or hurts political stability is clearly a key question in many countries, and one that cannot be answered in the abstract. As in the case of the economic arguments for and against decentralization, something like the Scottish legal decision of 'not proven' is perhaps the best that can currently be offered with respect to the political arguments. Nonetheless, political factors are clearly leading even long-centralized countries like the United Kingdom to decentralize, particularly with respect to Scotland. Similar decentralization can be seen in many other countries to varying degrees, for example, Finland (Aland Islands), Italy (South Tyrol), and even France (Corsica). Ethnic groups in countries as diverse as China (Tibetans and Uighurs, see Chapter 9), Georgia (Abkhaz and Ossetians), Nigeria (Ogoni) and Turkey (Kurds) are seeking similar or greater territorial autonomy.

Whether the long-term (or even the not so long-term) results of greater decentralization in response to such pressures is likely to be political stability or increased instability is, however, far from clear. Certainly many past examples are not particularly encouraging, such as the former Czechoslovakia, Federation of the West Indies, Rhodesia and Nyasaland, Soviet Union and Yugoslavia, along with Pakistan (Watts 1999). By contrast, counter examples exist where one could argue that decentralizing policies are one factor holding together countries that might otherwise have fragmented, for instance, Belgium (Chapter 6), Canada (Chapter 3), India (Chapter 10) and Malaysia (for some discussion of the Malaysian case see Holzhausen 1974; Mahbob and others 1997). Annett (2000), who focuses on countries in which he assumes budgetary institutions are too weak to support increased intergovernmental transfers, suggests that the success of such attempts may depend on such nations' ability to deliver higher levels of public services. As yet, however, the empirical evidence in support of such a proposition remains tenuous.

An additional important political concern is that excessive decentralization may unduly restrict a country's ability to take decisive action in the face of crisis. While most commonly manifested in the form of concerns about stabilization policy (Tanzi 1996), the problem is actually more general. Some argue that all countries face a fundamental trade-off between the extent to which their political systems represent different local points of view and their capacity for effective political action in the face of economic crisis. Some degree of decentralization may be needed in some circumstances to maintain the nation state, but too much decentralization might render that state ineffective in coping with crisis. While one could argue that such apocalyptic conclusions seldom pay sufficient attention to the details of precisely how decentralization institutions are designed and implemented, the effect of fiscal decentralization on stabilization policy remains a controversial issue that cannot be discussed in detail here.[10]

More pertinent to this volume is the fact that the trade-off between effectiveness and decentralization also manifests itself with respect to redistributive policy, whether interregional or interpersonal. It is not by chance, many argue, that the so-called welfare state was a centralizing state, because only at the national level could the interests of the disadvantaged receive sufficient weight to overcome the influence of local elites (Wilensky 1975). To the extent that effective decentralization implies local autonomy in relation to revenue and expenditure policy, there may seem to be an inherent conflict between subsidiarity and solidarity, between local autonomy and national redistribution. The case studies in this volume, however, show clearly that the precise terms of any such trade-off, and the related question of whether a breakpoint exists beyond which a country cannot both have its autonomous cake and eat its redistributive one, appear to depend on too many details of local institutions and circumstances to permit easy generalizations.

Paul Spahn and Jan Werner in Chapter 4, for example, suggest that the incorporation of its much poorer eastern regions may have pushed Germany closer to this breakpoint. If even a country as essentially homogeneous as Germany has a point beyond which those in richer regions are not prepared to expand their span of concern (Breton and Scott 1978) to encompass those in poorer regions within their distributive concerns, other countries—in Europe, Belgium (Chapter 6) comes to mind—may perhaps reach such a point at considerably lower levels of redistribution. The redistributive question is particularly difficult, because it encompasses both interpersonal and interregional redistribution. Canada has to some extent bypassed this problem at the provincial level by carrying out most interpersonal redistribution at the federal level, but, as Chapter 3 notes in passing, it too faces the problem of group versus individual redistribution with respect to its large aboriginal population (for different perspectives see Cairns 2000; Flanagan 2000). Other countries face similar problems.

FISCAL DECENTRALIZATION: GLUE OR SOLVENT?

Whatever its rationale or form, decentralization has often changed a state's fiscal structure, and hence may be expected to affect the nature and scope of state activities. Often the most critical and disputed questions with respect to decentralization are fiscal: who gets what and who pays for it? Fiscal changes may feed back upon and strengthen—or weaken—the political and economic pressures leading to decentralization in the first place. A key question explored in this volume is thus the nature and strength of the interactions between changes in intergovernmental fiscal relations in response to changing economic and political factors and the creation or continued maintenance of an effective public sector. Under what conditions does increased subsidiarity foster solidarity, and under what conditions might increasing the autonomy of subnational governments have the opposite result of fostering not national integration, but perhaps the disintegration of a nation? That is, when is decentralization a glue that holds countries together and when is it a solvent that results in their disintegration?

The key fiscal aspects of decentralization are

- Who determines who gets what revenues?
- Who is responsible for what expenditures?
- How do intergovernmental transfers work?
- How much freedom do subnational governments have with respect to borrowing?
- Who determines the institutional setting within which the preceding questions are answered?

The extensive literature on this subject suggests a number of key fiscal rules that should bind the various players in the intergovernmental game if the outcome is to be efficient and responsible provision of public services in an equitable and stable way (see, for example, Bahl 2002; Bird 2001). These include such things as providing clear expenditure assignments, giving responsibility for determining the rates for some major revenues to subnational governments, and distributing transfers by means of a predetermined formula. Properly designed, an intergovernmental fiscal regime set up along these lines in effect imposes a hard budget constraint on subnational governments, and hence provides an appropriate incentive structure for ensuring economically efficient outcomes.

The transfer system may also provide a certain degree of equity, at least in the sense of interregional equity, although to extend it very far in the direction of attempting to achieve interpersonal equity, some direct central intrusion into subnational decisions generally seems to be necessary (Bird and Rodriguez 1999; Ravallion 2000). In addition, to ensure macroeconomic stability, hierarchical controls may initially have to constrain subnational borrowing, although in the longer run it should ideally become subject primarily to market constraints (Rodden, Eskeland and Litvack 2003).[11] Finally, to make the whole system work, not only must the central government keep to the rules, but an adequate institutional structure needs to be in place to ensure the development of sufficient local capacity, the initiation of periodic adjustments to meet changing circumstances and the provision of a forum for resolving the disputes that inevitably arise in any intergovernmental system (Bird 2001).

Such rules do not, however, describe reality in most countries. Moreover, the relationship between such institutional rules and the political issues that appear to motivate much of the current concern with decentralization seems to be, at best, remote. How may this gap be closed?

ASYMMETRIC DECENTRALIZATION

One way to close the gap between theoretical prescriptions and institutional reality is by taking into account some important aspects of decentralization that are not encompassed in such simple rules and then considering how, in practice, the rules have been bent to accommodate deviations (Agranoff 1999). Rules such as those found in the economic literature explicitly recognize only one element of the heterogeneity that characterizes most countries, namely, that some territorial units are richer than others. They neglect the important role ethnic, linguistic and cultural differences play in explaining the nature of political institutions. Some of these differences, such as language-specific investment in human capital, can readily be placed in a purely rational economic framework (Vaillancourt 1992), but others cannot, such as different groups' various perceptions of history and current reality.

Nonetheless, countries containing diverse groups, particularly those that are territorially concentrated, need to find some way for the groups to work together if the countries are to provide public services effectively. In this connection, the extent and nature of tolerable or necessary asymmetry becomes a key issue.

Traditionally, in part perhaps because symmetrical constitutional status for all basic territorial units was the norm in such 'classic' federations as Australia, Switzerland and the United States, most discussions of federalism—and indeed, often of decentralization more generally—have implicitly assumed that symmetry was the rule. Some formal asymmetry has always been present even in the most classical federal countries, for instance, the District of Columbia and the territories in the United States and the Northern Territory in Australia. In many other federations, as Watts (2000) emphasizes, a degree of formal constitutional asymmetry has been around from the beginning, for example, in Belgium, Canada, India, Malaysia, Russia and Spain. Indeed, as mentioned earlier, even such traditionally unitary countries as the United Kingdom, which has always included distinctly different regimes for

Northern Ireland, the Isle of Man and the Channel Islands, have moved in the direction of still greater asymmetry in recent years. As Bernard Dafflon shows in Chapter 5, even the Swiss have, in their usual deliberate and pragmatic way, gradually introduced many asymmetrical elements into their system of fiscal federalism (see also Basta and Fleiner 1996; Stauffer 2001).

When examined closely, virtually every country, whether federal or unitary, large or small, appears to offer some evidence of asymmetry in practice between rich and poor, urban and nonurban, capital cities and frontier territories and territorial or nonterritorial groupings based on race, religion or language. Such asymmetry illustrates the adaptive nature of political institutions: it may be imposed from above, agreed to by all parties or chosen by particular communities.

Wehner (2000) suggests that such asymmetrical arrangements may arise for political reasons to diffuse ethnic or regional tensions, or for such efficiency reasons as to achieve better macroeconomic management and administrative cohesion or to enable subnational governments with differing capacities to exercise the full range of their functions and powers. The former type of asymmetry, which could be referred to as political asymmetry, is clearly driven by noneconomic concerns. By contrast, the latter, which could be termed administrative asymmetry, is fully consistent with a top-down approach to decentralization and might, for example, be implemented bilaterally through a staged or contract approach, under which those units that met certain standards (size, budget, institutional development) might be granted greater autonomy than others. (For an example of such an approach in Colombia with respect to education, see Bird and Fiszbein 1998).

Such administrative asymmetry might be applied either on a discretionary basis or, more desirably (to reduce the scope for short-run political manoeuvring), in accordance with some predetermined rules. Either type of asymmetry might be either transitional or permanent in nature and might have functional as well as financial manifestations. Asymmetry might be established constitutionally or by law (*de jure*) or simply by administrative practice or political agreement (*de facto*). It may be manifested through different degrees of autonomy or powers, through different degrees of representation in federal (or central) institutions or through differential application of central laws. Asymmetry might be confined to peripheral units, such as the various types of territories in the United States, or it might apply to some of the principal constituent units of the country, as in Canada and Spain, for example.[12]

In fiscal terms, our central concern here, asymmetry may be manifested in differential direct central spending patterns, in differential central taxes, in differential subnational functional or revenue responsibilities or in differential transfers. It may result in more or less equal treatment in certain respects. It may improve or worsen the efficiency and effectiveness of the public sector as a whole, for example, improving or worsening the uniformity of service delivery or macroeconomic balance. In addition, critically, it may sometimes strengthen and sometimes weaken the allegiance of differentially treated communities to the nation state. Outcomes may vary with the relative size and strength of the units affected, the precise nature and extent of their fiscal autonomy, the structure of intergovernmental transfers, the manner in which regional interests are represented in both central and intergovernmental political institutions, the nature of regional and national party systems and many other factors.

In Chapter 3, for example, Richard Bird and François Vaillancourt discuss the important role linguistic and cultural differences play in explaining the nature of Canadian fiscal federalism. In a recent paper, Simeon (2000, p. 15) suggests that to some extent Canadians may be thought of as two peoples divided by a misunderstood word: sovereignty. To English Canadians, he says, sovereignty tends to be interpreted 'in its classical sense of a fully independent state', while to many Quebecois the term evokes not a black or white, in or out meaning, but rather a fluid concept of 'a sense of national identity, and a sense that this is a community with a right to make a choice'. Such differences in perception, as Simeon stresses, are dangerous and may result in outcomes that neither group really desires.[13] Canada is, of course, not the only country suffering from such communication difficulties.

Fragmented societies will not necessarily become more coherent simply by ensuring that everyone really understands what everyone else wants. Real and fundamental conflicts may exist that are not resolvable without major political concessions by one side, or perhaps by both. Improved information and communication, like any other possible solution to the perceived problems of fragmented societies, may help, or it may hurt. Once again, it depends. As the tortured recent history of the Balkans clearly shows (see, for example, Chapter 13), bygones are never bygones if some version of history, however distorted, remains alive in the minds of significant groups of the population and motivates them to take political action. As much recent analysis suggests, and contrary to a key assumption in much economic discussion, ethnic identities and loyalties are not constants, but are subject to dynamic formation and reformation and may often be as much state-cued, that is, developed in response to policies and pressures, as they are in any sense inherent (Esman and Herring 2001).

Fiscal rationality may seem to be an irrelevant concern in the face of emotionally laden symbolism. Nonetheless, even though communication alone cannot achieve the consensus or trust that is the essential ingredient of any democratic polity, unless all major players in the political game communicate in the sense of getting the right information to the right people at the right time, clearly outcomes that will be both politically relevant and administratively feasible are unlikely to emerge. In the words of Chwe (2001, p. 111): 'When we face each other, when we are both awake, that fact is common knowledge, and successful coordination, although not guaranteed . . . is at least possible. When you are facing away, successful coordination is not possible, even when both of us get the message'. Fiscal institutions thus serve best if they deliver the message of accountability clearly (Kopits and Craig 1998), but whether the message will be received and acted upon will, as always, depend on whether other institutions allow the message to be heard.

In any case, as a minimum condition for operating an effective nation state, countries containing diverse groups, particularly those that are territorially concentrated, need to find some way for these groups to work together if they are to provide public services effectively. Canada has employed many approaches for this purpose over the years, ranging from introducing formal constitutional amendments through changing the judicial interpretation of the constitution, so-called executive federalism and formal intergovernmental agreements and, of course, the use of federal funds for both direct spending and intergovernmental transfers (see Boadway and Watts 2000 for an overview). Each of these approaches seems sometimes to have helped and sometimes to have exacerbated matters. On the whole, by changing the mix of instruments and policies employed, to date Canada has managed quite well, although as Chapter 3 indicates, whether it will be able to continue to muddle through without considering more fundamental political changes is not clear.

An important question that has constantly emerged in Canada, and that appears to resonate much more widely, relates to the underlying rationale and acceptability of asymmetry.[14] In Canada, for example, as Chapter 3 shows, Quebec is not a province *comme les autres* in a number of important ways. Over time, this difference has been recognized by the creation of a number of asymmetries in Canadian political and fiscal institutions. Nonetheless, as in other countries, an inherent tension remains between asymmetry and the common view that, to paraphrase Gertrude Stein, a province is a province is a province, that is, all provinces should be treated equally before the law (for a recent Canadian example in relation to the regulation of financial markets, see Vaillancourt and Bird 2002). Such tension exists even if one can argue that asymmetry is necessary not only to maintain the integrity of the nation state, but also to ensure that the intended results of national policies are indeed achieved in the varied circumstances of different regions.

Whether viewed in political or economic terms, the nature and effects of asymmetrical fiscal policies can, as a rule, only be understood in terms of each country's concrete and specific circumstances. Only then does it become clear whether such differentiation has made maintenance of the nation state and the effective provision of public services more feasible, that is, has it acted as glue to hold the state together, or on the contrary, has it induced regional appetites to grow so that those regions that are treated differently decide to go further and opt out completely, transforming the intended glue into a solvent. The most important questions about asymmetrical decentralization thus relate to its effect on the dynamics of political equilibrium, something that appears to be context dependent and not easily reducible to simple generalizations. A particular recent concern in this respect relates to the much discussed phenomenon of globalization.

GLOBALIZATION, REGIONALIZATION AND FISCAL DECENTRALIZATION

As noted earlier, asymmetrical policies may sometimes be required to elicit uniform responses to central policies from differently advantaged regions (see Feldstein 1975 for a classic illustration of this proposition). Similarly, differentiation may seem to be needed to soothe disaffected regions sufficiently to maintain political stability, even if doing so risks increasing the disaffection of those regions that see themselves as paying the price of such special treatment. In many countries, the economic and political factors giving rise to such policies have recently been accentuated by the phenomenon of globalization.

While scholars dispute just what globalization means and the extent to which it has increased much more than casual readers might expect, the world has clearly changed enormously over the last century: empires have risen and fallen, new countries have been created, old countries have disintegrated, wars have been fought, population has soared, living standards have risen enormously for many and technology has changed the world in many respects. Much has been said and written recently about the resulting 'new economy'; however, much less has been said about the 'new polity', perhaps because at first glance there seems to be much less to say.

In the political sphere life has certainly changed in many respects during the last century. Many more people around the world now live in some kind of democracy and have, at least occasionally, some limited say in how they are governed. As in the 19th century, however, the most important political institution everywhere continues to be the nation state. Moreover, while at first glance surprisingly little has changed in the basic structure of political democracies, closer examination reveals that many variants exist in democratic institutions around the world: different voting systems; different legislative structures; different types of party organization; different roles for different levels of governments; different relations between the legislative, executive and judiciary branches of government; different levels of popular participation in the political process; and so on.

The world thus offers a potentially rich laboratory of experiments in different governance structures that may be associated with different policy outcomes. Sorting out which differences in political institutions matter, how they matter and to what extent in affecting such outcomes as economic growth and the distribution of income and wealth is a complex analytical task that social scientists have only recently begun to untangle (see Persson and Tabellini 2000 for an overview and Alesina and Spolaore 2003 for a number of illuminating illustrations). The relevant point here is that pressures on the nation state from above may, at least in some instances, increase pressures from below, and thus bring to the fore the latent interregional tensions that lie below the surface in many countries. Such tensions are politically explosive when they reflect ethnic, linguistic or other potentially fragmenting characteristics, that is, when the boundaries of a single country contain more than one 'nation', a theme that William Fox and Christine Wallich develop in Chapter 13. Similar tensions may arise even in ethnically homogeneous countries, when, for example, one result of increased openness to the world economy is to exacerbate existing regional economic inequalities, or even to create them.

Such pressures and their political and economic consequences have been clearly manifested in Canada. Even though intranational trade remains vastly more important than international trade (Helliwell 1998), the increasing integration of both the industrial heartland (Ontario in particular plus Quebec) and the west, which is rich in raw materials (primarily Alberta, but also British Columbia) with the United States has profoundly altered the character of Canadian federalism. Quebec's disenchantment with some aspects of the existing political system is well known, as is the role that the internationalisation, or, more appropriately, the Americanization, of Canada's economy has played in strengthening the hand of those who argue that Quebec is as economically viable on its own as it is as part of Canada. Similarly, the rise of western Canada as a separate and important player in the federal game, with its own axes to grind, has been well documented in recent years. However, the key change in Canada is the increasing self-definition of an Ontario interest as separate from that of Canada, in contrast to the long-standing perception that, to paraphrase a well-known saying, what is good for Canada is good for Ontario, and vice versa (Courchene and Telmer 1998).

A central problem in any federation is to explain why rich regions are willing to support poor regions, whether such support is instituted through formal equalization systems, through favourable treatment in federal investment and other policies, through the tolerance of discriminatory barriers or through other means. In the absence of monetary, exchange and tariff policies, regions within a country are severely constrained in the extent to which they can, in the words of the Swiss constitution, 'attain the economic and political sovereignty of the people'. Regional regulatory barriers, discriminatory federal expenditures and regulations and differential tax and spending policies are the principal instruments open to regions that wish to make their mark, for good or ill, on economic decisions. The government may give richer regions, namely, those that are expected to be the source of redistribution, more autonomy to keep them in the country. Sometimes, however, centralizing pressures are exerted through both economic markets (factor mobility) and political markets (for instance, harmonization in the name of a common economic union) to discourage such 'disintegrating' policies. Alternatively, as appears to occur with small natural resource-rich regions in particular, they may be explicitly exempted from making their 'full' contribution to regional redistributive policy. (For an interesting early attempt to analyse some of these conflicting choices, see Milanovic 1996.)

Viewed from the recipient's side, interregional transfers permit regions to behave badly, for example, by implementing beggar-my-neighbour policies, without paying the full economic penalty for their misbehaviour. Economists have frequently criticized transfers for this reason. Conversely, however, such economic efficiencies might be considered a necessary cost of political stability. Indeed, at the extreme, the total rents created and distributed through economically inefficient policies could be used as a measure of the stock of political capital that has been created (Wintrobe 1998). Treisman (1998) rationalizes the inequality characterizing Russian interregional transfers in this fashion: with the notable exception of Chechnya, the larger transfers went to those regions that could most credibly threaten to damage the nation state by seceding and/or withholding revenues. He might also have treated the sum of such inefficient transfers as an investment by the central government in securing the loyalty of recalcitrant regions.

To the extent that regional transfers can be viewed as constituting payments in exchange either for yielding constitutionally entrenched authority (Breton and Scott 1978) or for adhering to the existing framework of the nation state (referred to as profitable federalism in Canada),[15] globalization may have an important impact. If the result of growing connections between foreign interests and local economies is to strengthen the latter in relative terms, centrifugal forces, such as those mentioned earlier with respect to Canada, may be strengthened.

By contrast, if the resulting strengthening of the national economy as a whole results in increasing central government revenues, the central government may be able to increase its 'buyout' package and maintain political stability, a task that will obviously be easier if more fundamental political forces, such as linguistic distinctiveness, do not strengthen the economic incentives. Naturally, if the major new revenues accruing to the state from globalization accrue to provincial governments, whether because they own natural resources (Alberta in Canada or Alaska in the United States) or simply have the first kick at the revenue can (Russia, and to some extent China), centrifugal pressures may be exacerbated rather than alleviated.[16] As a result, regional differences are accentuated, while at the same time the central government's capacity to level them out, whether through transfers or repression, is diminished.

If increasing openness to the world economy exacerbates regional economic disparities, poor regions in which exportable resources are located may generally be expected to increasingly assert their claim to a larger share of the growing rents yielded by such resources. Aceh in Indonesia (see Chapter 11) is an obvious example (see also Bahl and Tumennasan 2002). At the same time, even though they may themselves benefit disproportionately from increased trade, rich regions may become decreasingly inclined to support their poorer neighbours though interregional transfers. The bonds of common nationhood that were previously strengthened by the market dependency of the rich on the poor—for instance, in most countries the majority of transfers probably quickly flow right back to the so-called donor provinces through trade patterns—and the income dependency of the poor on the rich may thus erode from both sides as the world becomes the relevant market.

Broadly speaking, there are only three ways for political institutions to be sustainable, so that people not only believe in their credibility, but are willing to act on this belief. First, most people may simply share the underlying values, that is, they are pre-committed to the maintenance of the institution through a common ideology or belief system. If such a system does not exist, the state may attempt to create it through such means as the heavy use of political symbolism, for example, the flag in the United States, or perhaps in some countries the role of political parties and associated ideologies.

Another way to create a credible degree of pre-commitment is to put a series of checks and balances in place, for example, through a constitution that is not easy to amend and is interpreted by a credibly independent judiciary, as in the United States, or that can be changed only by a very direct democratic process, as in Switzerland. A different approach is to limit the power of the leviathan through such devices as a free press that can not only criticize the actions of those in political power, but also, and equally important, serve as an important means of informing those in power of what citizens really want. Combined with the existence of a credible constitutional means of removing leaders from power, such information systems may both enable commitments to be more credible and serve as an important transmitter of signals between citizens and leaders. Indeed, as Wintrobe (1998) argues, such considerations suggest that no matter how inadequate democratic systems may sometimes seem to be in practice, they are theoretically always superior to dictatorial alternatives. As Winston Churchill once said, 'Democracy is the worst form of Government except all those other forms that have been tried from time to time' (as cited in Lindert 2003, p. 315, note 1). Alternatively, the integrity of the nation state may be maintained by fear of the consequences of its failure. While most obviously at play in nondemocratic systems, the 'fear card' is certainly not unknown elsewhere. In Canada, for example, some observers believe that the fear of adverse economic consequences is the main deterrent to Quebec's separatism.

Finally, the loyalty of potential territorial dissidents may simply be bought, at least for a time. Pork barrel politics, as this process has been labeled in the United States, may serve not only to grease the wheels of politics, but may even provide some glue to hold the country together. Granting monopoly privileges or rent to one's supporters not only pays for their support, but also tends to deter shirking, because what has been given can be taken back. Sometimes, however, those who feel that their support has been bought may actually be reinforced in their dissident views.[17] Similarly, those who feel they are paying may become increasingly resentful of the burden over time, as seems to have occurred in Germany (Chapter 4). To the extent that significant groups see a country as being worthwhile only so long as it is profitable for them, by turning glue into solvent, increased global pressures may have serious implications for the continued existence of some countries.

By contrast, in some instances globalization may strengthen the centre at the expense of regions. For example, if the central government's revenue base is improved as a result, it may be able to increase transfers and strengthen the effectiveness of the state as a whole (see Wildavsky 1977 for an argument along these lines). If, however, the result is that regions gain new economic and fiscal strength while the central treasury is weakened, centrifugal pressures may be exacerbated rather than alleviated (see Davis, Ossowski and Fedelino 2003 for a discussion of the most dramatic instances, which relate to sudden infusions of mineral wealth, and their implications). Either some regions will feel more able to stand alone or, alternatively, they may want to break away more to hide their heads from the winds of global change than to flourish independently. If globalization weakens the domestic political bargains that have been struck over time to enable different groups to live together, the result may be increased tension that might perhaps be alleviated in part by directing anger at some foreign villain, at the extreme through what Barber (1995) labelled *jihad.*

To sum up, if the result of globalization is increased economic growth concentrated in a certain region, the effects will vary from country to country depending upon a variety of factors, such as:

- whether the region that benefits the most was previously rich or poor;
- whether the region is large or small;
- whether the region is actually or potentially disaffected, for instance, on historical or ethnic grounds;

- what the effects are on fiscal revenues at both the regional and central levels;
- what the nature of the intergovernmental fiscal system in place is and how it is affected;
- whether all parties are willing and able to adjust to the new circumstances in a timely fashion.

Listing such factors simply sets up a research agenda. It is far too soon to ascertain the importance of particular factors in different countries or how a country might resolve any problems that emerge, let alone whether the result will be the introduction of more asymmetrical policies than those already in place.

Yet no reward comes without risk. Increased economic openness may raise income levels, but it also often increases volatility. Considering the negative aspects of increased economic volatility suggests a quite different way of looking at the potential impact of globalization on regionalization. Some form of fiscal decentralization—used here loosely as a generic term for some degree of power division and separation—may be a sensible way to cope with risk by achieving a certain degree of risk pooling (von Hagen and Hepp 2000). Decentralization within a national framework may thus be viewed to some extent as a defensive manoeuvre to protect congruent regional and national interests.

All in all, both general considerations and the detailed examination of diverse national experiences recounted in this volume suggest that we should remember, to paraphrase Charles Darwin, that it is not always the strongest species that survive, nor the most intelligent, but the ones most responsive to change (Katzenstein 1985 develops this idea). With respect to decentralized political and fiscal institutions, as many of the cases in this book suggest, the interaction of globalization and decentralization may put this view of evolution to another test.

NOTES

1. With apologies to William Shakespeare, *Twelfth Night,* II.v.
2. Bird and Stauffer (2001) contains earlier versions of two of the case studies in this volume (Canada and Bosnia and Herzegovina).
3. Even with respect to the United States, however, there are many asymmetrical relationships, for example, Puerto Rico. Indeed, Elazar (1957) identifies 2 federacies, 3 associated states, 3 home rule territories, 3 unincorporated territories and 130 distinct 'first nations' with asymmetrical relations to the federal government. For a brief overview of the racial and economic diversity of Brazil, see Avelar (1999). Affonso (2001) provides a useful recent review of decentralization and reform in Brazil. Watts (1999) provides a useful categorization of different forms of association between territories.

4. For a discussion of the role of fiscal factors in sustaining political equilibrium, with particular reference to Latin America, see Bird (2003b). Winik (2002) in his brilliant account of the resolution of the American Civil War, provides an excellent recent reminder of how precarious the political balance may be at critical moments in a country's history.
5. The discussion here focuses on fiscal decentralization. While it notes the relationships between fiscal, administrative and political decentralization, it does not discuss the subject in detail. For further discussion see, for example, Rondinelli, Nellis and Cheema (1983).
6. Bird and Chen (1998), however, note the sharp contrast between delegation at the provincial and local level and devolution at the federal and provincial level in Canada.
7. See World Bank (2000) for citations to the relevant literature, much of which is also reviewed in Bird and Vaillancourt (1998).
8. For another, quite different, case of attempting to construct a new government from a scattered, though not ethnically diverse, population, see Ford and Litvack (2001) on the West Bank and Gaza. On Ethiopia, see World Bank (1999).
9. For a quite different version of the Colombian case, see Acosta and Bird (2004) and Bird and Fiszbein (1998). A more appropriate example might be Bolivia, which adopted a municipalization program in the early 1990s in part to strengthen the state by positioning it as the main lifeline of local development, while at the same time countering the centrifugal tendencies that a more federal decentralization program, focusing on the provincial level, would have fostered (Grindle 2000). As Faguet (2004) reports, the Bolivian experiment appears to have succeeded in making the government more responsive to local wishes and needs. For another discussion of Bolivia see Arze and Martinez-Vazquez (2003).
10. For a book length review focusing on the macroeconomic aspects of decentralization, see Rodden, Eskeland and Litvack (2003), whose book contains case studies of this question in two of the countries covered in this volume (Canada and Germany), as well as studies of a number of other industrial, developing and transition countries.
11. While macroeconomic equilibrium might have some asymmetrical aspects, whether small or large subnational governments are most likely to breach macroeconomic balance is not clear either analytically or empirically. The case for small subnational governments is that they are more susceptible to external shocks and are cheaper to bail out (Pisauro 2001), while the case for large subnational governments is that they are too big to fail in the sense of the negative externalities if they do, with the result that they may therefore be able to expect to be bailed out and thus feel that they can get away with worse behaviour (Wildasin 1997).
12. See Watts (2000) for an extensive discussion of all these possible classifications, with examples. The Spanish case is particularly interesting. In addition to Chapter 7 in this book, see Castells (2001), Ruiz Almendar (2002) and Vinuela (2001).
13. There can be few more telling political slogans in this respect than the slogan displayed on every automobile license place in the province of Quebec: the motto of what was once *la belle province* has, since the rise of separatist sentiments, become *je me souviens.* For an idiosyncratic but telling consideration of this and many other relevant issues, see Saul (1997).
14. In the context of the European Union, essentially the same issue is often discussed under the label of 'variable geometry', or the extent to which and the time span within which different member states take part in different aspects of European Union policy, for example, the Monetary Union or defence.
15. See Bird (2003a) for a criticism of the usual political misuse of numbers that purport to show which regions gain from fiscal flows and which lose.
16. Alesina and Spolaore (2003) provide a useful review of the empirical and theoretical literature on the trade-offs between political heterogeneity and the economic gains of market size. They conclude that, on the whole, globalization fosters political separatism.
17. As Hirschman (1971) notes with respect to foreign aid, people may take your money, which is explicitly given for purposes with which they do not agree, rationalize the apparent betrayal of their beliefs by doing so in some way and continue to hold their beliefs.

REFERENCES

Acosta, Olga Lucia and Richard M. Bird (2004), 'The Dilemma of Decentralization in Colombia', Paper no. 0404, International Tax Program, Rotman School of Management, University of Toronto, Toronto.

Affonso, Rui de Britto Alvares (2001), 'Decentralization and Reform of the State: The Brazilian Federation at the Crossroads', in Richard M. Bird and Thomas Stauffer (eds), *Intergovernmental Fiscal Relations in Fragmented Societies,* Fribourg, Switzerland: Institut du Federalisme, pp. 319–47.

Agranoff, Robert, (ed.) (1999), *Accommodating Diversity: Asymmetry in Federal States,* Baden-Baden, Germany: Nomos Verlagsgesellschaft.

Ahmad, Junaid (1998), 'South Africa: An Intergovernmental Fiscal System in Transition', in Richard M. Bird and François Vaillancourt (eds), *Fiscal Decentralization in Developing Countries,* Cambridge: Cambridge University Press, pp. 239–70.

Alesina, Alberto and Enrico Spolaore (2003), *The Size of Nations,* Cambridge, MA: MIT Press.

Annett, Anthony (2000), 'Social Fractionalization, Political Instability, and the Size of Government', Working Paper no. WP/00/82, International Monetary Fund, Washington, DC.

Arze, Francisco Javier and Jorge Martinez-Vazquez (2003), 'Descentralizaciòn en Latinoamérica desde una perspective de paises pequeños: Bolivia, El Salvador, Ecuador y Nicaragua', Working Paper no. 03-03, International Studies Program, Andrew Young School of Policy Studies, Georgia State University, Atlanta.

Avelar, Lucia (1999), 'Citizenship and Social Diversity: The Aspect of Regional Diversity', background paper for the International Conference on Federalism, Mont-Tremblant, Quebec.

Bahl, Roy W. (1997), 'Fiscal Federalism in Uganda', World Bank, Washington, DC, processed.

——— (2002), 'Implementation Rules for Fiscal Decentralization', in M. Govinda Rao (ed.), *Development, Poverty, and Fiscal Policy: Decentralization of Institutions,* New Delhi: Oxford University Press, pp. 253–77.

Bahl, Roy W. and Paul Smoke (eds) (2003), *Restructuring Local Government Finance in Developing Countries: Lessons from South Africa,* Cheltenham, UK and Northampton, MA, USA: Edward Elgar.

Bahl, Roy W. and Bayar Tumennasan (2002), 'How Should Revenues from Natural Resources Be Shared?', Working Paper no. 02-14, International Studies Program, Andrew Young School of Policy Studies, Georgia State University, Atlanta.

Barber, Benjamin (1995), *Jihad vs. McWorld: How Globalism and Tribalism are Reshaping the World,* New York: Times Books.

Basta, Lifija R. and Thomas Fleiner (1996), *Federalism and Multiethnic States: The Case of Switzerland,* Fribourg, Switzerland: Institute of Federalism, University of Fribourg.

Bird, Richard M. (2001), *Intergovernmental Fiscal Relations in Latin America: Policy Design and Policy Outcomes,* Washington, DC: Inter-American Development Bank.

——— (2003a), 'Fiscal Flows, Fiscal Balance, and Fiscal Sustainability', Working Paper no. 03-02, International Studies Program, Andrew Young School of Public Policy, Georgia State University, Atlanta.

——— (2003b), 'Taxation in Latin America: Reflections on Sustainability and the Balance Between Efficiency and Equity', Paper no. 0306, International Tax Program, Rotman School of Management, University of Toronto, Toronto.

Bird, Richard M. and Duanjie Chen (1998), 'Federal Finance and Fiscal Federalism: The Two Worlds of Canadian Public Finance', *Canadian Public Administration*, 43 (1), 51–74.

Bird, Richard M. and Ariel Fiszbein (1998), 'The Central Role of Central Government in Decentralization: Colombia', in Richard M. Bird and François Vaillancourt (eds), *Fiscal Decentralization in Developing Countries,* Cambridge: Cambridge University Press, pp. 172–205.

Bird, Richard M. and Edgard Rodriguez (1999), 'Decentralization and Poverty Alleviation: International Experience and the Case of the Philippines', *Public Administration and Development*, 19 (3), 299–319.

Bird, Richard M. and Thomas Stauffer (eds) (2001), *Intergovernmental Fiscal Relations in Fragmented Societies,* Fribourg, Switzerland: Institut du Federalisme.

Bird, Richard M. and François Vaillancourt (eds) (1998), *Fiscal Decentralization in Developing Countries,* Cambridge: Cambridge University Press.

Boadway, Robin and Ronald Watts (2000), 'Fiscal Federalism in Canada', Institute of Intergovernmental Relations, Queen's University, Kingston, Ontario, processed.

Breton, Albert and Anthony Scott (1978), *The Economic Constitution of Federal States,* Toronto: University of Toronto Press.

Cairns, Alan (2000), *Citizens Plus: Aboriginal Peoples and the Canadian State*, Vancouver: University of British Columbia Press.

Castells, Antoni (2001), 'The Role of Intergovernmental Finance in Achieving Diversity and Cohesion: The Case of Spain', *Environment and Planning C: Government and Policy*, 19 (April), 189–206.

Chwe, Michael (2001), *Rational Ritual: Culture, Coordination, and Common Knowledge,* Princeton, NJ: Princeton University Press.

Courchene, Thomas J. and Colin R. Telmer (1998), *From Heartland to North American Region State: The Social, Fiscal and Federal Evolution of Ontario,* Toronto: Centre for Public Management, Faculty of Management, University of Toronto.

Davis, Jeffrey, Rolando J. Ossowski and Annalisa Fedolino (eds) (2003), *Fiscal Policy Formulation and Implementation in Oil-Producing Countries,* Washington, DC: International Monetary Fund.

Ebel, Robert D. and Serdar Yilmaz (2003), 'On the Measurement and Impact of Fiscal Decentralization', in James Alm and Jorge Martinez-Vazquez (eds), *Public Finance in Developing and Transitional Countries,* Cheltenham, UK and Northampton, MA, USA: Edward Elgar, pp. 101–20.

Elazar, Daniel J. (1957), *Exploring Federalism,* Tuscaloosa, AL: University of Alabama Press.

Esman, Milton J. and Ronald J. Herring (2001), *Carrots, Sticks, and Ethnic Conflict: Rethinking Development Assistance,* Ann Arbor, MI: University of Michigan Press.

Faguet, Jean-Paul (2004), 'Does Decentralization Increase Responsiveness to Local Needs? Evidence from Bolivia', *Journal of Public Economics*, 88 (March), 867–94.

Feldstein, Martin (1975), 'Wealth Neutrality and Local Choice in Public Education', *American Economic Review*, 65 (1), 75–89.

Flanagan, Tom (2000), *First Nations? Second Thoughts,* Montreal: McGill-Queens University Press.

Ford, James Fitz and Jennie Litvack (2001), 'Intergovernmental Fiscal Relations and Nation Building: West Bank-Gaza Case Study', in Richard M. Bird and Thomas Stauffer (eds), *Intergovernmental Fiscal Relations in Fragmented Societies,* Fribourg, Switzerland: Institut du Federalisme, pp. 365–96.

Grindle, Merilee (2000), 'Designing Reforms: Problems, Solutions, and Politics', Faculty Research Working Paper Series no. RWP01-20, John F. Kennedy School of Government, Harvard University, Cambridge, MA.
Helliwell, John (1998), *How Much Do National Borders Matter?,* Washington, DC: The Brookings Institution.
Hirschman, Albert O. (1971), *A Bias for Hope,* New Haven, CT: Yale University Press.
Holzhausen, Walter (1974), *Federal Finance in Malaysia,* Kuala Lumpur: Penerbit Universiti Malaya.
Katzenstein, Peter J. (1985), *Small States in World Markets,* Ithaca, NY: Cornell University Press.
Kopits, George and Jon Craig (1998), *Transparency in Government Operations*, Occasional Paper no. 158, Washington, DC: International Monetary Fund.
Lindert, Peter (2003) 'Voice and Growth: Was Churchill Right?', *Journal of Economic History*, 63 (2), 315–50.
Litvack, Jennie, Junaid Ahmad and Richard Bird (1998), *Rethinking Decentralization,* Washington, DC: World Bank.
Mahbob, Sulaiman, Frank Flatters, Robin Boadway, Sam Wilson and Wlayne Yee Siew Lin (eds) (1997), *Malaysia's Public Sector in the Twenty-First Century: Planning for 2020 and Beyond,* Kingston, Canada: John Deutsch Institute for the Study of Economic Policy, Queen's University.
Martinez-Vazquez, Jorge and Jamie Boex (2001), *Russia's Transition to a New Federalism,* Washington, DC: World Bank.
Milanovic, Branko (1996), 'Nations, Conglomerates, and Empires: The Trade-Off Between Income and Sovereignty', Policy Research Working Paper no. 1675, World Bank, Washington, DC.
Persson, Torsten and Guido Tabellini (2000), *Political Economics: Explaining Economic Policy,* Cambridge, MA: MIT Press.
Pisauro, Giuseppe (2001), 'Intergovernmental Relations and Fiscal Discipline: Between Commons and Soft Budget Constraints', Working Paper no. WP/01/65, International Monetary Fund, Washington, DC.
Ravallion, Martin (2000), 'Monitoring Targeting Performance When Decentralized Allocations to the Poor Are Unobserved', *World Bank Economic Review*, 14 (2), 331–45.
Rodden, Jonathan, Gunnar S. Eskeland and Jennie Litvack (eds) (2003), *Fiscal Decentralization and the Challenge of Hard Budget Constraints,* Cambridge, MA: MIT Press.
Rondinelli, Dennis, J. Nellis and G. Cheema (1983), 'Decentralization in Developing Countries', Staff Working Paper no. 581, World Bank, Washington, DC.
Ruiz Almendar, Violet (2002), 'Fiscal Federalism in Spain: The Assignment of Taxation Powers to the Autonomous Communities', *European Taxation*, 42 (November), 467–75.
Saul, John Ralston (1997), *Reflections of a Siamese Twin: Canada at the End of the Twentieth Century,* Toronto: Penguin Books.
Simeon, Richard (2000), 'Let's Get at the Basic Question Indirectly', *Policy Options*, 21 (January–February), 11–16.
Simeon, Richard and Christina Murray (2000), 'Multi-Level Governance in South Africa: An Interim Assessment', University of Toronto, Toronto, processed.
Stauffer, Thomas P. (2001), 'Intergovernmental Relations in Fragmented Societies: The Case of Switzerland', *Environment and Planning C: Government and Policy*, 19 (April), 207–22.

Tanzi, Vito (1996), 'Fiscal Federalism and Decentralization: A Review of Some Efficiency and Macroeconomic Aspects', in Michael Bruno and Boris Pleskovic (eds), *Annual World Bank Conference on Development Economics 1995,* Washington, DC: World Bank.

Treisman, Daniel (1998), *After the Deluge: Regional Crisis and Political Consolidation in Russia,* Ann Arbor, MI: University of Michigan Press.

Vaillancourt, François (1992), 'English and Anglophones in Quebec: An Economic Perspective', in *Survival—Official Language Rights in Canada,* Toronto: C. D. Howe Institute, pp. 63–94.

Vaillancourt, François and Richard M. Bird (2002), 'Changing with the Times: Success, Failure, and Inertia in Canadian Federal Arrangements, 1945–2001', Working Paper no. 151, Center for Research on Economic Development and Policy Reform, Stanford University, Stanford, CA.

Vinuela, Juan (2001), 'Fiscal Decentralization in Spain', International Monetary Fund, Washington, DC, processed.

von Hagen, Jurgen and Ralf Hepp (2000), 'Regional Risksharing and Redistribution in the German Federation', Working Paper, Centre for European Integration Studies, Rheinische-Friedrich-Universitat, Bonn.

Watts, Ronald L. (1999), *Comparing Federal Systems,* 2nd ed., Montreal and Kingston, Canada: McGill-Queen's University Press.

——— (2000), 'Asymmetrical Decentralization: Functional or Dysfunctional?', Queen's University, Kingston, Ontario, processed.

Wehner, Joachim H.-G. (2000), 'Asymmetrical Devolution', *Development Southern Africa,* 17 (June), 249–62.

Welikala, Asanga (2003), 'Fiscal and Financial Arrangements in a Federal Sri Lanka: Some Issues for Discussion', Centre for Policy Alternatives, Colombo, processed.

Wildasin, David (1997), 'Externalities and Bailouts: Hard and Soft Budget Constraints in Intergovernmental Fiscal Relations', Policy Research Working Paper no. 1843, World Bank, Washington, DC.

Wildavsky, Aaron (1977), *Budgeting,* New Brunswick, NJ: Transaction Publishers.

Wilensky, Harold (1975), *The Welfare State and Equality,* Berkeley, CA: University of California Press.

Winik, Jay (2002), *April 1865: The Month that Saved America,* New York: Harper.

Wintrobe, Ronald (1998), *The Political Economy of Dictatorship,* Cambridge: Cambridge University Press.

World Bank (1999), *Regionalization in Ethiopia,* Washington, DC.

——— (2000), *World Development Report 1999/2000: Entering the 21st Century,* Oxford: Oxford University Press.

2. The Country Studies: Comparisons and Conclusions

Richard M. Bird, Robert D. Ebel and Sebastiana Gianci

Many countries around the world are decentralizing to various degrees, in various ways and for various reasons. No matter the form that the decentralization takes, its fiscal aspects are always important and are sometimes dominant in determining outcomes. This book explores the idea that the design of a country's intergovernmental fiscal relations may play an especially critical role in 'fragmented' nations, namely, those in which territorially-based linguistic or ethnic groups live together within the boundaries of a single nation state. In some circumstances, granting such groups greater authority to raise and spend revenues as they see fit may enhance social and political harmony. In other circumstances, however, freeing such groups from central government control may encourage separatist tendencies and ultimately the nation's disintegration. Of course, even though many other factors also affect how subsidiarity in the fiscal sphere relates to national solidarity, money definitely matters. How funds are raised, distributed and spent is an important determinant of the extent to which fragmented societies are able to sustain a viable and effective national government.

This book focuses on fiscal relations between the central governments of nation states and major regional or intermediate governments. This emphasis omits some points of interest. For example, one can argue that that the more important economic questions relate to lower-tier governments, such as local or municipal governments, especially with respect to service delivery.[1] Others have noted that even the most established and representative democracies many not recognize politically many 'fragments' of a population—aboriginal peoples, Romanies and certain ethnic groups—because they do not have an established territorial basis. (Biro and Kovacs 2001). That said, this volume concentrates on relations with regional governments because the conflict inherent in recognizing diversity through subsidiarity and national solidarity is generally strongest when it arises at this level. Moreover, the relevant analytical and theoretical issues can be discussed without the additional complexities of three, or often four or more, levels.

The fiscal window on a country's situation is an important one, in that it reflects fundamental political, historical, physical and institutional realities, and to some extent shapes them, but it is never the whole story. Some of the case studies therefore consider not just the traditional fiscal triumvirate of expenditure assignment, tax assignment and transfer level and design, but also the regional impact of direct central government expenditures, the regional impact of central government regulations, the regional barriers to trade and factor mobility and so on. The emphasis, however, is essentially on intergovernmental fiscal relations, with particular attention to the extent to which fiscal (and political) institutions explicitly take regional asymmetries into account and the extent to which such symmetrical (or asymmetrical) treatment may accentuate or work against national solidarity.

Even though all the authors of the country studies were given the same instructions, the countries covered are so diverse that the results are, unsurprisingly, themselves diverse. Moreover, as is inevitable, some divergences emerged in how each chapter treats asymmetry. In principle, each chapter attempts to provide both sufficient detail on the nature of social and territorial fragmentation and the related intergovernmental finance structures to elucidate the key issues linking fiscal structures and political outcomes in the country concerned. Such institutional details are needed to understand and appraise the nature of the problems and the likely sustainability of particular solutions. Some chapters, however, are inevitably much more detailed and comprehensive than others. Moreover, some authors take a different and narrower focus than others, in some instances reflecting the relative importance or unimportance of formal fiscal asymmetry. Unsurprisingly, the most detailed chapters are those that deal with formally federal countries with marked asymmetric elements, namely, Belgium, Canada, Russia and Switzerland.

THE COUNTRIES STUDIED

As Table 2.1 shows (see Box 2.1 for definitions of the terms used in Table 2.1), the 11 countries included in this book encompass not only a large proportion of the world's population, but also a wide variety of circumstances. The case studies include spatially small countries (Bosnia and Herzegovina, Switzerland) and large ones (China, India, Russia), rich and highly developed countries (Canada, Switzerland) and poor ones at different levels of development (India).[2] Income is distributed more equally in some countries than in others (the Gini index). Some are 'old' federal states (Canada, Switzerland),

Table 2.1 Basic characteristics of the case study countries

Country	Population (millions, 2003)	Area (thousands of square kilometres)	Gross domestic product/capita (constant local currency units, 2003)	Growth of gross domesitc product/capita (%, 2003)	Gini index of distribution of household income	Percentage of adults literate	Life expectancy (years)	Human development index (2004)	Fractionalization[a]		
									Ethnic	Linguistic	Religious
Belgium	10.3	33	22 898	0	25 (1996)	98	79	6	0.5554	0.5409	0.2127
Bosnia and Herzegovina	4.1	51	1986	2	—	—	74	66	0.6300	0.6751	0.6851
Canada	31.4	9971	32 376	2	32 (1997)	97	79	4	0.7124	0.5772	0.6958
China[b]	1281.0	9598	4394	7	40 (1998)	86	71	94	0.1538	0.1327	0.6643
Germany	82.5	357	24 039	0	38 (1998)	99	78	19	0.1682	0.1642	0.6571
India	1048.3	3287	2670	3	38 (1997)	59	63	127	0.4182	0.8069	0.3260
Indonesia	211.7	1904	3230	2	30 (2000)	88	67	111	0.7351	0.7680	0.2340
Philippines	79.9	300	4160	2	46 (2000)	95	70	83	0.2385	0.8360	0.3056
Russia	144.1	17 075	8230	5	46 (2000)	99	66	57	0.2452	0.2485	0.4398
Spain	41.2	505	21 460	2	33 (1990)	98	78	20	0.4165	0.4132	0.4514
Switzerland	7.2	41	30 010	0	33 (1992)	99	80	11	0.5314	0.5441	0.6083

Note: — = not available. See Box 2.1 for definitions of the Gini index, human development index and fractionalization.

a. Alesina and others (2003).

b. Only mainland China is included.

Sources: Unless otherwise noted, Central Intelligence Agency (2005); World Bank statistical information management and analysis database (August 2003).

BOX 2.1 DEFINITIONS

The Gini index measures the degree of inequality in the distribution of family household income in a country. It is also the most widely used summary measure of the degree of inequality in household income distribution. It is calculated by plotting cumulative family income against the cumulative number of families arranged from the poorest to the richest and taking the ratio between the resulting area and a 45-degree line from the origin to the entire triangular area under the 45-degree line. The more nearly equal a country's income distribution is, the closer the plotted (Lorenz) curve will be to the 45-degree line and the lower its Gini index. A Lorenz curve is a geographical representation of the proportionality of a distribution. The more unequal a country's income distribution is, the farther its Lorenz curve from the 45-degree line and the higher its Gini index. If income were distributed with perfect equality, the Lorenz curve would coincide with the 45-degree line and the index would be zero. If income were distributed with perfect inequality, the Lorenz curve would coincide with the horizontal axis and the right vertical axis and the index would be 100.

The human development index is a ranking compiled by the United Nations Development Programme in which 1 is the best ranking possible of the 162 countries included. The index measures a country's achievements in three aspects of human development: longevity as measured by life expectancy at birth; knowledge as measured by a combination of the adult literacy rate and the combined gross primary, secondary and tertiary enrolment ratios; and standard of living as measured by gross domestic product per capita (purchasing power parity US dollars).

The fractionalization index (Alesina and others 2003) reflects the reflects the probability that two randomly selected individuals from the population belong to different groups. The lower the number, the less fractionalization, on a scale from 0.0001 to 1. The goal of the index is to distinguish clearly between ethnic, religious and linguistic heterogeneity. The index is calculated as

$$\text{FRACTj} = 1 - \sum_{i=1}^{N} sij,$$

where *sij* is the share of group; *i* (*i* = 1 . . . N) in country *j*.

some are new federations (Belgium, Spain), some are explicitly nonfederal countries (China, Indonesia) and some are in effect new countries emerging from conflict (Bosnia and Herzegovina).

As Table 2.1 shows, the countries' rankings on the human development index, which examined 162 countries, vary dramatically. Table 2.1 also provides indexes of the degree of ethnic, linguistic and religious fractionalization, elements of diversity that emerge as a policy consideration in some of the case studies in this book. However, sweeping conclusions regarding 'obvious' links between policies on ethnic, linguistic and/or religious diversity and the likelihood of conflict or decentralization cannot be made based on the fractionalization indexes alone because those indexes do not take into account the critical territorial dimension of ethnic diversity within countries.

Political Structures

Political structures, number of subnational governments and regional differences also vary significantly from county to country, ranging from the huge regions and marked differences in regional income levels of Indonesia to the tiny regions and relative regional equality of Switzerland (Table 2.2). Their political and governmental configurations range from federal parliamentary monarchies (Belgium) to unitary communist states (China). The indicator of the relative level of voice and accountability in governance, while subjective, is perhaps more revealing. As one might expect, the five industrial countries all rank high on this indicator, followed by the two most democratic of the developing countries included (India and the Philippines), and then the countries that may be considered as in transition to democracy (Bosnia and Herzegovina, Indonesia, and maybe Russia), with China bringing up the rear.

Degree of Fiscal Imbalance

As discussed in detail in the country chapters, the intergovernmental fiscal arrangements in this mélange of countries are equally complex and varied. All decentralized countries have in common, however, some degree of concern with regional imbalance. As a rule, central governments tend to collect the most taxes while state and local governments are often responsible for more expenditures than they can finance from sources of revenue directly under their control. The resulting difference between expenditures and own source revenues at different levels of government is referred to as the vertical fiscal imbalance (VFI). At the same time, within each subnational level of government some jurisdictions are invariably richer than others. The resulting difference in the resources available to governments at the same level is referred to as the horizontal fiscal imbalance (HFI). Each of these concepts carries with it a fair amount of philosophical baggage and each is also difficult to measure in an unambiguous way. Countries use a wide range of fiscal instruments, including taxes and fees, transfers, grants, revenue allocations and expenditure responsibility rules, to deal with such imbalances.

The concepts of VFI and HFI cannot be cleanly separated. One way to think of VFI, for example, is that it might be considered to be eliminated—that is, vertical fiscal balance has been achieved—when expenditures and revenues (excluding transfers) are balanced for the richest local government, measured in terms of its capacity to raise resources on its own. Even then, however, a VFI will remain for all poorer local governments. As a rule, such gaps are treated as HFIs, that is, as a problem of achieving horizontal fiscal balance within the regional or local government sector rather than vertical balance between levels of government. However 'imbalance' may be defined, whether and to what extent fiscal imbalances are considered to be a problem is, of course, invariably a highly political issue.

A simple way to measure VFI is simply as the ratio of transfers to subnational expenditures. This measure has the considerable virtue of being easy to calculate, but it reveals nothing about the extent to which the fundamental concerns about political accountability and economic efficiency that underlie the concept of VFI are legitimate. The transfer to expenditure ratio does not get to the heart of the problem because it does not take into account the extent to which transfers, other subnational revenues and even subnational expenditures reflect federal or subnational policy decisions. Recognizing this problem, analysts have developed more refined measures of VFI and Table 2.3 presents two such measures. Essentially, the idea in constructing these measures is to distinguish between revenue sources that are under the central government's control and those that are under subnational control. Although any such distinction is inevitably somewhat subjective and suffers from both conceptual and empirical problems, such measures may nonetheless provide some useful comparative information.

The first VFI measure reported in Table 2.3 is a ratio of the budget balance to expenditures for regional governments and then for all subnational governments. A larger negative value indicates a higher degree of vertical imbalance, while a positive value means that that level of government is running a surplus. On this measure, for the year shown and for the limited data available, Canada and Spain appear to have the highest degree of regional VFI, as do Indonesia and India for subnational governments as a whole. The final column of Table 2.3 shows the shares of subnational expenditures that are covered by intergovernmental transfers. Again, a higher value corresponds to a higher degree of vertical fiscal imbalance and reflects a higher level of dependence by

Table 2.2 Political characteristics of the case study countries

Country	Type of government	Number and name of regional or state divisions	Subnational breakdowns	Ratio of gross domestic product/ capita in the largest state to that in the smallest state	Ratio of gross domestic product in the largest state to that in the smallest state	Average population/ state or region (millions)	Degree of political democracy (percentile ranking of voice and accountability)[a]
Belgium	Federal parliamentary democracy under a constitutional monarch	10 (9 provinces and Metropolitan Brussels)	589 communes	2.13	9.68	1.03	93.4
Bosnia and Herzegovina	Emerging federal democratic republic	2	10 cantons	—	—	2.05	43.9
Canada	Federation with parliamentary democracy	13 (10 provinces and 3 territories)	5600 municipalities[b]	1.99	250.56	2.4	94.9
China[c]	Communist state	30 (27 provinces and Beijing, Shanghai and Tianjing)	151 prefectures, 479 cities, 1894 counties, 60 000 townships, 804 153 villages	2.77	16.05	42.7	10.1
Germany	Federal republic	16 states (*länder*)	Approximately 15 000 municipalities and municipal associations	2.93	17.83	5.2	95.5

India	Federal republic	26 (25 states and 1 union territory)	602 municipalities[d]	9.27	210.00	40.3	60.6
Indonesia	Republic	30 (27 provinces, the capital and 2 special districts)	277 municipalities and 65 198 villages[e]	17.77	39.38	7.84	34.8
Philippines	Republic	13 regions and 76 provinces	64 cities, 1541 municipalities, 41 924 *barangays* (municipal subunits)	5.45	33.27	6.1	54.0
Russia	Federation	89 regional governments	12 903 municipalities	2.81	4.06	0.9	33.8
Spain	Parliamentary monarchy	17[f]	Approximately 8000 municipalities and municipal associations	2.19	24.94	2.4	87.9
Switzerland	Federal republic	26 cantons	Approximately 3000 communes	2.59	124.78	0.3	97.5

Note: — = not available.

a. Kaufmann, Kraay and Mastruzzi (2003). Rankings range from zero to 100. The higher the figure, the more democratic the country.
b. Statistics Canada: http://www.statcan.ca/english/census2001/dict/geo012.htm.
c. Only mainland China is included.
d. Indian government: http://districts.nic.in/dstats.asp.
e. Indonesian information system: http://202.159.18.43/english/Geography.htm.
f. Spain's Canary Islands and Basque Country are included. Not included are Ceuta and Melilla, two enclaves within Morocco's borders that gained limited autonomous status in 1994. Also not included are three small Spanish possessions located off the coast of Morocco: Islas Chafarinas, Penon de Alhucemas and Penon de Velez de la Gomera.

Sources: Unless otherwise noted, Central Intelligence Agency (2005); International Monetary Fund (2002); European Union and Organisation for Economic Co-operation and Development data.

Table 2.3 Measures of vertical fiscal imbalance in the case study countries

Country	Statistics of VFI (type I)		
	Regional (measure for state or provincial governments)	Subnational (consolidated measure for regional and local governments)	Coefficient of VFI (type II)
Belgium (1998)	—	1.26	0.5291
Bosnia and Herzegovina (1999)	—	—	—
Canada (1999)	–3.95	0.56	–0.1256
China (1999)[a]	—	1.10[b]	—
Germany (1999 for type I, 1998 for type II)	–2.06	4.88	0.0874
India (1999)	—	–3.15	0.2737
Indonesia (1993)	—	–4.17	—
Philippines (1992)	—	8.70	0.8067
Russia (1999)	—	1.52	0.0928
Spain (1997)	–5.21	–2.22	0.0172
Switzerland (1999)	1.30	1.62	0.1134

Note: — = not available. VFI type I refers to unrestricted budget balances for the central, local, regional and subnational governments (sum of regional and local governments). VFI type II refers to the shares of subnational expenditures that are covered by intergovernmental transfers.

a. Only mainland China is included.

b. Denotes a break in the comparability of data. Data appearing after this entry do not form a consistent series with data for earlier years.

Source: Authors' calculations derived from International Monetary Fund (2002).

subnational governments on transfers from the central government. The broad conclusion emerging from these latter calculations is that VFI is especially high in Belgium and the Philippines and appears to be low in most of the other countries. More detailed studies over a longer period reveal, however, that while VFI is consistently low in Germany and Switzerland, it is highly variable in Spain and usually moderately variable in Canada (Bird and Tarasov 2004).

Turning to HFI, the picture is even more complicated both conceptually and empirically, and no simple comparative measures can be calculated. Instead, Table 2.4 shows, for the countries for which data were available, four different measures of regional disparity. Maximum/minimum as a percentage of the national average is the ratio of the per capita value of the variable indicated for each country in the second column of the table in the poorest/richest region to the national per capita average. A high degree of deviation from the average in either direction relative to 100 per cent signals the presence of either extremely rich or extremely poor regions, while a low degree of horizontal imbalance in either direction—values of, say, plus or minus 5 to 10 percent (around 100 per cent)—indicates that all regions are relatively homogenous in terms of the selected measure. By this measure, as already suggested in Table 2.1, all the countries included in this volume appear to have significant regional variations.

The other indicators in Table 2.4 reveal much the same picture. The maximum to minimum ratio is the per capita value of GDP or income, depending on the country, for the richest region divided by the per capita value for the poorest region. A value of 1 for the maximum to minimum ratio would represent perfect equality, but none of the countries comes close, though note that many countries have exceptional cases, such as city states (Germany) or sparsely populated poor territories (Canada), that may affect the results. The unweighted and weighted coefficients of variation show dispersion around the mean. The value of the unweighted coefficient of variation would be zero with perfect equality, but this statistic is not really appropriate for cross-country comparisons, because its value depends on a number of regions in a sample. The weighted coefficient is better suited for cross-country comparisons, because it reflects the relative population of the different regions within a country, not just the number of regions. Nevertheless, all the measures show both that considerable regional variations exist within all the countries and that regional disparities across countries vary considerably.

OVERVIEW OF THE CASE STUDIES

This section underscores some themes that seem to be common to a number of the countries discussed in this book and a few others that appear to be unique. To orient and focus the discussion, Table 2.5 is a somewhat subjective attempt to summarize some of the key points, and the balance of this section outlines a few aspects of the various country chapters.

A common theme that emerges from Table 2.5 is that regional fiscal issues matter primarily for political reasons, usually spurred by pressures in particular regions that are in some way 'different'. Another theme is that academic observers, including many of those represented in this volume, often express concerns about the possibly undesirable effects of current intergovernmental fiscal arrangements on economic incentives. With respect to most of the issues noted in the table, however, patterns in different countries differ

Table 2.4 Measures of horizonal imbalance in the case study countries

Country	Regions and type of data[a]	Years data[b]	Maximum/ minimum as a percentage of average for the type of data	Maximum/ minimum ratio	Coefficients of variation	
					Unweighted	Weighted
Belgium	10	1990–95	80–162	1.89–2.02	0.2671–0.3021	0.1962–0.2209
	Per capita GDP		80–151	1.89	0.2671	0.1962
Canada	13	1961–99	48–173	1.84-2.87	0.2011–0.3571	0.1232–0.2330
	Per capita GDP		69–168	2.44	0.2699	0.1434
	Personal income	1926–99	44–139	1.48–2.93	0.1227–0.3392	0.0795–0.2702
			73–139	1.90	0.1862	0.0911
China[c]	30	1990–98		3.1		
	Per capita income					
Germany	16	1991–95	29–198	3.23–6.94	0.3538–0.5208	0.2496–0.3656
	Per capita GDP		55–176	3.23	0.3538	0.2496

Indonesia[d]	30	2002				
Russia	89 Per capita regional income	1992–97	Mean 18.9 (1992), 3762.6 (1997)	1.93	0.83	
Spain	17 Per capita GDP	1981–99	58–139 63–135	1.85–2.31 2.15	0.1760–0.2082 0.2074	0.1745 – 0.2316 0.2308
Switzerland	26 Personal income	1980–98	68–173 73–165	1.88–2.45 2.26	0.1720–0.2419 0.2260	0.1565 – 0.2087 0.2087

Note:
GDP Gross domestic product.
The reported ranges reflect the data for all regions. The statistical columns reflect overall ranges in numerical values over corresponding sample time periods.
a. The number of regions refers to the total number of regions (states, provinces) in each country.
b. The column shows a sample time range for each time series.
c. Only mainland China is included.

Source: For Organisation for Economic Co-operation and Development countries: Bird and Tarasov (2004); for Russia, Martinez-Vazquez and Boex (2001); for China and Indonesia, World Bank data.

Table 2.5 Selected themes that emerge from the case studies

Country	Age of relevant political structure	Rationale for regional fiscal concern	Government's administrative approach is top-down or bottom-up?	Importance of language factor	Degree of regional disparity	Degree of equalization	Degree of regional fiscal autonomy	Fear of separatism	Explicit fiscal asymmetry	Importance of regional administration	Special concerns	Special features
Belgium	New	Political	Bottom-up	High	Moderate	Moderate	Increasing	Low	Some	Low	Incentives	Dual structure
Bosnia and Herzegovina	New	Political	Bottom-up	Low	Moderate	Low	Very high	Very high	Yes	Very high	Recent war	Weak centre
Canada	Old	Political	Bottom-up	High	Moderate	Moderate	High	Moderate	Some	Moderate	Incentives	Size
China	Moderate	Economic	Top-down	Not important	High	Low	Low	Low	Low	High	Growing imbalance	Border regions
Germany	Moderate	Economic	Top-down?	Not important	Moderate	High	Low	None	Low	Moderate	Incentives	Reunification
India	Moderate	Political/economic	Both?	Moderate	High	Moderate	Low	Low	Moderate	Moderate	Numerous	Size
Indonesia	New	Political	Bottom-up	Low	High	Low	Low	High	Some	Moderate	Natural resources	Adjustments to re-centralize
Philippines	Moderate	Political	Bottom-up	Low	High	Low	Low	High	Some	Low	Incentives	Own local taxes
Russia	New	Political	Bottom-up	Low	High	Low	Low	Moderate	Low	Moderate	Incentives, resources	Size, history
Spain	New	Political	Bottom-up	High	Moderate	Moderate	Increasing	Low	Moderate	Low?	Incentives	Transitory measures
Switzerland	Old	Political	Bottom-up	High	Moderate	Moderate	Very high	Low	None	Very high	Ongoing adjustments	Direct democracy

Source: Editors.

widely. Consider, for example, the extent of explicit fiscal asymmetry found in the five industrial federal countries. Chapter 3 notes some minor asymmetries in the assignment of both revenues and expenditure powers, as well as in intergovernmental transfers, in Canada. Similar asymmetries, though to some extent transitional, are apparent in Spain (Chapter 7) and to a lesser extent in Belgium (Chapter 6). By contrast, Germany (Chapter 4) has only a possibly transitional asymmetry with respect to transfers. Finally, Switzerland (Chapter 5), probably the most resolutely federal country in the world, appears to have no explicit fiscal asymmetries at all.

Numerous other interesting peculiarities and similarities emerge from the case study chapters. Chapter 3 on Canada, for example, emphasizes the importance of the evolution over time of intergovernmental fiscal relations, something that is not always evident in the newer governmental structures reviewed in most other chapters. While the authors emphasize that the system has emerged from ongoing political bargaining, they indicate that some explicitly differential regional policies, such as equalization transfers, are needed to ensure acceptably equal results across a diverse country. In their view, some degree of asymmetry has to date probably aided rather than weakened national solidarity. They are not so sanguine about the future, however, and caution that the evolutionary and bargaining process inherent in Canadian federalism is a never-ending story.

In sharp contrast to Canada (and also to Australia and the United States), Chapter 4 stresses the strength of the central government in Germany and the extent to which subsidiarity in the sense of regional autonomy has been suppressed in the interests of national solidarity. The reunification of Germany greatly accentuated the stress on the country's fiscal system, however, and the authors suggest that one result may be a weakening of the current high degree of equalization. What the authors seem to be suggesting is that the emphasis on solidarity in Germany may have to be weakened in the face of global competitive pressures, while the authors of Chapter 3 suggest that Canada may have to weaken its opposite emphasis on subsidiarity if it is to cope adequately with its changing economic setting. Both chapters may have got it right—or wrong.

Chapter 5 on Switzerland, like some of the other chapters on federal states, may seem to those not familiar with the subject to provide almost excessive detail, but as the saying goes, the devil is in the details, and nowhere more so than in federations. Those who wish to understand the realities of decentralized fiscal systems in any country in which such systems have existed for some time must reconcile themselves to dealing with myriad details. All countries are in a sense unique, but perhaps none more so than Switzerland, one of the smallest, oldest and most complex federal states. Thus close consideration of the many ways in which the Swiss have managed to cope so successfully with their unique and difficult internal and external situations may have much to offer others. A common fallacy is that the large (China, India, Indonesia, Russia and so on) can learn only from the large (for example, the United States, the European Union [EU]). In reality, however, despite the improbability that some key aspects of the Swiss experience, such as direct democracy, will be scaled up elsewhere, large countries could likely learn much from Switzerland. Such features as firm rules, institutions designed to foster consensus politics and emphasis on horizontal cooperation among regions could be profitably emulated on a much wider scale.

Belgium, along with Germany and Spain, is a member of the EU. Like Spain it is a relatively new federal state, and its intergovernmental fiscal structure is still evolving. Like Canada and Switzerland, the primary, but not only, regional divide is linguistic. Belgium's political structure is, however, uniquely its own in terms of the overlay of dual linguistic and territorial units, and the stability of its current arrangements has not yet been proven. Belgium's apparently limited degree of equalization, for example, combined with its high degree of formal asymmetry and recently increased regional fiscal autonomy may not augur well for the future. In contrast to the foregoing argument with respect to Canada, Belgium's asymmetry may prove to be a case in which the 'appetite grows with the eating', and Flanders may continue to march towards an increasingly separate existence.

To some extent, one might be inclined to make a similar judgment with respect to the Spanish case, which involves a partly linguistic fragmentation bolstered by both formal asymmetrical arrangements and increasing regional fiscal autonomy, as well as the cushion EU membership may provide for smaller nations. However, some aspects of Spanish fiscal asymmetry appear to be diminishing over time. Where all this will end is, as for all the other countries considered here, not something that can easily be predicted. The authors of Chapter 7 note that one troubling feature of Spanish fiscal federalism is the lack of any explicit discussion of what degree of regional redistribution is 'proper'. Indeed, such ambiguity seems to be a common theme in all the countries. Perhaps the major exception has been Germany, where a high and virtually uniform level of public services has long been explicitly taken as a national goal, but even there, as noted in Chapter 4, this apparent certainty in relation to distributive objectives has recently been called into doubt by the economic and fiscal stresses resulting from reunification.

Turning from developed federations to the two huge transition countries featured in this book, China and Russia, is to turn to two examples that present parallels and differences both from the preceding case studies and from each other. Chapter 8 on Russia argues that some degree of asymmetry was a necessary element in constructing a new country out of the ruins of the Soviet Union. Even though the lack of transparency with respect to what was actually done in Russia is unique, the author notes a number of obvious parallels with experience elsewhere: the importance of natural resources, of 'titular nationals' (similar to 'aboriginal populations'), of *de jure* and *de facto* aspects of asymmetrical arrangements and the transitional nature of some of them and so on. As in the case of Spain, the overall assessment is that whereas asymmetry may have been an initial necessary evil, its long-run costs are likely to outweigh any short-run benefits. Those who make the decisions in Russia would appear to agree, as formally asymmetrical arrangements seem to have been diminishing in importance, in contrast to the apparent upward trend in Belgium and, to some extent, in Canada and even Germany.

China started its 'leap to modernity' with essentially a soviet-style fiscal system. In recent years it has, like Russia, moved a long way from its starting point, but unlike Russia, China's changes have been driven largely by economic and not political motives. To the extent that any formal fiscal asymmetry has occurred in China, Chapter 9 shows, first, that it has been related mainly to small minority populations, who in some instances occupy large and important border regions, and second, that it has been diminishing over time. China is unique among the countries included here in the extent to which regional interests cannot be heard openly in the national political arena essentially because no such arena exists. Nonetheless, as in other countries, ethnicity, natural resources and border regions continue to exert some influence on fiscal arrangements in China.

After China, India is the world's most populous country. Unlike China, however, India has an open, vibrant and complex political system, one that history launched with an explicitly asymmetrical fiscal system. Although India's initial asymmetrical arrangements were soon muted, its intergovernmental arrangements continue to reflect the extremely varied conditions of the subcontinent's regions and peoples. As in the case of Spain with its foral system, for example, historical traces remain in, for example, Sikkim's income tax, and as in China, border issues continue to be important. As Chapter 10 emphasizes, however, over the years India's intergovernmental fiscal arrangements have become increasingly discretionary, reflecting political and administrative expediency rather than principled adjustment to differential realities.

Chapter 11 on Indonesia takes a more historical approach than many of the other country chapters, explaining in detail how Indonesia's current system evolved from colonial arrangements (as in India, though quite differently) through a highly centralized period, to more decentralized administration, to its current exploration of slightly more autonomous regional fiscal arrangements. Uniquely among the countries covered here, Indonesia has recently lost part of its territory with the separation of East Timor, something Russia, for example, has long fought with respect to Chechnya. Also as in Russia (as well as Canada and to some extent China), the geographical locations of abundant natural resources have become a critical factor in Indonesia, with the problems being accentuated by ethnic differences in West Papua and Aceh. The result, as in India and the Philippines, has been the recent adoption of some explicitly asymmetrical fiscal arrangements, although some of them are intended to be temporary.

The Philippines, another Pacific island archipelago country, had an even more centralized colonial tradition than Indonesia and one that carried on largely unchanged until a decade or so ago when, as in Indonesia, political unrest in a fragmented part of the country led to the introduction of a formally asymmetrical fiscal system for a newly designated autonomous region. Collier and Hoeffler (2000) argue that secessionist political communities invent themselves when doing so is economically advantageous, for example, when natural resource rents are available for capture. Unlike the situation in Indonesia, however, territorial ethnic and religious differentiation in the Philippines is not accompanied by access to rich natural resources. Perhaps in part for this reason, as Chapter 12 shows, in reality the so-called autonomous region appears in many respects to have less fiscal autonomy than local and regional governments in the rest of the country have achieved in recent years.

Turning finally, to the two most 'broken' countries covered in this volume, Chapter 13 first considers in some detail the Dayton Accords, which established the country of Bosnia and Herzegovina from the wreckage of the former Yugoslavia. Many of the countries considered here—India, Indonesia, the Philippines, Russia—have experienced violent conflicts in some regions. Only in Bosnia and Herzegovina, however, have the warring parties been reconciled, at least in part, by a complete restructuring of the state, in effect, weakening the central authority considerably and bestowing almost complete authority on the component regions. While some structural asymmetry is apparent, in general, the situation in Bosnia and Herzegovina is perhaps better described as one with a high degree of formal asymmetry (full assignment of both revenues and expenditures to regions) with highly asymmetrical outcomes (because of regional differences) virtually unmodified by transfers. Unlike the equalization concerns so prominent in countries like Canada and Germany, in Bosnia and Herzegovina, the principal concern appears to be not so much to uplift the poor as to ensure that as few resources as possible flow from one region to another. The chapter on Indonesia discusses the concept of the 'we': the span of concern for fellow citizens prevailing in the country and its regions. In Bosnia and Herzegovina, the span of concern is ethnically delimited and likely to remain so. Thus the authors' conclusion that the permanence of the current arrangements remains in question is not surprising.

CONCLUDING COMMENTS

One obvious conclusion drawn from the consideration of the many issues discussed in this book is that virtually all 12 countries recognize diversity to some extent in practice (if seldom in law or by means of their constitutions for federal countries) in the way they establish and run their intergovernmental fiscal systems. Such asymmetrical arrangements may in many cases be both economically and politically efficient. An economic analogy might be to something like the Ramsey rule, whereby differential incentives are needed to elicit uniform responses. That is, differentiation may be needed to attain uniform service delivery, if that is the desired objective. As noted earlier, in political terms, differentiation may be needed to uplift the poor or assuage the disaffected sufficiently to maintain political stability. In some instances, of course, asymmetrical treatment may accentuate rather than alleviate tensions, as poor regions feel badly treated or inadequately compensated for some present or past occurrence or rich regions become decreasingly willing to extend what they see as largesse to their less-favoured fellows.

The various case studies in this volume cast varying shades of light on these and many other questions, although none of these studies considers all of these issues. Switzerland offers perhaps the world's best example of decentralized, diverse and (perhaps not coincidentally) direct democracy at work. Its use of federalism as an explicit strategy to deal with a multicultural society may offer a model for such places as Bosnia and Herzegovina. Switzerland's long experience with federalism is currently under renewed strain, however, reflecting both its uncomfortable dependence on immigrant labour and its uneasy place in the new Europe (see also Stauffer 2001, and for a more general perspective, Basta and Fleiner 1996). Canada provides another classic case of an old federal country with much relevant experience in accommodating diversity through fiscal and other policies, although one that is now facing new problems in the context of the North American Free Trade Agreement. It offers an interesting parallel to and contrast with the Swiss case.

Two newer European federations, Belgium and Spain, are also discussed, along with the quite different and considerably more homogeneous case of Germany. Spain has one of the most explicitly asymmetrical constitutions of any federal state (see also Castells 2001; Ruiz Almendar 2002), while Belgium has one of the most complex, incorporating both regional and community differentiation in fiscal and other dimensions. By contrast, Germany is the paradigmatic case of a symmetrical federation, with its strong commitment to consensus and uniform treatment. As Chapter 4 discusses, the great disparities in living standards between states that resulted from reunification put Germany's federal system under considerable strain, because such a system leaves little room for accommodating diversity beyond a modest level. Finally, all three of these countries are members of the EU, and the widened economic opportunities afforded by the EU may to some extent have encouraged exporting regions such as Catalonia to seek greater independence, especially if they are linguistically or in some other way distinct. The same phenomenon has often been noted in Canada with respect to Quebec.

The five studies of developed federal states in this book thus encompass a wide range of experiences, lessons and solutions and strongly reinforce the general message about the importance of diversity. Even though this book does not discuss the founding federation, the United States, no doubt many readers will have a number of its key features in mind when they read about the experiences of other countries (for two earlier comparisons that include the United States, see Bird 1986; Bird and Tarasov 2004). Uniquely among developed federations, the United States, in part perhaps reflecting the huge upheaval of the Civil War in the mid-19th century, stresses bottom-up institutions and judicial oversight rather than regional governments as the critical element in its version of federalism. However, further consideration of possible US parallels to and divergences from the cases discussed here would complicate the already complex task of this book even more.

Similar variety emerges with respect to the developing and transition countries included here. Indonesia offers a postcolonial history of a strongly unified state that is now under great pressure to decentralize. In this case decentralization may threaten to spiral out of control in some regions as has already occurred with respect to East Timor. Indonesia may therefore offer a warning of what many of the other nation states created in the 20th century probably fear the most as a consequence of decentralization, for example, those in Sub-Saharan Africa. The Philippines faces somewhat similar pressures in some areas, but its experience to date demonstrates how reality can diverge from 'labels', as its only avowedly autonomous region is, in practice, less autonomous in most respects than other regions. India, by far the largest federal country in the world, provides a particularly interesting test case of the strengths and limitations of the asymmetrical federal approach.

The two giants of the transitional world offer some further interesting contrasts. Russia is the only formally federal transition state, while China is formally strongly unitary. Both are, however, so large and diverse that considerable economic and fiscal autonomy is inevitable in practice. Both central governments appear to be threatened by such autonomy and take quite different steps to restrain and control it, with China to date clearly being much more successful than Russia in this attempt.

Finally, Bosnia and Herzegovina offers a fascinating test case of the limits to which fiscal ingenuity can be substituted for political consensus. Given its weak central government Bosnia and Herzegovina seems to be an example of subsidiarity supplanting solidarity.

As previous work suggests (Bird 2002), even though relevant universal principles that should be taken into account in designing intergovernmental fiscal arrangements undoubtedly exist, the local context invariably dominates what any particular country can and will do. None of the cases discussed in this book paints either a clear, or often a pretty picture of the workings of fiscal federalism in the different countries. Such, however, is the nature of reality in fragmented societies. Generally applicable answers may be hard to find, but a close reading of the case studies contained in this book will undoubtedly provide considerable food for thought for anyone concerned with decentralization in any country, fragmented or not.

NOTES

1. See, for example, Freire and Stren (2001), who emphasize the importance of municipal government. For constitutional recognition of this fact, see the discussion in Chapter 5 of recent events in Switzerland.
2. Of course, population and territory are not the same thing and have different implications for fiscal federalism. The fact that most extremely large countries in territorial terms are also large in population does not mean that the two categories overlap, for example, consider Australia and Canada as compared with China and Russia.

REFERENCES

Alesina, Alberto, Arnaud Devleeschauwer, William Easterly, Sergio Kurlat, and Romain Wacziarg (2003), 'Fractionalization', Working Paper no. 9411, National Bureau of Economic Research, Cambridge, MA.

Basta, L. and T. Fleiner (eds) (1996), *Federalism and Multiethnic States: The Case of Switzerland,* Fribourg, Switzerland: Institute of Federalism.

Bird, Richard M. (1986), *Fiscal Federalism in Comparative Perspective,* Toronto: Canadian Tax Foundation.

——— (2002), 'Intergovernmental Fiscal Relations: Universal Principles, Local Applications', in M. Govinda Rao (ed.), *Poverty, Development and Fiscal Policy,* New Delhi: Oxford University Press, pp. 192–223.

Bird, Richard M. and Andrey V. Tarasov (2004), 'Closing the Gap: Fiscal Imbalances and Intergovernmental Transfers in Developed Federations', *Environment and Policy C: Government and Policy*, 22 (1), 77–102.

Biro, Anna-Maria and Petra Kovacs (eds) (2001), *Diversity in Action*, Budapest: Open Society Institute.

Castells, Antoni (2001), 'The Role of Intergovernmental Finance in Achieving Diversity and Cohesion: The Case of Spain', *Environment and Policy C: Government and Policy,* 19 (2), 189–206.

Central Intelligence Agency (2005), *World Factbook 2005,* McLean, VA: Office of Public Affairs, available at http://www.cia.gov/cia/publications/factbook/index.html.

Collier, Paul and A. Hoeffler (2000), 'Greed and Grievance in Civil War', Development Research Group Working Paper no. 2355, World Bank, Washington, DC.

Freire, Mila and Richard Stren (eds) (2001), *The Challenge of Urban Government*, Washington, DC: World Bank Institute.

International Monetary Fund (2002), *Government Finance Statistics Yearbook*, Washington, DC.

Kaufmann, Dani, A. Kraay and M. Mastruzzi (2003), *Governance Matters III: Governance Indicators for 1996–2002*, Washington, DC: World Bank.

Martinez-Vazquez, Jorge and Jameson Boex (2001), *Russia's Transition to a New Federalism*, Washington, DC: World Bank.

Ruiz Almendar, Violeta (2002), 'Fiscal Federalism in Spain: The Assignment of Taxation Powers to the Autonomous Communities', *European Taxation*, (November), 467–75.

Stauffer, Thomas (2001), 'Intergovernmental Fiscal Relations in Fragmented Societies: The Case of Switzerland', *Environment and Policy C: Government and Policy*, 19, 207–22.

PART II

Federal Industrial Countries

3. Reconciling Diversity with Equality: The Role of Intergovernmental Fiscal Arrangements in Maintaining an Effective State in Canada

Richard M. Bird and François Vaillancourt*

Many countries contain diverse regions within their boundaries, and regional diversity may influence the nature and effectiveness of public sector activities through many economic and political channels. Few industrial countries offer clearer examples of this phenomenon than Canada. The most important and prominent manifestation of diversity in Canada has been the rise to dominance of a political party advocating secession in the largely francophone province of Quebec, but regional differences and tensions are by no means confined to Quebec. In particular, the rise of the western provinces, particularly Alberta and British Columbia, as separate and important players on Canada's political and economic scene was almost as marked a feature of the last third of the 20th century as the consequences of Quebec's so-called Quiet Revolution since the 1960s. More recently, since about 1990, the key central province of Ontario has also begun to act to some extent differently from Canada as a whole in a way that it has never done before (see Courchene and Telmer 1998 for a detailed discussion). Thus the last half of the 20th century was a turbulent period in Canadian politics. The first part of the 21st century seems unlikely to be calmer, as the continental integration of the Canadian and US economies continues to re-orient Canadians in a north–south rather than east–west direction.

One way that the federal government has attempted to accommodate the rise of Quebec's, and to a much lesser extent western, unrest is through changes in intergovernmental fiscal arrangements. This attempt was relatively successful in the early postwar years, when the cornucopia of funds flowing through Ottawa was easily redirected into provincial coffers, but it became increasingly strained as federal deficits accumulated for more than 20 years after 1974.

*This is a substantially revised and updated version of Bird and Vaillancourt (2001a, b).

Various attempts to reorganize political institutions more directly during this period, such as the Meech Lake Accord and the Charlottetown Agreement, failed. Only towards the end of the century, when federal budgetary prospects improved, was the new Social Union Agreement signed between the federal government and most provinces.[1] Nonetheless, much remains to be done in relation to Canadian fiscal federalism to deal with the problem of financing the welfare state, an issue that is increasingly affecting most modern states

The next section of this chapter looks at the nature and size of the fragmentation problem in Canada, tracing how some of the key dimensions of regional diversity have evolved over the last half-century or so. The chapter then turns to some developments in Canadian fiscal federalism during this period that both reflected and shaped the factors discussed in the previous section. Finally, the chapter attempts to assess whether the intergovernmental fiscal arrangements developed in the last half of the 20th century have helped or hindered the maintenance of an effective state in Canada.

Naturally, the process of federal fiscal evolution did not stop with the new century. Indeed, in some important ways Canada has entered a new and largely unexplored world, and whether Canadian federalism will succeed in adapting as well to the changes of the 21st century as, on the whole, it managed to do in the 20th century remains to be seen. The chapter concludes by suggesting that Canada may require more than changes in fiscal institutions if it is to continue to cope with the problems regional diversity creates for maintaining an effective state in its vast and diverse territory. Money alone seems unlikely to be enough to overcome the underlying problems of political legitimacy that arise at least in part from the tension of maintaining Canada's uniquely strong form of a centralized 'Westminster democracy' in an inherently nonuniform country.

REGIONAL DIVERSITY

Canada is the second largest country in the world, with an area of 10 million square kilometres. This immense and varied territory may be roughly divided into five regions: the Atlantic coastal area, which in turn is divided into four small provinces; the central heartland along the Saint Lawrence River and the upper Great Lakes, which is divided between the huge central provinces of Quebec and Ontario; the great plains, beginning in the province of Manitoba and extending through Saskatchewan to Alberta; the mountain region, which ends on the coast of British Columbia; and the great northern expanse, which extends from the northern sectors of most provinces (except the three small Maritime provinces of New Brunswick, Nova Scotia, and Prince Edward Island) into the treeless reaches of the three sparsely populated northern territories of Yukon, the Northwest Territories, and Nunavut (Figure 3.1).

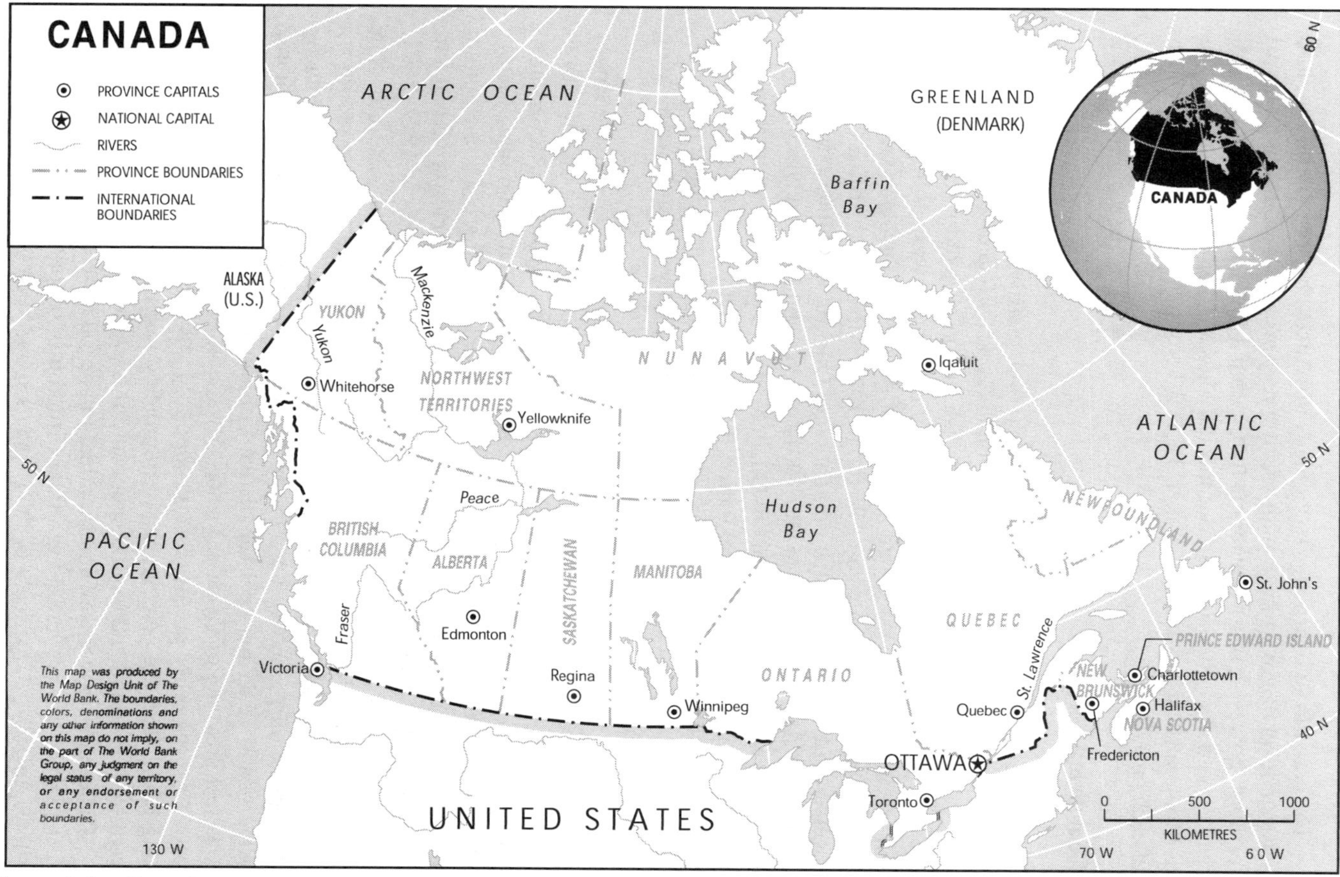

Figure 3.1 *Canada*

The constitution formally recognizes provinces, but not territories, as a separate level of government with specific responsibilities. Despite their vast territory, however, most Canadians live within a few hundred kilometres of the US border and in urban areas, especially in such major metropolitan areas as Montreal, Toronto and Vancouver. Table 3.1 summarizes some key features of each province.

Demographic Factors

Table 3.2 shows the changes in population distribution among the ten provinces from 1926 to 2001.[2] Even though Canada's population grew significantly from 1926 to 1951, its regional distribution changed little. In contrast, the even greater growth in the latter half of the century was accompanied by a major shift in population, with the biggest gainers by far being Ontario and British Columbia, followed by Alberta. In 1926, Alberta and British Columbia together had less than half the population of Quebec, and Ontario was only a fifth larger than its neighbour. By 2001, Alberta and British Columbia were home to almost as many people as Quebec, while Ontario had more than one-and-a-half times Quebec's population. In relative terms, however, Quebec's population share declined only marginally, with the four Atlantic provinces and the western provinces of Manitoba, and especially Saskatchewan, being the big losers.

Changes in relative population can result from demographic changes (births and deaths) or from migration. There are no significant differences in provincial death rates. Birth rates were somewhat higher in Quebec until 1961, but thereafter fell below the national average, so demographic factors play some role in explaining that province's declining share. On the whole, however, the key factor has clearly been migration, both interprovincial and international. According to data from Statistics Canada, during 1972–2001, Ontario, Alberta and British Columbia, the provinces that had gained most in terms of the relative share of population, were also three of the four provinces that gained, on balance, from interprovincial migration, with the percentages of population gained being 1.05 per cent for Ontario, 10.95 per cent for Alberta and 12.41 per cent for British Columbia. (The other gainer was the smallest province of Canada, Prince Edward Island, with a gain of 4.03 per cent.) All the other provinces lost population as a result of interprovincial migration, with the percentages of population lost ranging from –20.38 per cent for Newfoundland to –0.09 per cent for Nova Scotia.

Differential patterns of international migration have also been important. Canada has always had a significant immigrant population. As Table 3.3 shows, in 1931, 22 per cent of the population had been born abroad, with the proportion of immigrants being highest in the western provinces. In the latter

Table 3.1 Key features of Canada's provinces and territories, 2001

Feature	Canada	Newfoundland	Prince Edward Island	Nova Scotia	New Brunswick	Quebec	Ontario	Manitoba	Saskatchewan	Alberta	Britsh Columbia	Yukon	Northwest Territories	Nunavut
Area (square kilometres)	9 984 670	405 212	5660	55 284	72 908	1 542 056	1 076 395	647 797	651 036	661 848	944 735	482 443	1 346 106	2 093 190
Population (thousands)	31 082	534	139	943	757	7411	11 873	1150	1016	3064	4096	30	41	28
Population density (people/square kilometre)	3.2	1.3	24.6	17.1	10.4	4.8	11.0	1.8	1.6	4.6	4.3	0.1	Sparse	Sparse
GDP (Can$ hundred thousands)	1 085 141	13 916	3423	24 917	20 211	228 516	440 051	35 084	33 059	150 284	130 396	1131	2920	912
GDP per capita (Can $)	34 912	26 060	24 626	26 423	26 699	30 835	37 063	30 508	32 538	49 048	31 835	37 700	71 219	32 571
Percentage of area	100	4.1	0.1	0.6	0.7	15.5	10.7	6.5	6.5	6.6	9.5	4.8	13.4	21.0
Percentage of population	100	1.7	0.4	3.0	2.4	23.8	38.2	3.7	3.3	9.9	13.2	0.001	0.001	0.001
Percentage of GDP	100	1.3	0.3	2.3	1.9	21.1	40.6	3.2	3.0	13.8	12.0	0.1	0.3	0.1

GDP Gross domestic product

Source: Statistics Canada data.

Table 3.2 Population by province, selected years

Province	1926 Number (thousands)	1926 Share (%)	1951 Number (thousands)	1951 Share (%)	1961 Number (thousands)	1961 Share (%)	1971 Number (thousands)	1971 Share (%)	1981 Number (thousands)	1981 Share (%)	1991 Number (thousands)	1991 Share (%)	1996 Number (thousands)	1996 Share (%)	2001 Number (thousands)	2001 Share (%)
Newfoundland	n.a.	n.a.	361	2.6	458	2.5	533	2.4	576	2.3	580	2.1	561	1.9	534	1.7
Prince Edward Island	87	0.9	98	0.7	105	0.6	113	0.5	124	0.5	131	0.5	136	0.5	139	0.4
Nova Scotia	515	5.4	643	4.6	737	4.0	799	3.6	856	3.4	918	3.3	931	3.1	943	3.0
New Brunswick	396	4.2	516	3.7	598	3.3	644	2.9	708	2.8	749	2.7	753	2.5	757	2.4
Quebec	2603	27.5	4056	29.0	5259	28.8	6156	27.9	6569	26.4	7081	25.2	7274	24.5	7411	23.8
Ontario	3164	33.5	4598	32.8	6236	34.2	7868	35.7	8839	35.5	10 471	37.2	11 101	37.4	11 873	38.2
Manitoba	639	6.8	776	5.5	922	5.1	1001	4.5	1038	4.2	1113	4.0	1134	3.8	1150	3.7
Saskatchewan	821	8.7	832	5.9	925	5.1	934	4.2	978	3.9	1006	3.6	1019	3.4	1016	3.3
Alberta	608	6.4	939	6.7	1332	7.3	1672	7.6	2304	9.3	2601	9.2	2781	9.4	3064	9.9
British Columbia	606	6.4	1165	8.3	1629	8.9	2250	10.2	2836	11.4	3380	12.0	3882	13.1	4096	13.2
Canada	9451	100.0	14 009	100.0	18 238	100.0	22 026	100.0	24 900	100.0	28 120	100.0	29 672	100.0	31 082	100.0

n.a. Not applicable.

Sources: Statistics Canada data.

Table 3.3 Shares of foreign born population, selected years (per cent)

	Share of population foreign born			Share of Canada's total foreign born population		
Province	1931	1961	2001	1931	1961	2001
Newfoundland	n.a.	1.4	1.5	n.a.	0.2	0.1
Prince Edward Island	3.2	2.9	3.0	0.1	0.1	0.1
Nova Scotia	8.2	4.6	4.4	2.1	1.3	0.8
New Brunswick	6.0	3.9	3.0	1.2	0.9	0.4
Quebec	8.8	7.4	9.5	11.5	14.6	13.0
Ontario	23.4	21.7	25.5	37.0	50.7	55.6
Manitoba	33.8	18.4	11.6	10.8	6.4	2.5
Saskatchewan	34.6	16.1	4.7	14.2	5.6	0.9
Alberta	41.8	21.7	14.3	12.7	10.8	8.0
British Columbia	46.0	26.0	24.7	6.7	9.5	18.5
Canada	22.2	15.6	17.5	100.0	100.0	100.0

Note: The sum of the provincial share differs from 100 per cent because territories are included in the total but not accounted for here.
n.a. Not applicable.

Source: Census data.

part of the century, however, even though the immigrant population as a whole remained high, the Prairie provinces lost their attractiveness and relatively more immigrants settled in Ontario and British Columbia, particularly in the urban areas of Toronto and Vancouver.[3]

These changes in population size and shares were accompanied by significant changes in population composition. As in most of the western world, Canada's population has aged, with the proportion older than 65 increasing from 5.6 per cent in 1931 to 7.6 per cent in 1961 and 13 per cent in 2001. Because immigrant populations tend to be younger, however, this aging effect has been less apparent in the more rapidly growing provinces such as Ontario than in those that have expanded more slowly, notably Quebec, where the effects have been exacerbated by the fall in the birth rate. Marked changes also occurred in the ethnic and linguistic composition of provincial populations during the last half of the 20th century. Two particular aspects of these changes deserve special attention here.

The first, and politically by far the most important aspect, is language, which in Canada is now normally defined in terms of mother tongue, that is, the language first learned and still understood at the time of the census.[4] The most important distinction has traditionally been that between English speakers and French speakers (anglophones and francophones), but the continuing importance of immigrants means that a third and important category exists, namely, the so-called allophones, who may have any of dozens of other languages as their mother tongue. Table 3.4 shows that, as might be expected, allophones are most important in the provinces with the largest immigrant populations and have recently become much more important in Canada's largest province, Ontario. The table also clearly shows that francophones are a majority only in Quebec, where about three-quarters of all Canada's francophone population live, constituting about four-fifths of the province's population. Even though more than 2 million francophones live outside Quebec, they constitute a substantial proportion of the population only in neighbouring New Brunswick. In absolute numbers, however, by far the most important francophone population outside Quebec is in Ontario, although they account for less than 5 per cent of the population and are much less numerous than the province's allophone population.

Outside Quebec, and to a lesser extent northern New Brunswick, the francophone share of the population has been reduced in part as a result of linguistic assimilation, just as most allophones have in time joined the majority anglophone population in the provinces that have received the most immigrants. The assimilation rate (the proportion of those whose mother tongue is French that no longer report French as the household language most often used) of francophones in 2001 ranged from 75 per cent in British Columbia to 40 per cent in Ontario and 9 per cent in New Brunswick, with an average value of 38 per cent outside Quebec.

A second ethnic dimension of Canada's population that has become increasingly important in recent years relates to the aboriginal population. Even though Canada has fewer than a million people with aboriginal status, they are, as Table 3.5 shows, heavily concentrated in the western provinces of Manitoba and Saskatchewan, the same provinces that have generally lost population share in recent years. In all provinces, the aboriginal people are, as a rule, a low-income group, in part because of the unpromising parts of the country to which they moved, voluntarily or otherwise, as European settlement expanded. Moreover, they are constitutionally a federal responsibility, and are thus heavily dependent on federal support for their subsistence, health and education. Indeed, in recent years such support has been the most rapidly expanding component of federal program spending (Waslander 1997).

Economic Factors

Gross domestic product (GDP) per capita provides a useful indication of the level of economic activity within different regions, while personal income per

Table 3.4 Provincial populations by mother tongue, selected years (per cent)

	1931			1961			2001		
Province	Anglo-phone	Franco-phone	Allo-phone	Anglo-phone	Franco-phone	Allo-phone	Anglo-phone	Franco-phone	Allo-phone
Newfoundland	n.a.	n.a.	n.a.	98.6	0.7	0.7	98.5	0.4	1.1
Prince Edward Island	86.6	11.3	2.1	91.3	7.6	1.1	94.2	4.3	1.5
Nova Scotia	84.1	7.7	8.2	92.3	5.4	2.3	93.2	3.8	3.0
New Brunswick	68.1	30.3	1.6	63.3	35.2	1.5	65.4	32.9	1.7
Quebec	16.4	77.8	5.8	13.3	81.2	5.5	8.8	81.2	10.0
Ontario	81.9	6.4	11.7	77.5	6.8	15.7	71.9	4.4	23.7
Manitoba	58.2	5.7	36.1	63.4	6.6	30.0	76.1	4.1	19.9
Saskatchewan	56.4	4.5	39.1	69.0	3.9	27.1	85.9	1.9	12.2
Alberta	63.1	3.8	33.1	72.2	3.2	24.6	82.0	2.0	16.0
British Columbia	75.8	1.2	23.0	80.9	1.6	17.5	74.3	1.5	24.3
Canada	58.5	25.6	15.9	58.5	28.1	13.4	59.7	22.7	17.3

n.a. Not applicable.

Sources: 1931 and 1961: Marmen and Corbeil (1999, Table A-1); 2001: Census data.

Table 3.5 Share of aboriginal population by province, 2001

Province	Aboriginal share of national population	Aboriginal share of provincial population
Newfoundland	1.92	3.70
Prince Edward Island	0.14	1.01
Nova Scotia	1.74	1.90
New Brunswick	1.74	2.36
Quebec	8.13	1.11
Ontario	19.29	1.67
Manitoba	15.37	13.60
Saskatchewan	13.33	13.50
Alberta	16.00	5.31
British Columbia	17.42	4.39
Canada	100.00	3.29

Note: The sum of the provincial share differs from 100 per cent because territories are included in the total but not accounted for here.

Source: 2001 Census data.

capita provides a measure of the standard of living enjoyed by the inhabitants of those regions. Unfortunately, while provincial personal income data are available since 1926, provincial GDP data are available only since 1961. Table 3.6 depicts trends in per capita provincial income from 1926 to 2001. The most important conclusion to emerge from this table is that regional incomes converged significantly during the 20th century (see Coulombe 1999 for a summary of recent empirical evidence in this area). In 1926, per capita incomes in the richest province (British Columbia) were 2.2 times that in the poorest (Prince Edward Island). By 2000, this ratio had decreased to 1.4, with Alberta being the richest province and Newfoundland being the poorest.

Since the 1950s, incomes in the poorer Atlantic provinces have steadily improved relative to the national average. The extent to which incomes in the Prairie provinces are affected by agricultural conditions is also evident from Table 3.6, with Manitoba and Saskatchewan changing from relatively rich to relatively poor over the period. Alberta would probably have suffered the same fate had it not been for the discovery and development of substantial oil reserves beginning in the late 1940s. These reserves make Canada self-sufficient overall, with exports from western Canada to the United Sates counterbalancing imports to eastern Canada. Alberta now accounts for more than 80 per cent of Canada's petroleum and natural gas production, and in 1996 this sector accounted for 27 per cent of the province's GDP. While

Table 3.6 Per capita income by province, selected years (ratio to the mean for Canada as a whole)

Province	1926	1931	1941	1951	1961	1971	1981	1991	2001
Newfoundland	n.a.	n.a.	n.a.	0.48	0.60	0.64	0.69	0.78	0.79
Prince Edward Island	0.56	0.51	0.47	0.55	0.60	0.62	0.69	0.78	0.81
Nova Scotia	0.68	0.76	0.78	0.69	0.77	0.76	0.80	0.85	0.88
New Brunswick	0.65	0.67	0.64	0.67	0.67	0.72	0.74	0.80	0.87
Quebec	0.65	0.95	0.87	0.84	0.90	0.90	0.93	0.95	0.93
Ontario	0.85	1.28	1.29	1.18	1.18	1.17	1.04	1.09	1.08
Manitoba	1.14	0.91	0.93	1.01	0.94	0.93	0.91	0.89	0.93
Saskatchewan	1.08	0.45	0.59	1.08	0.72	0.79	0.98	0.83	0.85
Alberta	1.14	0.78	0.80	1.11	1.00	0.96	1.16	1.02	1.10
British Columbia	1.22	1.30	1.21	1.19	1.15	1.06	1.12	1.03	0.96
Canada (mean, Can$)	429	354	516	1210	1676	3418	11 776	21 549	27 756

n.a. Not applicable.

Sources: Statistics Canada data.

British Columbia was the richest province in 1926 using personal income, its relative income converged to the mean over the period, while both Ontario, and especially Quebec, improved their relative positions considerably during 1926–2001 as a whole, with Quebec continuing to improve even after 1971, when Ontario began to lose ground.

This marked convergence in income levels across the provinces reflects two quite different forces: the market and government policy. The latter is discussed in the next section. With respect to the former, Table 3.7 shows that at least after 1961, provincial per capita GDP levels also converged substantially, although not nearly to the same extent as personal incomes. In 1961, for example, the ratio of per capita personal incomes in the richest province (Ontario) to the poorest (Newfoundland) was 1.97, compared with only 1.33 in 1996. In contrast, the equivalent ratios in terms of per capita GDP were higher and decreased less, from 2.39 in 1961 to 1.97 in 2001, with Alberta being the richest province in these terms in the latter year and Prince Edward Island the poorest.

Another striking feature of the GDP data compared with the personal income data is the relative trend in the two key central provinces of Ontario and Quebec. As already mentioned, during 1961–96, per capita incomes converged significantly in these provinces: in 1961, the average per capita income in Ontario was 31 per cent higher than that in Quebec, but by 1996 it was only 10 per cent higher. Per capita GDP also converged in these provinces, but much less dramatically. In 1961, Ontario's per capita GDP was 33 per cent above that in Quebec, that is, the differential was approximately the same as for personal income. Even though the difference declined over the next few decades, Ontario was still 20 per cent above Quebec's level in 2001.

An important determinant of convergence between regions (or countries) can be the mobility of goods and services (trade), of capital (financial and physical) and of individuals (labour). Canada is not, and never has been, an internal common market. Provincial governments play an important role in both labour and capital markets and can and do erect various barriers to factor mobility (for an extensive, albeit somewhat outdated, treatment of this issue, see Trebilcock 1983). The following are specific aspects of provincial policies:

- With respect to the capital market, Canada does not have a national securities commission but ten provincial commissions, of which four (Alberta, British Columbia, Ontario and Quebec) are active and supervise Canada's four stock exchanges.[5]
- A number of provinces offer special tax incentives to residents who purchase financial instruments (such as shares) from issuers who are active or will invest in their province of residence, following the pattern

Table 3.7 GDP per capita by province, selected years

	1961		1971		1981		1991		2001	
Province	Can$	Ratio	Can$	Ratio	Can$	Ratio	Can$	Ratio	Can$	Ratio
Newfoundland	1118	50.2	2450	56.0	8411	58.8	15 783	65.8	26 060	74.6
Prince Edward Island	1095	49.2	2274	52.0	8000	56.0	16 550	69.0	24 626	70.5
Nova Scotia	1453	65.3	2986	68.2	9027	63.1	18 949	79.0	26 423	75.7
New Brunswick	1339	60.2	2831	64.7	8725	61.0	18 015	75.1	26 699	76.4
Quebec	2017	90.6	3943	90.1	12 176	85.2	21 887	91.2	30 835	88.4
Ontario	2674	120.2	5157	117.8	14 705	102.9	26 497	110.4	37 063	106.2
Manitoba	2003	90.0	3933	89.8	12 612	88.2	20 522	85.5	30 508	87.3
Saskatchewan	1735	78.0	3694	84.4	15 211	106.4	20 606	85.9	32 538	93.2
Alberta	2420	108.7	4657	106.4	22 473	157.2	27 497	114.6	49 048	140.5
British Columbia	2480	111.4	4600	105.1	15 591	109.1	24 066	100.3	31 835	91.2
Canada	2225	100.0	4378	100.0	14 297	100.0	23 996	100.0	34 912	100.0

Note: The ratio is calculated as (provincial GDP per capita/Canadian GDP per capita) x 100.

Source: Statistics Canada data.

initially set by the Quebec Stock Savings Plan introduced in 1979 and the first Labour Sponsored Venture Capital Fund created in 1983 (Vaillancourt 1997).

- Provincial policies can also significantly affect labour markets. For example, because provinces are responsible for postsecondary education, they can levy differential tuition fees on out-of-province students. Again, Quebec is the only province to do so at present.
- As the provinces are responsible for regulating and accrediting professions and some occupational trades, they can impose different standards. Quebec, for example, requires all professionals not schooled in French to pass a French language test before they can be licensed. At times interprovincial wrangles about employment have arisen, for instance, with respect to the relative freedom with which construction trades workers from Quebec and Ontario can work in the other province. Newfoundland gives priority to Newfoundland firms and workers in the offshore oil industry.
- Even with respect to trade in goods and services, observers have voiced some concerns about provincial procurement policies favouring in-province suppliers.

In an attempt to address some of these issues, in July 1995, the provinces and territories signed the Agreement on Internal Trade (AIT), whose aims are to reduce existing barriers, prevent the creation of new ones and harmonize standards.[6] The AIT is based on six general rules: nondiscrimination, right of entry and exit, no obstacles, legitimate objectives, reconciliation and transparency. Both the importance and impact of the AIT are debatable, however, for several reasons.

For example, few goods and services were subject to interprovincial trade barriers before the AIT and the proportion of the labour force in occupations subject to restrictions is small. The only notable changes since the AIT have been the use of open tendering with no place of business clause by provincial governments in 1995, extended to the important municipal, academic, schools and hospitals sector in 1999, although with British Columbia and Yukon not agreeing. Little has changed in the areas of public enterprise procurement, energy trade, processing of natural resources or transportation. Schwanen (2000) sums up by saying that 'some of the oldest of interprovincial barriers have so far survived the AIT very well' (p. 52). Indeed, a 1999 court decision in Quebec that upheld the rights of that province to impose margarine colouring rules different from those in the rest of Canada explicitly states that the agreement is a political and not a legal one.[7] The court concluded that Quebec was therefore free to renege on its signature at no cost.

Thus even though Schwanen (2000) praises the AIT's dispute settlement mechanisms, in particular, their accessibility by individuals and firms, and the Code of Conduct on Incentives, his comment that 'a new impetus is needed if the Agreement is to better realize its objectives' (p. 54) is not surprising. One issue is who should provide any such impetus: the federal government using its exclusive constitutional powers in relation to trade and commerce, the provincial governments or both? If this is not addressed, other agreements may replace the AIT. For example, while the AIT calls for labour mobility, not much has happened as a result. However, the 1999 Social Union Agreement (which Quebec did not sign) set a deadline of 1 July 2001 for implementing the AIT's provisions with respect to labour mobility.[8]

Despite such minor obstacles to mobility, people do move about a lot within Canada and, for the most part, as economic incentives would suggest, they move from poorer to richer areas. Two aspects of internal migration deserve special mention. First, the existence of large-scale public programs that to some extent sever the connection between market-generated output and personal income has reduced the level of interprovincial migration and has led, in particular, to the retention of larger populations in the poorer regions, notably the Atlantic provinces, than would otherwise have been the case.[9]

Second, language affects migration. The out-migration of some anglophones from Quebec following the activities (bombings, kidnappings) of the Front for the Liberation of Quebec in 1966–70 and the election of the first Quebecois Party (the secessionist party) government in November 1976 was important. Net interprovincial migration was –18 544 from 1 July 1968 through 30 June 1969 and rose to –35 813 in 1969–70. It fell to as low as –10 389 in 1975–76 but rose sharply to –45 748 in 1977–78. More important, however, is that Quebec francophones, most of whom are unilingual, are much less likely to migrate to the rest of Canada—to them a 'foreign' country—than are anglophones or allophones. During 1966–86, the out-migration rate of Quebec anglophones was about 15 times higher than for francophones (Vaillancourt 1992).

This has two important consequences. The first is that policies redistributing income regionally would, in principle, seem to be more important to people in Quebec than to those in other provinces, because the latter have more and less costly opportunities to move.[10] The second, and more politically prominent, consequence is that, for the same reason, the economic consequences of Quebec's policies matter more to Quebec residents than is true in other provinces, that is, francophone Quebec residents are to a considerable extent a captive audience. Quebec thus is not, and cannot be, a province *comme les autres*.

FISCAL MECHANISMS FOR DEALING WITH DIVERSITY

We have mentioned some of the regulatory devices that Canada has used to differentiate provinces by enabling provincial governments to act independently in what they consider to be the interests of their constituents. Over the years Canada has employed many other mechanisms, notably fiscal, at both the federal and provincial levels to try to manage or accommodate diversity. This section will first discuss policies that explicitly reduce interregional income disparities and then turn to policies that have specifically affected the two main outlier provinces, namely, Alberta and Quebec.

Transfers

Provinces are constitutionally able to tax anything they want except international and interprovincial trade. Indeed, they raise most of their considerable resources from the same sources as the federal government, that is, taxes on income and sales. Of course, as noted earlier, provincial tax bases vary widely, as indicated roughly by the differences in per capita GDP shown in Table 3.7.[11] Therefore corresponding differences exist in provinces' capacity to finance public services out of their own resources.

Even though this problem was first formally recognized in 1938 by the Rowell-Sirois Report, nothing was explicitly done about it until the 1950s, when the first important federal-provincial transfer programs were established. Over the years these transfers have been simplified to the point where at present there are essentially only two: the Canada Health and Social Transfer and the equalization transfer. In 2004–05, the Canada Health and Social Transfer is expected to account for 77 per cent of federal transfers to provinces and the equalization transfer for another 19 per cent.[12] Essentially, these major transfers are largely unconditional in the sense that provinces can spend them as they see fit. In recent years, however, as the federal government has increasingly provided special additional funding for health, it has stipulated that these funds should indeed be spent on health. Moving still further in this direction, as of April 2004, health finance has recently been separated from other 'social' transfers, and a new Canada Health Transfer has been created with additional stipulations with respect to both how some of the new funding can be spent and to provincial reporting of such expenditures. However, if these recent developments are a reversal of the long-term trend noted earlier or an exception to it is not yet clear.[13]

Table 3.8 depicts the changing importance of transfers over the last four decades, singling out the equalization transfer. Equalization, which is essentially intended to enable all provinces to provide a comparable level of services while imposing a comparable tax effect, as mandated by the 1982

Table 3.8 Equalization and total transfers by province, selected years

Province	1961			1971			1981			1991			1996			2001		
	Total (Can$ hundred thousands)	Per capita (Can$)	Provincial shares (%)	Total (Can$ hundred thousands)	Per capita (Can$)	Provincial shares (%)	Total (Can$ hundred thousands)	Per capita (Can$)	Provincial shares (%)	Total (Can$ hundred thousands)	Per capita (Can$)	Provincial shares (%)	Total (Can$ hundred thousands)	Per capita (Can$)	Provincial shares (%)	Total (Can$ hundred thousands)	Per capita (Can$)	Provincial shares (%)
Equalization																		
Newfoundland	11.2	24.45	6.8	120.6	226.27	11.5	466.6	810.07	10.4	910.4	1569.66	11.3	967.0	1696.49	11.0	1163	2177.9	12.2
Prince Edward Island	2.8	26.67	1.7	23.2	205.31	2.20	111.5	899.19	2.5	179.0	1366.41	2.2	196.4	1433.58	2.2	275	1978.4	2.9
Nova Scotia	18.2	24.69	11.1	93.8	117.40	8.9	554.6	647.90	12.4	960.2	1045.97	11.9	1147.9	1218.58	13.1	1394	1478.3	14.6
New Brunswick	16.0	26.76	9.7	97.2	150.93	9.2	437.7	618.22	9.8	810.0	1081.44	10.0	931.6	1224.18	10.6	1217	1607.7	12.8
Quebec	62.6	11.90	38.0	543.6	88.30	51.6	2399.6	365.29	53.6	3547.0	500.92	43.9	4074.9	550.96	46.3	5615	757.7	59.0
Ontario	n.a.	n.a.	n.a.	n.a.	n.a.	n.a.	n.a.	n.a.	n.a.	n.a.	n.a.	n.a.	n.a.	n.a.	n.a.	n.a.	n.a.	n.a.
Manitoba	11.9	12.91	7.2	58.6	58.54	5.6	404.6	389.79	9.0	1046.6	940.34	13.0	1054.8	927.70	12.0	1306	1135.7	13.7
Saskatchewan	21.2	22.92	12.9	115.6	123.77	11.0	103.7	106.03	2.3	622.0	618.29	7.7	423.3	416.22	4.8	377	371.1	4.0
Alberta	14.9	11.19	9.0	n.a.	n.a.	n.a.	n.a.	n.a.	n.a.	n.a.	n.a.	n.a.	n.a.	n.a.	n.a.	n.a.	n.a.	n.a.
British Columbia	5.9	3.62	3.6	n.a.	n.a.	n.a.	n.a.	n.a.	n.a.	n.a.	n.a.	n.a.	n.a.	n.a.	n.a.	n.a.	n.a.	n.a.
Canada	164.7	9.03	100.0	1052.5	47.78	100.0	4478.2	179.85	100.0	8075.1	287.17	100.0	8795.7	293.59	100.0	9522	306.4	100.0
Total transfers																		
Newfoundland	58.9	128.60	5.1	239.4	449.16	5.6	774.0	1343.75	5.4	1439	2481.03	5.2	1586	2874.27	5.1	1770	3450.76	5.6
Prince Edward Island	12.2	116.19	1.1	52.8	467.26	1.2	190.5	1536.29	1.3	320	2442.75	1.2	317	2355.88	1.0	397	2934.35	1.3
Nova Scotia	67.8	91.99	5.9	229.3	286.98	5.4	971.6	1135.05	6.8	1660	1808.28	6.0	2000	2199.54	6.4	2075	2285.22	6.5
New Brunswick	58.0	96.99	5.0	223.0	346.27	5.2	815.4	1151.69	5.7	1495	1995.99	5.4	1618	2192.02	5.2	1904	2610.01	6.0
Quebec	237.4	45.14	20.7	1288.7	209.34	30.3	4429.5	674.30	30.9	7410	1046.46	27.0	9047	1267.3	28.8	9634	1331.13	30.4
Ontario	313.0	50.19	27.2	1105.5	140.51	26.0	3137.5	354.96	21.9	6116	584.09	22.3	8034	747.1	25.6	6360	557.4	20.1
Manitoba	73.4	79.61	6.4	231.5	231.27	5.4	835.4	804.82	5.8	1833	1646.9	6.7	1985	1782.03	6.3	2022	1806.03	6.4
Saskatchewan	72.8	78.70	6.3	253.4	271.31	6.0	567.7	580.47	4.0	1508	1499.01	5.5	1039	1049.24	3.3	1039	1061.36	3.3
Alberta	103.8	77.93	9.0	272.6	163.04	6.4	896.7	389.19	2.7	2369	910.8	8.6	1750	648.91	5.6	1755	589.95	5.5
British Columbia	149.4	91.71	13.0	288.5	128.22	6.8	1129.5	398.27	2.8	2071	612.72	7.5	2483	666.67	7.9	3156	807.63	10.0
Canada	1149.0	63.00	100.0	4252.2	193.05	100.0	14 340.6	575.93	100.0	27 482	977.31	100.0	31 388	1088.09	100.0	31 716	1056.95	100.0

n.a. Not applicable.

Sources: Canadian Tax Foundation (2002); Perry (1997); census data; Statistics Canada data.

constitution, is naturally much larger in per capita terms in the poorer Atlantic provinces than in the other recipient provinces (currently Manitoba, Quebec and Saskatchewan), although in absolute terms by far the largest share flows to Quebec. While a similar relationship holds for total transfers, it is less marked because the Canada Health and Social Transfer, like its main predecessors, is paid on an equal per capita basis to all provinces.[14] While still interregionally redistributive, the result is that while Quebec still receives the largest transfer share of any province and the Atlantic provinces remain by far the largest winners in per capita terms, Ontario has also been a large transfer recipient in recent years. Nonetheless, as Table 3.9 shows, in 2001, federal transfers accounted for only 9.2 per cent of provincial revenue in Ontario (and even less in Alberta), compared with 16.4 per cent in Quebec and as much as 41.6 per cent in Newfoundland.

A second important component of differential federal payments to different provinces takes an alternative form: the federal government makes the major transfers to individual. Income-tested child benefits (through the tax system) and, in particular, universal old-age pensions, are paid federally, while a major public sector pension system based on payroll tax funding is formally a joint federal-provincial responsibility with two independent programs, one in Quebec by the Quebec Pension Board and one in the rest of the country by the Canada Pension Plan. While none of these programs have any explicit regional differentials, clearly those parts of the country with, for example, relatively more older inhabitants, such as the Atlantic and Prairie provinces, will be net fiscal gainers from such programs.

This feature is even more obvious with respect to the federal unemployment insurance program, euphemistically renamed employment insurance a few years ago. Like the Canada Pension Plan/Quebec Pension Board program, employment insurance is funded by payroll taxes, so the degree of self-funding of benefits by workers in different provinces will vary with both the level of insurable unemployment and the level of taxable wages in the province. Poor provinces with high unemployment will fund relatively smaller shares of the benefits paid than rich provinces with high wages. In 1996–97, for example, Newfoundland received Can$543 net per capita in regionally sensitive unemployment benefits (the difference between benefits received and contributions paid), while Ontario paid Can$74 per capita more than it received (Boothe 1998).

Several important features of Canada's employment insurance account for these results. These features specifically favour certain seasonal industries, such as forestry, and especially fishing, that have strong regional impacts. No similar special provisions are in effect for the equally seasonal agriculture that is the mainstay of the Prairie provinces (other than Alberta), though a look beyond the scope of the employment insurance act indicates that some special

Table 3.9 Total and transfer revenues by province, selected years

Province	1961			1971			1981			1991			2001		
	Total (current Can$ hundred thousands)	Transfer (current Can$ hundred thousands)	Transfer/total (%)	Total (current Can$ hundred thousands)	Transfer (current Can$ hundred thousands)	Transfer/total (%)	Total (current Can$ hundred thousands)	Transfer (current Can$ hundred thousands)	Transfer/total (%)	Total (current Can$ hundred thousands)	Transfer (current Can$ hundred thousands)	Transfer/total (%)	Total (current Can$ hundred thousands)	Transfer (current Can$ hundred thousands)	Transfer/total (%)
Newfoundland	92	58	63.0	417	244	58.5	1542	746	48.4	3196	1412	44.2	4346	1808	41.6
Prince Edward Island	20	12	60.0	89	53	59.6	340	178	52.4	713	304	42.6	1044	400	38.3
Nova Scotia	133	69	51.9	496	228	46.0	1957	922	47.1	4245	1,583	37.3	6522	2196	33.7
New Brunswick	114	57	50.0	477	231	48.4	1750	779	44.5	3906	1414	36.2	5715	1927	33.7
Quebec	878	208	23.7	4407	1288	29.2	18 930	4354	23.0	39 033	6909	17.7	60 205	9888	16.4
Ontario	1172	304	25.9	5565	1087	19.5	18 428	3215	17.4	43 559	6347	14.6	74 313	6830	9.2
Manitoba	163	73	44.8	689	241	35.0	2450	829	33.8	5948	1892	31.8	8686	2070	23.8
Saskatchewan	209	73	34.9	637	239	37.5	2902	550	19.0	5602	1621	28.9	7764	1138	14.7
Alberta	296	107	36.1	1202	273	22.7	10 569	838	7.9	14 444	1974	13.7	30 240	1885	6.2
British Columbia	424	147	34.7	1535	326	21.2	7205	1134	15.7	16 439	1994	12.1	29 789	3325	11.2
Canada	3506	1110	31.7	15 591	4274	27.4	66 603	13 955	21.0	138 693	26 789	19.3	230 462	33 073	14.4

Source: Statistics Canada data.

help for these provinces exists in the form of various crop insurance and stabilization schemes. To paraphrase Ecclesiastes, it seems that that for every region there is a program.[15]

Taxes

As noted earlier, provinces have access to most tax fields. They can set their own base and rates and, if they wish, collect their taxes themselves. Table 3.10 shows that significant differences exist with respect to most taxes, with tax rates sometimes, but not always, being higher in the poorer provinces.

Total (federal + provincial) personal income tax rates at higher income levels, for instance, are 25 per cent higher in Newfoundland than in Alberta. Quebec's own personal tax rates are the highest, but this is offset somewhat by the lower federal rates in Quebec than elsewhere. Currently the federal government collects personal income taxes for all provinces except Quebec, which collects its own personal income tax on its own tax base, although the differences from the federal system are relatively small except in the treatment of children. Until 2000, the nine other provinces levied their personal income taxes as a percentage of the federal tax. Since 2001, their personal income taxes are levied as a tax on income using the federal taxable income as the base.

One consequence of this change was that some provinces changed their tax rates from those used previously, for example, both Manitoba and British Columbia reduced the middle bracket rate of their three-bracket structure. More important, Alberta imposed a flat rate tax of 10 per cent on personal income. Because the previous system of a flat rate surtax on the federal tax was in effect progressive (and indeed accentuated the progressivity of the underlying federal rate structure), the new Alberta system constitutes a major change in provincial tax policy. Although this change is within the spirit of the Tax Collection Agreement in that it uses the federal definition of income, the degree of harmonization of provincial personal income taxation is less now than it was before 2000.

The federal government also collects corporate income taxes for all provinces except Ontario, Quebec and Alberta. Table 3.10 shows that provincial rates vary considerably, with both the second highest and the lowest rates found in neighbouring Atlantic provinces, and with Quebec having by far the lowest rate among the major provinces. Provinces also impose different rates on small and nonmanufacturing businesses, with the differences between these different categories varying from province to province. (For recent discussions of provincial business taxes, see Bird and McKenzie 2001; Chen and Mintz 2003.)

All the provinces except Alberta impose sales taxes. In New Brunswick, Nova Scotia and Newfoundland, the federal government collects a harmonized

Table 3.10 Main features of provincial taxes, 2002

	Provincial personal income tax brackets			Federal and provincial personal income tax[a]		Corporate income tax (manufacturing)		Sales taxes			
Province	Minimum rate (%)	Maximum rate (%)	Maximum rates applicable above (Can$)	Can$ 10 000 (%)	Can$ 200 000 (%)	Provincial (%)	Total (%)	Rate (%)	Type	Payroll tax (%)	Capital taxes[b] (%)
Newfoundland	10.57	18.02	59 180	24.74	48.64	5.0	27.12	8.0	HST	2.0	0/4
Prince Edward Island	9.80	16.70	61 509	14.90	47.37	7.5	29.62	10.0	Prov.	n.a.	0/3
Nova Scotia	9.77	16.67	59 180	14.90	47.34	16.0	38.12	8.0	HST	n.a.	0.25–0.50/3.00
New Brunswick	9.68	17.84	103 000	14.90	46.84	14.5	36.62	8.0	HST	n.a.	0.3/3.0
Quebec	16.00	24.00	53 405	27.06	48.21	9.04	31.16	7.5	QST+	4.26	0.64/1.55
Ontario	6.05	11.16	63 786	14.90	46.41	11.0	33.12	8.0	Prov.	1.95	0.3/0.6–0.9
Manitoba	10.90	17.40	65 000	26.04	46.40	16.5	38.62	7.0	Prov.	2.15	0.3–0.5/3.0
Saskatchewan	11.25	15.50	60 000	25.37	44.50	10.0	32.12	6.0	Prov.	n.a.	0.60/0.70–3.25
Alberta	10.00	10.00	Flat tax on taxable income	14.90	39.00	13.0	35.12	0	n.a.	n.a.	n.a.
British Columbia	6.05	14.7	86 785	20.53	43.70	13.5	35.62	7.5	Prov.	n.a.	0/1–3

HST Harmonized sales tax.
QST+ Similar base to federal gross sales tax.
Prov. Provincial.
n.a. Not applicable.

a. Personal income tax rates are for a single taxpayer with assessed income of either Can$10,000 or Can$200,000.
b. Capital taxes are general/bank rates.

Source: Canadian Tax Foundation (2002).

sales tax—a value added tax (VAT)—at a rate of 15 per cent, of which 8 per cent is a provincial tax that is allocated between provinces on the basis of consumption. In Quebec, the provincial government collects both the federal sales tax (the goods and services tax at 7 per cent) and its own VAT, the Quebec sales tax, at a rate of 7.5 per cent on almost the same base. The other five provinces impose their own retail sales taxes on a substantially different base that includes a significant proportion of business inputs.

Finally, provinces impose a variety of payroll and capital taxes on businesses at varying rates and on varying bases. As indicated in Table 3.10, such taxes are particularly important in Quebec, which thus stands out among the provinces with respect to the extent to which its taxation of business takes the form of taxes not related to profits (which are, incidentally, much less cyclically sensitive).

As even this condensed account shows, Canadian provinces not only have considerable discretion as to how they tax, but how they use this discretion to impose a variety of taxes and rates, both to reflect differences in local circumstances and to attempt to influence where business locate, as well as decisions by individuals on how to save, invest and spend through various incentives. Table 3.11 presents evidence on the provinces' use of this discretion to attract new businesses. Quebec is the most active province in the field, while Ontario, its immediate neighbour, prefers to use an overall lower tax burden.

In addition, certain federal tax policies have had significantly different effects on different provinces. Let us consider two examples. First, as noted earlier, the production of oil and gas is concentrated in Alberta. This concentration produced considerable strains on Canadian fiscal federalism during the era of high oil prices from 1973 to 1985. As late as 1974, Alberta, despite its above average per capita GDP level, had been a recipient of equalization transfers (Perry 1997). With the surge in oil prices, however, Alberta's per capita GDP quickly rose to unprecedented heights (see the figures for 1981 in Table 3.6). For the most part, provincial governments own natural resources, thus provincial policy has traditionally controlled the access to, the removal of and the price of natural resources. Understandably, therefore, the Alberta government attempted to capture the vastly increased resource rents through its royalty policy.

Unfortunately, from the federal point of view, this attempt had a potentially disastrous financial effect. Because the equalization system responded to changes in the level of provincial revenues, the resulting surge in provincial revenues raised the level of required equalization payments. However, these payments actually come entirely from federal revenues, and because royalties are a deduction for purposes of calculating corporate income taxes, federal revenues were lower, not higher. Confronted with these unpalatable facts, and coupled with its desire to shield the oil consuming—and politically

Table 3.11 Provincial programs aimed at attracting new businesses, 2000

Province	Program	Details
Alberta	None	
British Columbia	Small business tax holiday	Two-year CIT holiday for small businesses
	Corporation capital tax holiday	Four years for qualifying businesses
Manitoba	None	
New Brunswick	None	
Newfoundland	Economic Development and Growth Enterprises program	Ten-year tax holiday on CIT and payroll tax; ten-year tax holiday on property taxes
Nova Scotia	Small business tax reduction	Two-year CIT credit of 5%
Ontario	None	
Prince Edward Island	None	
Quebec	New business tax holiday	Ten-year tax holiday on CIT, capital tax and payroll tax for large investments, in other words, creating at least 350 jobs or 100 jobs for an investment of Can$300 million or more
		Five-year tax holiday for small businesses (CIT—first Can$200 000, capital tax—first Can$3 000 000, payroll tax—first Can$500 000).
	Information technology development centres	Five-year tax holiday on same three taxes + 40% wage tax credit maximum of Can$15 000 per employee
	Cité du Multimedia (Montreal); Centre National des Nouvelles Technologies (Quebec); Carrefour de la nouvelle économie (everywhere else)	40% (60% first year) wage tax (Can$15 000/Can$25 000 maximum) (60% only in Montreal)
	Foreign expert tax holiday	Five-year holiday of personal income tax
Saskatchewan	None	

CIT Corporate income tax.

Sources: Commerce Clearing House (1999); Vaillancourt (2001).

dominant—provinces of Ontario and Quebec from some of the effects of the world price rise by setting a lower Canadian price, which would benefit Ontario, and by using the revenue from a tax on oil exports to subsidize oil imports, thereby benefiting Quebec and the Atlantic provinces, the federal government proposed the National Energy Policy to share the resource rent from taxation. Even though the crisis dissipated with the fall in oil prices before the National Energy Policy really came into effect, the resulting political bitterness has lingered in Alberta to this day, and some of the other ameliorative policies undertaken at the time, such as the limits on deductions of royalties for federal tax purposes and the redesign of the equalization formula to, in effect, eliminate Alberta's revenues from the base, largely remain in place.

Second, as already noted, in several significant respects federal-provincial fiscal arrangements are different in Quebec from those in other provinces. For example, only in Quebec does the provincial government collect the federal sales tax (for how this system works, see Bird and Gendron 1998). When the federal government introduced the harmonized sales tax in 1996, the three small eastern provinces that signed on to this system received a special 'compensatory' payment of around Can$1 billion for doing so. The rationale for this payment was that in these provinces, unlike in most others, the move to a VAT required them to lower their previously extremely high retail sales taxes. Quebec, which had adopted the VAT base in 1992 without financial compensation, naturally protested, but the federal response, which does not seem unreasonable, was that Quebec had not faced a similar revenue loss. However, the federal government clearly agreed to Quebec's price, namely, provincial administration of the federal tax, only because it was so eager, after years of fruitless discussion in the 1980s, to get one province to sign on to the VAT approach on any terms. Despite the subsequent recriminations, this seems to be a good example of an exchange in which both parties essentially got what they wanted at the time.

An even more interesting example relates to the personal income tax. The federal personal income tax incorporates a special 'Quebec abatement' that reduces the federal income tax charged in that province by 16.5 per cent of the basic federal tax, that is, federal tax less certain credits. The result is that a Quebec taxpayer with a given income pays less federal tax than a taxpayer elsewhere in the country with the same income. This explicitly asymmetric treatment dates back to some acrimonious and extensive discussions that took place between the federal and Quebec governments in the early 1960s concerning the propriety of certain federal conditional transfers that, the province contended, intervened in spheres of action that were constitutionally explicitly provincial. Quebec's basic argument was that provinces should be permitted to opt out of such federal programs in areas in which provinces had their own programs and in exchange should be compensated by some appropriate combination of reduced federal taxes and, where necessary, additional equalization payments to make up for the forgone federal transfer.

After much discussion, the federal government offered a program broadly along these lines to all provinces in 1965. It was no surprise that only Quebec accepted the arrangement and opted out of a number of federal programs. Various alterations were made to the details over the years as a result of subsequent changes in both federal transfers and federal taxes, but since 1977, Quebec taxpayers have received abatements from the federal personal income tax of 8.5 percentage points for hospital insurance; 5 percentage points for a welfare cost-sharing transfer (the Canada Assistance Plan, now part of the Canada Health and Social Transfer); and 3 percentage points for so-called youth allowances, a program that has since been abolished.[16] Taxpayers have not noticed this federal reduction, because an offsetting rise in provincial taxes more than made up for it.

Other Policies

Some degree of asymmetry also exists in relation to several other policy areas. The first three listed here relate mainly to Quebec, while the last one has much wider ramifications.

- Quebec is constitutionally required to provide some services in English to its anglophone minority. This obviously entails certain special costs for the province. New Brunswick, which is the only constitutionally bilingual province, and Manitoba, which must provide some services in French, face some similar costs.
- Quebec has taken advantage of the fact that pension policy is constitutionally a concurrent field to maintain a distinct pension fund financed by the payroll tax. Moreover, it has used the funds thus accumulated to promote both provincial economic development and francophone ownership, for example, by means of voting agreements with francophone entrepreneurs that allow them to control their firms while owning a lower percentage of shares than they would otherwise require (see Vaillancourt 2000b for details).[17]
- Quebec is the only province that has exerted its right to separately screen and approve immigrants and receives some compensation from the federal government for related expenditures. This policy has aroused some resentment in the main immigrant receiving provinces of Ontario and British Columbia, which have argued that they too should receive additional federal funding for immigrants.[18]
- As in all countries, federal expenditures have frequently been spread about the country in asymmetrical ways, and to some extent this is

> inevitable, for example, expenditures on naval bases will be concentrated in coastal provinces. Because the federal capital, Ottawa, is located in Ontario, obviously many federal expenditures take place in that province, though to reduce this impact, for some years the federal government has followed a deliberate policy of locating an increasing proportion of its facilities in Hull, the neighbouring Quebec city.

In addition, the federal government has often attempted to build up the economy of one region or another, most notably in the Atlantic region. Both expenditure programs and tax incentive programs have frequently had explicit regional dimensions. Leblanc and Vaillancourt (1995) find that the Atlantic and Prairie provinces gained from both direct and tax expenditures in 1990. Despite their obvious political attractiveness, however, most such federal regional policies have tended to be ineffective and to have gradually spread to encompass a wider region. (For reviews of earlier experience with regional policy, see Lithwick 1978; Savoie 1986.)

Finally, the regional location of such 'footloose' federal expenditure, such as that for back-office facilities for tax administration and research facilities, often appears to have been decided—and more important, perceived as having been decided—on explicitly political grounds. When, for example, the federal government decided to locate its space research facilities in Montreal or to give the maintenance contract for warplanes to Montreal-based Bombardier, Toronto and Winnipeg, respectively, perceived the decisions as unwarranted favouritism, throwing yet another marker on the table around which the ongoing federal-provincial negotiations that have long characterized Canadian federalism take place.

As mentioned earlier with respect to the National Energy Policy, regionally selective memories of such events seem to be common, whether with respect to expenditure or regulatory policy. For instance, an earlier national oil policy had divided the Canadian oil market into two by a line (the so-called Borden line) that ran close to the Quebec border, with markets to the east being served by imported oil and markets to the west by higher-priced Canadian oil. One might have expected the Ontario industrial heartland, which was thus in effect forced to subsidize western oil production, to be the most resentful of this policy. In reality, however, the main residual effect of this policy appears to have been resentment by some politicians in Quebec of the resulting growth of a petrochemical complex in southwestern Ontario that rivalled the existing complex established on the basis of foreign crude in Montreal (Éthier 1986). Listening to the protagonists in the never-ending federal-provincial debate, Santayana's famous saying to the effect that those who recall (some version of) their history seem all too likely to repeat it appears to be appropriate.

ASYMMETRY: SOLUTION OR PROBLEM?

As discussed earlier, geography, demography and economics have ensured that Canada's regions are diverse. History and politics have both bestowed a considerable degree of autonomy on the provinces and ensured that the federal government is highly sensitive to diverse regional needs. At the same time, as in most federations, there is also a strong tendency to expect the federal government to treat all provinces equally. Reconciling the norm of equal treatment with diverse reality has not been an easy task.

We have sketched some of the fiscal ways in which Canada has tackled this task, ranging from explicitly asymmetric treatment to formally equal treatment. The distinction between the recipient and other provinces in the equalization system and the extent to which federal relations with Quebec often differ from those with other provinces illustrate the first of these approaches. The second is illustrated by the existence of a formula used to determine which provinces are the recipients of equalization measures and the provinces' ability to follow the same path as Quebec, or at least to do so at the time when the opting out option was available.

Has Canada's approach to reconciling diversity with equality, perhaps the central problem in any federal state, worked? We think that it has to a significant extent. Fiscal arrangements have helped to maintain an effective, if complex, state, though not without problems.

We first approach this question in an economic framework. In terms of the economic effects of Canada's intergovernmental fiscal arrangements, they have, on the whole, been successful in maintaining a fairly even provision of public services throughout a diverse country in which the major services (education, health and social assistance) are constitutionally in the hands of provincial governments with very different financial capacities. Moreover, Canada has accomplished this without impinging unduly upon provincial freedom to act fairly autonomously in most regards. The major exception to this relates to the aboriginal population, which is clearly much worse off than Canadians in general. This problem is not really related to intergovernmental arrangements, however, because aboriginal welfare is entirely a federal responsibility. Although it is by no means certain that matters would be much different if the provinces were responsible, federal performance in this area is not much of an advertisement for the virtues of more centralized provision of social services.

If an effective state is defined as one that can effectively deliver desired services in a flexible way to a diverse population, then Canada has done fairly well. However, if an effective state is considered to be one that, over time, develops more or less evenly throughout its territory, or, in other words, maintains or increases regional balance, then Canada has not done so well (though as Bird 2003 notes, one should be sceptical of balance as a policy objective). Indeed, as mentioned earlier, Canada's success in maintaining living standards in poorer regions through interpersonal and intergovernmental transfers may actually have perpetuated rather than reduced regional economic inequality. If solving one problem has exacerbated another, then how one evaluates the situation depends in part upon the relative weights to be attached to each of these goals, and because such weights can realistically only be assessed through the political process, judgment becomes not a matter of economics, but of political economy (for a simple example of such a policy matrix approach, see Bird 1982).

Even within this broader framework, however, assessment of the performance of Canada's intergovernmental system in reconciling provincial and national interests yields mixed results.[19] Viewed from one perspective, the evolution of Canadian intergovernmental fiscal arrangements over the last half of the 20th century offers a masterly demonstration of what Simeon (1972) calls federal-provincial diplomacy at its best—and its worst. The best is that it worked. The country has stayed together, grown respectably and, in general, treated most citizens fairly well and surprisingly uniformly, especially given the dominance of the provinces as providers of public services. The worst is that the process has been an unruly and noisy one that has consumed enormous political energies. In the long run, it may thus have reduced Canada's ability as a state to cope effectively with the changing world in which it exists, although, paradoxically, it may also have increased the regions' ability to deal on their own with north–south links and issues.

In any case, an important outcome of this process was some asymmetry in some federal-provincial arrangements, in particular, to allow Quebec to satisfy its expressed need for more autonomous policy. To some extent, at times occasional fiscal benefits may have flowed in the same direction in excess of those that would be expected in a completely uniform federal system, although those who think, on the contrary, that Quebec has been unfairly treated, would no doubt hotly dispute this assertion (for a discussion of the much-disputed area of fiscal imbalance in Canada, see Bird 2003). Nonetheless, let us assume, as Vaillancourt (1998) argues, that Quebec is a net fiscal gainer from intergovernmental finance. Is this a problem? It may not be, for at least the following three reasons:

- Fiscal gains may offset current or historical federal policies that have led to real, or at least perceived, regional losses. Quebec, with its motto of *je me souviens*, may excel in this respect, but it is by no means alone in Canada in viewing current intergovernmental finance in the context of its view of history. Recall the earlier example of Alberta in relation to natural resource policy. We could also mention the long-standing belief of many in the Maritime provinces that the industrial heartland of central Canada (Ontario and Quebec) was built at their expense by forcing them to buy high-priced 'upper Canadian' goods after confederation in 1867 rather than buying from their traditional and cheaper suppliers in the northeastern United States. Regions, like people, usually have no difficulty in justifying their favourable treatment, and indeed, sometimes such arguments may resonate even outside the region in question.

- Differential treatment may be required to achieve uniform results. Canada's equalization system is erected on precisely this argument, because its design ensures that provinces incapable of financing services at a certain level from their own resources receive sufficient funds to enable them to do so. However, this is still not enough to provide a level playing field for Quebec because of the special characteristics of that province's population, notably the relatively lower mobility of the francophone population.
- To some extent, differential fiscal (or other) treatment may at times be required simply to 'buy off' regional discontent and hold a country together. There is nothing unique or wrong about this approach. Since time immemorial politicians have traded favours for support, and probably every federal state in the world has at one time or another cut deals with particularly disaffected regions to reconcile them to staying within the system.[20] In any case, to the extent that such forces have been at play, it should come as no surprise if the regions with the most credible threat potential—primarily Quebec—have made the most of this process.

Suppose that any or all of these reasons explain why Quebec is treated asymmetrically in the Canadian federation. Did it work? That is, have the people of Quebec been reconciled to living in Canada as a result of Canada's flexible federalism? Or has the result been instead, as opponents of special treatment for Quebec commonly assert, that appetite grows with eating, and that the increased provincial autonomy that has resulted from the evolution of intergovernmental fiscal and other arrangements has led to demands for increasingly more powers up to the point of declaring an independent and sovereign state. Given that the support for sovereignty in Quebec—admittedly not a clear concept the way the issue has often been discussed in the province—increased from 10 per cent of the popular vote in the 1966 election to 49 per cent in the 1995 referendum, perhaps the second, more pessimistic, assessment is more accurate.

In addition, because one way that the conflict between the need for asymmetry and the desire for equal treatment has been reconciled has been to reduce federal controls over all provincial actions, this choice may have even more pernicious ramifications, in effect reducing the ability of Canada as a whole to do anything very effectively. For example, an articulate strand of Canadian opinion has long thought that a much stronger and more direct federal role is both appropriate and needed in areas such as health, education and welfare policy if all citizens are really to be treated as equally as they should be (see, for example, Hall 1980; Johnson 1985).

Nonetheless, through much intergovernmental manoeuvring, over the last 50 years Canada has managed both to hold the country together and to provide a relatively uniform package of public services to citizens. But how much longer can the centre hold before it breaks under the combined stress of strengthened provincial assertiveness, especially in Quebec, and the evolution of a continental common market? The next section presents a few preliminary comments on what the future may hold for Canada, and specifically for its intergovernmental fiscal arrangements.

WHAT MIGHT THE FUTURE HOLD?

Can Canada continue its fiscal juggling act of the last half-century in this century? The impact of globalization—or 'continentalization'—on Canada's diverse regions suggests that it probably cannot. More fundamental political changes may be called for in the decades to come than Canadians have been willing to accept in recent decades. We think that Canada will be unlikely to be able to continue 'muddling through' the next half-century. We say this for several loosely related reasons.

First, despite its current fiscal surplus, the federal government is unlikely to again come into funds on the scale it did after World War II, when the combination of economic growth and a generalized progressive income tax permitted an unprecedented expansion of intergovernmental transfers, thereby reconciling the fundamental misalignment of central finances and the provinces' newly expanding social functions (for details, see Bird 1970, 1979). For the same reason, in the future, the federal government is unlikely to be able to use its financial resources to 'buy' tranquillity in restless regions to the same extent as it did in the past.[21] One reason for this assertion is that we think Canada will not find it easy to maintain, let alone expand, its fiscal base in the face of increasing global competition, particularly situated as it is next to the relatively low-tax United States (see, for example, the recent discussions by Courchene 2000; Mintz 2000). The economy may continue to expand, in large part as a result of increasing integration with Canada's neighbour to the south, but provincial governments' relative ability to extract more resources is more likely to diminish than to expand as a result.

Second, such an externally driven growth process is itself likely to exacerbate matters for several reasons. To the extent that one result is to increase demand for Canada's resources—whether oil or water—the regional effects will be diverse. Because resources are basically controlled by the provinces, the effect will be to strengthen some provincial treasuries, thereby increasing regional diversity. In addition, the north-south orientation of provincial economic activity has increased dramatically. As Table 3.12 shows, the share of interprovincial exports in GDP declined from 24 per cent in 1984 (before the North American Free Trade Agreement) to 16 per cent in 2001 (after the North American Free Trade Agreement) overall, with a decline in all provinces, while the share of international exports grew from 27 per cent in 1984 to 35 per cent in 2001. Both the increasing north-south orientation of provincial policymakers coping with such trends and the resulting increase in competitive pressure on provincial policies seem likely to reduce the willingness of the 'winning' provinces—most likely those that are already relatively the best off—to provide increased support to, as they see it, losers elsewhere.[22] In other words, the impact of globalization on Canada's current intergovernmental arrangements seems likely to be negative: the underlying economic disparities are likely to widen, the support of the winning areas for transfers to the losers seems likely to diminish and the federal government is unlikely to have sufficient additional funds to deal with the problem.

Table 3.12 Importance of interprovincial and international trade, by province, selected years (per cent)

	Interprovincial exports/GDP			International exports/GDP		
Province	1984	1990	2001	1984	1990	2001
Newfoundland	10.35	10.67	8.97	28.71	29.19	26.30
Prince Edward Island	30.93	27.77	23.68	14.63	13.23	22.02
Nova Scotia	22.66	20.31	17.21	17.66	15.66	19.44
New Brunswick	28.71	27.46	25.85	30.69	26.91	29.18
Quebec	22.94	21.72	16.57	21.39	19.41	30.01
Ontario	23.15	20.71	15.97	33.03	27.19	41.41
Manitoba	29.23	27.47	25.70	19.33	18.07	26.08
Saskatchewan	24.03	22.86	21.16	38.03	25.81	34.25
Alberta	36.69	26.38	15.92	23.03	23.36	23.77
British Columbia	13.79	13.81	11.64	28.29	24.76	25.83
Total	24.02	21.02	16.18	27.49	24.05	34.77

Sources: Statistics Canada data; GDP data from Table 3.7.

Third, to some extent Quebec remains a wild card in the Canadian deck. In economic terms, it may not be one of the big winners from continental integration, but at the same time, the process also means that it probably has less to gain from remaining part of Canada. As 'Canada' becomes a relatively less important economic factor in people's lives and the popular perception of its political reality becomes even vaguer in the Quebec milieu, the likelihood of a popular vote for permanently opting out seems more likely to increase than to diminish.[23]

What would happen if Quebec did secede is completely unpredictable. Perhaps eventually the whole system would shake down and life would go on much as before both for Quebecois and those in the rest of Canada. Or perhaps years of acrimonious debate and much bad feeling on both sides may ensue, with either or both sides ending up much worse off. All we can say here is that no jiggling of intergovernmental fiscal arrangements will be able to put Humpty Dumpty together again if either Quebec or the rest of Canada decides not to play the game any more.

Fourth, to be less dramatic, possibly a new form of intergovernmental arrangements will instead gradually emerge over the next few decades. In the negotiations surrounding the Charlottetown Agreement (a constitutional revision that was rejected in 1992), the Ontario government put forward the idea of a social charter. In 1998, all ten provinces signed an agreement on social policy that included a provision for provincial opting out of federal social programs with compensation. However, when the federal and (nine) provincial governments signed the Social Union Framework Agreement in 1999, this provision was omitted and Quebec refused to sign.

An agreement covered by the Social Union Framework Agreement is the national child benefit, which was introduced in 1998 following several years of negotiation. Under the national child benefit, the federal government increased its payment to low-income families through the Canada child tax benefit. At the same time, the provinces and territories agreed that that they would spend any reduction in their own welfare payments resulting from this increase to benefit recipients in programs chosen by the province. For example, British Columbia created the British Columbia earned income benefit to facilitate employment, Alberta set up supplementary health insurance under the Alberta child health benefit and Nova Scotia offered a mix of prevention and child care initiatives. This form of fiscal federalism is innovative. It is not a shared cost program or a block funding transfer, but rather a flexible arrangement that may allow better use of both an existing federal program and various provincial programs.

More generally, the Social Union Framework Agreement (a) calls for more funding predictability by requiring consultation with the provinces one year prior to major social policy changes by the federal government, (b) indicates that the federal government will not introduce new programs without the agreement of a majority of provinces and (c) states that provinces not needing a new transfer in full because of existing programs can use the funds in related areas. Just how these provisions will work in practice remains to be seen, however. Many observers are not optimistic. Maioni (2000) writes that 'the real effect of the Social Union on policy outcomes is limited by the political conflict imbedded in the framework agreement and by unresolved issues surrounding health reform' (p. 41). Boychuck (2000) reminds us that 'federal-provincial agreement on the NCB [national child benefit] was a relatively modest achievement . . . [that] . . . entailed the enrichment and reworking of an existing federal program [and] did not require any provincial financial commitment' (p. 46). Finally, McIntosh (2000) writes that 'the debate about the nature of the Canadian social union has been about the health of the health system . . . the risk is that other aspects of the social union could find themselves orphaned' (p. 48).

One thing seems clear, however. To a considerable extent, as evidenced by some of the recent discussions about the heath system, the focus of discussion has shifted from the traditional federal-provincial forum to an interprovincial forum. Alternatively, or in a complementary fashion, some government functions may increasingly come to be seen as joint responsibilities of both levels of government. Given Canada's somewhat chequered recent history of constitutional reform, should this form of intergovernmental cooperation develop to any extent, it will likely happen informally as governments at both levels attempt to cope with the pressures they will all be facing.

To be still more speculative, even in the relatively favourable circumstances envisaged in the preceding paragraph, with everyone in an unusually cooperative mood (though Quebec's failure to sign the Social Union Framework Agreement does not indicate that this is likely to be the case), the problems that the Canadian federation may face in the next few decades are most unlikely to be readily resolved within the existing political structure. The virtually complete absence of any formal mechanism for provincial representation at the federal level, combined with the strong federal party system, the executive dominance of the legislature and the lack of any integration between federal and provincial parties, means that virtually every issue in Canadian politics sooner or later becomes a matter for federal-provincial conflict and confrontation. Thus approaches to cooperative solutions like those just mentioned are unlikely to emerge easily in a system in which the other side is almost invariably seen as the enemy. How this problem can be resolved, if at all, is not clear, because the foxes who would lose power if it were resolved are currently in control of the relevant hen houses.

Another emergent problem that is poorly dealt with in the current Canadian political structure is local government. As Table 3.13 shows, the size of

Table 3.13 Size of the federal, provincial and territorial governments, 2000

Item	Canada	New-foundland	Prince Edward Island	Nova Scotia	New Bruns-wick	Quebec	Ontario	Mani-toba	Saskat-chewan	Alberta	Britsh Columbia	Yukon	North-west Terri-tories
Total government spending (Can$ hundred thousands)	396 925	7849	2121	14 161	10 953	98 996	141 080	16 231	14 218	35 142	49 698	870	1283
Total governement spending as a percentage of GDP	37.3	57.0	62.5	58.5	54.7	44.2	32.5	48.5	42.2	24.3	38.4	75.3	47.8
Total government spending per capita (Can$)	12 900	14 616	15 370	15 049	14 507	13 418	12 074	14 163	13 912	11 679	12 244	28 065	31 293
Ratio of federal to total spending (%)	44.0	60.5	64.7	60.7	55.9	42.4	40.7	51.8	47.2	39.1	40.1	81.3	72.3
Ratio of provincial to total spending (%)	49.4	50.4	45.4	41.6	51.2	53.3	45.1	49.1	47.4	55.6	54.0	58.7	70.1
Ratio of local to total spending (%)	15.9	10.9	8.4	11.0	4.1	14.9	19.5	13.4	14.1	17.9	14.0	4.5	7.4
Ratio of local to local and provincial spending (%)	24.3	17.7	15.7	20.9	7.5	21.8	30.2	21.5	22.9	24.3	20.5	7.1	9.6

Note: Nunavet was created in 1999. No data were available at the time of writing.

Sources: Statistics Canada data.

the local sector varies considerably from province to province. Everywhere, however, local governments are entirely the creatures of provincial governments and are frequently treated with the disregard, even contempt, this label may suggest (Bird and Chen 1998). Yet it is local, not provincial governments, that are in many ways most relevant to people's lives, and their importance may increase as a result of the probable weakening of Canada's higher-tier governments as continental integration proceeds, as it is likely to do, albeit perhaps with some hiccups from time to time. One result, for instance, might be the need to finance and control a wider range of activities at the local level in accordance with diverging local circumstances—in effect a logical extension of the traditional Canadian argument for decentralization to the level of government that really is closest to the people. Whether this happens or not, the particular problems of the larger metropolitan areas—Montreal, Toronto and Vancouver—none of which currently has either a particularly effective or efficient government structure, will need close attention. Perhaps, as some have suggested, one possible development in the future might even be the development of some city-region as provinces or, more likely, quasi provinces (Bird and Slack 2004 consider this question in more general terms). Again, however, given the dominance of provincial politicians, it is hard to see how this could happen without a more basic political upheaval than seems likely short of something as drastic as the break-up of the country.

One possible factor that might cause such upheaval is the creation of a third order of government as a result of agreements between aboriginal tribes and the federal and relevant provincial governments. The first such agreement was ratified in 2000 with the Nisga'a people with respect to a rural area of northwest British Columbia.[24] This agreement distinguishes between Nisga'a citizens and noncitizens, that is, aboriginal and white residents of Nisga'a lands, with the former having more political powers than the latter in deciding on issues that affect both groups of residents. This new level of government has more power than any municipal government, though less power than any provincial government. How all these governments coexist, resolve their differences and deliver services will surely help shape Canadian federalism in the 21st century.

Finally, another possible revolution that may change everything could be the emergence of what can be referred to as transparent government. Recent or imminent developments in information technology make it increasingly possible to return to the state of the Greek *polis*, in which every citizen was able to have his or her say with respect to every important issue. Such a land of perpetual referendums would clearly be the total antithesis of Canada's present Westminster system, with its strong transitory dominance by the winning party. Obviously, how or to what extent the country may move in this direction in the coming century is far from clear, and whether the results will be good or bad is equally unclear: plausible arguments can be made in both directions (see Bird 2004). What is clear is that all bets would then be off. The rules of the game would be drastically changed, as would the relative power of the various players. We doubt that anyone can predict what developments in such directions might mean for the ability of Canada as it is currently structured to continue to be an effective state.

NOTES

1. The Federal-Provincial-Territorial Council on Social Policy Research was created in November 1996. All Canadian governments except that of Quebec are members of this council. In February 1999 its members reached agreement on the Framework to Improve the Social Union for Canadians, the text of which is available at http://www.socialunion.gc.ca.
2. The analysis of population diversity in this section has to some extent been shaped by the data available. Censuses have been carried out every ten years since 1871, and partial censuses have been carried out since 1906, also every ten years. Since 1986, the questions asked in both types of censuses have been identical. In general, the information content of the censuses has improved over time. National accounts information at the provincial level is available on a detailed annual basis since 1961, but some information, such as personal income, is available since 1926. Since Newfoundland joined Canada in 1949, data from 1951 onwards include that province. The chapter does not take the territories into account.
3. As only Canadian citizens can vote, one result is that a smaller proportion of the residents of the faster growing provinces can vote.
4. Until 1971, the traditional definition of an ethnic group was based on ethnicity, a self-defined trait supposedly based on the ethnic group of the first male ancestor to arrive in North America. Since then, the definition of ethnicity has changed, thus intertemporal comparisons cannot be made. We therefore use mother tongue to define the groups relevant for our discussion and the percentage of a mother tongue group that uses the same language at home-another census question—to measure assimilation.
5. In November 1999, Canadian stock exchanges were rationalized. The Vancouver and Alberta exchanges, where junior stocks were traded, merged into the Canadian Venture Exchange (the Winnipeg exchange joined the Canadian Venture Exchange in March 2000) and the Toronto Stock Exchange became the sole Canadian exchange for senior stocks, giving up derivative trading to the Montreal stock exchange in exchange for its delisting of these stocks. A small market for junior stocks was also kept in Montreal. In May 2000, the Quebec government announced that it would welcome NASDAQ in Montreal. The exact impact of this has yet to be seen, but some observers believe this could weaken the Toronto Stock Exchange, which has already suffered from the migration of important companies to the New York exchanges. For further discussion of securities market regulation, see Vaillancourt and Bird (2002).
6. See http://strategis.ic.gc.ca/epic/internet/inait-ac.nsfvwGeneratedItnerE/Home. The Canada-US Free Trade Agreement was signed on 1 January 1989 and the North American Free Trade Agreement was signed on 1 January 1993. Some analysts have argued that these agreements played a role in convincing provinces to sign the AIT.
7. Quebec dairy farmers are an important political force. This colouring rule requires margarine sold in Quebec to be coloured to make it look different from butter. The judgment is being appealed as of September 2004.
8. The 2001–02 annual report (p. 69) at http://www.intrasec.mb.ca/index_he.htm reports that by that date, 42 out of 51 professional associations had achieved ‘full or substantial compliance’ with this requirement.

9. As Day and Winer (1994) show in their review of the empirical evidence on the effects of public policy on internal migration, the issues are complex and the evidence is far from clear. Nonetheless, it seems clear that 'persistently applied inducements to migrate to, or remain in, a particular location may be effective in altering the regional allocation of labour and the nature of regional disparities over long periods' (p. 51). In the absence of the public policies discussed later, outflows out of poorer regions would probably have been even greater.
10. Of course, no one likes to move, and people (not to mention their governments) in poor anglophone areas like the Atlantic region are equally, or perhaps even more, happy to receive federal money for staying home than those in Quebec. But the point is that in the end, the welfare gain of an extra dollar transferred to Quebec is presumably greater because of the more restricted opportunities for francophones.
11. While provinces' expenditure needs also obviously differ, as indicated, for example, by the variations in the demographic structures discussed earlier, these differences are not further discussed here, for two reasons. First, to a considerable extent they are dealt with by direct federal spending, and second, they are not taken into account in the determination of transfers from the federal government to the provinces.
12. Other small transfers are in the fields of housing (public, social not-for-profit), income support for farmers, teaching official languages, and disabled workers (Vaillancourt 2000a).
13. For the federal view of recent developments, see http://www.fin.gc.ca/access/fedprove.html. According to press reports, some provinces disagree with the federal interpretation of recent discussions. But note that as of September 2004, a new health financing accord was signed with the provinces with some reporting conditions. See Laurent and Vaillancourt (2004) for a detailed description of federal funding of social policies in Canada since 1997.
14. This is not as clear-cut as it may sound, because the equal per capita payments include both cash and so-called tax transfer equivalents. The latter refer to taxes raised by the provincial governments as a result of their increasing income tax rates by the same amount as the federal government reduced its own rates, which in Canada is referred to as an exchange of tax room. Clearly a given tax rate will produce less revenue in poorer than in richer provinces, so an additional cash payment is made to produce what are called equalized tax points. Finally, to add to the confusion, the system works somewhat differently in Quebec, where federal and provincial tax systems have a different relationship in some respects than in the other provinces. Thus even though Canada has only two important transfers, this does not mean that the system is simple. For a complete description of the evolution of transfer programs, see Perry (1997).
15. For more information on the interprovincial redistributive consequences of individual transfers, see Vaillancourt and Rault (2003).
16. As a result, the value of the income taxes thus collected is deducted from federal transfers; hence the Quebec government collects a small amount of federal personal income tax, but using its own base, deductions, rates and so on.
17. Of course, other provinces have also attempted to promote provincial economic development in a variety of ways ranging from tax incentives to direct provincial investments.
18. Slack and Bird (2004) argue that such funding should go directly to the major immigrant receiving areas, namely, the major metropolitan areas, although actually implementing such an arrangement could be problematic.
19. You may have noticed that at various points we have shifted between discussing 'regional' and 'provincial' interests. As an informed observer of the Canadian scene noted many years ago, separating the two in a federal setting like Canada's is difficult, and indeed, the very existence of provinces makes them the relevant region from a policy perspective (Hodgetts 1966). Indeed, all provinces, whatever their size, appear to be entitled to federal aid ensuring their existence (Economic Council of Canada, 1977).
20. For a particularly recent and dramatic example of this process, see the analysis of the Russian Federation in Treisman (1999). As he notes, bribery may not seem attractive, but it looks a lot better if the alternative is likely to be war.
21. Bird, Bucovetsky and Foot (1979) make a similar argument based on an analysis derived from Wildavsky (1977). Because the country survived the next two decades in the face of

increasing stress, Canadian politicians obviously proved to be more adept managers than this analysis assumed. Nonetheless, past success does not necessarily augur future success in the face of what we think will be even more difficult times for those who would solve problems by spending public money.

22. Incidentally, to the extent that one rationale underlying the apparent generosity of the rich regions in supporting Canada's present redistributive system is to discourage people from migrating from poor regions, this rationale would seem to provide relatively less support for transfers to Quebec, because, as we have argued, francophones are less likely to migrate in any case.
23. Indeed, the passage in June 2000 of the so-called Clarity Bill by the federal government may increase this. This law, put forward as an implementation mechanism for a recent Supreme Court judgment on Quebec's right to secession, states that the federal government will determine at the beginning of the next Quebec-organized referendum if the question is clear. If it determines that the question is not clear, it will announce that it will not negotiate even should the referendum pass with a clear majority. Paradoxically, because this law reduces the risk of voting in favour of secession for swing voters, it may end up increasing the odds that more than 50 per cent of Quebecois will support some kind of sovereignty.
24. The text of the agreement may be found at http://www.ainc-inac.gc.ca.

REFERENCES

The word 'processed' describes informally reproduced works that may not be commonly available in libraries.

Bird, R. M. (1970), *The Growth of Government Spending in Canada*, Toronto: Canadian Tax Foundation.

——— (1979), *Financing Canadian Government*, Toronto: Canadian Tax Foundation.

——— (1982), 'Expenditure Policy and Regional Development', *Rivista di diritto finanziario e scienza delle finanze*, 41 (3), 483–503.

——— (2003), 'Fiscal Flows, Fiscal Balance and Fiscal Sustainability', Working Paper no. 03-2, International Studies Program, Andrew Young School of Public Policy, Georgia State University, Atlanta.

——— (2004), *Who Decides?*, Toronto: C. D. Howe Institute.

Bird, R. M. and D. Chen (1998), 'Federal Finance and Fiscal Federalism: The Two Worlds of Canadian Public Finance', *Canadian Public Administration*, 42 (1), 51–74.

Bird, R. M. and P.-P. Gendron (1998), 'Dual VATs and Cross-Border Trade: Two Problems, One Solution?', *International Tax and Public Finance*, 5 (3), 429–42.

Bird, R. M. and K. J. McKenzie (2001), *Taxing Business: A Provincial Affair*, Toronto: C. D. Howe Institute.

Bird, R. M. and E. Slack (2004), 'Fiscal Aspects of Metropolitan Governance', Paper no. 0401, International Tax Program, Rotman School of Management, University of Toronto, Toronto.

Bird, R. M. and F. Vaillancourt (2001a), 'Fiscal Arrangements for Maintaining an Effective State in Canada', *Environment and Policy C: Government and Policy*, 19 (2), 163–87.

——— (2001b), 'The Role of Intergovernmental Fiscal Arrangements in Maintaining an Effective State in Canada', in Richard Bird and Thomas Stauffer (eds), *Intergovernmental Fiscal Relations in Fragmented Societies*, Basel and Fribourg, Switzerland: Helbing & Lichtenhahn and Institut du Fédéralisme, pp. 189–229.

Bird, R. M., M.W. Bucovetsky and D. Foot (1979), *The Growth of Public Employment in Canada,* Montreal: Institute for Research in Public Policy.
Boothe, P. (1998), *Finding a Balance: Renewing Canadian Fiscal Federalism*, Benefactors Lecture, Toronto: C. D. Howe Institute.
Boychuck, G. W. (2000), 'SUFA, the Child Benefit and Social Assistance', *Policy Options Politiques,* 213 (April), 46–47.
Canadian Tax Foundation (2002), *Finances of the Nation 2002*, Toronto.
Chen, D. and J. Mintz (2003), 'Assessing Ontario's Fiscal Competitiveness', report for the Institute for Competitiveness and Prosperity, Toronto.
Commerce Clearing House (1999), *Government Assistance Manual*, Toronto.
Coulombe, S. (1999), 'Economic Growth and Provincial Disparity: A New View of an Old Canadian Problem', Commentary 122, C. D. Howe Institute, Toronto.
Courchene, T. J. (2000), 'A Mission Statement for Canada', *Policy Options Politiques*, 21 (6), 6–14.
Courchene, T. J. and C. R. Telmer (1998), *From Heartland to North American Regional State: The Social, Fiscal and Federal Evolution of Ontario*, Toronto: Centre for Public Management, Faculty of Management, University of Toronto.
Day, K. M. and S. L. Winer (1994), 'Internal Migration and Public Policy: An Introduction to the Issues and a Review of Empirical Research on Canada', in A. M. Maslove (ed.), *Issues in the Taxation of Individuals*, Toronto: University of Toronto Press, pp. 3–61.
Economic Council of Canada (1977), *Living Together*, Ottawa: Department of Supply and Services.
Éthier, M. (1986), 'Regional Grievances: The Québec Case', in K. Norrie (ed.), *Disparities and Interregional Adjustment*, Toronto: University of Toronto Press, pp. 159–84.
Hall, E. M. (1980), *Canada's National-Provincial Health Program for the 1980s*, Ottawa: Health and Welfare Canada.
Hodgetts, J. E. (1966), 'Regional Interests and Policy in a Federal Structure', *Canadian Journal of Economics and Political Science*, 32 (1), 3–14.
Johnson, A. (1985), *Giving Point and Purpose to the Federal Financing of Post-Secondary Education and Research in Canada,* Ottawa: Secretary of State.
Laurent, Stephen and François Vaillancourt (2004), 'Federal-Provincial Transfers for Social Programs in Canada: Their Status in May 2004', Institute for Research on Public Policy Working Paper, available at http://www.irpp.org/fr/wp/index.htm.
Leblanc, M. and F. Vaillancourt (1995), 'Les milliards de dollars non imposables: le coût des dépenses fiscales', *Policy Options Politiques*, 16 (1), 18–23.
Lithwick, N. H. (1978), *Regional Economic Policy: The Canadian Experience*, Toronto: McGraw-Hill Ryerson.
Maioni, A. (2000), 'The Social Union and Health Care', *Policy Options Politiques,* 213 (April), 39–41.
Marmen, L. and J. P. Corbeil (1999), *Languages in Canada, 1996 Census,* Ottawa: Supply and Services Canada.
McIntosh, T. (2000), 'Is the Social Union too Healthy? Rethinking Labour Market Policy', *Policy Options Politiques,* 213 (April), 48–49.
Mintz, J. M. (2000), 'Competitive Government: A Framework for Winning Economic and Social Policies', C. D. Howe Institute, Toronto, processed.
Perry, D. B. (1997), *Financing the Canadian Federation, 1867–1995*, Toronto: Canadian Tax Foundation.
Savoie, D. J. (1986), *The Canadian Economy: A Regional Perspective*, Toronto: Methuen.

Schwanen, D. (2000), 'Happy Birthday, AIT', *Policy Options Politiques*, 216 (July–August), 51–55.
Simeon, R. (1972), *Federal-Provincial Diplomacy*, Toronto: University of Toronto Press.
Slack, E. and R .M. Bird (2004), 'The Fiscal Sustainability of the Greater Toronto Area', Paper no. 0405, International Tax Program, Rotman School of Management, University of Toronto, Toronto.
Trebilcock, M. J. (1983), *Federalism and the Canadian Economic Union*, Toronto: University of Toronto Press and Ontario Economic Council.
Treisman, D. (1999), *After the Deluge: Regional Policy and Fiscal Transfers in Russia,* Ann Arbor, MI: University of Michigan Press.
Vaillancourt, F. (1992), 'English and Anglophones in Quebec: An Economic Perspective', in *Survival: Official Language Rights in Canada,* Toronto: C. D. Howe Institute, pp. 63–94.
——— (1997), 'Labour Sponsored Venture Capital Funds in Canada: Institutional Aspects, Tax Expenditures and Employment Creation', in P. Halpern (ed.), *Financing Growth in Canada*, Calgary: University of Calgary Press and Industry Canada, pp. 571–92.
——— (1998), 'The Economics of Constitutional Options for Quebec and Canada', *Canadian Business Economics,* 6 (2), 3–14.
——— (2000a), 'Federal-Provincial Small Transfer Programs in Canada, 1957–1998: Importance, Composition and Evaluation', in H. Lazar (ed.), *Canada: The State of the Federation 1999/2000*, Kingston, Ontario: Institute of Intergovernmental Relations, pp. 189–212.
——— (2000b), 'The Quebec Pension Plan: Institutional Arrangements and Lessons for Alberta', in P. Boothe (ed.), *A Separate Pension Plan for Alberta*, Edmonton, Canada: Edmonton Institute for Public Economics, pp. 23–40.
——— (2001), 'Les gouvernements sous-nationaux au Canada: quelques aspects financiers et fiscaux', *Economie Publique Études et recherches,* 8 (2), 41–60.
Vaillancourt, F. and R. M. Bird (2002), 'Changing with the Times: Success, Failure, and Inertia in Canadian Federal Arrangements, 1945–2001', Working Paper no. 151, Center for Research on Economic Development and Policy Reform, Stanford University, Palo Alto, CA.
Vaillancourt, F. and Stéphanie Rault (2003), 'The Regional Dimension of Federal Intergovernmental and Interpersonal Transfers in Canada, 1981–2001', *Regional and Federal Studies,* 13 (4), 130–52.
Waslander, B. (1997), 'Government Expenditures on Aboriginal People: The Costly Status Quo', *Canadian Tax Journal*, 45 (5), 959–78.
Wildavsky, A. (1977), *Budgeting,* New Brunswick, NJ: Transaction Publishers.

4. Germany at the Junction Between Solidarity and Subsidiarity

Paul Bernd Spahn and Jan Werner

The modern German federation was established only after World War II—for the western states in 1949—and half a century after its inception it appears to be strong and more robust than ever despite unification with the formerly socialist East Germany (see Figure 4.1 for a map of Germany). Germany is widely seen as having acquired functioning democratic institutions and a reliable political system that has even influenced the design of intergovernmental relations at the supranational level in Europe. Nevertheless, Germany, perhaps more so than many other nations, now finds itself at the junction of a historic choice between solidarity and subsidiarity. This is because, over the years, Germany has consistently sacrificed subsidiarity, and hence regional diversity, in favour of national solidarity. Solidarity has now attained a level at which the flexibility and responsiveness of subnational governments, notably the 16 states, have been severely impaired. In particular, interregional equalization appears to be grossly inflated—conspicuously so since Germany's unification—an assertion that even the Constitutional Court has supported in a recent ruling on the Equalization Law.

HISTORICAL BACKGROUND AND SETTING

The present state of German federalism can only be understood against its historical background. During most of the 19th century, Germany consisted of a patchwork of mini-states subject to the hegemonic interests of both the German-speaking superpowers, such as Austria and Prussia, and the centrally controlled European nation states, such as France, Russia and the United Kingdom. The German ambition at that time was to create a strong nation state to match competing European interests both politically and economically. The unifying force was clearly German language and culture, as well as economic motives, notably the creation of a common market without barriers among German states. The language criterion was so decisive that unification

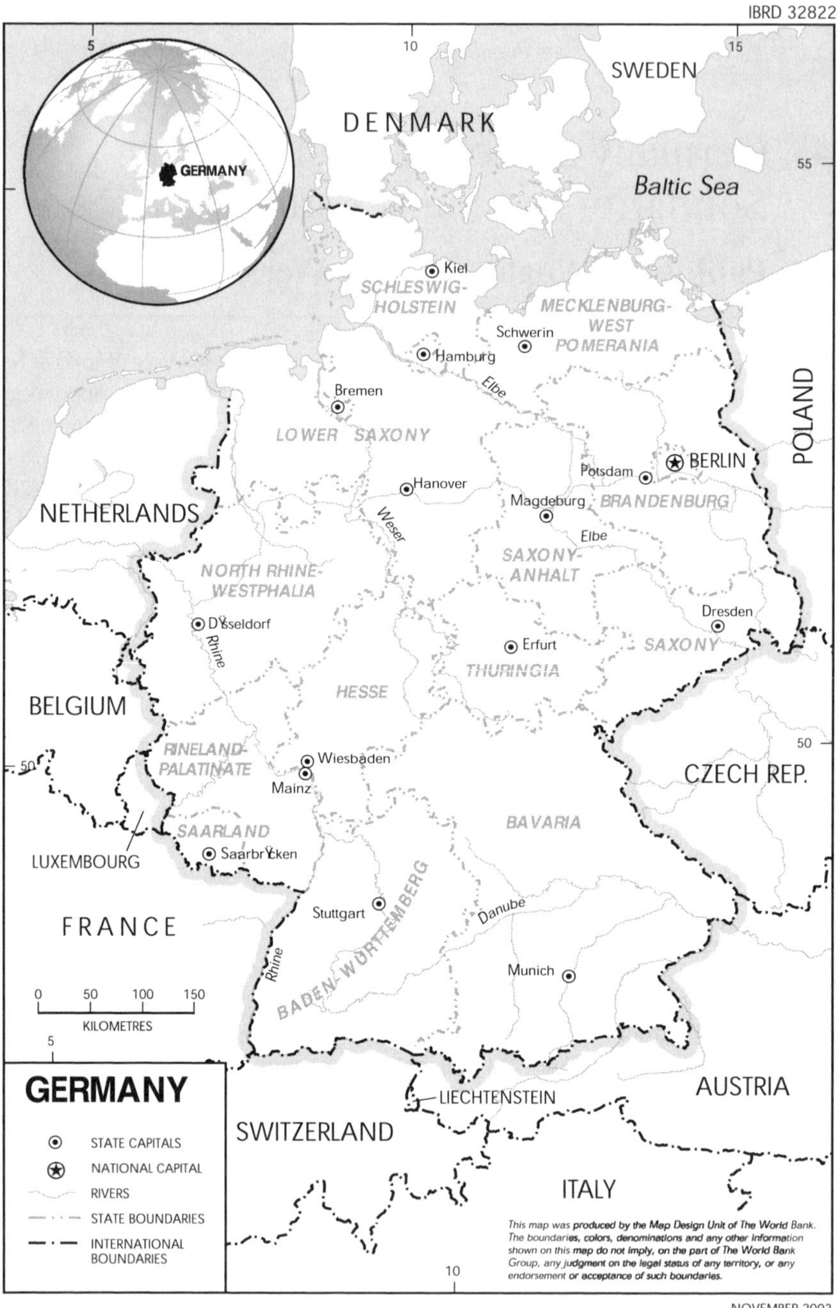

Figure 4.1 Germany

was impossible under Austrian rule, a monarchy that, at that time, had different aspirations in the non-German speaking Balkans and southern Europe. When the German Reich was finally established in 1871, Prussia controlled about two-thirds of economic resources in Germany, truly a highly asymmetric construct that would render the federation vulnerable to centripetal tendencies and abuse of power.

Although formally a federation, with representatives of the constituent German states cooperating in a similar way to today's European Union Council, the system had all the characteristics of a monarchy, with the emperor and his nominated cabinet exerting the sovereign power of the Reich. While there was an elected parliament, which became a source of continuing political quarrels, especially after the opposition to the ruling parties had won a significant majority, it remained virtually powerless and without significant political influence.

After World War I, the Weimar constitution aspired to establish the accountability of government to an elected parliament, but failed to render the latter politically viable. A highly fragmented party system, which represented a rickety society at a time of major social and political upheavals, and the national parliament eventually fell prey to the ploys and threats of the Nazis, which ended the short-lived democracy between the two wars. Hitler's ascendance to power had proceeded via Berlin and through Prussian institutions, with the other states of the federation being impotent or unwilling to counterbalance his usurpation of power. This is why the Allies abolished the state of Prussia immediately after World War II, thereby eliminating one important asymmetry and source of political instability.

The newly created zones, later *länder* or states, did not necessarily respect historic boundaries and, after the Nazi experience, regional balance and symmetry became guiding principles for the reconstruction of postwar Germany—at least in the former West Germany. However, a concession to German history was the creation of so-called city states, Hamburg and Bremen—the Hanse cities[1]—and after unification Berlin, which introduced a minor asymmetric element into intergovernmental fiscal relations that has more recently attracted the attention of the Constitutional Court. But as a general rule, as the devastation of World War II had left all regions equally poor and deprived of economic resources, balanced regional development and uniform living conditions became attractive features for policymaking and institution building. These principles were not only incorporated in the new federal constitution, but they became so entrenched in people's minds and penetrated all domains of collective decisionmaking—including nongovernmental decisions such as collective bargaining—that they would survive even the quandary of unification in 1990. Indeed, German unification, with the formerly socialist East Germany representing roughly 20 per cent of the population, but only less than 6 per cent of total value added, was, and still is, a major challenge for the political system and the economy.

This brief historic overview may help explain some key elements of the German national character and institutions: the desire to regroup the nation in line with its language and cultural heritage; the readiness to share the fruits of national economic development and growth on an even footing (interpersonal, sectoral and regional solidarity); the joint representation of state governments in the upper chamber of the federal parliament (the Bundesrat); and the acceptance of uniform standards and harmonized taxes throughout the nation, including a homogeneity of policies at lower tiers of government. Therefore the philosophy of the German brand of federalism is highly symmetrical in relation to potential outcomes. It may, however, imply vast asymmetries in inputs, in the functioning of institutions and in the workings of political and bureaucratic procedures.

To achieve the uniformity of living conditions and homogeneity of policies, for instance, uniform, typically centralized,[2] guiding principles must be in place for the entire nation. This by itself introduces a new type of asymmetry at the vertical level. While other federations such as Canada or the United States accept concurring sovereignties at various levels, with full taxing and expenditure powers for each tier, the German model of federalism can be characterized as asymmetrical power sharing. In this model, aside from its exclusive competencies such as foreign affairs and defence, the federation sets out a general framework for policymaking for all states (and eventually municipalities), while the states implement and administer such policies within this general setting. The historic roots of this form of power sharing can also be found in the German Reich, where the states (and municipalities) had already had a long tradition of administration that the centre could build upon, while the Reich itself had no comparable infrastructure on its own except for such exclusive responsibilities as defence.

Moreover, history explains why modern German states exert their sovereignty only conjointly at the national level, through the Bundesrat, the upper house, which consists of representatives of state governments, not elected officials like in the US Senate. No individual state is accorded privileges in the Bundesrat other than its vote, which is exerted *en bloc* and weighted roughly by population.[3] The result of the majority vote is binding for all, and the policy outcome is uniform across the nation. In particular, the tax law is identical, even for state and municipal taxes (though municipalities are accorded some discretion in setting tax rates for municipal taxes), and the states are denied any form of own taxation. Tax revenue is typically shared and apportioned among layers of government according to the constitution for income taxes or law for the value added tax (VAT), and is disbursed horizontally among regional entities according to formulas with strong equalization components.

Homogeneity of policies is also fostered at the national level through the voting mechanism for the national parliament (Bundestag), which follows the model of proportional representation and excludes all parties that fall below 5 per cent of the vote. This provision tends to neutralize extremist and factional parties, which had played a key role in destroying the Weimar democracy. This mechanism represents another example of asymmetric institutions designed to foster homogeneity and ultimately the symmetry of outcomes at the national level.

However, the rules equally protect minorities rather effectively through various asymmetric provisions: direct mandates according to majority voting are combined with proportional representation whereby the majority voting system favours singular, and even nonpartisan, candidates, and parties that attain at least three direct mandates will be represented in parliament even though their proportional vote may fall below the margin. This provision has worked mainly in favour of the Democratic Socialist Party, the successor party of the former communists, and hence in favour of East German citizens.

Although Germany's political landscape has varied considerably in recent years, with new entrants in parliament, such as the Green Party in the 1980s and the former Communist Party since reunification, the political system and its institutions rely heavily on achieving consensus according to the preferences of the median voter. He or she will ultimately determine the pace of politics at the national level, with the states and municipalities being compelled to implement and administer such policies within a common national framework.

A host of intergovernmental transfers that aim at fostering national homogeneity and uniformity of living conditions, combined with the states' inability to use own tax instruments, exacerbate the almost complete lack of policy discretion at lower tiers of government and the emptiness of the agenda of state parliaments. The transfer process begins with the formula apportionment of the jointly appropriated VAT, which is mainly population based and highly equalizing, to regions; proceeds through the horizontal redistribution of resources among states according to the Equalization Law; and is completed through a number of vertically asymmetrical grants from the federal government in favour of states in need, however defined, which are mainly, though not exclusively, states in eastern Germany. This interregional solidarity is pushed to a point where the average command of public resources per capita is now higher in the needier states than in some of the richest states in the west. It is this outcome that has spurred a constitutional challenge by three more affluent states in southern Germany: Baden-Wuerttemberg, Bavaria and Hesse. Thus the issue of solidarity versus subsidiarity has officially been raised for the first time, although it had been discussed in academic circles for a while.

SOLIDARITY VERSUS SUBSIDIARITY: WHAT IS AT STAKE?

Solidarity is a sacred cow in Germany, in particular as regards the new states of eastern Germany. This is less for moral than for political reasons: voters in the former German Democratic Republic have now become a decisive influence, even more so than Hispanic voters in the United States. The costs of this solidarity represent an enormous volume of yearly transfers of resources from west to east: the amount corresponds to more than twice the annual official development assistance provided by all industrial countries to all developing countries. This has introduced new asymmetries in intergovernmental relations that will continue to haunt German politics and affect regional economic development.

The authorities expected that solidarity with those in the former German Democratic Republic would produce two types of immediate benefits, one political (national integration and political stability), the other economic (the alignment of productivity levels and employment opportunities between regions). Even though the two parts of Germany were reunited 15 years ago, enormous inequalities persist between the west and east German states in many aspects of everyday life. For example, employment rates differ significantly: in mid-2004, the unemployment rate was 9.4 per cent in western Germany, but 20 per cent in eastern Germany. Enormous differences in private wealth and income are also apparent. In 1998 the average household in western Germany possessed average assets of about €131 000, while the assets of the average household in eastern Germany were worth only €45 000 (Federal Ministry of Labour and Social Security 2001a, p. 67). The gross annual income of a salaried west German employee averaged €27 300, while that of an east German averaged only €20 450 (Federal Ministry of Labour and Social Security 2001b, pp. 42–46). Even though large transfers have evened out regional income differentials, they have failed to spur significant productivity increases and growth in the east. Some observers even suspect that the transfers perpetuate existing gaps by preserving outdated economic structures, by discouraging entrepreneurship and by inducing moral hazard.

Irrespective of the asymmetries in favour of the east—which no German politician would dare to censure—interregional solidarity had already come under attack before unification. On the one hand, the donor states criticize the equalization system as being overly burdensome; on the other hand, economists emphasize the inherent economic inefficiencies of the grants system. In particular, the equalizing effects of the Equalization Law have been criticized. Critics see excessive solidarity as dampening accountability, regional growth initiatives and interest in developing own resources and as encouraging moral hazard and waste at the state level. Economists and public finance experts have increasingly taken the view that Germany's 'corporatist' approach to federalism is not only outdated, but is risky in a globalizing environment. According to this view, a modern government should meet the challenge of markets in the same way as the private sector and must accept competition among public entities and institutions (see, for instance, Kronberger Kreis 2000).

European integration has already induced the strengthening of regions, both economically and politically and has fostered a process of decentralization even in unitary states. Elements of 'competitive federalism' are now increasingly being discussed throughout Europe, and in Germany in particular, not only by academic economists, but also by politicians and lawyers. In particular, the concept of subsidiarity—cherished in the Maastricht Treaty as protecting the sovereignty of nation states and lower tiers of government against supranational interference—has become an attractive guiding principle for reorganizing the relationship between the German federation and its states. In this vein of competitive federalism, the governments of some states, notably Bavaria, have begun to question existing financial arrangements, asking for less intergovernmental solidarity and greater autonomy at the state level, in particular, the right to levy some own taxes. The ruling of the Constitutional Court on the November 1999 Equalization Law is pertinent here. Obviously this particular court cannot override the constitution or unilaterally revise it in the spirit of competitive federalism; however, its verdict has given some support to an in-depth revision of the general philosophy of the constitution and has spurred far-reaching discussions about intergovernmental fiscal relations. The following aspects of the court's ruling are noteworthy:

- The arguments in support of the ruling underline 'the preservation of the historic individuality' of the states and 'a degree of competition among the individual states as secured by the federal principle' (section 213) as well as the 'innovation-fostering function of political competition among the states and in relation to the federation' (section 214).[4] This addresses some fundamental criticisms by competitive federalism theorists.
- The verdict requests legislators not only to revise the existing Equalization Law, but insists on a law on general standards that is to specify the basic principles that would govern the equalization process (section 277).
- The law would attain almost constitutional rank, and is supposed to be drafted in the spirit of Rawls's 'veil of ignorance' (section 282), albeit this is too intricate to be realized in practice.

- The court has expressed its unwillingness to tolerate legislation that, in practice, makes the Bundesrat the only entity responsible for equalization (section 284). A simple parliamentary majority would not justify equalization at the expense of a minority of states. The court ascribes a responsible, balancing and neutrally appraising role to the federal government, a duty that is confined by elementary, general and overarching legal principles.

The conflict about equalization, and hence the degree of interregional solidarity, as opposed to lower tiers of government having more autonomy, and hence subsidiarity, is illustrative of the fundamental issues currently under review in Germany. If the public sector at lower tiers of government is to become more active, entrepreneurial, and creative, the federal government should not only rethink its approach towards equalization in light of the court's ruling, but should also tackle more fundamental issues that go beyond the constitution and introduce stronger competitive elements into the German federation.

FISCAL EQUALIZATION AMONG STATES: PROBLEMS AND STRUCTURAL CHANGES TO DATE

At the international level, interregional equalization schemes have adopted varying philosophies. The United States, for instance, does not have explicit regional redistribution programs, but implicit equalization effects result from such things as the progressive national income tax. In addition, regional asymmetries are entrenched in the multitude of federal programs entailing categorical grants to individuals or specific-purpose or bloc grants to regional jurisdictions and government agencies. Moreover, the regional pattern of equalization fluctuates in accordance with variations in local take-up rates of programs and grants.

By contrast, Australia has put in place an explicit and ambitious equalization scheme that aims at full, standardized budget equalization. In establishing a point of reference for such a scheme, Australia not only attempts to evaluate the standardized taxing capacity of its states, but also of standardized expenditures adjusted for needs and cost differentials among jurisdictions.

In Germany, like in Canada, the focus of equalization is on taxable capacity only, with little or no concern for specific burdens. As the tax law is uniform throughout Germany (except for some limited discretion of municipalities to vary their tax rates), standardizing taxable capacity among regions (as in Canada) is unnecessary, because effective tax collections can be considered to reflect regional variations in tax potentials.[5]

Fiscal equalization has both a vertical and a horizontal dimension. Horizontal equalization is typically combined with asymmetric vertical grants designed to close vertical fiscal gaps and to correct regional fiscal imbalances. Once vertical fiscal balance has been achieved, fiscal equalization among Germany's states consists largely of a pure horizontal reallocation of funds among states. However, there is also a vertical allocation of additional funds by the central government that has won prominence as a corrective measure to close remaining gaps and to foster economically weak regions.

Figure 4.2 illustrates the different approaches to interregional fiscal equalization. Australia has a strong, vertical fiscal imbalance in favour of the central government. It corrects this imbalance by using asymmetric vertical grants (based on the goods and services tax) with an implicit equalizing effect. The same is true for the European Union, but the direction of resource flows is upwards, not downwards as in Australia. Germany uses a share of the VAT to establish vertical fiscal balance between the federal government and the states. From this position it organizes the horizontal redistribution of resources among states to achieve regional equalization.

Germany's fiscal equalization among the states is based on the constitution and consists of several steps. Generally, horizontal fiscal equalization among the states can be broken into

- the distribution of corporation tax and income tax,
- the distribution of VAT,
- a narrow definition of fiscal equalization among the states,
- the allocation of additional funds by the federal government.

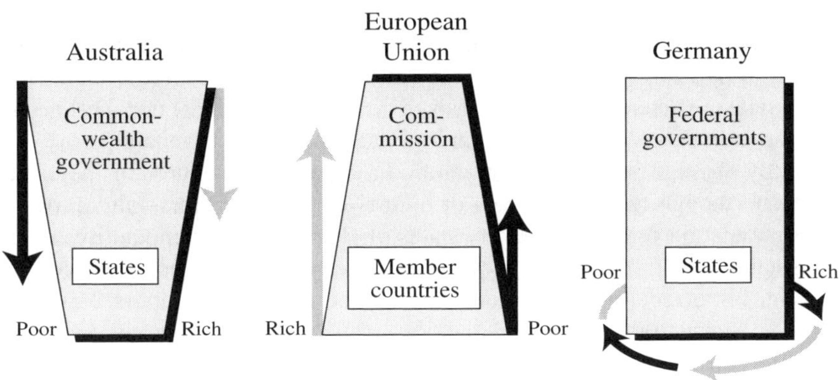

Source: Authors.

Figure 4.2 Approaches to regional equalization in Australia, the European Union and Germany

Generally, fiscal authorities in the respective states are entitled to receive all tax revenue from states' own taxes and a fixed share of both personal and corporate income taxes based on residence and derivation principles. The derivation principle deviates from the residence principle for corporate income tax. A company might have several outlets in different states, but it pays taxes only to the state where its head office is based. This requires a regional re-apportionment of the tax proceeds, which is effected according to the location of business or production units using a formula. However, the regional apportionment of income taxes is more or less in line with regional tax capacity, and no significant equalization effect is implied.

VAT is used for achieving both horizontal and vertical fiscal balance. As regards the regional allocation of VAT revenue, at least 75 per cent of VAT has to be distributed among the states according to the number of inhabitants. The remaining 25 per cent is distributed among the financially weak states. As Figure 4.3 demonstrates, the equalizing effect of this additional distribution is extremely significant.

The figure clearly shows that the allocation of additional VAT entitlements brings the new eastern states (Saxony-Anhalt, Mecklenburg-Western Pomerania, Thuringia, Saxony and Brandenburg) and financially weaker states close to the average level of financial capacity for all the states. Nevertheless, this mechanism for allocating VAT is not officially considered to form part of the equalization process because fiscal equalization is much more narrowly defined as direct, horizontal transfer payments among the states.

To determine the financial capacity of each state, an indicator of financial strength is first calculated by the federal Ministry of Finance that consists of the total of a state's taxes and 50 per cent of its municipal taxes. The states of Bremen, Hamburg, Lower Saxony and Mecklenburg-West Pomerania are allowed to reduce their financial capacity indicator on account of costs incurred by running seaports for the nation.[6] The financial requirements of each state are determined on the basis of an equalization indicator. This equalization indicator is calculated by multiplying the number of inhabitants of that state by average per capita state and municipal tax revenues for the entire country (though only 50 per cent of municipal taxes are taken into account). The population figures of the city states of Hamburg, Bremen and Berlin are adjusted by multiplying them by a factor of 1.35, which has become a controversial issue recently. (For more details, see Baretti and others 2001, pp. 16–18; Hickel 2001, p. 4.) Like the city states, states with densely populated regions can 'adjust' their population in the formula and are allowed to multiply their metropolitan population by a factor of 1.06.

If a state's equalization indicator is larger than its financial capacity per capita, it will receive equalization funds from the financially stronger states, that is, those whose financial capacity per capita is greater than their equalization

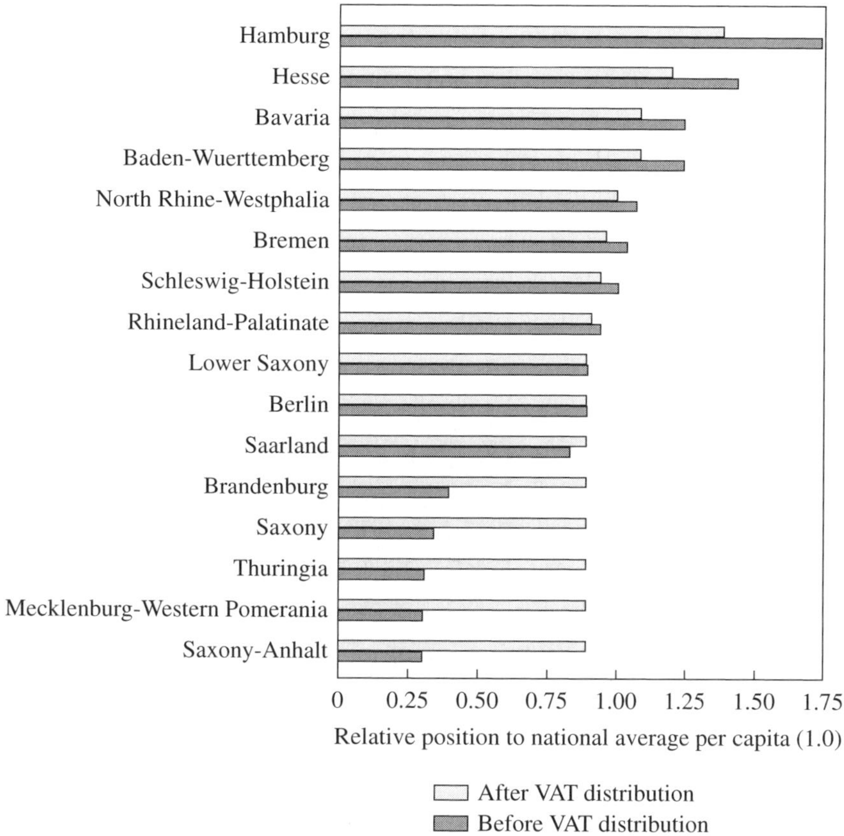

Source: http://www.laenderfinanzausgleich.com.

Figure 4.3 Redistribution effect of VAT allocations to the states, 2001

indicator. Through these equalization funds, the recipient states are able to attain at least 95 per cent of the national average of financial capacity per capita. At the same time, the financial capacity per capita of donor states must not fall below 100 per cent of the nationwide average. Figure 4.4 depicts the effect of horizontal fiscal equalization in 2001.

In addition to the horizontal transfers among states, the states receive additional funding from the central government in the form of federal grants. In 2001 these grants amounted to a total of about €12.6 billion. They are of two kinds: deficit coverage funds and special requirement funds. The deficit

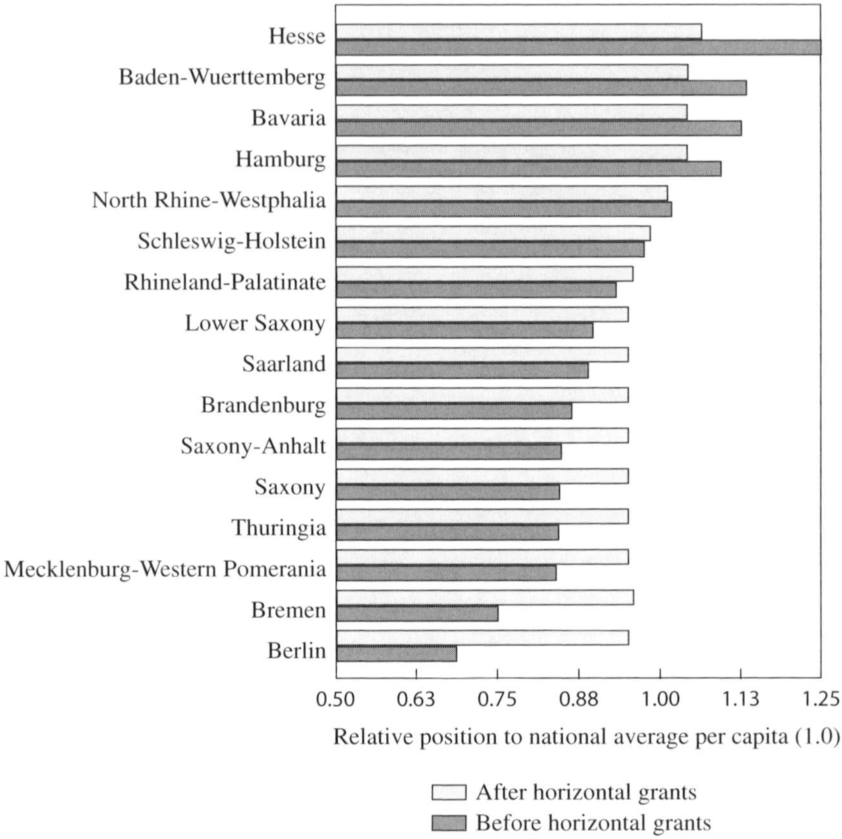

Source: http://www.laenderfinanzausgleich.com.

Figure 4.4 Effect of horizontal fiscal equalization, 2001

coverage funds enable financially weak recipient states to reach 99.5 per cent of the average financial strength per capita of all states. The special requirement funds are targeted to some states for specific purposes. Thus, for example, the central government provides around €0.75 billion a year to all states with fewer than 4 million inhabitants to compensate them for their disproportionately high political and administrative costs per capita. In addition, the central government has provided federal grants for budgetary crises (Bremen and Saarland), for the abolition of special burdens relating to Germany's division (Berlin and all new states) and for compensating western states for adverse effects resulting from unification (Bremen, Saarland, Rhineland-Palatinate,

Lower Saxony and Schleswig-Holstein). Figure 4.5 illustrates the redistributive effect of the vertical grants in 2001.

In its current form, the fiscal equalization system remains a highly contentious issue. As noted earlier, the states of Baden-Wuerttemberg, Bavaria and Hesse filed successful lawsuits with the Constitutional Court, which ruled on them in November 1999. As a result, a reform of the fiscal equalization system had to take place before the end of 2002, because the Constitutional Court declared current practices unconstitutional from 2003 onwards. In June 2001, the states and the central government agreed on a reform—known as the Solidarity Pact II—that came into effect in 2005 and will last until 2019.

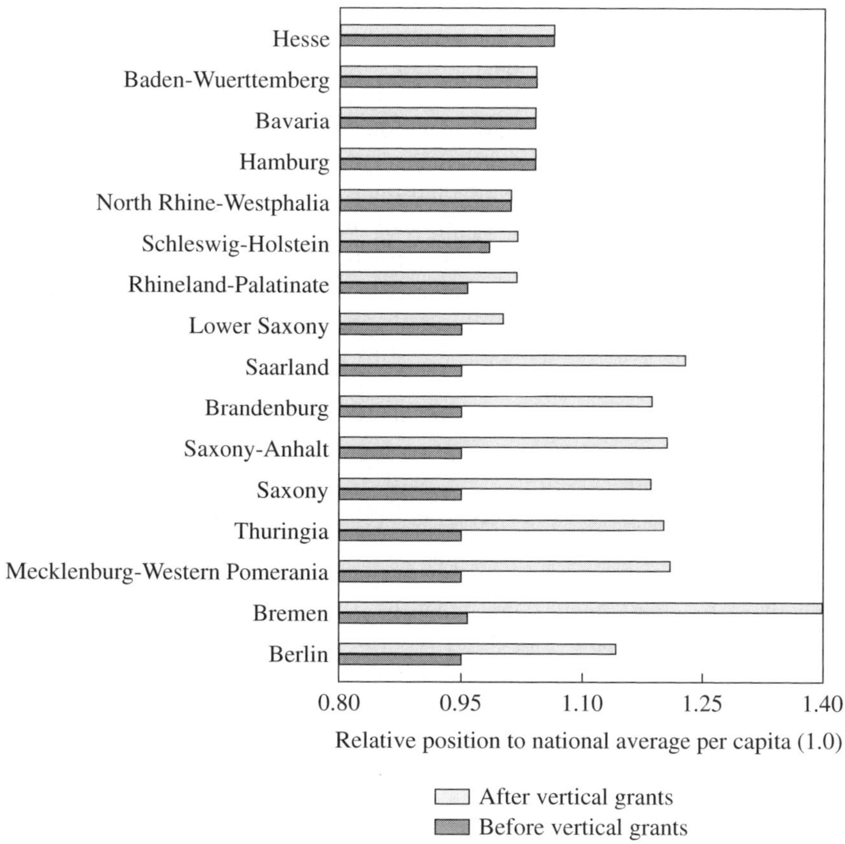

Source: http://www.laenderfinanzausgleich.com.

Figure 4.5 Redistribution effect of vertical federal grants, 2001

THE SOLIDARITY PACT II

The Solidarity Pact II and the corresponding changes to the law have reformed numerous interconnected elements of Germany's fiscal machinery, namely:

- the allocation of the share of VAT to the states,
- the fiscal equalization among the states in a narrow sense (horizontal equalization),
- the allocation of additional funds by the federal government,
- the German Unity Fund.[7]

As concerns fiscal equalization among the states, some parameters will be redefined. As a result, the coastal states of Hamburg, Mecklenburg-West Pomerania, Bremen and Lower Saxony will no longer be able to claim the burden of running ports as a factor that reduces their tax capacity. At the same time, the central government will allocate vertical grants of around €35 million per year to compensate the affected states for the loss of revenue.

The weighing of inhabitants by a factor of 1.35 for the three city states of Hamburg, Bremen and Berlin will persist; however, thinly populated states will also be taken into account when assessing municipal taxes. At the same time, the current municipal weighing of inhabitants, which depends on the size of the municipality and the density of its inhabitants, will be scrapped.

Another change is the increase from 50 to 64 per cent of municipal taxes in calculating a state's financial capacity. This penalizes the financially strong states, because it increases the weight of their financially stronger municipalities. Thus the bonus given to states with financially strong municipalities under the previous system has been reduced, but not completely abolished (Lenk 2002, p. 15).

A so-called premium model will be introduced to give positive incentives to both donor and recipient states under the fiscal equalization system. By disregarding a flat percentage of 12 per cent of above average tax receipts and below average tax shortfalls, which is low compared with the old scheme, states will be rewarded for increasing their tax revenues.

The rates governing horizontal equalization among the states have also been modified, and the graduated tariff or marginal rate of compensation will change to a steadier linear tariff with considerably lower siphoning-off rates as far as donor states are concerned. Consequently, donor states no longer face a marginal siphoning-off rate of up to 80 per cent, but only of 75 per cent.

Figure 4.6 depicts the marginal rates of compensation before the Solidarity Pact II and from 2005 onwards. The dotted line represents the old regime and the continuous line represents the new regime. The left side of the figure

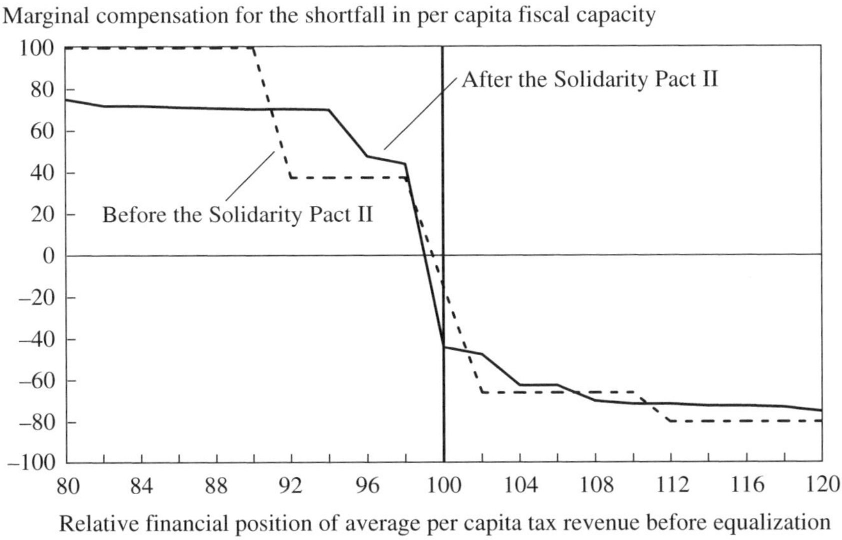

Source: Authors' calculations based on the 2001 and 2005 Equalization Laws.

Figure 4.6 Marginal rates of compensation before and after the Solidarity Pact II (per cent)

portrays the marginal rates of compensation for the receiving states (positive sign). For instance, before 2005, states whose fiscal capacity per capita is below 92 per cent of the national average obtain full compensation under the old regime, so no state can ever fall below this mark. For average fiscal capacity per capita between 92 and 100 per cent, these states obtain only 37.5 per cent marginal compensation, which adds another 37.5 per cent of 8 per cent (the maximum differential remaining), or 3 percentage points. This results in a maximum equalization of 95 per cent relative to the average. The right side of the chart shows the marginal rates of compensation for the contributing states (negative sign). Contributing states may see their marginal tax revenue per capita siphoned off by 80 per cent as they exceed the national average by 10 per cent. From 2005 onwards the formula is more complicated, in that there is no full or proportional compensation for given brackets. Indeed, the formula varies within brackets.[8]

A number of new regulations also affect the vertical allocation of additional funds from the central government. For example, the vertical allocation of federal grants of €770 million per year to go towards the costs of political administration and to assist thinly populated states will be lowered to €520 million per year, and Saxony will be added to the nine states that already receive these grants. The vertical grants for budgetary crises and the federal grants for the integration of the new states into the fiscal equalization system will no longer be provided. The allocation of federal grants for the east German states to compensate them for the burden imposed by the division of Germany will be €10.5 billion in 2005 and will gradually be reduced to €2 billion per year by 2019. (For a discussion of possible contortions of aged population data, see Kitterer 2002, p. 8.)

Overall, the Solidarity Pact II places an additional financial burden on the federal government, and for this reason the federal government and the states have agreed on annual compensations of around €1.32 billion to be paid to the central government from VAT revenues. Figure 4.7 illustrates the impact of horizontal and vertical equalization before and after the Solidarity Pact II based on tax receipts for 2001. It shows clearly that the removal of the vertical allocation of funds for budgetary crises from Bremen and Saarland and the inclusion of Saxony as a recipient of vertical funds to help defray its political administration costs will have significant effects.

THE CONFLICT BETWEEN SOLIDARITY AND SUBSIDIARITY

German decisionmakers are increasingly realizing that achieving homogeneity of outcomes has its price. The ensuing degree of regional redistribution has clearly been pushed beyond its limits: not only has fiscal capacity per capita been totally evened out at a level of 99.5 per cent of the national average, but when taking all federal grants into account, the variations among states will enlarge again, because states with low fiscal capacity per capita before grants will then exceed the per capita fiscal capacity of richer states after the grants.

While interjurisdictional solidarity through equalization certainly facilitates consensus in an intergovernmental framework, it does entail severe political and economic costs. The process of redistribution among states and between the federal government and lower tiers of government breaks necessary links between decisions about expenditures and the financing of those expenditures. This reduces policymakers' accountability and diminishes voters' influence on politicians. Moreover, the states lose interest in developing their own tax bases, for instance, through more effective tax administration or better economic policies. In a formal sense, interregional solidarity reduces the states' financial autonomy even further, an autonomy that is, in any case, already severely curtailed by the constitution. This jeopardizes the independence of their budgeting, and hence of their policies. Moreover, equalization

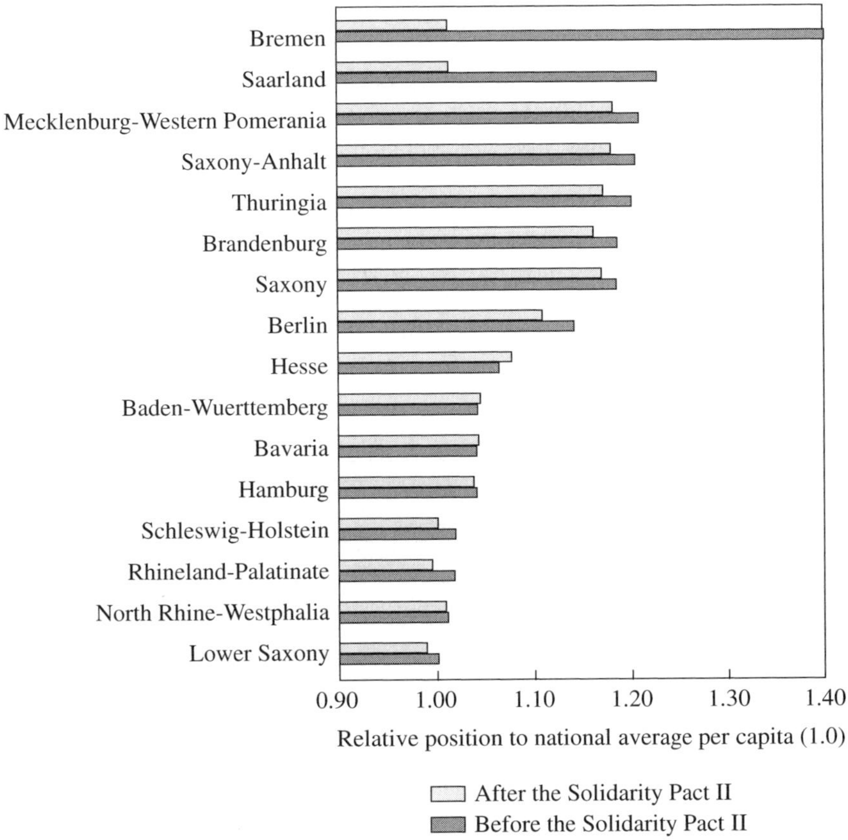

Source: http://www.laenderfinanzausgleich.com.

Figure 4.7 Effects of horizontal and vertical equalization before and after the Solidarity Pact II based on 2001 tax revenues

arrangements that penalize excess fiscal capacity relative to the national mean tend to encourage inefficient budget behaviour, especially if combined with a federal grants scheme that effectively bails out nonperforming state governments.

An analysis of the implicit marginal burden inherent in the system of interstate equalization indicates how much of the additional own revenues will ultimately remain at the disposition of a state, and conversely, what the implicit marginal burden would be on incremental own revenue. If a state is guaranteed a minimum level of resources, and if that state's resources fall below that minimum, the entirety of a tax increase is absorbed by the equalization system. This entails a lack of interest in developing own tax bases by these states. Figure 4.8 indicates the high degree of implicit marginal burden on own taxes inherent in the German system of intergovernmental grants.

A further aspect of the system is related to potential moral hazard by state authorities. A grants system that takes actual revenues and expenditures into account favours irresponsible budget behaviour. If the principle of intergovernmental solidarity means that the budget deficit of any one state is to be carried collectively, states have no incentive to avoid such deficits. While identifying such moral hazard behaviour in practice is not easy, observers suspect that the Equalization Law and federal grants soften hard budget constraints at the state level, resulting in economic inefficiencies and a waste of public resources.

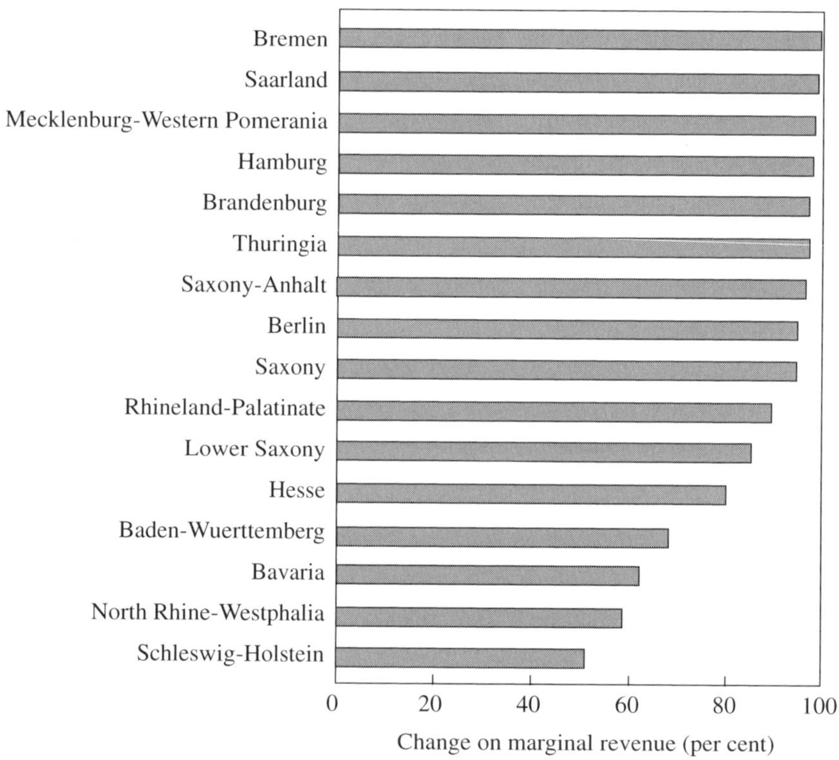

Source: Ebert and Meyer (1999, p. 108).

Figure 4.8 Marginal burden imposed on states' own fiscal resources

States' debt ratios provide an indirect indicator of the inherent drift toward moral hazard. If the consolidation of state budgets through compensating grants would lessen the need for state borrowing, then those states benefiting the most from equalization could perform at least as well as other states in terms of their debt per capita ratio. To examine this proposition, we derived an indicator for the eight states (which include all the eastern states) that top the list in terms of fiscal capacity after redistribution, and compared the result with the same indicator for the poorest eight states after redistribution, which ironically include the more affluent states before redistribution. Figure 4.9 depicts the results.

The eight states that are more affluent before equalization but comparatively poor after federal grants increased their debt per capita ratio continuously during 1991 through 2002, albeit modestly, from €2559 to €4109.

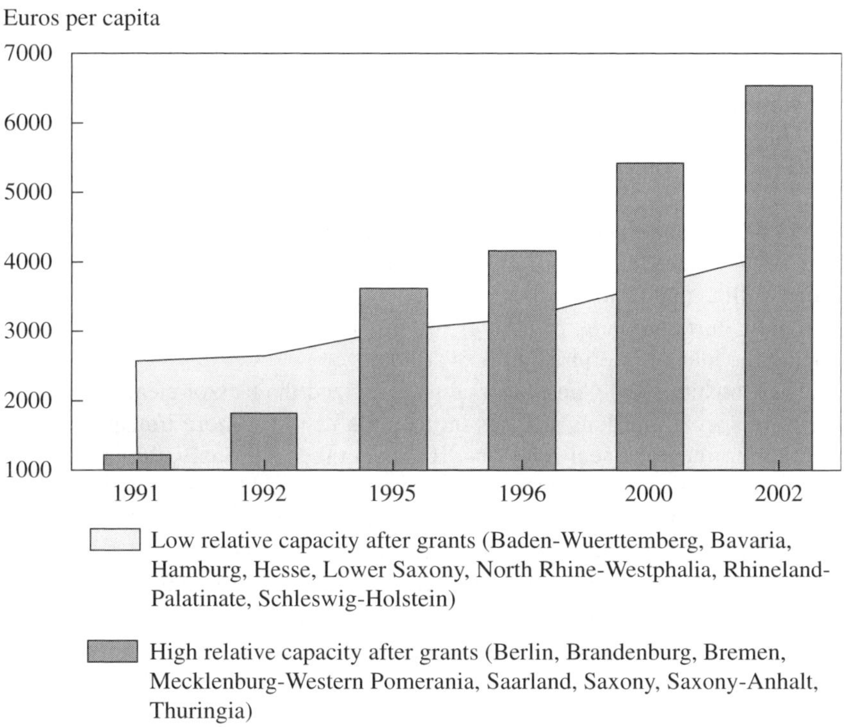

Source: Federal Ministry of Finance data; authors' calculations.

Figure 4.9 State indebtedness per capita for two groups of states, selected years

However, their poorer counterparts before equalization, yet comparatively rich after grants, exhibited a much stronger dynamic in relation to their debt per capita ratio during the same period. This is understandable to some degree, because the group includes the formerly socialist states, which had no debt following unification. Nonetheless, it is puzzling how the other group of states could have expanded their debt in an almost unbridled manner without the incentives embedded in intergovernmental fiscal relations. This suggests the need for a fundamental review of the bond between interregional solidarity and subsidiarity, and between equalization and moral hazard behaviour in particular.

STRIKING A BALANCE BETWEEN SOLIDARITY AND SUBSIDIARITY

Given the mounting criticism of the Equalization Law and the equalizing federal grants programs, the existence of a large number of reform proposals is not surprising. However, given the political significance of this issue, reforms are unlikely to gain broad support.

This is not the place to discuss reform proposals at length (see, for instance, German Council of Economic Experts 1992, 2001; Huber and Lichtblau 1997; Kronberger Kreis 2000; Peffekoven 1994; Renzsch 1999; Rosenfeld 1999; Scientific Council of the Ministry of Finance 1992). However, the broad outline that follows takes into account both the criticisms of the Constitutional Court and some principles of competitive federalism without abandoning the idea of interjurisdictional solidarity.

The Constitutional Court has mainly criticized the lack of clear criteria for defining special burdens and has indicated a need for more transparency in intergovernmental fiscal relations. If this is taken seriously, the authorities will need to define clear criteria for both vertical and horizontal equalization. The current definition of criteria for sharing resources between the federal government and the states is particularly unclear. The court believes that this would be possible on the basis of objective data, which is unlikely to be possible in reality. For example, how does the government evaluate the need for defence at the central level versus needs for education at the state level? Needs criteria are more easily established at a given subnational level for entities with similar responsibilities. For instance, defining criteria for distributing resources for primary education among states is feasible based on the number of school-age children, on student-teacher ratios, and so forth.

However, a clear constitutional dilemma arises here: the constitution mandates a quantitative approach for sharing resources at the vertical level, where it is virtually impossible, and prescribes population as the sole criterion for distributing resources horizontally,[9] where a quantitative, needs-oriented approach would in principle be possible. Moreover, because horizontal equalization is confined exclusively to fiscal capacity, not to expenditure needs, the court has asked that alien elements that have crept into the system, such as bonuses for states with seaports, should either be eliminated, or if accepted in principle, be rendered more general. In this case, other types of special burdens would have to be considered, and would ultimately lead to the adoption of the Australian philosophy of equalization.[10] However, given the tradition of intergovernmental fiscal relations in Germany, for the legislature to follow this avenue and adopt a more comprehensive approach is highly unlikely.

Nevertheless, if Germany were to follow the Australian system, equalizing grants would have to be designed to take into account (a) the relative fiscal position per capita for all current revenue, (b) the states' relative needs criteria and (c) the impact of specific federal transfers that affected the states' relative positions as defined in (a). Moreover, the first two elements would have to be standardized rather than be based on effective revenue or expenditure. In Germany some standardization already occurs in relation to the revenues of municipalities, where an average tax rate is used rather than an effective rate. For the remainder of fiscal revenue, fiscal capacity is already largely standardized by the fact that the tax law is uniform throughout the country. However, this is confined to the legal aspects of taxation. In principle, standardization would have to take into account such factors as regional differences in the tax base or in the effectiveness of tax administration and collection, which is indeed possible as the Australian example demonstrates. If the view is taken that such differences are negligible in Germany, then standardizing revenue beyond the current provisions for municipalities is unnecessary. However, the need to standardize will grow if states and municipalities have greater taxing autonomy.

Relative needs criteria should be translated into necessary expenditures, again at a standardized level. The basic approach is to define the costs of providing standard public services by various governments at any one level. An ideal procedure would be to devise appropriate expenditure categories for which needs are quantified in accordance with statistical methods, which could vary among categories. This is easier in countries with vertical power sharing than in the context of Germany's highly entangled fiscal arrangements, which would seem to call for a certain degree of disentanglement, a notion that is popular is Germany (see Rosenfeld 1999; Scharpf, Reissert and Schnabel 1976). However, despite entangled expenditure functions and a complex web of financial arrangements, including cofinancing, such problems could readily be solved if element (c) were taken into account properly. The solution would imply that the various forms of federal grants would have to be viewed as a way of strengthening states' own fiscal capacities, thus some of the federal grants that are now granted outside the Equalization Law would have to be accounted for prior to horizontal equalization.[11]

If defining a standardized deficit for each state were possible, which would correspond to

$$\text{state population} \times \text{sum of standardized expenditures} - \text{standardized revenue} + \text{grants and cofinancing from the central government,}$$

this would establish a neutral and fair basis for the horizontal equalization. In this context, neutral means that no receiving jurisdiction has an incentive to neglect its own revenue potential or to manipulate its budget, for instance, by increasing its expenditures in the expectation of an automatic bailout.

How far interregional solidarity should go is a matter of political choice. The Constitutional Court has sanctioned a levelling off of 95 per cent of the national average as conforming to the constitution, but has expressed qualms about further compensation that goes beyond that target. This should suffice to guide politicians in reviewing the law. Moreover, the population criterion mandated by the constitution as the guiding principle for interregional equalization could then be employed without further corrections of the interstate equalization system, where special burdens—which would now have been taken care of by specific federal grants at an earlier stage—would no longer play any role. In practice, it would relieve the states from compensating states for special burdens within the interregional equalization mechanism.

The amount the financially stronger states would be asked to contribute to interregional solidarity would depend on the implicit tax rate that reflects the compensation rate depicted in Figure 4.8. Public finance experts have typically expressed the view that this schedule should be linear rather than highly progressive as is currently the case. The rationale for this is mainly to avoid abrupt increases in marginal fiscal increments or siphoning-off rates. What the level of this schedule could be is, again, a political choice.

More competitive elements could easily be introduced into and reconciled with this approach, although they would imply a constitutional amendment. Competitive elements could enhance subsidiarity, and hence strengthen local and regional administrations both politically and economically without jeopardizing interregional solidarity, in particular, states' rights to levy some own taxes. An autonomous tax policy is an essential and constituent element of state sovereignty. It strengthens the accountability of politicians and bureaucrats in relation to their citizens and thus helps make state budget policies more responsive, effective and efficient.

Own taxing rights could simply be introduced in a form analogous to municipalities' rights to vary their tax rates on businesses and land. In particular, allowing states to levy a surcharge on the national income tax collected in their jurisdictions or, preferably, an own tax based on the federal income tax, would be both feasible and equitable. (For a detailed description of this proposal and some suggestion for reforming local taxation in Germany, see Werner 2003, pp. 87–108.) This would be administratively easy to implement and would render the state's tax share more visible to voters, thereby strengthening accountability. Of course, the resulting revenues would have to be exempt from any form of interregional redistribution and remain exclusively available to state authorities to dispose of as they saw fit. The federal government would have to make the necessary adjustments to accommodate such a state surcharge to keep the total tax burden constant. The implementation of this proposal would require a constitutional amendment to allow states to levy such taxes and would also affect the current 50:50 division rule for the vertical distribution of income taxes.

If states continue to be denied the right to levy their own taxes, this could lead to serious pressure to raise revenues through alternative means, which would undermine interregional solidarity in other ways. New methods for raising own revenue are likely to emerge and expand. This would entail a continuing dilemma. If such extra revenues remained excluded from the current equalization mechanisms, debate will continue on what the constitution means by 'current revenue', which is the basis for equalization. The poorer states would put pressure on the richer states to have such revenue included in the interregional solidarity mechanism.[12] However, if such revenue was to be integrated in the interregional solidarity programs—in other words, the states would forego this revenue that they derived from taxing their own citizens on the understanding that it would benefit their communities—this would externalise the lack of incentives for mobilizing own resources and managing regional budgets more efficiently at the state level. Given the history of German federalism and the reluctance to change rules that might be perceived as dismantling interregional solidarity, Germany is likely to choose the latter option.

Given this prospect, whether Germany will be in a position to compete with other nations and regions in a globalizing world is questionable. Excessive solidarity at the expense of regional diversity and freedom to act could jeopardize Germany's ability to meet the challenges imposed by the new economy. To the extent that regional decisionmaking affects economic development and growth, this could affect the welfare of the entire nation.

NOTES

1. During the Middle Ages, the Hanse was a successful organization of merchants in north Germany whose members founded a large number of coastal cities bordering the Baltic Sea and the North Sea.

2. Indeed, centralizing such principles is the rule, but uniform principles can also be established through horizontal coordination among states. This is effected in conferences of state ministries and conforming treaties among governments. One prominent example is the cooperation in education and culture through the interstate Conference of Ministers of Education.
3. Despite these constitutional provisions, some successful incidents of 'pork barreling' have occurred between the federal government and some states with decisive votes, most visibly in the context of securing support for the 2000 tax reform.
4. The quotations in this list have been translated by the authors.
5. A uniform state tax regime is, of course, immune from horizontal tax competition among states in a legal sense; however, states might have incentives to relax their tax administration in an effort to attract and foster regional economic activities. Such incentives are to be expected if the shortfall of revenue resulting from lenient tax administration is fully compensated through equalizing grants, which is true for a number of German states. While leniency has been suspected in some cases, proving its existence in practice is difficult.
6. This reduction amounts to a yearly total of around €150 million, which breaks down as follows: Lower Saxony €9 million, Mecklenburg-West Pomerania €25 million, Hamburg €71 million and Bremen around €45 million.
7. In the wake of German reunification, the central government introduced a number of off-budget funds, such as the German Unity Fund. This was a transitory scheme, funded by borrowing, to channel resources to eastern German states before they were included in the equalization machinery.
8. The explicit formula (for receiving states) is

$$F = \frac{3}{4} \times \left(X - \frac{317}{20\,000}\right) \text{ for a per capita fiscal capacity above 80 per cent,}$$

$$F = X \times \left(\frac{5}{26} \times X + \frac{35}{52}\right) - \frac{2121}{260\,000} \text{ for a per capita fiscal capacity above 80 per cent but below 93 per cent, and}$$

$$F = X \times \left(\frac{13}{7} \times X + \frac{11}{35}\right) \text{ for a per capita fiscal capacity above 93 per cent.}$$

where X is the shortfall of the per capita fiscal capacity below 100 per cent.
9. This is the reason why the legislature weights populations in favour of city states, a procedure criticized by the court.
10. The Australian approach involves standardizing budgets—fiscal capacity as well as revenue needs and costs—to determine the relative position of any one state relative to the average for the assignment of general revenue grants (see, for instance, Rye and Searle 1997; Spahn and Shah 1995).
11. Federal grants as the final step of equalization make sense only if they are understood to compensate for temporary, special burdens. This is true for the transfers destined to alleviate the special situation of the eastern states. These transfers should be retained as a last (fourth) step in correcting states' fiscal capacity. However, they should be phased out over time to underscore their temporary nature.
12. This corresponds to the actual situation in Germany, which the Constitutional Court has expressly sanctioned. Note that in Canada, new tax bases are regularly added to the equalization formula as provinces start to use them, with recent examples being revenue from video lotteries and casinos.

REFERENCES

Baretti, Christian, Bernd Huber, Karl Lichtblau and Rüdiger Parsche (2001), *Die Einwohnerveredelung auf Länderebene im Länderfinanzausgleich: Gutachten im Auftrag der Länder Baden-Württemberg, Bayern, Hessen und Nordrhein-Westfalen*, Munich: IFO Institut für Wirtschaftsforschung.

Ebert, Werner and Steffen Meyer (1999), 'Die Anreizwirkungen des Finanzausgleichs', *Wirtschaftsdienst*, 80 (2), 106–114.

Federal Ministry of Labour and Social Security (2001a), *Lebenslagen in Deutschland: Der erste Armuts- und Reichtumsbericht der Bundesregierung,* Berlin.

——— (2001b), *Lebenslagen in Deutschland: Der erste Armuts- und Reichtumsbericht der Bundesregierung: Daten und Fakten,* Berlin.

German Council of Economic Experts (1992), *Für Wachstumsorientierung: Gegen lähmenden Verteilungsstreit, Jahresgutachten 1992/93*, Stuttgart: Metzler-Poeschel.

——— (2001), *Für Stetigkeit: Gegen Aktionismus, Jahresgutachten 2001/02*, Stuttgart: Metzler-Poeschel.

Hickel, Rudolf (2001), *Einwohnerwertung: Ausgleich für Stadtstaaten als Landeshauptstädte ohne Umland,* Bremen: Fachbereich Wirtschaftswissenschaften der Universität Bremen.

Huber, Bernd and Karl Lichtblau (1997), 'Systemschwächen des Finanzausgleichs: eine Reformskizze', *Wirtschaftsdienst*, 78 (1), 142–47.

Kitterer, Wolfgang (2002), *Die Ausgestaltung der Mittelzuweisungen im Solidarpakt II*, Cologne: Finanzwissenschaftliches Forschungsinstitut an der Universität zu Köln.

Kronberger Kreis (2000), *Die föderative Ordnung in Not: Zur Reform des Finanzausgleichs,* vol. 36, Bad Homburg: Frankfurter Institut.

Lenk, Thomas (2002), *Die Neuregelung des bundesstaatlichen Finanzausgleiches – auf Basis der Steuerschätzung Mai 2002 und einer aktualisierten Bevölkerungsstatistik,* Leipzig: Institut für Finanzen der Universität Leipzig.

Peffekoven, Rolf (1994), 'Reform des Finanzausgleichs: eine vertane Chance', *Finanzarchiv*, 51 (1), 281–311.

Renzsch, Wolfgang (1999), 'Finanzreform 2005: Möglichkeiten und Grenzen', *Wirtschaftsdienst*, 80 (1), 156–63.

Rosenfeld, Martin T. W. (1999), 'Mehr Eigenverantwortung durch Entflechtung?', in Christoph Hüttig and Frank Nägle (eds), *Verflochten und verschuldet: Zum (finanz-) politischen Reformbedarf des deutschen Föderalismus in Europa,* Rehburg-Loccum: Evangelische Akademie Loccum.

Rye, C. Richard and Bob Searle (1997), 'The Fiscal Transfer System in Australia', in Ahmad Ehtisham (ed.), *Financing Decentralized Expenditures,* Cheltenham, UK and Brookfield, US: Edward Elgar, pp. 144–83.

Scientific Council of the Ministry of Finance (1992), *Gutachten zum Länderfinanzausgleich in der Bundesrepublik Deutschland*, vol. 47, Bonn: Ministry of Finance.

Scharpf, Fritz W., Bernd Reissert and Fritz Schnabel (1976), *Politikverflechtung: Theorie und Empirie des kooperativen Föderalismus in der Bundesrepublik*, Kronberg: Scriptor.

Spahn, Paul Bernd and Anwar Shah (1995), 'Intergovernmental Fiscal Relations in Australia', in Roy Jayanta (ed.), *Macroeconomic Management and Fiscal Decentralization*, Washington, DC: World Bank, pp. 49–72.

Werner, Jan (2003), 'El federalismo Alemán: en Estado de Fluctuación', *Zergak Gaceta Tributaria del Pais Vasco*, 25 (3), 81–114.

5. Accommodating Asymmetry Through Pragmatism: An Overview of Swiss Fiscal Federalism

Bernard Dafflon

This chapter deals with issues of symmetry and asymmetry in the Swiss federal system. It begins by addressing three crucial issues of fiscal democracy that have relevance for Switzerland's system of decentralized public finance: the vertical division of power; the institutional background of direct democracy; and the generally cooperative, but in some aspects competitive, behaviour of governmental actors. The following section explains the structure and volume of Switzerland's public sector. This lays the foundations for an analysis of another three issues closely connected to public expenditures and revenues: the application of the subsidiarity principle, the recent phenomenon of creeping centralization and the efforts made towards tax harmonization. The chapter then tackles the issues of subnational budget balance and debt control and their impact on national macroeconomic policy before concluding.

Switzerland is a small country located at the heart of Europe without being a member of the European Union (see Figure 5.1 for a map). The population, 7.2 million in 2000, consists mainly of German-speaking (63.7 per cent), French-speaking (20.4 per cent), Italian-speaking (6.5 per cent) and Romansh-speaking (0.5 per cent) people. All four languages are national languages entrenched in the constitution (Article 4 in the new constitution of 18 April 1999). Some 42 per cent of the population is Roman Catholic and 35 per cent is Protestant. Of the 26 cantons, 14 cantons have a Catholic majority, 9 of which are more than 70 per cent Catholics, and 7 cantons have a Protestant majority, but in none of these cantons does the share of Protestants exceed 70 per cent. In the remaining five cantons, none of the denominations of Christianity is dominant (Swiss Federal Statistical Office 2003, pp. 129 and 166). Languages and denominations are cross-cutting over the territories of the cantons.

Since the 1848 constitution, Switzerland has had a relatively complex system of three layers of government: (a) the communes at the local level, (b) the

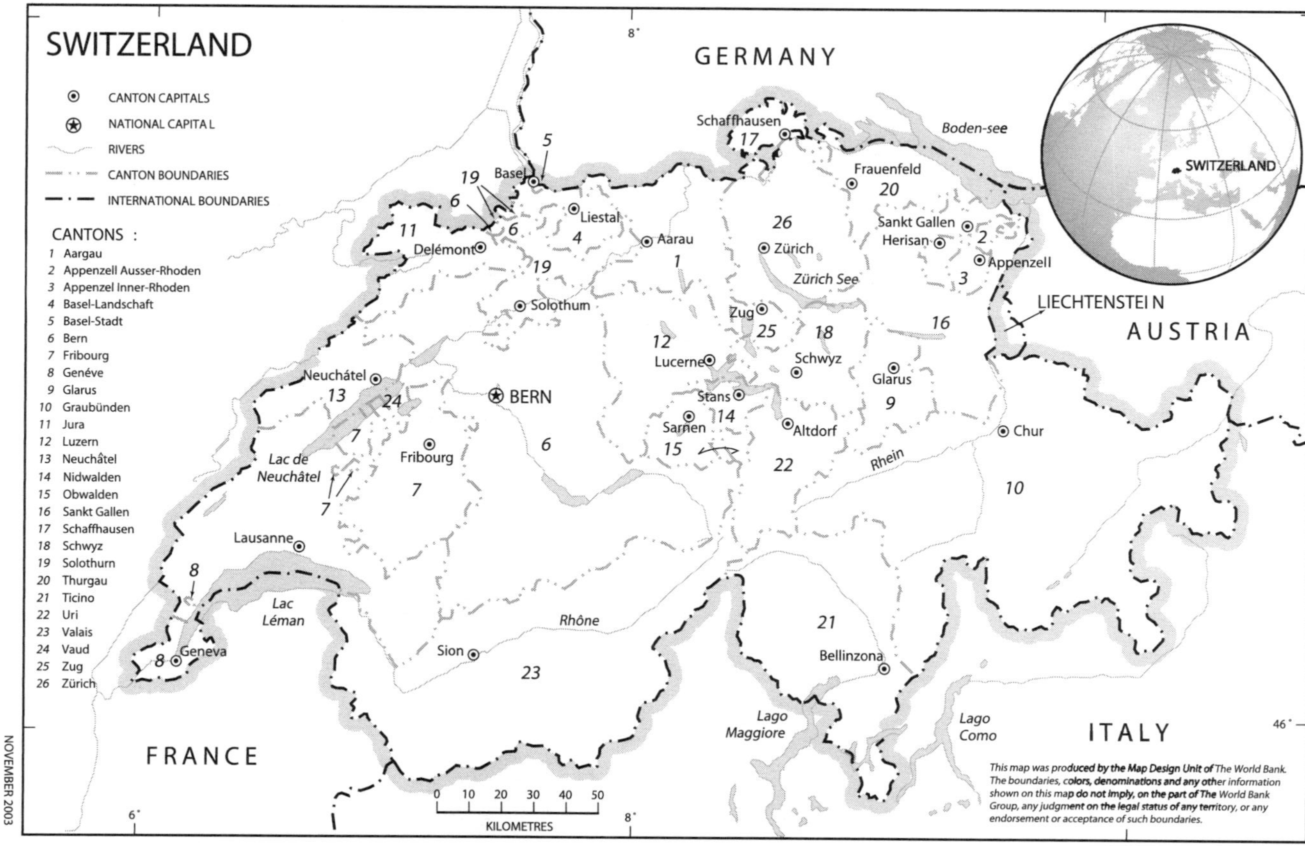

Figure 5.1 *Switzerland*

cantons at the intermediate level and (c) the confederation at the national level, all which are interconnected by many vertical and horizontal relationships. As of the end of 1998, Switzerland had 26 cantons and 2880 communes (see Table 5.1 for some general indicators about Swiss cantons).

Swiss fiscal federalism can be characterized in terms of overall fiscal restraint and minimal centralization of fiscal power. It is traditionally viewed as bottom-up federalism, but in practice, relations between the various levels of government are significantly more complicated than this, largely because of constitutional arrangements at both the federal and the cantonal levels. Several concomitant reasons account for this. One is that the federal government is not as strong as in other European countries. The Swiss political system is consensus government. The federal government consists of a cabinet of seven ministers chosen by the parliament (the National Council and the Council of States) according to an institutionalized but unwritten arrangement that ensures representation of the main political forces, regions and languages. Since 1959, the so-called magic formula has applied to the cabinet: it always consists of two members of the Radical Free Democratic Party, two of the Christian Democratic People's Party, two of the Social Democratic Party and one of the Federal Democratic Union (the agrarian popular party) (Klöti 1999, pp. 165–66). Several other small political parties are found in cantonal governments but are not included in the federal government.

Switzerland has probably respected the subsidiarity principle, which recommends that competencies in the provision of public services should be vested in the lowest possible level in the fiscal hierarchy, more scrupulously than many other federations, both because of constitutional guarantees and because of a traditional mistrust of nationwide policies. In addition, the cantons and communes are seen as public policy and management laboratories carrying out policy innovations without great risk of damaging the overall economy, because it is absolutely certain that the upper-level government (the confederation or the canton) will not provide a bailout. As a consequence, the power to decide and finance the provision of public services has remained largely in decentralized hands in either the cantons or in the communes.

Many forms of cooperative federalism have flourished in recent decades, whether in formal institutions like the intercantonal treaties and various forms of cooperation among communes, or informal institutions, like the intercantonal conferences of ministers or senior civil servants for various functions. The aim of such cooperation has always been pragmatic, that is, to reach certain economies of scale in the provision of public services without undue centralization or to solve local or regional spillover effects. However, it has also served to organize strong pressure groups and lobbying of the federal government by the cantons and of the cantonal authorities by the communes.

The Swiss model of federalism can be characterized by both symmetry and asymmetry. Many of the disparities can be explained by the position of a canton in the global market economy. In addition, while the constitution regards all cantons as perfectly equal,[1] the extensive territorial devolution of powers in practice results in a great deal of asymmetry. Thus the economic positions of the cantons and local choices both induce disparities. In any case, because the equalization system irons out excessive disparities in financial capacity, decentralized governments are virtually encouraged to act diversely. But how can growing imbalances be accommodated in a system in which canton-commune relations are beyond the federal government's reach?

One would expect that the extensive devolution of taxation powers and expenditure decisions to subnational levels, combined with internal control mechanisms, like the institutions of direct democracy and interjurisdictional mobility (voice and exit, in Hirschmann's [1970] terminology), is an efficient incentive for responsible financial behaviour. Nevertheless, horizontal and vertical fiscal equalization is indispensable for attenuating extreme disparities that are beyond the control of subnational governments. This inevitably leads to two questions. First, can or does this induce the cantons to play a strategic game whereby they overspend and undersave in the hope that the federal government will bail them out through grants? Second, could the federal government's intervention to equalize disparities be reduced if cantons and communes themselves attempted to harmonize those fiscal parameters over which they have control?

On the one hand, differences in the budgetary choices and other aspects of policy decisions of cantonal and local governments are scrupulously respected not only as a necessity, but also as a fundamental part of sovereignty. On the other hand, in the end the federal government assumes the consequences of cantonal and communal sovereignty.[2] Can the federal government share this burden with subnational governments, and if so, how?

The fairly extensive autonomy of cantonal and communal governments in relation to finance is not unlimited. Competition between jurisdictions is a first limit. Second, many cantons have introduced their own constitutional rules with regard to balanced budgets and debt limitations. Fiscal competition is partly softened by rules governing tax coordination and harmonization. However, autonomy in public expenditures, direct access to many revenue sources and, above all, differences in the cantons' economic potential (see Table 5.1, columns 6–8) have led to relatively important regional disparities, expressed in the fiscal burdens of the cantons and in their financial capacity. These disparities lie at the core of Swiss equalization policy, although Switzerland makes no claims about achieving perfect equality between the cantons or the communes.

Table 5.1 General indicators, by canton, 2000

Canton	Number of communes	Area[a] (km^2)	Population: Total	Population: Density (people/km^2)	Cantonal revenue: Total (Sw F) millions	Cantonal revenue: Sw F per capita	Cantonal revenue: Per capita variation 1980–2000[b] (%)	Cantonal revenue: Current and capital expend-itures	Public finance (Sw F thousands)[c]: Revenues	Public finance (Sw F thousands)[c]: Balance	Public finance (Sw F thousands)[c]: Per capita public expend-itures	Public finance (Sw F thousands)[c]: Public sector size (%)
1	2	3	4	5	6	7	8	9	10	11 (10 – 9)	12	13 (9/6)
Zurich	171	1729	1 211 647	701	78 683	64 378	10.5	9 212 598	10 171 845	959 247	7603	12
Bern	400	5959	943 696	158	37 396	39 339	–27.9	7 276 607	7 586 625	310 018	7711	19
Lucerne	107	1493	347 209	233	13 553	39 285	–18.4	2 390 186	2 583 984	193 798	6884	18
Uri	20	1077	35 246	33	1440	41 854	–14.6	450 169	437 857	–12 312	12 772	31
Schwyz	30	908	130 232	143	6106	47 544	20.8	694 075	780 534	86 459	5330	11
Obwald	7	491	32 414	66	1057	32 872	–18.2	256 506	262 927	6421	7913	24
Nidwald	11	276	38 000	138	2262	61 360	59.6	262 669	267 199	4530	6912	12
Glaris	29	685	38 546	56	2207	57 763	47.0	342 160	371 582	29 422	8877	16
Zug	11	239	99 388	416	7875	79 962	132.9	764 337	787 258	22 921	7690	10
Fribourg	226	1671	236 339	141	8763	36 954	–5.1	2 017 039	2 023 978	6939	8535	23
Solothurn	126	791	244 015	308	9874	40 769	18.2	1 503 452	1 518 836	15 384	6161	15
Basel-City	3	37	187 667	5072	16 865	88 477	142.4	3 608 973	3 827 612	218 639	19 231	21
Basel-Land	86	517	260 036	503	13 275	51 654	49.2	2 110 118	2 222 891	112 773	8115	16

Schaffhausen	34	299	73 305	245	3596	49 364	51.9	493 935	511 040	17 105	6738	14
Appenzell Outer Rhodes	20	243	53 515	220	2209	41 544	–6.3	348 059	366 525	18 466	6504	16
Appenzell Inner Rhodes	6	173	15 021	87	646	44 023	17.7	107 606	112,929	5323	7164	17
St. Gall	90	2026	449 399	222	18 347	40 983	24.3	3 323 806	3 681 058	357 252	7396	18
Grisons	212	7105	186 744	26	7834	41 650	34.1	1 757 974	1 752 615	–5359	9414	22
Argovie	232	1404	544 306	388	25 358	46 920	30.4	3 261 720	3 317 233	55 513	5992	13
Thurgovie	80	991	227 306	229	9146	40 285	18.9	1 316 280	1 381 017	64 737	5791	14
Tessin	245	2812	310 215	110	11 659	37 795	20.7	2 376 150	2 526 819	150 669	7660	20
Vaud	384	3212	620 294	193	31 150	49 562	38.5	5 741 052	5 552 903	–188 149	9255	18
Valais	160	5225	276 170	53	9325	34 216	6.3	2 231 634	2 212 551	–19 083	8081	24
Neuchâtel	62	803	165 731	206	7184	43 250	34.1	1 606 753	1 584 059	–22 694	9695	22
Geneva	45	282	408 820	1450	23 987	58 641	86.9	6 005 193	6 268 416	263 223	14 689	25
Jura	83	839	68 794	82	2295	34 174	7.3	692 308	707 491	15 183	10 063	30
Total	2880	41 287	7 204 055	174	352 092	48 840	23.1	60 151 359[d]	62 817 784	2 666 425	8350	17

a. Excludes lakes and glaciers.
b. Rate of growth of per capita revenue between 1980 and 1999 in real values. Current cantonal revenue values have been deflated by the indexes of consumption prices.
c. Values for the cantons only. The public expenditures of the communes amount to 67 per cent of the cantons' total.
d. Total current expenditures is Sw F 52 683 million and total capital expenditures is Sw F 7468 million.

Sources: Federal Department of Finance (2002, p. 59); Ladner and others (2000); Swiss Federal Statistical Office (2002, p. 66).

FISCAL DEMOCRACY

In fiscal federalism, institutions play an important role in shaping the relationships between the various layers of government. This section therefore looks at the workings of institutions in Switzerland, particularly the rules and principles, that govern the assignment of functions and revenue sources to decentralized jurisdictions. Three institutional characteristics are essential to the functioning of Swiss federalism: (a) the vertical division of power in the federal constitutions; (b) direct democracy, initiatives and referendums; and (c) horizontal cooperation between governments at the cantonal and communal levels.

Vertical Division of Power

The Swiss federal system emphasises the sovereignty of subcentral jurisdictions, namely, the cantons and communes. This sovereignty is derived from the federal and cantonal constitutions, which not only list the tasks of each level of government, but also fix their right to levy some sorts of taxes. Thus the assignment of competencies and revenue sources is guaranteed at each level of government. The vertical division of power, intended to prevent stable majorities from being able to exploit minorities, is strongly safeguarded in the federal constitution (Knapp 1986; Zimmermann 1987).

Article 3 of the 1999 federal constitution guarantees the cantons' sovereignty in all the spheres in which the constitution does not explicitly provide for the federal government's competence. Article 42 defines the assignment of functions to the confederation in a restrictive manner as follows: 'It shall accomplish the tasks which are attributed to it by the Constitution'.[3] Therefore each new competence of the federal government requires a constitutional amendment, which requires the consent of both a majority of the voters and a majority of the cantons. In contrast, article 43 stipulates that 'the Cantons shall define the tasks which they shall accomplish within the framework of their powers'. At the cantonal level, an explicit clarification in their constitutions is unnecessary. The autonomy of the cantons is also guaranteed by the legislative authority of two chambers that have equal power (article 148). The National Council (House of Representatives) is elected based on population in the cantons according to a system of proportional representation. The Council of States (the Senate) consists of 46 delegates of the cantons, two for each canton and one for each half canton (Appenzell Inner Rhodes and Appenzell Outer Rhodes, Basel-City and Basel-Land and Nidwald and Obwald) whatever its population, size or economic and financial power. The cantons regulate the elections of their senators.

This description also corresponds to the basics of the 1848 constitution; however, the 1999 constitution introduced considerable changes in the vertical division of power. Until 1999, fiscal and financial arrangements were discussed either at the federal-cantonal levels or at the cantonal-communal levels. The federal government could not bypass cantonal governments to address communal governments, either in relation to fiscal or financial matters or to the provision of public services. The inverse was also true: communal governments could not bypass cantonal authorities and had no direct access to federal bureaus or institutions. In this way, federal decisions concerned the cantons only and each canton organized communal competencies on its own.

This vertical division of power leaves the cantons with a high degree of autonomy, but also creates problems for the larger municipalities. On the one hand, the cantons have their own fiscal systems, which are independent of the federal system. The cantons are therefore able to set their own tax rates, and they decide on the provision of public goods and services on their own. Even though the procedures of direct democratic participation are long and complex, each voter/taxpayer in a canton or a commune is able to compare the costs and benefits of the public activity under consideration and decide on the amount of public expenditure in a vote or referendum. On the other hand, cantons that are large municipalities or agglomerations, like Zurich, which has more residents than the six neighbouring cantons put together, create spillovers over cantonal boundaries, but do not have the ability to negotiate directly across those boundaries.

Even though agglomerations have a statistical definition, and have been an expanding economic reality for the last three decades, only the 1999 federal constitution recognizes them as institutions. Article 50 envisages that for its activities, the confederation 'shall take into account the special situation of cities, agglomerations and mountainous regions'. This supplement to the constitution is the outcome of a long process whereby large cities and the Union of Swiss Towns have been increasingly claiming the right to participate directly in federal decisions that could affect the cities and their agglomerations and in the elaboration of federal policy on urban areas. This demand has come about because the share of the population living in urban areas has increased rapidly in recent years, reaching 75 per cent in 2000 according to census data from the Federal Office of Statistics. In addition, direct contacts between the confederation and the communes exist in a number of policy fields, for example, social policy and the environment. Article 50 is now being put into practice on the basis of a directive issued by the federal government in October 2002. This stresses that direct contact between the confederation and the communes is possible in a tripartite framework constituted by the three levels of government whenever anticipated measures by the Federal Council are likely to affect some or all communes, or when federal legislation directly charges the communes with executing a new public task. As a general rule, in such cases the federal government is to address itself to the communes' umbrella organizations, namely, the Association of Swiss Communes, the Union of Swiss Towns and the Swiss Grouping for Mountainous Regions. In matters concerning large urban areas, the forum for decisionmaking is the Tripartite Conference on Agglomerations. Direct contacts between the confederation and the communes should be the exception rather than the rule. Recognizing that the establishment of direct contacts between the highest and lowest tiers of government that circumvent the cantons is a politically sensitive issue, the Federal Council has decreed that with regard to the elaboration, implementation and evaluation of federal policy measures, the canton shall always be the confederation's main partner. In addition, any direct participation by communes in decisionmaking must always be transparent in relation to the cantons. Whatever the intent, the actual realization of these new intergovernmental relations and their impact on decisionmaking processes remains to be examined in the coming years.

Figure 5.2 illustrates this new vertical division of power. The black arrows drawn from the bottom to the top on the left-hand side illustrate the direction in which responsibilities were transferred from one government level to another. According to the 1848 constitution, all power and competence emanated from the people, who were free to concede any areas of power to higher levels of government. Such transfers always resulted in certain repercussions for the lower levels, signalled by the dashed arrows going from the top to the bottom.

This mechanism has not ceased to work under the 1999 constitution; however, it is accompanied by two recent phenomena that can be observed on the right-hand side. First, as noted earlier, the new constitution has granted cities and agglomerations the right to address themselves directly to the federal government, circumventing the cantons as intermediate authorities, and to participate in the decisionmaking process under certain conditions. This relationship is indicated by the upward arrow pointing from the urban communes to the federal government. Of course, agglomerations still have the right to address themselves to the canton, as indicated by the solid arrow from the urban communes to the cantons. Second, there is a creeping tendency towards centralization, as the federal government is transforming its partnership with the cantons into what one could refer to as executive federalism. The federal government has a growing preference for issuing framework regulations whose implementation it then delegates to the cantons, thereby limiting the cantons' room for making their own policy choices. The cantons, for their part, apply many of the same methods in relation to the communes. This is certainly not a consequence of the 1999 federal constitution, but is a tendency that complicates the vertical division of power between the tiers of government. The downward arrows pointing from the federal government to the

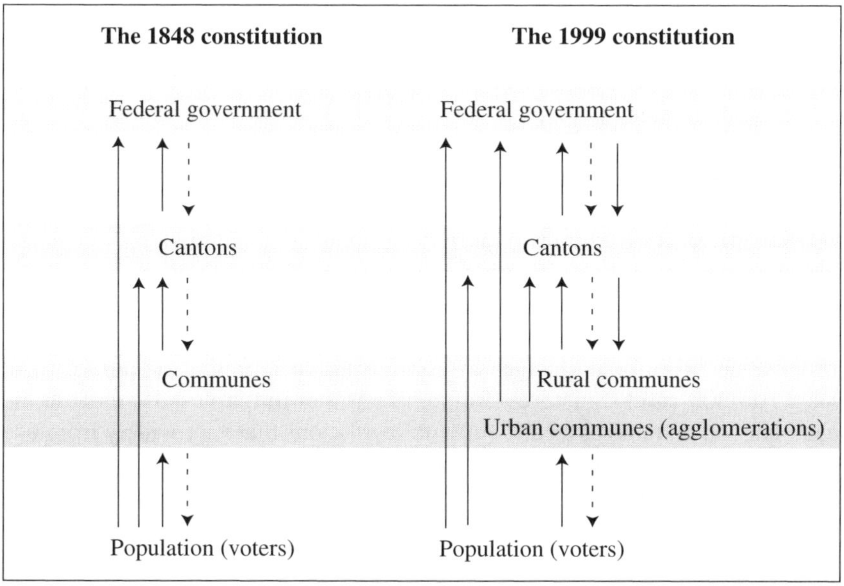

Source: Author.

Figure 5.2 The vertical division of power in the 1848 and 1999 constitutions

cantons and from the cantons to the communes on the right-hand side illustrate this new type of interaction.

Direct Democracy, Initiatives and Referendums

Most cantonal constitutions provide for direct participation in democracy by the communes so that citizens can take part in the decisionmaking on all important political and economic issues. In local public finance, this competence concerns current budgets, individual investment items from the capital budget, annual tax coefficients, regulations governing user charges, local public property sales or purchases, horizontal cooperation in the form of intercommunal association or special purpose districts for the joint provision of public facilities and amalgamation of communes. In addition to participation, control and audit competencies of some sort also exist. The communal assembly of citizens, or the communal parliament where it exists, elects a finance committee for a particular term. This committee not only has traditional audit competencies, but must also report to the assembly on the financial aspects of capital expenditures and changes in taxation. In addition, it has the power to investigate financial matters without warning if necessary. In some cantons, it may lodge complaints against individual members of the local authorities about any misuse of public funds.

When democracy is representative, which is the case in most cantons and in large cities, voters express their preferences about political and economic issues mainly via referendums, which may be brought up for a vote several times a year. Every federal bill may be submitted to a referendum if at least 50 000 citizens or 8 cantons require it (optional referendums). Any constitutional changes and the ratification of international treaties are automatically submitted to a compulsory referendum and can be enacted only if the majority of the voters and the majority of the cantons accept them. Citizens may also propose constitutional changes by submitting an initiative supported by at least 100 000 valid signatures. Referendums and initiatives also exist at the cantonal and communal levels, but with regulations that vary widely from one canton or commune to another (Novaresi 2001).

These institutions play the role of moderator for cantonal and local governments, because all important public decisions are usually subject to approval by voters. At the communal level, the most common items that might be included in an initiative or referendum procedure are much the same as those subject to voter approval at the cantonal level.

Obviously these institutions do not have the sole purpose of assuring economic efficiency in relation to expenditures and taxation. The more direct and democratic the institutions are, the better is their general capacity to strengthen the system of checks and balances, by both dividing and sharing political decisionmaking power. They give voters/taxpayers access to government, increase their capacity to control budgets and reduce political and bureaucratic leeway in rent-seeking behaviour. In Hirschman's terminology, they not only have the exit solution, but also the voice solution. The result is that the growth of government activity has been significantly lower than in representative democracies (Pommerehne and Schneider 1978), the size of government is limited (Pommerehne 1978) and public expenditures are demand-driven (Kirchgässner and Pommerehne 1990).[4] Other things being equal, jurisdictions with direct democracy also demonstrate a higher degree of economic efficiency (as measured by cantonal revenue per capita) and budget responsibility than those with purely representative democracy (Feld and Savioz 1997).

Cooperative Federalism

The federal and cantonal constitutions permit intensive horizontal cooperation at the cantonal and communal levels of government. This horizontal cooperation is important for the principle of fiscal equivalence (Olson 1969), so that the circles of decisionmakers, beneficiaries and payers coincide. The cantons and communes are free to conclude agreements with each another on cooperation in the most varied areas and so establish for themselves the optimum area necessary for the performance of government tasks, for example, university funding (intercantonal cooperation) or the maintenance of school districts and water provision (intercommunal cooperation) (new forms of intercantonal cooperation are described in Frey and Eichenberger 1999). Cooperation is not just permitted by the constitution, but in several policy areas is actively sought by cantons and communes.

The Swiss have an inherent tendency towards compromise and consensus and a strong commitment to safeguarding the interests of small groups (Spahn 1997), which helps them preserve a high degree of diversity. Yet even though intercantonal agreements are quite successful for several cantonal public policies and functions (university financing is a good example), they have failed with regard to taxation. In this policy area, harmonization has generally been formal, under the pretext that tax competition and regional growth policies should be promoted. Another reason why cooperative federalism should not be idealized is the simultaneous tendency to executive federalism mentioned in connection with Figure 5.2, that is, the creeping centralization of regulations and norms for public expenditures and tax resources.

Horizontal face-to-face cooperation between the cantons has taken another form that the constitution did not foresee. When the need for a nationwide steering policy arises, fiscal federalism in theory suggests that this should be realized at the centre by the federal government. This is not always the case in Switzerland, where the cantons have organized themselves horizontally in a set of powerful committees, the so-called conferences of cantonal ministers, one for each government function, of which the Conference of Cantonal Governments and the Conference of Cantonal Ministers of Finance are the most influential.

From a constitutional point of view, fiscal and financial relations between the federal government and the cantons cannot be tailored according to individual canton's characteristics or wishes. Equality of treatment applies, except within the Equalization Law. Although each canton could challenge fiscal and financial arrangements or negotiate them individually with the federal government, a single canton would stand little chance of modifying fiscal and financial arrangements to meet its own objectives, because any change has to be acceptable to the other cantons.

Within the conferences, the cantons negotiate common policies without interference from the centre, then present a common package to the federal government. The objective of the Conference of Cantonal Ministers of Finance is to discuss fiscal and financial matters that are of common interest to all or many of the cantons. It has been organized as much to coordinate and harmonize the fiscal and financial affairs of the cantons (horizontal relations) as to intervene more persuasively in federal-cantonal relations and to interfere sometimes in federal fiscal and financial matters. The conferences are not a constitutional institution. Yet fiscal matters cannot be decided at the federal level without previous consultations with the Conference of Cantonal Ministers of Finance. It is a powerful pressure group that the federal Finance Administration regularly consults. It has been successful in negotiating financial packages in which the point of view of the cantons differs from that of the federal government; has played an important role in shaping federal finance, the federal tax system and tax harmonization; and has a dominant position in federal equalization policies (Dafflon 1995). The Conference of Cantonal Governments exerts a powerful counterbalance against federal policy proposals. The entire process for a new fiscal equalization package, which is currently under discussion and is expected to enter into force in 2006, is a joint venture of the federal Ministry of Finance and the Conference of Cantonal Ministers of Finance.

The high degree of cantonal influence on federal decisionmaking makes the implementation of structural reforms fairly difficult. In the 1990s, experts from the Organisation for Economic Co-operation and Development found that the policies the cantons pursued were too often uncoordinated and marked by undesirable competition (Spahn 1997). In addition, intercantonal negotiations are seldom marked exclusively by cooperation. In a number of policy fields competitive elements dominate the consultations, even though there seems to be an accord about cooperation. Taxation is a good example. The 1990 federal law on the harmonization of direct taxation by the cantons and communes provides a comprehensive list of tax deductions and exemptions, but does not fix any amount. Cantons are free to offer generous deduction rules, competing with one another for the benefit of the most mobile taxpayers and to the detriment of immobile ones. A 1948 intercantonal agreement regulates tax competition, but as the sanctions for noncompliance are somewhat derisory and without any practical use (for example, a sanction procedure can be initiated only if one canton brings a lawsuit against another), the cantons have considerable room for manoeuvre. This reinforces competitive rather than cooperative behaviour between the cantons. In recent years, voters in federal and cantonal referendums have systematically rejected the idea of unifying tax rates. At the same time, however, the increasing fiscal competition between the cantons creates disparities that more and more people are perceiving to be unacceptable.

At the local level, the main incentives for intercommunal cooperation are, traditionally, low economies of scale; regional spillover effects; and, more recently, limited managerial skills in several small municipalities, especially when local governments function as production agencies for cantons or the confederation as, for example, in the field of national environmental policies.

Contrary to other federal countries, Switzerland has no de-concentrated federal agencies that act as regional public service providers that have to respect minimum standards set by the central government. As agents, the cantons decide how they will provide public services and usually assign them to the communes. There is no duplication of public service providers at the decentralized levels.

The communes have taken advantage of the opportunity to create intercommunal institutions, which has improved their efficiency in producing and delivering local public services. However, the multiplicity of intercommunal special-purpose districts has also created many institutional problems, such as the democratic deficit in the political decisionmaking procedures of the communes; the higher information and participation costs for individual citizens who belong not only to one commune, but to several groupings of communes; the strategic blockages of votes by negotiating communes when a qualified majority is required; and the like (Della Santa 1996). Despite these inconveniences, this executive flexibility of federalism may be precisely what has long made federalism resistant to attempts at centralization by the federal government in relation to the cantons or on the part of the cantons in relation to the communes. It also explains why so many small communes can survive without merging and why citizens do not readily accept the compulsory merging of extremely small communes (Dafflon 1998).

PUBLIC EXPENDITURES

The institutional arrangements presented in the previous section result in a price to be paid in terms of economic efficiency and equity. The solutions and practical arrangements do not conform to the textbook canon of fiscal federalism, nor do they permit a levelling out of all differences in the economy and the public sector. Marked differences exist between the cantons with regard to the organization of local government; to the number of communes; and to size, population and income (Table 5.1). Similarly, the growth of per capita cantonal revenue also varies considerably across the cantons. A comparative analysis of the cantons' positions with regard to the size and growth of their cantonal revenue per capita shows that, despite some 30 years of national fiscal equalization policy and as many years of regional development policies, the position of most of the poorest cantons has not improved significantly and the richest cantons have generally maintained their relative position. Thus neither equalization nor regional development policies appear to have been particularly effective (Federal Council 2002; Frey and others 1994), although in the absence of such policies, the disparities would probably have become even more acute and may eventually have jeopardized the basic structures of solidarity and social peace in the federation. Note also that the federal equalization policy has not had a completely gap-filling objective in setting revenue sharing formulas or equalizing grants.

In the urban cantons, like Basel-City or Geneva, where the volume of per capita public expenditures is considerably higher than the national average, the cantonal tier plays a central role compared with that of the communes. A more centralized delivery of public services internalizes urban benefit spillovers and reduces coordination and information costs. By contrast, in rural cantons with a relatively large number of communes and low financial capacity, such as Jura, an equivalent volume and quality of services weighs heavily on communal budgets: cantons and communes thus play an almost equal role in the provision and financing of public services. Nevertheless, there is no significant inverse correlation between the financial capacity of a canton and the size of its per capita public expenditures.

In relation to gross national product, the size of the public sector is still quite low—some 30 per cent in recent years—compared with other European countries. In 2000, the actual shares of the confederation, the cantons and the communes in total public expenditures were 32, 40 and 27 per cent, respectively, and have remained fairly stable in recent decades (Table 5.2). In times of economic downturns, like between 1990 and 2000, a slight trend towards centralization at the cantonal and federal levels is perceptible at the expense of the communes.

Exclusive Functions and Shared Responsibilities

Table 5.3 summarizes total expenditures for each function performed by the three levels of government. In almost all fields of public intervention, responsibility is shared to some extent. Obviously, the confederation is solely responsible for foreign affairs and for a significant portion of national defence (90 per cent), but the cantons and communes are primarily responsible for other items, such as education, culture, sports and recreation, health, the environment and roads.

Table 5.4 indicates the respective shares of public expenditures in the budgets of the three tiers of government. The table reveals the following in relation to horizontal shares:

- The communes have the highest share of expenditures in relation to the environment (62 per cent); culture, sports and leisure (54 per cent); and administration (42 per cent).
- The cantons have the highest share of expenditures in relation to public order (67 per cent), health (56 per cent) and education (54 per cent).

Table 5.2 Growth of the public sector, selected years

Tier of government	1970 Sw F millions	1970 Share of total (%)	1980 Sw F millions	1980 Share of total (%)	1980 Growth rate 1970–80 (%)	1990 Sw F millions	1990 Share of total (%)	1990 Growth rate 1980–90 (%)	2000 Sw F millions	2000 Share of total (%)	2000 Growth rate 1990–2000 (%)	2000 Growth rate 1970–2000 (%)
Confederation	7834	32	17 532	32	1.24	31 616	31	0.80	48 208	32	0.52	5.15
Cantons	9533	39	21 926	39	1.30	41 116	40	0.88	60 151	40	0.46	5.31
Communes	6840	29	16 476	29	1.41	30 245	29	0.84	40 599	27	0.34	4.94
Total (less social security expenditures)	24 207	100	55 934	100	1.31	102 977	100	0.84	148 958	100	0.45	5.15
Percentage of GNP	22.0	n.a.	29.8	n.a.	n.a.	29.5	n.a.	n.a.	30.6	n.a.	n.a.	n.a.

n.a. Not applicable.
GNP Gross national product.
Note: All figures in Swiss francs are in current values.

Source: Federal Department of Finance (2002, pp. 2–3).

Table 5.3 Public expenditures by tier of government, 2000 (Sw F thousands)

Function	Confederation	Cantons	Communes
Administration	1 651 665	3 007 253	3 417 301
Public order	548 548	4 832 425	1 833 573
Police	150 851	2 239 186	751 721
Justice	85 714	1 041 110	38 451
Fire fighting	0	61 768	487 272
Other	311 983	1 490 361	556 129
National defence	5 004 615	285 750	249 256
Army	4 912 655	176 830	53 498
Civil defence	91 960	108 920	195 758
Foreign affairs	2 273 607	0	0
Education	3 456 539	14 673 954	9 282 751
Kindergartens	0	367 458	702 111
Public schools	15 943	5 544 493	7 067 112
Special schools	0	507 662	541 546
Professional teaching centres	445 048	2 541 627	793 992
Colleges	11 438	1 859 926	82 822
Higher technical schools	18 826	415 271	18 172
Universities, research facilities	2 212 344	3 094 379	11 683
Other	752 940	343 138	65 313
Culture, sports and leisure	572 911	1 236 885	2 158 088
Culture	299 872	625 149	843 363
Sports	134 122	126 536	723 845
Leisure	138 917	485 200	590 880
Health	212 647	9 836 196	7 393 097
Hospitals	7 996	7 555 460	5 287 317
Other	204 651	2 280 736	2 105 780
Social affairs	12 273 563	10 700 206	6 013 066
Old-age pensions	4 582 728	1 062 103	209 877
Insurance for the disabled	3 331 381	1 106 561	173 206
Illness insurance	1 738 249	2 586 864	371 561
Other social insurance	951 613	2 151 333	899 625
Public housing	272 522	184 661	53 071
Homes for old-age pensioners	0	36 710	901 159
Individual social aid	1 397 070	2 843 749	2 845 323
Other	0	728 225	559 244

Table 5.3 (continued)

Function	Confederation	Cantons	Communes
Transportation	7 400 807	6 198 380	2 913 108
Roads	2 859 966	4 527 888	2 333 681
Railways	3 204 536	0	0
Regional public transportation	1 044 501	1 207 314	554 594
Others	291 804	463 178	24 833
Environment	745 624	1 413 412	3 530 432
Water	0	39 839	284 264
Sewage and water purification plants	176 569	493 679	1 554 346
Garbage collection and disposal	46 076	162 756	894 569
Land planning, zoning	319 756	472 430	222 229
Other	203 223	244 708	575 024
Economy	4 654 329	4 008 272	850 022
Agriculture	3 727 490	2 735 406	115 017
Foresty	341 450	587 914	368 357
Other	585 389	684 952	366 648
Finance	9 413 168	3 958 627	2 958 347
Equalization	0	705 010	388 327
Revenue sharing	5 709 507	625 154	0
Public debt interest and management	3 703 661	2 493 293	2 543 110
Other	0	135 170	26 910
Total	48 208 023	60 151 360	40 599 041

Source: Federal Department of Finance (2002, pp. 24, 44, 76).

- The confederation has exclusive responsibility for foreign affairs (100 per cent), a dominant position in relation to national defence (90 per cent) and assumes more than half of public expenditures in relation to finance (58 per cent) because of soaring debt service requirements. Its share is also predominant in the economy (49 per cent) and transportation (45 per cent).
- Although the cantons and the communes together spend more, the confederation has the largest single share in social affairs (42 per cent).

Table 5.4 Shares of public expenditures by tier of government, 2000 (per cent)

	Proportion of the function for the tier of government (vertical)			Proportion of the function within the tier of government (horizontal)		
Function	Confed-eration	Cantons	Com-munes	Confed-eration	Cantons	Com-munes
Administration	3	5	8	20	37	42
Public order	1	8	5	8	67	25
National defence	10	0	1	90	5	4
Foreign affairs	5	0	0	100	0	0
Education	7	24	23	13	54	34
Culture, sports, leisure	1	2	5	14	31	54
Health	0	16	18	1	56	42
Social affairs	25	18	15	42	37	21
Transportation	15	10	7	45	38	18
Environment	2	2	9	13	25	62
Economy	10	7	2	49	42	9
Finance	20	7	7	58	24	18
Total	100	100	100	32	40	27

Source: Author's calculations from Table 5.3.

In only a few cases does one tier of government have exclusive responsibility for a function. Otherwise the division of powers and the principle of subsidiarity apply. Thus general functions are subdivided, for example, as concerns social affairs, the federal government plays an important but not dominant role. Table 5.3 shows that it has the primary role only for old-age pensions, insurance for the disabled and public housing. Both the cantons and communes are primarily responsible for illness insurance and individual social aid, while cantons bear the brunt of other social insurance items, mainly family allowances. This type of vertical assignment exists for almost all subfunctions, but differs within each canton between the cantonal and communal layers.

In contrast with shares in total public expenditure, the assignment of functions between the three tiers of government has changed continuously over the 150 years of the confederation's existence. The optimum division of competencies is certainly never definitive, and the question of which tasks should be assigned to which level of government has been answered only provisionally to date (Dafflon 1992). Nevertheless, during the past three decades no major adjustments have been implemented. The current division of public expenditures may be explained in terms of subsidiarity and centralization; however, the process as a whole has been laborious and somewhat conservative, with political strategies and bureaucratic blockages often jeopardizing the results.

Articles 54 to 125 of the 1999 federal constitution contain an exhaustive and detailed enumeration of federal competencies. The constitution always specifies whether the federal level or cantons are responsible for a particular a function, and in the case of shared responsibilities, it defines the extent of central government involvement in cantonal affairs. However, as Table 5.3 indicates, the three layers of government share responsibility to some extent for almost all fields of public intervention.

The relative stability of the division of responsibilities in the last 30 years is largely due to a somewhat conservative evolution of public spending practices. When a particular function requires more resources compared with others, the growth of expenditures for that function runs almost parallel at the three levels. Various attempts to modify the existing constitutional division of tasks between the federal government and the cantons have either failed or produced negligible results. Changes in the relative positions of the three tiers may, however, occur, usually because of external circumstances. For instance, with the economic crisis of the 1990s and the concerns about high unemployment, the participation of the cantons in the distribution of individual social aid increased significantly, and by 2000 their level of participation was virtually commensurate with that of the communes. In other words, the burden of social aid financing has shifted from the communal to the cantonal level.

Subsidiarity

The fundamental principle in the distribution of tasks between the various levels of government is subsidiarity. Competencies are vested at the local level and can be transferred to the cantonal level only if the lower level is no longer in a position to provide a service efficiently. In most cantons, a constitutional amendment decided by popular vote or, at least a law passed by the cantonal parliament, which is sometimes subject to referendum, is necessary. The same principle is valid between the cantonal and federal levels. A transfer of competence from the cantons to the federal government must be accompanied by the passage of a constitutional law, with a majority of both voters and cantons agreeing to the transfer.

Reaching agreement on the concept of subsidiarity has not been difficult. The key questions are not semantic, but concern (a) the definition and measurement of efficiency, (b) the determination of who decides when the provision of a local (decentralized) public service is no longer efficient and (c) the level at which the responsibility should be centralized.

However, opinions diverge about which efficiency criteria are appropriate for the organization and reorganization of functions within the three layers of government (see Walsh 1993, pp. 32–35 for a summary of the normative arguments). Economies of scale, homogeneity of preferences, spillover effects and congestion costs are generally accepted as efficiency criteria (Dafflon 1992), but relatively poor governments, which argue that they ought to receive more equalization payments, dispute the criteria of financial capacity and budgetary resources. At the local level, implementation criteria are also fiercely debated. The issues are (a) whether the subsidiarity principle should take small communes' low technical capacity to manage their own responsibilities into account; (b) whether the amalgamation of communes is a prerequisite for more equalization; or (c) whether it is expedient to set minimum requirements at a level that small communes find difficult to comply with so as to stimulate them to amalgamate with each other, to establish special districts of cooperation for particular services or to shift the competence to the canton. Wiseman (1989) argues that efficiency criteria must be related to the capability to strengthen political checks and balances through appropriate procedures and not to tax and expenditure outcomes as such. This is probably the theoretical argument that most closely corresponds to Switzerland's situation. The resulting allocation of expenditure functions and of policymaking within the communes, the cantons and the confederation does not correspond to simple rules that ensure neatness and smoothness. Instead, an elaborate system of compromises limits horizontal and vertical coercion, which has led to the budgets of the different levels of government becoming increasingly entangled.

Education is a good example of how the subsidiarity principle is being applied. Table 5.4 shows that the cantonal level has the prime responsibility for education, with around 54 per cent of total public outlays, followed by the communal level (34 per cent) and the confederation (13 per cent). However, when the levels of education are broken out, the picture is quite different. Kindergartens (66 per cent) and public schools (56 per cent) are principally in local hands. For public schools, the communes have command mainly over school buildings and equipment. They are also responsible for teachers' salaries, but the cantons set salary levels. The cantons are also primarily responsible for decisions about teachers' qualifications and curricula (for the latter, sometimes in coordination with other cantons within the Conference of Cantonal Ministers of Education). Special schools are a communal responsibility in some cantons and a cantonal responsibility in others. Professional schools, teacher training centres, colleges and technical schools are predominantly at the cantonal level and are run with little intervention by the federal government. Except for the federal polytechnics, universities are cantonal, but are partly financed by all the cantons through horizontal transfers per student according to their place of residence and through federal grants-in-aid.

The subsidiarity principle implicitly carries with it the acceptance of asymmetry in the provision of public services. Indeed, it creates a melange of homogeneity and asymmetry between the autonomous subnational government units. In the field of education, examples of asymmetry include the following:

- Some variations are apparent in curricula, for example, schools in the canton of Zurich and several other cantons in east Switzerland prefer to teach English as a second language rather than French as a second national language, whereas French-speaking cantons continue to teach German as a second national language. Because of a significant dispute about what second language should be taught in the schools, a federal parliamentary proposal is now being considered to oblige all the cantons to teach another national language as a first priority. If this succeeds, it will be another step towards creeping legal centralization.
- The size of primary school classes varies between 18 and 29, with consequently different implications for pupils.
- Classes with a relatively high proportion of foreign language students may or may not receive special pedagogical support, usually depending on the canton's budgetary constraints.
- While all the cantons have free public schools plus private schools for which parents pay fees, a few cantons provide vouchers for private schools.

Whether the asymmetry is an appropriate tool for recognizing diversity and whether differentiation is needed to attain somewhat uniform service delivery or whether it will foster national integration or disintegration is unclear. Consider the case of primary schools. Subsidiarity and asymmetry are certainly needed and useful if the objective is to preserve or promote cantonal historical and cultural diversity, for example, Geneva and Zurich have neither the same approach towards nor the same tradition in teaching history, which in turn differs in a bilingual canton like Valais or Fribourg. There is no objective necessity for uniformity, but the cantons have to harmonize their public school programs to some extent, because of parents' increasing mobility among the cantons. This has been achieved and through intercantonal agreement. Nevertheless, the cantons were unable to agree on, for instance, whether the school year was to start in spring or autumn, to the point that the start of the school year had to be mandated by the constitution.

Creeping Centralization

Even though statistical data show that the relative shares of public expenditures by each tier have not much changed during the past 30 years (Table 5.2), creeping centralization is apparent in the ways in which cantonal and communal governments perform. A distinction, described in the fiscal federalism literature as agency or choice models, may be useful for understanding the issue. In the last three decades, the federal government has increasingly confined itself to issuing framework laws and has delegated the implementation of national functions to the cantons, which in turn have often transferred the tasks to their communes. This is the agency model.

As explained earlier, the federal government has few exclusive functions. The cantons are responsible for a number of tasks for which they receive financial support and guidance from the federal government. The centre seldom acts directly when implementing policies. Instead, it passes legislation that the cantons then implement. This corresponds with the Swiss notion of executive federalism, sometimes also referred to as administrative federalism (Germann 1986).

Both the functional and economic classification of public expenditures at the three levels of government reflect the confederation's limited participation in policy implementation (Tables 5.3, 5.4 and 5.5). In the functional classification of public expenditure at the various government levels, as already noted, a marked difference is apparent between the confederation and the other two tiers with respect to their participation in expenditures on education, the environment and health care (Tables 5.3 and 5.4). In the field of environmental policy, regulations are federal, while the executive agencies are mainly the communes, and their environmental expenditures amounted to some 62 per cent of total public outlays for this function in 2000. In health care, the federal government is responsible for only around 1 per cent of total expenditures, even though the health insurance system is governed by a federal framework law. The health system and the financial consequences of the law remain in the hands of the cantons (56 per cent) and of the communes (43 per cent). In the economic classification of public expenditures, the federal budget is a budget of transfers (Table 5.5). Transfer payments represent 54 per cent of total current plus capital expenditures.

Debate in the cantons about the effective extent of autonomy in local public expenditures is ongoing, first and foremost because no single measure of independence is appropriate (Wolman 1990). A second difficulty in measuring decentralization is that fiscal and financial relationships between communal and cantonal governments vary from one canton to another depending on the 26 cantonal constitutions. Yet the general trend in all the cantons has been that first, under the constraint of a current balanced budget, the communes' choice role has made increasing room for the agency role, and second, the change in the relative weights of the two roles is inversely related to the population of the communes, in that larger municipalities have been better able to maintain a higher proportion of the choice role (Dafflon and Perritaz 2000).[5]

Other researchers, for example, Wälti and Bullinger (2000), believe that administrative federalism was more a phenomenon of the 1970s and 1980s, and that it gave way to a more complex system of dual federalism from the 1990s onwards. The economic crisis of the 1990s and the growing pressure from the European Union to harmonize legislation in fields of common interest has forced the federal government to take a leading role in a number of policy areas. Yet the institutions of direct democracy and the traditions of consensus seeking limit the federal government's scope of action.

In any case, recent decades have revealed a clear tendency towards centralization. In relation to the tension between subsidiarity and centralization, two points deserve attention.

First, a higher level of government cannot readily impose its own ideas of efficiency upon a lower level of government, because it must respect democratic procedures. The difficulties inherent in amalgamating two or several communes is a good example: this has proved almost impossible on a compulsory basis despite the argument that communes are often too small to correctly perform the functions assigned to them. The voluntary amalgamation of communes occurs in response to other than strict fiscal considerations (Dafflon 1998). The thesis on the limited influence of higher-level governments on lower levels also applies to the relations between the confederation and the cantons. Wälti and Bullinger (2000) analyse the extent to which federalism matters in designing and implementing policies in Switzerland. They conclude that in several policy fields where decisions are taken jointly by the federal and cantonal governments, the predominant power of the cantons during implementation often constrains the federal government's ambitions. The ongoing reform of fiscal equalization is a good example.

Second, if a function needs more centralization, the impetus will come not from agencies of the higher-level government, but by lower-level tiers of government acting as agencies. Thus the communes will first organize in special intercommunal jurisdictions rather than give up a function to the canton. In addition, the cantons implement many federal standards mainly through bylaws or cantonal court decisions. In general, duplication of service provision precincts is absent, for instance, federal agencies acting in the cantons or cantonal agencies acting in the communes. The communes act as implementation agencies of the canton or the confederation, most often with the capacity to provide more than the required minimum service level if they want to, with the additional difficulty (from an analytical point of view) of distinguishing what is the required standard and what is the choice component.

Finally, figuring out how the centralization tendencies fit with the nontrivial asymmetry of Swiss federalism is not straightforward. Creeping centralization might indicate that asymmetric federalism has its limits. The federal government is not as powerful at mastering and fostering diversity and maintaining

Table 5.5 Economic classification of public expenditures by tier of government, 2000

	Confederation		Cantons		Communes	
Type of public expenditures	Sw F thousands	Percentage of total federal expenditure	Sw F thousands	Percentage of total canton expenditure	Sw F thousands	Percentage of total communal expenditure
Current account						
Personnel	5 278 947	11.0	21 793 860	36.2	15 494 725	38.2
Consumption	5 113 649	10.6	6 999 639	11.6	8 538 853	21.0
Interest	3 489 181	7.2	2 341 108	3.9	2 092 731	5.2
Revenue sharing and block grants	5 709 507	11.8	1 330 164	2.2	388 327	1.0
Grants-in-aid and reimbursements	22 066 144	45.8	20 218 584	33.6	8 849 069	21.8
Public sector						
Confederation	0		11 748		0	
Cantons	7 911 822		686 818		3 982 545	
Communes	0		4 658 108		1 536 150	
Semipublic sector	9 777 201		3 615 054		596 557	
Foreign countries	1 705 798		0		0	
Private sector	2 671 323		11 933 674		4 269 967	

Capital account						
Own investments	739 211	1.5	4 814 712	8.0	4 624 969	11.4
Loans and contributions	1 691 027	3.5	935 092	1.6	254 000	0.6
Grants-in-aid and reimbursements	4 120 358	8.5	1 708 580	2.8	356 336	0.9
Public sector						
Confederation	0		2729		0	
Cantons	2 590 365		6386		80 472	
Communes	0		809 230		99 507	
Semipublic sector	1 427 197		333 266		49 267	
Private sector	102 796		563 355		226 597	
Other	0	0.0	9619	0.0	30	0.0
Total	48 208 024	100.0	60 151 358	100.0	40 599 040	100.0

Note: Transactions between jurisdictions of the same government tier (canton-canton and commune-commune) are eliminated from the total to avoid double counting. We strictly followed the methodology of the Federal Department of Finance.

Source: Federal Department of Finance (2002, pp. 20, 40, 72, 74).

symmetry as one might expect. In some policy fields, especially where the protection of citizens' basic interests or the provision of a standard minimum level of service is deemed appropriate, the federal government should dictate the rules and enforce their implementation. However, it cannot always direct instruction and carry out enforcement, as proven by the fact that the large cities are fairly successful in backing out of their agency role in a number of policy fields.

PUBLIC REVENUES

In 2000, public revenues of the confederation, the cantons and the communes amounted to Sw F 156 879 million (Table 5.6). Since 1990, total revenues have been sufficient to cover total public expenditures at each level of government. Table 5.6 provides details of public revenue sources. Taxation is the most important single source of revenue for all three levels of government (Table 5.7).

The federal constitution organizes taxes in the following way:

- The federal government can levy federal direct tax on personal income and corporate profits, but in doing so it has to bear in mind that direct taxation is also the main source of finance at the cantonal and communal levels and that it must refund 30 per cent of the federal direct tax to the cantons, 17 per cent of it according to the derivation principle and 13 per cent for equalization purposes based on the cantons' fiscal capacities.
- The cantons have no access to value added tax, special sales and excise taxes, stamp duties (on certain capital and insurance transactions), withholding tax and customs tariffs, which are strictly federal.

Vertical Tax Coordination

Vertical coordination concerns the assignment of tax authority to the various levels of government. Which jurisdiction is entitled to tax which items from which taxpayer needs to be clear and attention must be given to the geographical distribution of tax yields. A good tax under subcentral authorities should have a tax base that is widely and evenly distributed throughout the country (King 1984, pp. 210–11). In general, Switzerland fulfils the objectives of vertical tax coordination in that

- the three levels of government have stable and predictable revenue sources,
- a high proportion of total cantonal and communal revenue is own revenue,

Table 5.6 Public revenues by tier of government, 2000 (Sw F thousands)

Sources	Confederation	Cantons	Communes
Taxes on income and wealth	21 032 541	26 771 016	20 165 057
Income of individuals	5 712 618	17 329 024	14 283 324
Wealth of individuals	n.a.	2 207 290	1 723 152
Corporate profits	4 891 385	3 934 369	2 377 805
Corporate capital	36 541	807 249	457 808
Immovable property	n.a.	186 519	548 327
Capital gains	44 170	474 338	415 752
Inheritance and gifts	n.a.	1 114 689	97 140
Transfer of immovable property	n.a.	717 538	261 749
Withholding tax	6 202 061	n.a.	n.a.
Stamp tax	4 145 766	n.a.	n.a.
Consumption or expenditure taxes	25 459 674	1 740 501	60 641
VAT	16 593 820	n.a.	n.a.
Tobacco	1 671 797	n.a.	n.a.
Customs and import duties	1 089 146	n.a.	n.a.
Petrol and other fuel oils	4 974 761	n.a.	n.a.
Motorway vouchers	643 167	n.a.	n.a.
Motor vehicles	n.a.	1 669 910	n.a.
Entertainment	n.a.	27 033	26 348
Dogs	n.a.	9 199	21 236
Other	486 983	34 359	13 057
Fiscal monopolies, licences	871 144	696 927	124 977
Revenues from public property	1 994 617	3 523 418	3 000 436
Interest, dividends	693 279	845 370	596 302
Rents	43 818	397 595	1 297 360
Others	1 257 520	2 280 453	1 106 774
Revenue sharing	5 687	4 186 365	1 324 477
Federal direct tax	n.a.	3 224 573	n.a.
Withholding tax	n.a.	616 386	n.a.
Military tax	n.a.	32 625	n.a.
Other	5 687	312 781	n.a.
Grants-in-aid	14 477	15 099 660	5 961 658
Federal grants-in-aid	n.a.	10 310 796	16 883
Cantonal	14 477	693 204	5 467 338
Communal	n.a.	4 063 017	1 635 657
Other	n.a.	725 847	477 437

(continued)

Table 5.6 (continued)

Sources	Confederation	Cantons	Communes
Indemnities and sales	2 616 226	10 799 901	11 430 338
Administrative fees	326 775	1 362 125	390 164
Sales of products and services	386 624	4 931 815	7 730 848
Sales of property	40 707	63 482	70 517
Reimbursements	1 210 915	1 912 901	563 167
Other	651 205	2 529 578	2 675 642
Total	51 994 366	62 817 788	42 067 584

n.a. Not applicable.
Note: Transactions between jurisdictions of the same government tier (canton-canton and commune-commune) are eliminated from the total to avoid double counting. We strictly followed the methodology of the Federal Department of Finance.

Source: Federal Department of Finance (2002, pp. 22, 26, 42, 74, 137, 139 and 141).

- the cantonal and communal levels have significant tax scope,
- the taxation system and accountability mechanisms are decentralized and efficient.

Table 5.6 indicates that vertical coordination is obtained partly through the allocation of exclusive tax sources to each level of government according to the doctrine of the separation of sources. This is clear for consumption and expenditure taxes, where no overlapping of tax bases occurs between the confederation, the cantons and the communes.

By contrast, direct taxation—personal income, corporate profits and corporate capital—are taxed at all three levels.[6] The vertical apportionment between the three levels of government is somewhat complex and often left implicit. It is obtained in two ways: moderate taxation at each level so that no single level of government exhausts taxpayers' entire tax capacity and an unwritten assignment of priority, with taxes assigned first to the cantons, then to the communes and finally to the confederation. Traditionally, the federal share of direct taxation does not exceed a quarter of the total.[7] The minimum taxable income is higher at the federal level than in the cantons and the tax rate schedule is more progressive.

One of the unique features of Switzerland's tax system is that vertical tax coordination is written into the constitution and the federal direct tax is supposed to be a temporary tax. According to article 196 of the 1999 constitution, the federal direct tax may only be levied until the end of 2006. Thus some years before this limit, the federal government is having to justify the further need to levy a direct tax at the central level in concurrence with the cantons

Table 5.7 Revenue sources by tier of government, 2000 (per cent)

Source	Confed-eration	Cantons	Com-munes	Total
Direct taxation	40	43	48	43
Consumption and expenditure taxes	49	3	n.a.	17
Fiscal monopolies, licences	2	1	n.a.	1
Public property	4	6	7	5
Revenue sharing	n.a.	7	3	4
Grants-in-aid and reimbursements	n.a.	24	14	13
From the Confederation	n.a.	16	0	n.a.
From the cantons	0	n.a.	13	n.a.
From the communes	0	6	n.a.	n.a.
Indemnities and user charges	5	17	27	16
Total	100	100	100	100

n.a. Not applicable.

Source: Author's calculations from Table 5.6.

and the communes and explain its motives. The decision to continue to levy a federal direct tax requires the agreement of a majority of voters and of cantons, which gives the cantons powerful leverage for obtaining compensatory advantages, notably, by means of the equalization policy.

Vertical coordination between the cantons and their communes is secured, because local governments have no sovereignty in these matters, but only tax flexibility. The most debated question is whether communal governments can tap this source in priority to the detriment of the cantons. The usual solution is that communal tax coefficients are subject to an upper limit fixed in cantonal law in proportion to cantonal taxes, for example, in the canton of Fribourg, this limit is fixed at a maximum level of 125 per cent of cantonal taxes.

Tax Harmonization

The tax system contains a certain degree of flexibility. Tax variables are largely under the control of the cantons and the communes, and consequently determine the volume of financial resources at their disposal, and thus the extent of their autonomy. Except for consumption taxes, which are exclusively federal, an important characteristic of the system is cantons' and communes' direct access to a number of fiscal (tax and nontax) resources. This secures regular annual receipts, compared with a situation where a government must rely on a single tax. It enables better distribution of the fiscal burden and avoids burdening particular categories of taxpayers in case fiscal needs are higher than expected. This can also be understood in the light of the cantons' low dependence on transfer payments from the federal government and the communes' low dependence on transfer payments from the cantons. Table 5.7 shows the percentages of various categories of revenue for the three levels of government.

Debate about the exact definition of tax sovereignty is never-ending. Tax sovereignty concerns a government's ability to decide what to tax, its direct access to taxation and the management of taxes. This can be summarized by the formula

$$T = t \times [B - (D_1, D_2, D_3, \ldots D_l, \ldots D_n)] \times (K_{fed} + K_{canton} + K_{commune}),$$

where T is the revenue from a tax, t is the tax rate schedule, B is the gross tax base, D is the possible deductions from the tax base and K is the annual coefficient aiming at a balanced current budget (or a balanced overall budget in the case of the confederation). Referring to this formula, the extent of tax sovereignty can be indicated by the following sequence of choices: (a) the use of the ability to pay principle (taxes) versus the benefit principle (user charges); (b) the object of taxation, implicit in [. . .] in the foregoing formula; (c) the group of taxpayers, including the definition of the taxpaying unit; (d) the computation of the tax bases, for example, for the taxation of income, the definition of gross taxable income B and specific deductions and exemptions, that is, D_1, D_2 and so on; (e) the tax rate schedules t, including the amount of deductions and exemptions in (d); (f) the annual coefficient of taxation K in the canton or the commune; (g) the tax collection; and (h) the procedure in case of disputes.

Full tax sovereignty comprises letters (a) to (h) in the foregoing list. Partial tax sovereignty exists where a government can decide (a) and some, but not all, of items listed between (b) and (e). Tax flexibility means that a government can at least decide on the coefficient of taxation—(f)—but cannot define the kinds of taxes it can raise. Compulsory taxation is where a government has no choice over (a) through (f) and must raise taxes or impose user charges according to the regulations set by a higher level of government.

In Switzerland, tax sovereignty lies primarily in the cantons and secondarily in the confederation to such an extent that it is stated in articles 128–34 of the 1999 federal constitution. Cantons are largely free to structure and frame their tax systems and determine the tax burden. This freedom is restricted only by the Federal Court's jurisprudence, which prohibits double taxation. In addition, the cantons are bound by three articles in the federal constitution that allocate indirect taxation (value added taxes and special consumption taxes) exclusively to the centre and another that forbids taxes to take the form of tariff barriers, which could impede the free movement of goods between cantons. In this situation of joint taxation, tax sovereignty means that 27 laws govern taxes, with the obvious consequent problems of competition, coordination and harmonization (Dafflon 1986).

The communes' autonomy to manage their finances varies from one canton to another. In principle, the cantons regulate the financial room for manoeuvre of their communes by establishing budget principles, uniform accounting models, taxation rules and debt limits. Local governments have limited tax sovereignty in that they can choose between ability to pay taxes and user charges where appropriate. They are, however, tied to their cantons' tax systems. For many taxes, local governments have only tax flexibility: they must apply cantonal laws and limit their decisions to an annual coefficient of taxation [$K_{commune}$] as a percentage of the canton's taxes. Local taxation is also compulsory for a limited number of taxes. If a commune chooses to raise user charges and fees, it can also define the main components (object of taxation, group of users and thus payers, computation of the user charge base and the tariff); however, these must fall within the limits set by the case law of the Federal Court of Justice (Knapp 1994, pp. 250–57). In addition, in most of the cantons the local parishes of the main national churches may charge their members (and eventually legal persons located in their jurisdictions) with a church tax to cover their expenditures. The level of taxation is determined by the annual coefficient of the cantonal tax rate.

The objectives of fiscal sovereignty are dual. The first objective is to enable each level of government and each government within a level to finance its own budget independently and according to its own criteria. This includes the capacity to finance public services in response to their electorates' preferences (the choice model), as well as those expenses that correspond to a minimum standard of goods and services as set by a higher level of government (the agency model), net of conditional grants. The second objective is to decide on redistributive policies, first in selecting ability to pay or benefit taxation, and second, in choosing the magnitude of redistribution, for example, through tax rate schedules or the amounts of exemptions and deductions applicable to income taxes.

Different jurisdictions at the same level of government will generally find that adopting at least roughly similar systems of taxation is desirable. Three reasons account for this, two of which pertain to fiscal neutrality criteria. First, where the interjurisdictional mobility of certain economic units is high, if such units are taxed, the taxes should take a similar form across the jurisdictions. Second, the rates at which these units are taxed locally should not vary greatly among the jurisdictions except to the extent that differences in rates correspond to differences in benefits to these units from the services provided.

In this way, allocative distortions in both resource use and incidence resulting from the tax system itself can be kept to a minimum consistent with other fiscal objectives of the individual jurisdictions (Oates 1972, p. 147). Third, harmonization promotes the transparency of the tax system, facilitates tax collection and minimizes administration and implementation costs, but note that tax harmonization can be formal or real. Formal tax harmonization concerns any attempt to align the various tax systems decided on independently by each jurisdiction towards a uniform system and towards a unitary definition of tax bases (letters [b] to [d] in the foregoing list). As a result, information and transaction costs are reduced for those who pay taxes in several cantons, administrative and implementation costs are reduced for the cantons' tax departments and the number of disputes decreases. Real tax harmonization is obtained when allowances, deductions, exemptions and tax rate schedules are identical in all jurisdictions. Such harmonization is at variance with the federal principle and has never been on Switzerland's political agenda.

The problem of tax harmonization arises exclusively for those taxes that the three levels of government levy simultaneously (shown as taxes on income and wealth in Table 5.6, excluding withholding tax and stamp tax, which are raised by the confederation only). Up to now, tax harmonization has remained fully and exclusively formal. The Federal Council has never envisaged more than a formal harmonization of direct taxes. Its sole aims were to enhance the transparency and coherence of the fiscal system and to establish the rules of fiscal competition. The arguments against real harmonization include the risks inherent in reducing competition between the cantons and suppressing incentives for cantons to be efficient and effective in their provision of public services (Federal Council 2002, pp. 18–20).

At the cantonal level, formal tax harmonization has been realized over the years for two reasons. First, collection of the federal direct tax is assigned to the cantons. Consequently, to reduce administrative and implementation costs, and because of bureaucrats who have arbitrarily reduced their workloads by not checking different tax return forms from the same taxpayer in every single case, the cantons had strong incentives to adopt rules and concepts similar to those of the federal direct tax. Second, increasing numbers of taxpayers, whether corporate or individual, are active outside their canton or own immovable assets in another canton, and are therefore pushing for uniformity of the various rules of taxation (and of tax return forms) to reduce their administrative and legal costs.

Formal harmonization is achieved by the 1990 federal law on the harmonization of direct taxation at the cantonal and communal levels, which came into effect in 1993. It provides a framework within which the cantons (and the communes insofar as the respective cantonal law provides for fiscal competences at the local level) must define their direct taxation laws, particularly with regard to assets, tax periods and the tax liability of persons and legal entities. Standardized tax declaration forms are being introduced, much to the relief of people liable for taxes in more than one canton, and income and wealth taxes have been annualized (they were previously based on a two-year assessment). The cantons were obliged to adjust their tax legislation by 31 December 2000 or else the law would automatically apply by that date. However, as the cantons still define their own tax rate scales and the amounts of allowances and deductions, wide variations in cantonal taxation levels persist. Thus formal harmonization solves problems relating to administrative costs, but not those pertaining to tax neutrality. Table 5.8 provides an overview of the tax burdens in the cantons and the communes.

At the communal level, formal and real tax harmonization has almost been achieved (even though real harmonization was not a goal) except for the annual coefficient of taxation, which depends on balanced budget requirements. However, differences in tax coefficients leave open the question of tax competition, which is on the agenda of most communes, primarily because of interjurisdictional mobility among urban areas.

Tax Competition

Tax competition between regional or local authorities within a decentralized, multilevel government system has long been an issue for policymakers. This is particularly the case in a federal system like Switzerland, where differences in business taxation between and within cantons have been an issue for the last 30 years (for a survey covering 1970–90, see Federal Tax Administration 1990, pp. 63–68). In the 1980s, the tax burden on firms' profits varied considerably between the cantons, with maximum to minimum ratios ranging from 2 to 4 depending on the amount of profits and the formula used to compute them for taxation purposes. Some empirical evidence also seems to indicate that the situation was similar in the communes, though to a lesser extent (Dafflon 1991, pp. 55–65). In the last decade, these differences have neither disappeared nor diminished, despite the federal law on the harmonization of direct taxation by the cantons and commune.

A recent survey indicates that the average tax rate on business profits varies from 13 to 31 per cent when taxation by all three levels of government is taken into account (OECD 1999, p. 109). Table 5.8 shows the general situation in 2000 for business profits and capital: the index of the tax burden on profits in the cantons and communes ranges from 59.7 in Zug to 157.8 in Neuchâtel, a maximum to minimum ratio of 2.64. For taxes on capital, the disparities are even larger, with the maximum to minimum ratio standing at 4.34. Such a relatively large discrepancy in business taxation between subnational governments results in a situation in which tax competition and actual

Table 5.8 Tax burden in the cantons, 2000
(index, 100 = average cantonal + communal taxes for Switzerland as a whole)

	Individual		Legal entities		Motor	Global
Canton	Income	Wealth	Profits	Capital	vehicles	index
Zurich	81.6	54.6	106.2	89.1	97.0	83.3
Bern	127.1	105.6	93.8	112.7	139.0	124.2
Lucerne	116.2	160.7	93.7	102.8	97.2	117.0
Uri	96.1	74.4	107.0	104.2	81.2	95.0
Schwyz	74.4	70.2	74.9	77.3	96.8	75.3
Obwald	111.8	89.7	99.0	78.3	90.5	108.2
Nidwald	72	39.4	88.9	42.7	82.3	71.1
Glaris	97.4	97.2	110.2	104.2	104.9	99.1
Zug	54.6	63.8	59.7	60.7	83.5	58.2
Fribourg	112.3	181.7	104.5	108.7	104.2	116.4
Solothurn	101.2	86.7	100.5	106.7	89.1	100.1
Basel-City	109.5	125.4	107.1	128.8	108.5	111.3
Basel-Land	86.9	92.1	103.9	185.5	110.9	91.1
Schaffhausen	102.7	90.1	111.7	81.6	65.1	101.4
Appenzell Outer Rhodes	106.7	86.6	112.4	130.1	117.1	105.8
Appenzell Inner Rhodes	90.4	79.5	85.4	84.5	98.2	89.1
St. Gall	104.2	98.9	102.1	49.3	104.8	102.3
Grisons	81.1	89.7	107.9	153.9	137.9	92.1
Argovie	95.6	98.5	104.3	115.1	75.3	96.5
Thurgovie	107.0	119.8	92.4	119.0	71.1	106.0
Tessin	90.5	77.9	94.8	87.8	93.6	90.4
Vaud	103.1	155.8	108.4	110.5	125.4	109.8
Valais	116.8	232.4	103.7	147.7	54.1	123.0
Neuchâtel	122.7	131.1	157.8	121.0	101.0	126.7
Geneva	99.5	120.9	120.9	98.3	69.3	103.8
Jura	128.5	132.1	103.7	119.4	119.2	126.3
Average	100.0	100.0	100.0	100.0	100.0	100.0
Ratio of maximum to minimum rates	2.35	5.90	2.64	4.34	2.57	2.18

Note: The tax burden indexes are computed in the following way. For each tax, several standard specifications are assessed. For example, for personal income tax, four categories are considered: single people, married people without children, married people with two children and old-age pensioners. For each category, the amount of cantonal, communal and church taxes paid in the capital town are computed. Each category is weighted in the global index according to the importance of this source to the total revenue of each canton. The average is given a value of 100. All indexes are proportionally calculated.

Source: Federal Tax Administration (2001, pp. 62, 76 and 89).

practices may eventually impinge on the implementation of fiscal policies at the subnational level, because governments may begin granting ad hoc tax advantages to particular firms. Empirical evidence for 1985–2001 suggests that tax reductions cannot attract firms to a specific location, because the ongoing process of tax competition eventually removes any comparative advantage one subnational government might have one over another.

Translated into the terms of game theory, the outcome is a noncooperative solution of the prisoner's dilemma. This classical dilemma exists for any canton considering the possibility of entering into tax competition with other governments at the same level and is applicable to its entire business sector. From a canton's perspective, it implies analysing the potential costs and benefits of changing the canton's tax regime and reducing its tax rates on business profits and capital for any firm situated within the canton during a particular fiscal year.

By contrast, cantons must also carry out case by case analysis when considering tax competition. Such analysis concerns firms that actively engage in negotiating particular tax arrangements with a number of competing governments under the threat of moving their activities to the fiscally most advantageous political jurisdiction. If successful, the bargaining strategy of such firms allows them to obtain more generous tax reductions than those already available to the business sector as a whole. In other words, competition between cantons acting individually and with no coordination opens the way for some firms to negotiate ad hoc tax arrangements. Whenever a canton's tax strategy succeeds in attracting a particular firm by granting it an additional tax bonus, another canton will soon respond by doing the same, but to a larger extent (in terms of the value and/or duration of the tax bonus), until the lack of coordination among decentralized governments will eventually result in all the cantons reducing their business taxes to a minimum. This situation is exacerbated by the problem of asymmetric information. When a firm is seeking tax advantages it often starts negotiations with more than one subnational authority. Thus the firm is aware of and can compare the different tax packages offered by competing governments, whereas none of the latter knows what its competitors are offering.

This kind of lowering of taxes means that all fiscal authorities lose a portion of their revenues, giving rise to a resource allocation problem. Furthermore, a race-to-the-bottom tax policy gives rise to a fiscal equity problem when associated with a balanced budget requirement: it forces subnational governments to transfer part of the tax burden to other, less mobile factors or activities, such as labour and consumption. Fiscal sovereignty or partial fiscal sovereignty is important at the cantonal level, but creates more and more problems over time. The difficulties Switzerland has experienced for the last three decades—since direct taxation became a major revenue source for the cantons—suggest the need for some kind of central tax law. The cantons now recognize that tax competition has had undesirable consequences for regional development policies and that economic disparities between the regions and the cantons have not been reduced despite federal equalization policies (Rossi and Dafflon 2004). The debate is ongoing (Feld 2000).

BUDGETARY POLICY

The cantons have their own constitutions, autonomy over their budgets and their own financial resources and, above all, power to tax. Cantonal autonomy in the area of fiscal policy contrasts with the budget principles and rules of taxation to which member states in other federations are subject. Legislative authorities at the federal level, in the 26 cantons and in every commune must decide on their budgets for revenues and expenditures before the beginning of the year and keep track of their revenues and expenditures. Since the mid-1980s, budgeting and bookkeeping techniques have been harmonized and all budget items must conform to applicable laws.

The federal constitution does not impose budget principles on the cantons. There are no federal constraints to deficit financing, except that none of the tiers of government can borrow from the central bank. The main external limitation on the cantons' budgetary sovereignty is competition with other cantons: if a canton pursues an inefficient fiscal policy with a poor correlation between costs and benefits, it will price itself out of the market. Individuals and firms will move to other cantons (exit in Hirschman's terminology), or voters will use initiatives and referendums to modify the mix of public goods and taxes (voice). Competition is even more important at the local level, particularly between communes in the same urban agglomeration.

Budget Orthodoxy

The autonomy of cantonal and communal governments in relation to their finances is not unlimited. Cantons' constitutions or laws impose some internal limitations, and the cantons and those communes that are under cantonal supervision generally respect two rules (Dafflon 2002).

The first rule requires a more or less balanced budget for providing goods and services. Financial regulations mean that running or accumulating deficits in their current budgets is difficult for most communal and cantonal governments. If a large budget deficit were to occur, taxation would have to be increased. As concerns loans, in many cantons, the loan amortization must not only be recorded, but must also correspond to the effective pace of the repayment. At the communal level, if a local authority does not follow this rule, the cantonal government may decide to raise the annual coefficient of taxation in the commune. In general, the cantons apply the so-called golden rule: communes' current revenues net of current expenditures must be sufficient to cover interest for any debt incurred and the running costs of past and new investments. Whether this rule includes annual reimbursement of the debt on a pay-as-you-go basis for capital expenditures financed by borrowing varies from one canton to another. This also necessitates a clear demarcation between current and capital expenditures and separation of the current from the capital budget. Again, the definition of such expenditures is not identical from canton to canton, in particular, with regard to their ability to transform capital expenditures into current outlays or to contract out certain services to private or semiprivate enterprises. The second rule concerns borrowing and debt limitations. Many cantons only permit public debt for financing capital expenditures, and if the communal and/or cantonal government has the financial capacity to pay the interest and amortization of the debt out of its current budget. Amortization rates are fixed according to the kind of investment and its possible length of use (pay-as-you-go finance). This requires a distinction between the current budget, which must be balanced, and the capital budget, which can be financed by borrowing. In addition to the liabilities recorded on the balance sheet, the cantons and communes also have significant contingent liabilities for which the government is not actually responsible, but may become responsible if some future event does or does not occur. These are guarantees of borrowing by institutions that provide public services in place of a cantonal or a local government or money borrowed by agent enterprises that is fully backed by a canton or a commune.

These two requirements address accountability and must be viewed in the perspective of the cantons' and communes' financial autonomy and access to own revenue sources. On the one hand, cantonal and communal governments have a fairly large, though diminishing, amount of autonomy to decide on and offer public services and direct access to taxes. On the other hand, these governments are expected to act in a responsible way and to finance what they are asked to produce without excessive borrowing. This is a classical approach to fiscal federalism (Tollison and Wagner 1986).

Debate is extensive about the effectiveness of financial referendums on the size of the public sector and on the reinforcement of budget discipline. The institutions of direct democracy seem to have the general capacity to strengthen the system of checks and balances. Indeed, the existence of referendums as part of the budgetary procedure implies that the Swiss generally follow a bottom-up approach, with the 'bottom' consisting of voters (Feld and Kirchgässner 1999). In reality, the picture is much more colourful. While most cantons follow a bottom-up budgetary procedure, top-down rules predominate in some cantons. Because the rules on initiatives and referendums differ from one canton to another, some cantonal governments are extremely restrictive in their requirements for balancing the budget and ensure easier access by voters to referendums and initiatives. The literature of the 1990s (see, for example, van Hagen 2002, pp. 468–71) holds that top-down budgetary procedures work better than bottom-up procedures, but they neglect the voters' power, which, according to Hirschmann's exit and voice theory, could effectively control the government's behaviour. The polemic on the relative effectiveness of top-down versus bottom-up procedures seems to have reached a compromise: top-down rules might work better in those countries where the institutions of direct democracy are not anchored in society. In such countries, a top-down approach might be preferable as a second-best option. In countries with direct democratic traditions, however, bottom-up procedures explain to a large extent why extensive devolution is possible without jeopardizing macroeconomic stability.

Macroeconomic Policy

The decentralization of government functions raises problems for macroeconomic control at the national level. This is because cantonal and communal accountability involves access to own revenue sources together with the right of the cantons and the communes to borrow. Uncontrolled access to capital markets and mismanagement of budgets by cantonal and communal governments could jeopardize any efforts to stabilize the economy. For this reason, so the textbook argument runs, central governments ought to have some monitoring or control power. But in the case of Switzerland, one must determine whether the assignment of responsibilities and revenues to the cantonal and communal tiers is in balance and regular or volatile and subject to strong cyclical variation. In the first case, control could be restricted to the golden rule, that is, borrowing is allowed only for infrastructure and for the duration of capital investment. In the second case, borrowing may be needed not only for investment, but also to compensate for cyclical variations in the budget, namely, higher social assistance expenditures with fewer revenues during cyclical downwards.

Yet effective decentralized public finance may be somewhat distant from textbook theory in the Swiss situation: the electorate has to vote in the tax law at the cantonal level or the tax coefficient at the communal level. While it may accept variation in taxation, whether to restore a balanced current budget or for new investments, it is unlikely to do so just for macroeconomic reasons. In addition, the time path required for such a decision is probably unrelated to upward or downward changes in macroeconomic trends.

Furthermore, the economic classification of public expenditures, as shown in Table 5.5, is revealing in relation to macroeconomic policy. At the federal level, current and capital grants-in-aid account for 54 per cent of total expenditures and revenue sharing for 12 per cent, whereas expenditures for personnel and interest payments correspond to 11 and 7 per cent, respectively. This means that about 84 per cent of the total budget falls in expenditure categories that are difficult, if not impossible, to modify in the short term for macroeconomic purposes. Consumption (11 per cent) and investments (2 per cent) amount to as little as 13 per cent of the total federal budget. This is by no mean sufficient for any kind of functional finance. With 20 per cent of their total expenditure going toward consumption (12 per cent) and investment (8 per cent), the cantons are in a similar position. Not surprisingly, the communes spend much more, about 32 per cent of their total expenditures, for consumption (21 per cent) and investment (11 per cent).

Because of the difficulty of adjusting personnel expenditures and transfers in the short term, macroeconomic policy cannot be a concern of the central government alone: it requires some form of consensus between the three tiers of government and vertical cooperation. This is not an easy matter, because regional and local interests differ. In particular, investment projects are increasingly requiring significant financial resources and long-term planning, and when such projects are ready to be voted on, governments are unlikely to agree to postpone them for macroeconomic reasons. Conversely, accelerating projects for macroeconomic reasons without taking the time to present a detailed investment programme is also problematic. Cantons or communes may be reluctant to abandon or postpone investments for the sake of a centrally coordinated macroeconomic policy. This also explains why fiscal and budgetary policy plays only a limited role in stabilization, compared with the position of the monetary authorities through the Swiss National Bank.

Another issue pertinent to macroeconomic policy that might also be interpreted in terms of symmetry and/or asymmetry is the federal government's recently announced policy on debt containment introduced to adhere to article 126 of the 1999 constitution. The basic idea behind this plan is to consolidate federal finances while taking the macroeconomic cycle into consideration. The rule would allow the confederation to run into the red during an economic recession, but in exchange it would require a budgetary surplus in the years of recovery that followed. By means of this rule the federal government hopes to stabilize the nominal level of public debt and reduce the rate of indebtedness in a progressive manner.

Cantons and communes are not required to or supposed to participate in the federal government's debt containment policy. Given that the allocation of public revenues and expenditures between the three tiers of government is somewhat entangled, and given the subtle tendency towards centralization at both the federal and cantonal levels, assessing whether the debt containment policy can be successful without the involvement of the lower levels of government will be an interesting exercise in the coming years.

EQUALIZATION

The differences in the cantons in terms of their size, geography, population and economic potential are so great that without equalization measures, fiscal federalism would function under intolerable disparities. Thus the federal government intervenes to balance the primary distribution of resources between the cantons by means of three main policy measures—fiscal equalization, agricultural aid policy and assistance to mountainous areas—with the aim of strengthening structurally weak regions.[8] Note that Switzerland has no constitutional provisions that equalization measures should compensate entirely for the differences between the cantons in order to realize identical economic or fiscal conditions. The pragmatic objective is to render regional disparities politically acceptable so that the remaining differences do not endanger the cohesion of the confederation.

According to the 1959 federal law on equalization, the original objective was to enable the cantons to provide minimum acceptable levels of certain public services without having much heavier tax burdens in some cantons than in others. Equalization related to policies aimed at correcting fiscal imbalances, whether resulting from differences in the cantons' revenue raising capacities or from above average unit costs of providing some defined levels of services. Eventually, fiscal capacity dominated unit costs, mainly because of the difficulty of defining needs, average versus minimum provision and relative costs, which induced strategic behaviour by recipient governments. As a result, three out of the four components in the formula for computing cantons' financial capacity (see the next section) now refer to revenue raising abilities. From the beginning, equalization has excluded differences in cantonal outlays for services other than those absolutely required or above minimum standards and differences in the progressiveness of the tax rate schedules, which reflect the concept of income redistribution or the mix between benefit taxes and ability to pay taxes at the cantonal level. At the local level, many cantons have introduced intercommunal equalization, with similar objectives.

The most direct way to reduce cantonal disparities is through fiscal equalization measures, that is, payments from the federal government to the cantons with the purpose of reducing differences in fiscal capacity. Switzerland currently has three sets of policies that include equalization components, but for the last 20 years they have not proved particularly efficient (Dafflon 1995). Discussions to reform the entire system are currently taking place.

Cantons' Financial Capacity

All equalization programmes have in common the fact that they relate to the financial capacity of the cantons. The actual formula for computing the financial capacity of the cantons has the following four components (Table 5.9):

- The per capita revenue in the individual cantons as a measure of each canton's financial resources. This component is weighted by a factor of 1.5 in the computation of the total index.
- The inverse of the tax burden of the cantons and the communes, weighted by a factor of 1.0.
- The per capita tax revenues of the cantons and their communes from different tax sources weighted by the tax burden indexes to obtain comparable values. This component is also weighted by a factor of 1.5 in the total index.
- An approximation of the cantons' expenditure requirements, taking into account their population densities and the relative importance of certain aspects of each canton's agricultural potential, weighted by a factor of 1.0.

The total index for each canton is the weighted average proportionally corrected in such a way that the lowest single index is given a value of 30. Those cantons with a score of more than 120 are considered as having a high financial capacity, those scoring 60 or less as having a low financial capacity and those scoring between 61 and 119 as having a medium capacity.

Using this formula, the maximum to minimum ratio was 7.3 in 2000/2001, ranging from Valais with 30 points to Zug with 218 points. The formula results in a relative expansion of the financial capacity scale. As long as only the per capita cantonal revenue is considered, the maximum to minimum ratio is 2.3; however, the introduction of the three additional indices in the formula results in an increased ratio: the difference between the actual highest and lowest financial capacity is more than sevenfold.

Federal Equalization Programmes

Since 1959, the federal government has developed three sets of federal equalization programmes for the benefit of the cantons: (a) conditional federal grants-in-aid, (b) revenue sharing of certain federal tax revenues and (c) contributions by the cantons to certain federal social security expenditures.[9]

Conditional federal grants-in-aid

Many cantonal expenditures benefit from federal specific grants. For most aided functions, the grants have the following two components: a basic rate,

Table 5.9 Index of the cantons' financial capacities, 2000–01 (index, 100 = average value for each component)

Canton	Per capita cantonal revenue 1996/97 × 1.5	Inverse of tax burden 1995–98 × 1	Tax revenues 1996/97 × 1.5	Expenditure requirements × 1	Weighted average	Total index
Zurich	125.15	118.22	126.56	108.95	120.95	157
Bern	88.50	83.25	84.99	94.18	87.53	66
Lucerne	88.82	87.75	83.36	102.09	89.62	72
Uri	86.81	113.89	81.17	73.61	87.89	67
Schwyz	97.49	118.71	94.20	85.49	98.35	96
Obwald	77.47	89.06	70.99	76.76	77.70	40
Nidwald	115.81	128.85	105.77	83.38	108.92	124
Glaris	113.65	90.98	80.86	77.30	92.01	78
Zug	158.32	142.23	161.02	96.63	143.57	218
Fribourg	84.63	70.00	78.09	97.00	82.21	52
Solothurn	91.51	102.51	88.46	103.52	95.20	87
Basel-City	141.00	89.93	129.60	111.10	121.39	158
Basel-Land	107.22	107.21	109.39	105.52	107.53	120
Schaffhausen	102.29	102.93	95.53	111.06	102.14	106
Appenzell Outer Rhodes	80.79	95.45	83.43	82.25	84.81	59
Appenzell Inner Rhodes	83.36	105.49	82.49	71.39	85.13	60
St. Gall	86.48	101.13	91.74	98.58	93.41	82
Grisons	87.12	100.89	101.52	70.00	90.77	75
Argovie	98.80	105.99	90.33	110.46	100.03	100
Thurgovie	86.31	102.42	89.40	110.44	95.28	87
Tessin	84.06	96.67	100.53	85.96	91.90	78
Vaud	98.77	87.80	98.47	106.17	97.96	95
Valais	74.23	71.99	70.00	81.19	73.90	30
Neuchâtel	87.53	76.48	84.35	88.65	84.59	58
Geneva	112.65	85.49	126.35	111.10	111.02	130
Jura	70.00	73.41	72.27	84.98	74.36	31
Switzerland	100	100	100	100	100	100
Ratio of maximum to minimum capacity	2.26	1.98	2.30	1.35	1.94	7.27

Note: The computed indexes are not directly comparable with the corresponding figures in tables 5.1 and 5.8, because for each series, the lowest result is given the value of 70 and all the other numbers are proportionnally computed through a specific formula. One cannot say *a priori* whether this adjustment reinforces or reduces equalizing effects. It depends on whether the original differences in the relative position of the cantons were higher or lower.

Source: Federal Council (1999).

S^j_{min} in the following formula, which represents the federal interest in minimum standard requirements for cantonal public services and which varies according to incentive or some other technical criteria (economies of scale, spillovers, congestion costs); and an equalization supplement, the second part of the following formula, which is inversely related to the recipient canton's index of financial capacity.

This type of fiscal equalization is mainly vertical, from federal to lower levels of government, and is regulated by many special laws. The general grant formula is

$$S^j_I = S^j_{min} + [(120 - E_I)/60 \times (S^j_{max} - S^j_{min})],$$

where S is the rate of the grant, j is the aided function, i is the canton ($i = 1 \ldots 26$), E is the index of financial capacity, *max* is the maximum rate of the grant and *min* is the minimum rate of the grant. For cantons with an actual financial capacity above 120 points, E_1 is brought back to 120, whereas for cantons with an actual capacity between 30 and 60, their E_1 value is corrected upwards to 60.

As an example, consider a basic grant rate of 30 per cent for function j and a maximum rate of 45 per cent. This means that a canton with less than a high financial capacity would be entitled to receive, at best, an additional 15 per cent of the basic rate to equalize its position. The exact additional grant rate is proportional to the difference between the two rates, here 15 per cent, weighted by the relative position of the cantonal index of financial capacity between 120 and 60 points. A canton with a capacity of 100 would receive $(120 - 100)/60 \times 15 = 5$ per cent in addition to the basic rate of 30 per cent, or 35 per cent of the recognized expenditure for the particular project in function j.

Revenue sharing

The share of the cantons in the federal government's tax revenue derives from several sources, but three revenue sharing programmes only have equalization components: for the federal direct tax, the withholding tax and part of federal customs duties on petrol and other fuel oils. Historically, revenue sharing was generally implemented to compensate for fiscal imbalance when a cantonal revenue source was centralized (customs duties, alcohol monopoly, coinage, stamp duties) or partly shared with the centre (direct and withholding taxation). With time, the main revenue sharing programmes have been linked to equalization payments.

The cantons receive 30 per cent of the federal direct tax (income, corporate profits and corporate capital), of which 17 per cent is allocated on the basis of origin, defined as the residence of the taxpayers, and 13 per cent according to financial capacity with the size of the population serving as the multiplicand (see Dafflon 1995, pp. 99, 112 and 131 for detailed revenue sharing formulas). They also receive 10 per cent of the withholding tax net of collection costs: 5 per cent is allocated according to population and 5 per cent is reserved for cantons with capacity indexes of $E_I < 100$. The formula takes the forms $[100 - E_I]$ and $[(100 - E_I)^2]$, with the size of the population serving as the multiplicand.

The federal government reimburses part of its revenue from customs duties and excise taxes on petrol and other fuel oils to the cantons. Half of the receipts from 'normal' duties and all so-called 'supplementary' duties are devoted to road expenditures, of which 12 per cent is reimbursed to the cantons. The equalization formula takes the form $[(100 - E_I)^{1.4}]$ with total cantonal expenditures on roads serving as the multiplicand.

Cantonal contributions to social security

The third category of transfer payments that includes equalizing components concerns the cantons' contributions to three federal social security programmes: old-age pensions and survivors insurance, pensions for the disabled and family allowances for those in agriculture. Total payments by the public sector are

Programme	Public sector participation	Federal	Cantonal
Old-age pensions and survivors insurance	20% of total expenditures	17.0%	3.0%
Pensions for the disabled	50% of total expenditures	37.5%	12.5%
Family allowances for those in agriculture	Total annual deficit	66.7%	33.3%

For the old-age pensions and survivors insurance and the pensions for the disabled, the formula for the cantonal payment, CONT (for contribution), is based on the total amount of pensions paid in a canton, *i*, weighted by the financial capacity of the canton in the form $[5/7\ (E_I - 100) + 100]$.

$$\mathrm{CONT}_i^{\mathrm{AVS}} = 0.03\ \Sigma_i\ \mathrm{AVS}_i \times \frac{\mathrm{AVS}_i \times [\frac{5}{7}(E_i - 100) + 100]}{\Sigma_i \mathrm{AVS}_i \times [\frac{5}{7}(E_i - 100) + 100]}.$$

For the family allowance for those in agriculture, those cantons with a federal direct tax per capita lower that four-fifths of the national average benefit from a reduction in their contribution proportional to the difference between this average and their own score (federal direct tax_I/H_I).

Importance of the Transfer Payments

Table 5.10 shows the importance of the three equalization programmes in 2000. Payments from the federal government to the cantons were Sw F 8916 million or 18 per cent of total federal expenditures. This amount corresponded to 14 per cent of the cantons' total public resources, that is 6 per cent for specific grants and 9 per cent for revenue sharing. Cantonal contributions to the three federal social security programmes amounted to Sw F 2141 million or 4 per cent of the cantons' total expenditures. However, only parts of the payments include equalization, also shown in Table 5.10. In total, they represent Sw F 3163 million or 35 per cent of total transfer payments from the federal government to the cantons and Sw F 171 million or 8 per cent of total cantonal contributions to federal social security expenditures. For the 26 cantons, the net equalizing part amounts to Sw F 6774 million and corresponds to 11 per cent of total cantonal revenues.

CONCLUSION

Based on the foregoing, we can conclude that intergovernmental relations in Switzerland—as in most 'classical' federal countries—exhibits characteristics of both political and administrative asymmetry as follows:

- Political asymmetry (originally *de facto* and recently also *de jure*) favours cities and agglomerations, at least since the adoption of the new federal constitution. The direct participation of urban area governments in federal decisionmaking is contrary to the logic of Swiss federalism, as it implies circumvention of the cantonal level. However, it might be interpreted as a necessary compromise to diffuse regional political tensions, even though these tensions have never really threatened the federation with disintegration. Because it is anchored in the constitution, the political favour accorded to these units may provoke permanent asymmetry in the Swiss federal system.
- In all other institutional and political aspects of intergovernmental relations, symmetrical or quasi-symmetrical relations prevail.
- Administrative asymmetry (both *de jure* and *de facto*) takes various forms and covers nearly all fields of intergovernmental fiscal relations. For example, differences in the fiscal burden and in the transfer dependency ratios across cantons suggest that cantons with strong financial capacity enjoy larger fiscal autonomy, even though the law accords the same rights to all cantons (the same applies to the communal level). Mountainous regions receive special attention in federal

Table 5.10 Transfer payments, 2000

Programme	Transfer payments (Sw F thousands)	Equalizing portion	
		Per cent[a]	Sw F
1. *Federal specific grants*[b]	3 486 966	25.0	886 648
2. *Revenue sharing*	5 428 788	41.0	2 276 168
Federal direct tax	3 224 573	43.0	1 386 566
Withholding tax	616 386	50.0	308 193
Customs duties	523 191	40.0	209 276
Transfers from the Swiss National Bank[c]	1 005 763	37.0	372 132
Military tax	32 625	0	0
Tax on alcohol	26 250	0	0
Confederation ➔ cantons (1 + 2)	8 915 754	35.0	3 162 816
3. *Cantonal contributions*	2 141 315	8.0	171 305
Old-age pensions and survivors insurance	1 009 077	8.0	80 726
Pensions for the disabled	1 089 735	8.0	87 179
Family allowances for those in agriculture	42 503	4.5	1913
Total (1 + 2 – 3)	6 774 439		

a. Equalizing proportions are evaluated on the basis of estimated results for 1991 (Dafflon 1995, p. 198) because the revenue sharing formulas have not changed.

b. Only federal specific grants paid to the cantons that contain an equalization supplement have been taken into consideration. The equalization proportion has been provided by the Federal Finance Administration from its own calculations. It corresponds to the results that the author has obtained for 1991 from his own estimation (Dafflon 1995, p. 299).

c. According to the constitution, at least two-thirds of the net profits of the Swiss National Bank shall be credited to the cantons.

Sources: Federal specific grants: Federal Department of Finance data; revenue sharing items: Federal Department of Finance (2002, pp. 26–27); Swiss Federal Roads Authority (2001, p. 30); Swiss National Bank (2000); Swiss Alcohol Board (2001); cantonal contributions: Federal Department of Social Insurance data.

decisionmaking, which is also manifested in federal grant supplements or reduced cantonal contributions to federal expenditures. In view of the significant interregional disparities, the uniformity of service delivery throughout the country and an overall macroeconomic balance at federal level can only be ensured by the unequal treatment of unequal regions in line with the principle of vertical equity.

- Administrative asymmetry is generally based on predetermined rules, namely, the constitution and other laws. Discretionary arrangements are the exception rather than the rule.
- Administrative asymmetry is not a transitional phenomenon. As perfect equalization of all existing disparities has never been an objective of the confederation, asymmetric legal arrangements are to be permanent.
- The existing asymmetries of intergovernmental fiscal relations result to a large extent from the sovereignty of constituent units. Asymmetry in this case is an indirect consequence of a federal constitutional principle. This is clearly illustrated by the sovereignty of cantons with regard to direct taxation and the lack of real tax harmonization. As this chapter has shown, the cantons' virtually unlimited fiscal sovereignty has provoked fierce tax competition in recent years, leading to substantial differences in cantonal tax burdens, thereby further widening the horizontal fiscal gap across jurisdictions. By contrast, institutions of horizontal cooperation, such as the Conference of Cantonal Governments, can effectively reduce the asymmetries resulting from the competitive behaviour of the cantons, even though intercantonal negotiations are not always marked by purely cooperative efforts. Similarly, all cantons have been accorded the right to organize local government as they wish. As a consequence, today the communal level demonstrates substantial asymmetries in terms of fiscal autonomy and public service delivery. These examples show how even formally symmetric relations may lead to *de facto* asymmetries because of an extensive devolution of powers and responsibilities.

With regard to the nature and effects of asymmetrical policies, the Swiss case confirms that asymmetry is an indispensable feature of federal fiscal systems. The asymmetric treatment of constituent units with weak financial capacity has proved to be a crucial policy element both with regard to the maintenance of the nation state and to the effective provision of public services. As for the quasi-preferential treatment of rich, urban regions, the consequences of this particular asymmetric arrangement cannot yet be foreseen.

NOTES

1. Two important exceptions to this rule are the representation of half cantons in the Council of States and the value of their votes during referendums.
2. For example, in 1999, 43 per cent of the total budgetary resources of Uri came from federal grants, as did 41 per cent for Grisons and Jura.
3. Official translation from the Web site of the Swiss confederation: http://www.admin.ch/ch/itl/rs/1/index.htm.
4. In most cantons, constitutional or legislative initiatives are possible on taxation and current or capital expenditures, which require a minimum number of citizens' signatures. Referendums

against capital, one-time or recurrent expenditures are also possible. The institutional and legal conditions governing the distinctions between compulsory or optional referendums, one-time and recurrent expenditures, capital or current expenditures, the number of signatures required and the time allowed for collecting signatures differ widely from one canton to another. While the influence of referendums in general on the outcome of the public budget is known, the influence of individual cantons' referendum conditions, as a measure of budget orthodoxy, on public deficits and the cantons' indebtedness are analysed by Kirchgässner, Feld and Savioz (1999) and Novaresi (2001).

5. In the canton of Fribourg, for example, around 20 per cent of total local current expenditures are made in response to standards set by higher levels of government (Dafflon 2004), fewer than a quarter correspond to ad hoc intercommunal institutions coordinating particular functions, leaving about half to be spend in line with local residents' preferences.
6. An October 1997 law suppressed the federal direct tax on business capital as of 1998.
7. This unwritten rule results from historical considerations whereby the cantons have always succeeded in limiting federal direct taxation to a strict minimum (Federal Council 2002; Weber 1969). At the federal level, a direct tax on wages and corporate profits was first introduced in 1915 under emergency rights in effect because of war. It was thereafter levied intermittently and was known at different times as the war tax, crisis tax, amortization tax and, since 1941, national defence tax.
8. However, Blöchliger and Frey (1993, p. 231) note that there is no overall coordination of regional equalization measures and that a number of measures have indirect redistributive effects that exacerbate regional disparities. For example, even though central government procurement is not intended to be redistributive in nature, it benefits mainly industrialized cantons that already have an above average cantonal revenue per capita (Jeanrenaud and Meyer 1985).
9. Intercantonal equalization also exists, principally as contributions for regional spillovers. One example is contributions by cantons without universities to cantons with universities in the form of a fixed annual sum per student. At the local level, many systems of revenue sharing and grants-in-aid function between various cantons and their communes. A number of cantons have also developed horizontal equalization mechanisms in which the fiscally strong communes provide direct support for the fiscally weak ones.

REFERENCES

The word 'processed' describes informally reproduced works that may not be commonly available in libraries.

Blöchliger, H. and R. L. Frey (1993), 'The Evolution of Swiss Federalism: A Model for the European Community?', in *The Economics of Community Public Finance*, Commission of the European Communities, European Economy: Reports and Studies no. 5, Brussels and Luxembourg: Directorate-General for Economic and Financial Affairs, pp. 213–42.

Dafflon, B. (1986), 'Fédéralisme, coordination et harmonisation fiscales: étude du cas suisse', *Recherches économiques de Louvain*, 52 (1), 3–43.

——— (1991), 'Local Business Taxation in Switzerland: Assessment, Strategies and Conflicts', in G. Pola (ed.), *Local Business Taxation: An International Overview*, Milan: Vita e Pensiero, pp. 41–66.

——— (1992), 'The Assignment of Function to Local Government: From Theory to Practice', *Environment and Planning C: Government and Policy*, 10 (3), 283–98.

——— (1995), *Fédéralisme et solidarité: étude de la péréquation en Suisse*, Studies and Colloquiums no. 15, Fribourg, Switzerland: University of Fribourg, Institute of Federalism.

——— (1998), 'Les fusions de communes dans le canton de Fribourg (Suisse): analyse socio-économique', in *Annuaire des collectivités locales 1998*, Paris: CNRS éditions, pp. 125–66.

——— (2002), 'Capital Expenditures and Financing in the Communes in Switzerland', in B. Dafflon (ed.), *Local Public Finance in Europe: Balancing the Budget and Controlling Debt*, Cheltenham, UK and Lyme, US: Edward Elgar, pp. 209–30.

——— (2004), *La péréquation intercommunale dans le canton de Fribourg: bilan et enjeux,* Fribourg, Switzerland: University of Fribourg, BENEFRI Centre for Studies in Public Sector Economics.

Dafflon, B. and S. Perritaz (2000), 'L'influence de la taille des communes sur leur degré d'autonomie budgétaire: présentation d'une méthode d'analyse et application aux communes fribourgeoises', Working Paper no. 336, University of Fribourg, Faculty of Economic and Social Sciences, Fribourg, Switzerland.

Della Santa, M. (1996), *Dalla collaborazione alla fusione: analisi degli aspetti economici, istituzionali e sociologi del commune,* doctoral dissertation, Faculty of Economic and Social Sciences, University of Fribourg, Fribourg, Switzerland.

Federal Council (1999), 'Ordinance of November 17, 1999, Concerning the Financial Capacity of the Cantons for the Years 2000 and 2001', Official Collection of Federal Laws, 1999 (51), Bern, pp. 3545–49.

——— (2002), 'Draft Law of November 14, 2001, Concerning the Reform of Fiscal Equalisation and the Assignment of Expenditures Between the Confederation and the Cantons', *Federal Bulletin,* (12), pp. 2155–2414.

Federal Department of Finance (2002), *Finances publiques en Suisse 2000,* Statistical Series of Switzerland no. 18, Neuchâtel, Switzerland: Swiss Federal Statistical Office.

Federal Tax Administration (1990), *Charge fiscale en Suisse 1989*, Statistical Series of Switzerland no. 18, Neuchâtel, Switzerland: Swiss Federal Statistical Office.

——— (2001), *Charge fiscale en Suisse 2000,* Statistical Series of Switzerland no. 18, Neuchâtel, Switzerland: Swiss Federal Statistical Office.

Feld, L. (2000), 'Steuerwettbewerb und seine Auswirkungen auf Allokation und Distribution: Ein überblick und eine empirische Analyse für die Schweiz', *Beiträge zur Finanzwissenschaft* no. 10, Tübingen, Germany: Mohr Siebeck.

Feld, L. P. and G. Kirchgässner (1999), 'Public Debt and Budgetary Procedures: Top Down or Bottom Up? Some Evidence from Swiss Municipalities', in J. Poterba and J. von Hagen (eds), *Fiscal Institutions and Fiscal Performance,* Chicago and London: University of Chicago Press, pp. 151–79.

Feld, L. P. and M. R. Savioz (1997), 'Direct Democracy Matters for Economic Performance: An Empirical Investigation', *Kyklos*, 50 (4), 507–38.

Frey, B. and R. Eichenberger (1999), *The New Democratic Federalism for Europe: Functional, Overlapping, and Competing Jurisdictions*, Cheltenham, UK and Northampton, MA, USA: Edward Elgar.

Frey, R. L., A. Spillman, B. Dafflon, C. Jeanrenaud and A. Meier (1994), 'Der Finanzausgleich zwischen Bund und Kantonen. Expertise zu den Finanzhilfen und Abgeltungen des Bundes an die Kantone im Auftrag der Eidgenössischen Finanzverwaltung und der Konferenz der kantonalen Finanzdirektoren', research report, Federal Department of Finance, Bern.

Germann, R. E. (1986), 'Die Beziehungen zwischen Bund und Kantonen im Verwaltungsbereich', in R. E. Germann and E. Weibel (eds), *Handbuch politisches System der Schweiz,* vol. 3, *Föderalismus,* Bern: Haupt Verlag, pp. 343–69.

Hirschmann, A. O. (1970), *Exit, Voice and Loyalty: Responses to Decline in Firms, Organizations and States,* Cambridge, MA: Harvard University Press.

Jeanrenaud, C. and D. Meyer (1985), *Marchés publics et économie des régions,* Lausanne, Switzerland: Presses Polytechniques et Universitaires Romandes.
King, D. (1984), *Fiscal Tiers: The Economics of Multi-Level Government*, London: Allen and Unwin.
Kirchgässner, G. and W. Pommerehne (1990), 'Evolution of Public Finance as a Function of Federal Structure: A Comparison Between Switzerland and the Federal Republic of Germany', International Institute of Public Finance, Brussels, processed.
Kirchgässner, G., L. Feld and M. Savioz (1999), *Die direkte Demokratie: Modern, erfolgreich, entwicklungs und exportfähig,* Bern and Munich: Helbing and Lichtenhahn, Vahlen.
Klöti, U. (1999), 'Regierung', in U. Klöti, P. Knoepfel, H. Kriesi, W. Linder and Y. Papadopoulos (eds), *Handbuch der Schweizer Politik,* Zürich: Verlag Neue Zürcher Zeitung, pp. 159–85.
Knapp, B. (1986), 'Etapes du fédéralisme suisse', in *Handbuch Politisches System der Schweiz*, vol. 3, *Föderalismus,* Bern: Haupt Verlag, pp. 31–53.
——— (1994), *Cours de droit administratif*, Basel and Frankfurt am Main: Helbing and Lichtenhahn.
Ladner, A., D. Arn, U. Friederich, R. Steiner and J. Wichtermann (2000), 'Gemeindereformen zwischen Handlungsfähigkeit und Legitimation', research project on the framework of the Swiss Priority Programme Switzerland: Towards the Future, Swiss National Science Foundation, Bern, processed.
Novaresi, N. (2001), 'Discipline budgétaire: éude de l'influence du référendum financier et des regles d'équilibre budgétaire sur les finances publiques des vingt-six cantons suisses', doctoral thesis, Faculty of Economic and Social Sciences, University of Fribourg, Fribourg, Switzerland.
Oates, W. (1972), *Fiscal Federalism*, New York: Harcourt Brace Jovanovich.
OECD (Organisation for Economic Co-operation and Development) (1999), *Economic Survey. Special Feature: Tax Reform in Switzerland*, Paris.
Olson, M. (1969), 'The Principle of "Fiscal Equivalence": The Division of Responsibilities Among Different Levels of Government', *American Economic Review,* 59 (2), 479–87.
Pommerehne, W. (1978), 'Institutional Approaches to Public Expenditures: Empirical Evidence from Swiss Municipalities', *Journal of Public Economics*, 9 (2), 255–80.
Pommerehne, W. and F. Schneider (1978), 'Fiscal Illusion, Political Institutions and Local Public Spending', *Kyklos*, 31 (3), 381–408.
Rossi, S. and B. Dafflon (2004), 'Tax Competition Between Subnational Governments: Theoretical and Regional Policy Issues with Reference to Switzerland', in E. Hein, A. Heise and A. Truger (eds), *Finanzpolitik in der Kontroverse,* Marburg, Germany: Metropolis-Verlag, pp. 227–49.
Spahn, P. B. (1997), 'Switzerland', in T. Ter-Minassian (ed.), *Fiscal Federalism in Theory and Practice*, Washington, DC: International Monetary Fund, pp. 324–41.
Swiss Alcohol Board (2001), *Rapport de gestion 2000,* Bern.
Swiss Federal Roads Authority (2001), *Informations 2001,* Bern.
Swiss Federal Statistical Office (2002), *Annuaire statistique de la Suisse 2002,* Zurich: Verlag Neue Zürcher Zeitung, available at http://www.statistik.admin.ch/stat_ch/ber01/fufr01.htm.
——— (2003), *Eidgenössische Volkszählung 2000: evölkerungsstruktur, Hauptsprache und Religion,* Neuenburg.
Swiss National Bank (2000), *93rd Annual Report,* Bern.

Tollison, R. D. and R. E. Wagner (1986), 'Balanced Budgets and Beyond', in J. M. Buchanan, C. K. Rowley and R. D. Tollison (eds), *Deficits*, Oxford, UK: Basil Blackwell, pp. 374–90.

Van Hagen, J. (2002), 'Fiscal Federalism and Political Decision Structures', in R. Blindenbacher and A. Koller (eds), *Federalism in a Changing World: Learning from Each Other*, Conference Reader, International Conference on Federalism, St. Gallen, Montreal and Kingston, Canada: McGill-Queen's University Press, pp. 443–77.

Walsh, C. (1993), 'Fiscal Federalism: An Overview of Issues and a Discussion of Their Relevance to the European Community', in *The Economics of Community Public Finance*, Commission of the European Communities European Economy Reports and Studies no. 5, Brussels and Luxembourg: Directorate-General for Economic and Financial Affairs, pp. 25–62.

Wälti, S. and A.-B. Bullinger (2000), 'Regional Policy and Energy Policy in the Light of Swiss Federalism', in D. Braun (ed.), *Public Policy and Federalism,* Aldershot, UK: Ashgate Publishing, pp. 78–107.

Weber, M. (1969), *Geschichte der schweizerischen Bundesfinanzen*, Bern: Haupt Verlag.

Wiseman, J. (1989), 'The Political Economy of Federalism: A Critical Appraisal', in *Cost, Choice and Political Economy*, Aldershot, UK and Brookfield, US: Edward Elgar, pp. 71–111.

Wolman, H. (1990), 'Decentralization: What It Is and Why We Should Care', in R. J. Bennett (ed.), *Decentralisation, Local Governments, and Markets: Towards a Post-Welfare Agenda*, Oxford, UK: Clarendon Press, pp. 29–41.

Zimmermann, H. (1987), 'Föderalismus und Einheitlichkeit der Lebensverhältnisse', in K. Schmidt (ed.), *Beiträge zu ökonomischen Problemen des Föderalismus*, Berlin: Duncker and Humblot.

PART III

New Federal Countries

6. Belgium: A Unique Evolving Federalism

Benoît Bayenet and Philippe de Bruycker

Article 1 of the Belgian constitution of 5 May 1993 states that 'Belgium is a Federal State made up of communities and regions'.[1] Even though Belgium has become a true federation, its federalism takes a unique style because of the significant characteristics of its institutional structure compared with those of the typical federal state.

ORIGINS OF BELGIAN FEDERALISM

A question that remains to be answered is whether a unitary state created in 1830 has, over a period of 30 years, transformed itself into a federal state after 140 years of constitutional stability. (For a short history of Belgium see, for example, Fitzmaurice 1983, 1996; Senelle 1989; Witte, Craeybeckx and Meynen 2000. For a bibliography about Belgium history, see Bayenet and others 2000.) The 1830 constitution envisaged a strong, centralized national government. The provinces and local authorities, known as communes, enjoyed a constitutional right to exist. Their powers, financial resources and legal instruments were nevertheless limited, and their actions were subject to administrative oversight by the central government. The constitution recognized neither regions nor communities (Fitzmaurice 1996).

We can analyse the history of Belgium under the assumption that the foundation of the new state relied on a double consensus. First, inside Belgium the major social, philosophical and political components of society were unified against the Netherlands,[2] and second, outside Belgium the dominant European powers recognized the new state. However, this consensus slowly disappeared because of three kinds of internal tensions, namely:

- Philosophical conflicts between members of the secular world and the Catholic church. This left a deep imprint on the country's history, including, for example, a number of 'school wars' about the respective places of public and denominational education that concluded in 1958 with a 'school pact'.

- Political gaps between capital and labour, highlighted by the leading role played by a third party. Even though Belgium was one of the most industrialized powers in the world in the mid-19th century, the gap between the middle classes, which became increasingly richer, and the working classes grew. The increasing strength of the workers' party, later called the socialists, disrupted the opposition between the Christians and the Liberals, the two main political parties. The outcome was a series of changing coalitions. The Christians played a pivotal role on the political stage, sometimes making alliances with the liberal right, sometimes with the socialist left, until they were finally removed from power after the June 1999 elections.
- Linguistic tensions that set Dutch-speaking Flanders in the north against French-speaking Wallonia in the south, with Brussels being the main area for clashes between the two languages.[3] The language factor has undermined Belgium's unity since its foundation. Initially, the state was unilingual, with the official language being French, and the ruling classes in Flanders, Brussels and Wallonia all spoke French. In Flanders, Dutch was spoken by the disenfranchised. The first Flemish demands for the Dutch language to be used surfaced as long ago as 1840, despite the agreement by the bourgeoisie and the nobility that French would be the sole official language. For the next 100 years, Dutch speakers fought to gain recognition of their language, and finally did so through a number of pieces of legislation that eventually resulted in the creation of single-language regions in 1930. These were included in Article 4 of the constitution in 1970, when four language regions were created: the French-speaking region (Wallonia), the Dutch-speaking region (Flanders), the bilingual region (Brussels capital region) and the German-speaking region (the German-speaking community).

The first two kinds of tensions are aligned roughly along the same geographical lines as the language divide, for example, Catholic Flanders is dominated by the Flemish Christian Social party, as opposed to the more secular Wallonia dominated by the Socialist Party. The divisions explain the complexity of Belgian society, which is organized in 'pillars' comprising the institutions (parties, trade unions, mutual benefit societies and organizations, youth associations and a series of other diverse organizations) of the three main political groupings (Catholics, Socialists and Liberals) and functions through the conclusion of major compromises between these various interest groups. Belgium is thus a consensus democracy as opposed to a conflict democracy (Lijphart 1981; McRae 1986).

Of the three divisions, the language split that played the largest part in Belgian political life, ultimately affecting many social, economic, financial, administrative and legal issues and culminating in a clash between two blocs, the Dutch speakers and the French speakers. Some observers interpret Dutch speakers' demands as the expression of a new nation that has gradually been created within the Belgian state that some regard as a state artificially created by the main European powers for diplomatic reasons, but one that lacks any true national foundation. Despite all that could potentially unite them in terms of their way of life, two communities that hold different views on a number of issues have thus been created that are attempting to continue their coexistence through a federal organization intended to give them the greatest possible measure of autonomy while enabling them to maintain a single state.

The transformation of a state from a centralized, unitary state into a decentralized and finally a federal state is a long, gradual process. Constitutional reforms became inevitable when, in the 1960s, Belgium had to admit that a unitary state was an inappropriate framework for resolving the coexistence difficulties of the two major linguistic communities.[4] The Flemish Belgians were the first to demand linguistic and cultural autonomy on the grounds that they had been dominated by the French speakers since the 19th century, and in the end they succeeded in getting the communities set up in 1970. Walloon demands came later, when Walloons perceived that their region's economic decline was partly due to the dominant position gradually won by the Flemings in central government circles because of their demographic strength. Wallonia and Brussels were traditionally economically superior to Flanders, but this started to change after 1945, and in the 1960s Flanders surpassed the rest of the country in economic terms. As a result, a Walloon movement developed that demanded the devolution of economic competencies so that it could undertake economic reform and industrial conversion policies. This situation explains the origins of Belgium's unique institutional arrangement with a double layer of federal entities. Note that today the pressures for more economic and fiscal autonomy come from the Flemish Community. The reform of the state has not been the result of any master plan, but a gradual process that has taken place by means of five sets of institutional reforms as follows:

- In 1970, the communities and regions gained constitutional recognition and the central government's institutions were reorganized based on equal representation.
- In 1980, the communities and regions were effectively 'liberated' from central government structures.
- In 1988–89, significant transfers of powers and funds considerably increased the hitherto limited autonomy of the communities and regions.

- In 1993, federalism was officially recognized, essentially through the transformation of the unitary Senate into an assembly intended to represent the various federal entities.
- On 1 January 2002, communities' funds and regions' fiscal autonomy increased following lengthy negotiations.

CHARACTERISTICS OF BELGIAN FEDERALISM

This section describes the institutional structure of new federal Belgium, Belgian society and the economy, the political structure and the assignment of competencies.

The Institutional Structure of New Federal Belgium

In 1993, Belgium officially became a federal state. Belgium is made up of three regions and three communities: Flanders, the Dutch-speaking region and the Flemish-speaking Community in the north (which includes the Dutch-speaking inhabitants of the Brussels capital region); the bilingual French and Dutch Brussels capital region in the centre of the country; Wallonia, the French-speaking region in the south; the German Community in the east; and the French-speaking Community, which includes Wallonia and the French-speaking inhabitants of the Brussels capital region. Flanders preferred the community option, absorbing the Flemish region into the Flemish-speaking Community, leading to references being made only to the latter institution. Thus the Flemish parliament and the Flemish government deal with both community and regional affairs. A similar merger has not occurred between the French-speaking Community and the Walloon region.

These three communities—the Dutch speaking, the French speaking and the German speaking—and the three regions—Flanders, Wallonia and the Brussels capital region—coexist within the Belgian state, resulting in a total of six federal entities superimposed on geographical areas that are largely, but not completely, identical to the language areas (Figure 6.1). The country is further divided into 10 provinces and 589 municipalities or communes (see Figure 6.2 for a map of Belgium).

Belgian Society and the Economy

This section compares the different Belgian institutions in terms of population, budgets, surface area, economy and employment. Belgium's total surface area is 30 528 square kilometres. Flanders accounts for about 44.3 per cent of the land area, Wallonia for 55.2 per cent and Brussels for 0.5 per cent.

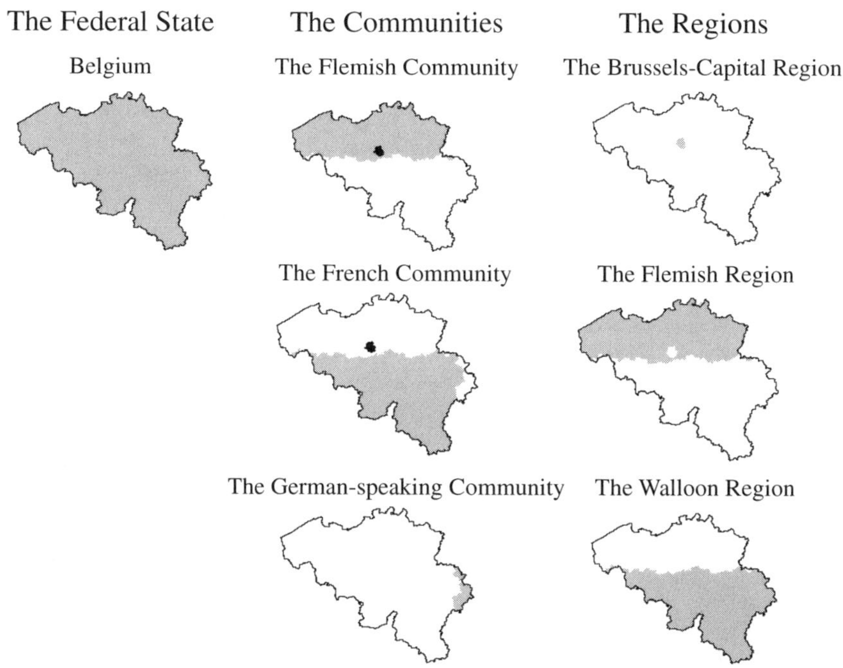

Source: Authors.

Figure 6.1 Divisions of the federal state of Belgium

In 2002, the total population was 10.3 million, resulting in a population density of 338 inhabitants per square kilometre, with 57.9 per cent of the population living in the Flemish region, 32.6 per cent in the Walloon region and 9.5 per cent in Brussels. The population of the German-speaking Community (included in the Walloon region) was 71 036 (National Institute of Statistics 2004b). Estimating the population of the French and Flemish communities is more difficult, because no official statistics exist. Some studies estimate that 85 to 90 per cent of the Brussels region are French speaking and 10 to 15 per cent are Flemish speaking. Thus the French-speaking Community accounts for about 40 per cent of Belgium's population, the Flemish-speaking Community for about 60 per cent and the German-speaking Community for less than 1 per cent.

Gross domestic product (GDP) was €253.8 billion in 2001, with the Flemish share being 57.3 per cent, the Walloon share 23.5 per cent and the Brussels share 19.2 per cent (National Bank of Belgium 2004b). Table 6.1 shows the unemployment rate, GDP per capita in euros and using an index based on per

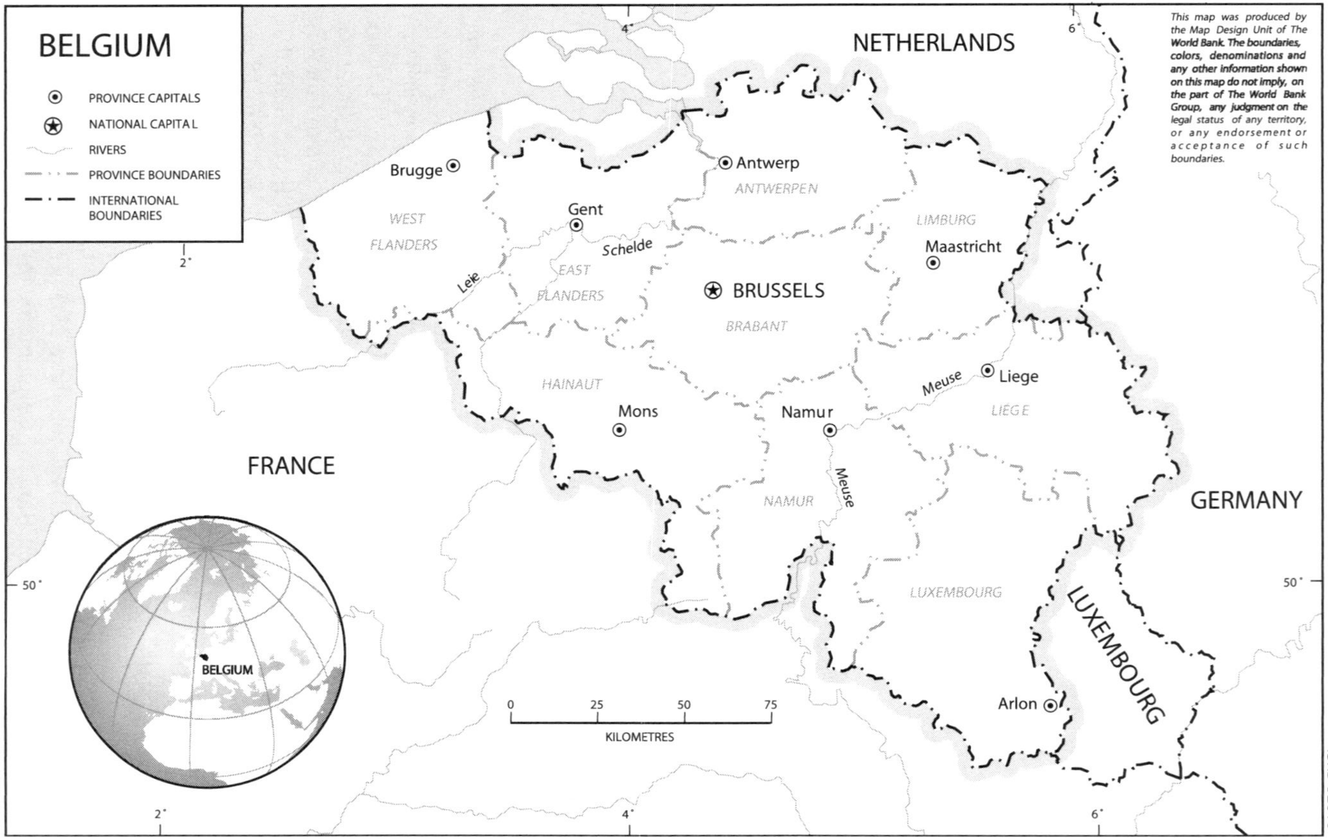

Figure 6.2 *Belgium*

Table 6.1 Economic statistics by region, selected years

Region	Unemployment rate, 2002 (%)	GDP per capita, 2001 €	GDP per capita, 2001 Index (Belgium = 100)	Average net taxable income per capita, 2000 €	Average net taxable income per capita, 2000 Index (Belgium = 100)	GDP growth rate 1991–98 %
Brussels region	14.5	50 090	203	9961	90	0.8
Flemish region	4.9	24 329	99	11 788	107	2.3
Walloon region	10.5	17 827	72	10 088	91	1.3
Belgium	7.5	24 673	100	11 062	100	1.8

Sources: Capron (2001); Eurostat (2003); National Bank of Belgium (2004a); National Institute of Statistics (2004a, b).

capita GDP in Belgium as a whole, average net taxable income per capita in euros and index form and the GDP growth rate for 1981–98.

As concerns value added by kind of activity, in 2001, the Brussels and Walloon regions realized the greatest value added from real estate, rental and business activities and the Flemish region from manufacturing (Table 6.2). Other important differences between regions are also apparent. These differences are reflected in employment by activity (Table 6.3).

Political Structure

Belgium's double layer of federal entities results in an exceptionally complex institutional structure (Figure 6.3). Belgium is a hereditary, constitutional monarchy within a bicameral parliamentary system.

The federal parliament consists of two chambers, the Chamber of Deputies (House of Representatives) and the Senate. The Chamber of Deputies, along with the king, are the sole repositories of legislative power, that is, they initiate and make the final decisions on laws. The Senate is essentially a chamber (or body) of reflection, that is, it intervenes, reviews and recommends as necessary. Nevertheless, in relation to anything concerning the constitution or special majority laws, the Chamber of Deputies and Senate continue to act equally. Special majority laws mean a majority of each language group plus a two-thirds majority of all votes in each chamber of parliament.

The Chamber of Deputies consists of 150 directly elected deputies and represents all citizens of the federation. The structure of the Senate is different and reflects Belgium's federal structure. Some members of each community's parliament are designated by their respective parliament to be members of the

Table 6.2 Value added by kind of activity and region, 2001 (percentage of all activities)

Activity	Brussels region	Flemish region	Walloon region	Belgium
Agriculture, hunting, forestry, fishing	0.0	1.8	1.6	1.4
Mining, quarrying	0.0	0.1	0.4	0.1
Manufacturing	8.0	23.6	17.9	19.1
Electricity, gas, water supply	3.2	2.4	2.9	2.7
Construction	2.4	5.8	5.6	5.1
Wholesale and retail trade	11.0	13.3	10.4	12.1
Hotels, restaurants	2.0	1.7	1.5	1.7
Transport, storage, communication	9.4	6.7	6.3	7.1
Financial intermediation	15.5	3.3	2.9	5.5
Real estate, rentals, business activities	25.3	23.5	22.1	23.5
Public administration, compulsory social security	11.7	5.8	11.1	8.3
Education	5.3	6.0	9.3	6.7
Health, social work	4.9	7.1	8.7	7.1
Other community, social, personal service activities	4.1	1.9	2.0	2.4
Private households with employed people	0.8	0.4	0.9	0.6
Financial intermediation services indirectly measured	–3.6	–3.6	–3.6	–3.6
Total	100.0	100.0	100.0	100.0

Source: National Bank of Belgium (2004b).

Table 6.3 Employment by kind of activity and region, 1998 (percentage of total employment)

Region	Agri-culture	Manu-facturing	Business services	Non-business services
Brussels region	0.2	15.1	58.2	26.9
Flemish region	2.4	30.3	47.9	18.2
Walloon region	2.6	24.5	46.5	26.0
Belgium	2.2	27.2	49.7	20.9

Source: Capron (2001).

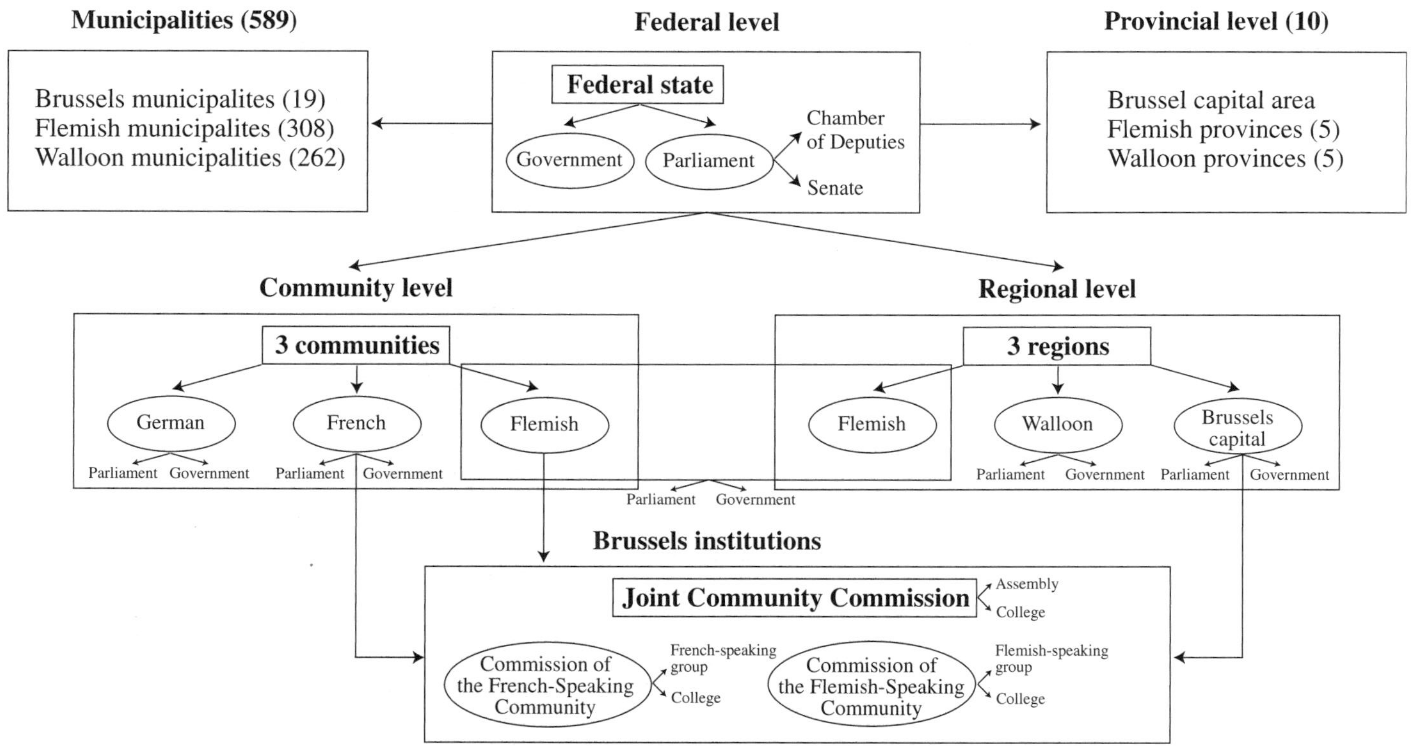

Source: Bayenet and others (2000).

Figure 6.3 Structure of the federal state

senate (10 French-speaking senators, 10 Dutch-speaking senators and 1 German-speaking senator). Other senators are directly elected by the voters (25 Dutch-speaking senators and 15 French-speaking senators) and they co-opt the remaining senators (6 Dutch-speaking senators and 4 French-speaking senators). Thus the 71 senators consist of 29 French-speaking senators, 41 Dutch-speaking senators and 1 German-speaking senator. Thus the Senate has become the chamber that represents the federal entities with a concomitant reduction in its powers in comparison with those of the Chamber of Representatives. It is an imperfect institution, in that only some of the senators represent the communities and the rest represent the various components of the Belgian state, with the numbers weighted by population, that is, 58.6 per cent of the senators are Flemish and 41.4 per cent are French-speaking, roughly corresponding to the current distribution of the population.[5] Furthermore, some entities are not represented in the Senate. This applies to all the regions, but is particularly true for the Brussels capital region, which is pulled in both directions by its two communities.

The Senate's working methods reflect the extent of the failure of its 1993 reform. Its members are still divided according to language, and voting on the basis of language spoken is the only means of protecting minorities. Thus the new Senate reflects the bipolar nature of a country divided into two main communities more than it represents a federal state actually made up, in functional terms, of the Flemish-speaking Community, the Walloon region, the Brussels capital region and the German-speaking Community.

The regional assemblies are directly elected in Brussels (89 deputies),[6] Flanders (118 deputies)[7] and Wallonia (75 deputies). The 89 deputies of the Brussels capital region are divided into two groups: a French-speaking group of 72 deputies and a Flemish group of 17 deputies. With the exception of the assembly of the German-speaking Community (25 deputies), also directly elected by the residents of the nine municipalities of the German-speaking region,[8] the members of the regional assemblies are required to form the community assemblies. The 118 members of the Flemish regional assembly and the 6 deputies directly elected by Dutch-speaking people living in the bilingual Brussels capital region come together in the assembly of the Flemish-speaking Community, and the 75 deputies elected to represent the Walloon region join 19 of the 72 French-speaking regional representatives of the Brussels capital region in the assembly of the French-speaking Community.

Note that both French- and Flemish-speaking people live in the Brussels capital region. The Flemish and French communities are therefore responsible for community matters for the Brussels capital region. Thus the Brussels capital region has three commissions (Figure 6.3): the Commission of the French-Speaking Community, the Commission of the Flemish-Speaking Community and the Joint Community Commission. The Commission of the French-Speaking Community and the Commission of the Flemish-speaking Community are, respectively, responsible for French or Flemish single community institutions of the Brussels capital region and community matters, for example, education. The Joint Community Commission is responsible for community matters that are common to both communities of the Brussels capital region, for instance, some health competencies.

Assignment of Competencies

The main difficulty in understanding the structure of the Belgian state is that it consists of two different kinds of federated entities, regions and communities, whose territories partly overlap, but with each entity responsible for different matters. (For an economic analysis of Belgian federalism, see Bayenet, Gilbert and Thys-Clément 1999; Bayenet and others 2000.) The federal state retains control over such important competencies as foreign affairs, defence, justice, social security, some important aspects of public health and domestic affairs, economics, research, finance (including the federal public debt) and the Belgian federation's economic and monetary union.

The communities' powers are grouped into four main areas: the use of language in relation to culture, education (and research), welfare and health. Note that health is a community competence with the exception of the numerous matters still within the competency of the federal government because of the existence of a federal social security scheme. Note also that welfare competence concerns various powers, all involving contact between the authorities and citizens who need assistance: family policy (other than family benefits, which come under social security), immigrant reception policy (other than basic legislation on nationality and entry, residence and expulsion, which are still matters for the federal government), certain aspects of policy on the disabled, policy on senior citizens (with the exception of the guaranteed minimum income), protection of young people (other than the civil law rules relating to minors and the rules of criminal law and civil procedure) and social welfare (except the guaranteed minimum income).

The regions focus on two main areas. The first is management of the environment in which people live, that is, spatial and urban planning, rural renewal and nature conservation, the environment, housing (except for leases) and the supervision and financing of municipalities and provinces (with the exception of the rules on their organization, which are still within the federal competency, but have been devolved to the regions since 2002). The second is the economy, that is, economic expansion, public industrial initiatives, exploitation of natural resources, regional planning, market and export policies, employment, public works, applied research, foreign trade, transport, water policy, agriculture and energy (except for the electricity facilities plan; nuclear energy; major storage infrastructure; and energy pricing, production and transport). The latter is carried out within a general framework of economic union; monetary union; freedom of trade and industry; and free movement of people, services, goods and capital.

Note that in relation to research, the federal state, the communities and the regions carry out research that is pertinent to their specific competencies.

To clarify the substance of these principles, the federal state may legislate in a number of areas and maintain a single, homogeneous set of standards, laying down, for example, the general rules applicable to public contracts, consumer protection and economic organization, to which the regions may add their own rules. By contrast, a number of areas are wholly the preserve of the federal government, namely, internal and external monetary policy, financial policy, savings protection, credit, banking and insurance legislation, prices and incomes policy, competition law, laws regulating commercial practice, business law, company law, conditions governing access to occupations, industrial and intellectual property, quotas and permits, weights and measures and their standardization, the national investment company, labour law and social security.

Table 6.4 shows the respective financial weights of the various entities of the Belgian federal state in 2002. To manage these competencies, the federal state had a budget of €44.9 billion in 2002. Note that the federal budget as shown in the table does not include funds for the social security system (€49.3 billion in 2002). While Flanders is undeniably the largest federal entity, as 57.9 per cent of the population lives there, compared with 32.6 per cent for Wallonia and 9.5 per cent for Brussels, note that the figure of €16.8 billion encompasses the Flemish-speaking Community and the Flemish region, because the two have merged, while the French-speaking Community and the

Table 6.4 Budgets of the various components of the federal state, 2002 (€ millions)

Category	Federal government	Flemish community and region	French-speaking community	Walloon region	Brussels capital region	German-speaking community
Resources	45 189.4	16 718.4	6 458.5	4 782.5	1 732.0	128.8
Expenditure	44 894.5	16 812.7	6 631.5	5 283.6	1 899.6	128.6
Budgetary surplus or deficit	294.9	–94.3	–173.0	–501.1	–167.6	0.2

Sources: Ministry of Finance (2003); Supreme Financial Council (2003).

Walloon region remain separate entities and the bilingual Brussels capital region is only about 10 per cent Flemish.

Communities and regions singularly restricted freedom to determine their own organization contrasts with their freedom of action. Nevertheless, the institutional reforms of 1993 gave them some limited scope to organize as they choose by enabling them to decide freely about their electoral constituencies, the size of their assembly and government and the rules about these bodies' operations.

Two rules seem vital for conferring true autonomy to the regions and communities. The first is the principle of sole power, that is, only one authority has the power to deal with particular matters. The second is equivalence between the standard-setting power of communities and regions and that of the federal government, meaning that community and regional decrees would have the same force as federal law. In practice, regulations lay down which entities are responsible for which competencies; however, even if one authority is given a particular power, other authorities may also have a certain level of power over the same area. Furthermore, the large extent of opinion giving, association and coordination procedures between the various tiers and the institutionalization of cooperation agreements bear witness to the fact that exclusive powers *de jure* nevertheless often remain highly complementary *de facto*.

A constitutional court, the Court of Arbitration, was created in 1984. The court respects parity between Dutch-speaking and French-speaking people. Its members are legal experts and former members of parliament to ensure that judges are not oblivious to the political logic underlying the constitutional reform. It is a genuine court, responsible for resolving disputes about powers that may arise between the federal government, communities and regions. Even though the court does not yet have the power to verify compliance with all the provisions of the constitution despite the extension of its jurisdiction to disputes relating to equality and to education, the imperatives of constitutional reform have overcome policymakers' traditional hesitancy about supervision of the constitutionality of legislation. A consultation committee made up of representatives of the federal, regional and community governments has been set up to rule on conflicts of interest, which refer to any political disputes that do not involve disputes about the powers of federal, community and regional authorities.

PECULIARITIES OF BELGIAN FEDERALISM

While Belgium's structures comply with the classic rules of federalism, namely, autonomy, equality, participation and cooperation, Belgian-style federalism nevertheless has at least five atypical features.

The first peculiarity is the way in which power is distributed among federal institutions. In the early 1970s, before federalism was on the agenda and when the aim was only cultural autonomy and the introduction of regions, which many people viewed as just a form of decentralization, Belgium attempted to strike a new balance in relation to conflicts between communities and regions by rearranging the institutions of the central government. The idea was to acknowledge the existence of two main linguistic communities, the Dutch speakers and the French speakers, and particularly to avoid making the French speakers a minority within the structures of the central government, heretofore dominated by Dutch speakers. This is why the Federal Council of Ministers is now required to have equal numbers of ministers from each community and why the members of both chambers of the federal parliament were divided into two main groups by language (French and Flemish).

The adoption of legislation on institutional reform requires a special majority (a majority of each language group plus a two-thirds majority of all votes in each chamber of parliament are required for any constitutional reform). These unusual features convey a confederal aspect to the federal government, which operates on the basis of consensus between the two main linguistic communities represented within it, thereby bearing witness to the still profoundly dualistic nature of the Belgian state. The important question is the extent to which federalism based upon recognition of a third, bilingual region around Brussels and, to a lesser degree given its extremely small political weight, of the German-speaking community, will generate the multilateral dynamics that will make overcoming the opposition between Dutch and French speakers possible.

The second peculiarity is the asymmetric nature of Belgian federalism. Flanders preferred the community option, absorbing the Flemish region into the Flemish-speaking Community, to the extent that when referring to northern Belgium, people tend to refer just to the Flemish Community, not the region. Thus Flanders has only one parliament and government (Figure 6.3), but different deputies vote on regional as opposed to community laws. Those deputies of the Flemish parliament who come from the Brussels capital region cannot vote on laws concerning regional competencies, but only on laws concerning community competencies. In contrast, the southern part of the country relies on the distinction between the two existing regions, the Walloon region and the Brussels capital region, rather than referring to the French-speaking Community.

These contrasting institutional choices correspond to the different circumstances in northern and southern Belgium. Faithful to its initially cultural and linguistic claims, Flanders presents itself as a community anxious to maintain its firm links with the Brussels capital region, whose autonomy is accepted only reluctantly, and which remains its capital, and which Dutch speakers sometimes still regard as a Flemish city. This contrasts with the lack of unity of French speakers who, increasingly divided into Walloons and residents of Brussels, opted to deprive the French-speaking Community of part of its substance by dividing some of its powers between Brussels and Walloon institutions. This institutional development in southern Belgium, reflecting the increasingly strong affirmation of Walloon regional awareness, has been fuelled by the recurrent budgetary problems of the French-speaking Community, which have weakened it institutionally and are now among the major elements of the development dynamics of Belgian federalism.

The third peculiarity is the incompleteness of the federal entities' legal systems. They lack constitutions of their own, their status being determined—subject to the highly limited powers granted to them to create or alter their status—by the federal government. Furthermore, while they do enjoy legislative powers and governments of their own, they lack judicial bodies and use the federal government's courts. Finally, residual powers are still held by the federal government, while communities and regions hold only those powers explicitly vested in them until Article 35 of the constitution, which allows this system to be reversed, is operationalized. The only explanation for this situation is that Belgian federalism is a centrifugal movement derived from the break-up of a unitary state and not the product of the association of formerly independent components.

The fourth peculiarity is the extremely complex institutional arrangements in the Brussels area. Brussels is a city region with a population of 1 million and the capital of Belgium. The Brussels capital region consists of the city of Brussels and 18 other municipalities. The region was granted autonomy because neither Dutch speakers nor Walloons could bring themselves to leave such a small but symbolically and politically important region (because of the numerous international institutions, including those of the European Community located there) to the other group. While Brussels is effectively a region, it does not constitute a Community,[9] with the French-speaking Community holding power there with respect to cultural, social and educational institutions that use the French language and the Flemish-speaking Community where the language used is Dutch.

Note that the official bodies of the Brussels capital region are organized in the same way as the Federal Council of Ministers and parliament at the federal level so as to protect the Flemish minority in the region. The complex tangle of institutions is the result of Brussels' position in the area, which has seen the toughest competition between the French and Dutch languages. This multicultural city, now largely French speaking, was historically a Flemish city, but has become increasingly French speaking over time.

The fifth peculiarity concerns international relations. Federal Belgium resolutely followed the path of removing foreign policy from the federal sphere when it carried out its 1993 institutional reforms. A new article of the constitution recognizes the capacity of community and regional governments to conclude treaties on matters for which they are responsible under domestic law, subject to safeguards to ensure consistency in the federation's foreign policy. The special legislation of 5 May 1993 also empowers regions and communities to represent Belgium at international organizations under the same conditions. Cooperation agreements are to be concluded to address the difficulties that arise under two kinds of circumstances. The first is when organizations recognize only states. The second is to decide what line is to be taken if the members of a Belgian delegation that consists of representatives of several tiers of authority cannot reach consensus, because the subjects under consideration relate to matters for which, under domestic law, both the federal government and the communities and/or regions are responsible.

Belgium has thus defied the classic rule of the federal state acting as a single entity in international relations, taking its federal logic to the point where communities' and regions' internal powers are extended into international law. This is undeniably a peculiarity that some people will interpret as an increase in the autonomy of federal entities, whereas others will regard it as presaging a form of confederacy.

FINANCING FEDERATED ENTITIES

Under the Ordinary Institutional Reform Act of 9 August 1980, the financing of federated entities essentially depended on the central budget (for more details about the financing of federation entities, see Bayenet 2003a,b; Bayenet and others 2000). The funds provided to the communities by the central government were divided so that 55 per cent went to the Flemish-speaking Community and 45 per cent to the French-speaking Community. Federal grants were shared among regions on the basis of a scale that gave equal weight to the following three factors:

- the population of each region, a criterion that benefited Brussels;
- the proceeds from income tax in each region, a criterion that benefited Flanders;
- the surface area of each region, a criterion that benefited Wallonia.

This system was dubbed consumer federalism, because the overall amount of money that regions and communities had available to spend and how it was distributed among them was not their responsibility. The federal parliament took advantage of the sweeping transfer of powers introduced by the August 1988 law to review these financial arrangements. The current system is governed by the Special Law on Community and Regional Financing Bases of January 1989 (modified in 1993 and 2001), which replaced the August 1980 law. The German-speaking Community is covered by a special system that will not be discussed here.

As Table 6.5 shows, Belgian federalism was extremely modest before 1980 and remained relatively insignificant in financial terms under the 1980 law. The financing of federal entities did not become significant until after the institutional reforms of 1989, which entailed major transfers of law making and budgetary powers. Table 6.5 presents total financial transfers from the federal state to regions and communities (excluding specific regional taxation). Two figures are provided for each period because reform of the state is a gradual process that involves the introduction of laws at various stages.

As shown in Table 6.5, the real turning point came in 1989. The January 1989 law (modified in 1993 and 2001) established a series of sources of revenues for communities and regions (Table 6.6). Even though the resources of communities seem to be fairly similar to those of regions, in practice, the resources of communities and regions vary significantly. The following sections analyse the major resources of communities and regions, that is, the taxes collected at the national level and allocated to regions and communities (the share of the federal income tax and the federal value added tax proceeds)

Table 6.5 Financial transfers from the federal level to federated entities since federalization

		Absolute figures	
Period	Years	€ millions	As a percentage of the federal budget
Start of federalization	1972	171.2	2
	1981	2394.9	9
Intermediate situation (the Ordinary Institutional Reform Act of 9 August 1980)	1982	2568.7	9
	1988	4177.9	10
Current system (Special Law on Community and Regional Financing Bases of 16 January 1989)	1989	14 199.3	35
	2002	27 963.3	60

Sources: Bayenet and others (2000); Chamber of Deputies (2002).

Table 6.6 Revenue sources for communities and regions until 2001

Type of resource	Regions	Communities
Fiscal resources	Share of federal income tax Regional taxes Regional taxing power	Share of federal income tax Share of the value added tax Radio and television licences Community taxing power
Nonfiscal resources	Nonfiscal taxes Loans Specific federal grants Solidarity contribution	Nonfiscal taxes Loans Specific federal grants

Source: Authors.

and the fiscal power of regions (regional taxes and regional taxing power) and communities (radio and television licences). In 2001, these resources represented 85.9 per cent of the resources of the Brussels region, around 83.7 per cent of the resources of the Walloon region, 94.8 per cent of the resources of the French-speaking Community and 96.9 per cent of the resources of the Flemish-speaking Community (Table 6.7)

Regions and communities also receive specific federal grants. Regions receive federal grants to manage agriculture competencies transferred in 1993 and to manage job creation programmes. Communities receive federal grants to finance the higher education of foreign students. The Brussels capital region receives a special grant to compensate it for the loss of real estate tax receipts resulting from the number of national and international institutions located in Brussels, which do not pay this tax. (The German-speaking Community is essentially financed by a federal grant that accounts for 71 per cent of its resources.)

The Brussels capital region also benefits from specific taxes inherited from the former province of Brabant and the Brussels agglomeration. The institutional reform of 1993 split the bilingual province of Brabant into Flemish Brabant and Walloon Brabant as of 1995. The provincial competencies (including fiscal power) were transferred to the Brussels capital region. The principle of agglomeration was introduced in the constitution in 1970 to provide for broader planning and transport coordination in Brussels, Antwerp, Charleroi and Namur. However, such an agglomeration was only established in Brussels (Fitzmaurice 1996). The competencies of the Brussels agglomeration were transferred to the Brussels capital region.

The Walloon region also receives financial compensation from the French-speaking Community. Indeed, this community, which had no fiscal autonomy at all, faced recurring financial difficulties since responsibility for the education system was transferred to it in 1989, causing major political problems throughout the 1990s. In 1993, the financial problems of the French Community resulted in some amendments to the January 1989 law. The lack of resources for education in Flanders was less worrying because of the merger of the budgets of the Community and the region.

To save the French Community from bankruptcy, the institutional reform of 1993 allocated new resources to communities without changing the principles introduced in 1989 and allowed the Walloon region and the Commission of the French-speaking Community in the Brussels capital region to help the French-speaking Community financially. The French-speaking Community transferred some competencies to the Walloon region and the Commission of the French-speaking Community, but without transferring all the resources linked to these competencies. The compensation from the French-speaking Community to the Walloon region shown in Table 6.7 is the result of this arrangement. The financial crisis that the French-speaking Community experienced affected the development of federalism by helping to strengthen regional federalism on the French-speaking side, because no other solution was found to relieve the pressure on its budget than to divest the community of some of its powers in favour of the regional institutions of Wallonia and the Brussels capital region.

Table 6.4 indicates the deficit or surplus situation of the budget for each entity; however, the need to protect the federation's economic and monetary union led to the introduction of supervisory machinery to monitor the debt situation at the different levels of government. The federal minister of finance and the Federal Council of Ministers have been vested with various powers that give them a degree of control over the loans taken out by regions and communities. To analyse the situation, a new unit has been set up in the Supreme Financial Council that consists of equal numbers of members representing the federal government and entities and equal numbers of French and Flemish speakers. Its task is to recommend whether or not the borrowing capacity of an entity of the federation should be limited.

A major political agreement was concluded in October 2000 between the representatives of the two main linguistic communities and was further refined by the federal government in January 2001. This agreement was converted into the two 'special' laws of July 2001. It amended the law of January 1989 by attempting to satisfy the demands of both communities and regions. One part of the agreement concerned greater fiscal autonomy for regions, which headed the list of demands drawn up by Flanders for a new round of state reform. The second part concerned the refinancing of communities, in particular, for education. Even though both communities benefit from these new revenues, they were necessary to save the French-speaking Community from bankruptcy.

Table 6.7 Resources of communities and regions, 2001 and 2002

Resource	Brussels capital region € millions	%	Walloon region € millions	%	French-speaking community € millions	%	Flemish region and Flemish-speaking community € millions	%	German-speaking community € millions	%
2001										
Taxes collected at the national level										
Shares of income tax allocated to regions	974.2	59.6	3609.5	71.2	n.a.	n.a.	6258.9	37.3	n.a.	n.a.
Shares of income tax allocated to communities	n.a.	n.a.	n.a.	n.a.	1634.0	25.7	2886.7	17.2	n.a.	n.a.
Shares of value added tax allocated to communities	n.a.	n.a.	n.a.	n.a.	4151.0	65.3	5457.2	32.5	n.a.	n.a.
Specific federal grants	55.7	3.4	154.3	3.0	57.6	0.9	249.6	1.5	93.3	70.6
Regional taxes	343.9	21.0	511.1	10.1	n.a.	n.a.	1193.8	7.1	n.a.	n.a.
Regional taxing power	86.9	5.3	122.6	2.4	n.a.	n.a.	0.7	0.0	n.a.	n.a.
Radio and television licences	n.a.	n.a.	n.a.	n.a.	268.7	4.2	468.7	2.8	4.9	3.7
Specific taxes of the Brussels region	130.3	8.0	n.a.	n.a.	n.a.	n.a.	n.a.	n.a.	n.a.	n.a.
Specific compensation from the French-speaking Community	n.a.	n.a.	301.2	5.9	n.a.	n.a.	n.a.	n.a.	n.a.	n.a.
Other resources	44.6	2.7	369.6	7.3	241.0	3.8	272.3	1.6	33.9	25.7
Total	1635.6	100.0	5068.3	100.0	6352.3	100.0	16 787.8	100.0	132.1	100.0

2002										
Taxes collected at the national level										
Shares of income tax allocated to regions	555.1	32.0	2642.4	55.3	n.a.	n.a.	4275.0	25.6	n.a.	n.a.
Shares of income tax allocated to communities	n.a.	n.a.	n.a.	n.a.	1558.8	24.1	2916.9	17.4	n.a.	n.a.
Shares of value added tax allocated to communities	n.a.	n.a.	n.a.	n.a.	4282.3	66.3	5689.1	34.0	n.a.	n.a.
Specific federal grants	87.8	5.0	177.6	3.7	58.4	0.9	283.7	1.7	99.1	76.9
Regional taxes	712.2	41.1	1394.0	29.1	n.a.	n.a.	2750.78	16.5	n.a.	n.a.
Regional taxing power	133.9	7.7	116.3	2.4	n.a.	n.a.	21.1	0.1	n.a.	n.a.
Radio and television licences	n.a.	n.a.	n.a.	n.a.	273.0	4.2	455.3	2.7	4.9	2.9
Specific taxes of the Brussels region	126.7	7.3	n.a.	n.a.	n.a.	n.a.	n.a.	n.a.	n.a.	n.a.
Specific compensation from the French-speaking community	n.a.	n.a.	291.3	6.1	n.a.	n.a.	n.a.	n.a.	n.a.	n.a.
Other resources	116.3	6.7	160.8	3.4	285.9	4.4	326.8	2.0	24.7	19.2
Total	1732.0	100.0	4782.5	100.0	6458.5	100.0	16 718.4	100.0	128.8	100.0

n.a. Not applicable.

Source: Ministry of Finance (2003).

As Table 6.7 shows, the most recent reform has modified the relative importance of the major resources of communities and regions, but without affecting the principles of the financing system introduced in 1989. In comparison with 2001, the share of regional taxes increased and the share of income tax allocated to regions and communities decreased.

Fiscal Resources of Federated Entities

This section analyses the major fiscal resources of federated entities: taxes collected at the national level and allocated to federated entities and the fiscal powers of federated entities.

Taxes collected at the national level and allocated to federated entities

The law of January 1989 introduced a system of distribution of some of the resources derived from two national taxes, personal income tax and value added tax (VAT), to the regions and communities. These taxes represent a major resource of regions and communities (Table 6.7). The basis on which the proceeds from these taxes are shared vertically between the state and the regions and communities is the budget resources associated with the powers that have been successively transferred from the state to the regions and communities. The amount of income tax proceeds allocated to the regions and communities is intended to finance competencies transferred from the federal state except for education, which is financed by a share of the proceeds from the VAT. The amounts were determined in 1989 and are indexed independently of the total national proceeds of these taxes.

The special law of January 1989 on community and regional financing broke with the pattern of the 1980 law with regard to the sharing of financial resources among federal entities. The horizontal distribution of income tax proceeds between the regions and between communities is no longer based on the scales mentioned earlier, but on the so-called fair returns principle, whereby the funds allocated to each region and community are proportional to the revenues produced by income tax in each entity. To determine the share of income tax proceeds granted to each region, we first estimate the income tax proceeds collected in each region as a percentage of total income tax proceeds. We then apply this percentage to the amount of income tax proceeds devoted to the regions and fixed by law (for example, €10.33 billion in 2002). Thus for 2002, the Brussels capital region share was 9.03 per cent (€932.90 million), the Walloon share was 28.54 per cent (€2949.00 million) and the Flemish share was 62.43 per cent (€6450.80 million).

In 2002, an amount of €4.6 billion was granted to communities following the same principle. In the Brussels capital region, 80 per cent of funds went to the French Community and 20 per cent to the Flemish Community. The share of the Flemish Community was 64.57 per cent and the share of the French Community was 35.43 per cent (Chamber of Deputies 2002).

This new distribution pattern is meant to make the entities more responsible, because how much they have to spend depends largely on the tax revenues generated by those living in their territories. This creates a problem for the Brussels capital region, which is financially penalized, because 300 000 workers commute there every day to work and generate costs linked to their use of the public services provided for them, but the proceeds from the income taxes they pay go to their regions of residence.

The change in 1989 from distribution according to needs to distribution according to means has led to a redistribution of financial resources between the components of the federal state to the advantage of Flanders. To avoid too harsh an impact on the Walloon region and the French-speaking Community, the law provided for a ten-year transition period from 1989 to 1999, so the system did not come into complete effect until 2000. This ten-year period also served to involve the entities in the effort to restore equilibrium to public spending, although Belgium's huge public debt burden is a federal government responsibility. Indeed, while Belgium satisfied the convergence criteria imposed by the Maastricht Treaty for entry into the euro zone by bringing the budget deficit to less than 3 per cent of GDP, its gross debt amounted to 100.8 per cent of GDP in 2002 (Ministry of Finance 2003), which is much higher than the 60 per cent stipulated in the treaty.

The distribution of the proceeds from the VAT to communities to pay for education departs from the fair returns principle, forging a sort of implicit solidarity among the communities. Until 2000, these resources were shared between communities based on the number of school-age children in each community. In 1988, 57.55 per cent went to the Flemish-speaking Community and 42.45 per cent to the French-speaking Community. Before education was transferred to the communities, the French-speaking community received 43.51 per cent of the total amount allocated to education (Flemish and French), that is, a 1.06 per cent surplus in comparison with the estimation based on the number of school-age children. Thus to avoid too brutal a loss to the French-speaking Community, the new method of calculation was gradually put into effect during the 1989 to 1999 transition period.

The January 1989 special law stipulates that as of 1999, the amounts 'will be adjusted in accordance with the numerical distribution of pupils on the basis of objective criteria laid down by law'. In 1999, this adjustment to the distribution of VAT proceeds was to the advantage of the French-speaking Community and to the detriment of the Flemish-speaking Community, giving rise to a dispute between these two main linguistic communities that was solved only through negotiations between French-speaking and Dutch-speaking members of the federal government. These led to the eventual passage of a law in May 2000. As of 2000, the distribution of VAT proceeds between communities is adjusted annually according to the number of pupils age 6 through 17 enrolled in primary and secondary schools in each community. The headcount gave a coefficient of 57.06 per cent for the Flemish-speaking Community and 42.94 per cent for the French-speaking Community, which thus gained 0.49 percentage points, or €45.1 million, over what it received before, and Flanders automatically lost the equivalent amount. However, the political agreement allocated new transfers of funds from the federal budget to cover the costs of foreign students in the case of the communities and job creation programmes in the case of the regions. As a result, the overall budget of the Flemish-speaking Community did not sustain a loss.

In 2002, the amount of VAT receipts transferred to communities was estimated at €10.0 billion and the shares of pupils age 6 through 17 were, respectively, 56.97 per cent for the Flemish Community and 43.03 per cent for the French Community (Chamber of Deputies 2002).

The means for indexing the resources allocated to communities and regions in 1989 have been at the heart of political debate in recent years. Under the original provisions of the January 1989 special law, the amounts awarded to regions and communities were pegged to the retail price index, so they decreased as a proportion of overall public spending. Thus at the time of the 1993 reforms, the reformers decided that the share of income tax revenues allocated to regions and communities would be pegged to the rate of economic growth. According to the July 2001 law, a similar mechanism will start operating in 2007 to index the share of VAT allocated to communities to finance spending on education. The amount of VAT granted to communities also depends on changes in the birth rate, in that a decrease in the birth rate induces a decrease in the amount transferred to communities.

Following the last institutional reform of June 2001, the amount the federal state assigns to communities will increase overall by €1.1 billion over a period of ten years (2002–12), but these new revenues are shared between communities following the fair returns principle and over a gradual transition period between 2002 and 2011. Evidently this agreement was largely facilitated by the restoration of economic growth in 2000.

The small number of new powers decentralized to the regions in June 2001 in the fields of municipal and provincial organization, election spending, agriculture, foreign trade and development cooperation does not give rise to budget transfers between the federal government and regions comparable to those brought about by the previous reforms. In 2002, the federal state transferred €76.5 million, €14.9 million and €6.1 million, respectively, to the regions in accordance with the new powers in agriculture, foreign trade and municipal and provincial organization.

Fiscal powers of federated entities

Regional taxes represent the regions' other major resource (Table 6.7). Even if the January 1989 special law qualifies those taxes as regional taxes, until 2001 not all the proceeds went towards regional budgets. Moreover, the fiscal power of regions was limited. For some regional taxes the federal government laid down the tax base and/or the rate and/or exemptions and penalties. The taxes concerned were the gaming and betting tax, the tax on automatic entertainment machines, the tax on the licensing of bars, death duties, ecotaxes (taxes on products deemed harmful to the environment), the real estate income tax, stamp duties on property transfers and the road tax. In the last institutional reform of June 2001, other federal taxes were 'regionalized', namely, the new vehicle tax, radio and television licences, registration tax on all real estate transfers, taxes on mortgages and other transactions and the Eurotax (paid by heavy goods vehicles for the right to use the road network).

All the regional taxes were fully regionalized as of 1 January 2002 with the exception of ecotaxes, which have been transferred to the federal state. This complete transfer of regional taxes should help shake off the inertia generated by the splitting of powers between the federal government and the regions with respect to certain taxes. The impact of the full regionalization of regional taxes results in an estimated increase in the amount going to the regions of about €3.5 billion, but this transfer of resources to regions is neutral for the federal state, because the increase in regional taxes is offset by a decrease in the share of income tax revenue allocated to the regions.

Tax administration is mainly organized at the federal level. Under the January 1989 special law, the federal government continues to collect regional taxes free of charge on behalf of and in cooperation with the regions, unless they wish to collect them themselves, which the Flemish region decided to do in 1998 for the real estate tax.

Following the July 2001 law, regions are authorized, within limits fixed by the federal government, to levy increases or reductions on the federal income tax. This fiscal power was still allowed in the January 1989 special law, but it had not been used. A plan by the Flemish region to award a tax rebate to its residents because of the increasingly large budget surpluses it had registered in recent years caused a dispute with the Walloon region in 2000, which blocked the plan under the consultation procedures provided for by law. It was undoubtedly in order to render this possibility operational, previously cramped by a vague legal framework, that the institutional reform of June 2001 provides for amendment of the January 1989 special law. This allows regions to increase and reduce the income tax within certain limits provided that the progressive nature of income tax is not affected and that no unfair fiscal competition results. Any region taking such an initiative must inform the other regions and the federal government and submit the measure to the Auditor General's Department for an opinion. The latter must give its opinion within a month on whether the limits imposed by the law have been respected, stating its reasons. The Jurisdiction and Procedure Court may then take the opinion into account in the event of an lawsuit brought against a region for failure to observe the statutory limits of its fiscal powers.

Article 170 of the constitution also gives the regions the power to raise their own taxes while leaving it to the federal government to determine the necessary exceptions to this rule. The federal government immediately restricted this large degree of freedom that the entities were to enjoy. To ensure that the regions' new taxing powers did not result in an increase in the tax burden that might make Belgium less competitive than its European neighbours, the government passed a law in January 1989 prohibiting the entities from levying taxes on anything the federal government already taxed except in the fields specifically listed in the January 1989 special law, plus water and refuse management policies, which the regions tax. This boils down to the regional tax authorities having to engage in the difficult task of finding new things to tax.

Table 6.7 indicates the degree of fiscal autonomy enjoyed by the regions and the impact of the June 2001 reform. A comparison of regional taxes in 2001 and 2002 shows that the share of the regions' taxes derived from regional taxes increased dramatically. The share of the proceeds of regional taxing power in the regional resources is less important. However, the lack of proceeds for the Flemish-speaking Community does not mean an absence of regional taxing in Flanders. The receipts for these taxes, which amounted to €332.2 million in 2001, are directly passed on to special public organizations that are responsible for water and refuse management policies.

It is too early to pass judgement on a system that is already being amended, even before it has become fully functional. The fiscal autonomy of regions, which most observers consider to be limited to date, will increase considerably. This is undeniably a step forward that will enable the entities of the federation to pursue their own policies and adjust their taxes in response to their financial needs. In the present budgetary context of regions, only Flanders is able to reduce some taxes. The Flemish-speaking Community suppressed the radio and television licence and the tax on the licensing of bars in 2002 and reduced stamp duties on property transfers; however, the Walloon region and the Brussels capital region have few opportunities to reduce taxes.

The future will tell what effect this increase in fiscal autonomy will have on the equilibrium of the federation. During the debates on giving some fiscal power to the regions to reduce or increase the income tax, opinions differed concerning the degree of leeway the regions should enjoy. Some insisted on percentage limits to the raising and lowering of income taxes and on the obligation to respect the progressive nature of the tax imposed on the regions to minimise the risk of unfair fiscal competition between them. Others argued that substantial inequalities in the tax burden could arise if taxes were reduced in the wealthier regions and increased in the poorer ones, and that variations in taxes affecting businesses could distort the economy because of their effects on people's purchasing power, and perhaps even on salaries. Looking beyond this worst case scenario, the risks of fiscal competition seem fairly slight because of the limits to mobility imposed by the language difference between the Walloon and Flemish regions, but which tends not to apply in the Brussels capital region because of its various compensating advantages. Moreover, some important differences between municipalities still exist in relation to the possibility that municipalities will impose additional income and real estate taxes. For example, concerning variations in additions to the income tax, the gap between municipalities varies from zero to 8.5 per cent, but to date there are no indications that this gap has induced migration from municipalities with high taxes to municipalities with lower taxes.

The consequences of the complete regionalization of regional taxes should not be ignored. Risks of harmful fiscal competition between regions exist, and its effects have indeed been felt with respect to death duties. Just how serious the threat is will depend on the efficacy of the machinery devised to thwart it. For example, the January 1989 special law is to be amended by a provision stipulating that applicable death duties are those of the location where the deceased was resident for the longest period during the last five years of his or her life, which will make last minute changes of residence for inheritance tax purposes more difficult. In the same spirit, regions will not be able to use their powers concerning vehicle taxes with respect to car hire firms without previously concluding a cooperation agreement.

Communities enjoy no fiscal autonomy at all, and this is unlikely to change with the exception of the German-speaking Community, which enjoys a slight degree of autonomy. Even if the constitution gives the communities the power to raise taxes, the development of proper community taxes has been hindered by uncertainty as to how they would be levied in the bilingual Brussels capital region. In the bilingual Brussels capital region there is no way to distinguish between French-speaking and Flemish-speaking residents, and thus no way to impose a tax only on one group or the other. The radio and television licence fee was thus the only community tax under the January 1989 law. Even though communities receive the proceeds, they have no power to regulate the tax: the federal government determines the assessment base, rate and exceptions, while the power to increase this tax was awarded to the regions. The proceeds from the licence from the Brussels capital region were shared on an 80 per cent–20 per cent basis between the French-speaking and Flemish-speaking communities, respectively. It benefits the latter, however, as only 10 per cent of the population is estimated to be Flemish according to the votes obtained by the Flemish-language candidates in the regional elections in Brussels. The last institutional reform in June 2001 drew the logical conclusion from this situation and programmed the regionalization of the radio and television licence (except in the German-speaking Community). As compensation, the communities receive a new federal grant.

Fiscal federalism has therefore taken a distinctly regional turn to the detriment of the communities. In practice, however, this lack of fiscal autonomy at the community level is only felt by the French-speaking Community, because the Flemish-speaking Community benefits indirectly from the fiscal autonomy of the Flemish region, with which it merged, and the German-speaking Community, which has no boundary problems with Brussels, has a different system. The financial situation of the French-speaking Community, which is one of the factors determining the shape of federalism, will gradually improve with the financial reshuffle resulting from the June 2001 reform and with the indexing of its finances to economic growth.

Solidarity Between the Federation's Entities

As the January 1989 special law on community and regional financing bases distributes funds on the principle of fair returns, a logical step was that it should at the same time provide for solidarity between the federation's entities. This is done by means of the January 1989 Special Law on Community and Regional Financing. It works only between regions as follows: a region of the federation where the mean per capita proceeds from income tax are lower than the average for Belgium as a whole receives the equivalent of €11.6 per inhabitant and per percentage point difference between its mean income tax proceeds and the national average. €11.6 is an estimate of the surplus the Walloon region received under the old 1980 system. This figure is pegged to the retail price index and adjusted annually.

The Walloon region has benefited from national solidarity from the start, and received €657.52 million in 2002 (12.9 per cent of its resources). This amount is included in the share of income tax receipts allocated to regions. The Brussels capital region has benefited from national solidarity since 1997. Table 6.8 shows the divergence between the three regions in terms of their inhabitants' income.

On average, the inhabitants of the Flemish region are better off than those of the Walloon region, with Brussels somewhere in between the two. In the 1990s, the Flemish population's income increased substantially, while the Walloon population grew somewhat poorer, though the trend seemed to have eased in the late 1990s. The most spectacular change concerns the population

Table 6.8 National solidarity mechanism between regions, 1990 and 2002

Year	National solidarity data	Brussels capital region	Flemish region	Walloon region
1990	Per capita income tax deviation from national average in 1989 (%)	+13.75	+2.42	–8.46
	Solidarity payments (€ millions)	0	0	376.80
2002	Per capita income tax deviation from national average in 1999 (%)	–3.63	+7.61	–12.49
	Solidarity payments (€ millions)	54.95	0	657.52

Sources: Bayenet and others (2000); Chamber of Deputies (2002).

of the Brussels capital region, which was wealthier than the Flemish population in 1989 but gradually grew poorer to drop below the national average in 1997. This is largely due to the exodus of people in the higher income brackets towards the outer reaches of the city in the neighbouring Flemish or Walloon regions.

The national solidarity mechanism is simple and transparent, but does have some specific characteristics. Cattoir and Verdonck (1999) point to what they refer to as a receipts paradox: the national solidarity mechanism induces an inversion of the relative taxes per capita of regions. Moreover, the total revenues of a region that benefits from national solidarity decrease when the amount of taxable income increases more in this region than in others. In other words, any economic improvement in this region that increases taxable revenues immediately leads to a loss of the region's total revenues.

There is no solidarity mechanism between communities, but the proportion of VAT receipts allocated to communities, which is their main source of revenue and serves to finance their responsibilities in the education sector, is not calculated according to the principle of fair returns but is based on the number of pupils in each community in 1988. This distribution method based on the needs of the education system in the two communities rather than on the proceeds from income tax in their respective territories was chosen with the aim of guaranteeing equality of opportunity to all children in the federation, irrespective of which linguistic community they belong to. It is a form of implicit solidarity with a special subsidy for the French-speaking Community. Note, however, that the additional means earmarked for communities as a result of the June 2001 reform will be progressively apportioned in the same way as the proceeds from income tax, that is, according to the principle of fair returns.

SOLIDARITY AND SUBSIDIARITY

Compared with the redistribution carried out by means of national solidarity, which may appear relatively modest given the amounts involved, one feature of note is the scale of transfers made via the social security system. These two different forms of solidarity should not be confused. National solidarity affects relations between federated entities, whereas social security is a form of interpersonal solidarity between inhabitants regardless of which region or community they belong to. This issue lies at the core of one of the most deep-seated controversies surrounding the state reform. Before going into the details of this matter, let us examine how the social security system can be defined and describe how various powers are allocated. Note that compared with neighbouring countries, Belgium's poverty rate and degree of income inequality are low. According to Lipszyc and Pestieau (1998), this can be explained by a generous and efficient social security system.

Organization of the Social Security System

The social security system consists of a series of social insurance schemes that vary according to those covered. For employees, social security covers sickness and disability benefits, unemployment benefits, old-age and survivors' pensions, benefits for industrial and occupational diseases, reimbursement of medical expenses and family benefits. The system for self-employed workers is both more limited in scope and less generous in terms of payments, providing only sickness and disability benefits, reimbursement of medical expenses, old-age and survivors' pensions, family benefits and benefits in the event of bankruptcy. Special schemes also exist for such categories of people as seamen, miners and, above all, civil servants.

One characteristic of the social security system is its funding system: up to 70 per cent of the system is funded from employers' and employees' contributions. A single body, the National Social Security Office, is responsible for collecting contributions, whereas a whole range of different institutions make payments. With a budget of €49.3 billion in 2002, the social security system is a giant apparatus for the redistribution of funds between the young and the old, the sick and the healthy, the employed and the unemployed and households with and without children. Alongside the social security system, various social assistance schemes—minimum subsistence income, guaranteed income for the elderly, guaranteed family benefits, various allowances for the disabled and social welfare—are also in place that are financed by taxes and are accessible to anyone living in Belgium who is in need.

Assignment of Social Protection Powers

Part of the federal government's residual powers concern social security. This exclusive area of competence is made explicit in the August 1980 special institutional reform act. This was supplemented by a special law in August 1988, which stated that 'the Federal authority also has sole jurisdiction over labour law and social security'. The same law also makes the federal government responsible for the minimum incomes awarded to those in need, which are traditionally referred to as social assistance.

The distribution of powers in the social protection field has the appearance of a jigsaw puzzle, as many of the responsibilities inextricably associated with social security or social assistance have been assigned to communities. For instance, communities are responsible for

- social assistance policy, except for minimum subsistence income;
- policy on the elderly, except for their guaranteed income;
- policy on the disabled, except for the allowances paid.

Interpreting the rules on the apportionment of powers in this area has created difficulties when plans to set up new forms of social protection have been devised, and deciding on whether the federal authority or the communities are to exercise a power implies distinguishing between social security and social assistance, which is not easy, and the special institutional reform acts fail to resolve this issue.

The problem now arises in practice with a March 1999 decree of the Flemish Community on the organization of health insurance so as to provide non-medical services and support without means testing, for those unable to support themselves (and not only in financial terms), particularly the very old, via the Flemish medical insurance fund. The latter is financed by a grant from the Flemish Community budget and by contributions from everyone living in Flanders, for whom it is now compulsory to join a medical insurance fund. Following an application by the French-speaking Community for setting aside this measure, the Jurisdiction and Procedure Court resolved the controversy in March 2001. Strangely, the court did not attempt to define and circumscribe the notions of social security and social assistance, but it did confirm the Flemish Community's powers by stating that 'a community does not exceed its powers if, in exercising its power to assist individuals, it grants some of them special assistance, distinct from any support provided under the federally-organised social security system and without impinging on an area over which the federal government has exclusive powers'. This is only an initial judgement that, in particular, fails to convey a precise idea of the extent of the federal government's social security powers. However, this judicial decision will probably be crucial for the future of social protection, because it paves the way for a separate Flemish social security system covering new risks that the federal level does not cater for. But the controversy over social security is not confined to the interpretation of rules on the apportionment of powers between communities and the federal government. The Flemish Community also contests the original apportionment of powers established by the special institutional reform act of August 1980.

Flemish- Versus French-Speakers' Demands

From the mid-1990s onwards, the Flemish authorities gradually clarified their social security demands in various documents that are included in five resolutions adopted by the Flemish parliament in March 1999. In relation to social security, the Flemings' claims were 'law-making, executive and financial responsibility for health and family policy as a whole shall be transferred entirely to federal entities, including responsibility for health insurance and family benefits'. These demands are based on a proposed new distinction between two categories of social security: (a) replacement benefits aiming at offsetting the loss or absence of income from employment and including unemployment benefits, old-age and survivors' pensions and sickness and disability benefits; and (b) supplementary or compensatory benefits intended to reimburse specific costs, including health insurance and family benefits.

Income replacement benefits would continue to be a matter for the federal government. As they are linked to people's occupational activity and financed by employers' and employees' contributions, thereby forming a direct component of production costs, the economic and monetary unity of Belgium requires that these benefits be organized at the federal level. This argument does not apply to the compensatory benefits that the Flemings would like to decentralize. The proposed transfer of powers to communities in keeping with the Flemish vision of state reform would be accompanied by standardization of both funding and benefits. In 1999 figures, it would involve €16.3 billion, or 40 per cent of the total social security budget.

The main argument of those who advocate such reform is that the current apportionment of powers is incoherent. They maintain that even though communities are responsible for family affairs, they cannot pursue any real policy in this area as long as such a major mechanism as family benefits remains under federal control in the social security system. The same argument applies to the health sector. As described in the special institutional reform act of August 1980, communities are in charge of 'the policy for the provision of care inside and outside health care establishments'. However, the subsequent list of exceptions over which the federal level holds power, including sickness and disability insurance, are so numerous and extensive that they represent the rule rather than the exception. The Flemish idea is to re-establish homogeneous sets of powers to enable the communities to pursue policies that would be more efficient because they would facilitate reform more easily than at the federal level and closer to the concerns of the Flemish and the French speakers, whose needs are regarded as partially divergent (for critiques of this concept of a homogeneous set of powers, see de Callatay and Savage 1998; Roland, Vandeveld and Van Parijs 1999).

The French-speaking Community remains resolutely opposed to any form of decentralization of social security, because of a desire to preserve the existing solidarity within the Belgian state. It views the splitting of the social security system as among the excesses of a form of Flemish nationalism that would result in Flanders withdrawing into its own ethnic shell and as a challenge to the very existence of federal Belgium. The French-speaking authorities' desire to preserve the federal nature of social security originates from a fear of the major impoverishment that complete decentralization of the system would cause in the French-speaking Community. Some economists predict that it would result in a 50 per cent rise in poverty in Wallonia (Delhausse and Perelman 1998).

The Flemish parliament's plan is regarded as opportunistic, because it does not contemplate the decentralization of sectors other than health care and family allowances, such as pensions, which could be detrimental to Flanders in the long term because of its ageing population. French-speaking authorities stress that most of the transfers carried out implicitly through the social security system are objectively justified and stem from the distinctive characteristics of the populations of federal entities.[10] The French-speaking authorities acknowledge the need to ensure that legislation is applied as uniformly as possible so as to avoid transfers governed by subjective choices, particularly in the health field; however, they point out that there are also subregional differences in health expenditure between the provinces and between urban and rural areas, so that the matter cannot be interpreted merely in terms of which federal entity people belong to.

Note that the decentralization of social security to communities as conceived by the Flemings would cause major organizational problems in the bilingual territory of the Brussels capital region, because it would force inhabitants to choose between the Flemish and French-speaking systems. This would inevitably rekindle the debate about the recognition of Flemish- and French-speaking subnationalities and could be perceived by some of the people concerned as a form of apartheid.

CONCLUSIONS

The year 1999 was particularly meaningful for Belgian federalism. In March 1999, the majority and the opposition of the Flemish parliament joined forces and voted almost unanimously in favour of five resolutions. These called for the continuation of state reform and entailed another total upheaval of the structure of the Belgian federation. These resolutions focused on the following issues:

- reorganization of federalism on a dual basis centring on Flemish- and French-speaking federated entities,
- special status for the Brussels capital region and the German-speaking Community,
- greater fiscal and financial autonomy for federated entities,
- partial decentralization of social security,
- further transfers of large-scale powers from the federal government to federal entities over a range of fields.

In response, all French-speaking parties formed a united front against what they regarded as steps along the road to confederalism. In this context, Dutch and French speakers could not agree on the adoption of a declaration by means of which the newly elected chambers of the federal parliament might have been able to proceed with constitutional reform, namely, a declaration containing the express condition that the reform would not relate to the institutional clauses of the constitution. This raised questions as to whether the representatives of the two main communities would still be able to reach sufficient agreement to form a federal government after the elections, giving rise to fears of a major political crisis that might threaten the survival of the federation.

The political landscape was reshaped by the parliamentary elections of June 1999, which were marked by the advance of the Greens and the subsequent party political negotiations. A coalition of the liberal right, the socialist left and the Greens swiftly reached agreement in July 1999 and the Christian centrist party, which had been in power for the preceding 40 years, was relegated to the opposition. The new political climate resulted in a truce between Dutch and French speakers supported by declarations of friendship between the new regional and community governments. The federal coalition agreement was based on the premise that everyone must be loyal to the federation, stating that improvements must be made to the structures of the Belgian Federal State so that tension between communities is eliminated once and for all and harmonious relationships are established between regions and communities. To realize this goal, the federal government set up an intergovernmental and interparliamentary conference for institutional renewal that consisted of representatives of the governments and parliaments of the federation, the regions and the communities and was presided over by two chairs, one for each language. A government agreement of 14 July 1999 described it as 'a place for calm analysis of the present operating machinery of the state, providing an opportunity to anticipate means by which these can be enhanced so as to improve the functioning of the federal institutions'.

The only aims of the conference that the government will admit to seem to stem from a concern with tinkering with existing institutions to improve their functioning rather than a desire to take constitutional reform any further. In reality, the institutional issue was delegated to a committee to ensure that it would not hamper the formation of a new federal government. The question of the need to refinance the French-speaking Community has, however, re-emerged as one of the main concerns of French-speaking politicians, prompting them to negotiate a new round of constitutional reform measures with the Flemings. This is what led to the amendment of the special law on the financing of communities and regions. On the one hand, this June 2001 agreement increases community funds and enables the French-speaking Community to preserve its education system. On the other hand, it meets the Flemish parliament's desire for more fiscal independence. This is an initial response, and the future will tell whether it is sufficiently balanced or is likely to undermine Belgium's economic union, bearing in mind that a key factor in the future of the federation will be whether the differences between the economic development of Flanders and Wallonia continue to increase or begin to diminish.

Whereas the laws passed in July 1993 during the fourth stage of constitutional reform pursued the explicit goal of creating a federal state structure, recent events appear to bear out the changing nature of Belgian federalism. We welcome the genuine and much-vaunted ability of Belgians to reach peaceful compromises calculated to appease conflicts between the various groups that make up this multi-ethnic state, whose institutional structures have been adapted to achieve this goal in a manner that may appear to be extremely complicated, but that reflects reality. This method is characteristic of the way in which Belgian federalism functions, enabling both Dutch and French speakers to find reasons for satisfaction in what they have negotiated and ensuring that neither side loses face. Nevertheless, issues arise in connection with the durability of this system. Indeed, when Belgium was a unitary state, the method used to settle disputes between communities in the 1960s and 1970s was such that spending in Flanders was automatically offset from public finance by equivalent spending in Wallonia and vice versa. In the new federal system, the method used to solve disputes between entities is based on the possibility of transferring federal government competencies to regions and communities and redistributing the fruits of economic growth between the different levels of power.

As successive reforms are introduced, the day may come when the federal government has given all that it can possibly give and will have no more money to redistribute. At this point, the problems of implementing a form of federalism that leans strongly towards dualism and in some respects resembles a confederate system could suddenly become painfully obvious.

The distribution of wealth among federated entities has clearly become the main focus of recent negotiations on state reform. The Flemings' claims in relation to the decentralization of health care insurance and family allowances seem to stem from a desire to redistribute powers between the federal authorities and communities in a supposedly more appropriate way rather than from a desire to end the financial transfers deriving from the social security system. However, the question of solidarity will arise when the powers are actually transferred, as will what should happen to financial flows between the different parts of the country in these sectors. The coalition agreement of July 1999 contained a sentence on this subject that was as fundamental as it was succinct. One of the tasks of the conference on institutional renewal was defined as 'proposing solutions to future major problems over functioning of the Federal State at all levels, taking the principle of interpersonal solidarity as a starting point'. This idea was echoed in the section of the text on social security: 'The government intends to modernise the social security system to meet new needs. It wishes to guarantee the necessary means with the sole aim of preserving a system of insurance and interpersonal solidarity.' This reassertion of the principle of interpersonal solidarity that underpins Belgium's current federal social security system was absolutely crucial. However, the calls for more autonomy expressed by the Flemish parliament in 1999, which will not have been satisfied by the political agreement of October 2000, are likely to re-emerge in future discussions between Dutch and French speakers.

Solidarity can, of course, be secured in various ways, and in Belgium the social security system seems to be a much more important means of redistributing wealth than the tax system. The Flemish parliament is not against preserving solidarity between federated entities, but would like it to be organized according to an objective, clear, transparent and reversible procedure. Any decrease in interpersonal solidarity could then be offset by an increase in solidarity between the entities. This prompts the question whether the explicit solidarity that the Flemish parliament wishes to establish between the federated entities would reach the same level as that which currently implicitly unites all inhabitants of Belgium. However, this raises philosophical and ethical considerations that are much more fundamental than the mere financial question. Bearing in mind that Flemish political leaders are not unanimous on this point, the real question is whether Flanders distinguishes between solidarity among a single people (in this case the Flemings) and solidarity between different people (Dutch and French speakers). In the future, this question is likely to divide the two main linguistic communities. The debate to which it might give rise is liable to be fiercer than the current one about fiscal autonomy. Indeed, it will pose a direct threat to solidarity among Belgians. Moreover, it is related to Belgium's economic union, because the calculation of labour costs includes both tax payments and social security contributions. French speakers view social security as the cement that holds the federal state together. This means that the success of attempts to reconcile greater decentralization in favour of the federal entities with the preservation of genuine solidarity among the inhabitants of the federation will be as crucial to the future of federal Belgium as restoring economic balance between Flanders and Wallonia.

NOTES

1. Authors' translation.
2. In 1815, following Napoleon's defeat at Waterloo, Austria, England, Prussia and Russia decided at the Congress of Vienna that a greater united Netherlands should be created as a buffer state between France and northwestern Europe, and Belgium was annexed by the Netherlands.
3. Note that in Belgium, Dutch speakers and Flemish speakers are the same group. The official language is Dutch, of which Flemish is a dialect, but most Dutch speakers use Flemish in their day-to-day lives.
4. Constitutional reforms is a term routinely used in Belgium to describe the institutional process leading to federalism through greater autonomy for regions and communities.
5. Note that the senator of the German community does not belong to the Flemish-speaking group or the French-speaking group of the Senate, so we estimate the percentage based on a total of 70 senators (without the senator of the German Community). The result corresponds to the distribution of the population.
6. Before the institutional reform of July 2001, the number of deputies in the Brussels' region was 75 and the new legislation will be in effect for the June 2004 elections. For a specific analysis, see Bayenet and others (2001, 2002).
7. All 118 deputies are directly elected by people living in the Flemish region and 6 are directly elected by Flemings living in the Brussels capital region. The direct election of Flemish deputies from the Brussels capital region was introduced by the July 2001 institutional reform and was in effect for the June 2004 elections.
8. The German-speaking people represent a mere 0.7 per cent of the population, making this linguistic minority one of the world's best protected.
9. Unlike the German speakers, who enjoy autonomy through their community, but fall under the Walloon region with respect to regional powers.
10. The controversy caused by the Flemish plan for partial decentralization of the social security system pertains to the broader issue of financial transfers between federal entities. Since the end of the 1980s, the transfer issue has been the focus of a highly emotionally charged political and media debate, with contrasting images of a Wallonia subsidized by Flanders and a nationalist Flanders increasingly less inclined to show solidarity. Both sides carried out many analyses of the problem (for a survey, see Bayenet and others 2000). A review of these analyses shows that except for Van Rompuy and Bilsen (1993), most of them consider only social security expenditures and not receipts. Van Rompuy and Bilsen (1993) conclude that there were social security transfers from the north to the south of Belgium, but that these came essentially from social security receipts and not from expenditures. Studies have also shown that most social security-related transfers are based on objective criteria. For Wallonia to benefit more from social security expenditures despite contributing less than Flanders arises naturally because of the demographic and economic differences between the two regions.

REFERENCES

Bayenet, B. (2003a), 'Impacts des derniers accords institutionnels de 2001 sur les finances des entités fédérées', in *Année sociale*, Brussels: Free University of Brussels, Institute of Sociology, pp. 25–43.

——— (2003b), 'Les conséquences des accords institutionnels 2001 sur les finances du pouvoir fédéral', *Administration publique*, T 2-3-4/2002, 254–61.

Bayenet, B., V. Gilbert and F. Thys-Clément (1999), 'Analyse économique du fédéralisme belge', *Revue de droit de l'ULB*, 19 (1), 9–52.

Bayenet, B., M. Feron, V. Gilbert and F. Thys-Clément (2000), *Fédéralisme budgétaire: mode d'emploi*, Brussels: University of Brussels Press.

Bayenet, B., E. Gassner, E. Lentzen and F. Thys-Clément (2001), 'Les accords du Lombard', in *Année sociale*, Brussels: Free University of Brussels, Institue of Sociology, pp. 25–43.

——— (2002), 'Les conséquences électorales de l'accord du Lombard sur les institutions communautaires et régionales belges', Cahiers du Cevipol, Free University of Brussels, Brussels.

Capron, H. (2001), 'L'économie wallonne: du déclin au redéploiement économique', in M. Germain (ed.), *La Wallonie à l'aube du XXIe siècle*, Charleroi, Belgium: Jules Destrée Institute.

Cattoir, P. and M. Verdonck (1999), 'La péréquation financière. Analyse de quatre pays', in F. Docquier (ed.), *La solidarité entre les Régions*, Brussels: DeBoeck University, pp. 51–97

Chamber of Deputies (2002), *Budget des Voies et Moyens de l'Etat fédéral 2002*, Ordinary session 2002–03, document 50-1447/001, Brussels.

de Callatay, E. and R. Savage (1998), 'Fédéralisme et choix budgétaires', *Reflets et perspectives*, XXXVII (2), 101–122.

Delhausse, B. and S. Perelman (1998), 'Inégalités et pauvreté: Mesures et déterminants', *Wallonie et Bruxelles: Evolutions et perspectives*, paper presented at the Congress of French Language Economists, Centre interuniversitaire de formation permanente, Charleroi, Belgium, 26–27 November.

Eurostat (2003), 'Les taux de chômage régionaux varient entre 2.0% et 29.3% dans l'UE en 2002', European Communities press release number 131/2003, 17 November.

Fitzmaurice, J. (1983), *The Politics of Belgium: Crisis and Compromise in a Plural Society*, London: C. Hurst.

——— (1996), *The Politics of Belgium: A Unique Federalism*, London: C. Hurst.

Lijphart, A. (1981), *Conflict and Coexistence in Belgium*, Berkeley, CA: University of California.

Lipszyc, B. and P. Pestieau (1998), 'Pauvreté et exclusion et politiques sociales', paper presented at the Congress of French Language Economists, Centre interuniversitaire de formation permanente Charleroi, Belgium, 26–27 November.

McRae, K. D. (1986), *Conflict and Compromise in Multilingual Societies: Belgium*, Ontario: Wilfrid Laurier University Press.

Ministry of Finance (2001), *Bulletin de documentation*, Brussels.

——— (2003), *Bulletin de documentation*, Brussels.

National Bank of Belgium (2004a), *Indicateurs clés pour la Belgique*, Brussels.

——— (2004b), *Regional Accounts*, Brussels.

National Institute of Statistics (2004a), *Niveau de vie*, Brussels.

——— (2004b), *Structure de la population*, Brussels.

Roland G., T. Vandeveld and P. Van Parijs (1999), 'Repenser (radicalement?) la solidarité entre les Régions', in F. Docquier (ed.), *La solidarité entre les Régions, Bilan et perspectives,* Brussels: De Boeck University, pp. 99–112.

Senelle, R. (1989), 'Constitutional reform in Belgium: from Unitarism Towards Federalism', in M. Forsyth (ed.), *Federalism and Nationalism*, Leicester: Leicester University Press.

Supreme Financial Council (2003), *Rapport annuel 2003 sur les Besoins de financement des pouvoirs publics*, Brussels.

Van Rompuy, P. and V. Bilsen (1993), 'Regionalisering van de sociale zekerheid', Leuvense Economische Standpunten no. 68, Leuven, Belgium.

Witte, E., J. Craeybeckx and A. Meynen (2000), *Political History of Belgium*, Brussels: University Press.

7. Fiscal Decentralization in Spain: An Asymmetric Transition to Democracy

Teresa Garcia-Milà and Therese J. McGuire

Asymmetric fiscal decentralization, that is, different fiscal arrangements between the central government and different groups of or individual lower-level governments, may be justified from an economic efficiency perspective. As Oates (1972), Tiebout (1956), and others argue, a decentralized system of regional and local governments is better able to accommodate differences in tastes for public goods and services. This efficiency argument calls for decentralization of fiscal authority to regional and local governments, but not necessarily asymmetric decentralization. However, when the differences in tastes for public goods and services arise out of differences in history, culture and language across regions of a country, asymmetric treatment may be justified. History, culture and language may influence how a group of people (a region) views autonomy, independence and fiscal authority. Some regions may have had experience with autonomous government in the past. They may have a culture that is strongly reliant upon or wary of the central government or they may be fearful of losing their separate languages if they do not have special arrangements. To accommodate differences in taste for independence, autonomy and fiscal authority, having different fiscal arrangements between the central government and the different regions comprising the country may be necessary (see Petchey, Shapiro and Walsh 1997 for a discussion of differences across subnational governments in values and in preferences for political structures).

Another efficiency argument for asymmetric decentralization centres on differences among regions in their capacities for public administration. Efficient provision of public goods and services and efficient decisionmaking rely on a well-functioning bureaucracy and supportive political institutions. If some regions have greater capacities for running governments and public agencies than other regions, perhaps because these regions have historical experience with autonomy, devolving fiscal authority to these regions alone, or at least more quickly to these regions than to regions without sufficient administrative capability, may be more efficient.

Neither of these efficiency arguments for asymmetric devolution may hold in perpetuity. If fiscal authority is devolved in stages more or less quickly to different regions because of their different capacities, even the regions with less authority will, over time, develop administrative capabilities. In the limit, administrative know-how should be similar across the regions and an asymmetric system may not be needed to achieve efficiency. Similarly, as regional governments gain experience and as mutual trust between the central government and its regions develops, in other words, as a formerly centralized system matures into a decentralized one, differences in taste for independence and fiscal authority may dissipate, and the rationale for asymmetric treatment, embedded in historical and cultural differences, may become less compelling.

This chapter explores the implications of these theoretical arguments for the case of Spain. It begins by arguing the relevance of these theories in relation to Spain. The next section presents information about Spain's economic, historical and cultural diversity. The following two sections are devoted to a description and evaluation of Spain's system of fiscal decentralization before the chapter concludes with a discussion of the relevance of Spain's experience for emerging democracies.

THE RELEVANCE OF THEORY TO THE SPANISH CASE

In many respects, the two economic efficiency reasons for asymmetric decentralization were present in Spain at the time the decentralization process began in the late 1970s. Spain had, and continues to have, regions with a strong sense of nationality, that is, of identity differences in terms of language, culture, laws and even economic relationships. Most individuals in these regions have clear preferences for deciding and administering many aspects of public intervention without having to follow centrally decided policies. The Basque Country, Galicia and Catalonia, the so-called historic nationalities in Spain, are clearly identified in this group.

Differences in public administration know-how were also present in Spain at the time the current decentralized system was discussed and established. For centuries, Navarra and the Basque Country had a particular political and fiscal arrangement (*fueros*) that survived centralizing attempts by different kingdoms. Indeed, Navarra and álava, one of the Basque Country provinces, kept part of this special arrangement even during Francisco Franco's dictatorship, while Vizcaya and Guipuzcoa, the other two Basque provinces, which had not supported Franco's movement, had their special regime abolished during that period. Catalonia established an autonomous regional government in 1932 that endured through the short-lived Second Republic and the three-year civil war that started in 1936. Galicia adopted an autonomous system in 1936 that was never implemented because of the eruption of the civil war.

These three regions, the Basque Country, Galicia and Catalonia, with different degrees of intensity, have both preferences and experience favouring decentralization from an economic efficiency perspective. Navarra also has relevant experience related to a long history of self-government, the existence of specific laws developed locally and a preference for autonomy, although possibly to a lesser extent given its lack of a strong national identity.

Thus at first glance, designing a decentralization process that would be asymmetric for different regions, taking into account their preferences and their experience, would seem to have been appropriate. We analyse whether the design and degree of asymmetry were indeed appropriate and the extent to which asymmetry eased or fuelled the tensions that were present when Spain was designing not only a decentralized system, but also a democratic system that would enable the country to move away from a dictatorship that had endured for almost 40 years. When analysing these issues we cannot forget that in addition to the cultural and historical differences across regions, there were, and still are, economic differences. Because of these differences, some regions were concerned about what fiscal decentralization would imply for the regional solidarity that is built into the centralized system.

REGIONAL DIVERSITY

Spain is divided into 17 regions known as autonomous communities (Figure 7.1), with regional governments that were created following guidelines established in the democratic constitution ratified in 1978 (the fiscal decentralization model—the different regimes referred to in the figure—is explained later). These regions are diverse from many perspectives, including history, culture, language and economic conditions. An understanding of these differences may help explain the asymmetric fiscal decentralization model that was established in the late 1970s.

The existence of Spain as a country dates back several centuries and is the result of a long process that combined several kingdoms and other forms of political organization. One important step towards the creation of Spain was the unification by marriage of the Kingdom of Castilia with the Kingdom of Aragon (which includes Aragon, Catalonia, the Balearic Islands and Valencia) in the late 15th century. The Spanish kingdom expanded and grew strong in Europe and America, though many local laws and autonomous forms of government prevailed for at least two centuries. In the early 1700s, Felipe V established a new

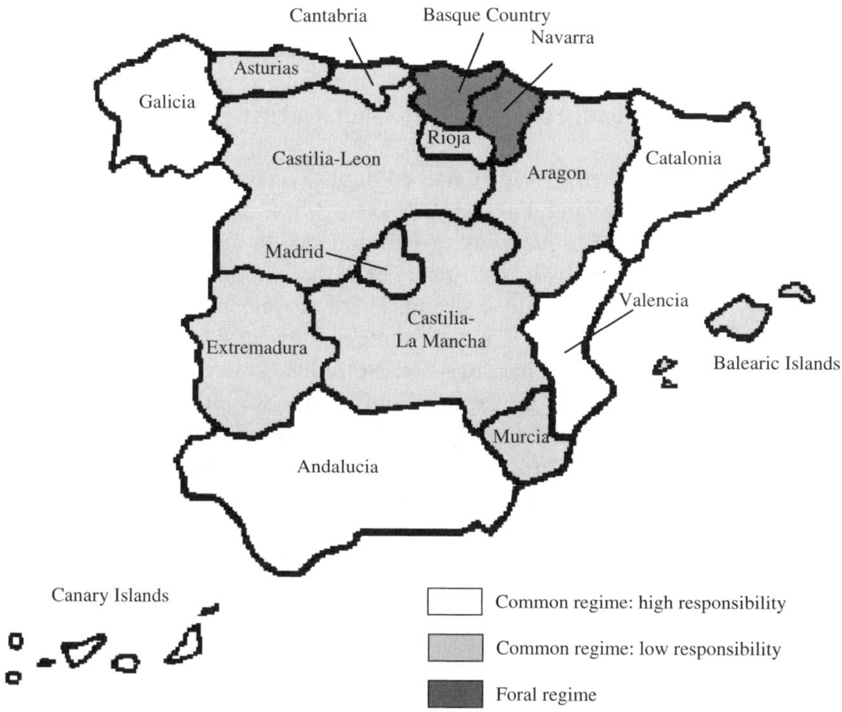

Source: Author.

Figure 7.1 Asymmetric fiscal decentralization

regime (Nueva Planta) that abolished the political and administrative autonomy of Aragon, Catalonia, the Balearic Islands and Valencia with the purpose of centralizing and unifying political power. This was especially painful for Catalonia, which had a long history of community and self-government, had been an important political and economic power in the Mediterranean and had conquered the Balearic Islands and Valencia in the early 1200s. Even though Catalonia unified with the Kingdom of Aragon by marriage in the early 1100s, the organization was a confederation rather than a centralized kingdom, and therefore Catalonia had retained its autonomy and identity.

The special political and economic organization, the *fueros*, of the three provinces of the Basque Country and of Navarra survived this centralizing attempt by the Spanish kingdom. The reasons seem quite clear and are linked to the support that these provinces provided to the king in his political conflicts. The special arrangement for these provinces allowed them to remain autonomous in many respects, with an independent fiscal authority, and even a free trade area that prevailed until the mid-1800s. While they lost some of their political autonomy in the late 1800s, they kept a special fiscal arrangement that prevailed until Franco's dictatorship, and even beyond for Navarra and álava.

In some regions, their historical and cultural diversity is enhanced by their own languages. Four languages are spoken in Spain: Castilian (Spanish), Catalan, Galician and Basque, plus several dialects. In the late 19th and early 20th century, the nationalistic sentiments of Galicia, the Basque Country and especially Catalonia became quite strong. These movements cannot be considered in isolation from the fact that these three regions each have their own language, a major identifying characteristic. Note that these three regions either established an autonomous government during the Second Republic or their autonomous status had been approved and they were in the process of establishing an autonomous government when the civil war broke out in 1936. (For a comprehensive historical analysis of Spain and its regions, see Fusi 1989; for a map of Spain indicating political jurisdictions, see Figure 7.2. Please note that Figure 7.2 does not show the Canary Islands, which are in the Atlantic, southwest of the Spanish mainland.)

Spain is also a diverse country economically. Per capita gross domestic product (GDP) differs across regions, although the differences are not as large as in other European countries, such as France, Germany or Italy (Esteban 1999; Hall 1999). As Table 7.1 shows, the richest region, Madrid, has a GDP per capita about twice that of the poorest region, Extremadura. Differences were even larger in the 1950s, with the richest regions having a GDP per capita three times that of the poorest, but the differences had fallen to a factor of a little over two by the mid-1970s and have remained essentially unchanged ever since.

In the 1970s, Spain's industrial mix was quite diverse, with the north, mainly the Basque Country, and northeast having most of the manufacturing, while the centre (with the exception of Madrid), the south and the northwest relied primarily on agriculture. As in most industrial countries, the manufacturing and agriculture sectors have decreased in favour of the services sector, but the strength of the regional economies is, in most cases, still related to the initial industrial mix. Some regions, like the Balearic Islands, have benefited strongly from the tourism boom that Spain experienced in the last third of the 20th century. Madrid has taken advantage of being the political capital, building a strong economy and becoming the main financial centre, the centre for telecommunications and the Spanish headquarters for many large international firms.

Through public investment, and in some cases detailed development plans, the central government has attempted to help poor regions grow faster and approach the rich regions in terms of GDP per capita. The effectiveness of these public actions for long-run growth has not been demonstrated, although

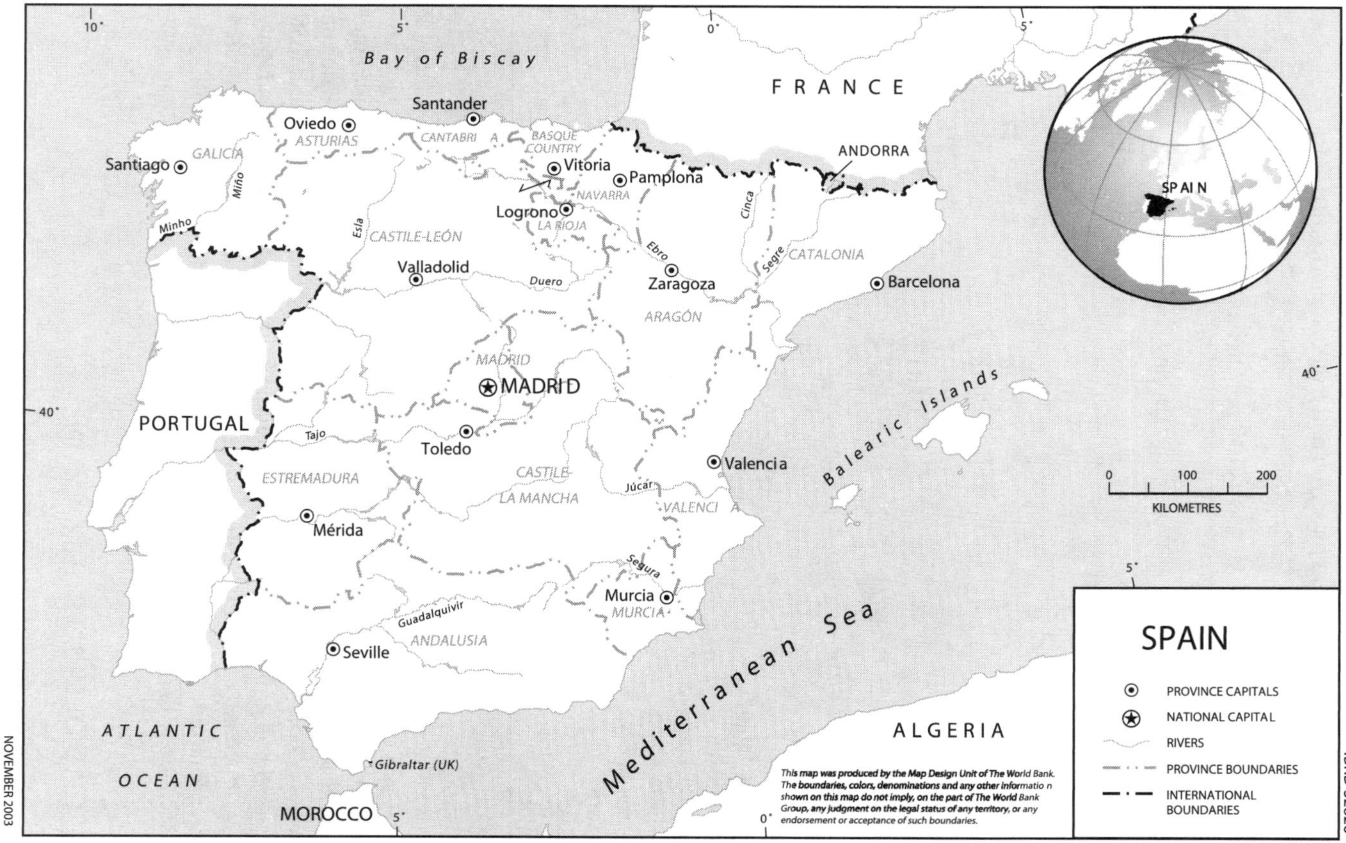

Figure 7.2 *Spain*

Table 7.1 GDP per capita by region and fiscal responsibility, 2001

Regime and region	GDP per capita (€)	Relative to Spain (Spain = 100)
Foral regime		
Basque Country	16 692	126
Navarra	16 881	127
Common regime		
High responsibility		
Andalucia	10 165	77
Canary Islands	12 442	94
Catalonia	15 687	118
Galicia	10 812	81
Valencia	12 752	96
Low responsibility		
Aragon	14 204	107
Asturias	11 451	86
Balearic Islands	14 924	112
Cantabria	12 948	97
Castilia-La Mancha	10 584	80
Castilia-Leon	12 609	95
Extremadura	8987	68
Madrid	17 302	130
Murcia	10 789	81
Rioja	14 766	111

Source: National Statistics Institute (Spain) data.

short-run effects were noticeable (Garcia-Milà and Marimon 1999; Garcia-Milà and McGuire 2001). Some regional solidarity was likely built into the central government's public investment policy before the decentralization process took place, which could explain why some regions feared that regional redistribution might vanish with the advent of decentralization. However, once the decentralization process began, fears based on opposite grounds arose, because regions did not want to miss out on any advantages associated with the decentralized system.

FISCAL DECENTRALIZATION

Economic, cultural and historical diversity influences and constrains the form of the decentralization system. This section analyses how the diversity of the

Spanish regions influenced the decentralization system adopted in the late 1970s. Democratization and decentralization processes cannot be separated in Spain. The basic structure of the autonomous communities is contained in the constitution, which was ratified by referendum in December 1978 and defines the start of democracy in Spain. While the concept of asymmetry is established in the constitution, its details are developed in the Fundamental Law on the Financing of the Autonomous Communities. The third set of legal arrangements is the Statutes of Autonomy, developed and approved by each region in accordance with the general principles of the constitution.

The constitution establishes two possible layers of asymmetry. The first and most important enacts two completely different systems of decentralization, the foral and the common regimes. The foral regime is in place only for the Basque Country and Navarra, while the common regime applies to the other 15 regions (Table 7.1). The primary difference between the two is that regions in the foral regime have the authority to raise taxes locally, whereas regions in the common regime have limited local taxing authority.[1] In terms of spending responsibilities, the regions of the foral regime have similar responsibilities to five regions under the common regime, that is, those within the common regime with high responsibility.

Under the foral regime, most taxes, including income, corporate, wealth, inheritance and wealth transfer taxes, are ceded, giving the regions the responsibility for tax administration and, subject to certain constraints, the autonomy to set rates and tax bases. Some of these constraints were eased in the 1997 reform. The regional governments collect the value added tax, but without any authority to set rates or define the base. Thus in the foral regime, residents do not pay any part of these taxes to the central government.

To compensate for the services that the central government provides to the regions, the regional government pays a certain amount to the central government (*cupo* for the Basque Country and *aportación* for Navarra). The cupo and aportación are essentially grants or transfers from the regional government to the central government. The central government directly raises some minor taxes in the two regions, and these revenues are taken into account when the cupo and aportación are calculated.

In contrast to a cost-accounting basis, the cupo and aportación have not been calculated according to the effective cost of the services that the central government provides to, and the effective revenue that the central government raises in, the two regions under the foral regime. Instead they have been calculated as a percentage of the difference between the national cost of those services not devolved and the national revenue of the taxes not devolved (and the national deficit imputable to expenditures in the Basque Country is also subtracted). In effect, this formula allocates some percentage of an artificially and narrowly defined national deficit to the regions in the foral regime. The percentage is a function of the region's income share. Even though the percentage was to have been updated as those shares changed over time, it has not been changed since it was first established in 1981.

The foral regime regions also contribute to the central government's solidarity fund. The Interterritorial Compensation Fund, a conditional grant that supports investment spending and is designed to help poor regions grow, is considered a national service, and therefore the foral regime regions contribute to the solidarity fund through the cupo or aportación.

Agreed upon in July 2001 and effective as of January 2002, the common regime underwent a substantial change that ceded substantial taxing authority to the regional governments. However, understanding the initial arrangement is important, as it was the basis of the system for more than 20 years and conditioned the reforms undertaken. Initially the common regime was characterized by having a fair amount of expenditure responsibility, but little revenue autonomy. The regions in this regime were mainly financed by central government transfers, which accounted for more than 75 per cent of the revenues of these regions. The regions of the common regime also had ceded taxes, although this was largely an administrative role because, unlike the foral regime regions, they had no authority to set tax rates and bases for these taxes.[2] In addition, revenues raised under ceded taxes resulted in nearly equal reductions in central government grants, and thus for regions to affect a change in revenues through a change in ceded taxes was practically impossible. The ceded taxes included the wealth tax, the inheritance tax, a tax on wealth transfers and taxes on gambling, and accounted for approximately 10 per cent of the revenues of the regions. Finally, regions in the common regime could initially, and still can, impose some taxes and fees for which they have complete authority to set rates and bases, although these revenue sources represent only some 4 per cent of regional revenues.

The second layer of asymmetry established by the constitution concerns only the 15 regions of the common regime. The constitution defines two alternative paths for devolution of spending responsibilities, one slow and one fast. This is set out in articles 143 and 151, which is how the two sets of regions are sometimes referred to. In effect, the two groups were given different amounts of spending responsibility. The high responsibility regions make spending decisions about health and education in addition to all of the spending areas held by the ten low responsibility regions.[3] The constitution specifies that eventually the two paths will meet, whereupon all the regions in the common regime would have identical spending responsibilities. That eventuality occurred in January 2002, when the final transfer of health responsibilities was agreed upon. Health and education account for the largest part of the budget, representing more than 80 per cent of the total spent by the high responsibility regions (for more details, see Monasterio and Suarez 1998).

As already mentioned, the largest revenue source for regions in the common regime has been transfers from the central government. The unconditional grant was distributed according to formulas that differed for the high and low responsibility regions, but the most important factor for both was population. Those regions responsible for health expenditures received a separate conditional health grant as well.[4] The regions with lower per capita income also receive a solidarity grant (Interterritorial Compensation Fund) and funds, mainly development funds under the European Regional Development Fund, from the European Union.

The way the transfers are determined has changed over time. The initial method was based on cost, that is, the central government would transfer an amount equal to the historical cost (before decentralization) of the services that were devolved to each region. This method assumed that the regional allocation of spending made by the central government before the decentralization process had started was adequate. This criterion was meant to be temporary, covering only the transition period, and in 1986 was changed to a distribution formula. The idea was to have an allocation mechanism that would be a function of some indicators of need. A weighted formula based on several variables was adopted: population, insularity or not, area, separate provincial governments or not, relative wealth and fiscal effort (calculated as the gap between the region's share of revenues from personal income tax and the region's share of GDP). The weights were set not according to general economic principles, but rather to reproduce as closely as possible the distribution that had existed previously under the effective cost allocation, ensuring that all regions received at least as much as under the previous allocation.

Starting in 1986, financing agreements lasting for five-year periods were established. Every five years a revision would take place and a new agreement would be established for the following period. Few changes were introduced at the end of the first period (1987–91), with only a small revision of the weights in the distribution formula incorporated into the agreement for the second period (1992–96). The negotiations in 1996 for the 1997–2001 period agreement led to fairly significant changes with respect to local revenue raising authority. Regions were granted some authority over rates for all previously ceded taxes as well as an additionally ceded 15 per cent of the income tax. Out of fear that the new changes would diminish the total funds available, Andalucia, Castilla-La Mancha and Extremadura opted out of this reform, introducing additional complexity to an already cumbersome setup. The latest reform, effective January 2002, established a financing system applicable to all 15 regions under the common regime. As the differences between high and low responsibility regions have vanished, and as health is no longer financed by a specific grant, the financing system has become more uniform and transparent.

In 1993, two years into the second five-year period, a substantial revision of the system, at least in spirit, was implemented. The revision established a new approach that would be continued with the changes introduced in 1997 and in 2002. The reform of 1993 ceded to the autonomous communities an initial 15 per cent of the income tax, but with no authority to set tax rates. The idea behind the reform was to involve the regional governments more deeply in the revenue process. It gave them an incentive to be more efficient in the collection of the tax, as the region would keep 15 per cent of the fiscal effort above a reference value. After negotiations, final changes were introduced that limited possible gains and provided guarantees for minimum revenues.

The reform of January 2002 was not restricted to a five-year period like the previous reforms were. This reform unified the financing scheme for all 15 regions in the common regime, a task that was eased by the convergence of responsibilities for the high and low responsibility regions. It further simplified and clarified the model by eliminating the conditional grant for health, which is now financed within the general system. Finally, it significantly increased the revenue authority of the regions. The central government has ceded approximately one-third of both the personal income tax and the value added tax, as well as special taxes on gas, alcohol and tobacco. It has also eased many of the restrictions on establishing rates and exemptions for the ceded taxes (except for the value added tax and the special taxes that are regulated by the European Union).

These changes in the system tried to accommodate criticisms about the lack of autonomy in revenue within the common regime. The term used in Spain has been co-responsibility, meaning a sharing of responsibility for revenues between the central and regional governments. As we have seen, the process towards higher regional responsibility in revenues has been slow, limited and extremely complicated, as not all the regions initially participated. It is possible that the latest reform will lead to gains in efficiency, because it resulted in regions gaining revenue raising authority.[5] However, as an important motivation behind the changes was to try to keep more tax revenues in the regions where the taxes were generated, it is too soon to tell whether the reform will succeed. A tension remains as rich regions aim to redefine the system in a way that reduces their contributions to solidarity, while poor regions try to avoid losing funds.

EVALUATION OF THE DECENTRALIZATION PROCESS

While the two groups of regions under the common regime—the high and low responsibility regions—started quite far apart, but eventually converged to identical circumstances, the foral and common regimes are intended to remain under different financial arrangements with the central government. This section explores the basis for such differential treatment.

Given the revealed differences in preferences and in administrative know-how, asymmetric decentralization was probably a good economic decision for Spain in the late 1970s to early 1980s. It probably also helped to ease some of the political tensions expressed by nationalists, mainly of the Basque Country, Catalonia and to a lesser extent Galicia. Establishing a flexible system that could be revised was also important given the lack of experience in these matters on the part of many regions and of the country as a whole.

After 20 years, regions have caught up in knowledge, and perhaps also in preferences for autonomy, although the latter is more questionable.[6] Under the new circumstances whereby regional governments have matured and citizens have gained experience with decentralized government, moving towards a system that gives up asymmetry for gains in simplicity, clarity, revenue autonomy, certainty and transparency in solidarity may be more efficient.

Spain has partly moved in this direction. Within the common regime, convergence in spending responsibility has occurred: responsibilities in education were devolved to all regions in 2000 and devolution of responsibility for health was agreed upon in January 2002.[7] Spain has also introduced some changes to the financing scheme, slowly moving towards a per capita distribution of grants and greater revenue authority for the regions. The recent changes towards higher revenue autonomy have been applied to all 15 autonomous communities under the common regime, a step in the direction of simplicity and clarity.

In one respect, the system's complexity and transparency have not improved much. Little has been done to discuss openly the degree of solidarity that regions can agree upon or to establish clear and transparent equity criteria. The need for an open discussion about solidarity is revealed by the fact that rich regions sense they are contributing too much, while poor regions believe they receive too little. Not surprisingly perhaps, given the lack of open discussion concerning solidarity, regions have tried to push each new revision of the system in favourable directions.

The most important asymmetry built into the system—the large difference between the foral and the common regimes—has remained unchanged, and appears not to be subject to change for the foreseeable future.

As several authors have pointed out, generalizing the foral regime to other regions would not be sustainable. If all the regions were under the foral regime and payments to the central government (cupo or aportación) were similar to the ones set for Navarra and the Basque Country, all regions except Extremadura and Andalucia would retain more money than they receive under the present system (Zubiri 2000; Zubiri and Vallejo 1995). Castells (2000) estimates that the ratio of per capita funds for the regions under the foral regime was 1.8 times that of the five regions in the common regime with high spending responsibilities, these being the regions with expenditure responsibilities comparable to those of the foral regions.

The asymmetry is not only in terms of the degree of revenue autonomy, but also in the regions' contributions to centrally provided goods and services and to redistribution. While one can argue that the foral regime had strong historical, political and cultural reasons to prevail in the past, from an economic efficiency perspective, arguing that such disparate treatment is justified in the future or, indeed, in the present, is difficult.

If asymmetric treatment is no longer justified, how should Spain move towards a more symmetric system? The most crucial asymmetry in the system—the different systems applied to the Basque Country and Navarra on the one hand and to the other 15 regions on the other—will be difficult to remove. Applying a reformed common regime to the two regions of the foral regime would likely improve efficiency and transparency, and possibly political acceptability, at least among the 15 regions of the common regime. As this change may be difficult to implement for historical reasons, if the foral regime prevails, the revenue advantages given to this group should be re-evaluated.

Within the common regime, the 15 regions should be given greater revenue raising authority, especially for revenues at the margin. Any justification for current restrictions on regional taxing authority, such as lack of administrative know-how at the regional level or lack of trust by the central government, is no longer relevant given 20 years of experience with a decentralized system (see Garcia-Milà and McGuire 2004 for another argument for restricting regional taxing authority based on solidarity).

While the Spanish system of decentralization needs flexibility and the possibility of revision, as do all political systems, it also would benefit from a more solid foundation grounded in basic principles so that there is less uncertainty about the future. When regions are uncertain about the amount and source of funds and about the future rules of the game, they may engage in strategic behaviour, face perverse incentives and make inefficient decisions. Certainty, but not lack of flexibility, is needed to achieve efficiency.

A move towards symmetry does not necessarily mean that all regions end up with identical revenue and expenditure responsibilities. Because of historical, cultural and language differences, some regions may choose to go further down the path of autonomous government than others. If the choice of degree of autonomy is available to all, and if greater expenditure responsibilities are linked to greater revenue raising authority, then different choices about the degree of autonomy should not lead to economic inefficiencies.

RELEVANCE FOR EMERGING DEMOCRACIES

The Spanish decentralization system is often presented as an example for emerging democracies to follow, probably because in Spain, the democratization and decentralization processes were tightly linked. There is no question that Spain's peaceful and rapid transition from a dictatorship to a democracy is a model for emerging democracies to follow. Few other examples of comparably calm and successful transitions exist. It is also true that the establishment of a decentralized state by the constitution eased some nationalistic tensions and helped to accomplish the transition to a democratic system. Thus while Spain is clearly a model to follow in a broad sense, not all details of the decentralization process and system are worthy of imitation.

Initial asymmetry may be justified if the emerging democracy has regions with cultural, ethnic or historical differences that are related to differences in taste for autonomy, or if some regions have some experience of decentralization while others do not. Under such circumstances, starting with asymmetric decentralization may be economically efficient. However, asymmetry builds in complexity, is sometimes linked to a lack of transparency and may hide perverse economic incentives, resulting in inefficient regional decisionmaking. Asymmetry may also build up regional tensions over time as regions become more alike in their preferences for autonomy and in their knowledge of autonomous administration, thereby weakening the rationale for an asymmetric system. What may be appropriate in the beginning may not be desirable in the long run, but once asymmetry has been established, moving to a more symmetric system may be difficult.

Spain significantly reformed its fiscal system in 2002. Under the new system, regions were given significant taxing authority, and all regions under the common regime were given essentially the same level of spending responsibility. It is too soon to assess whether this latest reform will live up to its promises. We close with a summary of problems that characterize the system that prevailed for the two decades leading up to the recent reform.

- Persistent asymmetric treatment over time, both in the financing regime and in the details of implementation, with differences in revenues per capita that were not justified by economic or solidarity arguments. These differences in treatment need to vanish over time so that the regions come to trust the system and do not engage in perverse behaviour to obtain more from the central government. Attempts to negotiate better deals with the central government arise not only because the regions perceive a need for more funds, but also from a desire to be treated fairly.

- Limited taxing authority of the 15 regions in the common regime. Such an arrangement breaks the link between the costs and the benefits of a public decision and likely induces inefficient local public spending and excessive borrowing. It also limits the regions' choices and creates unsatisfied needs that could be avoided if the regions' residents are willing to finance local spending with regional taxes.
- Continuous evolution of the system without clear rules. Constant renegotiation of the system adds complexity and introduces uncertainty about the future. It may trigger perverse strategic behaviour on the part of the regions and result in political dissatisfaction.
- Absence of an explicit discussion about regional solidarity. Lack of agreement among regions on the proper level or range of redistribution creates numerous problems, adds instability and a lack of transparency and creates incentives for inefficient economic behaviour.

Asymmetric fiscal decentralization has satisfied some nationalistic claims, eased tensions among the regions and provided an important foundation for a stable transition to democracy. However, if certain aspects of the system had been designed differently, the economic outcome would have been more efficient and Spain would have a system that the regions would find more satisfactory. Perhaps emerging democracies can learn from the Spanish experience and design decentralized systems that achieve autonomy and solidarity at a lower cost.

NOTES

1. Taxes have been partially ceded over the years as explained later. During the first several years, however, regions in the common regime had virtually no autonomous taxing authority.
2. In the 1997 reform, some limited authority to set parameters of the ceded taxes was devolved.
3. Common responsibilities are forestry, agriculture, livestock and fisheries in internal waters; urbanism and housing; roads; ports and airports without commercial activity; hydraulic exploitation, channels and irrigation; environmental protection; historical preservation, cultural promotion of the regional languages, libraries, museums and conservatories; self-government institutions; internal commercial fairs, sports promotion and tourism.
4. In 2002, health financing was integrated into the general financing scheme and the conditional grant was abolished.
5. The lack of local revenue authority together with the continuous renegotiation of the system over the past 20 years created a situation whereby regions may have had incentives to borrow in excess, because they did not bear all the costs of such decisions (see Garcia-Milà, Goodspeed and McGuire 2002 for an elaboration of this argument).
6. A sense of regional identity has developed in many autonomous communities. This sense of identity is linked to the existence of and experience with autonomous government rather than strong cultural or language differences.
7. The 2002 reform responded to some of the demands of health economics experts (López Casasnovas 1999) that had been calling for incorporating the health transfer into the general system and including additional parameters besides population to take into account characteristics of the population and the services provided.

REFERENCES

Castells, A. (2000), 'Autonomía y solidaridad en el sistema de financiación autonómica', *Papeles de Economía,* (83), 37–59.

Esteban, J. M. (1999), 'Un análisis de las desigualdades interregionales en Europa: la década de los ochenta', in Antoni Castells and Nuria Bosch (eds), *Desequilibrios territoriales en España y Europa*, Barcelona: Ariel, pp. 58–93.

Fusi, Juan Pablo (ed.) (1989), *España Autonomías*, Madrid: Espasa-Calpe.

Garcia-Milà, T. and R. Marimon (1999), 'Regional Integration and Public Investment in Spain', in John Adams and Francesco Pigliaru (eds), *Economic Growth and Change*, Cheltenham, UK and Lyme, USA: Edward Elgar, pp. 349–416.

Garcia-Milà, T. and T. J. McGuire (2001), 'Do Interregional Transfers Improve the Economic Performance of Poor Regions? The Case of Spain', *International Tax and Public Finance,* 8 (3), 281–95.

——— (2004), 'Solidarity and Fiscal Decentralization', in *Proceedings of the 96th Annual Conference of the National Tax Association,* Washington, DC: National Tax Association, pp. 152–56.

Garcia-Milà, T., T. Goodspeed and T. J. McGuire (2002), 'Fiscal Decentralization Policies and Subnational Government Debt in Evolving Federations', unpublished manuscript.

Hall, R. (1999), 'Disparidades regionales en Europa durante los años noventa. Una referencia a España y sus regiones', in Antoni Castells and Nuria Bosch (eds), *Desequilibrios territoriales en España y Europa*, Barcelona: Ariel, pp. 21–57.

López Casasnovas, G. (1999), 'Los problemas de la financiación sanitaria en España. Especial referencia a su descentralización autonómica', in *Financiación Autonómica. Aspectos Económicos y Debate Político*, Madrid: Foundation for Applied Economic Studies and the Andalucian Entrepreneurs' Confederation, pp. 99–119.

Monasterio, C. and J. Suarez (1998), *Manual de hacienda autonómica y local*, Barcelona: Ariel.

Oates, Wallace E. (1972), *Fiscal Federalism*, New York: Harcourt Brace Jovanovich.

Petchey, Jeffrey, Perry Shapiro and Cliff Walsh (1997), 'Transfers in Federal Systems: A Critical Survey', in Ronald C. Fisher (ed.), *Intergovernmental Fiscal Relations*, Boston: Kluwer Academic Publishers.

Tiebout, Charles M. (1956), 'A Pure Theory of Local Expenditure', *Journal of Political Economy,* 64 (October), 416–24.

Zubiri, I. (2000), 'La capacidad normativa de las comunidades forales. Su extensión al esto de Comunidades Autónomas', *Papeles de Economía*, (83), 127–46.

Zubiri, I. and M. Vallejo (1995), *Un análisis metodológico y empírico del sistema de cupo*, Bilbao: Fundación Banco Bilbao Vizcaya.

PART IV

Countries in Transition

8. Asymmetric Federalism in Russia: Cure or Poison?

Jorge Martinez-Vazquez

The Soviet Union disintegrated in 1991 for several fundamental reasons, including the failure of planned socialism to improve people's standard of living. One less anticipated, but also fundamental, reason for the disintegration of the Soviet state was the diversity and pluralism of the Soviet republics, which included countries as diverse as Estonia, Latvia and Lithuania in the Baltics; republics such as Tajikistan, Kazakhstan and the Kyrgyz Republic in Central Asia; and Armenia, Azerbaijan and Georgia in the Caucasus. To the surprise of many, one of the leading supporters of this separation was the Russian Federation that, until then, had been perceived as the ruling centre of a vast empire put together during many centuries of war by czarist Russia and the Soviets.

The birth of the Russian Federation in the agony of the disintegration of the Soviet Union marked the young country from the start with a fear of its own disintegration. The fears were justified: the Russian Federation was formed of 89 very different regions. From the start, several of these regions rushed to declare their sovereignty and independence from the Russian Federation. In many ways, therefore, the new country was subject to centrifugal forces similar to those that had led to the disintegration of the Soviet Union.

Nation building, indeed, keeping the nation together, took first priority in the national agenda in the early years of the transition (1992–93). One of the most important tools used in this effort was the design of a new system of intergovernmental fiscal relations between the federal and regional governments and, to a lesser extent, between regional and local governments, capable of accommodating the diversity of Russian regions and ethnic groups. The new Russian government theoretically had the choice of building a homogeneous system of intergovernmental fiscal relations that treated all regions exactly the same or an asymmetric system, which would have given advantages to some regions over others.

In reality, in 1992–93 the federal government did not have much of a choice but to accept an asymmetric system of intergovernmental relations, which was rapidly being shaped by the demands of a small number of ethnic republics. Indeed, it was the regions that early on dictated the agenda of the federal contract, that is, the shape and form the Russian Federation should assume. During the early years of the transition, the federal government remained reactive and tried to adapt to the agenda set by the maverick regions. The 1993 Russian constitution recognized the possibility of an asymmetric configuration of intergovernmental relations between the regions and the federal government.

In the eyes of many, the asymmetric design of the system of intergovernmental fiscal relations saved Russia from falling into an abyss of civil wars as in Chechnya, and thus kept the country from disintegrating. However, asymmetric federalism has not been without its costs. A number of observers have explained many of the problems and tribulations Russia has faced in the last decade—lack of fiscal discipline, economic stagnation and so on—as having roots in asymmetric federalism and the federal government's inability to enforce federal laws throughout the Russian Federation. In 1997–98, the administration of President Boris Yeltsin started a campaign to rein in the regions. This policy was significantly increased by the new administration of President Vladimir Putin, who, since he took over in 2000, has made gaining control over the regions and enforcing federal laws a cornerstone of his administration.

The trademark of the early years of the Yeltsin administration was to accommodate the demands for more autonomy with concessions to the most aggressive regions that basically gave them more favourable treatment within the framework of intergovernmental fiscal relations. Leaving aside the issue of Chechnya, this special treatment did not succeed in quieting those demands. Part of the problem was self-inflicted, in that early on, Yeltsin saw the regional demands as a strategic weapon that he could use in his fight for political dominance with the legislative branch, the Supreme Soviet. Yeltsin eventually prevailed over parliament, but things got too far away from Yeltsin for him to reclaim control over the powerful and now democratically elected governors he had created. During the Yeltsin years, many regions behaved as if they saw little benefit from being part of the federation and acted preponderantly with a narrow, selfish view and not in the national interest. This scenario changed radically with Putin's election as president in March 2000. Putin was elected with a wide margin and his popularity allowed him to immediately take on the regional governors and reduce their power.

The objective of this chapter is to evaluate the role, significance and effects of asymmetric federalism in the Russian Federation to draw a number of useful lessons in relation to those things that have worked and others that have not. The organization of fiscal federalism in Russia continues to evolve. Where President Putin and his administration actually want to take fiscal federalism is uncertain, but more central control from Moscow and a strengthened state appear to be high on the policy agenda. This does not necessarily mean that sustained fiscal recentralization will occur. However, the most recent changes in 2004 following the Beslan school hostage crisis in southern Russia signal a further swing toward centralization in the country. The most significant of these changes is President Putin's call for the elimination of democratic elections for regional governors and having them directly appointed from Moscow.

The next section describes the significant economic, geographic and ethnic diversity of Russia's regions in some detail. This is followed by a discussion of the principles and theory of asymmetric federalism. The next section reviews the nature and extent of asymmetric federalism in Russia (I do not discuss in any depth the conflict in Chechnya; for this see Lapidus 1998). The chapter then examines how well the asymmetric design of intergovernmental fiscal relations has worked before turning to a discussion of the future of fiscal decentralization in Russia and what role asymmetric policies are expected to play.

REGIONAL DIVERSITY

Russia is the largest country in the world, spanning 11 time zones and 17 million square kilometres (see Figure 8.1 for a map of Russia). It encompasses 89 regional autonomous governments (grouped into 11 areas for statistical purposes) with a total population of 145.9 million in 2000. Russia's regions are diverse in terms of economic conditions, ethnic composition, language and religious and historical differences. The 1993 constitution states that of the 89 'subjects of the federation', which I will refer to as regions, 21 are republics, made up of the former autonomous republics and most of the autonomous *oblasts* in the former Soviet Union; 55 are regular Russian oblasts and *krays*; 2 are the city regions of Moscow, the capital, and St Petersburg, the capital from the time of Peter the Great until the Soviet era; and 11 are autonomous *okrugs* (AOs), including the Jewish autonomous oblast.[1] Even though the Russian Federation theoretically consists of 89 regions, because of the ongoing civil war in one of its regions, Chechnya, statistics and reports often refer to only 88 regions.

Many of the ethnic republics tend to be quite poor and are often located on the periphery of the country, with higher transportation costs to main markets and alienation from the country's mainstream. This group includes the republics of Tuva, Buryatia, Karelia, Chechnya and Dagestan. At the same time, several ethnic republics are rich in natural resources and have been at the vanguard of demands for autonomy and separatist threats. This group includes Tatarstan, Bashkortostan and Sakha (Yakutia).

Figure 8.1 The Russian Federation

Main Regional Features

Table 8.1 presents the main features of the regions for the 11 geographical areas, and the appendix shows the feature for all 89 regions. The most striking feature is the unevenness of the distribution of land and population. For example, the East Siberia Area and the Far Eastern Area combined represent more than 60 per cent of the territory of the country but barely over 11 per cent of the population. By contrast, the Central Area, which includes Moscow, represents 2.8 per cent of the area of the country but 20 per cent of the population. In terms of population density, it is less than 0.1 person per square kilometre in Taimyrsky AO in East Siberia and 8631 people per square kilometre in Moscow.

The regions also differ in the vertical structure of government. The budgetary system across regions is quite diverse, with regions having three to five levels of government, but not all of them with a separate budget (Kurlyandskaya 2001). In some regions, the regional authorities have a two-tier government structure. This typically happens in regions where municipalities are subordinated to *rayon* (county) governments. This second tier of regional government typically has a purely executive function and the authorities are appointed by the regional centre, which is, however, assigned its own operating budget.

Demographic Changes

During the last decade of economic transition, Russia has lost population. The country's population stood at 148.7 million in 1992, but was down to 145.9 million in 2000 (Table 8.2). Most regions suffered population losses from 1991 to 1999 that were as high as 6.6 per cent in the Central Area, which includes Moscow. The notable exceptions were several ethnic republics and AOs that experienced natural increases in population during the period, for example, Dagestan, Chukotskiy AO, Ingushetiya and Yamalo Neteskiy AO. Those experiencing the largest negative natural changes in population were the regions in the corridor between Moscow and St. Petersburg (Tver, Novgorod, Pkov and Leningrad oblasts).

The areas have varied much more widely in terms of changes in population caused by net migration. The two main migration processes during the transition years were the return of Russians from other former Soviet republics and out-migration from the more inhospitable regions in the north and far east to the western and southern parts of Russia (Heleniak 1997). The big losers were the Far Eastern Area, which lost 10.7 per cent of its population in 1991–99, and the Northern Area, which lost 5.1 per cent (Table 8.3). These area averages conceal some dramatic differences within the areas. For example, in the

Table 8.1 Key features of areas, selected years

Name of area	Area, 2000 (thousands of km^2)	Population, 2000 (thousands of people)	Population density, 2000 (people per km^2)	GRP, 1998 (Rub thousands)	GRP per capita, 1998 (Rub thousands)	Percent-age of area	Percent-age of population	Percent-age of GDP
Northern Area	1466.3	5668	3.9	110 383	19.1	8.59	3.88	4.59
Northwestern Area	197.1	7898	40.1	126 866	15.9	1.15	5.41	5.28
Central Area	484.0	29 361	60.7	615 670	20.8	2.83	20.12	25.63
Volgo-Vyatsk Area	265.4	8292	31.2	97 686	11.7	1.55	5.68	4.07
Central Chernozem Area	167.7	7781	46.4	87 858	11.2	0.98	5.33	3.66
Povolzhsk Area	536.4	16 805	31.3	240 021	14.2	3.14	11.52	9.99
North Caucasian Area	374.4	17 677	47.2	148 653	8.4	2.19	12.11	6.19
Ural Area	824.0	20 321	24.7	306 038	15.0	4.83	13.93	12.74
West Siberia Area	2427.2	15 040	6.2	356 823	23.6	14.21	10.31	14.85
East Siberia Area	4122.8	8973	2.2	158 566	17.5	24.14	6.15	6.60
Far Eastern Area	6231.0	7160	1.1	153 717	21.0	36.49	4.91	6.40
Russian Federation	17 075.4	145 925	8.5	2 402 280	16.3	100.00	100.00	100.00
Maximum	3103.2	8631	8 631.0	362 520	62.7	18.17	5.91	15.09
Minimum	0.6	18	0.0	1053	3.4	0.00	0.00	0.00

GDP Gross domesitc product.
GRP Gross regional product.

Source: Goskomstat data.

Table 8.2 Population by area, selected years

Area	1986 Number (thousands)	1986 Percentage share	1992 Number (thousands)	1992 Percentage share	1994 Number (thousands)	1994 Percentage share	1996 Number (thousands)	1996 Percentage share	1998 Number (thousands)	1998 Percentage share	2000 Number (thousands)	2000 Percentage share
Northern Area	5959	4.1	6136	4.1	6023	4.1	5889	4.0	5785	3.9	5668	3.9
Northwestern Area	8091	5.6	8270	5.6	8136	5.5	8052	5.4	7989	5.4	7898	5.4
Central Area	29 821	20.7	30 363	20.4	30 099	20.3	29 883	20.2	29 651	20.2	29 361	20.1
Volgo-Vyatsk Area	8372	5.8	8503	5.7	8483	5.7	8444	5.7	8376	5.7	8292	5.7
Central Chernozem Area	7702	5.4	7762	5.2	7840	5.3	7880	5.3	7846	5.3	7781	5.3
Povolzhsk Area	16 035	11.1	16 641	11.2	16 808	11.3	16 920	11.4	16 886	11.5	16 805	11.5
North Caucasian Area	16 347	11.4	17 246	11.6	17 518	11.8	17 738	12.0	17 707	12.0	17 677	12.1
Ural Area	19 882	13.8	20 475	13.8	20 465	13.8	20 461	13.8	20 406	13.9	20 321	13.9
West Siberia Area	14 364	10.0	15 122	10.2	15 093	10.2	15 128	10.2	15 109	10.3	15 040	10.3
East Siberia Area	8834	6.1	9260	6.2	9200	6.2	9144	6.2	9071	6.2	8973	6.1
Far Eastern Area	7581	5.3	8032	5.4	7788	5.2	7505	5.1	7336	5.0	7160	4.9
Russian Federation	143 835	100.0	148 704	100.0	148 366	100.0	147 976	100.0	147 105	100.0	145 925	100.0
Maximum	8740	6.1	8957	6.0	8793	5.9	8664	5.9	8629	5.9	8631	5.9
Minimum	21	0.0	25	0.0	23	0.0	20	0.0	20	0.0	18	0.0

Source: Census data reported by Goskomstat.

Table 8.3 Net changes in population by area, 1991–99 (per cent)

Area	Natural changes	Change from migration
Northern Area	–1.9	–5.1
Northwestern Area	–6.7	2.5
Central Area	–6.6	3.6
Volgo-Vyatsk Area	–4.3	2.5
Central Chernozem Area	–6.0	6.8
Povolzhsk Area	–3.0	4.6
North Caucasian Area	–0.7	4.7
Ural Area	–2.6	2.3
West Siberia Area	–1.8	1.8
East Siberia Area	–0.4	–1.8
Far Eastern Area	0.7	–10.7
Russian Federation	–3.3	2.1

Source: Author's computation based on Goskomstat data.

Far Eastern Area, the Chuotsky AO lost more than half of its population and Magadan oblast lost 40 per cent. These are remote, isolated areas with harsh living conditions that lost strategic military value with the end of the Cold War.[2] Another big loser in net migration was Chechnya because of its secessionist war.

The big winners in net migration were warmer and more hospitable parts of the country, such as the Central Cherzozem (Black Soil) Area, with the population of Belgorod oblast, for example, increasing by 11.8 per cent, and the North Caucasian Area, with the population of Krasnodar kray increasing by 11.4 per cent. Kaliningrad oblast, a western enclave in the Baltic Sea between Poland and Lithuania, was also a big winner in net migration, up 10.8 per cent in 1991–99.

An interesting observation is that Moscow, by far the richest and most attractive destination in economic terms, did not experience much net migration: 2.2 per cent during 1991–99. This may have been due to Mayor Yuri Luzhkov's illegal demands that would-be residents apply for residency permits,[3] but also by the scarcity and high cost of housing. In St. Petersburg, where there has been no highly publicized enforcement of residency permits, but where the cost of housing is high and which experienced much less economic growth than Moscow, net migration was a negative 0.1 per cent. Note that the oblasts surrounding the two cities, Leningrad oblast and Moscow oblast, experienced much higher net migration during the period, 8.3 per cent and 4.3 per cent, respectively.

Ethnic Diversity and Relative Geographic Remoteness

The Russian Federation has significant ethnic diversity, but much less than in the former Soviet Union. Lapidus (1999, p. 75) describes the 21 ethnically defined republics of the Russia Federation as 'islands in an ethnically Russian sea.' As Table 8.4 indicates, in 1989, 88 per cent of the country's population was ethnic Russian. The ethnic nationalities tend to be concentrated along the periphery of the country, such as the North Caucasian Area, but even here some three-quarters of the population are ethnic Russians. However, in 11 regions, ethnic nationalities account for more than half the population. These are the Chuvasia republic, the Kalmikya republic, the Tatarstan republic, the Dagestan republic, the Ingushetiya republic (which includes Chechnya), the Kabardino-Balkaria republic, the Karachaevo-Cherkesskaya republic, the North Osetia

Table 8.4 Shares of Russian and other populations by area, 1989 (per cent)

Area	Russian	Main ethnic group	Other ethnic groups[a]
Northern Area	89.5	6.2	4.2
Northwestern Area	97.6	0.0	2.4
Central Area	98.4	0.0	1.6
Volgo-Vyatsk Area	79.2	18.7	2.0
Central Chernozem Area	97.4	0.0	2.6
Povolzhsk Area	78.9	16.9	4.2
North Caucasian Area	76.1	22.6	1.3
Ural Area	83.0	10.8	5.4
West Siberia Area	95.1	1.0	4.0
East Siberia Area	86.3	8.0	5.7
Far Eastern Area	85.5	4.9	9.7
Russian Federation	88.3	8.0	3.6
Maximum	100.0	80.2	28.4
Minimum	19.8	0.0	0.0

a. Others may include Ukrainians, Belorussians, Tatars, Armenians, Germans, Jews and other nationalities that are not Russians and not part of the main ethnic group.

Source: Census data reported by Goskomstat.

republic, Komi-Permyatskaya AO, the Tuva republic and Aginskiy Buryatskiy AO. In some of these regions 'titular' nationals (or the main ethnic group) constitute a majority of the population. In addition to titular nationals, Goskomstat, the statistical office, also records other nationalities, such as Ukrainians, Belorussians, Armenians, Tatars and Jews. Even though these groups constitute minorities in the country as a whole, the various ethnic groups are concentrated enough in a number of regions to make ethnic demands an important issue in the design of intergovernmental fiscal relations.[4]

Another significant factor of diversity, and possibly of conflict and frustration between the regions and the centre, involves time zones and geographical distance between the federal capital and the regions. Because Russia has 11 time zones, many regions are unable to communicate with Moscow during regular working hours. The average distance between the capitals of the regions in the Far Eastern Area and Moscow is 9355 kilometres and the average time difference is eight hours. The average distance between regional capitals and Moscow for the entire Russian Federation is 2633 kilometres and the average time difference is two hours.

Economic Disparities

Russia's regions are significantly disparate in industrial development and natural resource endowments. This has led to extremely high differences in gross regional product (GRP) per capita across the regions. In 1998, the difference between the region with the highest GRP per capita (Tyumen oblast, which has the largest deposits of oil and gas in Russia) and that with the lowest (Ingushetia republic) was 18-fold, with areas' ratios to the mean GRP per capita for Russia ranging from 3.8 to 0.2 (Table 8.5). The area averages for GRP per capita shown in the table hide some large disparities. For example, regions with high GRP per capita are Moscow and the republic of Sakha (Yakutia) in Siberia, which is rich in mineral deposits, while extremely poor regions include the Dagestan republic and other peripheral ethnic republics.

The transition period has done little to erase disparities, and if anything, economic disparities have become worse (see Sutherland and Hanson 1996 for a discussion of growing economic disparities in the early years of the transition). As Table 8.6 shows, the ratio between the maximum and minimum values for regional personal income per capita, themselves expressed as ratios to the overall mean for Russia, increased from 3.8 in 1985 to 18.5 in 1999, an almost 500 per cent increase. This trend has added to the challenge of designing the right system of intergovernmental fiscal relations, especially the system of equalization transfers.

Economic disparities are aggravated by significant differences in the cost of living across the regions, for instance, in 1999, the cost of the minimum

Table 8.5 GRP per capita by area, 1998

Area	GRP per capita (current Rub)	Ratio to the mean for Russia
Northern Area	19 081	1.17
Northwestern Area	15 880	0.97
Central Area	20 764	1.27
Volgo-Vyatsk Area	11 663	0.71
Central Chernozem Area	11 198	0.69
Povolzhsk Area	14 214	0.87
North Caucasian Area	8395	0.51
Ural Area	14 997	0.92
West Siberia Area	23 617	1.45
East Siberia Area	17 481	1.07
Far Eastern Area	20 954	1.28
Russian Federation	16 330	1.00
Maximum	62 661	3.80
Minimum	3365	0.20

Source: Author's computation based on Goskomstat data.

Table 8.6 Personal income per capita by area, selected years (ratio to the mean for Russia)

Area	1985	1990	1995	1999
Northern Area	1.19	1.12	1.17	1.04
Northwestern Area	1.04	1.06	1.07	0.93
Central Area	1.07	1.12	1.54	1.74
Volgo-Vyatsk Area	0.92	0.88	0.67	0.58
Central Chernozem Area	0.90	0.87	0.67	0.66
Povolzhsk Area	0.92	0.91	0.71	0.75
North Caucasian Area	0.77	0.81	0.57	0.61
Ural Area	0.92	0.91	0.78	0.78
West Siberia Area	1.10	1.10	1.15	1.12
East Siberia Area	0.98	0.94	1.01	0.87
Far Eastern Area	1.30	1.28	1.24	1.07
Russian Federation	1.00	1.00	1.00	1.00
Maximum	2.18	2.12	3.50	4.26
Minimum	0.57	0.60	0.23	0.23

Source: Author's computation based on Goskomstat data.

regional subsistence basket was 470 per cent higher in Chukotskiy AO than in Ulyanov oblast. The most expensive regions are in the Far Eastern Area and the least expensive are in the Povolzhsk area.

The disparities have arisen primarily because economic growth has increasingly been concentrated in a handful of regions and foreign direct investment (FDI) has been concentrated in an even smaller number of regions. Some areas that in the past depended more heavily than others on Moscow for transfers and subsidies, such as the Far Eastern and Northern areas, have suffered disproportionately from budget cuts and from the end of the Cold War era and the subsequent closing of many military facilities. In addition, changes in revenue sharing arrangements between the centre and the regions have allowed more income to stay in the resource-rich regions.

With the exception of growth of 0.5 per cent in 1997, the growth rate for Russia as a whole was negative during 1995–98, though it has improved in recent years. Area average growth rates followed much the same pattern, ranging from growth of 1.9 per cent in the Northern Area in 1998 to –14.5 per cent in the West Siberia Area that same year despite significant positive growth in 1995 and 1996. The largest cities, Moscow and St. Petersburg, did well in terms of growth during this period, especially Moscow. Their surrounding oblasts did less well. Natural resource-rich regions like Tyumen oblast experienced ups and downs in real GRP depending on oil prices. Other regions experienced what seem to be extremely large fluctuations in real GRP, but whether these represent reporting anomalies or not is unclear.

Ahrend (2000) investigates a number of possible factors that could help explain the difference in economic performance across the regions during the transition years. He finds that the most robust explanatory variable is the initial competitiveness of a region's industry, measured as the share of exports in total regional output. Other important factors in explaining performance were industrial structure, natural resource endowment and human capital. What is most controversial in Ahrend's findings is that political, institutional and reform variables did not seem to matter in explaining different growth rates across regions. Despite the wide belief that the degree to which a region implemented economic reform measures should have played an important role in explaining economic performance, Ahrend (2000) finds that initial conditions at the start of the transition played a much more important role. Similarly, de Melo, Ofer and Yossifov (1999) find that economic performance of the regional capitals along the Volga River was associated with favourable initial conditions; however, they also give economic reform an important role in explaining differences in performance.

One possibility is that the impact of economic reforms on economic growth works with a lag and therefore takes some time to be detected statistically. Another possibility is that positive initial conditions tend to be positively correlated with economic reform, and therefore disentangling the two types of effects is hard. At any rate, with few constraints on their lawmaking powers, the regions have come up with quite different legal and regulatory regimes (Polishchuck 2000). These differences in economic and regulatory regimes are to a large extent manifestations of regional preferences and the autonomy the constitution provides to the regions. The starkest difference has been between a group of regions that have maintained intensive interventions in the economy through price controls, hurdles to interregional trade and the use of consumer subsidies, the so-called red belt regions, and many other regions that have followed liberal and more market-friendly policies.[5]

Foreign Direct Investment Patterns

To date the opening of the economy to foreign investors has done little to reduce economic disparities across the regions. Indeed, FDI appears to have contributed to the widening disparities.

Clearly Moscow has benefited from being the political capital of the country and is by far the most attractive destination for FDI. During 1995–99, the city of Moscow accounted for 44.1 per cent of Russia's total FDI and Moscow oblast, the regional ring around the city, came in second place among the regions, accounting for 9.8 per cent of total FCI. Together this represents more than half of all FDI in Russia, and according to Goskomstat, the trend seems to have continued in more recent years. By contrast, the city of Moscow and Moscow oblast together represent about 20 per cent of Russia's gross domestic product. Because it is the capital, some FDI that has been recorded as taking place in Moscow may actually have ended up elsewhere. Nevertheless, in addition to being the country's finance and communications centre, Moscow has built up a significant industrial and services base.

The next most important destination for FDI has been St Petersburg and its surrounding region, Leningrad oblast. The two combined represented almost 8 per cent of total FDI in 1995–99. FDI has also been significant in several other regions. In some cases, it is related to gas and/or oil projects, for example, in Sakhalinsk oblast and in Krasnoyarsk kray, but in other cases investments have been more diversified, as in Novosibirsk oblast with investments by Coca-Cola and other food processing enterprises and in Samara oblast with investments by the chemical, food processing and petroleum refining industries. Broadman and Recanatini (2001) analyse the distribution of FDI and find that the most important determinants are market size, infrastructure development and policy environment factors.

The Haves and the Have Nots

Disparities in economic conditions have led to a political split at the regional level, with two main coalitions lobbying the federal authorities in quite different directions. The first group consists of the rich or donor regions, that is, the regions that contribute in net terms to the federal budget. The second group consists of the poor or subsidized regions, that is, those that receive a net inflow of funds from the federal budget. The club of rich regions has had some mobility at the bottom, but permanent members include the city of Moscow, St Petersburg, Nizhny Novgorod, Samara, Sverdlovsk, Volgograd, Tyumen, Khanty-Mansi, Krasnoyarsk and Sakha (Yakutia).

Policies to Reduce Interregional Income Disparities

This section highlights some of the main policies concerning revenue assignments, federal expenditures and transfers that have had major impacts on regional disparities (see Martinez-Vazquez and Boex 2001 for more details). Revenue assignments have evolved significantly during the transition. At the start of the transition, and despite all the problems it represented in terms of bargaining and discretion, the practice of regulation (or adjusting tax sharing rates for individual regions in a discretionary manner) provided the federal authorities with the significant advantage of being able, at least in theory, to equalize fiscal disparities across regions by reducing the rates at which taxes are shared in richer regions and increasing them in poorer regions. The drive to improve predictability and transparency in revenue assignments meant that after 1994, the federal authorities attempted to keep sharing rates stable over time and to make them uniform across regions, with the implication that all regions, rich and poor, had to be treated the same. Table 8.7 summarizes revenue assignments between the federal government and the regions during 1991–2002.

Thus the attainment of more efficient and transparent revenue assignments resulted in even larger fiscal disparities between the regions and the federal government had to rely on a new system of equalization grants to offset some of the increased disparities in the distribution of fiscal resources. Whereas revenue sharing arrangements were relatively stable from 1994 through 1997, several substantial changes were made in revenue sharing arrangements before and after the economic crisis of August 1998. Changes in the assignment of revenues, especially the assignment of personal income tax collections, reflect a tug-of-war over resources between the federal and regional governments. As Table 8.7 shows, in recent years fiscal policy reforms have aimed at reassigning tax revenues away from subnational governments and towards the federal government. The federal government's share of overall tax collections reached 60 per cent in 2001, up from a low of 42.5 per cent in 1997.

As noted earlier, a particularly important source of fiscal disparities is the extremely uneven distribution of natural resources, especially oil and natural gas. The significance of uneven distribution was emphasized by tax reforms

Table 8.7 Legislated sharing rates for major taxes between the federal government and the regions, 1991–2002 (percentage of the total)

Tax	Law on basic principles of taxation, 1991		1992, Q1		1992, Q2–Q4		1993		1994, Q1		1994, Q2–Q4		1995		1996		1997		1998		1999, Q1		1999, Q2–Q4		2000		2001		2002	
	Federal government	Regions	Federal government	Regions	Federal government	Regions	Federal government	Regions	Federal government	Regions	Federal government	Regions	Federal government	Regions	Federal government	Regions	Federal government	Regions	Federal government	Regions	Federal government	Regions	Federal government	Regions	Federal government	Regions	Federal government	Regions	Federal government	Regions
VAT[a]	100	0	negotiable		80	20	80–50	20–50	75	25	75	25	75	25	75	25	75	25	75	25	75	25	85	15	85	15	100	0	100	0
Profit enterprise tax	0	100[b]	47	53	41	59	31	69	37–34[c]	63–66[c]	37–34[c]	63–66[c]	34	66	34	66	34	66	34	66	37	63	37	63	37	63	31	69[d]	31	69[e]
Personal income tax	0	100[b]	0	100	0	100	0	100	0	100	0	100	10	90	10	90	0	100	40	60	14	86[f]	14	86	16	84	1	99	0	100
Excise taxes on alcohol	50	50	50	50	50	50	50	50	50	50	50	50	50	50	50	50	50	50	50	50	50	50	50	50	50	50	50	50	50	50
Energy excise taxes	—	—	100	0	100	0	100	0	100	0	100	0	100	0	100	0	100	0	100	0	100	0	100	0	100	0	100	0	100	0
Excise taxes on domestic production	—	—	n.a.	n.a.	n.a.	n.a.	n.a.	n.a.	0	100	0	100	0	100	0	100	0	100	0	100	0	100	0	100	0	100	0	100	0	100

— Not specified in the law.
n.a. Not applicable.
Q = Quarter.
VAT Value added tax.

a. VAT on imports, precious metals and stones is assigned 100 per cent to the federal level.
b. These taxes could be shared with the federal government.
c. The federal profit tax rate was 13 per cent. Regional profit tax rates ranged up to 22 per cent of profits for most enterprises and 25 per cent of profits for banks and insurance companies. The sharing percentages in the table are calculated based on the 13/22 and 13/25 profit tax rates.
d. In 2001, a local enterprise profits tax rate of 5 per cent was introduced, therefore the regional share also includes the local 5 per cent.
e. In 2002, a local enterprise profits tax rate was 2 per cent, therefore the regional share includes the local 2 per cent.
f. The regional share is taken as equal to the average.

Source: World Bank (1996), updated by the author.

that, for the first time in Russia's history, gave the regions a significant share of the tax revenues from mineral resources beginning in 1992 and confirmed in the Tax Code in 2002.

Actual revenues may also differ across regions because subnational governments have been granted some degree of tax autonomy. This autonomy basically consists of the choice of tax rates up to a maximum rate for three taxes: the shared part of the enterprise profit tax, with different rates for financial institutions and other enterprises; the sales tax; and the enterprise assets tax.[6] However, with just a few exceptions, regional governments are making full use of their ability to raise taxes by charging the highest allowable rates for those taxes. Nevertheless, their ability to self-finance their budgets out of own and shared taxes varies considerably, ranging from 1 per cent in Madagasnk oblast to 100 per cent in the city of Moscow.

In addition to tax policy, the federal government's expenditure policies in the regions can increase or dampen fiscal disparities. One way to look at this issue is to observe direct expenditures by the federal government in the regions, which are difficult to calculate and involve some arbitrary assumptions (Table 8.8). Setting aside the extremely large figure for federal direct expenditures per capita in the city of Moscow, which reflects the allocation there of 'unallocatable' items (such as a large share of national defence expenditures, which cannot be easily identified with any particular area), the numbers in Table 8.8 tell two main stories. First, federal direct expenditures seem to help equalize fiscal disparities, because they are larger in poorer, remote areas in the Northern Area, the East Siberia Area and the Far Eastern Area. Second, though not shown in the table, is that those regional governments that by treaty or unilateral action tend to retain a higher portion of federal tax revenues, such as Tatarstan and Bashkortostan, do indeed account for the lowest federal direct expenditures per capita by a wide margin.

The most important tool the federal government uses to address the problem of fiscal disparity is the system of intergovernmental equalization transfers. This has been changing continuously during the transition as the formula used to allocate funds to the regions has continued to improve. After the 2000 reforms, the system improved in terms of its transparency, objectivity and minimization of negative incentive effects on revenue mobilization and expenditure efficiency by using measures of revenue capacity and expenditure needs to arrive at fiscal disparities. Table 8.9 shows total federal transfers by area for 1997–2000 and budgeted equalization transfers for 2001. As a percentage of the total, regions in the North Caucasian Area receive the largest amount of transfers, followed by regions in the Far Eastern Area. The Central Area is also an important recipient, as are West and East Siberia.

In per capita terms, the rankings are somewhat different, with the regions in the Far Eastern Area and the North Caucasian Area being significantly

Table 8.8 Federal direct expenditures by area, 1998

Area	Population (thousands)	Federal direct expenditure per capita (Rub)	Total federal direct expenditure (Rub thousands)
Northern Area	5785	526	3 043 922
Northwestern Area	7989	500	3 998 013
Central Area, of which	29 651	2057	60 988 759
city of Moscow	8629	6074	52 412 546
Volgo-Vyatsk Area	8376	280	2 342 736
Central Chernozem Area	7846	315	2 474 648
Povolzhsk Area	16 886	266	4 487 642
North Caucasian Area	17 707	388	6 862 222
Ural Area	20 406	260	5 299 156
West Siberia Area	15 109	544	8 219 592
East Siberia Area	9071	470	4 258 988
Far Eastern Area	7336	727	5 334 204
Russian Federation	147 105	731	107 605 984
Maximum	8629	6074	52 412 546
Minimum	20	43	20 826

Source: Goskomstat data.

ahead of the rest (Table 8.9). Note, however, that with some exceptions, federal transfers do not represent the largest share of areas' budgets,[7] for example, the share of transfers in the total revenues of the Far Eastern Area was 11.8 per cent in 2000 (Table 8.10). This share varied significantly for individual regions, for instance, for the same year, transfers represented 78 per cent of total revenues for the Tuva Republic in the East Siberia Area.

What Has Driven Federal Transfers to the Regions?

Investigators have carried out a considerable amount of research on the political economy and equity of federal transfers in Russia. The question most often asked has been whether the goal of federal transfers is to attain such economic objectives as the equalization of fiscal capacity and expenditure needs among different levels of governments, or whether they actually reflect political economy considerations and purely asymmetric treatment and are governed by the political forces of the moment. Popov (2002), Treisman

Table 8.9 Transfers to regions by area, 1997–2001

Area	1997			1998			1999			2000			2001[a]		
	Total (current Rub thousands)	Per-centage share	Per capita transfer (current Rub thousands)	Total (current Rub thousands)	Per-age share	Per capita transfer (current Rub thousands)	Total (current Rub thousands)	Per-age share	Per capita transfer (current Rub thousands)	Total (current Rub thousands)	Per-age share	Per capita transfer (current Rub thousands)	Total (current Rub thousands)	Per-age share	Per capita transfer (current Rub thousands)
Northern Area	951 685	2.6	163.0	972 611	3.6	168.1	1 337 117	3.0	233.2	2 219 859	3.4	391.6	2 207 666	2.4	389.5
Northwestern Area	1 200 274	3.3	149.6	730 690	2.7	91.5	1 083 963	2.4	136.2	1 579 343	2.4	200.0	2 216 091	2.4	280.6
Central Area	4 824 125	13.3	162.1	2 698 203	10.0	91.0	4 788 192	10.8	162.1	7 750 702	11.8	264.0	10 431 548	11.3	355.3
Volgo-Vyatsk Area	2 365 394	6.5	281.2	1 441 433	5.3	172.1	2 433 732	5.5	291.7	2 552 314	3.9	307.8	5 013 809	5.4	604.7
Central Chernozem Area	1 470 193	4.1	186.8	951 745	3.5	121.3	1 768 926	4.0	226.2	2 223 207	3.4	285.7	3 302 801	3.6	424.5
Povolzhsk Area	2 654 818	7.3	157.1	1 919 319	7.1	113.7	2 686 343	6.0	159.3	3 295 345	5.0	196.1	4 818 460	5.2	286.7
North Caucasian Area	6 499 136	18.0	300.2	5 766 562	21.4	239.9	9 866 039	22.2	403.2	13 965 098	21.3	613.2	20 612 228	22.8	1166.0
Ural Area	1 742 492	4.8	85.3	1 273 856	4.7	62.4	1 695 813	3.8	83.2	1 991 825	3.0	98.0	2 479 502	2.7	122.0
West Siberia Area	5 069 274	14.0	335.8	3 961 793	14.7	262.2	5 813 714	13.1	384.9	7 661 153	11.6	509.4	11 031 684	12.0	733.5
East Siberia Area	2 413 281	6.7	264.8	2 296 029	8.5	253.1	4 152 312	9.3	459.8	7 454 078	11.3	830.7	8 707 739	9.4	970.4
Far Eastern Area	6 661 508	18.4	897.7	4 970 332	18.4	677.5	8 510 621	19.1	1173.6	14 572 554	22.1	2035.3	18 971 945	20.6	2649.7
Russian Federation	36 076 529	100.0	236.5	26 982 573	100.0	173.1	44 415 103	100.0	284.2	65 683 354	100.0	428.7	90 430 398	100.0	619.7
Maximum[b]	1 838 827	5.1	6853.3	1 491 394	5.5	4721.6	2 878 355	6.5	7062.4	4 998 161	7.6	24 015.5	7 495 647	8.1	12 516.9
Minimum[b]	0	0.0	0.0	0.0	0.0	0.0	0.0	0.0	0.0	0.0	0.0	0.0	0.0	0.0	0.0

a. Preliminary figures. Population used is that for 2000.
b. These figures apply to the individual regions and not the areas.

Source: Goskomstat data.

Table 8.10 Share of transfers in areas' total revenues, 1997–2000 (per cent)

Area	1997	1998	1999	2000
Northern Area	5.1	5.3	3.8	3.3
Northwestern Area	5.9	3.2	2.9	0.7
Central Area	4.8	2.9	3.1	12.2
Volgo-Vyatsk Area	13.9	8.5	9.2	9.0
Central Chernozem Area	10.6	6.7	8.1	7.6
Povolzhsk Area	5.7	4.5	3.8	2.9
North Caucasian Area	25.0	21.6	21.8	25.2
Ural Area	3.4	2.5	1.8	2.2
West Siberia Area	6.7	5.7	4.8	4.8
East Siberia Area	10.0	10.0	8.4	9.3
Far Eastern Area	21.3	18.7	13.4	11.8
Russian Federation	8.4	6.6	6.2	6.3
Maximum	66.0	100.0	75.0	96.2
Minimum	0.0	0.0	0.0	0.0

Source: Goskomstat data.

(1996, 2000) and others find that politics have been a major force in defining federal transfers to the regions, though the relevant political factors may have changed over time. For example, Treisman (1996) concludes that early on, the central government used federal transfers to appease troublemaking regions. Between 1992 and 1994, the regions that got treated most favourably were those that had not supported Yeltsin's government in the dispute with parliament and those that had made separatist noises through such actions as issuing declarations of sovereignty. By contrast, during 1996–98, Popov (2002) and Speckhard (1998) find that the regions that got treated better in terms of federal transfers were those that had supported the Yeltsin government in the 1995 parliamentary elections and the 1996 presidential elections.[8]

However, other studies have emphasized that transfers have been roughly compatible with regions' fiscal needs, because the bulk of federal transfers has gone to the neediest regions, thereby partially accomplishing the desirable objective of equalization (Martinez-Vazquez and Boex 2001; McAuley 1997; Stewart 1996). But as Solanko (1999) points out, whether politics or economic and fiscal needs motivated transfers in the Yeltsin years may be hard to discern because of the correlation between poor socioeconomic conditions and the antireform and anti-Yeltsin sentiments among regions early on during the transition.

THE RATIONALE FOR ASYMMETRIC FEDERALISM

One of the ways the Russian Federation has managed to cope with such a high degree of diversity has been through the differential treatment of the regions, that is, the practice of asymmetric federalism. Russia is not alone in having adopted this approach. Many multinational democracies have done so (Stepan 1999).[9]

Concepts

Even though asymmetric federalism has become a commonly used term, its meaning is not always clear and several dimensions need to be considered. To begin with, one can distinguish between *de jure* asymmetric treatment as opposed to *de facto* asymmetric treatment. In the first case, decentralization laws treat some regions more advantageously, such as providing them with wider revenue powers than other regions. In the second case, the advantage comes from how laws are actually implemented, basically discriminating in favour of or against particular regions by, for example, channelling additional funds to some regions in an ad hoc or nontransparent manner.

Another useful differentiation is between asymmetric treatment *ex ante* versus asymmetric treatment *ex post*. Asymmetric federalism implies the unequal treatment of regions *ex ante*, with regions having different powers and privileges for being what they are. *Ex post* most regions will almost certainly fair differently, because of the many other factors that affect outcomes in addition to the institutional policy framework provided by the central government.

Asymmetric federalism can manifest itself in different aspects of decentralization. For example, as concerns political decentralization, some regions may have more autonomy than others to legislate and use the trappings of nationhood. In relation to administrative decentralization, regions may have different powers to set salaries and fire and hire personnel. In the case of fiscal decentralization, regions may have different revenue and expenditure assignments.[10]

Benefits

Asymmetric federalism can be used to accommodate diverse and more or less permanent preferences and appetites for autonomy across regions. Often the different demands for autonomy are based on regions' particular history (McLure, Wallich and Litvack 1996). Asymmetric federalism can also be used to accommodate different regional administrative capabilities and state of readiness for decentralized management (Garcia-Milá and McGuire, Chapter 7 in this volume). In the case of Russia, asymmetric fiscal arrangements appear to have arisen more from political considerations than from efficiency considerations. By accommodating different desires for regional autonomy and political independence, asymmetric federalism fit the early demands for independence by a number of ethnic republics. While Russian regions have quite different administrative capabilities, this never seemed to be a driving force for asymmetric federalism. Asymmetric federalism has also been explained as a way to address conflicts of interest and growing divergence between richer regions with stronger economic bases and more incentives to resist interregional distributions and poorer regions that are highly dependent on central transfers (Freinkman and Haney 1997). Naturally regions with fewer resources are more inclined to oppose asymmetric decentralization because the asymmetry will likely protect the interests of the wealthier regions. This process has no doubt played a role in Russia.

Stepan (1999) makes an interesting point from a cultural and linguistic perspective. He argues that some groups of individuals in a country may only be able to participate fully as individual citizens if they acquire particular rights as a group. For example, the rights to schooling, media access and freedom of religious practice correspond to the groups' rights to use its own language and culture, therefore these different needs and preferences give rise to asymmetric treatment in democratic environments. Initial conditions matter in these interpretations. For example, is the right to use a regional language an example of asymmetric treatment or is the prohibition against using a regional language an example of asymmetric treatment?

Costs

Asymmetric federalism obviously offers some advantages, whether temporary or more permanent, but not without costs. One cost is philosophical, in the sense that asymmetry means an absence of equal rights across the country. For example, if the republic of Tatarstan is allowed to retain a higher share of revenues than other regions, its citizens may receive a higher level of public services than residents in other regions. Asymmetry also tends to diminish the central government's ability to pursue national objectives, such as revenue mobilization for the delivery of services at the national level, or its ability to implement equalization at the subnational level. The asymmetric treatment of regions is often associated with a lack of transparency and with complex administrative relationships. A good example is the secret bilateral treaties the Russian federal government struck with many regions in the mid-1990s.

THE PRACTICE OF ASYMMETRIC FEDERALISM IN RUSSIA

Asymmetric federalism has played an important role in Russian federalism. From the start, asymmetric federalism played a crucial role in the struggle to keep the Russian Federation together. What followed were different manifestations of asymmetric federalism, including customized bilateral treaties between the centre and the regions and an intense constitutional debate about the nature of the Russian Federation (Lynn and Novikov 1997). Fundamentally, however, asymmetric federalism started for pragmatic reasons. De facto asymmetry arose simply from the fact that several regions were demanding more autonomy and disregarding federal laws and the central authorities were incapable of enforcing federal laws.[11]

The most intense demands and declarations of independence were coming from ethnic republics such as Tatarstan, Bahskiria and Chechnya. While in the case of Tatarstan and Bahskiria the situation was managed through the negotiation of treaties with the federal government as early as 1993, in the case of Chechnya it led to a bloody civil war. A number of natural resource-rich regions, for example, Sakha (Yakutia) and Tyumen, demanded special arrangements and treatment on the basis that they had been exploited for their natural resources, which had resulted in environmental degradation, and had never benefited from their wealth. Less aggressive in their demands, at least at the beginning of the transition, were the industrially well endowed and generally wealthier regions, but later on these regions joined the chorus of complaining regions, in their case arguing about being forced to subsidize poorer regions.

These different treatments became *de jure* asymmetric treatment when the new 1993 constitution made asymmetric treatment legal and standard. Legally, asymmetric arrangements were also formalized in the different charters and constitutions of the regions, and in the case of many republics, their national constitutions appeared to be at odds with the constitution of the Russian Federation (Lynn and Novikov 1997). The regional charters and constitutions used a different definition of the bilateral relationship between the regions and the centre, especially in relation to specific arrangements relating to revenue and expenditure assignments.

After some six or seven years of transition, asymmetric federalism was being slowly but surely dismantled, a trend that started in the closing years of the Yeltsin presidency and accelerated after Putin became president. Indeed, one of Putin's first important moves was to cut back the power of regional governors, including assigning himself the authority to remove incompliant governors from office. This section takes a closer view of how asymmetric federalism has evolved in the Russian Federation. Russia's experience may provide one of the richest examples of asymmetric federalism, with all the advantages and disadvantages that come with it.

Russia's Path to Asymmetric Fiscal Relations, 1992–93

In the early years of the Yeltsin presidency (1992–93), pressures to contain and mitigate powerful centrifugal forces dominated intergovernmental fiscal relations. Many regions were attempting to position themselves to benefit as much as possible from the political and institutional weaknesses of the centre at this stage of the transition. These same regions often flaunted federal laws, and by doing so, imposed explicit costs and negative externalities on other regions. The federal authorities' desire to find conditions acceptable to troublemaking regions inevitably led to different forms of asymmetric fiscal federalism.[12]

Regional assertiveness, especially on the part of the ethnic republics, reached its peak during 1992–93, when Yeltsin and the Supreme Soviet (parliament) were involved in a power struggle. Even thought the Federation Treaty of March 1992 gave the ethnic republics some additional powers, the 1993 constitution took these powers away. However, the constitution itself opened the door to new forms of asymmetric treatment by virtue of allowing bilateral treaties between the federation and regional governments.

To a large extent, the asymmetric federalism of the early years of the transition was *de facto*. The regions ignored or disobeyed federal laws, in particular, several important laws enacted during the early period of transition, such as the 1991 Law on the Foundations of the Tax System in the Russian Federation (Igudin 1998; Lavrov 1998; Wallich 1994). The ambiguity of the 1993 constitution about such fundamental questions as the inalienable rights of the regions did not help the situation (Teague 1996), and these important issues were left to be decided in practice.

By allowing the federal government to enter into secret bilateral treaties with regional governments, the 1993 constitution legalized the practice of asymmetric federalism, and this became reality through the allegedly favourable treatment given to the ethnic republics of Tatarstan and Bashkortostan in the first two treaties. This fits the view that the federal government provided systematically more advantages and privileges to the politically difficult regions to bribe the regional opposition and tame centrifugal forces. In short, Moscow has tended to reward rather than punish defiant regions. As Wallich (1994) and others argue, this type of response created an asymmetric federalist system starting in 1992 whereby, according to Lavrov (1995), a pattern was established that favoured the 21 ethnic republics over the other regions in the form of larger subsidies, permission to retain a higher share of tax collection, and special decrees granting economic benefits. While in early

1992 just a few regions had stopped or greatly reduced their remittances to the federal government, namely, Tatarstan, Chechnya, Sakha (Yakutia) and Bashkortostan, by the end of 1992 similar problems had arisen with 20 regions, and by 1993, this number had increased to 30 regions (Wallich 1994).

Asymmetric Relations in 1994–97

The 1993 constitution's formal acceptance of asymmetric relations through bilateral treaties—which covered such issues as budgetary relations, state property, ownership and use of natural resources and migration—restored some predictability and order to the system of intergovernmental fiscal relations. While confrontations between the federal government and some regions continued to test the federation's strength during this period, the nature of these confrontations tended to shift from centrifugal tensions towards a competition between the regions for special recognition and favourable fiscal arrangements.

The constitution declared all subjects of the federation equal, although it also granted the ethnic republics special rights, such as passing their own constitutions. However, the constitution gave basically the same rights in one form or another to all the regions.[13]

While the bilateral treaties provided an official acknowledgement of regional power, the general pattern of behaviour among the regions became less chaotic and threatening to Russia's unity with the notable exception of Chechnya. Another sign of the regions' power during this period was the regional governments' absolute discretion to organize their relationships with their local governments.

One central feature of the asymmetric treatment of the regions during this period was that not all the regions had a bilateral treaty with the federal government. Indeed, other regions' growing resentment against the ethnic republics had become apparent and not surprising. In 1995, many other regional governments tried and succeeded in getting bilateral treaties with Moscow. Although concessions granted to some regions affected bargaining with other regions, not all treaties came out the same (Solnick 1995).

Many observers have concluded that the problems with Russian federalism during this time were the manifestation of a weak federal government, the absence of cooperation between the centre and the regions and a common pool (or 'tragedy of the commons') problem. This is a main theme in Blanchard and Shleifer (2000); Lavrov, Litwack and Sutherland (2000); and OECD (2000). Blanchard and Shleifer (2000), in particular, emphasize that the contrast between the success of China's transition versus the failure of Russia's occurred because China was able to retain a strong political centre.

Mending Russia's fiscal federalism problems required strengthening the political and institutional power of the centre relative to the regions (see also the discussion in Martinez-Vazquez and Boex 2001; Shleifer and Treisman 2000), and Russia would have to wait until Putin's election as president for a significant turnaround in the relationships between the centre and the regions. However, the situation may have involved more than a weak centre. For example, de Figueiredo, Rui and Weingast (2001) observe that a problem with Russian federalism was the lack of appropriately defined limits on the central government. They maintain that in some way the federal government was too strong, given its ability to change rules pertaining to and extract rents from the regions, which detracted from the regions' perceptions of benefits resulting from participation in the federal relationship. From this perspective, solving the problem of noncooperation required not only more power for the centre, but simultaneously credible limits on the centre, which had acted and could continue to act without self-restraint in the pursuit of its own interests. For example, at the start of the transition the federal government dumped expenditure responsibilities on the regions without adequate funding and has continued to control virtually all tax and regulatory powers, while the regions depend on the centre for most of their budget funding and are therefore subject to the whims of federal authorities.

Retreat from Special Treatment: Yeltsin 1998–99

In addition to generating mistrust and resentment among the regions, asymmetric federalism in general, and the bilateral treaties in particular, had other significant costs. One of them was the mounting fiscal pressure on the federal budget that became increasingly noticeable during the first six months of 1998 (see, for example, World Bank 2001). The conflicting budget demands at the regional and federal levels and the federal government's inability to collect revenues eventually resulted in a federal deficit as high as 10 per cent of gross domestic product. At the same time, both the federal and regional governments continued to borrow heavily domestically and abroad. All levels of government also proceeded to accumulate payment arrears while becoming more frequent users of mutual settlements (noncash offsets) and barter. The combination of increased deficits, tight money supply and fixed exchange rates led to the August 1998 crisis, with the devaluation and floating of the ruble and the federal government's default of most of its domestic debt, which in turn precipitated a banking crisis.

The August 1998 crisis provided the federal government with an opportunity to re-evaluate its policies on many fronts, including its budgetary relationships with the regions. One of the issues examined was the role the bilateral treaties had played in the crisis. This examination showed that the special fiscal treatment provisions in the treaties had contributed to the mounting fiscal pressures that eventually led to the crisis. Undoing the damage caused by the bilateral treaties and special deals proved difficult. Nevertheless, the retreat from asymmetric treatment clearly started in the late Yeltsin years by the federal government simply not always complying with provisions in the treaties. At this time, the federal government also started a serious recentralization of fiscal resources (Martinez-Vazquez and Boex 2001). These efforts involved introducing deeper tax reforms that eventually included the Tax Code, the Budget Code, the Law on the Financial Foundations of Local Self-Government and the so-called concept of reform of intergovernmental relations in the Russian Federation for 1999–2001. Another law, the Law on the Principles for the Demarcation of Jurisdictions and Powers, enacted in June 1999, clearly restated the supremacy of the federal constitution, federal legislation and federal decrees over regional constitutions, legislation and decrees. One clear feature of all these documents was the new willingness of the federal government to intervene in fiscal arrangements between regional governments and their local governments.

The Putin Era: 2000–02

Putin came to power in March 2000 with what now seems a clear mandate to control the regional governments and re-assert the role of the federal authorities. For example, in May 2000, the Chief Prosecutor's Office declared that 60 regions had local laws, including regional charters or constitutions, that seriously contradicted federal laws, and in June 2000, Putin's appointed chief prosecutor gave the regions one month to synchronize their laws with federal laws.

This was just the beginning. Following his election, Putin took a number of steps to strengthen the federal position in relation to the regional governments. In May 2000, he issued a decree that divided Russia into seven groups of regions (the federal districts), each with a presidential envoy (or plenipotentiary) to monitor regional legislation and ensure that regional administrations were abiding by federal laws. Furthermore, the State Duma (or lower house of parliament) approved legislation that gave the Russian president the power to suspend regional legislation that conflicted with federal law, as well as the power to dismiss regional governors if their actions were judged to be in violation of federal statutes. The makeup of the Federation Council, the upper chamber of parliament, was redone by replacing the governors with regional representatives elected by the regional legislatures. In the past, as members of the Federation Council the regional governors had often played an obstructionist role. These legal changes gave the federal authorities effective instruments to deal with even the most recalcitrant regions, excluding Chechnya. The best evidence that the federal government has regained much authority is that Tatarstan is adopting amendments to its constitution to bring it closer in line with the Russian constitution and other legislation (East West Institute 2002a). Nevertheless, some regions are resisting, for example, Bashkortostan is holding on to its declaration of sovereignty and President Murtaza Rakhimov has run for office a third time on his sovereignty platform (East West Institute 2002b).

Putin's administration continued the recentralization of revenues that had started in the late years of the Yeltsin administration. Following his election to the presidency, Putin managed to get four chapters of the second part of the Tax Code approved by the State Duma, which had a profound impact on regional finances. Subnational government turnover taxes, which provided a substantial level of own source revenues for local and regional governments, were substantially reduced and are scheduled to be eliminated, and the overhaul of the personal income tax also reduced subnational revenues.

HOW WELL DID ASYMMETRIC FEDERALISM WORK?

Given the significant differences among Russia's regions, including different demands for fiscal and political autonomy, and the extremely weak institutions at the federal level, allowing asymmetric decentralization was the right thing to do. But what is interesting about Russia's experience with asymmetric federalism is that its practice was not at first a voluntary or conscious policy choice by the federal authorities. Instead, as noted earlier, asymmetric policies were forced onto the federal government by the unilateral actions of some regional governments. After a while, asymmetric federalism was formally adopted in the constitution approved in 1993 as an explicit and deliberate policy of the federal government. In recent years, the trend has been reversed, with deliberate efforts made to eliminate the most important manifestations of asymmetric federalism.

The difficult question is whether asymmetric federalism was a cure for national frailties or a poison of the national body politic. The answer is that it was probably both a cure and a poison at different times during the transition. Initially, the asymmetric treatment of regions served to stem the enormous centrifugal forces in operation at the start of the transition. The positive results occurred at a time when federal institutions were weak and unable to enforce its national laws (Solnick 1995). Its fear of being unable to enforce legislation may have caused the federal government to consider bilateral negotiations as a solution. Thus Moscow's strategy of buying consent from the regions was largely imposed by circumstances and was the only democratic way out. Prior to the introduction of the bilateral treaties, Moscow was having a hard time holding the country together. Separatist threats and resistance to federal policies by a group of regional governments were constant.

The bilateral treaties had the strategic effect of weakening any coordinated action and demands by the ethnic republics that had been most antagonistic to Moscow. The treaties are also widely acknowledged as having prevented the secession of some of those ethnic republics, such as Tatarstan.[14]

The net impact of asymmetric federalism in the first half of the transition decade was probably to rein in the powerful centrifugal forces that existed in Russia at that time.[15] Naturally, we cannot know how things would have developed if different decisions at been made at the time. For example, the conflict in Chechnya undoubtedly had a profound impact on the scope and depth of other regions' demands. Thus the moderating effects of asymmetric federalism may have resulted from how Moscow handled the Chechnya conflict. From early on, many in Moscow appeared to view the conflict in Chechnya as the line in the sand for the future viability of the Russian Federation. The supporters of armed intervention emphasized the need to bring the secessionist leadership to heel to prevent the break-up of the entire country (Lapidus 1999).

However, what had been a solution to a serious problem soon turned into a serious problem itself. Asymmetric treatment of what were supposed to be equal subjects of the federation rapidly gave rise to resentment, lack of solidarity and noncooperative behaviour by the regions, leading to a situation akin to the tragedy of the commons. A weakened federal government was unable to stop this process. By 1995–96, asymmetric federalism was increasingly poisoning the national fabric. Because of asymmetric federalism, almost all the regions had an incentive to deviate from cooperative behaviour and press for special treatment with the federal authorities or try to take matters into their own hands, such as illegally retaining federal revenues (see Eckardt 2002 for a discussion of some of these issues). For many observers, large and sustained federal budget deficits, the federal government's inability to impose fiscal discipline and the financial crisis of 1998 were all associated with the form of fiscal federalism practiced. The privileged treatment of some regions was an important flaw in Russia's federalism that had to be changed as disparities grew in terms of the quality and quantity of public services (Martinez-Vazquez and Boex 2001). In this respect, the dilemma the government faced is familiar to any country trying to develop its regions in a balanced way. Maintaining living standards in all regions may actually retard overall economic development. Perhaps a more important manifestation of the system's inadequate performance was the extensive failure to harmonize regional and national interests: a number of regions and their governors appeared to be willing to inflict high costs on the rest of the country for minimal gains to themselves.

Not long after the crisis of August 1998, consensus arose about the need to retreat from the asymmetric treatment of the regions and to rein in regional governors. Even though the federal government tried to do this in the later years of the Yeltsin administration, it did not happen until Putin's election as president.

WHAT DOES THE FUTURE HOLD?

Russia's system of fiscal federalism will continue to evolve in the future. The Russian Federation is still a young country, as reflected by its system of fiscal decentralization. Of course, international trends affect Russia as much as they do other countries, and one of these trends is globalization. As some regions increase their commercial links with other parts of the world, the value of the domestic market and other common domestic institutions may be diminished for these regions, resulting in more centrifugal pressures, especially in the far-flung areas such as the Far East, the North Caucasian and the Northwest areas, although for the present the main beneficiaries of globalization have been the city and oblast of Moscow, neither of which are likely to adopt a separatist agenda. At the same time, international trade increases the federal government's leverage through its control of customs, pipelines, railroads and so on. Thus, for example, shipments of oil from landlocked Tatarstan are entirely in the hands of the federal authorities. In the past, Moscow has refused to issue import-export licenses to companies headquartered in troubled regions or threatened to close oil pipelines.

On the domestic front, several important issues will take centre stage in the immediate future. How the federal government addresses these issues will define Russia's fiscal federalism in the decades to come. The first issue is asymmetric federalism and the status of the bilateral treaties. After several years of Putin's administration, as noted earlier, the need for asymmetric federalism has been put into question. When running for president in early 2000, Putin was clear about his intentions to restore and strengthen the authority of the federal government over the regions. He has kept this election promise. Most regions have ceased to act from a 'what can we get' perspective and have begun to ask 'what can we keep' from the concessions won during the past seven or eight years. Thus the regional mavericks are in retreat, but they are far from defeated. In relation to the bilateral treaties, the official view in Moscow during the Putin administration years has been that they are an important impediment to the rationalization and reform of intergovernmental fiscal relations. While some regional governors renounced their bilateral treaties with Moscow soon after Putin had made his opposition to them public, others adamantly refused to give them up. Not surprisingly, ethnic and richer regions have been more likely to try to keep their treaties with Moscow in place. In his annual address to the State Duma in April 2002, Putin reiterated his position that the bilateral treaties signed 'behind the backs' of the other regions have outlived their usefulness. He also made the point that if any of these treaties remain in place, they should be approved by the State Duma so that 'everyone knows who has what preferences and why'.

The second issue is the growing fiscal disparity and whether national solidarity can address this. Economic disparities will probably continue to increase, because of the sites selected for domestic and foreign investment and because of the concentration of natural resources. In turn, pressure on the federal budget to redress the imbalances will also increase. Inevitably, regardless of the form the equalization system takes, the additional resources will have to come from the better-off regions. The question is how much tolerance these regions will exhibit towards poorer regions, which in some cases the richer regions may perceive as inefficient or corrupt. Without support from the richer regions, it will become harder for the federal government to undertake effective equalization, but growing disparities and concentrations of poverty will pose political risks, especially at the periphery of the country. Putin's popularity and his ability to maintain good relations with the regions and the State Duma may stave off these tendencies for some time, but the underlying problems are unlikely to dissipate and could flare up.

The third issue is whether the federal government will intervene any further in the restructuring of the relationships between regional and local governments. The current administration continues to stress its strong support for local governments, and the federal government has worked on several proposals to provide separate assignments at the local level. How these will translate into concrete legislation on fiscal issues, such as separate revenue and expenditure assignments or mandated formula transfers, remains to be seen. Of course, if approved such changes would weaken the grip of regional governments and governors over local governments.

The fourth issue is whether the federal government will push for administrative and political reform in the regions. Consolidation of the regions into fewer regions, which would not only reduce administrative costs, but could also help address the need for asymmetric arrangements and for fiscal equalization, is an issue that has been discussed for some time. In particular, a series of proposals originating with the State Duma suggest either allowing regions to merge on a voluntary basis or forcing them to merge. The most repeated proposal is the elimination of the ten AOs and one autonomous oblast and their assimilation by the surrounding oblasts and krays. Many have interpreted Putin's recent creation of the seven federal districts headed by directly appointed plenipotentiaries as the first step towards regional consolidation. However, even more recently, Putin has made it clear that he does not want the federal districts to develop into quasi states or quasi republics. Thus far, the federal districts have been used to de-concentrate federal power and exercise more active and effective supervision of the regions' actions.

An important recent development in relation to fiscal federalism was Putin's appointment of a high-level commission in 2001, known as the Kozak Commission, to redefine and reform intergovernmental fiscal relations. The commission issued recommendations in September 2002, but Putin decided to send the recommendations to the State Council, a consultative body, for further consideration before sending any bills to parliament. These recommendations include the need to adequately fund each level of government according to its assigned expenditure responsibilities, which may be interpreted as more money and tax autonomy for subnational governments. The increase in revenue autonomy will not negate the need for transfers, because only a tiny minority of Russia's 13 000 local governments have enough money to meet or exceed their present expenses with their current revenue assignments).

One of the most divisive issues is the reassignment of revenues from taxes from natural resources. The Kozak Commission report appears to argue that these revenues should be recentralized and then redistributed more fairly among the regions. Furthermore, the commission recommends abandoning the so-called two key practice, whereby both federal and regional governments must provide licenses for the exploitation of natural resources, for full and exclusive federal control. Naturally the natural resource-rich regions are completely opposed to this suggestion.

Russia has made a remarkable journey over the past decade. It has returned from the brink of disintegration and chaos to become a young, but still fragile, democracy. The challenge for the future remains, however, to find the appropriate balance between the rights of the regions, including respect for and acceptance of their diversity, and a federal government capable of enforcing the law and protecting and defending common national interests. Whether this balance can be maintained in the future without the asymmetric treatment of the regions and with respect for basic democratic principles remains to be seen.

Appendix: Key features of regions, selected years

Name of area	Area, 2000 (thousands of km²)	Population, 2000 (thousands of people)	Population density, 2000 (people per km²)	GRP, 1998 (Rub thousands)	GRP per capita, 1998 (Rub thousands)	Percentage of area	Percentage of population	Percentage of GDP
Northern Area	1466.3	5668	3.9	110 383	19.1	8.59	3.88	4.59
Karelia	172.4	766	4.4	11 306	14.6	1.01	0.52	0.47
Komi	415.9	1135	2.7	28 350	24.4	2.44	0.78	1.18
Arkhangel oblast	410.7	1414	3.4	22 763	15.3	2.41	0.97	0.95
Nenetsky AO	176.7	46	0.3	—	—	1.03	0.03	—
Vologot oblast	145.7	1324	9.1	24 118	18.0	0.85	0.91	1.00
Murmansk oblast	144.9	983	6.8	23 847	23.4	0.85	0.67	0.99
Northwestern Area	197.1	7898	40.1	126 866	15.9	1.15	5.41	5.28
St Petersburg	0.6	4694	7823.3	89 781	18.9	0.00	3.22	3.74
Leningrad oblast	85.9	1674	19.5	21 171	12.6	0.50	1.15	0.88
Novgorod	55.3	729	13.2	9402	12.7	0.32	0.50	0.39
Pskov	55.3	801	14.5	6512	7.9	0.32	0.55	0.27
Central Area	484.0	29 361	60.7	615 670	20.8	2.83	20.12	25.63
Bryan oblast	34.9	1443	41.3	11 884	8.1	0.20	0.99	0.49
Vladimir oblast	29.0	1609	55.5	15 995	9.8	0.17	1.10	0.67
Ivanov oblast	21.8	1222	56.1	9050	7.3	0.13	0.84	0.38

Kaluzh oblast	29.9	1081	36.2	10 916	10.0	0.18	0.74	0.45
Kostroma oblast	60.1	786	13.1	8882	11.1	0.35	0.54	0.37
Moscow	1.0	8631	8631.0	362 520	42.0	0.01	5.91	15.09
Moscow oblast	47.0	6511	138.5	100 612	15.3	0.28	4.46	4.19
Orlov oblast	24.7	899	36.4	10 246	11.3	0.14	0.62	0.43
Ryazan oblast	39.6	1284	32.4	14 186	10.9	0.23	0.88	0.59
Smolensk oblast	49.8	1133	22.8	12 234	10.6	0.29	0.78	0.51
Tver	84.1	1602	19.0	17 747	10.9	0.49	1.10	0.74
Tul oblast	25.7	1746	67.9	19 051	10.7	0.15	1.20	0.79
Yaroslav oblast	36.4	1414	38.8	22 348	15.6	0.21	0.97	0.93
Volgo-Vyatsk Area	265.4	8292	31.2	97 686	11.7	1.55	5.68	4.07
Mariy El	23.2	759	32.7	6568	8.6	0.14	0.52	0.27
Mordoviya	26.2	929	35.5	9323	9.9	0.15	0.64	0.39
Chuvashiya	18.3	1357	74.2	12 123	8.9	0.11	0.93	0.50
Kirov oblast	120.8	1589	13.2	16 931	10.5	0.71	1.09	0.70
Nizhegorod	76.9	3658	47.6	52 741	14.3	0.45	2.51	2.20
Central Chernozem Area	167.7	7781	46.4	87 858	11.2	0.98	5.33	3.66
Belgorod	27.1	1497	55.2	19 609	13.2	0.16	1.03	0.82
Voronezh	52.4	2459	46.9	23 907	9.6	0.31	1.69	1.00
Kursk	29.8	1316	44.2	16 827	12.6	0.17	0.90	0.70
Lipetsk	24.1	1240	51.5	17 043	13.7	0.14	0.85	0.71
Tambov	34.3	1269	37.0	10 472	8.1	0.20	0.87	0.44

Appendix (continued)

Name of area	Area, 2000 (thousands of km²)	Population, 2000 (thousands of people)	Population density, 2000 (people per km²)	GRP, 1998 (Rub thousands)	GRP per capita, 1998 (Rub thousands)	Percentage of area	Percentage of population	Percentage of GDP
Povolzhsk Area	536.4	16 805	31.3	240 021	14.2	3.14	11.52	9.99
Kalmykiya	76.1	316	4.2	1704	5.4	0.45	0.22	0.07
Tatarstan	68.0	3779	55.6	67 700	17.9	0.40	2.59	2.82
Astrakhan	44.1	1024	23.2	10 773	10.5	0.26	0.70	0.45
Volgograd	113.9	2678	23.5	30 907	11.4	0.67	1.84	1.29
Penza	43.2	1531	35.4	11 131	7.2	0.25	1.05	0.46
Samara	53.6	3297	61.5	72 662	22.0	0.31	2.26	3.02
Saratov	100.2	2712	27.1	28 663	10.5	0.59	1.86	1.19
Ulyanov oblast	37.3	1468	39.4	16 482	11.1	0.22	1.01	0.69
North Caucasian Area	374.4	17 677	47.2	148 653	8.4	2.19	12.11	6.19
Adygeya	7.6	449	59.1	3384	7.5	0.04	0.31	0.14
Dagestan	50.3	2149	42.7	8652	4.1	0.29	1.47	0.36
Ingushetiya	19.3	488	25.3	1053	3.4	0.11	0.33	0.04
Chechnya	12.5	574	45.9	—	—	0.07	0.39	—
Kabardino-Balkar	14.1	792	56.2	6361	8.0	0.08	0.54	0.26
Karachaevo-Cherkes	8.0	435	54.4	2854	6.5	0.05	0.30	0.12
Alaniya	19.3	674	34.9	4142	6.2	0.11	0.46	0.17

Krasnodar	76.0	5067	66.7	53 732	10.6	0.45	3.47	2.24
Stavropol	66.5	2691	40.5	28 591	10.7	0.39	1.84	1.19
Rostov	100.8	4358	43.2	39 886	9.1	0.59	2.99	1.66
Ural Area	824.0	20 321	24.7	306 038	15.0	4.83	13.93	12.74
Bashkortostan	143.6	4117	28.7	64 191	15.6	0.84	2.82	2.67
Udmurtiya	42.1	1633	38.8	20 014	12.2	0.25	1.12	0.83
Kurgan	71.0	1097	15.5	9684	8.8	0.42	0.75	0.40
Orenburg	124.0	2224	17.9	28 770	12.9	0.73	1.52	1.20
Perm	127.7	2814	22.0	55 594	18.6	0.75	1.93	2.31
Komi-Permyatsky AO	32.9	152	4.6	—	—	0.19	0.10	—
Sverdlov	194.8	4612	23.7	80 675	17.3	1.14	3.16	3.36
Chelyabinsk	87.9	3672	41.8	47 110	12.8	0.51	2.52	1.96
West Siberia Area	2427.2	15 040	6.2	356 823	23.6	14.21	10.31	14.85
Altay	92.6	205	2.2	1634	8.1	0.54	0.14	0.07
Altaysky Kray	169.1	2653	15.7	22 411	8.4	0.99	1.82	0.93
Kemerovskaya oblast	95.5	2987	31.3	45 644	15.1	0.56	2.05	1.90
Novosibirk oblast	178.2	2744	15.4	35 231	12.8	1.04	1.88	1.47
Omsk oblast	139.7	2163	15.5	29 466	13.5	0.82	1.48	1.23
Tomsk	316.9	1067	3.4	21 232	19.8	1.86	0.73	0.88
Tyumen	161.8	1358	8.4	201 206	62.7	0.95	0.93	8.38
Khanty-Mansiysky AO	523.1	1368	2.6	—	—	3.06	0.94	—
Yamalo Nenetsky AO	750.3	495	0.7	—	—	4.39	0.34	—

Name of area	Area, 2000 (thousands of km²)	Population, 2000 (thousands of people)	Population density, 2000 (people per km²)	GRP, 1998 (Rub thousands)	GRP per capita, 1998 (Rub thousands)	Percentage of area	Percentage of population	Percentage of GDP
East Siberia Area	4122.8	8973	2.2	158 566	17.5	24.14	6.15	6.60
Buryatiya	351.3	1035	2.9	11 167	10.7	2.06	0.71	0.46
Tuva	170.5	311	1.8	1847	6.0	1.00	0.21	0.08
Khakassiya	61.9	581	9.4	8192	14.0	0.36	0.40	0.34
Krasnoyarsk kray	710.0	2978	4.2	71 548	23.2	4.16	2.04	2.98
Taimyrsk AO	862.1	43	0.0	—	—	5.05	0.03	—
Evenkiysk AO	767.6	18	0.0	—	—	4.50	0.01	—
Irkutsk Oblast	745.5	2604	3.5	52 620	19.0	4.37	1.78	2.19
Byryatsk AO	22.4	144	6.4	—	—	0.13	0.10	—
Chitinsk oblast	412.5	1180	2.9	13 191	10.3	2.42	0.81	0.55
Aginsky AO	19.0	79	4.2	—	—	0.11	0.05	—
Far Eastern Area	6231.0	7160	1.1	153 717	21.0	36.49	4.91	6.40
Sakha	3103.2	977	0.3	33 375	33.3	18.17	0.67	1.39
Evreyskaya AO	36.0	199	5.5	1832	8.9	0.21	0.14	0.08
Chukotsk AO	737.7	72	0.1	2593	32.0	4.32	0.05	0.11
Primorsk kray	165.9	2174	13.1	31 473	14.2	0.97	1.49	1.31
Khabarovsk kray	788.6	1518	1.9	30 073	19.5	4.62	1.04	1.25
Amursk oblast	363.7	1006	2.8	14 739	14.4	2.13	0.69	0.61

Kamchatska oblast	170.8	354	2.1	11 136	28.1	1.00	0.24	0.46
Koryaksk AO	301.5	29	0.1	—	—	1.77	0.02	—
Magadan oblast	461.4	233	0.5	6735	27.4	2.70	0.16	0.28
Sakhalin oblast	87.1	598	6.9	13 100	21.1	0.51	0.41	0.55
Kaliningrad oblast	15.1	949	62.8	8659	9.2	0.09	0.65	0.36
Russian Federation	17 075.4	145 925	8.5	2 402 280	16.3	100.0	100.0	100.0
Maximum	3103.2	8631	8631.0	362 520	62.7	18.17	5.91	15.09
Minimum	0.6	18	0.0	1053	3.4	0.00	0.01	0.04

— Not available.
AO Autonomous okrug.
GDP Gross domestic product.
GRP Gross regional product.

Source: Goskomstat data.

NOTES

1. Oblast is a name for the subnational entity in several Slavic languages. The word kray (which also means border or end), is used for regions located along the economic and geographic periphery. Okrug is a Slavic adaptation or translation from German kreis, a term that denotes administrative subdivision. The autonomous okrugs are administered as separate parts of the oblasts and krays, but for reporting and statistical purposes, the autonomous okrugs are often incorporated into the surrounding oblast or kray.
2. In June 2001, the federal government and the World Bank agreed to a loan of US$80 million to resettle inhabitants of the far north to reduce the needs for public support. Helping the same families in other parts of Russia with more moderate climates and better access to public services is definitely cheaper than helping them if they remain in the far north.
3. In Soviet times, the authorities enforced restrictions on internal mobility by issuing residency permits and internal passports.
4. There is, of course, rich history to accompany each ethnic republic and AO. For example, Tatarstan, one of the most colourful and assertive ethnic regions, has been part of Russia since 1552, when Czar Ivan the Terrible entered Kazan, the capital, defeating the khanate of Kazan.
5. The red belt consists of those predominantly agricultural and nonurban regions that consistently voted for the Communist Party during the transition. Berkowitz and DeJong (1998) find evidence of virtual internal borders in these regions, explained by their protective and centrally controlled economic policies.
6. Unlike the enterprise profit tax, which is a federal tax shared with subnational governments, the sales tax and the enterprise assets tax are 100 per cent local taxes (and therefore not shown in Table 8.7). The federal government eliminated the (local) sales tax in 2004.
7. Remember that tax sharing is not considered to be part of the equalization transfers.
8. Note that differences in findings may reflect the use of different definitions of transfers. For example, Popov (2002) uses a more comprehensive definition of transfers than Treisman (1996).
9. Some multinational democracies assign different legal, linguistic and cultural competencies to their regions, for instance, Belgium, Canada, India, Russia and Spain.
10. In the case of transfers, even under perfectly symmetric federalism, regions will receive different amounts, reflecting differences in need, capacity and so on. Transfers are a complex, grey area in terms of asymmetric federalism. Formula-driven and objective procedures to determine transfers may be considered symmetrical treatment *ex ante;* however, in many countries equalization formulas have been reshaped and twisted to accommodate the interests of particular regions.
11. McLure, Wallich and Litvack (1996) report that by mid-1992, some 20 regions had unilaterally declared that they alone would decide what portion of taxes their regions would share with the federal government, the so called single channel arrangement, and by mid-1993 some 30 regions had done so. Naturally these sharing rates were lower than those the Ministry of Finance had in mind.
12. To some extent, asymmetric federalism was also practiced in the Soviet Union, because subnational budgets were customized on the basis of negotiated expenditure norms, regulated revenue sharing rates and negotiated transfers.
13. In particular, article 77 of the constitution establishes that the regions will determine their system of government, but must follow federal principles of legislative and executive powers, which requires direct election of the head of government, something that many of the ethnic republics were already doing. In 2004, President Putin announced plans to return to the old system of having heads of regional governments appointed from the centre.
14. According to an article in the *New York Times* (9 March 2000), long-standing Tatarstan President Mintimer Shaimiyev maintains that the push towards sovereignty, and even the flaunting of the Russian constitution in the first years of the transition, defused Tatarstan's seething nationalist sentiment. That produced much better results than Chechnya's attempt to break away by means of armed resistance. See also the discussions in Freinkman and Haney (1997) and Treisman (1996).
15. However, not everyone agrees on the effectiveness of the asymmetric federalism as practiced. In the view of Ordeshook (1995) and Polishchuk (1996), the political system failed to

accommodate the regions' diverse economic and political interests, which during the Yeltsin years led to more political conflict and economic instability than was necessary.

REFERENCES

The word 'processed' describes informally reproduced works that may not be commonly available in libraries.

Ahrend, Rudiger (2000), 'Speed of Reform, Initial Conditions, Political Orientation, or What? Explaining Russian Regions' Economic Performance', Working Paper no. 2, Russian-European Centre for Economic Policy, Moscow.

Berkowitz, Daniel and David N. DeJong (1998), 'Russia's Internal Borders', University of Pittsburgh, Pittsburgh, PA, processed.

Blanchard, Olivier and Andrei Shleifer (2000), 'Federalism With and Without Political Centralization: China Versus Russia', Working Paper, Massachusetts Institute of Technology, Cambridge, MA.

Broadman, Harry G. and Francesca Recanatini (2001), 'Where Has All the Foreign Investment Gone in Russia?' World Bank, Washington, DC, processed.

de Figueiredo, Rui J. P. and Barry R. Weingast (2001), 'Constructing Self-Enforcing Federalism in the Early United States and Modern Russia,' Stanford University, Palo Alto, CA, processed.

de Melo, Martha, Gur Ofer and Plamen Yossifov (1999), 'Transition in Regional Capitals Along the Volga', *Post-Soviet Geography and Economics*, 40 (8), 553–616.

Eckardt, Sebastian (2002), 'Russia's Market Distorting Federalism: Decentralization, Governance, and Economic Performance in Russia in the 90s', Working Paper No. 42, Eastern Europe Institute of the Free University of Berlin, Berlin.

East West Institute (2002a), *Russian Regional Report,* 7 (7).

——— (2002b), *Russian Regional Report,* 7 (12) 7.

Freinkman, Lev and Michael Haney (1997), 'What Affects the Russian Regional Governments' Propensity to Subsidize?' Policy Research Working Paper No. 1818, World Bank, Washington, DC.

Heleniak, Timothy (1997), 'Internal Migration in Russia During the Economic Transition', *Post-Soviet Geography and Economics*, 38 (2), 81–104.

Igudin, Albert G. (1998), 'Analysis and Assessment of the Existing System of Intergovernmental Fiscal Relations in the Russian Federation', Ministry of Finance of the Russian Federation, Research Institute of Finance, Moscow.

Kurlyandskaya, Galina (2001), 'Budgetary Pluralism of Russian Authorities', Discussion Paper no.17, Open Society Institute, Local Government and Public Service Reform Initiative, Budapest.

Lapidus, Gail W. (1998), 'Contested Sovereignty: The Tragedy of Chechnya', *International Security,* 2 (Summer), 5–45.

——— (1999), 'Asymmetrical Federalism and State Breakdown in Russia', *Post-Soviet Affairs,* 15 (1), 74–82.

Lavrov, Alexei (1995), 'Russian Federation: First Steps, First Results', Segodnya, in Russian.

——— (1998), 'Intergovernmental Fiscal Relations in Russia: An Agenda for Reform', processed.

Lavrov, Aleksei, John M. Litwack and Douglas Sutherland (2000), 'Fiscal Federalist Relations in Russia: A Case for Subnational Autonomy', Working Paper, Organisation for Economic Co-operation and Development, Paris.

Lynn, Nicholas J. and Alexei V. Novikov (1997), 'Refederalizing Russia: Debates on the Idea of Federalism in Russia', *Publius: The Journal of Federalism*, 27 (2), 187–203.
Martinez-Vazquez, Jorge and Jameson Boex (2001), *Russia's Transition to a New Federalism,* World Bank Institute Learning Series, Washington, DC: World Bank Institute.
McAuley, A. (1997), 'The Determinants of Russian Federal-Regional Fiscal Relations: Equity or Political Influence?' *Europe-Asia Studies,* 49 (3), 431–44.
McLure, Charles E., Jr., Christine I. Wallich and Jennie I. Litvack (1996), 'Special Issues in Russian Federal Finance: Ethnic Separatism and Natural Resources', in Richard Bird, Robert Ebel and Christine Wallich (eds), *Decentralization of the Socialist State,* Washington, DC: World Bank, pp. 379–404.
OECD (Organisation for Economic Co-operation and Development) (2000), *Economic Surveys: The Russian Federation*, Paris.
Ordeshook, Peter O. (1995), 'Re-examining Russia: Institutions and Incentives', *Journal of Democracy,* (April), 46–61.
Polishchuck, Leonid (1996), 'Russian Federalism: Economic Reform and Political Behavior', Social Science Working Paper no. 972, California Institute of Technology, Division of Humanities and Social Sciences, Pasadena, California.
——— (2000), 'Legal Initiatives in Russian Regions: Determinants and Effects', University of Maryland, Center for Institutional Reform and the Informal Sector, College Park, MD, processed.
Popov, Vladimir (2002), 'Fiscal Federalism in Russia: Rules Versus Electoral Politics', Carleton University, Institute of European and Russian Studies, Carleton, Canada, processed.
Shleifer, Andrei and Daniel Treisman (2000), *Without a Map: Political Tactics and Economic Reform in Russia*, Cambridge, MA: MIT Press.
Solanko, Laura (1999), 'Regional Budgets and Intergovernmental Transfers in Russian North and Northwest Regions', Working Paper No. 99-6, Bank of Finland, Institute for Economies in Transition, Helsinki.
Solnick, Steven L. (1995), 'Federal Bargaining in Russia', *East European Constitutional Review*, 4 (4), 52–58.
Stepan, Alfred (1999), 'Federalism and Democracy: Beyond the U.S. Model', *Journal of Democracy*, 10 (4), 19–34.
Stewart, Kitty (1996), 'Are Intergovernmental Finances in Russia Equalizing?' European University Institute, Department of Economics, Working Paper ECO No. 97/22, Badia Fiesolana, San Domenico (FI), Italy.
Sutherland, Douglas and Philip Hanson (1996), 'Structural Change in the Economies of Russia's Regions', *Europe-Asia Studies,* 48 (3), 367–92.
Speckhard, C. (1998), 'The Political Economy of Institutional Asymmetry in the Russian Federation, 1990–1998', University of Texas, Austin, processed.
Teague, Elizabeth (1996), 'Russia and the Regions: The Uses of Ambiguity', in John Gibson and Philip Hanson (eds), *Transformation from Below: Local Power and the Political Economy of Post-Communist Transition*, Cheltenham, UK and Brookfield, USA: Edward Elgar.
Treisman, Daniel (1996), 'The Politics of Intergovernmental Transfers in Post-Soviet Russia', *British Journal of Political Science,* 26 (3), 299–335.
——— (2000), *After the Deluge: Regional Crises and Political Consolidation in Russia,* Ann Arbor: University of Michigan Press.
Wallich, Christine (1994), *Russia and the Challenge of Fiscal Federalism*, Washington, DC: World Bank.
World Bank (1996), *Fiscal Management in Russia*, Washington, DC.
——— (2001), 'Russian Federation Fiscal Federalism and Regional Fiscal Reform Loan', Washington, DC, processed.

9. Ethnic Minority Regions and Fiscal Decentralization in China: The Promises and Reality of Asymmetric Treatment

Christine Wong

At first glance, China does not seem to fit into the group of countries in which decentralization affects, and is in turn affected by, national cohesion and ethnic relations. After all, China has a population that is highly homogeneous, with more than 90 per cent belonging to the Han racial and ethnic group, which has a strong, unified cultural and linguistic identity developed over 1000 years and dating back to the Han Dynasty.

The reality is more complex. First, given China's enormous size, while only 8.4 per cent of the population is non-Han, these minorities numbered nearly 107 million people by the end of 2000. Second, the non-Han so-called minority nationalities occupy a large and strategically important territory: some two-thirds of the minority population resides within 200 kilometres of China's international borders, and more than 90 per cent of those borders lie along officially designated autonomous areas (see Figure 9.1; for a more detailed map of China see Figure 9.2). These areas contain more than 60 per cent of China's total land area and many natural resources, for example, oil, gas and uranium in Xinjiang. Third, the interaction between the minority groups and the Han has been complicated historically, and to varying degrees the minority groups exhibit some ambivalence towards the Han-dominated Chinese state. Some of the groups are descendants from formerly independent states, notably Manchus, Mongols, Tibetans and Uighurs (a Turkic group located mostly in Xinjiang). Two of them, Mongols and Manchus, have ruled China itself at times in the past.[1] Today many have significant cross-border links with modern nation states: the Koreans with North and South Korea, the Mongols with Mongolia, the Jings with Vietnam and various Turkic and Muslim groups with Central Asian and Middle Eastern states (Gladney 1999; Harrell 2001). This combination of factors means that the interaction between the

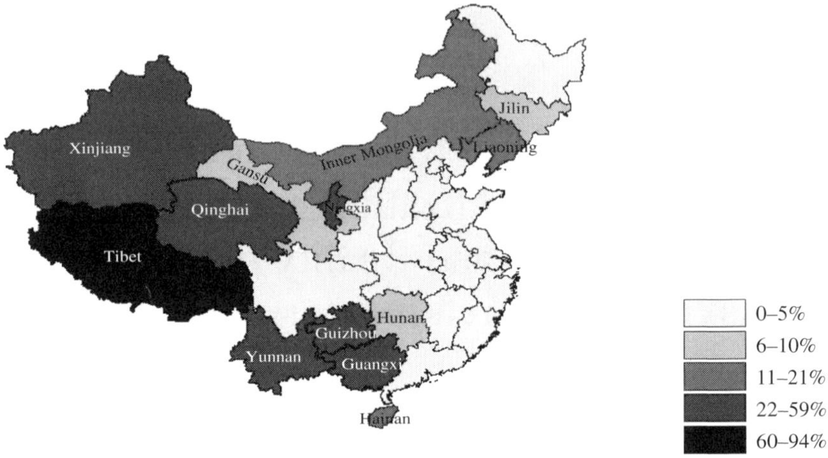

Source: National Bureau of Statistices (2001).

Figure 9.1 Share of minority nationalities in population, 2000

central government and the regional governments in minority areas, and how this treatment is perceived, can have a direct impact on the maintenance of national cohesion. Seen in this light, China appears to have much in common with the other countries in this volume.

However, these ethnic divisions should not be overemphasized, as the Chinese situation has some significant differences as well. First, the overwhelming numerical dominance of the Han means that many places have been extensively Sinicized. In the eight provinces designated as minority regions,[2] the Han are actually a minority in only two: Tibet and Xinjiang (Table 9.1). Moreover, many groups are culturally assimilated with the Han, including the three largest groups, the Zhuang, the Manchu and the Hui. The Zhuang were so little differentiated from the Han that in the 1950s many resisted being classified as a minority nationality, insisting instead that they were descendants of the Han who just happened to speak Zhuang (Kaup 2000). The second largest group, the Manchu, having ruled China for nearly 300 years during the Qing Dynasty, became so Sinicized that today they are virtually indistinguishable from the Han. The complexity and murkiness of cultural identity is probably most extreme for the Hui, Chinese-speaking Muslims. Living in every province and virtually every county in China, they are highly inter-married with the Han, speak Chinese almost exclusively and strongly resemble the Han physically and in their material lives. However, they remain distinct from their Han neighbours because of their practice of Islam and/or

Figure 9.2 China

their collective memory of a separate tradition and history.[3] Despite their apparent assimilation with the Han in so many ways, the Hui have a volatile relationship with the Han, with periodic flare-ups but without secessionist intent (Lipman 2004).

Nevertheless, strong separatist movements do exist among some ethnic groups, notably in Tibet and Xinjiang. Since the late 1980s, ethnic groups have rebelled against the government numerous times. Tibetans have rioted on several occasions, and several monks have immolated themselves in protest against Chinese rule. In Xinjiang, the government estimates that 200 attacks by separatists took place during 1990–2001, causing 162 deaths and 440 injuries. In the largest single incident, as many as 100 people were killed in a pro-independence uprising in the town of Ili in 1997 (Chung 2002), while others report that as many as 500 people were killed (Kaup 2000). In Inner Mongolia, Kaup (2000) claims that 200 people were killed in clashes in May 1990, when secessionists demanded independence for a Mongolian republic with Outer Mongolia. More recently, a group calling itself the Eastern Turkestan Islamic Movement has been active in Xinjiang and the former Soviet republics of Kyrgyz and Kazakhstan.[4]

These differences among China's ethnic minorities are rooted not only in history, but also in geography. China has a sharp northwest-southwest divide. The ethnic groups in the northwest are more clearly demarcated and separated from the Han. This is true of the Mongols, the Uighurs (in Xinjiang), and the Tibetans, who are linguistically unified internally and are different from the Chinese. They have centralized religions that provide leadership and organizational structures. They live in greater concentrations, and all three groups have actively petitioned for statehood since the People's Republic of China was founded (Kaup 2000). Among the regions in the northwest, Tibet is unique in that it was not annexed by China until 1959, and China did so under terms that the Tibetan leadership of the time disputed. The head of the Tibetan theocracy, the Dalai Lama, escaped and has been living in exile, and in the eyes of many Tibetans remains as their true spiritual and national leader.

In contrast to the northwest, the groups in the southwest are fragmented in their religions and languages, live in close proximity to the Han and are much less cohesive. In Yunnan and Guangxi, for example, few administrative districts contain people of just a single nationality.[5]

Table 9.2 presents some basic indicators for the eight minority nationalities regions. Inner Mongolia, Qinghai, Tibet and Xinjiang, all in the northwest, are vast, sparsely populated regions, whereas population densities in Guangxi and Guizhou in the southwest are above the national average. In terms of income levels, only Xinjiang is above the national average, all the others are below, most of them substantially. With a per capita gross domestic product (GDP) of Y 2856 in 2001, Guizhou is the poorest province in China.

Table 9.1 Proportion of minorities by province, end of 2000

Province	Population (millions of people)	Percentage of total population
Beijing	12.57	4.26
Tianjin	9.59	2.64
Hebei	66.14	4.31
Shanxi	32.04	0.29
Inner Mongolia	**23.62**	**20.76**
Liaoning	41.71	16.02
Jilin	26.58	9.03
Heilongjiang	37.92	5.02
Shanghai	14.74	0.60
Jiangsu	72.13	0.33
Zhejiang	44.75	0.85
Anhui	62.37	0.63
Fujian	33.16	1.67
Jiangxi	42.31	0.27
Shandong	88.83	0.68
Henan	93.87	1.22
Hubei	59.38	4.34
Hunan	65.32	10.21
Guangdong	72.70	1.42
Guangxi	**47.13**	**38.34**
Hainan	7.62	17.29
Chongqing	30.75	6.42
Sichuan	85.50	4.98
Guizhou	**37.10**	**37.85**
Yunnan	**41.92**	**33.41**
Tibet	**2.56**	**94.07**
Shaanxi	36.18	0.49
Gansu	25.43	8.69
Qinghai	**5.10**	**45.51**
Ningxia	**5.43**	**34.53**
Xinjiang	**17.74**	**59.39**
China	1265.83	8.41

Note: Provinces shown in bold are designated minority nationalities regions.

Source: National Bureau of Statistics (2001, Table 4-11).

Table 9.2. Basic indicators for minority nationalities regions, 2001

Region	Area		Population		Population density (number of people/km^2)	Gross domestic product		
	Thousands of square kilometres	Percentage of total	Millions of people	Percentage of total		Y hundred millions	Percentage of total	Per capita (Y)
Guangxi	236	2.5	47.88	3.8	203	2231	2.3	4660
Guizhou	176	1.8	37.99	3.0	216	1085	1.1	2856
Inner Mongolia	1201	12.5	23.77	1.9	20	1546	1.6	6503
Ningxia	66	0.7	5.63	0.4	85	298	0.3	5300
Qinghai	702	7.3	5.23	0.4	7	301	0.3	5754
Tibet	120	12.5	2.63	0.2	22	139	0.1	5275
Xinjiang	1600	16.7	18.76	1.5	12	1485	1.5	7918
Yunnan	395	4.1	42.87	3.4	109	2075	2.2	4840
China	9600	100.0	1276.27	100.0	133	95 933	100.0	7517
China net of nationalities autonomous areas	5104	53.2	1091.51	85.5	214	86 773	90.5	7950

Source: National Bureau of Statistics (2001).

This chapter examines the status of minority nationalities in China and how their treatment has changed in the two decades of the country's transition from a Soviet-type planned economy to a market economy. It focuses on the fiscal system, which is the channel through which the government can alleviate the locational and developmental disadvantages of the minority nationalities areas through transfers and expenditure policy. Historically poorer, China's ethnic minorities have also benefited less from China's recent growth spurt and increased participation in the global economy, because they are concentrated in the northwest, west and southwest parts of the country and are far from the coast.

To examine the evolution of intergovernmental fiscal relations in the past two decades, the chapter starts by providing some background on the ethnic minorities. The next section discusses the asymmetric treatment of minority regions under the pretransition fiscal system. This is followed by a summary of the evolution of fiscal decentralization during the two decades of transition to a market economy and how that has affected the treatment of the ethnic minority regions. The concluding section looks ahead to the next steps in interethnic relations and the limited role for intergovernmental fiscal relations in China.

HISTORICAL BACKGROUND ON CHINA'S ETHNIC MINORITIES

The categories of nationalities were established in the 1950s, when the government undertook a massive linguistic and ethnological effort to determine how many ethnic groups existed, how many members they had and where the groups ranked on the Marxist scale of evolution (this section draws heavily on Harrell and Gladney 1999). To this day, the personal identity cards of all Chinese citizens have an ethnic designation, for instance, Han, Hui or Tibetan (people can dispute their ethnic designation, but not escape it altogether, while children of mixed parentage can choose their ethnic designation).

The guidelines for the recognition of a minority group were patterned on those used in the former Soviet Union and were based on a proposal by Stalin in a 1913 essay on 'Marxism and the Nationalities Question' (cited in Harrell and Gladney 1999) that nationality be defined by groupings whose members historically share a common territory, language, economy and 'psychological makeup expressed in a common culture'. In the identification exercise, the application of these criteria was not always straightforward or easy, which is hardly surprising given that identity is such a complex and multifaceted concept. This was especially true for the Hui. Having committed early on to recognizing the Hui as a nationality, the government had to do contortions around the fact that, unlike the Mongols, the other group to receive early recognition with the creation of the Inner Mongolia Autonomous Region in 1947, the Hui lack a common language, territory or mode of production and the common culture they share is derived almost entirely from Islam and Islamic practices.[6] The government's ideological discomfort in legitimating religion as the basis for the Hui identity has led to inconsistencies in the treatment of mosques, imams and Islamic practices over the years that have contributed to ethnic antagonisms.[7]

In the nationalities identification exercise, administrative expediency also motivated the lumping together of some of the smaller ethnic groups, sometimes even when the groups did not identify with each other. For example, Harrell (2001) argues that the Yi nationality was created by amalgamating many subgroups in Yunnan, Sichuan and Guizhou who have different languages that are related, but are mutually unintelligible. The groups were culturally diverse and trace their origins to different kingdoms. Some had distinctive socioeconomic traditions not shared by other subgroups, for instance, the Nuosu in Sichuan had a caste system, and these subgroups had previously identified themselves differently, as Nasu, Nuosu, and so on. Similarly, Kaup (2000) notes that none of the 20 groups amalgamated to form the Zhuang had used the term to describe themselves in recent memory, and most felt no kinship ties to the other groups. The 1953 population census listed only 41 groups, although more than 400 had applied for the designation. Some refinements were made through the 1950s, so that a total of 56 nationalities came to be recognized, including the Han.

By the end of 2000, an estimated 107 million people belonged to the 55 officially designated minority nationalities, equal to 8.4 per cent of the total population (Table 9.1). They inhabit every one of the 31 provincial-level units, but some two-thirds of them are concentrated in the officially designated nationalities autonomous areas (NAAs). Table 9.3 shows the distribution of the major minority nationalities, including only those groups with a population of more than 1 million.

Early Minority Policy

The Chinese Communist Party came into contact with ethnic minorities and their aspirations for autonomy during the 1930s and 1940s, before coming to power in 1949. Forced to operate in frontier areas because of military pressure from the nationalist government and later the Japanese, the communists quickly saw the advantage of alliances with members of various ethnic groups. In opposition to the nationalist government policy of political and cultural assimilation, the communists embraced ethnic pluralism and hinted at the future possibility of a federal state in which the minority regions would exercise genuine autonomy, including the right of secession. The earliest ethnic

Table 9.3 Distribution of major minority nationalities by province, 1990

Nationality	Primary locations (provinces)	Number of people
Zhuang	Guangxi, Yunnan, Guangdong	15 555 820
Manchus	Liaoning, Hebei, Heilongjiang, Jilin	9 846 776
Hui	In 19 provinces including Ningxi, Gansu, Henan, Xinjiang, Qinghai, Yunnan, Hebei, Shandong, Anhui, Liaoning, Beijing, Inner Mongolia	8 612 001
Miao	Guizhou, Hunan, Yunnan, Guangxi, Chongqing	7 383 622
Uighur	Xinjiang	7 207 024
Yi	Yunnan, Sichuan, Guizhou	6 578 524
Tujia	Hunan, Hubei, Chongqing, Guizhou	5 725 049
Mongols	Inner Mongolia, Liaoning, Jilin, Hebei	4 802 407
Tibetans	Tibet, Sichuan, Qinghai, Gansu, Yunnan	4 593 072
Buyi	Guizhou, Hunan, Yunnan, Guangxi, Chongqing	2 548 294
Tong	Guizhou, Hunan, Guangxi	2 508 624
Yao	Guangxi, Hunan, Yunnan, Guangdong	2 137 033
Korean	Jilin, Heilongjiang, Liaoning	1 923 361
Bai	Yunnan, Guizhou, Hunan	1 598 052
Hani	Yunnan	1 254 800
Li	Hainan	1 112 498
Kazakh	Xinjiang	1 110 758
Thai	Yunnan	1 025 402

Source: 1990 census data.

autonomous region was set up in a county in Ningxia province, which was proclaimed the Yuhai Hui Minority Autonomous Government in October 1936. This was followed by a proclamation by Mao Zedong at the Sixth Plenum of the Sixth Central Party Congress in October 1938 supporting the establishment of ethnic minority autonomous regions under unified national rule. More autonomous regions were set up during the late 1930s and early 1940s in the areas ruled by the communists (Huang and Li 1993).

Even though it quickly revoked the policies permitting secession once it had assumed effective control over the whole country in 1949, in the 1950s the communist government reiterated its commitment to granting limited autonomy, and in the early years made a concerted effort to invite cooperation from the ethnic minority groups, sending delegations to the minority regions with messages of friendship. The communist government also tried to recruit members of local elites to positions of authority in the government. To create the foundations for future recruitment, the government established a large number of schools—from county-run secondary schools to nationalities institutes at the central, regional and provincial levels—to train members of ethnic minorities in the Chinese language, modern scientific topics and the political philosophy of Marxism-Leninism.

Legal Foundations of Autonomy

The legal foundations of the current system of limited autonomy for minority nationality areas were first laid down in the constitution and the 1952 implementation regulations for the autonomy of nationalities areas. These were solidified and expanded in 1984, when the National People's Congress passed the Law on Autonomy in Nationalities Areas (hereafter referred to as the Autonomy Law). The law was amended in 2001.

The law and the regulations preceding it provide for the establishment of NAAs on the basis of concentrated populations of national minorities. These autonomous areas exist at all four tiers of subnational government: at the provincial level there are five autonomous regions (Tibet, Xinjiang, Inner Mongolia, Ningxia and Guangxi). In 1980, Yunnan, Qinghai and Guizhou provinces were added to the list for receiving fiscal subsidies targeted to NAAs. Even though the latter three provinces were not officially labelled as NAAs, for the purposes of this chapter we will treat them as such, bringing the total to eight provincial-level units. At the next level were 30 autonomous prefectures in 10 other provinces. Below them were 121 autonomous counties (in 18 provinces). At the lowest tier were 1267 minorities townships. Because official aid is often targeted at areas rather than peoples, official designation as a minority area is important. In addition, because education in the minority languages is typically available only in NAAs, the designation improves the likelihood that minorities will be able to maintain their ethnic identities and privileges.

The designation of NAAs at multiple levels allows subordinate units located outside designated minority areas to apply for the label if their minority nationality group constitutes more than 30 per cent of the population (Dai 1997). For example, the Yi, who are the sixth largest minority nationality, have no autonomous region of their own, but have five autonomous prefectures (four in Yunnan and one in Sichuan province) and ten autonomous counties (seven in Yunnan, two in Sichuan and one in Guizhou) (Heberer 2001). Because the designations are group specific, NAAs can be layered. For example, within the Xinjiang Autonomous Region there are autonomous prefectures, autonomous counties and autonomous townships designated for the other 11 minority nationalities. Indeed, the Bayingguoleng Mongolian Autonomous Prefecture, where Mongols account for 35 per cent of the population, comprises nearly one-third of the land area of Xinjiang. Even with these different layers of NAAs, however, some 30 per cent of the members of minority nationalities reside in nondesignated areas. Table 9.4 shows the number and distribution of NAAs at the subprovincial levels.

In the NAAs, the Autonomy Law specifies the creation of a people's government and a people's congress, subordinate to the State Council. The head of the people's government must be a member of the nationality for whom the autonomous area is created, while the people's congress should represent this nationality, but should also reserve places for representatives from other nationalities residing in the area.

The Autonomy Law gives some guarantees of linguistic, educational, cultural and religious freedoms. Specifically, the law guarantees the freedom of

Table 9.4 Distribution of NAAs and populations at subprovincial levels, 1999

Provinces and autonomous regions	Number of prefectures	Number of counties	Number of cities at the county level	Total population in minority areas (10 000 people)	Number of minority population	Minority population as a percentage of the total population in minority areas
Hebei	0	6	0	189.80	108.70	57.27
Liaoning	0	8	0	333.47	167.07	50.10
Jilin	1	11	6	332.62	117.11	35.21
Heilongjiang	1	0	0	24.38	5.12	21.00
Zhejiang	0	1	0	17.55	1.76	10.03
Hubei	1	10	2	443.17	209.13	47.19
Hunan	1	15	1	470.57	320.26	68.06
Guangdong	0	3	0	45.68	16.08	35.20
Hainan	0	6	0	154.17	75.65	49.07
Chongqing	0	5	0	289.48	163.18	56.37
Sichuan	3	50	1	594.72	323.86	54.46
Guizhou	3	46	4	1475.07	833.64	56.52
Yunnan	8	78	7	2050.59	1109.39	54.10
Gansu	2	21	2	308.91	170.82	55.30
Qinghai	6	35	2	303.18	178.05	58.73
China[a]	77	635	70	16 682.55	7591.40	45.51

a. Including those in the provincial-level NAAs.

Source: National Bureau of Statistics (2001).

each nationality to use and develop its own language and script and the right to use local languages in administration, including in court proceedings. The law also provides for the use of minority nationalities' languages in schools at all levels, although all schools must also teach Chinese. In terms of religious freedom, the law guarantees the freedom to believe or not to believe and prohibits the use of religious activities to interfere with the education system. The party's basic document on religion (number 19, 1982) states as follows:

> [W]hile Party members cannot be members of religious organizations or engage in religious practices, certain exceptions may be made in minority nationalities areas where religion is part of the ethnic identity. There, Party members may participate in traditional ceremonies and show respect to religious leaders, as long as they continue to work to 'reform those customs and traditions which prove harmful to production or to the physical and mental health of the masses'. (Harrell and Gladney 1999)

These guarantees notwithstanding, the treatment of ethnic minorities has shifted over time with the ideological swings of the government. During the radical phases of the Maoist period, roughly 1958–78, the government sometimes reneged on its autonomy regulations and pursued hard line assimilationist policies committed to eliminating cultural differences. Religion and religious practices were vigorously suppressed, as were religious practitioners. In the late 1960s and early 1970s, at the height of the Cultural Revolution, rampaging Red Guards, claiming that they were cleansing the country of feudalism and a feudal mentality, destroyed many cultural artefacts, including sacred monuments in ethnic minority areas. Ethnic minority languages and cultures were held up to ridicule and vilification, and appointments of members of ethnic minorities to key government posts declined.[8]

However, with the beginning of reform and transition in 1978, the government has turned once again towards a more pluralistic, open policy towards minority languages, cultures and religions. The liberalizing climate has permitted a revival of ethnic values, and China's opening to the world has also brought increased contact with people of like ethnicity abroad. For Chinese Muslims, this opening up has brought new opportunities for study and travel to Islamic countries, and many have gone to study in the Middle East, Malaysia and Brunei. Many localities have also received contributions from abroad to build new mosques or refurbish old ones (Armijo 2001).

ASYMMETRIC TREATMENT OF NATIONALITY MINORITY AREAS IN THE FISCAL SYSTEM

Both the constitution and the Autonomy Law emphasize the principles of autonomy and preferential treatment. Article 117 of the constitution states that '[t]he government of the nationalities autonomous areas should have the authority for self-management of local finances. All revenues of the nationality autonomous areas collected in accordance with the national fiscal system should be allocated by the governments of the nationalities autonomous areas'. These principles are reiterated and expanded in the Autonomy Law, which states that 'the revenues and expenditures of nationality regions should be set according to the State Council's principle of preferential treatment'. This preferential treatment included some rights to petition the national government to waive implementation of national provisions that run against local customs or interests and special provisions for aiding the development of 'nationalities trades' (Dai 1997).

In practice, autonomy has always been highly constricted, creating a substantial gap between rhetoric and reality. Under the extremely centralized character of China's fiscal system, little autonomy existed for local governments in budget management throughout the Maoist period. The central government set all taxes and revenues, with revenues collected by local governments on behalf of the central government. The central government approved local budgets, with expenditures based roughly on national provision standards and spending norms. Revenue sharing was set annually, calculated to leave local governments with the revenues they needed to finance their approved budgets.

This system left little scope for granting autonomy to the NAAs except at the margins and on a case-by-case negotiated basis. Across the board, asymmetric treatment of the NAAs included the following so-called 'three preferences' conferred in 1963:

- A 5 per cent discretionary allowance was added to the annual fiscal allocation based on the final accounts for the past year's expenditures (excluding capital spending and working capital).
- A larger contingency allowance was granted. The autonomous regions were allowed to budget for 5 per cent of the total (compared with 3 per cent for ordinary provinces), autonomous prefectures could budget 4 per cent (compared with 2 per cent for ordinary prefectures) and autonomous counties could budget 3 per cent (compared with 1 per cent for other counties).
- A nationalities subsidy fund was provided for extraordinary expenses by the nationality areas.

During 1964–79, the NAAs received a total of Y 3.5 billion from these three preferences (Huang and Li 1990, p. 470), which provided an additional 10 per cent or so for local expenditures, a small but symbolically important gesture in relation to conferring some limited autonomy for the NAAs.

On the important issue of natural resource exploitation, the preferential treatment included a 20 per cent profit sharing arrangement for central government enterprises operating in the NAAs. This was an important concession to the many resource-rich NAAs, because the central government owns all large deposits of natural resources, and local governments did not normally share in the profits. In addition, the NAAs were also allowed some measures to aid the development of ethnic products and trades, mainly through the granting of some tax exemptions and price subsidies to so-called ethnic goods.

Overall, under the planned economy, the fiscal system was relatively generous to the NAAs. Per capita fiscal expenditures (after preferences and transfers) grew faster in the eight NAAs than the national average during 1952–70. Even though actual expenditure levels remained below the national average in all regions except Qinghai during this time (Table 9.5), they were catching up to the national average even while per capita GDP growth rates in the regions were below average (again except in Qinghai).

EFFECTS OF THE TRANSITION

The story of China's gradual transition to a market economy is well known (for a broad, comparative perspective on China's transition until 1995, see World Bank 1997). The process ushered in a period of dynamic growth and development that is virtually unprecedented in world history, accompanied by China's dramatic rise as a key player in the global economy. The NAAs have benefited from the accelerated economic growth over the past two decades, which was extraordinarily broadly based (Table 9.6), although the trends among the eight NAAs differed. From 1980 to 2000, per capita GDP grew faster than the national average in Xinjiang, Yunnan, Inner Mongolia and Guangxi, but slower in Guizhou, Ningxia, Qinghai and Tibet (Table 9.5). In terms of industrial growth, however, (as measured by the share of GDP derived from industry), six of the eight NAAs fell relatively further behind. Yunnan stayed in place, and only Guangxi gained slightly (Table 9.7).

The trend was more positive for the NAAs during 1980–90, when industrial growth was close to or above the national average in five of the eight NAAs. In the 1990s, all eight NAAs experienced below average growth rates. This is consistent with the overall picture of accelerating growth in the coastal regions that left inland provinces progressively further behind. With constraints on migration limiting the trickle-down effect on inland regions, the result was that during the 1990s, disparities in incomes and opportunities rose sharply across sectors and regions.

These trends are even more marked for fiscal revenues and expenditures. From 1980 to 1990, per capita revenue growth was significantly faster than

Table 9.5 Relative trends in NAAs, selected years (numeraire = fiscal national average)

Item	1952	1957	1970	1980	1990	2000
GDP per capita						
Guangxi	0.56	0.61	0.52	0.60	0.65	0.61
Guizhou	0.49	0.59	0.48	0.48	0.50	0.38
Inner Mongolia	1.45	1.38	0.96	0.78	0.90	0.83
Ningxia	1.06	0.88	0.88	0.94	0.85	0.68
Qinghai	0.85	1.15	1.10	1.03	0.95	0.72
Tibet	n.a.	n.a.	n.a.	1.02	0.78	0.64
Xinjiang	1.39	1.59	0.86	0.89	1.10	1.06
Yunnan	0.59	0.72	0.57	0.58	0.75	0.66
Revenue per capita						
Guangxi	0.37	0.30	0.33	0.30	0.43	0.31
Guizhou	0.27	0.28	0.19	0.21	0.43	0.23
Inner Mongolia	0.62	0.72	0.37	0.19	0.59	0.38
Ningxia	0.65	0.44	0.45	0.46	0.52	0.35
Qinghai	0.60	0.65	0.53	1.44	1.48	0.30
Tibet	n.a.	n.a.	–0.18	2.49	2.22	0.19
Xinjiang	0.53	0.86	0.46	0.27	0.55	0.39
Yunnan	0.36	0.33	0.40	0.31	0.81	0.40
Expenditure per capita						
Guangxi	0.29	0.34	0.42	0.40	0.57	0.46
Guizhou	0.15	0.21	0.32	0.37	0.55	0.46
Inner Mongolia	0.48	0.63	0.67	0.79	1.04	0.83
Ningxia	0.45	0.45	0.78	1.24	1.19	0.86
Qinghai	0.38	1.73	1.22	1.25	1.42	1.05
Tibet	n.a.	n.a.	0.90	2.02	2.16	1.82
Xinjiang	0.42	0.88	0.79	1.02	1.15	0.79
Yunnan	0.18	0.26	0.54	0.44	0.90	0.77

n.a. Not applicable.

Source: Author's calculations based on data from the National Bureau of Statistics.

average in all the NAAs except Qinghai and Tibet, and above average expenditure growth occurred in all but Ningxia. During 1990–2000, however, all the NAAs lost ground in terms of both revenues and expenditures. Some scholars have accused the government of abandoning equality as a social objective (Khan and Riskin 2000; Riskin, Li and Zhao 2001). An examination of the evolution of fiscal decentralization points strongly to the government falling captive to the interests of rich, coastal provinces (Wong 2000; World

Table 9.6 Growth rates of gross regional product per capita, selected years

Province	1975	1980	1985	1990	1995	1999
Northern region	8.09	4.55	10.04	2.27	11.78	6.21
Beijing	11.85	10.90	6.09	3.71	11.81	7.28
Tianjing	2.69	8.48	9.35	3.67	14.06	3.85
Hebei	9.38	1.94	11.25	1.02	13.03	8.41
Shanxi	6.14	0.78	5.41	3.34	9.95	–3.42
Inner Mongolia	9.22	1.16	19.72	3.22	7.98	6.99
Northeastern region	7.21	9.19	10.33	1.98	6.67	6.02
Liaoning	7.37	11.28	12.86	1.03	6.39	6.13
Jilin	11.17	5.40	7.38	1.17	4.61	5.91
Heilongjiang	5.23	8.22	8.42	4.27	8.74	5.63
Eastern region	6.51	7.87	15.01	3.53	14.33	8.29
Shanghai	3.82	7.04	12.29	4.57	13.87	–2.32
Jiangsu	4.80	4.08	17.67	1.48	14.66	9.65
Zhejiang	–4.87	15.06	21.50	3.74	15.94	9.32
Anhui	1.57	1.10	14.85	0.09	13.11	6.63
Fujian	0.55	17.90	16.42	6.37	13.71	6.75
Jiangxi	6.89	2.84	13.44	2.28	16.92	6.79
Shandong	27.44	11.89	11.40	7.58	13.70	9.59
Central south region	7.53	9.61	14.03	6.15	12.77	7.17
Henan	4.54	13.88	11.91	3.94	13.88	7.22
Hubei	9.95	5.22	14.82	3.17	13.55	7.70
Hunan	8.33	4.08	10.83	8.39	9.35	4.62
Guangdong	9.09	14.64	19.05	8.00	13.33	7.14
Guangxi	4.46	8.10	9.06	4.68	10.18	6.84
Southwestern region	9.63	7.07	12.63	4.22	7.94	5.33
Sichuan and Chongqing	12.72	7.98	14.44	4.09	7.67	4.91
Guizhou	7.68	2.71	6.45	3.28	5.97	6.83
Yunnan	2.78	7.22	11.51	5.35	9.78	5.99
Northwestern region	8.49	7.67	12.97	6.22	7.47	7.03
Shannxi	3.57	6.36	15.13	2.21	8.01	7.69
Gansu	14.76	7.74	11.69	6.20	7.21	7.34
Qinghai	5.27	25.20	2.99	7.48	6.43	6.67
Ningxia	2.08	6.39	14.89	1.23	7.19	7.41
Xinjiang	13.11	5.15	13.38	15.54	7.12	5.44
China	7.4	7.83	13.07	4.03	11.79	7.28
Mean	7.28	7.92	12.3	4.32	10.56	6.15
Maximum	27.44	25.20	21.5	15.54	16.92	9.65
Minimum	–4.87	0.78	2.99	0.09	4.61	–3.42
Coefficient of variation	0.79	0.70	0.36	0.71	0.33	0.46

Source: Bahl and Martinez-Vazquez (2003).

Table 9.7 Industry share in GDP relative to the national average, selected years
(numeraire = national average)

Province	1952	1980	1990	2000
Guangxi	1.10	0.65	0.63	0.72
Guizhou	0.89	0.82	0.86	0.77
Inner-Mongolia	0.54	0.97	0.77	0.78
Ningxia	0.22	0.94	0.94	0.89
Qinghai	0.35	0.91	0.92	0.85
Tibet	n.a.	0.52	0.31	0.46
Xinjiang	1.05	0.83	0.73	0.84
Yunnan	0.74	0.83	0.84	0.85

n.a. Not applicable.

Source: Bahl and Martinez-Vazquez (2003).

Bank 2002). These currents are clearly and specifically reflected in the fiscal treatment of the NAAs.

The Early Transition Period: 1980–87

When fiscal decentralization first began in the 1980s, the national leadership was eager to make amends for the treatment that many NAAs had suffered during the Cultural Revolution. The preferential treatment of NAAs was retained, with some of the previous provisions rolled into their base expenditure figures. Generous new subsidies were also introduced, and the central government committed to an annual increase of 10 per cent to the nationalities subsidy. At this time, coverage was expanded to add Yunnan, Qinghai and Guizhou provinces to the five autonomous regions eligible for the special nationalities treatment. During 1980–88, a total of Y 5.06 billion was distributed under the nationalities subsidy, accounting for around 5 per cent of budgetary expenditures in the NAAs.

In addition, two new subsidies were created that were earmarked mostly for the NAAs, namely:

- aid for the development of poor regions, 60 per cent of which was designated for NAAs, and which totalled Y 5.2 billion during 1979–88;
- subsidies for border regions, mostly for use in education and health in the NAAs, and which totalled Y 1.2 billion during 1978–88; special capital funds subsidy for the frontier regions that totalled Y 1.7 billion during 1978–88.

The effect of these more generous terms can be seen in Table 9.5, where in 1990 per capita fiscal expenditures (relative to the national average) were significantly higher in all NAAs than in 1980. In five of them, per capita expenditures were higher than the national average, attesting to the significant redistribution in favour of these NAAs. Central subsidies financed more than half of total expenditures in many NAAs, including Xinjiang, Guizhou and Tibet.

Abandonment of the Poor: 1988–2000

The 1990 numbers notwithstanding, achievements in relation to equalization were already being eroded in the mid-1980s. Through the 1980s, fiscal pressures on the central government intensified, as the dismantling of planning mechanisms and the end of the state monopoly over industry resulted in a collapse of the tax base, and revenues declined from more than 30 per cent of GDP in 1978 to less than 20 per cent in 1988 (Figure 9.3). First, the profits of state-owned enterprises, which had provided roughly half of all government revenues, declined precipitously as prices adjusted to market competition.[9] Concurrently, amid rapid changes in prices and market conditions, the central government lost its capacity to monitor tax efforts and enforce revenue remittance obligations from local governments. Fearing further erosion of its financial position, in 1988 the central government implemented the ill-fated fiscal

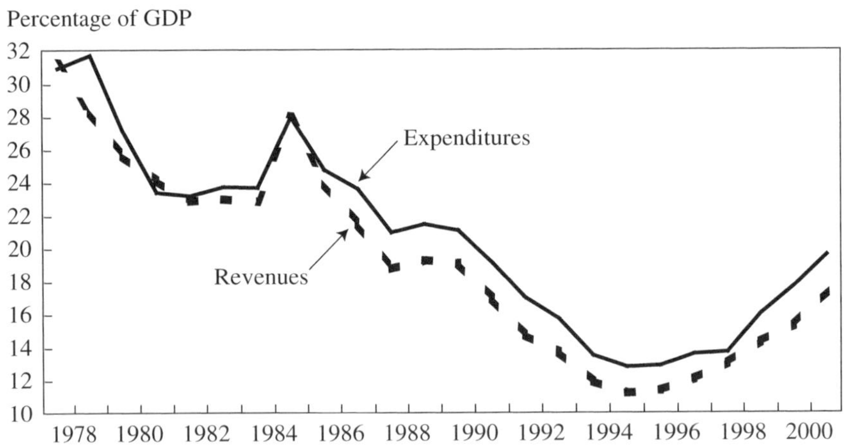

Source: World Bank (2002).

Figure 9.3 The long fiscal decline, 1978–2000

contracting system in revenue sharing. These contracts committed each provincial government to remitting a fixed amount—in nominal terms—to the central government each year, with some variations on the rate of growth of the remittance. With extremely favourable terms that ceded the bulk of new revenues to local governments, the central government's position quickly deteriorated to a low of 22 per cent of total revenues, while total revenues continued their decline to a low of just 11 per cent of GDP in 1995 (Wong, Heady and Woo 1995; World Bank 2002).

Fiscal stress and declining central government revenues led to cuts in intergovernmental transfers. When fiscal contracting was introduced in 1988, the central government froze all equalization transfers at the 1987 level and committed to no further increases over the medium term, including the nationalities subsidy. Given the double-digit rates of inflation during the late 1980s and early 1990s, freezing the subsidies in nominal terms meant that their real value declined rapidly during the decade.

Even more significant was the de-linking of expenditure needs from revenue considerations through the transition, so that local governments changed from being agents of the central government in carrying out delegated functions to bearing financial responsibilities, a genuine devolution of responsibilities. For transfer-dependent regions, which included virtually all the NAAs, the dwindling intergovernmental transfers meant a *de facto* gradual devolution of expenditure responsibilities. For the other provinces, the shift was formalized by the 1988 fiscal contracts and later codified in the 1994 Budget Law.

A watershed in intergovernmental fiscal relations occurred with the introduction of the tax sharing system in 1994. The tax sharing system involved a reform in tax policy that introduced the value added tax (VAT) and corporate and personal income taxes. It fundamentally altered revenue sharing by shifting from the negotiated, mildly equalizing system to a tax assignment system dominated by the sharing of VAT between the central and local governments by origin (75 per cent central, 25 per cent local). This system is inherently disequalizing, and to date the government has not fulfilled its promise to roll out a new equalization scheme to offset these effects. The reform also dramatically recentralized revenues, and the central government's share jumped from 22 per cent of total revenues in 1993 to 57 per cent in 1994. This created a huge, vertical fiscal imbalance, because the recentralization of revenues was not accompanied by an adjustment of expenditure assignments (Figure 9.4). The outcome was a marked deterioration in the public services provided in the poor regions and a significant rise in regional disparities (World Bank 2002). In effect, with the tax sharing system reform, the government had turned its back on poor regions.

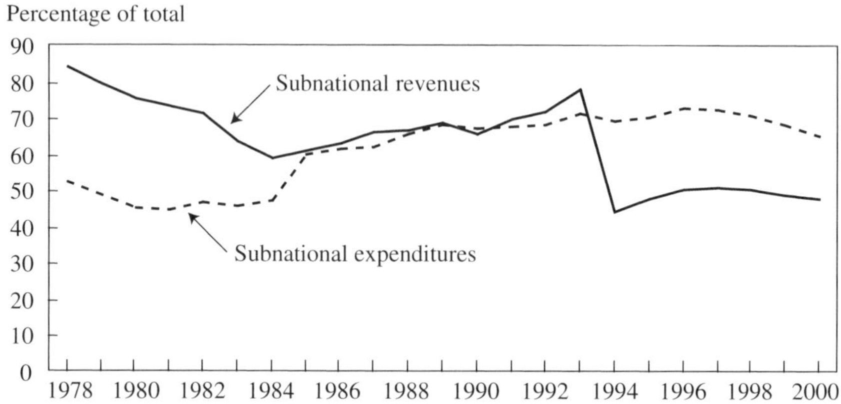

Source: World Bank (2002).

Figure 9.4 Subnational fiscal trends, 1978–2000

The combination of centralization and dis-equalizing changes in the intergovernmental system meant that by the mid-1990s, fiscal problems were serious in the NAAs. In Yunnan province, 106 of the 127 counties were unable to meet their budgeted expenditures in 1995, as were 66 of the 86 counties in Guizhou. Two-thirds of the minority nationalities counties had civil service wage arrears in 1995 (Dai 1997, p. 12). In the autonomous prefecture of Liangshan Yi in Sichuan province, the decentralization of responsibilities to the local level meant the elimination of free medical care and work to prevent epidemics and of free movies and cultural activities. Many clinics and health stations closed and epidemic diseases thought to have been wiped out reappeared. In 1996, only 40 per cent of Yi children attended school, a figure that dropped to 10 per cent in the poor villages (Heberer 2001).

Wang (1994, p. 11) complained that during the transition period

> [t]he prices for goods that are urgently needed in agriculture (such as means of production, diesel oil, chemical fertilizers, and insecticides) are rising faster than the prices for farm products, with the result that farm incomes are diminishing . . . State support monies for the agricultural sector in poverty areas (for the purchase of means of production . . .) come significantly late. They are often paid only after the agricultural season for which they were needed is already over . . . There are practically no agricultural experts in the rural areas of Liangshan Prefecture. . . . The medical network in the villages is practically shattered: there are hardly any doctors or medications, to the point where the death rates have begun to rise. . . . Drug taking, dealing, and addiction are rising drastically, without any intervention by the authorities.

While these problems are much the same as those farmers everywhere face, many Yi perceived them to be an outcome of Han policies (Heberer 2001).

NEXT STEPS IN RELATIONS WITH THE NAAS

The feeling among many in the NAAs that they are being short-changed by Han policies is buttressed by their perception that fiscal preferences for the NAAs have gradually been eliminated during the transition period. The changes include the abolition of the sharing of revenues from natural resource exploitation and of the special provisions that granted larger reserve and/or contingency funds to the NAAs. Xu and Qin (1991, p. 112) claim that in Guangxi, for example, the province received only Y 40 million in reserve funds and Y 60 million in contingency funds in 1987, compared with the Y 138.4 million and Y 160.2 million it would have received under the old rules. Moreover, many NAAs are saddled with heavy social protection expenditures (pension and unemployment outlays) associated with the decline of heavy industries built as part of the national defence effort during the early 1970s, when China felt itself to be under threat from both the former Soviet Union and the United States (Zhang 1998). Some scholars have even argued that the fiscal preferences given to the coastal provinces during the transition have come at the expense of the poor regions in the west. Pointing to the five-year exemption of revenue remittances from Shenzhen, the booming special economic zone contiguous to Hong Kong, Wang (2000) claims, '[I]n this process, the fiscal burdens increased correspondingly for the central and western regions. It can be said that the Central and Western provinces were sacrificed to enable the development of the Eastern regions'.

These critics are both right and wrong. The figures in Table 9.5 appear to support the government's claim that ethnic subsidies and preferences had been factored into the base expenditure figures for the NAAs when fiscal decentralization began in the early 1980s and supported improvements in the fiscal status of the NAAs until 1990. Similarly, the formula used for determining equalization grants contains a nationalities parameter. The NAAs were getting less in the 1990s, because the intergovernmental system had become less equalizing, and all the poor regions were getting less. The entire equalization scheme accounted for only 3 per cent of total transfers in 2001, even after growing rapidly for the previous four years. In addition, by embedding the earlier preferences into base expenditure figures, the system no longer has an explicit policy of treating the NAAs asymmetrically. In that sense the critics are right.

By the 1990s, the need to give special treatment to the NAAs was clearly not at the top of the policy agenda for China's leadership. A perusal of key government documents, including a report on the work of the government the premier delivered to the National People's Congress at its annual meeting and budget speeches by the minister of finance, reveals only perfunctory mentions of solidarity with minority nationalities. As no one sounded any alarm, the special treatment for ethnic minority regions was swept aside as part of the government's efforts during the transition period to move away from particularistic contracts to a more rules-based system of interaction with subnational governments. Factors that contributed to the downgrading or neglect of the special needs of the NAAs included the following:

- The easing of international tensions since the mid-1970s, which led to the downgrading of border issues. The end of the Vietnam War brought a gradual rapprochement with the United States, and the rise of Mikhail Gorbachev and the subsequent demise of the Soviet Union ended the threat from the north. As part of the intent of the special treatment had been to bolster the defence of frontier regions, the need for this had became harder to justify by the 1990s.
- The failure of fiscal policy. Because the government was slow to overhaul the tax system to adjust to changes brought about by an increasingly decentralized, market economy, the resultant steep fiscal decline forced deep cuts in spending and a reactive policy stance (Wong 1993).
- The erosion of the central government's fiscal position through the 1980s increased the relative power of the provinces, especially the rich coastal provinces. This has led to changes in the intergovernmental fiscal system since the mid-1980s that have been largely anti-poor (Wong, Heady and Woo 1995; World Bank 2002).
- The governing ideology. As in other transition countries, in China this has been characterized by a virulent rejection of the failed egalitarianism of the planned economy. This is epitomized by Deng Xiaoping's guiding principle for reform: letting some people (regions) get rich first.

By the late 1990s, the leadership finally began to focus on growing regional inequalities. With great fanfare, the government introduced the new Western Development Initiative (in 1999), which calls for making massive new investments to help the western regions catch up with the coastal regions. All the NAAs are included in this initiative. Given the weakness of the revenue mechanism—whereby the budget was equivalent to only 16 per cent of GDP in 1999, with the central government managing only half of it—large-scale redistribution through budgetary transfers is unlikely to be forthcoming. Instead, the government appears to be inclined towards treating NAA issues mainly as problems of poverty and underdevelopment whose solution lies in promoting economic development.

In 2001, the central government reaffirmed its commitment to recognizing the special status of the NAAs with an amended Autonomy Law that would help the NAAs gradually reduce the gap with coastal regions The law also introduced new fiscal preferences, including promising the NAAs that 80 per cent of their incremental VAT revenues would be returned as earmarked transfers, compared with less than 30 per cent for other provinces.[10] In addition, the law pledged to reduce the matching funds requirements for central government capital grants to ensure that the NAAs are not excluded from programs because of financing difficulties. However, the law did not set out a specific timetable for these concessions, leaving it to follow the 'development of the national economy and growth in fiscal revenues, [whereby] higher levels will gradually increase the amount of fiscal transfers to the NAAs' (Tiemur 2000).

The government's past efforts to develop the frontier regions do not inspire great confidence in the success of the Western Development Initiative in building solidarity with ethnic minorities. The history of Xinjiang over the past half century is illustrative: despite massive state investments that brought relatively rapid economic growth to the region, today Xinjiang is a hotbed of separatist sentiments. Xinjiang occupies a strategic position. It accounts for one-sixth of all Chinese territory and has borders with eight other countries.[11] It is also the site of large gas and oil deposits. During the early 1960s, numerous skirmishes with the Soviet Union took place in Xinjiang. Because of its strategic importance, the government has invested heavily in the province since 1949 (Bachman 2004). Bachman reports that except during 1971–75, per capita investment in Xinjiang has ranked among the top 10 of China's 31 provinces throughout the history of the People's Republic of China. As a result, Xinjiang enjoys higher than average per capita GDP (Table 9.5). The Western Development Initiative is projected to bring investments of Y 420 billion to Xinjiang during 2001–05, mostly for large-scale infrastructure projects, such as rail links, roads and telecommunications. A pipeline will also be built to bring gas from Xinjiang to Shanghai. More recently, China has been negotiating the building of a pipeline to bring oil from Kazakhstan to the Chinese heartland via Xinjiang.

However, many Uighurs in Xinjiang see industrialization and development as a Han intrusion that has brought more Han into the region and has benefited mainly the Han. The most visible symbol of this is the Production and Construction Corps. The corps was first established during the 1950s as a network of quasi-military Han settlements in the northern half of Xinjiang, staffed with demobilized soldiers, to help fortify the border region. Over the years the corps has established 170 urban settlements and 2000 villages across Xinjiang with a total population of 2.4 million, one-seventh of Xinjiang's total, with 90 per cent of them being Han. Today the corps is a so-called stand-alone planning unit, reporting to and taking orders from the State Council, China's cabinet. Since 1990 it has had provincial-level status. It is a huge military-industrial-agricultural complex that accounts for 20 per cent of Xinjiang's arable land under grain crops and more than one-third of the land under cotton. In 1995 the corps had nearly 3000 industrial enterprises that accounted for more than one-fifth of Xinjiang's total industrial output (Bachman 2004).

Because the Han and Uighur populations are highly segregated, with the Uighurs living mostly in the rural south and southwest and the Han in urban areas and areas under the Production and Construction Corps, Bachman (2004) could use county-level data to show a high correlation between the ratio of Han to the total population and per capita GDP across counties. This seems to support the charge that economic policies in Xinjiang have been tools of internal colonization. Many Uighurs resent the massive immigration that increased the Han population from 6 per cent of the total in 1949 to more than 40 per cent today.

Thus, paradoxically, the Western Development Initiative will make it more urgent for the government to reach out to ethnic minorities in Xinjiang rather than less. Even though ethnic tensions grew through the 1990s, exacerbated by the government's 'strike hard' campaign against terrorist groups, Xinjiang is not currently on the verge of making a bid for secession. If the 1000-mile oil pipeline to Kazakhstan is ever built, however, Xinjiang's strategic importance will be greatly elevated, and the Uighur separatists, who at present are just a prickly security problem for the government, could become a major security threat.

Thus the government may be forced to revisit the issue of asymmetric treatment for minority nationality regions, or at least for the most troublesome ones. In the post-911, post-Soviet world, the growing strength of Islamic cultural and religious movements worldwide has created new centrifugal forces, which presents a particular problem in Xinjiang given that the Uighurs are Moslems and that Xinjiang it located on the edge of Central Asia, making it a likely trouble spot for the indefinite future. With past policies of assimilation through economic growth and industrialization having failed, more explicit gestures to ensure inclusiveness and solidarity will be required.

NOTES

1. During the Yan Dynasty (1279–1368) and the Qing Dynasty (1644–1911), respectively.
2. Officially only five are designated as 'autonomous minority nationalities regions', but since 1980, Guizhou, Yunnan and Qinghai provinces have been included in the group entitled to subsidies for minority nationalities. This chapter will use this broader definition.
3. Most Muslims who do not speak Chinese are classified as members of other Muslim 'nationalities', of which there are nine, including Uighur. There are exceptions, however.

Muslims in Yunnan and Guizhou who speak Tibeto-Burmese languages and Malay-speaking Muslims in Hainan province are classified as Hui (Lipman 2004).

4. The government accuses the Eastern Turkestan Islamic Movement of having ties to al Qaeda. The US government added the group to its list of international terrorist organizations in August 2002 and froze their US assets. Since the Chinese government instituted its so-called strike hard campaign in 1996, many separatist groups have gone underground, but remain active and have claimed credit for several bombing incidents involving Chinese embassies and diplomats in the two republics. A recent terrorist attack was a bus bombing in the Kyrgyz Republic, in which 21 Chinese were shot dead on their tour bus headed to Kashgar and the bus was set on fire (Interfax, Bishkek, 2 April 2003).
5. The northwest has historically been more rebellious. Throughout the first half of the 20th century, ethnic nationalities in Tibet, Mongolia and Xinjiang repeatedly rebelled against central Chinese rule. The result was that the nationalist government (1911–49) paid little attention to the southwest. During 1935–47, for example, the southwest only received 16 per cent per cent of budgetary allocations for 'border education', even though it accounted for 56 per cent per cent of the population, and the bulk went to the northwest (Kaup 2000, p. 55).
6. In the 1982 census, Hui were living in 2308 of the 2372 counties and cities in China (Gladney 1999).
7. Lipman (2004) points out the irony that it was the creation of Hui as an ethnic identity in the 1950s that has created or enhanced the feeling of a collective memory for many Muslims, which did not exist previously.
8. Lipman (2004) recounts many horrific stories of abuse, including forcing Muslims to raise pigs in their courtyards and eat pork. In the village of Shadian in Yunnan province, local Han cadres placed pig bones in village wells to 'help' the Muslims get used to the taste of pork. The Muslim resistance eventually led to an armed struggle that brought the full force of the army into the village, and ended with the village being razed to the ground.
9. China had copied the Soviet model in rigging the price structure to transfer surpluses from the agriculture and mining sectors to the industrial sector, where the state monopoly on ownership ensured easy capture of revenues for state coffers. This revenue mechanism was unsustainable without the supporting mechanism of compulsory procurement at fixed prices, a component that was eliminated step by step during the first years of market reforms.
10. Even though tax rebates are the single biggest source of transfers, they are extremely biased towards the coastal provinces, because rebate amounts are pegged to local collections. Thus the NAAs are unlikely to benefit a great deal from this provision.
11. Afghanistan, Kazakhstan, the Kyrgyz Republic, Mongolia, Pakistan, Russia, Tajikistan and Uzbekistan.

REFERENCES

Armijo, Jacqueline (2001), lecture, University of Washington, Seattle May.

Bachman, David (2004), 'Making Xinjiang Safe for the Han?' in Morris Rossabi (ed.), *Governing China's Multiethnic Frontiers*, Seattle: University of Washington Press.

Bahl, Roy and Jorge Martinez-Vazquez (2003), 'Fiscal Federalism and Economic Reform in China', Working Paper, Georgia State University, Andrew Young School of Policy Studies, International Studies Program, Atlanta.

Chung, Chien-Peng (2002), 'China's "War on Terror"', *Foreign Affairs*, July/August: 8.

Dai, Xiaoming (1997), 'Concerning Fiscal Autonomy in Minority Nationalities Autonomous Regions and the Legal Issues', *Nationalities Research*, (6) 8–17, in Chinese.

Gladney, Dru (1999), 'The Hui', in Halsey Beemer and Sandra Erb (eds), *China: Minority Profiles*, Discussion Papers, Washington, DC: World Bank.

Harrell, Stevan (ed.) (2001), *Perspectives on the Yi of Southwest China*, Berkeley: University of California Press.

Harrell, Stevan, and Dru Gladney (1999), 'Background, Law and Policy', in Halsey Beemer and Sandra Erb (eds), *China: Minority Profiles*, Discussion Paper, Washington, DC: World Bank.

Heberer, Thomas (2001), 'Nationalities Conflict and Ethnicity in the People's Republic of China, with special reference to the Yi', in Stevan Harrell (ed.), *Perspectives on the Yi of Southwest China*, Berkeley: University of California Press.

Huang, Guangxue and Honglie Li (eds) (1993), *The Current Agenda for China's Nationalities*, 2 vols, Beijing: Current Chinese Press, in Chinese.

Huang, Wanlun and Wenchao Li (eds) (1990), *New Theories on the Economies of China's Minority Regions*, Beijing: Central Nationalities Institute Press, in Chinese.

Kaup, Katherine Palmer (2000), *Creating the Zhuang: Ethnic Politics in China*, Boulder, CO: Lynne Reiner.

Khan, Azizur Rahman and Carl Riskin (2000), *Inequality and Poverty in China in the Age of Globalization*, New York: Oxford University Press.

Lipman, Jonathan (2004), 'White Hats, Oilcakes and Common Blood: The Local and the National Among the Chinese-Speaking Muslims', in Morris Rossabi (ed.), *Governing China's Multiethnic Frontiers*, Seattle: University of Washington Press.

National Bureau of Statistics (2001), *Chinese Statistical Yearbook*, Beijing.

Riskin, Carl, Shi Li and Renwei Zhao (eds) (2001), *China's Retreat from Equality*, Armonk, NY: M. E. Sharpe.

Tiemur, Dawamaiti, deputy commission chair of the Standing Committee of the National People's Congress, (2000) 'On Explaining the Draft Proposal on the Revision of the Law on Autonomy of the Nationalities Regions in the People's Republic of China', speech, 23 October.

Wang, Changwu (2000), 'The Fiscal Policy Issues in the Western Development Strategy', *China Finance News,* 3 April, in Chinese.

Wang, Linlu (1994), 'Liangshan's Peasants Have Eight Hopes', *Nationalities,* 11

Wong, Christine P. W. (1993), 'Public Finance and Economic Decentralization,' in Walter Galenson (ed.), *China's Economic Reform in the 1990s*, Ann Arbor: University of Michigan Press.

——— (2000), 'Central-Local Relations Revisited: The 1994 Tax-Sharing Reform and Public Expenditure Management in China', *China Perspectives*, (31).

Wong, Christine P. W., Christopher Heady and Wing T. Woo (1995), *Fiscal Management and Economic Reform in the People's Republic of China,* Hong Kong: Oxford University Press.

World Bank (1997), *China 2020: Development Challenges in the New Century*, Washington, DC: World Bank.

——— (2002), 'China: National Development and Subnational Finance: A Review of Provincial Expenditures', Report No. 22951-CHA, World Bank, East Asia and Pacific Region, Poverty Reduction and Economic Management Unit, Washington, DC.

Xu, Jieshun and Naichang Qin (1991), *Nationality Autonomous Theory,* Nanning, China: Guangxi Education Press, in Chinese.

Zhang, Wenshan (1998), 'On the Legal Framework of China's System of Nationalities Laws', *Nationalities Research*, (3), 10–15.

PART V

Developing Countries

10. Asymmetric Federalism in India

M. Govinda Rao and Nirvikar Singh

A variety of motivations can account for various national units coming together to form a federation. Political and economic theories of federalism attempt to understand the rationale behind the formation of federations and, once they are formed, analyse the conditions under which they hold together. Issues of freedom, security, political stability and strength, while keeping a separate group identity that might be lost in a unitary system, account for the political impulse behind smaller units' desire to federate. Similarly, some of the economic reasons for smaller units coming together to form a federation are the resulting access to a larger common market, which allows reaping economies of scale in the provision of nation-level public goods, and the availability of wider choice of bundles of services to meet diverse preferences. In a situation of free association, each federating unit would try to bargain for terms advantageous to it when joining the federation, while an existing federation would try to attract entry and control exit. Given the unequal nature of interests and powers, symmetry in intergovernmental relationships may not be possible.

Asymmetric federalism is understood to mean federalism based on unequal powers and relationships in political, administrative and fiscal arrangements between the units constituting a federation. Asymmetry in the arrangements in a federation can be viewed in both a vertical sense (between the centre and the states that make up the federation) and a horizontal sense (among the states).[1] If federations are seen as an indestructible union of indestructible states (Wheare 1953) and the centre and states are seen to exist on the basis of equality, then neither has the power to make inroads into the defined authority and functions of the other unilaterally. However, such a purist view of federalism rarely, if ever, occurs in practice. Even when the constitution of federal systems guarantees almost equal powers to the states, the centre typically dominates in the political, administrative and fiscal spheres because of its greater control over resources or because of the natural assignment to the centre of such tasks as national defence.

A considerable volume of literature deals with the domination of the centre in Indian federalism, covering both the assignment system in the constitution and the centre's intrusion into the states' domains (for a survey of the relevant literature, see Rao and Chelliah 1997). Unlike classical federations like the United States, the Indian federation is not an indestructible union of indestructible states (see Figure 10.1 for a map of India). Only the Union is indestructible, but the states are not. Article 3 of the constitution vests parliament with the powers to constitute new states by separating territories from existing ones, altering their boundaries and changing their names. The only requirement for this is that the bill for the purpose must be placed before parliament on the recommendation of the president and following the solicitation of the views of the relevant state legislature (though its approval is not necessary). In addition, the federation is not founded on the principle of equality between the Union and the states. India's central government has the powers to invade the states' legislative and executive domains and does so (Chanda 1965; Rao and Sen 1996; Rao and Singh 2000).

However, a review of the nature and basis of the relationship between the centre and states is not the objective of this chapter. Rather, the chapter focuses on unequal arrangements and special treatment for some units within the Indian federation. Such an arrangement is quite feasible when it evolves from bargaining and accommodation. It may also be desirable to have special powers and asymmetric arrangements to be able to continually accommodate diverse groups' interests and identities, and therefore these asymmetries have an important role in both the coming together and holding together aspects of federalism. Nevertheless, such accommodation can only be at the margin and cannot violate the basic fabric of equality and fair treatment of jurisdictions, as perceived by constituents. This, in turn, requires arrangements to be transparent.

Therefore an important distinction is between unequal arrangements or asymmetries that are transparent and rules based, and which evolved to facilitate the smooth functioning of the federation, and those that are opaque and discretionary, and are caused by shifts in the balance of administrative and political power and by expediency. The former may be built into the constitutional arrangement itself or may have evolved through conventions for the smooth functioning of the federation. This type of asymmetry is transparent and rules based and plays an important role in building the nation in terms of imparting a sense of shared identity and self-identification. In contrast, the latter type of asymmetry can simply be an outcome of administrative and political power plays in a federation. In India, for example, the dynamics created by the end of single party rule in both the centre and the states, the emergence of coalition governments at the centre and the importance of regional parties in the central coalition as well as in the states can create asymmetries in the functioning of the federation because of short-run political considerations. This can have serious repercussions for the future of the federation.

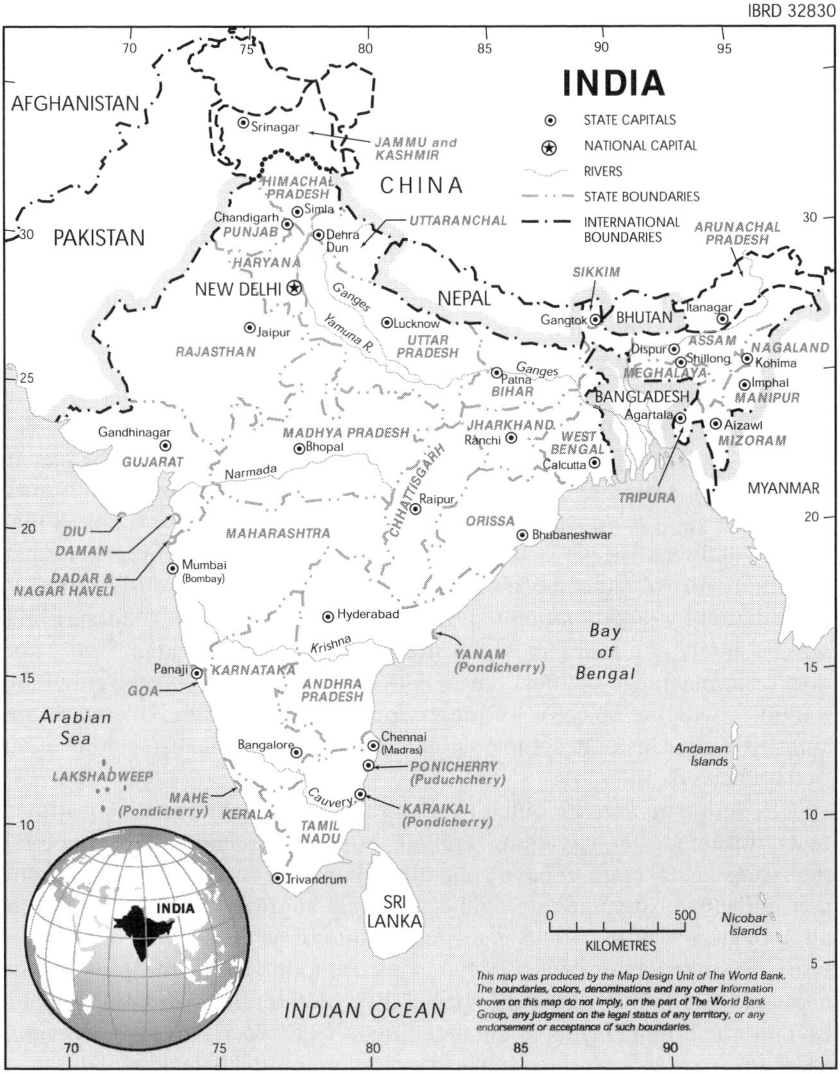

Figure 10.1 India

This chapter examines the asymmetric features of Indian federalism and evaluates their importance and impact. The next section explores the conceptual issues of asymmetric federalism. The chapter then traces some aspects of the evolution of Indian federalism and analyses the factors that contribute to the asymmetric arrangements in political, administrative and fiscal relations.

This is followed by a review of asymmetry arising from constitutional arrangements or conventions that have evolved over the years. The chapter then turns to recent political developments and asymmetric treatment resulting from administrative and political exigencies before concluding.

ASYMMETRIC ARRANGEMENTS: SOME CONCEPTUAL ISSUES

According to political scientists such as Riker (1975), federalism is an outcome of rational bargaining among various constituents. This bargain may concern political and/or economic gains, although Riker emphasizes the former. In the political bargain, the constituents give up political autonomy for security from external threats. The economic bargain is intended to enable a common market and to ensure optimal provision of public services by reaping economies of scale and catering to diverse preferences. However, while striking the bargain, the constituents try to preserve valued dimensions of their identity and seek special status. The motivation behind seeking special status may be purely to expand economic opportunities and secure freedom from exploitation by larger and more powerful members of the federation. It may also be purely political, that is, a desire to enhance the individual state's freedom or to maximize political power and influence. It may also be cultural or religious, with the objective of preserving groups' identities. Overall, it may simply be a means of accommodating diverse groups' interests within a unified framework.

If federalism were an outcome of a rational bargain among constituent units, differences in bargaining strength would be a source of asymmetry. If the issues at stake are to have general applicability to the majority of units, then collective bargaining strength could result in greater decentralization and all subnational units would get greater autonomy. If, on the contrary, the issues at stake were relevant only to specific units, and if the units had the necessary strength to secure the special dispensation, then this could result in asymmetric arrangements in the federation. Such special arrangements may be *de jure,* that is, enshrined in the constitution or established by tradition, or *de facto*, that is, observed in practice. Special arrangements may also evolve over time. In many cases, special arrangements are accorded only temporarily until units are assimilated into the federation, that is, coming together has been completed. In other cases, bargains may have to be struck by giving special status for holding the federation together. Yet other cases of asymmetry may arise purely through political alignments in a democratic polity. The ways in which bargains are struck and special demands by various constituents are accommodated through asymmetric arrangements have a vital bearing on the federation's stability.

Thus asymmetric arrangements need not necessarily be the outcome of constitutional arrangements and can also result from the way in which administrative, political and fiscal systems are implemented in a federation. *De facto* asymmetries can be desirable and can contribute to nation building if they are based on transparent principles. At the same time, special arrangements instituted to meet short-term political expediency needs or for reasons of administrative discretion can cause the progressive degradation of intergovernmental institutions. While some degree of discretion to meet special circumstances will always be desirable, one possible danger is that such arrangements can result in the arbitrary conferring of special favours and, in the long run, can increase disharmony and instability in a federation.

In a centralized federation, the central government has considerable scope to discriminate among the units, because it presumably has more and more effective policy instruments. The potential for discrimination may be particularly strong when the central government is weak and, at the same time, some states wield significant control over the centre, even when the formal structures are those of a centralized federation. This issue is pertinent in India, because regional parties in some states wield significant power over the coalition central government.

EVOLUTION OF ASYMMETRIC ARRANGEMENTS IN INDIAN FEDERALISM

Political bargaining between various national units for coming together is the essence of federalism. In this process, the bargaining powers of various parties are unequal, and therefore the terms of accession between different national units in a federation could differ considerably. In addition, during the course of the working of the federation, special features of different units and special circumstances may require differential treatments. Thus asymmetric arrangements are a common feature of federations. However, the nature and implementation of asymmetric arrangements is an issue critical not only to the working, but also to the stability, of federations.

Historical Background

The distribution of power between the centre and the states and the treatment of different states in the Indian constitution owe much to historical and political factors. The cabinet mission sent by the UK government in 1946 saw no virtue in partitioning India into two different independent nations based on religion. Instead it recommended that the independent country should be governed by a federal constitution with the central government dealing with only foreign affairs, defence and communications and with remaining powers vested with two groups of provinces, one predominantly Hindu and the other predominantly Muslim. This proposal for a decentralized federation was meant to provide sufficient guarantees of autonomy for the Muslims, who were in a minority at the national level, though not in all regions of India. However, the Muslim League's insistence of having a separate nation for the Muslims led to the formation of Pakistan, which comprised the Muslim majority regions of the northwestern part of the subcontinent and the eastern part of Bengal. As a result, creating a highly decentralized federation was no longer necessary. Instead, the founding fathers of independent India decided to have a federation with a strong central government to hold together the country's diverse economic, linguistic and cultural entities and to avoid fissiparous tendencies. They also believed that centralization was desirable to unify a country that consisted of the regions that had been directly ruled by the British and 216 princely states and territories (for a detailed account of the history leading to Indian independence, see Chanda 1965).

Asymmetric Structure at Independence

Asymmetric arrangements in Indian federalism have a long history and go back to the way in which the British unified the country under their rule, and later the way in which the territories under the direct control of the British and various principalities were integrated into the Indian Union. While the territories ruled directly by the British were easily integrated into the Union, the treaties of accession signed by individual rulers covered the integration of different principalities. The provinces ruled directly by the British had a modicum of autonomy and rudimentary forms of parliamentary government as the British gradually loosened their grip from 1919.

The constitution that was adopted in 1950 classified the states into four categories. The provinces that had been directly ruled by the British were classified as Part A states. The princely states that had a relationship with the central government based on individual treaties were classified as Part B states. These included the states of Hyderabad, Mysore, Jammu and Kashmir and five new unions of princely states. In the case of Jammu and Kashmir, the terms of accession gave the state special powers as discussed in more detail later. The remaining princely states acceding to the Union were grouped under Part C states. Finally, the territories gaining independence from other foreign powers (France and Portugal) and areas not included in the first three categories were brought under the direct control of the Union to form Part D states or Union territories.

Thus at the time of its formation in 1947, the Union of India began with a major asymmetry between British India and the princely states, and among the latter, the terms of accession differed depending on their bargaining strength. In almost all cases, the princely states surrendered whatever notional sovereignty they had to the newly independent country of India in exchange for a guaranteed revenue stream: their so-called privy purses. The nature of this bargain was clear: the princely states received security and money in exchange for giving up authority or residual control rights. This is close to the standard view of federation as a political bargain, with the difference being that the successors of the British in India, the Indian National Congress, were in an extremely strong bargaining position, even relative to the coalition of the princes. This was illustrated in the case of the exceptions to voluntary accession, such as Hyderabad, where military force (the authority over which was also inherited from the British) ensured integration into the new Union.

Assimilation of Units After Independence

While many of the former princely states, particularly the Part B states, continued to function as administrative units after their integration into India, this continuation was not an essential part of the bargain. Furthermore, the reorganization of state boundaries, which took place from 1953, and which the constitution freely permitted, gradually eroded their status as continuing subnational units. The constitution allowed substate structures for regions closely tied to some former princely states, but this had little practical import, as the states became almost the sole significant subnational units of governance. Thus, in general, the princely states ceased to matter as geographic entities. In this respect, the outcome was completely different from the standard case of federation, where the constituents of the federation would normally retain their identities. Broadly speaking, this aspect of the asymmetric arrangement was a recognition of the different sets of institutions and administrative standards, which were unified over the years. The asymmetries present in 1947 with respect to almost all the princely states disappeared from Indian federalism.

Special Position of Kashmir

The sole exception to the disappearance of asymmetries for the princely states was the state of Jammu and Kashmir (for a good discussion of the asymmetric arrangements in Jammu and Kashmir and the northeastern states, see Arora 1995). While this state included several diverse populations and regions, the overwhelming majority of the population in the Kashmir Valley was Muslim, and the state bordered the new nation of Pakistan. Despite the extensive literature on the history of the conflict over Kashmir, consensus on the interpretation of events in 1947–48 is lacking. Here we merely note that the state acceded to the Indian Union under special terms that were subsequently incorporated in Article 370 of the constitution. This article provided the state with a unique position in the Union, with its own constitution, a title interpreted as the equivalent of prime minister for its chief executive and a special assignment of functional responsibilities. Specifically, the centre's jurisdiction was restricted to foreign affairs, defence and communications, with the state's legislature having residuary powers. This was a striking contrast to the situation of other states, where the centre's assignment of responsibilities was much more extensive, and where the centre retained residuary powers.

Integration of Northeastern Hill States

India's administrative reorganization focused on the creation of new boundaries based primarily on language. Typically, separate religious, caste, ethnic or tribal identities within these boundaries were not the basis for further divisions. One major exception to this has been the northeastern part of India, where there is a distinct difference in ethnicity from the rest of India, and several strong divisions are based not only on language, but also on culture and tribal traditions. This part of India contains the states of Arunachal Pradesh, Assam, Manipur, Meghalaya, Mizoram, Nagaland, Sikkim and Tripura. Of these, only Assam has a population comparable in size to that of the typical Indian state, while the others are quite small. Most of these states were upgraded from the status of Union territories, this reclassification giving them, at one level, a political status equivalent to that of larger states such as Bihar, Madhya Pradesh and Uttar Pradesh (for a chronology, see, for example, Brass 1994). Each state carries equal weight when mustering the 50 per cent of states required to ratify an amendment to the constitution.

Furthermore, various clauses in Article 371 accord special powers to the northeastern states. These provisions have been introduced through amendments, typically at the time a Union territory converts to a state, or in the case of Sikkim, after its accession to India. The safeguards provided to these states through these special provisions include respect for customary laws, religious and social practices, restrictions on the ownership and transfer of land and restrictions on the migration of nonresidents to the state. State legislatures are typically given final control over changes to these provisions.

Thus various provisions in the Indian constitution protect groups' rights and compensate them for initial inequalities in the social system. While recognizing the idea of fundamental human rights at the individual level, the constitution does not assume an idealized initial condition of equality, either in pure economic terms or otherwise. Allowances are made for separate laws to govern different religious groups and provisions exist for various kinds of affirmative action programs for extremely disadvantaged groups. The former simply respect diversity (though this can create issues of unequal treatment across subgroups, for example, women, in different religious groups). The latter attempt to correct for specific inequities, recognizing that equal legislative treatment from extremely unequal initial conditions will not achieve desired equity goals. Conceptually, at this level of ethical or normative judgement, there is no difference between these provisions and the ones for the indigenous residents of northeastern states, except that the latter happen to be geographically concentrated into reasonable administrative units.

ASYMMETRIES IN PRACTICE

In every federation, the asymmetric arrangements are built into the constitution, and constitutions have evolved to ensure that the smooth working of the federation is formalized into rules and systems. In addition, the political arrangements made in the process of governing can also result in the asymmetric distribution of both political and economic powers among individual units in a federation. Thus the actual asymmetry in economic, administrative and political spheres may go farther than the *de jure* asymmetry in the constitutional arrangements.

Economic Asymmetry

The coming together of units with diverse histories, resources, policies and institutions in a bargain to form a federation would certainly entail *de facto* asymmetry in terms of differences between states in relation to their geography, demography and economies. India currently has 28 states and 7 Union territories. Union territories are governed directly by the central government, except for Delhi and Pondicherry, which have their own elected governments and legislatures.

Table 10.1 highlights the wide variations in the economic characteristics of the states. For example, the biggest state, Rajasthan, is 90 times bigger than the smallest state, Goa. Similarly, in terms of population size, Uttar Pradesh, the state with the largest population, has 308 times more people than Sikkim, the state with the smallest population. Meanwhile population density varies from 13 people per square kilometre in Arunachal Pradesh to 901 in West Bengal. In addition, Maharashtra, the state with the highest net state domestic product (NSDP), had 284 times the NSDP of Sikkim, the state with the lowest NSDP. Finally, significant variations are also apparent in per capita incomes: in 1999–2000 Goa, a small state on the west coast, had a per capita NSDP of Rs 44 613, which was almost nine times the per capita NSDP of Rs 4813 in Bihar.

For the sake of convenience, we have broken down the states into special category states and general category states. The former are those that are

Table 10.1 *Characteristics of Indian states*

State	Area (km^2)	Population, 2001 (thousands)	Population density (per km^2)	NSDP, 1999–2000 (Rs millions)	Per capita NSDP, 1999–2000 (Rs)	Percentage of total area	Percentage of total population	Percentage of total NSDP
High-income states	601 800	194 065	322.5	4 065 770	22 461	18.31	18.90	28.74
Goa	3800	1344	353.7	58 620	44 613	0.12	0.13	0.41
Gujarat	196 000	50 597	258.1	896 060	18 685	5.96	4.93	6.33
Haryana	44 000	21 083	479.2	424 880	21 551	1.34	2.05	3.00
Maharashtra	308 000	96 752	314.1	2 131 510	22 604	9.37	9.42	15.07
Punjab	50 000	24 289	485.8	554 700	23 254	1.52	2.37	3.92
Middle-income states	725 000	302 633	417.4	4 867 930	17 635	22.05	29.47	34.41
Andhra Pradesh	275 000	75 728	275.4	1 117 530	14 878	8.36	7.37	7.90
Karnataka	192 000	52 734	274.7	862 980	16 654	5.84	5.13	6.10
Kerala	39 000	31 839	816.4	569 260	17 709	1.19	3.10	4.02
Tamil Nadu	130 000	62 111	477.8	1 143 090	18 623	3.95	6.05	8.08
West Bengal	89 000	80 221	901.4	1 175 070	14 874	2.71	7.81	8.31
Low-income states	135 800	450 202	332.1	4 022 290	9013	41.30	43.83	28.44
Bihar	94 000	82 879	881.7	383 260	4813	2.86	8.07	2.71
Chattisgarh	135 100	20 796	153.9	213 310	10 405	4.11	2.02	1.51
Jharkhand	79 700	26 909	337.6	232 270	9223	2.42	2.62	1.64
Madhya Pradesh	308 000	60 385	196.1	677 780	11 626	9.37	5.88	4.79
Orissa	156 000	36 707	235.3	311 950	8733	4.75	3.57	2.21
Rajasthan	342 000	56 473	165.1	710 200	13 046	10.40	5.50	5.02
Uttar Pradesh	241 000	166 053	689.0	1 493 520	9323	7.33	16.17	10.56

General category states	2 682 600	946 900	353.0	12 955 990	14 605	81.66	92.20	91.59
Special category states	594 000	63 662	107.2	63 930	10 695	18.01	6.20	4.52
Arunachal Pradesh	84 000	1091	13.0	14 270	13 352	2.56	0.11	0.10
Assam	78 000	26 638	341.5	2 533 300	9720	2.37	2.59	1.79
Himachal Pradesh	56 000	6077	108.5	106 570	17 786	1.70	0.59	0.75
Jammu and Kashmir	222 000	10 070	45.4	121 820	12 373	6.75	0.98	0.86
Manipur	22 000	2389	108.6	28 580	12 721	0.67	0.23	0.20
Meghalaya	23 000	2306	100.3	29 040	12 063	0.70	0.22	0.21
Mizoram	21 000	891	42.4	12 880	14 909	0.64	0.09	0.09
Nagaland	17 000	1989	117.0	23 300	12 594	0.52	0.19	0.16
Sikkim	7000	540	77.1	7580	14 751	0.21	0.05	0.05
Tripura	10 500	3191	303.9	41 930	13 195	0.32	0.31	0.30
Uttaranchal	53 500	8480	158.5	—	—	1.60	0.83	—
All states	3 276 600	1 010 562	308.4	13 595 290	14 359	99.67	98.40	96.11
Union territories	10 974	16 453	1499.3	549 870[a]	31 211	0.33	1.60	3.89
Total	3 287 574	1 027 015	312.4	14 145 160	13 778	100.00	100.00	100.00

— Not available.
NSDP Net state domestic product.

a. Excludes state domestic product from the union territories of Dadra and Naga Haveli, Daman and Dieu and Lakshadweep..

Sources: Census data; Ministry of Finance (2001).

given special status in receiving plan assistance from the central government. The general category states are in turn classified into high-income, middle-income and low-income states based on their per capita NSDP: those with a per capita NSDP that is more than 15 per cent above the average for India as a whole are classified as high-income states and those with a per capita NSDP that is less than 10 per cent of the average are classified as low-income states.

Table 10.1 shows that the 11 special category states, cover 18 per cent of the geographical area of the country, have just about 6 per cent of the population and generate about 5 per cent of the NSDP. The importance of non-economic factors in determining the structure of federalism is underscored by the fact that most of the special category states are not economically viable in terms of providing standards of public services or livelihoods comparable with those in the rest of the Union. While the general category states (except for Goa) are large, there are significant interstate variations in size, resource endowments and developmental indicators.

Within the general category states, wide variations in area, population and income levels are apparent. The high-income states, which account for about 18 to 19 per cent of India's area and population, generated 29 per cent of NSDP whereas the low-income states, which represent some 43 to 45 per cent of India's geographic area and population, accounted for only 28 per cent of NSDP.

The foregoing discussion brings out the point that economic viability has never been a consideration in demarcating the states in India, nor has it been a factor in the reorganization of states. Thus intergovernmental relationships are placed on an uneven economic keel. Naturally a uniform assignment system in an unevenly endowed federal system results in large differences in fiscal capacities. Varying sizes of states in terms of area and population, differing demographic compositions and different terrain and topography cause significant variations in the unit cost of providing public services and varying expenditure needs and place a heavy burden of equalization on the intergovernmental transfer system.

Table 10.2 shows the implications of interstate differences in economic conditions on fiscal variables by bringing out some important fiscal features of Indian federalism. First, variations in economic characteristics have resulted in significant differences in the revenues collected in different states, caused partly by differences in the capacity to raise revenues and partly by differences in their collection efficiency. Generally, the ratio of revenues to NSDP is positively related to the level of per capita income. The low-income states had lower revenue ratios than the middle-income states, which in turn had lower ratios than the high-income states.

Second, the ratio of revenues to NSDP was much lower in special category states than general category states, even when the latter had comparable

Table 10.2 States' revenues and expenditures, 2000–01 (revised estimates)

States	Poverty ratio (percent)[a]	Per capita own revenue (Rs)	Own revenue as a percentage of NSDP	Per capita transfers (Rs)	Per capita current spending (Rs)	Percentage of own revenue in current spending
High-income states	17.83	2931.6	13.1	500	4386.6	66.8
Gujarat	14.07	2684.6	13.2	863	5167.6	52.0
Goa	4.4	14 310.3	15.8	588	11 904.8	120.2
Haryana	8.74	3209.7	12.1	502	4107.9	78.1
Maharashtra	25.02	2741.3	11.1	448	3852.6	71.2
Punjab	6.16	3333.2	10.2	494	4712.7	70.7
Middle-income states	20.3	1868.8	10.6	658	3400.4	55.0
Andhra Pradesh	15.77	1930.2	10.7	713	3320.2	58.1
Karnataka	20.44	2148.1	11.3	686	3580.9	60.0
Kerala	12.72	2295.8	10.2	690	3689.4	62.2
Tamil Nadu	21.12	2342.5	11.3	658	3594.3	65.2
West Bengal	27.02	1091.0	5.5	576	3092.7	35.3
Low-income states	34.28	858.5	9.3	673	2261.3	38.8
Bihar	42.6	338.2	8.9	724	1515.5	22.3
Chattisgarh	—	1264.0	4.9	—	2455.2	51.5
Jharkhand	—	1128.0	9.0	—	2229.4	50.6
Madhya Pradesh	37.43	1061.9	11.5	624	2695.5	39.4
Orissa	47.15	900.5	9.3	969	2785.3	32.3
Rajasthan	15.28	1297.2	10.4	693	2864.2	45.3
Uttar Pradesh	31.15	791.2	8.1	598	2135.6	37.0
General category states	25.97	1606.3	11.0	660	3060.9	52.5
Special category states	30.50	1032.2	9.7	2896	5126.7	20.1
Arunachal Pradesh	33.47	1067.8	5.3	7985	9992.3	10.7
Assam	36.09	798.7	7.2	1216	3317.0	24.1
Himachal Pradesh	7.63	1660.5	7.8	3070	7420.6	22.4
Jammu and Kashmir	3.48	1150.4	7.9	4602	6080.0	18.9
Manipur	28.54	406.0	3.1	3971	6032.3	6.7
Meghalaya	33.87	1066.8	6.3	3149	5878.4	18.1
Mizoram	19.47	679.0	3.8	9602	12 845.6	5.3
Nagaland	32.67	506.8	3.7	6332	7291.0	7.0
Sikkim	36.55	5998.1	15.9	7945	12 200.6	49.2
Tripura	34.44	729.6	4.8	3376	5838.9	12.5
Uttaranchal	—	1295.5	—	—	4912.7	26.4
All states	26.10	1570.1	10.9	768	3191.1	49.2

— Not available.
NSDP Net state domestic product.

a. 1999–2000.

Sources: Ministry of Planning data; Reserve Bank of India data.

NSDP levels. The singular exception to this is the case of Sikkim, which had retained the power to levy income taxes when acceding to the country. Thus unlike in other states, Sikkim has the power to levy income tax, and federal income tax cannot extend to Sikkim.

Third, the small size of jurisdictions in the special category states implies that they cannot reap economies of scale in providing services. In any case, the hilly and inhospitable terrain prevalent in these states means that the unit costs of providing public services are higher than in other states. Thus their overwhelming dependence on central transfers is not surprising. In 2001–02, general category states, on average, raised sufficient revenues to finance more than 52 per cent of their current expenditure, whereas in the special category states this figure was around 20 per cent, meaning that central transfers financed more than 80 per cent of the expenditures of special category states. In per capita terms, transfers to special category states are more than four times the average transfers received by general category states.

Asymmetric Design of the Transfer System

As noted earlier, the different position of special category states is reflected not only in structural asymmetries and fiscal arrangements, but in the methods and patterns of central transfers to the states. In some respects, the small size of the special category states—they account for about 6 per cent of India's population—is an advantage for the Union, because transfers that are high in per capita terms for these states are unlikely to place a significant burden on the rest of the nation. Their small size also encourages these states to combine politically for some purposes and to negotiate collectively with the centre.

Transfers from the centre to the states come from three sources. The first is the statutory transfers made on the recommendation of the Finance Commission appointed by the president of India every five years. The second channel for transfers is the assistance given for state plan schemes by the Planning Commission. Finally, the third channel is plan transfers given by various central ministries for specific purposes with or without matching requirements on the part of the states. Various central government ministries have initiated and administer more than 200 such schemes. The allocation of resources to different states is also influenced by the central government's regional policy in relation to such matters as direct investment by the central government.

The framers of the constitution intended that transfers to the states should be based on the recommendations of an impartial, semi-judicial body appointed by the president every five years, the Finance Commission. So far, 11 such commissions have made recommendations; however, given the increased emphasis on centralized development planning over the years, the Planning Commission has gained in importance as a dispenser of both grants and loans. Thus the Finance Commissions have been confined to examining the states' non-plan requirements and providing transfers to meet those requirements while the Planning Commission has been assigned to deal with plan requirements.

Initially, the volume of central assistance for state plans, as well as the grant versus loan composition of such assistance, was determined on the basis of approved plan projects in the different states, but since 1969, the allocation has been determined on the basis of a formula as calculated by the National Development Council (NDC). The NDC is an intergovernmental body presided over by the prime minister and composed of cabinet ministers, members of the Planning Commission and states' chief ministers. Over the years, with increased earmarking of central assistance for specific schemes, the formula-based component of central assistance for state plans has been reduced, and in 2002–03, it was estimated at about 46 per cent of total transfers to the states. In the early 1990s, the entire assistance under this category was formula based.

In addition, the central ministries exercised discretion in relation to transfers by increasing transfers under sectoral and centrally sponsored schemes. Thus, as shown in Table 10.3, Finance Commission transfers account for about two-thirds of total transfers, and this has remained broadly constant since the early 1970s. However, transfers given for state plan schemes and specific purpose transfers for central sectoral and centrally sponsored schemes have generally increased over time. More important, the discretionary element of the transfer system has increased steadily over the years.

Finance Commission Transfers

Finance Commission transfers consist of tax devolution and grants. The commission's methodology is to assess the fiscal position of the centre and the states in the absence of transfers, projecting the states' revenues and non-plan expenditures for the next five years, then augmenting the states' projected revenues by recommending what shares of central taxes should go to individual states based on general economic indicators and finally filling the remaining gap between non-plan expenditures and revenues with grants-in-aid. This is referred to as the gap-filling approach.

Discretionary elements enter into even the formula-based transfers of the Finance Commission. The commission determines the shares of the centre and the states in central taxes broadly on the basis of judgements pertaining to their relative requirements, but mostly on the basis of past shares. For example, for 2000–05, the Eleventh Finance Commission recommended that 29.5 per cent of the net collections from central taxes should be transferred to the states. The relative shares are determined on the basis of general economic

Table 10.3 Central transfers to the states, 1969–2002
(Rs billions)

Plan	Finance commission transfers			Plan grants			Other grants	Total
	Tax devolution	Grants	Total	State plan scheme	Central scheme	Total		
Fourth Plan (1969–74)	45.6 (54.2)	8.6 (10.2)	54.2 (64.6)	10.8 (12.8)	9.7 (11.6)	20.5 (24.4)	9.3 (11.0)	83.9 (100.0)
Fifth Plan (1974–79)	82.7 (50.2)	28.2 (17.1)	110.9 (67.3)	29.1 (17.7)	19.3 (11.7)	48.4 (29.4)	5.4 (3.3)	164.7 (100.0)
Sixth Plan (1980–85)	237.3 (57.0)	21.4 (5.1)	258.7 (62.1)	73.8 (17.7)	69.0 (16.6)	142.8 (34.3)	15.1 (3.6)	416.5 (100.0)
Seventh Plan (1985–90)	494.6 (54.2)	62.7 (6.9)	557.4 (61.0)	155.2 (17.1)	165.1 (18.0)	320.3 (35.1)	35.2 (3.9)	913.1 (100.0)
Eighth Plan (1992–97)	1318.5 (55.6)	147.2 (6.2)	1465.7 (61.8)	483.4 (20.4)	364.7 (15.4)	848.4 (35.7)	58.4 (2.5)	2373.1 (100.0)
Ninth Plan (1998–2002)	2300.9 (57.9)	239.9 (6.0)	2540.8 (64.0)	777.0 (19.6)	469.4 (11.8)	1146.3 (31.3)	189.5 (4.8)	3976.6 (100.0)

Note: Figures in parentheses are percentages of total transfers.

Source: Government data.

variables with weights assigned to population, income, area, an infrastructure index, tax effort and fiscal discipline, and it is the choices made in relation to variables and their weights that influence the relative shares of the states. This, however, need not necessarily be a source of unacceptable asymmetry, because the formulas the commission uses are transparent.

The need to avoid nontransparent discretion for large-scale transfers is precisely why the framers of the constitution intended that the distribution of transfers should be undertaken primarily through the Finance Commission and why the commission is supposed to be a statutory, semi-judicial authority. However, the formation of the commissions and the approach and methodology they adopt, as well as their recommendations, have recently been controversial. Notable among the criticisms was that levelled against the Ninth Finance Commission for its use of the poverty ratio as a criterion for ascertaining the states' tax shares (Bagchi 1988). Critics argued that poverty alleviation is not an objective of general purpose transfers, and that this should be taken care of by the direct anti-poverty interventions initiated by the rural development and urban development ministries. They also maintained that the transfer system should not be used to reward states that are not making sufficient efforts to alleviate poverty. An even more important criticism concerned the Ninth Finance Commission's discretionary transfer for slum clearance in Mumbai (Bombay) and Kolkata (Calcutta) (Bagchi 1988; Guhan 1989). Similarly, the Tenth Finance Commission was criticized for giving transfers to Andhra Pradesh to compensate the state for revenue it lost by following a prohibition policy, that is, prohibiting the consumption or sale of alcoholic beverages.[2]

The most serious criticism of the Finance Commission has been with respect to its gap-filling methodology. Critics allege that the fiscal dentistry practised by the various commissions has enlarged budgetary cavities, because the states can gain more by reducing their own tax efforts and indulging in profligate spending. Indeed, critics attribute some of the serious deterioration in states' finances observed in recent years to the transfer system (Rao 2004). This has resulted in the states resorting to frequent overdrafts. As the states have had to seek more assistance, the central government made each of the states sign a memorandum of understanding that they would initiate measures to correct the situation. Notably, the contents of these memoranda of understanding have not been placed in the public domain, thus whether the conditionalities differ for the different states remains unknown.

Yet despite the memoranda of understanding, the fiscal position has continued to deteriorate. Therefore when the 11th Finance Commission was about to submit its report, an additional term of reference was given to the commission to draw up a 'monitorable fiscal reform program aimed at reduction of revenue deficit of the states and recommend the manner in which the grants to states to cover the assessed deficit in their non-plan revenue account may be linked to progress in implementing the program'. Based on the commission's recommendation, the centre initiated the Medium-Term Fiscal Reform Programme. Accordingly, a small portion of the transfers has been earmarked for giving grants to those states that achieve a five percentage point reduction in revenue deficits.

Critics have pointed to a number of shortcomings in the scheme. To begin with, the amount earmarked for giving grants under the Medium-Term Fiscal Reform Programme constitutes less than 2 per cent of the transfers recommended by the Finance Commission. In addition, it has contributed to further segmentation in the transfer system. A more important criticism from the viewpoint of asymmetry is that in the case of special category states, more than 80 per cent of their revenues accrue from central transfers, thus an inability to reduce their deficits may be due to a reduction in central transfers, but this will be seen as poor performance by the states.

Asymmetry in State Plan Assistance

The transfer system's asymmetric design in favour of the special category states is apparent in relation to the distribution of plan assistance. Until 1969, plan assistance for state plan purposes was provided according to the various plan schemes approved. To impart greater objectivity, the NDC approved a transfer formula in 1969, and since that time plan assistance has been distributed to the states according to this formula, which the NDC has modified from time to time.

The asymmetry in the plan assistance is seen mainly between the special category states and the general category states. According to the current formula, first, 30 per cent of the central assistance for state plans is earmarked for the special category states despite their small population share. Second, 90 per cent of plan assistance to special category states is given as grants and the remainder as loans, compared with a 30/70 split for the general category states. The policy may by partly justified on the grounds that the unit cost of providing public services in the remote, mountainous states is higher and that the transfer system should neutralize this difference. In practice, per capita spending in the special category states is higher than even in the high-income states (Table 10.2). Higher transfers may also be needed to meet special expenditure requirements, such as higher levels of security, that are not required in other states. Thus these states may, to some extent, be acting as agents of the centre in the provision of the national public goods of strategic stability and defence. Another part of the reason for higher transfers to the special category states may be because the centre has not allowed foreign investment to flow into these regions because of their location along international borders, and therefore has the responsibility of strengthening the regions by means of domestic investment.

Perhaps the most important reason for the large transfers to the special category states is the political bargains that brought these areas firmly into the Union and keeps them there. This kind of reasoning is particularly clear for such formal, separate inductions into the Union as took place for Sikkim and for the case of Kashmir, but it also applies to such states as Nagaland, where a long insurgency after Indian independence was finally brought under some control through the granting of statehood with special provisions, and where an implicit political bargain may require continuing above average transfers.

A notable feature of the state plan assistance is the steady increase in its discretionary component. Even though plan transfers are supposed to take place according to the NDC formula, over the years an increasing proportion of the assistance has been earmarked for specific schemes and kept outside the formula-based assistance. The remaining portion included such earmarked assistance as schemes for hill, border and desert areas; assistance to the northeast and Sikkim; slum development; the accelerated power development scheme; the accelerated irrigation benefit program; and the prime minister's village development plan and rural roads program.

An important component of non-formula based assistance under state plan schemes is the pass-through assistance from multilateral and bilateral donors to the state governments. In recent years, lending by multilateral and bilateral donors to subnational governments has increased significantly, and some discussion of this is in order. According to the constitution, the states do not have the power to borrow from foreign agencies; however, in recent years the states have been allowed to negotiate directly with multilateral and bilateral donors, even though the loans are eventually routed through the central government. The central government has allowed some states to seek loans from multilateral donors, whereas others have been unable to access such assistance. This has naturally given rise to questions about propriety and partisanship in the selection of states for such assistance, for example, those states ruled by regional parties that support the coalition government at the centre may find that accessing such loans is easier than those states ruled by the main opposition parties. In a situation in which most of the states are ruled by the main opposition party, the central government seems to have adopted a policy of going slow on this aspect of liberalization.

The discussion of plan assistance is not complete without referring to the way in which the states' borrowing operations are conducted. Article 293 of the constitution empowers the states to borrow internally from the centre or from the market; however, it stipulates that they can borrow money from the market without referring to the central government only if they are not indebted to the centre. Centralized planning has ensured that all states are indebted to the centre, therefore market borrowing by the states simply implies an allocation of market loans by representatives of the central Ministry of Finance, the Planning Commission and the Reserve Bank of India. The stipulation of a statutory liquidity ratio for the commercial banks ensures that the state governments' bonds are subscribed to by the banking system.

The ways in which both central loans and market borrowing are allocated to states are not rules based and transparent, and therefore have resulted in resentment by some states. Generally, after meeting repayment liabilities, some additional resources are mobilized thorough these instruments for spending on plan schemes. Asymmetry can result from the volume of loans allocated to each state and the extent of interest rate repression. Until the early 1990s, the interest rates charged on states' market loans were substantially below the market interest rates, but since that time interest rates have been better aligned to market rates. The whole process is somewhat opaque, in that significant scope exists for favouring some states over others in the allocation of market borrowing.

Tremendous scope for discrimination among the states arises from the practice of rescheduling and writing off loans based on special considerations. In the past, a number of finance commissions were asked to look into states' indebtedness and recommend rescheduling and writing off, and based on their recommendations, rescheduling was carried out. This was not an action required by the constitution. In recent years the central government has written off states' loans in Punjab and Jammu and Kashmir and has proposed writing off Nagaland's loans solely on a discretionary basis, without referring the issue to any body. The reason given was that these states have fought terrorism and insurgency on behalf of the nation, and therefore needed to be compensated for the consequent loss of economic activity and revenues and the expenditures incurred. Whatever the merits of these arguments, such practices entail serious moral hazard problems, and the arbitrary manner in which the central government decides to write off states' loans creates asymmetry and scope for discrimination, which may not be in the long-term interests of the Indian federation.

Central Sectoral and Centrally Sponsored Schemes

The greatest scope for differential treatment lies in the assistance given to states under a variety of central sectoral and centrally sponsored schemes. The former are funded entirely by the central government, and the states are used merely as implementing agencies. The latter, however, are close ended, specific purpose transfer programs intended to influence states' priorities in areas the central government views as important. These are not sanctioned by the constitution and are given purely on a discretionary basis (see National

Institute of Public Finance and Policy 1993 in relation to an opinion that this is unconstitutional). Discretion enters into the choice of the schemes, their design and the way they are implemented.

Currently more than 200 central sectoral and centrally sponsored schemes are in operation, although just 10 schemes account for more than 75 per cent of the total assistance for such schemes. The schemes are introduced by various central ministries, and sometimes on the basis of announcements by the prime minister, for example, during the annual Independence Day speech. Once introduced, they are continued. While the central sectoral schemes are entirely funded by the centre, the centrally sponsored schemes are shared cost programs. The schemes are designed by the central ministries. There is scope for discrimination between states in the selection of schemes and in their design. Often new schemes can be introduced merely to favour a particular state or group of states. The strongest criticisms have been levelled against the transfers given under these schemes, but that has not deterred the central government from initiating more schemes, nor has the centre made any attempt to consolidate schemes to give the states greater say and flexibility in relation to scheme design and implementation. The ways in which these are introduced and designed continue to be opaque.

Other Sources of Asymmetry

In economies subject to centralized planning, particularly those that had to deal with acute scarcities, price and quantity controls on both inputs and outputs are common. Once introduced, such controls tend to persist even when they have outlived their usefulness, either because no one bothers to reassess them, or because they create strong vested interests for their continuance. In addition, support prices may be introduced for various commodities, and these tend to be much higher than border prices, introducing an element of implicit subsidy. All such price and quantity controls are sources of invisible transfers and can affect different states differently. A discussion of all such controls and invisible transfers in India is impossible, but some important and obvious sources of interstate discrimination can be noted.

The determination of procurement prices for food grains is an important source of invisible transfers. In an economy with high tariffs, when the support prices declared by the government are significantly higher than the prices that would have ruled in the market, and when the government-owned Food Corporation of India guarantees to purchase these commodities at the declared price, market prices will be higher than they would otherwise have been. As the support prices are fixed mostly for agricultural commodities that are relatively price inelastic, this tends to have significant regional redistribution impacts. This policy has a discriminatory impact on different states depending on the crop chosen for support pricing and the extent to which support prices vary from the border prices (international price + transportation cost). Not surprisingly, the determination of support prices on wheat, rice and other products is a matter of controversy. It is not uncommon to see some of the regional parties holding power in the states that are also partners in the coalition government at the centre using their positions to influence the determination of procurement prices.

Another recent example of a price and quantity control system affecting resource distribution in an asymmetric manner concerns the allocation of subsidized food grains to different states. The central government has the discretion to allocate food grains to states for distribution in fair price shops according to a formula that it determines, but it can exercise considerable discretion in distributing food grains for regions affected by droughts or floods. It can thus send substantial relief to states ruled by parties it perceives as friendly and provide only token relief to those ruled by parties it sees as unfriendly.

Another important instrument that can be used to discriminate between the states is regional policies, particularly those regarding the location of central public sector enterprises. In a planned economy, location decisions are not necessarily taken on the basis of economic considerations. In India during the first few plans, major investments in the steel and coal industries were made on the basis of backward and forward linkage considerations, but in more recent years, the issue of locating central industrial units has been subject to controversy. Similarly, the location of regional offices of railways has been subject to much discussion.

POLITICAL ELEMENTS OF ASYMMETRIC PRACTICES

A major source of asymmetric treatment of different states pertains to the nature of the Indian polity and the functioning of political institutions. In the initial years after independence, the issue of asymmetry did not come to the fore, because the Indian National Congress, which was in the forefront of the independence movement, had little opposition and a virtual monopoly on forming the government at the centre as well as in the states. There was thus little scope for disharmony between the centre and individual states and for discrimination between the states. However, the following five important developments have led to the asymmetric treatment of states:

- The increasing economic centralization. The 1950 constitution had a strong centripetal bias in its assignment of powers, enough to be considered quasi federal. This bias towards centralization became stronger with the adoption of a planned development strategy that required a concentration of economic powers and the centralized allocation of resources. The concentration of economic powers reached its pinnacle with the nationalization of insurance companies and the important commercial banks in 1969. The concentration of fiscal and financial resources at the centre greatly increased the scope for interstate discrimination in the allocation of resources.

- The end of single party rule at the centre and in the states. Single party rule for relatively long periods had two notable implications for intergovernmental relations. First, the strong authority of the party, especially the prime minister, had to be accepted, and any perceptions of discrimination were ignored in the larger euphoria of planning for economic progress. Second, the concentration of power in the party and the resolution of centre-state and interstate issues by informal means within party forums meant that sufficient scope for the development of formal and rules based intergovernmental systems did not exist.
- The emergence of parties with regional identities as ruling parties in some important states. In many states, from time to time the electorate perceived that their regional interests and their distinct identities would be better preserved if they voted regional parties into power. The emergence of two Dravidian parties alternating as ruling parties in Tamil Nadu; the *Telugu Desam* taking power in Andhra Pradesh; and other parties, such as the Haryana Development Party in Haryana and the People's Party of Biju with a distinct regional identity in Orissa, are all cases in point. This change has shifted the perspective of parties in power at the state level towards strongly safeguarding regional interests, even if at a cost to the rest of the country (Manor 1995; Rao and Singh 2001).
- The formation of coalition governments at the centre. As none of the national parties emerged with a simple majority of parliamentary seats during the last three general elections, they had to forge alliances with other parties, including regional parties, to form governments. As a result, the regional parties could force their agenda and try to extract the maximum returns in exchange for supporting the coalition.
- The decreased time horizon of politicians and parties in recent years. As electorates have become more cynical and their trust and faith in politicians have deteriorated, the probability of representatives getting re-elected has declined sharply. In the last general election, only 38 per cent of the members of parliament were re-elected, a lower percentage than in previous general elections. As a result, elected representatives find it more worthwhile to maximize their personal gains when in office rather than working for the welfare of their electorates.

Thus, on the one hand, the central government continues to have enormous financial strength to dispense favours to state governments, but on the other hand, it has lost much of its power to prevent strong states from bargaining and skewing the allocation of resources in their favour. The states ruled by regional parties with significant strength in parliament have become pivotal, and have been able to secure substantially higher resources relative to other states. They have managed to do so because a significant proportion of explicit and implicit transfers is discretionary.

CONCLUDING REMARKS

This chapter has attempted to bring out some important features of the asymmetric arrangements inherent in Indian federalism. Asymmetry in the administrative, political and economic spheres of federal systems is unavoidable, and may actually be necessary not only to bring individual states together, but to hold them together. However, while transparent asymmetric arrangements that can be justified on the grounds of overall benefits to the federation contribute to nation building, discriminatory policies followed purely because they can yield short-term political gains can be inimical to the long-term interests and stability of federalism.

The rationale for asymmetry arises from the premise that federalism is a rational bargain among various units. Thus the terms for joining the federation for constituent units depend on their bargaining strength. Furthermore, even in a federation with no provision for exit, political alignments determine the bargaining strength of governments of different units in their interaction with the centre, and this may result in discriminatory treatment of various units. The potential for discrimination is higher in more centralized federations and is inversely related to the political strength of the central government in relation to the various regional governments.

Making a clear distinction between asymmetric arrangements that are rules based and transparent and those resulting from political and administrative expediency is important. Asymmetric arrangements built into a constitutional framework and those that have evolved to ensure the smooth functioning of a federation belong to the first category. Over time, the initial arrangement may change depending on such factors as the extent to which various units assimilate themselves in the federation and their relative bargaining strength. In contrast, the asymmetric arrangements arising from political and administrative expediency are opaque and discretionary, can lead to the degradation of intergovernmental institutions and can be inimical to the federation's long-term stability.

NOTES

1. This chapter uses the words centre, union and federation interchangeably.
2. Gujarat has consistently followed such a policy since independence, while some states like Tamil Nadu and Andhra Pradesh have followed such a policy from time to time if perceived to be advantageous before elections.

REFERENCES

Arora, Balvir (1995), 'Adapting Federalism to India: Multilevel and Asymmetric Innovations', in Balvir Arora and Douglas Verney (eds), *Multiple Identities in a Single State*, New Delhi: Konarak Publishers, pp. 71–104.

Bagchi, Amaresh (1988), 'First Award of the Ninth Finance Commission: An Appraisal', *Economic and Political Weekly*, 3 December, pp. 2593–601.

Brass, Paul R. (1994), *The Politics of India Since Independence*, 2nd ed., Cambridge: Cambridge University Press.

Chanda, A. K. (1965), *Federalism in India*, London: George Allen and Unwin.

Guhan, S. (1989), 'The Norm and the Tilt: First Report of the Ninth Finance Commission', *Economic and Political Weekly*, 14 January, pp. 86–94.

Manor, James (1995), 'Regional Parties in Federal Systems', in Balveer Arora and Douglas Verney (eds), *Multiple Identities in a Single State*, New Delhi: Konark Publishers, pp. 105–35.

National Institute of Public Finance and Policy (1993), *The Ninth Finance Commission: Issues and Recommendations*, New Delhi.

Ministry of Finance (2001), *Economic Survey*, New Delhi: Government of India.

Rao, M. Govinda (2004) 'State Level Fiscal Reforms in India', in Kaushik Basu (ed.), *India's Emerging Economy: Performance and Prospects in the 1990s and Beyond,* New Delhi: Oxford University Press, pp. 115–50.

Rao, M. Govinda and Raja Chelliah (1997), *Survey of Research in Indian Fiscal Federalism*, New Delhi: Indian Council of Social Science Research.

Rao, M. Govinda and Tapas Sen (1996), *Fiscal Federalism in India: Theory and Practice*, New Delhi: Macmillan India.

Rao, M. Govinda and Nirvikar Singh (2000), 'The Political Economy of Center-State Fiscal Transfers in India', paper presented at the Columbia University and World Bank Conference on Institutional Elements of Tax Design and Reform, 18–19 February, Columbia University, New York.

Rao, M. Govinda and Nirvikar Singh (2001), 'India's Federal Institutions and Economic Reform', paper presented at the conference on India's Public Institutions, 9–10 February, Harvard University, Cambridge, MA.

Riker, William (1975), 'Federalism', in Fred I. Greenstein and Nelson W. Polsby (eds), *Handbook of Political Science*, vol. 5, Reading, MA: Addison-Wesley, pp. 276–90.

Wheare, K. (1953), *Federal Government*, London: Oxford University Press.

11. Intergovernmental Fiscal Relations and State Building: The Case of Indonesia

Bambang Brodjonegoro and J. Fitz G. Ford

This chapter briefly reviews the origins of the unitary Indonesian state, the attitudes and policies towards decentralization, the developments with regard to intergovernmental relations during the first two decades of independence and the changes in intergovernmental fiscal relations under the New Order government. It also speculates about what may be required as Indonesia contemplates substantial reform to its governance structures and explores the tolerance for asymmetry in intergovernmental fiscal relations.

ORIGINS OF THE INDONESIAN UNITARY STATE

Casual observers might be tempted to speculate that the existence of Indonesia as a unitary state is a recent and desperate attempt to hold disparate elements together. As MacAndrews (1986, p. 7) notes, 'In looking at Indonesia, one is struck more by the forces leading to fragmentation in the country than by the forces leading to unity'. As with many other aspects of Indonesia, reality is rather more complicated than surface appearances suggest.

Two major factors influenced Indonesia becoming a unitary state. The first lies in its colonial history. The Dutch, in their desire to pre-empt their European colonial rivals, progressively incorporated most of the islands of the Indonesian archipelago under the government they administered from their base in Java. This was a more manageable solution than establishing separate governments among the several cultures that occupied 3000 of the archipelago's 13 667 islands.

In the process of executing this strategy, the Dutch built an administrative structure that consisted predominantly of Javanese bureaucrats. However, they also created an outward-looking elite among the colonized islands, who associated themselves with the idea of a large, potentially dominant and important state that transcended the comparatively smaller territories from which they originated. Thus at the time when the politically active indigenous leadership began contemplating independence, they thought primarily in terms of Indonesia rather than of states limited to the lands of their various origins. This should not suggest that they ignored their origins; rather, they saw decentralization as an essential feature of a unitary Indonesia. For the majority of the largely uneducated population, affiliation was highly localized, and as a result, debate about independence and the concept of a state other than the Dutch-created Indonesia was rare. Nevertheless, the leadership understood that failure to account for the diversity of the country's regions would be disastrous for the nascent state.

The second factor was also a consequence of colonial history, in this instance, the events leading up to the end of the colonial period in Indonesia. The Dutch, ousted from their prized East Asian territory by the Japanese during World War II and contemplating its permanent loss to the independence movement, promulgated federation as the most appropriate constitutional governmental structure for their former colony. Indonesians viewed this as an attempt to divide and rule, and the Dutch approach made anything but a unitary state anathema to the great majority of those fighting for independence. Despite the sometimes vigorous debates about the desirable degree of centralization of the government, '[E]ven the severest critic of the centralization of authority ... made it clear that their complaints were not directed against the unitary state as such' (Maryanov 1958, p. 32).

THE FIRST TWO DECADES OF INDEPENDENCE

Indonesia proclaimed its independence on 17 August 1945, but it was not until five years later that the declaration remained undisputed. In the interim, the first law on decentralization of the Republic of Indonesia,[1] Law Number 22 of 1948,[2] the basic law on regional government, was passed. Shortly afterwards, the Dutch captured the republican capital and a year later the federal Republic of the United States of Indonesia came into being. Less than a year later it was replaced by the unitary state that has prevailed ever since. The Indonesian leadership of the time viewed the 1950 republic as a continuation of the 1945 republic.

An important development during those five years was the strengthening of decentralization sentiments among republicans. The new constitution (technically, amendments to the federal constitution) provided for

> The division of Indonesia into large and small regions with the right to govern their own affairs together with the form of government for these regions, shall be established by law, keeping in mind the basis of consultation and representation as in the system of government of the State . . . These divisions shall be given the largest possible measure of autonomy to manage their own affairs. (Official translation)

This provision was considerably stronger than that in the 1945 constitution, which provided for the division of the territory based on consultation, but without mentioning autonomy.

The political debates of that period left no doubt as to the recognition of the meaning and importance of decentralization to the success of the unitary state. This perspective may be best summarized by Mohammad Hatta (*Keng Po* newspaper, 27 April, 1957, p. 1), co-signer of the Declaration of Independence and vice president until December 1956: 'We were aware from the very beginning that democracy, as government by those who are governed, must be realized through decentralization'.

Dimensions of Diversity

Despite the commitment to the unitary state, widespread concern about decentralization was understandable. Indonesia was and is one of the most diverse countries in the world. It encompasses 13 667 islands, which if overlaid on a map of the United States would stretch from Seattle to Washington, DC, a distance of more than 3000 miles. The approximately 990 inhabited islands are grouped into four main areas: Greater Sunda (Sumatra, Java, Kalimantan and Sulawesi); Lesser Sunda (from Bali to Timor); the Maluku (scattered between Sulawesi and Timor to the west and New Guinea to the east); and Papua.

The population is currently 215 million, the fourth largest of any country. About 60 per cent of the population lives on Java, while 11 of the 31 provinces each have 1.5 per cent or less of the total population (see Figure 11.1 for a map of Indonesia). These 215 million people represent 52 indigenous ethnic groups plus 3 million Chinese who speak more than 200 languages, including four among the Chinese. At least 16 of these languages are spoken by more than 1 million people each. A notable success of the founders of Indonesia was with regard to language policy. The constitution recognized Bahasa Indonesia as the national language, although six 'culturally important' languages are also taught in primary schools. From 90 per cent illiterate in 1942, Indonesia's population became 60 per cent literate by 1975 to 86 per cent today, making it one of the most successful applications of language policy by any country.

Assessing Indonesia's regions from an economic perspective presents another dimension of diversity. Hill and Weidermann (1989) settled on five groupings of provinces (while acknowledging the validity of alternative arrangements) that took resource base, geographic location, population and history into account to produce the following classification: a group of five resource-rich provinces (Papua, Aceh, Riau, Jambi and East Kalimantan); a group of three isolated provinces (East and West Nusa Tengagara and East

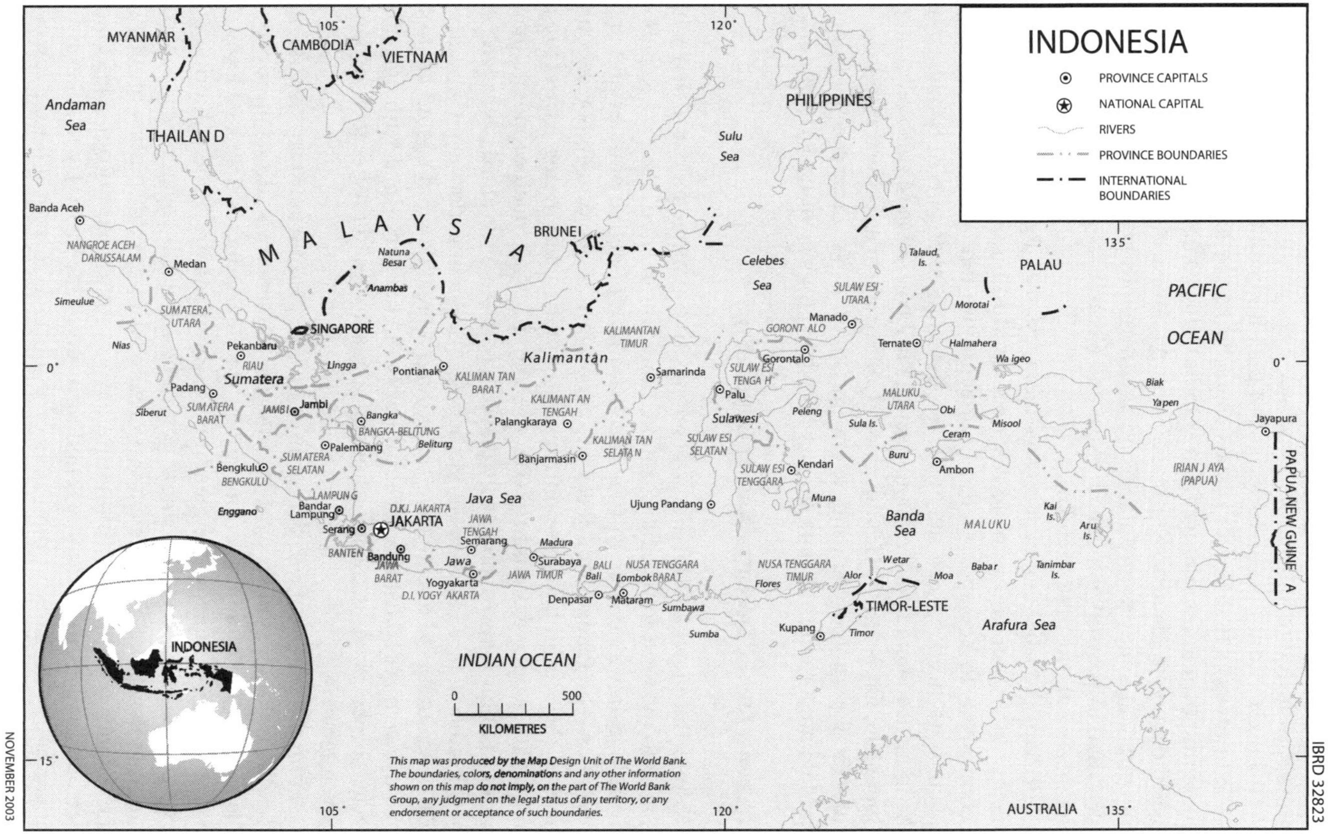

Figure 11.1 Indonesia

Timor, now no longer part of Indonesia); a group of densely populated provinces, including the heavily populated Java provinces (Jakarta, East and West Java, Central Java and Jogjakarta) plus Bali and Lampung; a group of settled provinces in the outer islands characterized by extensive international economic penetration dating from colonial times and possessing an established economic identity (North and South Sulawesi, North, South and West Sumatra and South Kalimantan); and an amorphous group of five provinces identified as sparsely populated (West and Central Kalimantan, Central and Southeast Sulawesi and Maluku).

Perhaps the label that appears to encompass the largest group of Indonesians is the 90 per cent who are described as Muslims, and even that classification needs to be subdivided, as a much more fundamentalist version of Islam is practiced in Aceh and to a lesser extent in other parts of Sumatra than the more accommodating version practiced in Java. Indonesia also recognizes Buddhism, Christianity, Hinduism and Confusianism as official religions. A substantial portion of the Chinese are Christians, as are those people resident in Maluku, portions of Papua and the erstwhile province of East Timor.

Responses to the Decentralization Imperative

Despite the views of Hatta and other positive sentiments expressed with regard to the need for decentralization, the government of the new Republic of Indonesia was unable to translate them into effective policies and programmes. The fundamental fact that Indonesia was one of the poorest countries in the world, but was confronting unrealistically rising expectations among its people, did not help (Booth 1996, p. 182). Macroeconomic management failures also undoubtedly played a part. An overvalued exchange rate penalized non-Java exporters to the benefit of Java importers and consumers. This eventually led to extensive smuggling, a breakdown of central controls and *de facto* federalism as local military commanders sided with and protected local officials in the imposition of illegal levies to finance their region's governments.

From the perspective of the focus of this chapter, the most striking failure was the lack of a well thought out intergovernmental fiscal system. Beyond the designation of a number of regions, no clear policies delineated governance systems, functions, expenditure assignments, revenue authority and expected transfers from the central government to local governments. Financing from the central government was largely ad hoc, with the usual results. In the absence of clear rules, administrative procedures were opaque and cumbersome, and regional leaders found themselves having to fly to Jakarta for minor policy decisions. Complaints of inadequate financing for the regions soon followed, to which was added dissatisfaction with bureaucrats from Java being sent to the regions to take posts for which locals felt that they were qualified.

The growing dissatisfaction reached the threshold of imminent crisis by early 1956. Local official and military-sanctioned barter trading of copra for imported food, automobiles and machinery in North Sulawesi spread to North Sumatra, where rubber and coffee were the prime exports. The crisis exploded in late 1956 and early 1957, with army-led rebellions in parts of Sumatra, Sulawesi and Kalimantan. The more successful of these rebellions (in Central and South Sumatra, East Indonesia and Kalimantan) resulted in some degree of regional control by army commanders superseding central control.

Despite this, the evidence indicates that these were not secessionist revolts, but a desire to replace the succession of failed governments with a more effective set of arrangements (Booth 1996, p. 184; Maryanov 1958, p. 35). Army commanders remained within the army and regional and central ministry officials continued to communicate. Nevertheless, the absence of a well-functioning intergovernmental system was severely testing, and in some cases, threatening the 'we' that had brought the disparate territories and language groups of the archipelago together as the unitary state of Indonesia.

Preoccupation with Political Debate

The absence of sound intergovernmental fiscal relations until that time was one of the consequences of the unresolved conflicts within the political leadership and between the political elite and the administrative elite. The political leaders had all recognized the need for decentralization and expressed support for it, and generally agreed on a structural model of provinces, districts and municipalities, subdistricts and villages. However, consensus was lacking as to what decentralization would mean in governance and fiscal terms.

The decentralization programme was based on two laws—Law Number 22 of 1948 and Law Number 44 of 1950, originally passed by the State of East Indonesia in preparation for unification. The country was divided into ten administrative divisions, of which three, plus the Special Region of Jogjakarta on Java and three special regions on Sumatra, were made autonomous. The 13 regions of the former State of East Indonesia also had autonomy. In addition, the four provincial-level regions on Java were subdivided into several autonomous districts and municipalities. The difficulties lawmakers faced included translating autonomy into operational meaning without making decisions that would be interpreted as concessions to federalism.

Another source of difficulties was encountered in arriving at much needed consensus on exactly what was meant by decentralization, namely: (a) a deconcentration of central administrative power; (b) a delegation of administrative responsibilities to somewhat autonomous and somewhat representative subnational authorities; and/or (c) a devolution of powers to elected, representative, self-governing entities. The Indonesian words *decentralisasi* and *otonomi* were often used interchangeably; however, to users the words had different emphases. Often political groups intended the terms to reflect the extent of popular participation in decisionmaking and management that their particular political party favoured.

Given Indonesia's physical, cultural and economic diversity, the mosaic of characteristics exhibited by its political parties is not surprising. The spectrum of the several political parties ranged from nationalist, such as the Democratic Party of Indonesia and the Nationalist Party of Indonesia; to ideological, for instance, the Indonesia Communist Party and the Socialist Party of Indonesia; to religious, including Islamic parties of different degrees of radical conviction and Catholic parties; to ethnic Chinese parties. To some extent, parties' affiliations tended to overlap with nationalist sentiment, and alliances were common and sometimes fluid.

Political parties' support for more representative local government reflected their view that local democracy was necessary to preserve national unity. Nevertheless, they continued to disagree on operational details. This inability to agree on the precise nature of democratic institutions may have had roots in the existing culture and interpretations of how far Western ideas of democracy were applicable to Indonesian circumstances.

For the administrative elite, that is, the national bureaucracy that managed the public sector at all levels, they clearly preferred a deconcentration of administrative powers, with local inputs through advisory committees. The members of the bureaucracy most committed to this approach were, not surprisingly, the field officials of the Ministry of Home Affairs. These were the experienced backbone of the civil service, with their origins in the colonial era, who viewed themselves as the glue that held the country together.

The divergent views and interests among and between these power groups naturally had a major impact on attempts to prepare and promulgate laws to implement a coherent decentralization programme. Disagreements between the political parties caused them to lose the initial advantage they had enjoyed immediately following independence. As notions of democracy took hold, local advisory councils were being strengthened at the expense of the Ministry of Home Affairs field officials. However, as the parties bickered about what democracy meant in the Indonesian context and how much of it the people could absorb, the bureaucracy regrouped.

In the first skirmish, the issue was how to appoint the regional executives who would replace the Ministry of Home Affairs field officials when decentralization was fully implemented. In what Walker (1960, p. 5) described as a decisive victory for the administrative elite, the government established that the regional executives would not be answerable to the elected legislature.

The bureaucrats consolidated this victory by appointing the principal Ministry of Home Affairs field officials as regional executives. Thus began a curious dualism under which individuals represented regional interests to themselves as agents of the centre. In this schizophrenic fray, the centre usually won (Walker 1960, p. 5).

The rivalry of national political parties extended to local levels of government to the detriment of the parties' shared broader agenda for democracy. The colonial hangover of a collegial executive had been incorporated in Law Number 22 of 1948. Under this arrangement, all major parties shared in executive decisionmaking in the mistaken notion that partisanship would not affect local-level issues. As a result, the local executive boards were ineffective decisionmaking bodies, which meant that most important matters were left to the regional executives, thereby further strengthening the administrative service.

Having failed to curb the power of the Ministry of Home Affairs field officials, the post-1950 parliament began work on a new law to replace or update Law Number 22 of 1948. Disagreements on policy between Muslim and secular blocs and the vigorous defence of a strong, central administrative service by parties composed of former civil servants prevented agreement. The weakening of this latter group because of substantial losses in the 1955 elections finally paved the way for the new law in 1956, after five years of debate.

Law Number 1 of 1957 was clearly the turn of the political elite. It anticipated the abolition of the Ministry of Home Affairs field officials, along with other centralized technical services. It also required the regional executives to be elected by popular vote (an interim provision allowed election by the legislative assembly) and to be answerable to the local legislature. However, the law included an interim period during which the Ministry of Home Affairs field officials would continue to carry out central functions, thereby creating a dualism in government structure and responsibilities. In addition, no timetable was attached to this interim status.

Unfortunately for the democracy movement, the law maintained the collegial executive system at the local level, with its inherent weaknesses intact. This undermined the effectiveness of local executives to the extent that control once again passed to the administration and the increasingly important military elite (Walker 1960, p. 8). Another failure for the political elite during this phase of the battle for local control was that they did not implement a representative system of administration at the village level as called for by law. Thus village administration remained in the undisputed hands of the Ministry of Home Affairs field officials.

From the perspective of intergovernmental fiscal relations, the outstanding weaknesses of Law Number 1 were: (a) the failure to provide meaningful taxing powers to local governments; (b) the absence of a meaningful system of local accountability; (c) the continuation of the separation of assignment of functions and revenue authority and (d) the high local dependence on a non-transparent central transfer system. The minor, mostly nuisance, taxes permitted to local governments resulted in local sources providing as little as 3 per cent of regional budgets. Thus while the regency of Sumenep on Madura generated Rp 1.6 million of its Rp 11.3 million budget in 1957, the province of East Java managed to provide only Rp 9 million of its Rp 300 million budget (Walker 1960, p. 9). East Java also refused to administer public forest lands because it was not allowed to collect harvesting fees.

Thus the bulk of budget requirements was provided by appropriations through the Ministry of Home Affairs. Walker (1960) attributed this unwillingness to provide meaningful taxing powers to local governments to the familiar central fears that local assemblies would use the revenue for personal gain rather than in the public's interests. Note that an alternative model was readily available in neighbouring Malaya, where the primary condition for granting autonomy to local governments was their ability to support themselves.

While this infighting played itself out at the central level, the frustration in the regions grew, finally erupting in the events of 1956 and 1957 mentioned earlier. When this escalated to genuine secessionist sentiments in 1958, the loyal military who were required to put down these revolts agreed with the view that corrupt and quarrelsome political parties were responsible. These events propelled the military further into civil administration, ultimately leading to its entrenched role in government.

A further consequence was a growing alliance between the military and the civil service. Under Law Number 1/1957, elections and the formation of new assemblies would have resulted in the transfer of powers and the central civil service personnel who administered them to the regional governments. Naturally, the Ministry of Home Affairs field officials resisted what they perceived as their demise, and found support among members of the military, who felt that national security and order would be better served by keeping executive powers out of the hands of the unreliable locally elected officials.

Parliament did not share these views, and in early 1959, in retaliation for the delaying tactics of the Ministry of Home Affairs field officials, passed a law requiring them to give up their sweeping, discretionary powers in local administration. It also called for the assignment of the Ministry of Home Affairs field officials to local governments. No implementation regulations were immediately forthcoming, and on 5 July 1959, before any could be enacted, President Sukarno decreed a return to the 1945 constitution in order to introduce guided democracy to Indonesia.

With a parliament based on Western principles, the national government had proved to be a squabbling body inept at governing, producing short-lived and ineffectual cabinets that failed to respond to priority issues. The most important of these were the promulgation of a policy and institutional framework that would provide for a locally satisfactory degree of regional autonomy, a strong and supportive central system and rapid and sustainable economic growth.

In February 1957, President Sukarno had presented his alternative governance model based on traditional Javanese culture, in particular, village-based institutions for debate and decisionmaking. Within this framework, debate would be guided by village headmen in order to reach consensus. As for the participants in these debates, partisanship would be replaced by the involvement of occupational groups that were to be considered natural stakeholders. This was the model of a village process in which the traditional headman engaged the village rice farmers, who shared common interests, to arrive at an acceptable agreement. If no consensus was possible, the issue was referred up to the subdistrict officer, the lowest level of the Ministry of Home Affairs field officials, for a decision.

However, attempts to arrive at consensus between the president and the political parties dragged on for two years. Meanwhile, relations between the centre and the regions continued to deteriorate, especially over the issue of revenue sharing. Ultimately this led to the loss of central control over parts of Sumatra and Sulawesi in 1958 as noted earlier.

Key interest groups saw the 1945 constitution as the most direct means of implementing guided democracy. It predated Japan's surrender at the end of World War II and the re-emergence of political parties and concentrated executive powers in the presidency and the president's hand-picked councils. Because it would replace political representation with representation by functional groups, Sukarno assured himself of the critical support of the administrative elite and the military.

Following the adoption of the 1945 constitution, the role of parliament was circumvented by the Supreme Advisory Council and the National Planning Council. In 1960, parliament was abolished. At the regional level, where political parties retained some strength, the regional executives reverted to being appointed positions, although supposedly selected from a list of candidates nominated by the elected assembly. The executive councils became advisory. The result was a return to bureaucratic control emanating from Jakarta to the regions, free from local political interference.

Walker (1960, p. 16) noted:

> Given the internal tensions of Indonesia's elite, given also the acuteness of regional tensions, it may be quite possible that a strong benevolent guided government may be the only alternative to the disintegration of this young republic, provided, and this can not be overemphasized, *sympathy for regional aspirations exists at the centre.* (Emphasis added)

This statement was to be prophetic for much of the subsequent period of Indonesia's history, but was not to be fulfilled in the remaining years of Sukarno's rule. Continued poor macroeconomic management resulted in rising inflation and a greatly overvalued exchange rate. The consequence was increased smuggling on a scale only possible with the support of the local military, whose anticommunist perspective led to alliances with regional dissidents against the centre. Bargains over the imposition of illegal taxes and imposts and revenue sharing from smuggling were struck between local officials, the military and civilian representatives of the central government (Booth 1996, p. 185).

Thus, ironically, a leadership that had fought for a unitary state was forced to accept *de facto* federalism as a consequence of its failure to implement an appropriate system that would give expression to its philosophy of decentralization within a unitary state.

THE NEW ORDER EXPERIENCE

The initial period of Indonesia's history with regard to central-local relations was characterized by an emphasis on public politics and an absence of effective intergovernmental fiscal instruments and macroeconomic management. The New Order period took the opposite tack. The alliance between the presidency, the military—which added an explicit civil role with its doctrine that permitted a formal civil role for the military in addition to national defence and allowed military officers to take up political and civil government positions without relinquishing their army status—and the Ministry of Home Affairs field officials was extended to a new intellectual elite brought in to manage the economy. Party politics was reduced almost to a ceremonial ritual.

The 1945 constitution and the nature and structure of government it implied remained in place, but the difference in economic management was striking. By 1969, inflation had been reduced to single digits and growth was discernable. Substantial foreign aid and growing oil revenues opened new options for central-local relations, and these began to be carefully utilized by the central government. A system of central government transfers to local government began to be put in place, consisting primarily of Instruki President (Presidential Instruction or INPRES) grants. Perhaps as important as the funds themselves was the transparency and efficiency with which they were transferred and the clear and effective accountability systems that accompanied them. These grants were, for the most part, accurately targeted at much needed infrastructure and other services. As a result, regional confidence in, and allegiance to, the central government was restored.

Other investments by the central government reinforced this resurgent sense of the Indonesian state. Transport and other communications improvements linked localities and regions. Labour mobility, encouraged by the transmigration programme—a major government-sponsored internal migration programme—and economic growth soared, although some tensions resulted from the introduction of largely Javanese populations into the outer islands. In the 1970s, migration from rural to urban areas accounted for 52 per cent of urban population growth and urban areas generated 45 per cent of all new jobs (World Bank 1984a, p. 20). All-in-all, the New Order government could justifiably claim to have knitted a tapestry of 'we'—a successful, diverse, important nation—that began to reflect the early vision of the state.

As the system of INPRES grants was expanded and deepened and communication links multiplied, including television coverage across the entire country, people in the regions apparently put aside their interest in political representation in exchange for growing economic benefits. By the end of the 1970s, infant mortality rates were dropping, and a decade later Indonesia achieved universal primary education.

Asymmetry in the treatment of troublesome and/or particularly poor regions by pouring in additional resources to convince them of their proper place within the large and diverse nation was tolerated without notable dissent.[3] The regional economic diversity of Indonesia is well illustrated by the classification of provinces presented earlier and Hill and Weidermann's (1989) review of regional economic performance from 1970 to the mid-1980s. In 1971, gross domestic product (GDP) per capita was Rp 31 500; however, regional gross domestic product (RGDP) per capita ranged from Rp 192 300 in Riau to Rp 13 800 per capita in East Nusa Tenggara (Table 11.1). By 1983, when the exploitation of natural resources had largely been responsible for raising the country's GDP per capita (in current prices) almost 14-fold to Rp 433 200, Riau's RGDP per capita had increased 19-fold to Rp 3.66 million, while East Nusa Tenggara's had increased to Rp 176 000, approximately 13-fold. Moreover, Aceh, South Sumatra, East Kalimantan, Central Kalimantan and Papua were also generating RGDP per capita well above the national average as a result of oil, natural gas, timber and mining activities.

Jakarta, which benefited from its role as the capital, was the only other province to maintain above average RGDP during 1971–83, as RGDP in all the other provinces declined in relative terms. According to Castles (1989, p. 233): '[N]early all its other remarkable features derive from that role. It is the outstanding centre of national and international communications, the largest centre of manufacturing (especially import substituting sectors), the largest port for imports, and the main seat of such cultural industries as research, publishing, film, radio-TV'.

The distribution of central resources, largely derived from the exploitation of natural resources, emphasized different messages depending on the analytic lenses through which it is viewed. Because central support of provincial routine expenditures was largely intended to support the basic administrative

Table 11.1 RGDP and RGDP per capita, 1971 and 1983 (current prices)

Province	1971				1983			
	Total RGDP (Rp billions)	RGDP per capita (Rp thousands)	Index of RGDP per capita with oil (Indonesia = 100)	Index of RGDP per capita without oil (Indonesia = 100)	Total RGDP (Rp billions)	RGDP per capita (Rp thousands)	Index of RGDP per capita with oil (Indonesia = 100)	Index of RGDP per capita without oil (Indonesia = 100)
Aceh	56.3	28.0	89	97	3470.5	1220.7	282	113
North Sumatra	305.7	46.2	147	159	3645.7	404.4	93	113
Riau	315.6[a]	192.3[a]	610	140	8687.9	3660.2[a]	845	110
West Sumatra	72.6	26.0	83	90	1251.6	344.6	80	101
Jambi	44.0	43.7	139	151	432.8	266.0	61	76
South Sumatra	212.9[a]	61.9[a]	197	164	3189.1[a]	625.4[a]	144	149
Lampung	74.0	26.7	85	92	999.2	182.8	42	65
Bengkulu	13.7	26.4	84	91	236.2	270.7	62	88
Jakarta	329.0	71.8	228	248	7192.5	984.3	227	276
West Java	550.1	25.4	81	88	9185.9	309.7	71	87
Central Java	470.4	21.5	68	74	6740.9	253.3	58	74

Yogyakarta	54.7	22.0	70	76	713.1	251.2	58	65
East Java	656.8	25.7	82	89	10 347.8	339.6	78	97
West Kalimantan	59.5	29.4	93	102	759.9	285.9	66	96
Central Kalimantan	23.8	33.9	108	117	483.6	458.6	106	129
South Kalimantan	54.7	32.2	102	111	842.1	383.1	88	88
East Kalimantan	58.4	79.6	253	248	3880.3	2697.1	623	206
North Sulawesi	61.2	35.6	113	123	715.3	316.2	73	112
Central Sulawesi	15.0	16.4	52	57	341.0	236.4	55	70
South Sulawesi	119.7	23.1	73	80	1684.5	264.2	61	81
Southeast Sulawesi	20.6	28.9	92	100	315.1	305.6	71	74
Bali	62.2	29.6	94	102	904.9	348.9	81	127
West Nusa Tenggara	33.6	15.2	48	52	525.4	180.1	42	52
East Nusa Tenggara	31.8	13.8	44	48	509.7	176.0	41	54
Maluku	33.8	31.0	98	107	536.1	349.4	81	100
Papua	26.6	28.8	91	99	892.4	703.5	162	120
Indonesia[b]	3757.0	31.5	100	100	68 483.5	433.2	100	100

a. Includes income from oil.
b. Reflects sum of provincial GDPs, not national income statistics.

Source: Hill and Weidemann (1989).

apparatus, poorer and smaller provinces received more support as a proportion of RGDP than richer and larger ones (Table 11.2). Routine expenditures as a proportion of RGDP were clearly greater in the poor provinces of East Nusa Tenggara (14.6 per cent), South Sulawesi (9 per cent), Central Sulawesi (9.4 per cent) and Benkulu (9.7 per cent) than for resource-rich Aceh (1.8 per cent), East Kalimantan (0.9 per cent) and Riau (0.9 per cent). However,

Table 11.2 Provincial and district expenditures as a percentage of RGDP, 1982/83

Province (ranked by population, largest first)	Routine expenditure		Development expenditure		
	Provincial	District	Provincial	District	Total
East Java	2.7	1.0	0.6	0.8	5.1
West Java	2.9	0.9	0.4	0.8	5.0
Central Java	4.2	1.2	0.5	0.9	6.8
North Sumatra	3.1	1.1	0.8	1.0	5.9
Jakarta	1.8	n.a.	1.6	n.a.	3.3
South Sulawesi	4.7	4.3	0.8	2.4	12.2
Lampung	3.6	0.9	1.4	1.2	7.0
South Sumatra	1.7	1.3	0.5	0.7	4.3
West Sumatra	3.8	0.8	1.1	1.4	7.1
Yogyakarta	6.5	1.4	1.5	1.8	11.1
West Nusa Tenggara	6.0	2.1	2.1	1.5	11.7
East Nusa Tenggara	9.0	5.6	1.7	1.5	17.8
Aceh	1.3	0.5	0.5	0.4	2.7
West Kalimantan	4.3	1.7	1.6	2.8	10.3
Bali	4.4	1.2	1.5	1.4	8.4
Riau	0.5	0.4	0.3	0.2	1.4
North Sulawesi	5.7	1.7	2.0	1.4	10.4
South Kalimantan	4.6	1.2	2.1	2.9	10.8
Jambi	5.7	4.0	3.5	2.9	16.1
Maluku	5.1	1.6	1.7	0.8	9.3
Central Sulawesi	7.2	2.2	3.1	1.3	13.8
East Kalimantan	0.6	0.3	0.6	0.2	1.8
Papua	5.2	3.4	1.0	1.0	10.7
Central Kalimantan	5.4	1.9	3.3	0.5	11.0
Southeast Sulawesi	6.3	4.5	4.1	1.8	16.7
Bengkulu	6.1	3.6	4.9	0.2	14.8

n.a. Not applicable.

Sources: Central Bureau of Statistics (1986a, b); RGDP: Hill and Weidemann (1989).

Papua, where the central government paid incentives to civil servants assigned there and where shipping and other logistics costs resulted in a higher cost of living, had routine expenditures totalling 8.6 per cent of RGDP. The same general broad pattern held for development expenditures.

This would seem to be consistent with a policy of redistribution according to need; however, if INPRES grants are assessed on a per capita basis, no such obvious bias is apparent (Table 11.3). On this basis, Central Sulawesi, East Nusa Tenggara, South East Sulawesi, Aceh and Riau seem to fall into one group, while East Kalimantan, Papua and Bengkulu fall into another group.

Similarly, an examination of total development grants (Table 11.4) shows a slightly different pattern that groups East Kalimantan, Papua, Central

Table 11.3 Total INPRES grants per capita, 1985/86

Province (ranked by population, largest first)	Rp
East Java	5193
West Java	5341
Central Java	5794
North Sumatra	9841
Jakarta	4067
South Sulawesi	10 475
Lampung	6930
South Sumatra	10 328
West Sumatra	14 121
Yogyakarta	8258
West Nusa Tenggara	12 959
East Nusa Tenggara	13 526
Aceh	15 605
West Kalimantan	16 407
Bali	10 004
Riau	15 025
North Sulawesi	14 406
South Kalimantan	13 210
Jambi	16 534
Maluku	19 884
Central Sulawesi	12 915
East Kalimantan	19 662
Papua	23 259
Central Kalimantan	32 005
Southeast Sulawesi	12 915
Bengkulu	24 953
East Timor	38 749

Sources: Hill and Weidermann (1989, Table 1.15); Department of Finance unpublished data.

Table 11.4 Central government regional development grants, 1983/84 and 1985/86 (Rp billions)

Province	1983/84				1985/86			
	Villages	Districts and sub-districts	Provincial govern-ments	Total	Village	Districts and sub-districts	Provincial govern-ments	Total
Aceh	7.0	3.6	9.0	19.6	7.6	4.0	10.0	21.7
North Sumatra	7.3	11.0	11.0	29.4	8.0	12.9	12.0	32.9
West Sumatra	4.6	4.9	9.0	18.5	5.0	5.5	10.0	20.5
Riau	1.4	2.8	9.0	13.2	1.7	3.3	10.0	14.9
Jambi	1.7	1.9	9.0	12.6	1.9	2.1	10.0	14.1
South Sumatra	3.1	5.8	11.0	19.9	3.4	6.7	12.0	22.1
Bengkulu	1.4	1.1	9.0	11.5	1.5	1.2	10.0	12.7
Lampsung	2.1	6.0	9.0	17.1	2.2	7.3	10.0	19.5
Jakarta	0.8	8.1	9.0	17.9	0.5	9.7	10.0	20.2
West Java	8.8	34.8	11.0	54.6	10.3	39.2	12.0	61.5
Central Java	11.5	31.8	11.0	54.3	12.3	35.4	12.0	59.8
Yogyakarta	1.0	3.4	9.0	13.4	0.9	3.9	10.0	14.8
East Java	11.6	36.5	11.0	59.0	12.4	40.7	12.0	65.0
West Kalimantan	6.0	3.1	9.0	18.1	6.5	3.6	10.0	20.1

Central Kalimantan	1.5	1.4	9.0	12.0	1.7	1.6	10.0	13.2
South Kalimantan	3.2	2.6	9.0	14.8	3.4	2.9	10.0	16.3
East Kalimantan	1.5	1.9	9.0	12.4	1.6	2.2	10.0	13.8
North Sulawesi	1.8	2.6	9.0	13.4	1.9	3.1	10.0	15.0
Central Sulawesi	1.7	1.7	9.0	12.4	1.9	2.0	10.0	13.8
South Sulawesi	1.9	7.9	9.0	18.8	2.0	8.8	10.0	20.8
Southeast Sulawesi	1.0	1.2	9.0	11.2	1.1	1.4	10.0	12.5
Bali	1.0	3.2	9.0	13.2	1.0	3.5	10.0	14.5
West Nusa Tenggara	1.0	3.4	9.0	13.4	0.9	3.8	10.0	14.7
East Nusa Tenggara	2.6	3.1	9.0	15.0	2.5	3.9	10.0	16.4
Maluku	2.4	1.8	9.0	13.2	2.4	2.0	10.0	14.4
Papua	1.4	1.8	9.0	12.2	1.5	2.0	10.0	13.5
East Timor	2.3	2.1	9.0	13.3	2.5	2.2	10.0	14.7
Central government[a]	n.a.	7.5	n.a.	7.5	0.1	1.0	n.a.	1.1
Total	91.6	197.2	253.0	541.8	98.6	215.9	280.0	594.5

n.a. Not applicable.

a. Refers to central government support activities.

Source: Azis (1989).

Sulawesi, Bengkulu and Riau together and Aceh and South East Sulawesi together, with East Nusa Tenggara falling between them.

Finally, as Table 11.5 indicates, the distribution system continues to show anomalies when subsidies from higher levels are compared with total revenues at the provincial and district levels. East Kalimantan, for example, shows relatively low levels of subsidy compared with Aceh and Riau.

Table 11.5 Subsidies from higher levels as a percentage of total revenues, 1982/83

Province (ranked by population, largest first)	Provincial revenues		District revenues	
	Routine	Development	Routine	Development
East Java	77.0	99.2	59.7	48.6
West Java	77.8	33.6	56.5	36.2
Central Java	84.8	56.2	65.5	46.4
North Sumatra	78.3	88.8	57.8	61.7
Jakarta	35.0	29.7	n.a.	n.a.
South Sulawesi	80.1	78.6	72.3	56.8
Lampung	72.8	61.8	64.8	77.0
South Sumatra	77.1	70.5	78.7	38.7
West Sumatra	78.6	88.0	53.7	65.8
Yogyakarta	74.2	77.5	67.8	86.9
West Nusa Teggara	86.9	70.8	70.2	10.4
East Nusa Teggara	88.7	59.8	60.9	81.4
Aceh	72.9	96.7	76.0	57.9
West Kalimatan	84.6	64.6	73.8	56.6
Bali	72.5	92.4	51.9	7.1
Riau	73.5	71.2	76.5	74.4
North Sulawesi	87.0	73.8	68.7	78.3
South Silmantan	77.1	66.3	56.5	66.5
Jambi	83.5	67.3	85.5	74.5
Maluku	80.4	84.9	70.8	62.1
Central Sulawesi	92.1	90.9	73.5	78.5
East Kalimantan	66.1	55.5	41.0	45.2
Papua	93.4	79.5	89.3	77.2
Central Kalimantan	90.8	75.5	81.3	27.0
Southeast Sulawesi	80.5	78.1	86.3	93.3
Bengkulu	74.1	84.3	88.1	90.1

n.a. Not applicable.

Source: Hill and Weidemann (1989, Table 1.16).

The data do show clear redistributive effects, in that resources were clearly not returned to their sources of origin in proportion to their contribution. However, the grant distribution criteria and outcomes suggest a tendency towards equalizing different types of infrastructure capacities: administrative capacity through the routine grants and physical and human resources through the development transfers. Azis (1989, p. 63) questions the clarity of the central government's allocation criteria and others, including Booth (1996), Ravallion (1988) and Shah and Qureshi 1994), have tried to decipher the impacts of the transfers. The consensus appears to be that despite its flaws, which include excessively centralized control and disincentives to local revenue raising, the system has had positive effects on growth and distribution.

Thus by the early 1980s, positive indicators of the broad distribution of the benefits of economic growth abounded, and Indonesia began to be extensively cited among the examples of successful development models. This perception was reinforced when Indonesia was one of the few developing oil-exporting countries to avoid the so-called Dutch disease during the good times and to adjust successfully when oil prices fell precipitously.

For almost three decades, Walker's (1960) prophetic comment cited earlier appeared to hold. Success at economic and intergovernmental fiscal management reinforced the underlying structure of government, and only cosmetic changes seemed to be needed to satisfy persistent, if muted, appeals for greater local autonomy. The distrust of public politics seemed justified by this period of stability and growth, in sharp contrast to the economic disarray of the era of rampant party politics.

Internal systems of accountability within the government seemed to work, even though there was little public accountability. An outstanding example was the reform of the grossly corrupt Customs Department during the mid to late 1980s. In this celebrated case, the military leadership and the economic ministries combined to remove the entire department and replace it with a private international company for a number of years until a new system and staff could be instituted.

When the economic and political system proved its ability to adjust the economy from a dependency on oil to broadly based sources of growth, the future seemed assured. The only sources of unease seemed to be centred around the president, especially the growing, blatant wealth of his family and business allies and the question of the succession. These concerns ultimately proved fatal to the regime and to the structure on which it depended.

The issue of Suharto's primarily ethnic Chinese business associates intersected with an uncomfortable reality of the Indonesian situation. The Chinese presented a dilemma with regard to the 'we' of Indonesia even before independence. Ironically, attempts by the colonial administration to improve the status of indigenous people at the expense of the Chinese by restricting their land ownership and employment in the government steered them almost exclusively towards commerce. As a group they did not endear themselves to indigenous leaders when at the time of independence, about half (400 000) of the resident Chinese rejected Indonesian citizenship.

The situation was complicated in the early days by mutual suspicion between Indonesia and China. China viewed Indonesia's leadership, as typified by Hatta, as imperialist tools, while Indonesians feared the promotion of communism through the local Chinese population. The Chinese government wanted to have particularly close ties with the local Chinese population to counter the strong inroads made by Taiwan among that group. Nevertheless, uneasy progress was made on both the domestic and international political fronts during the 1950s. Hatta, wanting to counter domestic criticism of being a capitalist tool, argued that Indonesia's foreign policy credibility required relations with China (Sukma 1994), and in the 1955 elections, members of Baperki, the Chinese-dominated political party, were elected to parliament.

Notwithstanding these developments, the integration of local Chinese into the Indonesian 'we' continued to be difficult. On the one hand, more Chinese were inclined to accept Indonesian citizenship when the opportunity arose between 1960 and 1962. On the other hand, Chinese were expelled from their homes in Banda Aceh in 1966 and from various parts of Kalimantan (where at least one Chinese community had been established for about 200 years) in 1967, as a result of the murder of Dayaks, an indigenous tribal group, by Chinese communist guerrillas. Chinese have also been the victims of periodic riots in Medan and Jakarta as recently as in the 1990s.

Ambivalence characterizes relations between the Chinese and indigenous populations in Indonesia. Chinese were said, for example, to resist assimilation into Indonesian society, because unlike the Indians and Arabs, they maintained their own schools and published their own newspapers, yet according to Mabbett and Mabbett (1982, p. 12), Chinese households were more likely than ethnic Indonesian households in the major Javanese cities of Jakarta, Bandung, Surabaya and Jogjakarta to use Indonesian as their everyday language. Although by far the largest Chinese communities are in Jakarta and Medan, the Chinese are dispersed throughout the archipelago, and Indonesian economic life has been permeated at all levels and dominated by ethnic Chinese since at least the 1960s. Although the majority of ethnic Chinese are small business people, it is the ownership and control of the major private conglomerates by a non-indigenous ethnic group that is the source of public resentment.

One of the consequences of the ousting of President Suharto from office has been a new and violent rise in expressions of dissatisfaction in the regions. This belies the notion that the intergovernmental fiscal system, which had been one of the sources of the regime's success, was adequate to satisfy the complex demands of central-local relations. Thus a closer examination of the system and its performance is useful.

Major Elements of the Intergovernmental Fiscal System

The first INPRES grants, aimed at villages, were initiated in the 1969/70 budget, and went to villages as lump-sum block grants to pay for construction materials for local development projects. The second INPRES grants, for districts and subdistricts, began being allocated as block grants to districts in 1970/71 on a per capita basis, but with a provision for a minimum grant for districts below a certain population level. The third and last transfer with block grant characteristics, the INPRES grants for provincial governments, started being distributed to provinces in 1972/73, mostly to replace a system for sharing export taxes that had benefited the provinces that did not export oil in particular. Although nominally block grants, the central government indicated that these funds would be primarily expended on roads, bridges and irrigation. The allocation criteria initially favoured the high population centres of Java and Sumatra, but the distribution was changed in the mid-1980s to an equal lump sum for every province. Central direction pertaining to the use of INPRES funds was also eventually relaxed.

The remaining six grants were specific grants to be used as determined by the central government. One, the subsidy to autonomous regions, supported recurrent expenditures, largely salaries, and another was actually a subsidized loan programme. The other four were for development expenditures: the first was initiated in 1973/74 to build facilities and purchase necessities in support of primary education, the second was implemented in 1974/75 for primary health care, the third was launched in 1976/77 and was aimed at reforestation and soil conservation and the fourth started in 1979/80 and was intended for provincial and district road building and maintenance. A new INPRES grant targeted at 'left behind' villages was introduced in 1994/95, reflecting 'growing official concern with spatial inequities in economic development' (Booth 1996, p. 188).

Economists in particular have examined and critiqued the design of these transfers from various points of view. The subsidy to autonomous regions, for example, essentially pays the salary costs of civil servants at the local level whose posts have been approved by the Ministry of Home Affairs. This means that the ministry exercises effective control over the size and composition of local government staff. From an efficiency perspective, this does not encourage local governments to seek cost-effective alternatives to managing their functions, because their incentives are to persuade the ministry to approve and fund additional staff positions.

Economists have criticized the sectoral development grants for not encouraging the growth of local revenues and local accountability to citizens. The transfers did build local capacity to implement investment projects and other activities for which local governments were answerable to the centre; however, the intergovernmental fiscal system did little to promote local capacity to decide on the quantity, quality and priority of public services local communities wanted and were willing to pay for. From the introduction of the INPRES grants for road improvement in 1979/80, for example, the block types of INPRES grants only exceeded the amount of specific grants in total INPRES grants once (1982/83) before the adjustment years of 1987/88 to 1989/90. In the following three years, block grants returned to their minority position (Wuryanto 1996, Table 3.7). In addition, with the emphasis on investment programmes financed by the centre, local governments had little incentive to focus on the operation of services and on the maintenance of assets built by central grants.

As noted earlier, a number of studies have tried to examine the impact of transfers on the relationship between the intergovernmental fiscal policies of the New Order government and economic growth and equity. Inherent technical and data difficulties make the derivation of unqualified results difficult, but the tendency has been to conclude that the policies may have facilitated growth. Azis (1989, p. 22), for example, notes that

> Regional finance is crucial to understanding the dynamics of provincial economic development in Indonesia up to the mid-1980s. It is no exaggeration to say that the economies of many provinces, particularly the poorer ones of eastern Indonesia, were driven by rapidly expanding expenditures by, or grants from, the central government.

With regard to equity (see Booth 1996), the story is complicated. Not all efforts at targeting have worked, but adjustments in allocations were made in the direction of increasing local options and expenditures on socially desirable services. Shah and Qureshi (1994, pp. 57–58) note that between 1986 and 1994, general-purpose transfers increased at an average annual rate of 22 per cent, while specific-purpose transfers averaged increases of 16 per cent per year. However, the relatively slower rate of growth of special-purpose transfers came at the expense of the subsidy to autonomous regions, which grew at 13 per cent, while other special-purpose INPRES grants increased at an average annual rate of 33 per cent.

At the same time, high levels of poverty, as measured by per capita consumption, coexisted alongside extremely high levels of per capita regional incomes (Booth 1996, pp. 199–200). This has been particularly the case in Papua, where in 1985, per capita consumption was US$167 while per capita income was US$620. Similar gaps between consumption and income were apparent during the same period in Aceh, where per capita consumption was US$282 and per capita income was US$1300, and in East Kalimantan, where per capita income was US$293 and per capita consumption was US$3319, although poverty is not as extreme.

The first-order problem is that the bulk of the resource-based revenues from which the income figures are derived accrues to the central government and the share of central revenues remitted as grants is substantially less. One could argue that leaving a greater share of revenues in their provinces of origin would remedy this problem; however, this presupposes that a local government closer to the people would spend the funds more wisely. Experience suggests that this is most likely to occur when that government is truly accountable and responsive to the people, and this is not the case. Two conclusions are evident. First, the current intergovernmental fiscal arrangements are not working well for those that Booth (1996, p. 199) characterizes as 'poor little rich provinces'. Second, fiscal reforms without more fundamental political and institutional reforms are unlike to be adequate (see Booth 1996, pp. 199–206 for a more detailed discussion of these issues).

Other aspects of the intergovernmental fiscal system also contributed to the undermining of local initiative and responsible governance. In addition to the fact that local revenues are by far the least significant public revenue source,[4] local governments have little control over the administration of the major sources of what are traditionally local revenues. The property tax, which accounted for about 8 to 9 per cent of total transfers from 1989/90 to 1992/93 (Wuryanto 1996, Table 3.9), is a central government tax and is administered by the Ministry of Finance. The ministry pays itself an administration fee of about 9.0 per cent of collections, transfers 18.2 per cent to the provinces and transfers the remaining 72.8 per cent to districts and municipalities. The central government sets the rates for user charges (for example, for water) and fees (such as for motor vehicle registration), which provide the bulk of the remaining own source revenues.

For more than two decades, however, the central government's dominance in public expenditure, even at the local level, was exemplified primarily by the deconcentrated activities of central ministries administered by their offices at the local level. These offices implemented the ministries' development budgets in the field. During the 1980s, the ministries' development budgets accounted for 84 per cent of development expenditures (Wuryanto 1996, p. 6); in 1993/94 total INPRES grants amounted to 18 per cent of the total development budget (Booth 1996, p. 188).

Thus for most of the New Order period, local governments were completely dependent on the central government for most of their revenues (67 per cent for districts and 69 per cent for provinces in 1988/89). In addition, local government expenditures remained a minor portion of total public expenditures—less than 21 per cent in 1991/92—though the good news was that this portion was growing.

Nonfiscal Issues: Local Government Structure and Representation

Publicly, the New Order government reiterated the desirability of some degree of decentralization. Indeed, in 1974, Law Number 5, which outlines the relationship between the central government and regional governments, articulated a decentralization framework with a three-tier (later expanded to four tiers in 1979 to accommodate villages) local government system and allocated functions among central and local governments, though as might be expected, responsibilities were heavily weighted towards the central government. Provincial governors, appointed by the Ministry of Home Affairs, were to have substantial powers. This included effective authority over assigned functions, budgets and borrowing (with Ministry of Home Affairs approval), as well as the ability to coordinate all activities of central government agencies in the province. All leadership positions at local levels were appointed, with the exception of the heads of neighbourhood associations and household associations in villages. These were the only elected positions in the management of the local government system; even their equivalents in municipalities were appointed. Nevertheless, as MacAndrews (1986, p. 16) writes:

> What was remarkable was that this was the first time in Indonesian post-independence history that it had a fully functional system of local government in which relationships, including the division of power and responsibility between the central government and the provinces, were spelled out. In practice, the central government retained much of the decision making power although in contrast to early periods in post-independence history, the provinces were finally given much greater authority over their own budgets and over many areas of decision making denied them previously. At the same time, they were given greater opportunities to recruit people from their own areas to the civil service and to build up stronger provincial identities. *Political power, however, remained in the hands of the central government.* (Emphasis added)

A fundamental problem was that the partially elected peoples' assemblies that existed at the central, as well as the provincial and district levels, had no policymaking powers. In effect, they just commented on government policies by means of one of the few mechanisms designed for the expression of public opinion.

The introduction of regulations that would give greater autonomy to non-provincial local governments under Law Number 5 of 1974 was slow. During discussions, officials frequently invoked the familiar arguments about the need to build local capacity before turning over greater responsibilities to local levels. When debating the relative merits of decentralization versus a high degree of central control, military officers appointed to governorships or as district heads would often cite the need to maintain the security of the unitary state. Undoubtedly, this was in recognition that ethnic differences, and especially some regions' strong dislike of the Javanese-dominated central government, were important factors to contend with. East Timor and Irian Java were the extreme, but not totally isolated, indicators of these issues. The challenge as the government perceived it was how to recognize these differences through the governance system without risking a fracturing of the state.

Important shifts in the tenure of discussions about decentralization began to take place beginning in the mid-1980s. Development programmes became more complex as the easier and more obvious investment programmes were completed. In addition, the multiplicity of programmes that were required increased the need for local discretion in priority setting or in designing the details of broad, centrally mandated programmes. Finally, the decline in oil prices reintroduced the risk that the central government could no longer meet the regions' income and economic growth expectations. The structural adjustment programmes that had responded to this last set of circumstances reduced or eliminated a number of the central government's big-ticket projects and focussed public expenditures on those areas of public investment that would best cushion the effects of adjustment on the majority of the population. As these investments were aimed primarily at local government services, inevitably, greater responsibility progressively accrued to local governments. The language of decentralization began to emphasize participation, but still within the existing governance framework.

Two examples illustrate how this concept of greater local participation played out in practice. The first concerns the Integrated Urban Infrastructure Development Programme of the Ministry of Public Works. Although cited as an example of a decentralized programme, the financing and management of all major aspects of the programme, from the technical assistance with the planning to the investments that resulted, emanated from the central ministry. Mayors whose municipalities were selected to benefit were grateful for this major grant-financed programme and the heightened degree of consultation it afforded them, but were under no illusion that they were in charge of it within their jurisdictions.

Another programme was the bottom-up process that was introduced into the preparation and implementation of the national five-year development plans during the 1980s. During the formulation of the annual development programmes that were within the five-year plans, no expenditure envelope was given to the subdistrict level at which the process starts. Proposals from the public were discussed at a meeting chaired by the head of the subdistrict at which district and central technical staff were present. The proposals were sent to the district, where they were competed before being sent further upward, along with proposals prepared by the technical staff. A meeting chaired by the district or municipality head determined the winning proposals, which then competed with more technical staff proposals at the provincial level. A meeting chaired by the governor decided which proposals would be presented to the National Planning Agency. A representative of the National Planning Agency chaired any meetings involving interregional proposals and the meetings at which the provincial proposals were presented. No political representatives were present at the meetings with the National Planning Agency and no decisions were taken at those meetings. Decisions were taken at subsequent meetings chaired by National Planning Agency representatives at the central government level without any regional government representation. As Wuryanto (1996, p. 6) notes: 'Although proposals from the provinces and district governments are allegedly taken into account during the formulation process [of the five-year plans], the province and district governments are unable to influence the final decision of sectoral allocations'.

During the late 1980s, pressure continued to grow for more responsibility to be decentralized. A milestone was achieved in 1990/91, when for the first time, total transfers exceeded ministries' development budgets, although the total INPRES programme still accounted for only 18 per cent of development expenditures in 1993/94.

Endgame

Eventually, the fatal weaknesses in the system began to be revealed, as corruption at the highest level of government appeared to be growing unchecked. Without an open electoral process, people had no way to express their dissatisfaction with this situation. Furthermore, the internal process of accountability that had served for other circumstances was not equipped either culturally or institutionally to deal with an errant leader in an orderly way. The catalyst for eruptive change was the 1997 economic crisis that began in Thailand and swept through Asia, and manifested itself uniquely in its impact on Indonesia. As the corruption around the president appeared to limit the government's ability to respond to the crisis, the long excluded political elite found a new opportunity for leadership. Not surprisingly, their agenda has not stopped at reform at the national level. A worldwide trend that has intertwined democracy and decentralization has again legitimized the view of early Indonesian independence leaders that democracy in the unitary state depends on representative local governments with meaningful degrees of autonomy.

THE DEMOCRATIZED AND DECENTRALIZED ERA

Indonesia has faced a number of crises since the economic collapse stimulated the student-led unrest that forced Suharto's resignation in May 1998. Most of these crises reflect the link between democracy and decentralization as well as fissures in the 'we' that had never been completely sealed. Indonesia was forced to relinquish control over East Timor, and the Muslim-Christian hostilities that underlay popular conceptions of the conflict spilled over to Maluku in long, bloody conflicts. Aceh's longstanding dissatisfaction with its relationship with Jakarta and its share in earnings from its resources erupted yet again into armed conflict and demands for independence. An independence movement has become prominent in Papua, encouraged by East Timor's success.

The secession of East Timor indicated that even disproportionate central-local transfers may not, by themselves, overcome deeply rooted antipathy in a community strongly committed to an identity that is substantially different from that of the dominant state. Catholic East Timorese, supported by the church and its strong external links, had never accepted their annexation by the largest Muslim population in the world. The Indonesian notion that by virtue of geography, East Timor was necessarily a part of the Indonesian 'we', had no standing with most East Timorese. As a result, there proved to be no basis for accommodation.

This may not necessarily be the case in the other regions of conflict, although those in Papua also point to racial and cultural divides that cannot be ignored. Any accommodation that is successful, however, will have to confront the issues of decentralization that result in relation to significant local autonomy, and thus control over the use of and proceeds from local natural resources.

Vice President B. J. Habibie, who inherited the presidency from Suharto, was therefore under great internal pressure to reform intergovernmental fiscal relations as part of the overall political reforms demanded by a newly broad-based opposition. Two new basic laws were hastily assembled in April 1999 and signed by Habibie in the following month. Critics immediately assessed the reforms indicated in the new laws as flawed (McBeth 1999). Habibie's failure at the polls a month later and his replacement as president by Abdurrahman Wahid in October 1999 was followed by a number of critical, in-depth reviews of the legislation, most notably by Alm, Aten and Bahl (2001) and Buentjen (1999).

Understandably, the new government is unwilling to see further defections from the state. To succeed in keeping the state together it will need to address the critical issues inherent in the implementation of the new laws. These include a familiar set of failings that derive from hastily assembled efforts to meet a short-term political timetable, namely, a lack of clarity with regard to the goals and priorities of the intergovernmental political, administrative and fiscal reforms; an unclear assignment of functions between different levels of government; a failure to determine whether transfers are sufficient to pay for critical functions; a lack of revenue decentralization; an absence of coordination between the Ministry of Local Government, which is responsible for political and administrative decentralization, and the Ministry of Finance, which is responsible for intergovernmental fiscal relations; the inadequate attention to transition issues involving the transfer of responsibilities and of civil servants; the inadequate capacities to take on their new roles in both the central and local governments; and the lack of a monitoring programme to keep what is clearly a work in progress on track.

The two laws that propose to reorganize the intergovernmental system are the 1999 Law on Fiscal Balance Between the Central Government and the Regions and the 1999 Law on Regional Government. The Law on Regional Government is intended to restructure the political and organizational arrangements of the subnational government system and subnational governments' relationships with the central government. The key features include greater autonomy of local governments (municipalities/districts or cities) by dissolving their hierarchical relationships with provinces. Local government heads would report to locally elected assemblies instead of to provincial governors. Provincial governments would continue to report to the central government. In addition, except for specific national responsibilities, deconcentrated units of central ministries would be transferred to the control of provinces or local governments as appropriate. National responsibilities are defence and security, foreign policy, monetary and fiscal policy, judiciary affairs, and religious affairs.

The Law on Fiscal Balance Between the Central Government and the Regions focuses on the intergovernmental fiscal system. Four categories of regional government revenues are now defined: own sources, the balance fund, regional loans, and others. The most significant changes are associated with the establishment of the balance fund. These changes arise from the introduction of the sharing of revenues from the exploitation of natural resources—not surprising given the political pressures—and the reorganization of the transfer system. The subsidy to autonomous regions and the block INPRES have been subsumed into a general allocation fund (from which the balance fund is financed), the total of which is set at 25 per cent of the central government's domestic revenues.

From a political perspective, perhaps the most significant changes concern the sharing of revenues derived from natural resources (Table 11.6). Obvious concessions have been made in relation to the distribution of natural resource

Table 11.6 Changes in the distribution of natural resource revenues

Revenue source	Old sharing arrangement	Major change	New sharing arrangement
Oil revenues	100% Central government	Assignment of revenues after tax deduction to regional governments	85% Central government 3% province of origin 6% districts/cities of origin 6% other districts/cities in the province of origin
Gas revenues	100% Central government	Assignment of share in revenues after tax deduction to regional governments	70% Central government 6% province of origin 12% districts/cities of origin 12% other districts/cities in the province of origin
Reforestation fee	100% Central government	Regional government component integrated into specific grants	60% Central government 40% regional governments of origin
Licence fee on forest enterprises	55% Central government 30% provinces 15% districts	Reallocation of fees	20% Central government 16% province 64% districts/cities
Forest Production Royalty	30% Central government 70% regional governments	Reallocation of royalties	20% Central government 16% provinces 32% districts/cities of origin 32% other districts in the provinces of origin
Mining land rents	65% Central government 19% provinces 16% districts/cities	Reallocation of rents	20% Central government 16% provinces 64% districts/cities
Mining royalties	30% Central government 56% provinces 14% districts	Reallocation of royalties	20% Central government 16% provinces 32% districts/cities of origin 32% other districts/cities in the provinces of origin
Fishery enterprises fee	None	Newly introduced	20% Central government 80% equally distributed to districts/cities
Fee on fishery income	None	Newly introduced	20% Central government 80% equally distributed to districts/cities

Source: Buentjen (1999, Table 3), reproduced and edited with the author's permission.

revenues to the locales of origin. Equally striking, however, is the favourable distribution to districts and cities.

How these new laws are implemented will determine the success or failure of the proposed reforms. On the positive side, the structural reforms that give substantial autonomy to local governments could have multiple benefits in strengthening the national fabric. As Alm, Aten and Bahl (2001, p. 86) point out, these benefits include bringing government closer to the people by making local officials accountable to their electorates, which could increase communities' satisfaction with government. To the extent that people perceive the central government as enabling local officials' responsiveness, dissatisfaction with Jakarta could also lessen. However, the new intergovernmental fiscal system must be supportive of these objectives and the transitional arrangements, in particular, the transfer of central government civil servants to regional governments will need to be well thought through and carefully executed.

The circumstances have changed since the first attempt to establish a decentralized system of government in the early years of independence, and certainly the understanding of and appreciation for intergovernmental instruments have increased substantially. Nevertheless, the complex history of intergovernmental relations affects the current situation. The new reforms were born out of crisis and were hastily conceived, and the legislation was written without clearly established objectives and with little consultation with or involvement by the public (Buentjen 1999, p. 2). The new Law on Fiscal Balance Between the Central Government and the Regions continues the reluctance to allow local governments to raise revenues locally to any meaningful extent, and this omission jeopardizes one of the key benefits of decentralization, that is, enforcing local governments' accountability to their constituencies. As long as local communities do not have to pay directly for the public services they receive, they have little incentive to focus on the performance of their elected officials (Alm, Aten and Bahl 2001, p. 89). The analytic underpinnings of key elements of the new intergovernmental fiscal system are also in question, for example, the pool for the balance fund has been set at 25 per cent of general revenues, but whether this amount is adequate or excessive is not clear (Alm, Aten and Bahl 2001).

In addition, experience with follow-up regulations and other actions to give effect to decentralization laws have an unpromising history. This is a concern, because so many critical issues require regulations or other follow-up (Buentjen 1999, p. 62). These include distribution formulas for revenue sharing and regulations for both the Law on Fiscal Balance Between the Central Government and the Regions and the Law on Regional Government to reconcile the transfer of management responsibilities and financial resources. As mentioned earlier, the Ministry of Home Affairs is responsible for the Law on Fiscal Balance Between the Central Government and the Regions, while the Ministry of

Finance is responsible for the Law on Regional Government. At least since Law Number 5 of 1974, the former ministry has tended to favour more decentralization, but the latter has not. Buentjen (1999, pp. 61–62) suggests that these disagreements have not been reconciled, and notes the lack of coordination between the two ministries and the inconsistencies in the regulations that are emerging. Finally, the unease of central government civil servants about being transferred to local governments has not been soothed by the lack of clarity about the details of the transfer process or its intended personnel management outcomes (Alm, Aten and Bahl 2001, pp. 91–92). Given the civil service's history of resisting decentralization, letting simmering dissatisfaction with elements of the process boil over would not be wise.

Quite surprisingly, the transfer of around 2 million civil servants in 2001, the first year of decentralization implementation, did not create many major problems; however, efficiency issues in the public sector began to emerge as a result of this massive transfer. Because most formerly central government civil servants had been transferred to the provincial level, this meant that the provincial governments ended up with many more civil servants than they needed. In addition, some resistance to just accepting the transferred civil servants has arisen at the municipality and district level because of the issue of hiring locals versus outsiders. However, municipality and district governments do need help in implementing the decentralization process successfully, and most of them are not helping themselves in terms of capacity building by giving priority to local officials.

As mentioned previously, the lack of coordination between central and local governments and between central government ministries has affected the decentralization process. One of the critical aspects of the decentralization process is the delegation of authority from the central to local governments. The Law on Fiscal Balance Between the Central Government and the Regions clearly emphasizes that municipality and district governments are primarily responsible for delivering public services, but implementation has been hindered by the failure, as in the past with other laws, to draft the pertinent regulations following enactment of the law. To be effective, the regulations should be drafted from the bottom up, that is, they should clearly define exactly what the municipality and district level is responsible for in terms of public service delivery, then assign duties at the provincial level, with the central government being responsible for the remainder. Instead, the regulations have been drafted in a top-down fashion, meaning that the municipality and district level has been assigned whatever is not done at the central and provincial levels.

After two years of implementing the intergovernmental fiscal reform mandated by the Law on Fiscal Balance Between the Central Government and the Regions and the Law on Regional Government, improvements are still needed in the design of the system and its implementation that could lead to both laws being amended. From the design point of view, the central government is decentralizing expenditures, but not revenues. Taxing powers at the local level are practically the same as before decentralization, and the central government still handles major tax revenues directly. Despite the reallocations mandated by the Law on Regional Government, the key issue remains the principle of tax authority rather than the amount of revenue. With fiscal decentralization led by transfers, creating a mechanism whereby local government officials are held accountable to local voters becomes difficult. Not only do local residents not pay local governments directly for public services, local members of parliament are elected not by voters, but by their political parties. Furthermore, district heads and mayors are elected solely by members of parliament. Thus the fact that most recent complaints about local governments and parliaments reflect the gap between elected officials and voters is not surprising.

From the implementation point of view, the first years of fiscal decentralization seemed to have created some degree of 'shock' both at the central and local levels. At the central level, the shock arises when different ministries and units within ministries have to collaborate in resolving issues pertaining to the balance fund. While some issues have been resolved successfully, such as the monthly disbursement of the general allocation fund, the fund has failed to perform its intended role as an equalization grant because of political interference in the allocation formula.

The so-called hold harmless provision guaranteed that every local government would receive the general allocation fund in an amount that was at least the same as the subsidy to autonomous regions and INPRES funds received in 2000. Because the provision still persists, the performance of the general allocation fund as an equalization grant is still suboptimal from a fiscal viewpoint, but may be necessary from a political perspective to maintain national unity.

A more critical problem seems to stem from the sharing of natural resource revenues, for which the schedule for revenue disbursement remains uncertain. Most of the regions rich in natural resources have encountered cash flow problems because of the late disbursement of natural resource revenues, which account for the bulk of their funds. In addition, local governments accuse the central government of not being transparent in calculating the portion of revenues to be shared. The calculation process is extremely complicated and involves more than one ministry. This accounts for both the disbursement delays and local government officials' difficulties in understanding the process.

The shock at the local level has occurred mostly in the regions rich in natural resources. The sudden influx of funds from the natural resources revenue sharing, especially for oil and gas, has created some significant changes in how these regions are planning for their economic development. They have tended to focus on large infrastructure projects and free public services, but they need to realize that the supply of natural resources is not indefinite and to plan for the future accordingly. In addition, while providing free public services may be a good thing, the effectiveness of free education is questionable. However, what worries most Indonesians is a perception that the natural resource revenues are not being spent wisely, or even worse, that the spending is being directed by corrupt local governments, as reflected in the coexistence of relatively unnecessary, prestigious projects and the continued persistence of large numbers of poor people.

Indonesia now consists of 31 provinces and 417 districts and municipalities, compared with 27 provinces and less than 300 districts and municipalities before the start of decentralization in 2001. Estimates indicate that the annual growth rate of new regions is 10 per cent. Two main reasons account for these rapidly growing new regions: an article in the Law on Fiscal Balance Between the Central Government and the Regions and the general allocation fund formula. The article clearly states that the formation of new regions is allowed if the original district government gives its approval. It also permits regions to merge, but this has not occurred. As for the general allocation fund, its guarantee of a lump-sum minimum allocation creates incentive for forming new regions.

Whether the formation of new regions will benefit both the political and economic goals of decentralization is debatable. From a political point of view, smaller local governments mean that they are closer to their residents and can therefore be held accountable more readily, but as noted earlier, accountability mechanisms are not yet in place. Whether the new general election law that permits the direct election of both local officials and local legislators will provide the initial conditions for such a mechanism remains to be seen.

From an economic point of view, more smaller regions could lead to diseconomies of scale and inefficiency in providing public services. Furthermore, the greater the number of regions, the less the average amount of the general allocation fund that the regions will receive.

In addition to the issues already discussed in connection with the reform of intergovernmental fiscal relations, others include the need to build strong central capacity to manage decentralization, including the intergovernmental transfer system; to oversee regional government borrowing; and to resolve disputes and design changes to the systems as necessary.

ASYMMETRIC DECENTRALIZATION: SPECIAL AUTONOMY FOR ACEH AND PAPUA

The Law on Fiscal Balance Between the Central Government and the Regions and the Law on Regional Government do not seem to have helped narrow the gap in understanding between Aceh and Papua and the central government, and separatist sentiments persist. In response, the central government has reacted quickly by proposing special autonomy for both regions by what amounts to an extension of the Law on Fiscal Balance Between the Central Government and the Regions and the Law on Regional Government. One obvious difference is the level of government that receives greater autonomy. Under the special autonomy law, the provincial governments are the most important ones rather than the district and municipal governments. Despite resistance and objections to the asymmetric decentralization both from residents in Aceh and Papua and people elsewhere, parliament finally approved laws enacting special autonomy for Aceh (Law Number 18 of 2001), now known as Nanggroe Aceh Darussalam, and Papua Law Number 21 of 2001.

The concept of special regions is not really new. Aceh was referred to as a special region beginning in 1959. Jakarta has been referred to as a special region in the 1960s and Yogyakarta since the 1950s. However, in these cases the definition of special regions only partially referred to local culture and history. Aceh was defined as a special region, but no special conditions accrued to it as a result. Jakarta achieved this status simply because it is the capital city, while Yogyakarta was considered different because of its long history as a Javanese kingdom. By contrast, the current concept of special autonomy tries to accommodate specific local characteristics and differences from the rest of the country in all aspects of life: religious, ethnic and cultural.

The laws of special autonomy give Aceh and Papua the right to use the symbols and identities of each region, for example, they can use their provincial flags and anthems as long as this use is not intended as a demonstration of sovereignty. The law also allows each region to set up an institution to protect and preserve local culture, local civil law, heritage and religion. That institution will be one of advisory local bodies in each region. Aceh has three such advisory bodies. Papua has a local peoples' assembly, as distinct from the local parliament. Papua also has the right to form a special human rights committee.

The special autonomy laws give Aceh and Papua the right to set up affirmative action programmes for indigenous people, especially in relation to government employment. In Papua, the governor and vice governor have to be indigenous Papua; however, to preserve national unity, governors and vice governors of both regions must be approved by the president and have to report to the president.

Among many privileges granted by the special autonomy laws, the most anticipated, and perhaps the most important, are those pertaining to fiscal matters, especially the balance fund. Both provinces and all districts and municipalities inside the provinces are still bound by the same Law on Regional Government provisions regarding the balance fund as other regions. As special autonomy regions, however, they receive extra funds from shared oil and gas revenue and Papua receives a special allowance of 2 per cent of the total general allocation fund. Aceh and Papua will receive an additional 55 per cent of oil revenue and 40 per cent of gas revenue as a special autonomy fund that will be part of the provincial budgets. The provincial governments must allocate this fund to all districts and municipalities according to an allocation formula, one of whose goals has to be to promote less inequality among districts/cities. The special autonomy fund will not, however, last forever. In Aceh, the extra oil and gas revenue is only forthcoming for 8 years, while in Papua it will be forthcoming for 25 years. After that time, each region will receive a smaller percentage of oil and gas revenue, but one that is still higher than the percentages other provinces receive. Papua's special allowance of 2 per cent of the total general allocation fund will be effective for 20 years.

Articles in the special autonomy laws mandate some expenditure for such basic services as education, health and nutrition. In Aceh, at least 30 per cent of the special autonomy fund must be spent for education, while in Papua, at least 30 per cent must be spent on education and at least 15 per cent on health and nutrition. Papua's 2 per cent of the general allocation fund is intended for education and health, but Papua can also propose infrastructure projects each year.

The implementation of the special autonomy fund in fiscal year 2002 significantly increased the balancing fund in Aceh and Papua compared with what they received in 2001 (Table 11.7). In Aceh, the additional revenue came from the additional percentage of oil and gas revenue, while in Papua, the additional revenue came from the additional 2 per cent of the total general allocation fund. Aside from these two provinces, no other provinces experienced such a dramatic increase in their balancing fund in 2002. However, what Aceh and Papua received from their special treatment does not amount to the highest balance fund amounts. As Table 11.7 shows, provinces in Java were still the biggest recipients of the balancing fund in total, though not per capita. In 2002, with the special autonomy fund, Aceh became the second richest province after Riau in terms of sharing revenue from natural resources. In the same year, Papua became the province with the highest special allocation fund.

The potential for internal conflicts within Aceh and Papua triggered by huge differences in natural resource reserves between districts has not disappeared. These differences could lead to the formation of new provinces in these two regions. Laws propagated in 1999 and 2000 have indicated that Papua will be divided into three separate provinces, but how these laws will affect Papua's special autonomy status is not clear. A proposal to break Aceh up into three separate provinces has also been floated.

Even though the special autonomy provisions have been in effect since 2001, the Aceh Freedom Movement and the Papua Freedom Organization are

Table 11.7 Provincial balance fund, 2001 and 2002 (Rp millions)

Province	2001					2002				
	Balance fund	Tax share revenue	Natural resources share revenue	General allocation fund	Special allocation fund	Balance fund	Tax share revenue	Natural resources share revenue	General allocation fund	Special allocation fund
Nanggroe Aceh Darussalam	3 071 787	206 915	744 612	2 080 333	39 927	4 459 002	152 968	2 139 942	2 105 200	60 892
North Sumatra	3 878 848	456 845	65 595	3 318 259	38 149	4 559 253	473 895	64 894	3 954 240	66 224
West Sumatra	2 021 200	150 223	17 137	1 842 720	11 119	2 362 682	135 182	18 802	2 199 580	9119
Riau	6 700 787	516 715	3 898 577	2 230 611	54 884	6 626 406	595 100	3 847 440	2 142 910	40 956
Jambi	1 253 890	127 449	51 279	1 062 010	13 152	1 589 023	105 086	74 307	1 397 040	12 589
South Sumatra	2 559 204	234 692	656 882	1 662 338	5291	2 386 171	222 715	482 609	1 678 740	2107
Bengkulu	748 686	43 001	1360	687 945	16 381	864 489	42 848	9552	809 890	2198
Lampung	2 104 760	143 619	208 159	1 740 770	12 212	2 434 919	121 135	210 637	2 096 281	6867
DKI Jakarta	3 684 456	2 726 741	184 652	773 064	0	3 731 073	2 767 655	190 400	773 018	0
West Java	7 766 052	1 175 357	257 783	6 323 208	9703	8 529 341	1 084 328	264 228	7 125 285	55 500
Central Java	8 858 456	597 910	20 340	8 217 279	22 926	9 127 851	546 465	22 952	8 558 435	0
Yogya	1 113 224	100 902	1730	988 655	21 937	1 404 859	80 075	2046	1 321 090	1648
East Java	10 036 135	989 467	124 555	8 879 775	42 338	10 064 675	839 594	128 943	9 087 643	8494
West Kalimantan	1 728 813	124 218	17 171	1 563 445	23 979	2 029 123	128 473	41 034	1 820 276	39 341

Central Kalimantan	1 487 611	147 890	76 164	1 068 419	195 138	1 669 618	117 864	320 791	1 219 043	11 920
South Kalimantan	1 559 343	175 339	226 356	1 150 372	7276	1 805 326	163 471	190 308	1 443 360	8187
East Kalimantan	6 521 859	433 754	4 153 883	1 736 561	197 662	3 504 253	261 478	1 960 844	1 245 440	36 491
North Sulawesi	870 178	62 061	8702	799 102	313	1 206 214	59 375	11 120	1 132 720	3000
Central Sulawesi	1 162 652	62 129	8223	1 057 704	34 596	1 456 397	63 314	14 724	1 364 309	14 051
South Sulawesi	3 240 510	295 020	65 303	2 860 991	19 197	4 008 524	288 834	46 598	3 613 805	59 286
Southeast Sulawesi	957 944	44 791	10 852	892 550	9750	1 156 904	39 302	14 116	1 099 120	4366
Bali	1 659 596	197 088	139 297	1 303 976	19 235	1 715 508	158 275	2551	1 554 682	0
West Nusa Tenggara	1 576 901	91 224	226 483	1 251 301	7894	1 685 994	89 876	103 646	1 468 070	24 403
East Nusa Tenggara	2 227 181	110 832	2557	2 110 654	3138	2 214 534	75 635	2676	2 136 223	0
Maluku	451 772	25 310	3052	419 134	4275	730 534	33 034	7515	683 890	6094
Papua	3 284 049	332 279	352 904	2 429 707	169 159	4 866 379	321 027	254 597	2 777 509	1 513 246
North Maluku	568 749	33 701	35 808	476 715	22 524	728 436	27 154	35 422	665 860	0
Banten	1 672 109	395 078	3447	1 272 546	1038	1 945 940	519 777	4748	1 421 416	0
Bangka Belitung	422 427	42 841	48 600	330 679	307	570 635	40 618	35 613	494 250	153
Gorontalo	421 555	23 704	107	392 405	5339	560 964	22 995	2740	534 520	709
Indonesia	83 610 733	10 067 094	11 611 572	60 923 229	1 008 838	89 995 027	9 577 547	10 505 794	67 923 845	1 987 841

Source: University of Indonesia, Institute for Economic and Social Research database.

still promoting secession, with 2001–December 2004 marked by martial law and violence, as the Papua Freedom Organization fighters hid in the mountains and the Aceh Freedom Movement terrorized most of Aceh, including urban areas. However, the death of 120 000 Acehnese in the 26 December, 2004, tsunami dramatically changed the politics of the situation, as both the government and the rebels lost the desire to continue the violence. Diplomacy moved quickly, and in August 2005 a peace deal was struck that ended 26 years of conflict when the two sides agreed upon a withdrawal of government groups, which was completed on 31 December, 2005; the establishment of a truth and reconciliation commission; and the implementation of a peace monitoring process. Nevertheless—as with any postconflict situation—major challenges lie ahead, including the nature of any special autonomy for Aceh and Papua.

The future of Aceh and Papua as special autonomy regions might go in different directions, especially from the fiscal point of view. The gas reserves in Aceh have been depleted and are unlikely to last for more than ten years. Without significant attempts to find new reserves, Aceh's future fiscal sustainability might have to depend on the general allocation fund or on a special allocation fund like Papua. Papua, by contrast, will be ready to take over Aceh's position as one of Indonesia's biggest liquid natural gas producers when production starts around 2010. An interesting observation is that both provinces are significantly dependent on a single multinational company, Exxon Mobil in Aceh and Freeport in Papua, although British Petroleum make take over the dominant role in Papua in the coming years.

CONCLUDING REMARKS

In relation to intergovernmental fiscal relations in Indonesia to date, eight issues appear to be important. The first is continued good economic performance. Indonesia has had three decades of experience with commendable economic management. Export-led growth will require continued sound management of the country's natural resources and labour endowments. The economy's shift away from overdependence on natural resources has increased the number of available options. Java and Sumatra are no longer net consumers and should shortly be net producers. Politically sensitive issues of the sources of private sector investment and management as well as their regional impacts will clearly be critical in terms of their implications for the 'we' that has been an ongoing part of this discussion. Can Indonesia accept its ethnic Chinese population as a permanent and benign group?

Second, participation by the people, especially at local levels, must be meaningful and multifaceted. Communities must have a real say in setting priorities and delivery standards with regard to the services that are important to them. However, for this involvement to be realistic, they must be informed about the available resources and the costs of the various choices open to them. Otherwise their expectations may become unrealistic, with the consequent negative effects. At the same time, informed participation is a sound basis for building a system of accountability to the public among local leaders and administrators.

Third, systems for participation, monitoring and accountability must be easily accessible and must operate efficiently if they are to be used effectively by a wide range of interests. To accomplish this, they must be designed and implemented bearing in mind the culture and experience of the Indonesian people. The central government has a crucial role in ensuring the integrity of the political system and the instruments for participation, transparency, monitoring and especially accountability. Its relationship with local governments is therefore crucial.

The choice of a basic constitutional structure should not be overemphasized. Internationally, both unitary and federal systems have worked well and badly. Much depends on what rights and responsibilities are defined and where they are built into the various elements of the constitutional and legal architecture. From the perspective of an intergovernmental fiscal system, at minimum this argues for broad consensus on the objectives and priorities of the transfer system, meaningful local tax regimes so that local choices about services and service levels are reflected in local taxpayers' willingness to finance these services and service levels, local governments' ability to borrow responsibly, avoidance of ambiguity in relation to the allocation of responsibilities between levels of government for services and avoidance of unfunded mandates from higher to lower levels of government. Public dialogue on these issues is incomplete at this time.

Fourth, the administrative elite has an important but redefined role to play that must be acknowledged and designed into the new systems. Critical features of this new role are preparing technical analyses to inform and educate the public and decisionmakers and making a wide range of reliable sources of information for decisionmaking, monitoring and evaluation accessible to the public. This means that incentive systems have to be designed that reward openness, transparency and accessibility, as well as effectiveness in educating the public and decisionmakers. This involves a fundamental reform of a civil service that has, from its earliest existence, operated best behind closed doors and according to the unwritten rules of a closed society. To help eliminate corruption, a difficult but necessary step on the part of the political leadership must be to design a compensation system that increases public servants' legitimately derived remuneration.

Fifth, the body of experience in political management and administration accumulated by the military should be exploited, not shunned. The requirement that military occupants of civilian posts must choose between one role or the other is to be applauded. The difficulty that invariably accompanies choices of this nature is to ensure that the candidates make the choices that best suit the public interest.

Sixth, it would have been desirable if the new intergovernmental fiscal instruments had not been redesigned in a rush to the exits at the end of the New Order political regime. It is already clear that complex interests must be balanced to ensure that the new intergovernmental system continues to build the state. Thus a more deliberate approach is called for to assess and take into account potential effects and ensure that the desired effects are dominant. The stakeholders must consider that, for example, if revenue flows go disproportionately to some provinces, as long as Indonesia is a single country with free, mobile labour markets, interregional migration will result. If that is widely regarded as positive, then this is an outcome to be desired. However, what are the associated steps that must be taken to mitigate the likely consequence that this interregional migration will exacerbate tensions between indigenous populations and newcomers? Given the history of Indonesia since the New Order government, this is not a trivial concern.

Two major factors have influenced population movements since at least the 1960s. One was the government-managed transmigration programme that resulted in more than 3 million mostly Javanese being dispersed to various provinces since Indonesia's beginnings in 1905. The other has been the lure of economic opportunity. Between 1971 and 1980, migrants were attracted primarily to Jakarta, Aceh, Riau, East Kalimantan, Central Kalimantan and Papua (World Bank 1984b, Table 4.3). From the perspective of an economic rationalist, Indonesia's policies with regard to internal population mobility have been at minimum sensible, and with regard to their proactivity, commendable. From that perspective, the transmigration programme was flawed only in terms of inadequately sensitive and thorough design and expensive, and sometimes poor, execution. From the perspective of local communities in the receiving areas and other Indonesian ethnic groups, Indonesia's policies, largely formulated and operated by Javanese officials, have sometimes been interpreted as attempts to Javanize other parts of Indonesia (Manning and Rumbiak 1989, p. 98). Clearly issues pertaining to internal migration have to be part of the public dialogue and a factor in the negotiation of details of the intergovernmental system.

There are many levels of 'we', and the closeness and degree of sharing desired among groups is a function of the meaning of 'we' to critical groups. Willingness to share and to be proximate is a function of the rewards that accompany differences between groups as well as the level of discomfort suffered as a consequence of such differences. The success of an intergovernmental fiscal system therefore depends on how effectively the system assigns the rewards and mitigates the discomforts. An even better response is to blur identification with narrower distinctions so as to broaden the self-definition of 'we'. For these reasons, an intergovernmental fiscal system must be negotiated, not imposed. The indications are that people in Indonesia still identify enough with a national 'we' to negotiate a consensus on intergovernmental fiscal relations; however, the instruments and processes have to be carefully thought through before embarking on negotiations.

The seventh consideration is that the political objectives and agreements that result from the negotiations must be clearly understood and documented before laws are written. Good laws codify understandings already reached. The failure of previous decentralization laws were partly the consequence of trying to write the laws before consensus on the system that those laws would describe had been reached.

Finally, as the relatively brief history of independent Indonesia illustrates, circumstances change, sometimes drastically. Indonesia should build a process of periodic review and orderly change of its intergovernmental operating systems and fiscal instruments into its institutional arrangements.

NOTES

1. The Dutch had promulgated laws on decentralization beginning in 1903 and again in 1926, 1929 and 1930.
2. Note that this chapter adopts the Indonesian convention of referring to laws by their number and year of promulgation.
3. Booth (1996, p. 198) notes that the considerable growth in INPRES grants in the early 1990s appears to have been biased towards the less populated and less prosperous provinces.
4. A district-level official once explained to one of the authors (Ford) the situation from his perspective as follows (translated): 'If it is fat, it belongs to the centre; if it has some meat, it's the province's; if it's really thin, it's mine'.

REFERENCES

Alm, James, Robert H. Aten and Roy Bahl (2001), 'Can Indonesia Decentralize Successfully? Plans, Problems, and Prospects', *Bulletin of Indonesian Economic Studies*, 37 (1), 83–102.

Azis, Iwan J. (1989), 'Key Issues in Indonesian Regional Development', in Hal Hill (ed.), *Unity and Diversity: Regional Economic Development in Indonesia Since 1970*, Singapore: Oxford University Press, pp. 55–74.

Booth Anne (1996), 'Intergovernmental Relations and Fiscal Policy in Indonesia: The National Impact of Equity and Inequity in the Provinces', in Christine Fletcher (ed.), *Equity and Development Across Nations: Political and Fiscal Realities*, New York: St Martin's Press.

Buentjen, Claudia (1999), 'Fiscal Decentralization Reform in Indonesia: A Critical Assessment of Law No. 25/1999 on the Fiscal Balance Between the Central and

Regional Government', report prepared for the German Technical Assistance Support for Decentralization Measures Project.
Castles, Lance (1989), 'Jakarta: The Growing Centre', in Hal Hill (ed.), *Unity and Diversity: Regional Economic Development in Indonesia Since 1970,* Singapore: Oxford University Press, pp. 233–53.
Central Bureau of Statistics (1986a), *Regional Government Financial Statistics, Districts and Municipalities, 1977/78–1982/83,* Jakarta.
——— (1986b), *Regional Government Financial Statistics, Provinces, 1977/78–1982/83,* Jakarta.
Hill, Hal and Anna Weidermann (1989), 'Regional Development in Indonesia: Patterns and Issues', in Hal Hill (ed.), *Unity and Diversity: Regional Economic Development in Indonesia Since 1970,* Singapore: Oxford University Press, pp. 3–54.
Mabbett, Hugh and Ping-Ching Mabbett (1982), 'The Chinese Community in Indonesia', in Charles A. Coppel (ed.), *The Chinese in Indonesia, the Philippines and Malaysia*, Report no. 10, London: Minority Rights Group, pp. 10–16.
MacAndrews, Colin (ed.) (1986), *Central Government and Local Development in Indonesia: An Overview*, New York and Oxford, UK: Oxford University Press.
Manning, Chris and Michael Rumbiak (1989), *Economic Development, Migrant Labour and Indigenous Welfare in Irian Jaya 1970–1984*, Canberra: Australian National University, Research School of Pacific Studies, National Centre for Development Studies.
Maryanov, Gerald S. (1958), *Decentralization in Indonesia as a Political Problem,* Interim Report Series, Modern Indonesia Project, Ithaca, NY: Cornell University, Department of Far Eastern Studies, Southeast Asia Program.
McBeth, John (1999), 'Too Little, too Late', *Far Eastern Economic Review* (Hong Kong), 13.
Ravallion, M. (1988), 'INPRES and Inequality: A Distributional Perspective on the Centre's Regional Disbursements', *Bulletin of Indonesian Economic Studies*, 24 (3), 53–71.
Shah, Anwar and Zia Qureshi (1994), *Intergovernmental Fiscal Relations in Indonesia: Issues and Reform Options,* Discussion Paper no. 239, Washington, DC: World Bank.
Sukma, Rizal (1994), 'Recent Developments in Sino-Indonesian Relations: An Indonesian View', *Contemporary Southeast Asia*, 16 (1), pp. 40–41.
Walker, Millidge (1960), 'Decentralization in a Guided Democracy: The Future of Local Government in Indonesia', paper read at a meeting of the Association for Asian Studies, 13 April, New York.
World Bank (1984a), *Indonesia: Policies and Prospects for Economic Growth and Development*, Jakarta.
——— (1984b), *Indonesia: Selected Aspects of Spatial Development,* vol. 1, Washington, DC.
Wuryanto, Luky Eko (1996), 'Fiscal Decentralization and Economic Performance in Indonesia: An Interregional Comparable General Equilibrium Approach', PhD thesis, Cornell University, Ithaca, NY.

12. Subsidiarity and Solidarity: Fiscal Decentralization in the Philippines

Christine Wallich, Rosario Manasan and Saloua Sehili

HISTORICAL BACKGROUND AND SETTING

The 84 million people of the Philippines include at least 77 major ethno-linguistic groups with more than 500 dialects and inhabit around 1000 of the more than 7000 islands constituting the archipelago (see Figure 12.1 for a map of the Philippines). Most Filipinos are of Malayan descent. Those of mixed Malay, Chinese and Spanish descent make up the country's business elite. Living in coastal and low inlands, Christian Filipinos are the largest and politically most powerful group, and account for 94 per cent of the population. The second largest group, which accounts for some 5 per cent of the population, consists of Muslim Filipinos or Moros, who live mainly in the southern islands. Both Christian and Muslim Filipinos include a number of major ethno-linguistic groups.[1]

In addition to being strongly defined along family, religious and ethnic dimensions, social ties are perpetuated by the Filipino tradition of debts of gratitude, whereby favours are extended and are expected to be reciprocated on demand. These personal relations have traditionally dominated both national and local politics, whereby officials are elected based on their family wealth and influence and the benefits of patron-client ties. Political loyalties are tied to specific politicians rather than to individual political ideologies. Local political alliances are often unstable and fraught with personal rivalries over votes and access to funding from the central government. These rivalries have sometimes translated into violent behaviour characterized as 'warlordism' or brigandage, which is still manifest, especially in the south.

For a country with such ethnic, religious and geographical diversity, the Philippines has had a surprisingly long history of highly centralized government administration. Although the decentralization process started as early as

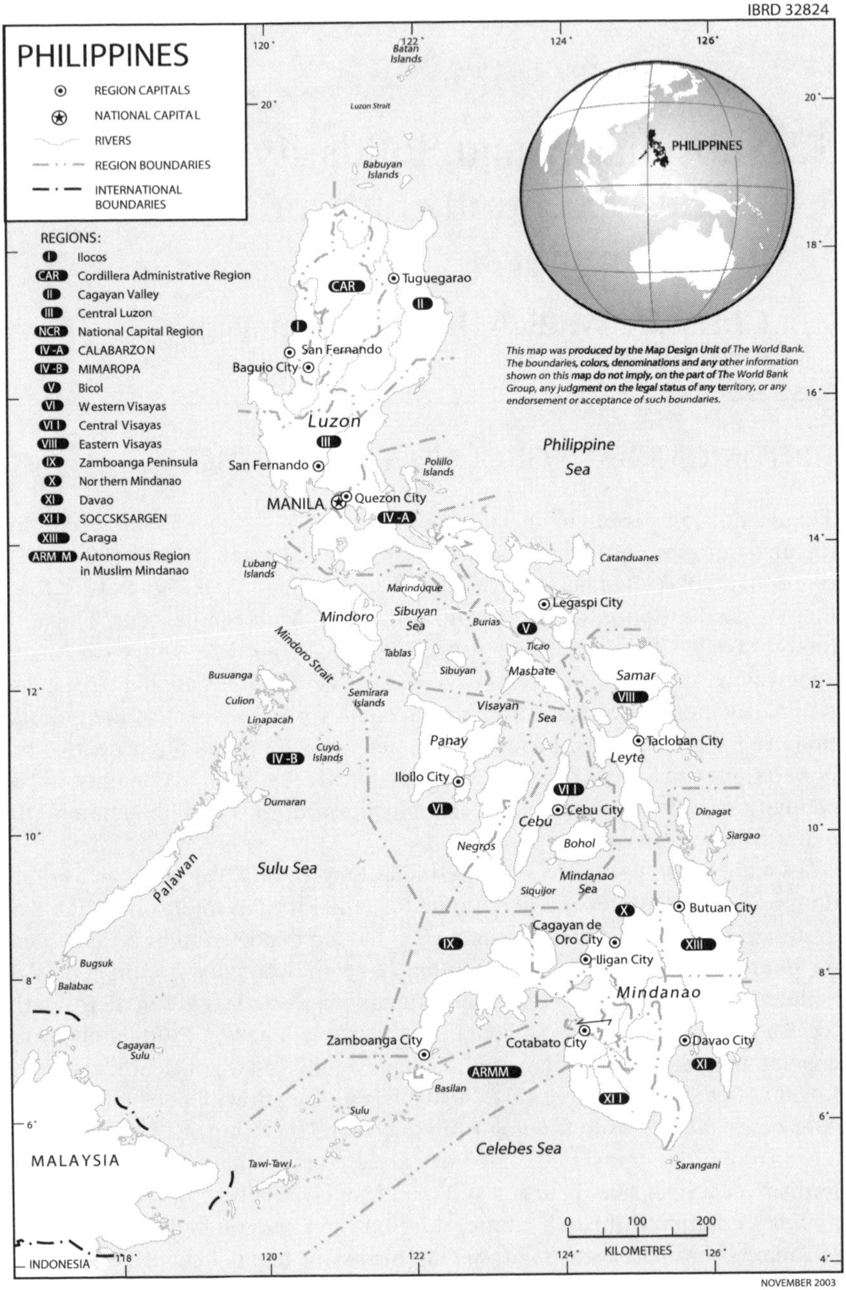

Figure 12.1 The Philippines

1898 with the country's first constitution, devolution, as opposed to administrative deconcentration, did not materialize until the implementation of the 1991 Local Government Code. This latest form of decentralization was fuelled by repeated demands from the citizenry for greater democratization and better economic conditions. The secessionist tendencies of Muslim ethnic minorities in the south further led to the enactment of the 1989 Organic Act for the Autonomous Region of Muslim Mindanao, which conceded powers to a new regional government. Thus efforts to maintain solidarity have given rise to asymmetric federalism.

Currently, the Philippines has a unitary form of government with a multi-tiered structure. It is a presidential republic with a bicameral legislature composed of the 24-member Senate and the 250-member House of Representatives. The president is chief executive, head of state and commander-in-chief of the armed forces. The judiciary consists of the Supreme Court and several layers of lower courts.

At the top is the central government, which operates through some 20 departments and agencies. The country is divided into 15 administrative regions, and most central government agencies maintain regional offices. In addition, there is one autonomous region, the Autonomous Region for Muslim Mindanao (ARMM). Note that with the exception of the ARMM, the regions are just administrative subdivisions and not regional governments with elected regional officials.

The second tier of government is composed of local government units (LGUs). The local government structure consists of three layers. The first layer is provinces and highly urbanized cities. Provinces are divided into municipalities and component cities, each of which is further subdivided into *barangays* (or *barrios*), the smallest political unit. While highly urbanized cities exist at the same level as provinces, that is, they share the same functions and authorities, they are partitioned directly into barangays.

At present, there are 79 provinces, 115 cities, 1495 municipalities and 41 945 barangays, amounting to a total of 43 634 LGUs. Each LGU is headed by an elected chief executive (governor, mayor or barangay captain) and has a legislative body composed of an elected vice governor or vice mayor and council members.

Antecedents of Decentralization Initiatives

For more than 300 years, the Philippines was under Spanish colonial rule with a highly centralized, hierarchical government system based in Manila.[2] The 1935 constitution mentioned the term local government in only one section and solely with reference to the president's power to 'exercise general supervision' over it (De Guzman and Tapales 1973).

Decentralization initiatives first surfaced in the 1950s, when democracy and development were put forth as a counterinsurgency response to the Huk rebellion (Carino 1998).[3] In 1959, city and municipal governments were given greater fiscal, planning and regulatory functions and were allowed to undertake any public works project they could finance themselves. The same year, the Barrio Charter gave the barangays a quasi-municipal corporate character with their own legislative and taxing authorities. The 1967 Decentralization Act further increased the share of provinces' in national taxes, allowed provinces and cities to supplement national programmes in agricultural extension services and transferred the authority to appoint certain local officials—who are paid out of local funds—to local chief executives. However, the central government continued to hold most of the powers, as many of the rural areas had poor tax bases and few ways to support their new fiscal responsibilities (Carino 1998).

The martial law era under Ferdinand Marcos's dictatorship was characterized by decentralization rhetoric. For instance, the 1973 constitution guaranteed the autonomy of local governments and called for the enactment of a local government code that did not materialize until a decade later. Similarly, even though the Marcos government articulated and legislated a number of ostensibly decentralist initiatives, such as the Local Tax Code and the Real Property Tax Code in 1973, Marcos concentrated decisionmaking powers in his hands by abolishing Congress, suspending both national and local elections, and abrogating the power to appoint local officials to himself. Furthermore, he concentrated the ownership and control of economic resources in the hands of his associates through government-mandated monopolies and special subsidies and privileges in what came to be known as crony capitalism.

Given its low level of public support, the Marcos government consolidated its position in the early 1980s and re-centralized local police and fire protection, physical planning and agricultural extension services (Brillantes 1987). In effect, Marcos promoted administrative deconcentration rather than devolution. The creation of administrative regions with regional development councils and the establishment of regional offices of central government agencies 'allowed some decisions to be made at lower levels, and for some services to be more accessible' (Carino 1998). For the most part, however, LGUs were treated as mere administrative arms of central government agencies.

Building Solidarity Through Local Autonomy

A four-day protest in Manila known as the People Power Revolution of 1986 toppled the Marcos regime and installed the Corazon Aquino administration, setting the stage for a radical departure from the centralist tendencies of the previous regime. To better appreciate the regime's dynamics, an understanding of the interplay between a number of economic, social and political factors as they defined the spirit and temperament of the decentralization movement in the late 1980s and early 1990s is helpful.

In the mid-1980s, catalysed by a worldwide economic recession, unsustainable debt and rampant corruption during the Marcos administration, the economy sank into a deep recession. Furthermore, economic growth in the preceding years, which had averaged a creditable 4.5 per cent annually, was unevenly distributed and benefited only a small segment of the population. Thus the country was characterized by considerable spatial diversity in the levels and rates of change in development and socioeconomic progress (Table 12.1). The regional income divide coincided with the religious and ethnic divide, as in the case of the Cordilleras and Muslim Mindanao.[4] In particular, the Muslim-dominated regions, Western Mindanao and Central Mindanao, were the most backward in terms of per capita income, functional literacy and infant mortality.

The struggle of the people of the Cordilleras and Muslim Mindanao for independence can be traced as far back as the 16th century, when the Spanish invasion overtook the Muslim principalities in the southern Philippines, giving rise to prejudice and hostilities between Christians and Muslims in the region. The rebel movement continued throughout Spanish rule, under American colonialism and into the postindependence era. Hostilities were further fuelled when the government opened Mindanao to Christian immigrants from the Visayas and Luzon, with the new settlers blatantly encroaching on what was considered to be Muslim territory and, in many places, transforming the Muslim majority into a minority.

Thus the underlying motivation of the people of the Cordilleras and Muslim Mindanao in their pursuit of autonomy and self-determination goes beyond the substandard income levels and human development outcomes prevalent in their areas. It is deeply rooted in their need to preserve their unique and distinct heritage, culture and religion and to re-establish their inherent rights to their ancestral lands. Put another way, Tanggol (1994) argues that the quest for autonomy has

> a dual significance to Muslim Mindanao and the Cordilleras. One concerns the imperative for an effective public administration where goods and services are efficiently delivered to the poor. Here, these two communities are similarly situated with the rest of rural and poverty-stricken Philippines. The second concerns the need to preserve the uniqueness of Muslim and Cordillera cultures, religions and ways of life. Here, these two communities are not similarly situated with the other Filipinos, the dominant majority.

Widening income disparities, increasing poverty and the repressive and corrupt political environment during the years of martial law fuelled armed resistance by both the leftist National People's Army—a wing of the Communist Party of the Philippines comprising former Huks—and the separatist

Table 12.1 Per capita regional gross domestic product and social development indicators, selected years

Region	1980					1988				
	RGDP per capita (₱)	Income per capita[a] (₱)	Functional iteracy rate (%)	Infant mortality (per 1000)	Poverty inci- dence[a] (%)	RGDP per capita (₱)	Income per capita (₱)	Functional literacy rate[b] (%)	Infant mortality rate[c] (per 1000)	Poverty inci- dence (%)
Metro Manila	32 202	10 797	97.2	48	27.2	26 090	11 826	90.60	46	25.2
Cordillera Autonomous Region	—	—	—	—	—	11 066	5140	73.70	63	50.7
Ilocos Region	6892	5733	84.5	58	43.5	5675	5236	75.10	56	51.7
Cagayan Valley	8189	5030	79.4	66	42.7	5942	5130	72.00	62	44.6
Central Luzon	12 271	6808	88.7	43	32.2	10 546	7543	84.10	45	33.8
Southern Tagalog	15 150	5514	85.8	60	45.7	12 784	5451	79.80	53	46.6
Bicol Region	6166	3446	85.1	67	67.6	4789	3937	68.80	64	61.4
Western Visayas	10 787	4295	81.8	60	66.5	8586	4470	71.30	61	56.6
Central Visayas	11 653	3878	76.3	51	61.9	9696	4337	70.60	55	52.1
Eastern Visayas	6228	3281	79.2	77	65.2	5334	3748	65.50	76	54.7
Western Mindanao	8061	4110	65.7	56	60.0	6393	4671	57.70	64	43.7
Northern Mindanao	11 059	4874	84.6	67	56.7	10 356	5320	76.50	57	50.2
Southern Mindanao	12 325	5190	81.1	51	49.7	11 784	5390	74.10	56	48.9
Central Mindanao	10 087	4088	64.1	80	56.3	8800	5085	63.10	56	41.0
ARMM	—	—	—	—	—	—	—	—	74	—
Correlation coefficient with RGDP per capita		0.8823	0.5728	–0.4810	–0.6449		0.8978	0.7455	–0.6538	–0.7198

Region	1998					2002				
	RGDP per capita (₱)	Income per capita[d] (₱)	Functional literacy rate[e] (%)	Infant mortality rate (per 1000)	Poverty incidence[d] (%)	RGDP per capita (₱)	Income per capita (₱)	Functional literacy rate[e] (%)	Infant mortality rate[f] (per 1000)	Poverty incidence (%)
Metro Manila	27 198	18 472	92.40	41.5	8.5	27 940	12 582	92.40	41.5	11.0
Cordillera Autonomous Region	15 295	8442	78.60	37.1	55.8	18 455	8371	78.60	37.1	40.3
Ilocos Region	6983	6821	86.40	28.7	44.1	7542	6468	86.40	28.7	40.9
Cagayan Valley	6441	6772	86.60	35.3	38.0	8589	6875	86.60	35.3	34.5
Central Luzon	10 962	11 088	87.30	31.4	18.5	11 233	9354	87.30	31.4	24.2
Southern Tagalog	12 924	10 072	88.00	26.0	30.0	13 370	9532	88.00	26.0	27.6
Bicol Region	5574	6034	82.80	23.6	57.0	6035	4716	82.80	23.6	59.3
Western Visayas	10 159	7075	80.90	60.8	45.9	11 505	6686	80.90	60.8	43.4
Central Visayas	11 417	6375	80.80	44.6	38.9	13 133	5271	80.80	44.6	40.4
Eastern Visayas	5891	4698	79.70	41.0	48.5	6160	4567	79.70	41.0	52.5
Western Mindanao	8391	6705	75.40	40.9	45.5	8744	5317	75.40	40.9	52.1
Northern Mindanao	11 400	5026	83.40	48.4	52.7	10 917	5324	83.40	48.4	49.3
Southern Mindanao	9712	5945	79.40	55.1	44.3	10 844	6281	79.40	55.1	45.5
Central Mindanao	9416	5344	77.40	53.2	50.1	9957	5113	77.40	53.2	57.2
ARMM	4120	4374	61.20	55.1	62.5	4747	4080	61.20	55.1	62.8
Correlation coefficient with RGDP per capita		0.8738	0.5340	–0.0102	–0.6854		0.8241	0.5095	–0.0040	–0.7635

— Not available.
RGDP Regional gross domestic product.

a. 1985 data. b. 1989 data. c. 1990 data. d. 1997 data. e. 1994 data. f. 1998 data.

Sources: Per capita RGDP: National Statistical Coordination Board (2004a); household income: National Statistics Office (1990, 1999, 2002); literacy rate, infant mortality rate and incidence of poverty: National Statistical Coordination Board (1996, 1999, 2004b).

Moro National Liberation Front throughout the archipelago. The National People's Army had built up considerable military strength in many parts of the country, notably the Cordilleras, the Bicol Region and Western Visayas. In 1974, they influenced the Cordilleras natives to launch violent resistance against the construction of hydroelectric dams and the intrusion of a logging concession for paper and pulp manufacturing (Buendia 1991). In 1968, the killing of 28 Muslim army recruits in the so-called Jabidah massacre in the south ignited Moro student activism. One month after the declaration of martial law in September 1972, Maranao Muslims staged a violent uprising in Marawi City, and the Moro National Liberation Front claimed leadership of the Moro secessionist movement. By 1975, the fighting between the Moro National Liberation Front and the armed forces had escalated into large-scale, conventional warfare. The conflict killed around 120 000 people and left more than a million people homeless (Muslim and Cagoco-Guiam 1999).

Realizing that a stalemate had been reached, and under pressure from the Organization of Islamic Conference, the Marcos government called for a ceasefire and started peace negotiations with the Moros. In December 1976, the Moro National Liberation Front and the Marcos government signed the Tripoli Agreement, which provided for autonomy in 13 provinces and 9 cities in the southern Philippines. The Muslims, however, were dissatisfied with the way Marcos implemented the agreement, and hostilities resumed. Disagreements inside the Moro secessionist movement caused the Moro National Liberation Front to split into two factions along ideological lines: the Moro National Liberation Front headed by Nur Misuari and the Moro Islamic Liberation Front headed by Hashim Salamat.[5] This split is along ethnic lines as well: Misuari and the Moro National Liberation Front are mainly Tausug having influence in the mostly Tausug provinces of Sulu and Tawi-Tawi; the Moro Islamic Liberation Front is mainly Maguindanaon.

Partly in reaction to the political repression evident during the period, the number and activities of nongovernmental organizations (NGOs) and peoples' organizations (POs) expanded markedly during the martial law years. NGOs and POs found ways to establish projects supporting participatory development strategies within the confines of the limited democratic space that was available at that time. The development-oriented NGOs and POs were largely based in barangays or villages, where they developed and implemented small-scale livelihood projects. To take advantage of economies of scale at the municipality, city and provincial levels, they broadened the scope of their projects and advocacies and started taking local elections seriously (Rocamora 1995).[6] NGOs' participation in public affairs has been widely recognized as one of the greatest successes of the 1990s.

For many local government officials, the concentration of political and economic power in the National Capital Region during the Marcos years was no better than the virtual colonization of the country by imperial Manila. Under both administrations, they had to spend more time lobbying for resources and following up on the concomitant paperwork with the central government than dealing with their own jurisdictions. Those politicians who actively pursued economic development for their localities were handicapped by their limited ability to raise local revenues and by their reliance on national funding, which was awarded primarily on the basis of political considerations. Patron-client relationships further fostered personalized, discrete services that benefited specific families. All these factors severely limited the implementation and maintenance of projects that promote sustainable growth of local communities.

Having remained resolutely committed to not seeking re-election and having no ambitions to stay in power beyond her six-year term, President Aquino was not afraid of the diminution of central government authority that greater local autonomy implies. Moreover, she looked at decentralization as a reform that would facilitate the transition to democracy, which she considers to be the main legacy of her government (Eaton 2000). Against this backdrop, Aquino adopted a policy of national reconciliation when she assumed office and focused on the peaceful settlement of armed conflicts through peace talks (Buendia 1991). Thus one of her first official acts was the release of political prisoners. The government then started peace talks with the National Democratic Front, the Cordillera Peoples' Liberation Army (a splinter group of the National People's Army) and with the Moro National Liberation Front.[7]

The new constitution, drawn up in 1987, contains more explicit provisions in support of decentralization than either the 1935 or the 1973 constitutions. Specifically, the 1987 constitution provides that (a) the territorial and political subdivisions of the state shall enjoy local autonomy; (b) the LGUs shall have a just share in national taxes and in the proceeds of national wealth within their respective jurisdictions; and (c) the LGUs shall have the power to create their own sources of revenues and to levy taxes, fees and charges subject to guidelines and limitations laid down by Congress.

For the first time, regional autonomy for the Cordilleras and Muslim Mindanao was enshrined in the constitution, which provides that autonomous regional governments shall be created in Muslim Mindanao and the Cordilleras, areas sharing a 'common and distinctive historical and cultural heritage'. In compliance with these provisions, the Organic Acts for Muslim Mindanao and the Cordilleras were legislated in 1989, predating the passage of the Local Government Code of 1991.[8]

DEFINING THE LIMITS OF SUBSIDIARITY

The 1991 Local Government Code and the 1989 Organic Act for Muslim Mindanao jointly define central-local relations. The Organic Act granted the regional government of the ARMM most powers that had previously been held by the central government. It provides for the ARMM's expanded share and automatic retention of national internal revenue taxes collected in the region, for significant regional discretion in development planning and for the regional government's primacy in the delivery of basic services as well as the utilization and management of natural resources. The Local Government Code, which is up for mandatory review and amendment after five years, represents a fundamental shift in local governance in that it includes far-reaching provisions that affect the assignment of functions across different levels of local government, revenue sharing between the central and local governments, resource generation and use by local governments and participation by civil society in various aspects of local governance.

Devolution of Functions

The Organic Act for Muslim Mindanao shifts to the regional government all powers, functions and responsibilities heretofore exercised by the central government except (a) foreign affairs; (b) national defence; (c) postal service; (d) fiscal and monetary policy; (e) administration of justice; (f) quarantine; (g) citizenship, naturalization and immigration; (h) general auditing, civil service and elections; (i) foreign trade; (j) maritime, land and air transportation and communications that affect areas outside the ARMM; and (k) patents, trademarks, trade names and copyrights.

The Local Government Code, by contrast, assigns a slightly narrower range of functions and responsibilities to non-ARMM local governments. Thus non-ARMM local governments are not responsible for providing agrarian reform and education services or promoting employment, workers' welfare, trade and industry. Specifically, the functions devolved from the central government to local governments are the delivery of basic services and the operation of facilities in the following areas: agricultural extension and research, social forestry, environmental management and pollution control, primary health care, hospital care, social welfare services, repair and maintenance of infrastructure facilities, water supply and communal irrigation and land use planning.

The devolution is substantial not only in terms of the sheer number of functions that were devolved, but also in terms of the number of personnel transferred (Table 12.2) and the corresponding reductions implied in the budgets of affected central government agencies (Table 12.3). The central government agencies that were most heavily affected by devolution were the Department of Agriculture, the Department of Health and the Department of Social Welfare and Development.

Even though the Organic Act allows the regional government of the ARMM to devolve some of its functions to local governments in its jurisdiction, the

Table 12.2 Number of devolved personnel, 1992

Department or agency	Number of personnel before devolution	Number of devolved personnel	Ratio of devolved personnel to pre-devolution personnel (%)
Department of Agriculture	29 638	17 673	59.63
Office of the Secretary	29 234	17 664	60.42
National Meat Inspection Commission	404	9	2.23
Department of Budget and Management	3532	1650	46.72
Department of Environment and Natural Resources	21 320	895	4.20
Department of Health	74 896	45 896	61.28
Department of Social Welfare and Development	6932	4144	59.78
Other executive offices	191	25	13.09
Philippine Gamefowl Commission	191	25	13.09
Total	136 509	70 283	51.49

Source: Department of Budget and Management (1993).

regional government has not done so. Thus LGUs in the ARMM did not receive any of the functions that were devolved to local governments outside the ARMM during the implementation of the Local Government Code.

With a few exceptions, the devolution of expenditure responsibilities to local governments and the ARMM is consistent with the decentralization theory. For the most part, these are activities that can be provided at low levels of government and have few important spillovers to a broader community that would indicate that they should be provided by a higher level of government. The functioning of the decentralization theory is enhanced by LGUs' tendency to organize themselves into larger cooperative units when significant spillovers do occur. Frequently, small LGUs team up to carry out their responsibilities jointly when economies arise from doing so and when interlocality spillovers are present. This development is highlighted in the emergence of metropolitan arrangements in many locations (Manasan and Mercado 1999).[9]

One important exception to the application of the decentralization theory remains. Except in areas covered by the ARMM, the central government still provides education. In 1997, central government agencies accounted for 92

Table 12.3 Agency budgets and devolution, 1992 (pesos thousands)

Devolved agency	Budget before devolution	Budget after devolution	Ratio of devolved budget to pre-devolution budget (%)
Department of Agrarian Reform	1 842 374	9389	0.51
Department of Agriculture	5 210 028	1 055 620	20.26
Department of Budget and Management	465 379	172 847	37.14
Department of Environment and Natural Resources	1 941 782	167 675	8.64
Department of Health	9 991 392	3 851 079	38.54
Department of Public Works and Highways	27 109 267	1 096 347	4.04
Department of Social Welfare and Development	1 320 708	866 420	65.60
Department of Tourism	207 721	2753	1.33
Department of Transportation and Communication	7 563 929	97	0.00
Philippine Gamefowl Commission	15 208	8705	57.24
Total	55 667 788	7 230 932	12.99

Note: Based on the 1992 expenditure programme and incorporates the full year impact of the functions, projects and activities devolved. Captures only the expenditures of devolving agencies.

Source: Budget before devolution: Department of Budget and Management (1991); budget after devolution: Department of Budget and Management (1993).

per cent of all education spending, although school construction and maintenance were devolved to local governments. Both school construction and maintenance are largely funded by the proceeds from an add-on to the real property tax. These proceeds are earmarked for the Special Education Fund, which is controlled by local school boards. Thus teachers' salaries and other education inputs are mainly funded by the central government, although many LGUs top-up central government allocations for these items.[10]

Expenditure assignments are generally clear and well understood by local governments and the regional government of the ARMM. The Local Government Code provides an explicit and clear delineation of functions across levels of governments except perhaps in the area of environment and natural resource management and public works.[11] However, some central government agencies continue to exercise undue influence on local governments in terms of how they should conduct their expenditure responsibilities. For instance, the Department of Interior and Local Government issued a number of circulars, rescinded in 2001, that imposed restrictions on the way local governments could spend their local development funds.

Tax Assignment

Various types of taxes are assigned exclusively to different levels of government. For instance, the income tax (both individual and corporate) and customs duties are reserved for the central government alone, while the real property tax and the community tax (poll tax) may only be imposed by LGUs. In addition, the value added tax and excise taxes on alcoholic beverages, tobacco products and petroleum products are off-limits to LGUs.

In contrast, the regional government of the ARMM is authorized to levy all types of taxes with the exception of the income tax and customs duties. In practice, however, the ARMM does not touch any of the taxes that the central government levies. Instead, it has chosen to impose a supplementary rate (that is, a surcharge) on taxes that are typically levied by LGUs, such as the real property tax and the franchise tax. The recently amended Organic Act for Muslim Mindanao formalizes the symmetrical treatment of the ARMM and other local governments with regard to the limitations on their taxing powers, which means that the ARMM can now only impose the taxes assigned to LGUs in the Local Government Code. Moreover, tax rates in the ARMM are typically 80 to 90 per cent lower than those of LGUs both inside and outside its jurisdiction.

Even though the Local Government Code raised the ceiling rate for real property taxation at the provincial level from 0.5 per cent to 1.0 per cent, it withdrew the power of municipalities (except for those in Metro Manila) to impose such a tax, thereby maintaining the effective real property taxation rate in provincial municipalities at the pre-Local Government Code level (Manasan 1992). In terms of real property assessment levels, the Local Government Code set maximum assessment rates for different classes of property, whereas the actual levels had been fixed in the pre-Local Government Code period. The new maximum assessment rates are no higher, and often significantly lower, than the preceding fixed assessment rates, with an effective reduction in the assessment levels of residential land, all types of buildings and all types of machinery, leading to a potentially substantial reduction in real property tax revenues. Changes in the sharing formula for real property tax revenues among the various levels of LGUs resulted in an overall decrease in such revenues for provinces, municipalities and cities and an increase in those of barangays.

Except for real property tax revenues, the major portion of local government tax receipts is derived from the local business tax, which is basically a turnover tax levied at an *ad valorem* rate on the gross receipts of businesses and traders. The base of each of these taxes is defined by central government legislation, which also limits (that is, sets floors and/or ceilings on) the tax rates that local governments may impose. Note that only cities and municipalities (but not provinces) are authorized to levy the local business tax and the community tax. In addition to the real property tax, provinces are allowed to levy a tax on the following: transfer of ownership of real property, franchises, printing or publication businesses, sand and gravel extraction, professionals, amusement places and delivery vans. The Local Government Code further expanded the tax base of LGUs to include products, activities and sectors—such as banks and other financial institutions and printing and publishing enterprises—that used to be outside the reach of local taxation. In practice, however, the size of the local tax base has not changed much. Moreover, with the exception of the real property tax and the local business tax, most local taxes have low yields.

Thus despite the changes, the bulk of productive tax bases still rests with the central government. Furthermore, many local governments have not made full use of their revenue-raising powers, a fact attributed to the disincentive effect of intergovernmental transfers on local tax efforts. Consequently, the contribution of local governments to total central and local government tax revenues remains low at 6 per cent in 1992–2002, compared with 4 per cent in the pre-Local Government Code period.

Intergovernmental Transfers

Under the Local Government Code, all LGUs are entitled to the internal revenue allotment (IRA), a fixed share of central government tax revenues, on the basis of a formula fixed by law. The aggregate IRA is set at 40 per cent of internal revenue tax collections three years prior to the current year (excluding national tariffs and customs duties). In contrast, prior to the Local Government Code, the aggregate share of LGUs in internal revenue taxes never exceeded 20 per cent, and was often less.

The IRA is transferred as a block grant from the central government to LGUs, which enjoy considerable discretion in how they use it. The share of each level of local government in the IRA pool is fixed in the code: 23 per cent to provinces, 23 per cent to cities, 34 per cent to municipalities and 20 per cent to barangays. In turn, the IRA share of each tier of local government is then apportioned to specific LGUs according to a predetermined formula based on population, land area and equal sharing.

Under the Local Government Code, provinces' and municipalities' shares decreased in favour of barangays, although no functions have been devolved to the latter. Furthermore, a larger weight was given to land area and equal sharing and a smaller weight to population (Table 12.4). Because the demand for social services is largely a function of population size while that for infrastructure depends on land area, the implication is that the Local Government Code gives more emphasis to the latter relative to the previous regime. More emphasis on equal sharing further implies that a disproportionate increase in LGUs' fixed overhead expenses is expected. This might be based in part on the sheer number of devolved personnel from central government agencies to the LGUs.

LGUs in the ARMM are not only entitled to their share of the IRA under the Local Government Code, but also to their share under the Organic Act for Muslim Mindanao. Actual collections of internal revenue taxes in the region are divided as follows: 40 per cent accrues to the central government, 30 per cent to the regional government and 30 per cent to the ARMM's local governments, all distributed according to the origin principle. The regional office of the Bureau of Internal Revenue, the collecting agent, automatically remits the region's own share together with the shares of its constituent LGUs to the regional government. Thus the regional government of the ARMM retains 60 per cent of the revenues collected in its jurisdiction, half of which is remittable to its constituent LGUs.

Note that the ARMM regional government's share in internal revenue taxes is small when compared with its expenditure responsibilities and with

Table 12.4 IRA sharing

Category	Pre-local government code (%)	Post-local government code (%)
Local government unit		
Provinces	27	23
Cities	22	23
Municipalities	41	34
Barangays	10	20
Apportionment basis		
Population	70	50
Land area	20	25
Equal sharing	10	25

Source: Republic of the Philippines (1991).

the aggregate IRA share of its component LGUs. In particular, the share of the regional government in internal revenue taxes is about 4 per cent of the cost of the functions devolved to it and averages less than 5 per cent of the IRA share of its constituent LGUs. This is partly because the regional government's share is computed on the basis of origin, and the tax base in the ARMM is lower than the average tax base for the country as a whole. In contrast, the IRA distribution formula is to some extent equalizing, that is, it transfers more money to poorer LGUs. As a result, the ARMM is dependent on yearly allocations from the central government's general appropriations to carry out its mandate.

Popular Participation

The Local Government Code provides that LGUs shall promote the establishment and operation of POs and NGOs so that they become active partners in the pursuit of local autonomy. In particular, the code mandates participation by POs and NGOs in such local bodies as development councils; school boards; health boards; and prequalification, bid and award committees. Civil society organizations played an extensive role in providing public services during the Marcos era, acquiring socio-political capital that could be tapped and integrated into the country's decentralization endeavour. By the late 1990s, 16 per cent of Filipino households declared that they were members of civil society organizations (Alba 1999).

ISSUES AND PROBLEMS

Analysis of the convergence of per capita incomes across the regions indicates that the dispersion of the log of regional gross domestic product per capita did indeed narrow, albeit slightly, between 1990 and 2000 (Figure 12.2). However, the speed of convergence slowed down relative to the previous decade (Manasan and Chatterjee 2003).

The ARMM continues to have one of the lowest levels of per capita income and the highest incidence of poverty in the country (Table 12.1), exacerbated by the ongoing conflict. In early 2000, fighting erupted once again in Muslim Mindanao, and President Joseph Estrada declared an all-out war policy. In January 2001, Estrada was impeached following allegations of corruption and was replaced by Gloria Macapagal-Arroyo, his vice president. She pursued a policy of reconciliation and negotiation with the Moro Islamic Liberation Front, with Malaysia acting as an intermediary. The government is, however, still cracking down on the secessionist militant group Abu-Sayyaf, which has been linked to terrorist activities.

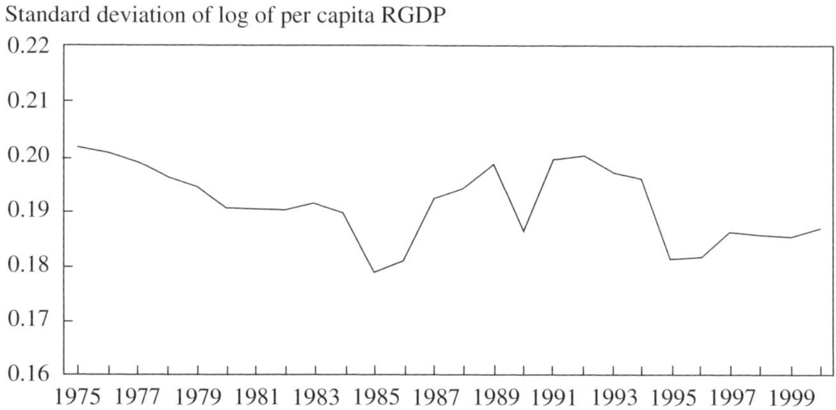

Source: Manasan and Chatterjee (2003).

Figure 12.2 Dispersion of log of per capita regional gross domestic product, 1975–2000

Local Government Units

President Aquino signed the Local Government Code into law in October 1991, but implementation did not start until after May 1992 under the administration of President Fidel Ramos. Developing the necessary organizational structures and processes to absorb the devolved functions and personnel and to start working towards effective decentralization took another two years (Rood 2000).

Filipinos welcomed the passage of the Local Government Code with great fanfare. Many viewed it as a landmark piece of legislation that genuinely vested LGUs with real local autonomy, because it devolved a significant number of functions and responsibilities to LGUs in addition to giving them a higher and more predictable share of national tax revenues. The process for releasing funds to the LGUs was relatively stable for the most part, but some initial scepticism about the actual disbursement of the IRA re-emerged in 1998–2000, when the national government's fiscal position became strained with the onset of the Asian financial crisis.[12]

Some evidence indicates that productive efficiency and allocative efficiency have improved since the implementation of the Local Government Code. Case studies have shown that local governments are able to deliver services more cheaply than the central government, especially in the case of the construction of roads, school buildings and other local structures (Loehr and Manasan 2001). Some LGUs have even started joint ventures with the private sector to deliver various services (see Box 12.1 for examples of such and

BOX 12.1 INNOVATIONS IN LOCAL GOVERNANCE

The following are some examples of initiatives at the local level brought about by the devolution of powers to local governments in 1992. These have helped improve the quality of life of local communities through better governance and pertain to local resource generation, environmental management, health services, housing, participation and livelihood generation. These programmes have won national recognition through the Galing Pook Awards Program.

Local Resource Generation

- Victorias, a small municipality in Negros Occidental, responded to its constituents' housing needs by floating bonds. The mayor initiated this with the assistance of such national government agencies as the National Home Mortgage Fund.
- After the city of Mandaluyong lost its public market to a fire, it reconstructed it using a build-operate-transfer scheme and joint venture with the private sector. This was initiated by the mayor, who was a former judge and therefore well versed in the law, who took advantage of the newly passed law governing build-operate-transfer schemes and the powers devolved to local governments under the Local Government Code.
- A small municipality, Ilocos Norte, built its public market stalls through a variation of the build-operate-transfer approach.

Environmental Management

- The Bais City Environmental Management Project was a showcase of ecological preservation that came about in response to a natural disaster that occurred in the nearby city of Ormoc and to concerns about soil erosion, flash floods, biodiversity loss and overall watershed degradation.
- The Save the Maasin Watershed Program in Iloilo mobilized more than 5000 participants from all sectors of Ilonggo society, who actively participated in the massive tree planting that took place at the start of every rainy season by enlisting the full support and cooperation of all sectors (corporations, private companies, NGOs, POs, schools, and so on) and the media.
- In the early 1960s, the Metro Iloilo Water District started its reforestation plan in response to the rapid deforestation caused by unrestricted entry of farmers into the watershed. The programme started in earnest in the mid-1980s, when the Department of the Environment and Natural Resources started its watershed protection and rehabilitation programmes. When Governor Arthur Defensor took over in the early 1990s, he immediately expanded the Maasin Watershed Program by appealing to all sectors of Iloilo society to participate in regenerating the watershed because of the role it plays in the area's survival.

Health Services

- The city of Surigao's Primary Health Care Program is a self-help programme that promotes community awareness of health issues and allows community participation in health programmes and activities using the primary health care approach in line with the government's People Empowerment Program.
- The provincial government of Negros Oriental set up a community primary hospital in the hinterlands of the province to provide basic health services and meet people's minimum basic needs, and in the process, this also became a counterinsurgency strategy.

Housing

- A low-cost housing programme in Puerto Princesa emerged in response to the city's squatter problem and the need to provide affordable housing alternatives to squatters. The programme also received support from the US Agency for International Development.
- Legaspi City floated bonds to meet the demand for housing. The bonds have been redeemed, and the LGU has identified other projects that could be supported by a bond flotation scheme.

Participation

- Despite the controversy it generated, the volunteerism programme in the city of Olongapo has demonstrated how people and the government can become partners in responding to crises, in this case the eruption of Mount Pinatubo, and work together to rehabilitate an area and generate livelihood projects.
- The mayor of Dumarao regularly holds so-called people's congresses. The people's congress is an expanded municipal development council that brings together the various sectors of the municipality to address pressing local issues and concerns and to map out common strategies to address them.

Livelihood Generation

- The city of Marikina provided livelihood opportunities to its residents, particularly young people, through the Shop in Every Village Program. Among other things, the programme makes tools available that people can borrow and use for livelihood generation activities, ranging from manufacturing, repair and renovation to sculpting.
- The municipal government of Guagua provided the framework for its residents to plant sampaguita flowers and supply various outlets in Metro Manila.

Source: Brillantes (2001b).

other innovations). Furthermore, the mix of local expenditures has changed, with the expenditure pattern shifting in favour of education, housing and general public services. However, some deficiencies are apparent with respect to the code's impact on fiscal efficiency.

Vertical balance

The implementation of the Local Government Code resulted in significant increases in LGUs' share of the IRA, with the proportionally largest increase going to barangays, followed by cities and municipalities. Hand-in-hand with the expansion in the IRA, other expenditure responsibilities were shifted to the LGUs under the devolution programme that was mandated by the Local Government Code.

Nevertheless, the perception is widespread that a vertical imbalance exists, in the sense that the LGUs' prevailing share in national taxes is insufficient to cover both the cost of devolved functions and the cost of unfunded mandates. These unfounded mandates include salary increases mandated by the Salary Standardization Law and additional personnel benefits provided under the Magna Carta for Health Workers. Indeed, citing the difficulties LGUs have experienced in paying the salaries of staff devolved from central government agencies, especially health workers, some people have called for recentralization of the health sector. Analysis shows that while these concerns were generally unfounded in the aggregate during the early years of implementation of the Local Government Code (1993, 1994 and 1995), this was not the case in 1996, 1997 and 1998. During this later period, the salary adjustments under the Salary Standardization Law were so hefty that the increases in the IRA were not enough to keep up with the rising costs of both devolved functions and unfounded mandates. However, a comparison of aggregate IRA levels with LGUs' expenditure responsibilities, including devolved functions, in 1999 and 2001 shows that the increase in the IRA arising from the implementation of the Local Government Code is now sufficient to cover the inflation- and population-adjusted costs of devolved functions and unfunded mandates.

Provinces absorbed 45.6 per cent of the total costs of devolved functions, municipalities absorbed 47.4 per cent, cities absorbed 7.0 per cent and barangays did not absorb any of the costs. When this is contrasted with the LGUs' mandated share of the IRA—provinces 23 per cent, cities 23 per cent, municipalities 34 per cent and barangays 20 per cent—it becomes clear that a mismatch exists between the resources transferred and the expenditure responsibilities devolved to the different levels of local government. This skewed distribution reflects the reality that in general, provincial governors present more of a threat to members of Congress than mayors. Thus by making provinces responsible for more services than they can pay for with automatic revenue transfers, Congress has ensured that governors would remain dependent on legislators, who could subsequently offer their services as brokers of additional revenues from the centre in a personalized function (Eaton 2000).

Horizontal balance

In addition to the vertical imbalance across different levels of local government, an imbalance also exists across LGUs within each level. Thus while the increase in the IRA share of some LGUs is not enough to finance the functions devolved to them, others have received resources that exceed their requirements. For instance, in 1993, the transfer of net resources per capita was negative in 37 out the 66 provinces for which data were available (that is, per capita transfers were less than mandated per capita expenses),[13] but in 1994, this figure was down to 3 provinces. However, the situation has worsened since then because of the huge size of the unfunded mandates, such as the Magna Carta for Health Workers and the Salary Standardization Law. Thus in 2001, 35 out of 79 provinces, 644 out of 1496 municipalities and 20 out of 113 cities suffered from negative net resource transfers. Clearly the IRA distribution formula needs to be improved so that the expenditure needs of the various levels of local government and the different units within each level are taken into account.

Augmentation funds

Section 17 (c) of the Local Government Code provides the basis for the continued involvement of central government agencies in functions that are primarily assigned to local governments. It allows central government agencies to implement 'public works and infrastructure projects and other facilities, programs and services *funded by the national government under the annual General Appropriations Act, other special laws, pertinent executive orders, and those wholly or partially funded from foreign sources'* (emphasis added). However, the Local Government Code and its implementing rules and regulations failed to define the mechanisms through which the central government could direct such assistance to local governments.

Meanwhile, Executive Order 53 mandates national government agencies to retain management control over all foreign-assisted projects and/or nationally funded projects, even if they involve devolved activities. Furthermore, because many of the devolved national government agencies are held accountable for the overall outcome in their respective areas, they deem it their responsibility to direct local government behaviour in support of national objectives. Thus most of them tend to make full use of Section 17 (c) of the Local Government Code and Executive Order 53 regarding augmentation. Consequently, the prevailing regulatory framework effectively permits, and may even encourage, the existence of a two-track delivery system, where both national government agencies and LGUs can initiate devolved activities (Gonzalez 1996).

Section 17 of the Local Government Code is also extremely useful to those in Congress, because it allows them easy access to 'pork barrel' funds. They can access such funds simply by inserting a special provision in the General Appropriations Act, which ordains that monies from the augmentation funds can only be released for 'projects that are identified by members of Congress'. Consequently, the budgets of devolved central government agencies have grown disproportionately relative to the IRA. For instance, while the IRA grew by an average of 15 per cent per year during 1994–97, the budget of the Department of Agriculture expanded by 48 per cent, that of the Department of Health by 25 per cent and that of the Department of Social Welfare and Development by 22 per cent. Although this trend has been reversed in recent years, the practice whereby members of Congress identify the types and locations of projects financed from augmentation funds continues and is a major source of discord between Congress and local government officials.

Thus while the augmentation fund provision of the Local Government Code presents a logical opening for the operation of a matching grants programme for devolved activities with significant externalities and spillover of benefits—as might be the case for environmental or basic social programmes—it has been used against the interests of local autonomy. The central government continues to interfere with and control local government operations in other ways as well (Brillantes 2001a). For example, the Department of Interior and Local Government has become increasingly aggressive in regulating and supervising local governments, while other national agencies use various issuances and circulars to dole out exemptions from local government regulations.

Fiscal inefficiency

The ratio of aggregate local tax revenues to gross national product rose from an average of 0.5 per cent of gross national product before the Local Government Code era to 0.9 per cent afterwards. Despite this positive development, however, the contribution of LGUs to total tax revenues of the general government remains low at 6 per cent. This is indicative of the low local tax effort. Anecdotal evidence suggests that many local officials tend to shy away from the imposition and effective collection of local taxes primarily because they equate increased tax effort with lower chances of winning an election. For instance, the collection efficiency for the real property tax has deteriorated since the introduction of the Local Government Code.

The IRA is by far the largest source of revenue for most LGUs. Indeed, it more than covers the cost of devolved expenditures for many of them. Given the considerable political cost to local government officials of raising revenues locally, their reliance on intergovernmental transfers for revenue and failure to engage in vigorous local tax efforts is not surprising. Empirical evidence seems to support this view. Manasan and Chatterjee (2003) and Manasan and Mercado (1999) find that in 1985, prior to the implementation of the Local Government Code, intergovernmental transfers had a neutral effect on local revenue performance, but in 1992, 1993, 1995 and 1997, they substituted for local tax revenues in all levels of local governments. This suggests a need to alter the IRA distribution formula so as to provide LGUs with incentives for enhancing local tax effort.

Equalizing revenue capacity

According to fiscal theory, intergovernmental transfers should help equalize disparities in income and economic opportunities among LGUs. Simple regression analysis of per capita IRA on per capita personal income reveals that these two variables are negatively related to one another. That is, localities with lower per capita personal income tend to receive higher per capita IRA, suggesting that the distribution formula tends to be equalizing. However, this equalizing effect is insufficient to compensate for the inherent disparities in the tax base, as per capita total LGU revenue—the sum of local own source revenue and IRA funds—is found to be positively related to per capita personal income. This apparent weakness in the IRA distribution formula in relation to equalizing fiscal capacity may explain the skewed distribution of LGU capital expenditures in favour of cities and the more developed LGUs, which further exacerbates existing disparities.

Local taxes and intergovernmental transfers are not the only means of finance available to local governments. The Local Government Code allows LGUs to borrow as long as their debt service is less than 20 per cent of local revenues. Thus local governments have started prudently exploring avenues of borrowing from government and private banks. Access to private funding sources is also increasingly available as a result of build-operate-transfer schemes. Some local governments have issued bonds, while others have explored options to access such external resources as official development assistance. With borrowing largely limited to better off LGUs, the Local Government Unit Guarantee Corporation was established in 1998 to enable poorer LGUs to borrow from private finance institutions by providing a 100 per cent credit guarantee for LGU debt and to stimulate the development of the municipal bond market .

Whether at the province, municipality, city or barangay level, local residents are increasingly involved in the provision of local services, thereby ensuring greater transparency and accountability of local governments. In turn, by means of such organizations as the League of Provinces, League of Cities and League of Municipalities, local governments have developed lobbying power to exert influence on the national government and protect their powers under the Local Government Code from being eroded during the periodic mandatory congressional reviews (Rood 2000).

Regional Government of the ARMM

Since the enactment of the Organic Act for Muslim Mindanao, both the Moro National Liberation Front and the Moro Islamic Liberation Front immediately rejected it and campaigned against its ratification in a November 1989 plebiscite. The objections were on the basis that both organizations had been excluded from the process of drawing up the said law and that the ARMM had been given little financial independence. A further concern was that the law did not include provisions that would enable the Muslim regions to overcome the effects of past deprivation (Muslim and Cagoco-Guiam 1999). Consequently, only 4 of the original 13 provinces identified in the act opted to be part of the ARMM.[14]

When Ramos assumed the presidency, he opened another round of peace negotiations with the Moro National Liberation Front, headed by Misuari. After four years of hard work on both sides, they signed the so-called Final Peace Agreement in 1996. The agreement had two phases. The first phase was intended as a three-year transition period of confidence building. The second phase involved amendment of the Organic Act for Muslim Mindanao to include provisions that would provide the ARMM with more substantial autonomy. The amended law would then be presented in a plebiscite to determine which areas would join the new autonomous region.

During the first phase, the Special Zone of Peace and Development was established in the 14 provinces (one of the original 13 provinces was later split into 2 provinces) and 9 cities that were included in the Tripoli Agreement. The Southern Philippines Council for Peace and Development was created to promote, accelerate, coordinate, supervise and monitor the implementation of peace and development projects in the Special Zone and the integration of Mindanao Muslims into the Filipino nation. However, a lack of funding and diluted powers prevented the Southern Philippines Council for Peace and Development from making a tangible impact. During this phase, the integration of Moro National Liberation Front elements into the armed forces of the Philippines was also set in motion. In the meantime, with the backing of President Ramos' Lakas party, Misuari ran for the post of ARMM governor in the 1996 elections and won. He was also appointed concurrent head of the Southern Philippine Council for Peace and Development, thereby paving the way for the absorption of many leaders and members of the Moro National Liberation Front into positions of power in the regional government and the council itself.

Hostilities with the Moro Islamic Liberation Front took on an intermittent character that provided the backdrop to the protracted peace negotiations. At the same time, the perceived exclusiveness of the ARMM and the Southern Philippine Council for Peace and Development's peace and development initiatives for the members of the Moro National Liberation Front and their families fuelled further uneasiness, if not mistrust and resentment, on the part of Christians and minority tribal groups towards the Final Peace Agreement. Meanwhile, many LGU officials in the Special Zone, who were already enjoying greater autonomy under the Local Government Code, viewed the regional government as another layer of bureaucracy.

In the 1998 elections, many politicians in the Special Zone who opposed the Final Peace Agreement won local and congressional elections to the detriment of Moro National Liberation Front leaders. During the August 2001 plebiscite for the amended Organic Act, which constituted the last item of the 1996 peace accord with the Moro National Liberation Front, one additional province (Basilan) and one additional city (Marawi) joined the ARMM, while the original four provinces were not allowed to vote out, which some analysts believe they would have done if they had been given the choice (Mercado 1998). Furthermore, Misuari, after being accused of rebellion following attacks by his supporters on security posts in Jolo, was suspended from his post as governor of the ARMM. With the support of the Macapagal-Arroyo administration, Parouk Hussin won the subsequent election and assumed the governorship in January 2002. Misuari's supporters retaliated and launched attacks against government forces.

Hussin, a former Muslim separatist guerrilla, was later recognized by the Organization of Islamic Conference as the legitimate head of the Moro National Liberation Front. Praised by the administration for his integrity, he has also been accused by the press and others of buying votes in anticipation of the 2001 elections. President Macapagal-Arroyo also did not escape allegations that she distributed funds to administration candidates to bolster their chances in the 2001 ARMM elections.

Vertical balance

Together, the Organic Act and the Local Government Code have resulted in a severe, vertical fiscal imbalance in the ARMM because of a mismatch between the expenditure responsibilities that were transferred and the level of the subnational government's revenues. On the one hand, the regional government's share in internal revenue taxes is not sufficient to cover the expenditure responsibilities assigned to it. In particular, the share of the regional government in internal revenue taxes is sufficient to cover a mere 3 per cent of the cost of devolved functions. This occurs largely because the ARMM's share in national taxes is computed based on where the tax is actually collected, but precisely because the ARMM is a less developed region, its tax base is lower than the average tax base for the country. On the other hand, the problem also partly stems from the fact that the regional government has not shifted any of the responsibilities devolved to it by the central government to the LGUs in its jurisdiction.

As a result, the regional government of the ARMM is dependent on yearly allocations from the central government's general appropriations to carry out its mandate. The regional government has little control over the size and composition of this funding. Indeed, the size of this direct funding support is entirely dependent on the central government, and the ARMM competes for these resources just like other central government agencies. Furthermore, the allocation of these transfers to various uses is *de jure* predetermined by the central government as these uses are represented by line items in the General Appropriates Act. This suggests that in effect, the regional government is basically an administrative arm of the central government that simply implements the latter's plans and programmes.

Since 1994, central government transfers in the form of General Appropriations Act allocations to the regional government have grown more rapidly than what would have been warranted if they had simply taken inflation and population growth into account. Indeed, central government allocations of ₱ 2.8 billion for the ARMM's regular operations in 1994–96 were almost triple the ₱ 1 billion spent in 1991–93. In 1997–99, central government appropriations for the ARMM expanded to an average of ₱ 4.2 billion yearly, but then started to contract in real terms from their peak in 2000 because of the re-emergence of severe fiscal problems at the centre. Some observers have attributed this to the central government's desire to make restitution to the Moros for its past negligence, while others view it simply as the price for maintaining a modicum of peace in the region.

In contrast to the regional government, the ARMM's local governments are entitled to the resources, but are not assigned the expenditure responsibilities. Local governments in the ARMM are entitled not only to their IRA share under the Local Government Code, but also to their share of the ARMM's internal revenue collections under the Organic Act. Consequently, aggregate intergovernmental transfers accruing *de jure* to ARMM LGUs are more than 20 times those of the regional government. However, no mechanism is in place to ensure that local governments actually have access to their share from the regional government.

Fiscal inefficiency

Existing intergovernmental relations with and within the ARMM are not conducive to realizing the expected efficiency gains from fiscal decentralization for a number of reasons. First, even though the regional government is vested with limited taxing authority, it has chosen not to make full use of it. Because the regional government can rely on the central government to directly fund the cost of devolved functions through the General Appropriations Act, it has little incentive to raise its own revenues locally. This situation effectively severs the link between expenditure decisions and local taxation that is expected to make local officials accountable to their constituents. Indeed, it seriously weakens the downward accountability of the regional government.

Second, the regional government cannot alter the expenditure mix in the ARMM to better correspond to local preferences for two reasons. The first reason is that the central government itself determines *de jure* how much is spent on what activities and programmes when it provides the ARMM with its line budget in the General Appropriations Act. However, the continued insurgency makes it difficult for the central government to monitor the regional government's expenditure activities. In this sense, the upwards accountability of the regional government is also severely limited. The second reason is that the regional government has retained all the responsibilities that the central government has devolved and has not passed any of them on to the local governments in its jurisdiction. They therefore cannot take advantage of the allocative efficiency that arises when subnational governments reallocate their resources to match the needs of their constituents. For instance, many of the functions that now rest with the regional government are better assigned to LGUs. These functions include construction and maintenance of local roads and other infrastructure, operation of rural health units and hospitals and delivery of social welfare services and agricultural extension. Elsewhere in the Philippines, LGUs bear the primary responsibility for these functions.

The *de facto* fiscal arrangements in the ARMM simply concentrate the decisionmaking powers in terms of resource allocation in the hands of the regional government, with complete lack of oversight from and accountability to both the central government and the local constituency. This lack of transparency lends credence to allegations of rent-extracting behaviour on the part of ARMM regional government officials. Misuari was openly accused of nepotism, corruption and incompetence by Hussin, his successor as governor. When 15 of his senior leaders, including Hussin, ousted Misuari from his position as chair of the Moro National Liberation Front in April 2001, they faulted him for wasting development funds and for his dictatorial and divisive leadership style. Upon taking over the governorship, Hussin requested an audit of the ARMM's remaining budget, suspecting that Misuari had misappropriated it to support his armed loyalists.

In this sense, Misuari appears to have been no different from the two ARMM governors before him, who were similarly tainted by charges of waste and corruption (Vitug and Gloria 2000).[15] On the one hand, close to 75 per cent of the ARMM's budget was allocated to personnel in 1997–2002, up from 54 per cent in 1992–96. Indeed, the ARMM's bureaucracy is bloated by 22 departments and agencies instead of the 9 provided for in the Organic Act, making it the largest employer in the region, most likely because many members of the Moro National Liberation Front expected employment as part of their share of the peace dividend (Vitug and Gloria 2000). As a result, development spending has been low, accounting for a mere 10 per cent of the ARMM's budget in 1997–2002. On the other hand, the regional governor is susceptible to corruption, because central appropriations for the regional government are released directly to the Office of the Regional Governor. For instance, the Commission on Audit reported that in 1993, 1995 and 2000, the Office of the Governor did not release all the funds appropriated for line agencies in the region. Another common finding for the ARRM is the liquidation of cash advances that are not supported by official receipts and other appropriate documents. Meanwhile, project monitors for the central government's Poverty Alleviation Fund noted that tracking the flow of money was difficult and that projects may be reported as completed even when they are not (Vitug and Gloria 2000). Thus the low impact of government expenditure in the ARMM on the level of human development in the region is not surprising (Table 12.1).

Although some political scientists have argued that as with other secessionist movements, the motive behind secession in Muslim Mindanao is rebels' pursuit of the right to self-determination and to preserve their heritage, recent research suggests that 'secessionist political communities invent themselves when part of the population perceives secession to be economically advantageous' (Collier and Hoeffler 2000). In most cases, the economic advantage is a high level of natural resources located in the minority's territory, and the true objective is simply resource capture. Access to natural resources provides short-term benefits in that they finance the rebel movement, as well as long-term benefits in that the minority becomes the owner of the resources if it achieves secession or some form of autonomy. Secession is also more likely to occur where the level of education is low, because politicians are better able to manipulate the population through 'identity politics'.

The circumstances surrounding the secessionist movement in Muslim Mindanao certainly suggest that the underlying motivation is resource capture by the movement's leaders. First, the education level is low, making the population susceptible to identity manipulation by political leaders. Second, unlike the rest of the Filipino population, which has had more say in the allocation of local resources since the enactment of the Local Government Code, Muslims in the ARMM have had a small voice in local politics and have experienced few improvements in their economic and social well-being, let alone in self-determination. Even though the region is poor, with a comparative advantage in agriculture and fisheries, there are indications of mineral and oil deposits in and around the ARMM, which prospectors have been unable to explore because of the continued insurgency.

Resource capture in the ARMM takes the form of rent extraction from the central government and from the local constituency in exchange for maintaining national unity, in addition to monetary contributions from oil-rich Islamic nations. This is easily done, because the ARMM governor's office has direct access to central government transfers and remittances as well as to all of the 60 per cent of tax revenue raised in the region, with little oversight by or accountability to either the central government or the local constituency. In addition to being engaged in the romantic pursuit of self-determination, the local population is pacified through lower regional tax rates and collection efforts and through highly visible, albeit sparse and poorly maintained, infrastructure projects such as Misuari's multilane highway.

Hussin's accession to the governorship brought with it pledges of up to US$100 million from the government of the United States and the World Bank and ₱ 750 million from the government of the Philippines for development projects, all votes of confidence in his integrity and ability to lead the ARMM in the right direction. The fact that he is the administration's candidate, however, portrays him to some Moros as the administration's henchman, and therefore as an encroachment on the ARMM's autonomy. This exacerbates the conflict that is still prevalent in the region.

The recent drive by Islamic militants to create an Islamic superstate spanning much of Southeast Asia and including Muslim Mindanao puts more pressure on the Philippine government to try and counteract further secessionist efforts. However, given the region's poverty and high level of illiteracy and the warlordism that is still deeply rooted in Muslim Mindanao, payments by the promoters of the Islamic superstate provide secessionist elements with the financial means they need to perpetuate the conflict.

In late 2001, measures supporting constitutional change to federalism were submitted to the Senate and the House of Representatives. A federalist system similar to that of the United States has been proposed as a potential solution to the conflict in Mindanao and the Cordillera. Under this system, exclusive Muslim Mindanao and Cordillera governments would function autonomously under a federal central government. In a bid for more autonomy, one proposed form of federalism would remove LGUs' reliance on shares in taxes collected by the central government. The House Committee on Constitutional Amendments, having reservations about the public's reactions to charter changes, is considering alternative options, such as provisions creating regional senate districts.

Even though the IRA formula has a disincentive effect on local tax effort, removing local governments' access to central government transfers is not a viable option, especially for poorer localities. Rather, altering the formula to reduce the disincentive effect and to increase equalization among localities would be a better alternative. Nonetheless, some scope exists for greater tax decentralization, that is, the assignment of greater taxing authority to regional governments so as to promote greater local accountability by making them less dependent on central government transfers. While a federalist system might well work better, it would not resolve any of the outstanding issues in the Cordillera and Muslim Mindanao as long as local political elites and erstwhile rebel leaders dominate the regional governments. Instead, this would perpetuate elite capture, deny local residents any form of democracy and provide a breeding ground for internal conflict. In this regard, it is important for ongoing development and peace building initiatives that the national government should adopt a more inclusive character, so that civil society, LGUs and other local stakeholders are drawn in from the periphery and encouraged to play a greater role in defining the course of these development and peace building initiatives (Aguja 2000).

CONCLUSION

Even though decentralization efforts started as early as 1898, devolution, as opposed to deconcentration, did not materialize until the enactment and implementation of the Local Government Code in 1991. Since then notable, albeit uneven, progress has been made towards effective decentralization through greater participatory governance. This in turn has great potential to improve transparency and help combat corruption, a well-recognized and endemic problem in the Philippines. Currently, expenditures are significantly more decentralized than revenues, with LGUs largely dependent on the yearly IRA from the central government. Greater accountability and transparency could be achieved by enhancing tax autonomy for local governments and by altering the distribution formula so as to provide incentives for local tax efforts.

The need to deflate secessionist tendencies by Muslim ethnic minorities in the southern Philippines has given rise to asymmetric federalism in the form of autonomy for the ARMM. Asymmetric fiscal arrangements usually favour resource-rich ethnic regions that seek autonomy so that they can lay claim to a higher portion of the natural resource rents. Despite strong suggestions of such resources in and around the ARMM and certainly in the area that is originally covered by the Tripoli Agreement, it is currently one of the poorest regions in the Philippines. Nevertheless, local political elites are able to extract rents from the local constituency and the central government through concentration of powers and lack of transparency and accountability. Despite higher real intergovernmental transfers to the region, income levels and other human development indicators are still the worst in the country. The region continues to be and is likely to remain torn by conflict as competing factions try to wrest power from one another.

NOTES

1. The dominant Christian Filipino groups are the Tagalogs, Cebuanos, Ilocanos, Ilongos, Bicolanos, Waray-Waray, Pampangans and Pangasinans. Muslim Filipinos are dominated by the Maguindanao, who live in Mindanao and are the largest Muslim group; the Maranao; the Tausug; and the Samal.
2. Spanish colonial rule of the Philippines started in 1565 and lasted until 1898, when the Philippines was transferred to the United States of America's control after the Spanish-American War. The Philippines became an independent democratic republic in 1946.
3. The Huks, or People's Anti-Japanese Party, were a guerrilla movement formed in 1942 to resist the Japanese occupation. The party consisted mainly of the rural poor of central and southern Luzon. By 1946, the rebellion had evolved into a movement for agrarian reform.
4. Prior to its creation, the provinces that make up what is now the Cordillera Autonomous Region were parts of the Ilocos Region and the Cagayan Valley.
5. The latter group staunchly stands for independence instead of autonomy, seeking to set up an independent state in Mindanao. This faction has been charged with protecting kidnappers and Abu Sayyaf members.
6. The local government structure is composed of three layers. Provinces are the first layer. In turn, provinces are divided into municipalities, each of which is further subdivided into barangays, the smallest political unit. At the same time cities, which are geographically smaller than provinces but typically more urbanized than municipalities, are at the same level as provinces, that is, they share the same functions and authorities. Cities, like municipalities, are partitioned directly into barangays.
7. While the National People's Army works for the armed overthrow of the government and the establishment of a communist state, the Cordillera Peoples' Liberation Army opts for the creation of an autonomous Cordilleran government within the confines of parliamentary struggle (Buendia 1991).
8. Because only one province (Ifugao) voted for the approval of the Organic Act for the Cordilleras in the plebiscite held in January 1990, the Supreme Court subsequently ruled that Ifugao alone cannot make up the Cordillera Autonomous Region. Ifugao lost the ratification of a second organic act for Cordilleras autonomy in 1997 as well. At present, the Cordilleras is run instead as a special administrative region.
9. For example, the Metro Naga Council was established to facilitate local cooperation for integrated planning, five municipalities in Capiz formed the Central Panay Economic Union to facilitate trade and several municipalities in Mindanao set up agro-industrial councils to facilitate cooperative arrangements (Brillantes 2001a).
10. The education sector was not devolved partly because of fears that the electoral process might be compromised if public school teachers who serve on the Board of Election Inspectors were appointed by LGU officials.
11. For instance, the Local Government Code gives municipalities implementing responsibility over community-based forestry and watershed projects, but allows the Department of Environment and Natural Resources to retain supervision and control over such projects. Similarly, LGUs are tasked with the primary responsibility for the construction and maintenance of local roads, but the Department of Public Works and Highways may continue to undertake similar activities if the funding comes from national funds.
12. In case of a national government budget deficit, the Local Government Code states that the IRA may be reduced, but to no less than 30 per cent of the Bureau of Internal Revenue's gross tax receipts.

13. The net resource transfer per capita in 1993 is defined as the 1993 per capita IRA less the 1992 per capita IRA less the per capita cost of devolved functions adjusted for inflation.
14. Part of the reason for the defeat of the Organic Act for Muslim Mindanao in many of the localities concerned was statistical, that is, Muslims are a minority in many of the areas included in the Tripoli Agreement. The Muslims are predominant only in about five provinces: Lanao del Sur, Maguindanao, Basilan, Sulo and Tawi Tawi (Tanggol 1990).
15. The first two governors of the ARMM belonged to the local political elite. While they have no formal links with the Moro National Liberation Front or the Moro Islamic Liberation Front, they were said to be sympathetic to them.

REFERENCES

The word 'processed' describes informally reproduced works that may not be commonly available in libraries.

Aguja, Mario (2000), *The Aftermath of Ethnic Violence: Post-War Reconstruction in Southern Philippines: A Preliminary Assessment of the Role of the International Community*', International Conflict Research Ethnic Studies Network, http://www.incore.ulst.ac.uk.home/esn/joyo.htm.

Alba, Michael (1999), 'Exploring the APIS Data on the Accessibility of Public Services', Manila, processed.

Brillantes, Alex, Jr. (1987), 'Decentralization in the Philippines: An Overview', *Philippine Journal of Public Administration,* XXXI (2).

——— (2001a), *Innovations and Excellence in Local Governance in the Philippines*, Manila: University of the Philippines, National College of Public Administration and Governance.

——— (2001b), 'Public Sector Reform and Poverty Reduction', paper presented at the Conference on Poverty, Growth and the Role of Institutions, 10–12 October, Asian Development Bank, Manila.

Buendia, Rizal G. (1991), 'The Cordillera Autonomy and the Quest for Nation-Building: Prospects in the Philippines', *Philippine Journal of Public Administration*, XXXV (4), 335–68.

Carino, Ledivina V. (1998), 'Governance in Local Communities: Towards Development and Democracy', paper read at the conference on the Nation and the University of the Philippines: 100 Years Hence, 25 May, University of the Philippines, Manila.

Collier, P. and A. Hoeffler (2000), 'Greed and Grievance in Civil War', Development Research Group, Working Paper no. 2355, World Bank, Washington, DC.

De Guzman, Raul P. and Proserpina D. Tapales (eds) (1973), *Philippine Local Government: Issues, Problems and Prospects,* Manila: University of the Philippines, College of Public Administration.

Department of Budget and Management (1991), *Fiscal Year 1992 National Expenditure Program*, Manila: Republic of the Philippines.

——— (1993), 'Cost of Devolved Function by LGU', Manila, processed.

Eaton, Kent (2000), 'Political Obstacles to Decentralization: Evidence from Argentina and the Philippines', *Development and Change* (February).

Gonzalez, Eduardo (1996), 'Intergovernmental Fiscal Relations: An Institutional Analysis', in Ruperto P. Alonzo, Emmanuel F. Esguerra, Raul V. Fabella and Felipe M. Medalla (eds), *Developing an Action Plan for the Financing of Local Government*

Projects with Social and Environmental Objectives, vol. 2, Institutional and Sectoral Studies, Quezon City, Philippines: University of the Philippines, School of Economics Foundation, pp. 234–79.

Loehr, William and Rosario Manasan (2001), 'Fiscal Decentralization and Economic Efficiency: Measurement and Evaluation', Consulting Assistance on Economic Reform II Project, Discussion Paper no. 38, Harvard Institute for International Development, Cambridge, MA.

Manasan, Rosario G. (1992), 'Fiscal Implications of the Local Government Code of 1991', *Journal of Philippine Development*, XIX (34), 1–58.

Manasan, Rosario G. and Shiladitya Chatterjee (2003), 'Regional Development', in Arsenio Balisacan and Hal Hill (eds), *Philippine Economy Development, Policies, and Challenges*, New York: Oxford University Press.

Manasan, Rosario G. and Ruben G. Mercado (1999), 'Regional Economic Growth and Convergence in the Philippines: 1975–1997', in Eduardo T. Gonzales (ed.), *Reconsidering the East Asian Economic Model: What's Ahead for the Philippines,* Pasig City: Development Academy of the Philippines.

Mercado, Eliseo (1998), 'Peace and Development: The MNLF and the SPCPD Experience', http://mindanao.com/kalinaw/peaceproc/pa-imp-mercado.htm.

Muslim, Macapado A. and Rufa Cagoco-Guiam (1999), 'Mindanao Land of Promise', in Mara Stankovitch (ed.), *A First Step to Peace: Mindanao in Transition,* Accord Issue 6, London: Conciliation Resources.

National Statistical Coordination Board (1996), *1996 Philippine Statistical Yearbook,* Manila: Republic of the Philippines.

——— (1999), *1999 Philippine Statistical Yearbook,* Manila: Republic of the Philippines.

——— (2004a), *The Gross Regional Domestic Product*, Manila: Republic of the Philippines.

——— (2004b), *2004 Philippine Statistical Yearbook,* Manila: Republic of the Philippines.

National Statistics Office (1990), *1988 Family Income and Expenditure Survey,* Manila: Republic of the Philippines.

——— (1999), *1997 Family Income and Expenditure Survey,* Manila: Republic of the Philippines.

——— (2002), '2000 Family Income and Expenditure Survey', Manila, processed.

Republic of the Philippines (1991), Republic Act No. 7160, Local Government Code of 1991, 10 October 1991.

Rocamora, J. (1995), 'Classes, Bosses, Goons, and Clans: Re-imagining Philippine Political Culture', in J. Lacaba (ed.), *Boss: Five Case Studies of Local Politics in the Philippines,* Manila: Institute for Popular Democracy.

Rood, Steven (2000), *Decentralization, Democracy, and Development*, http://www.asiasociety.org/publications/philippines/decentralization.html.

Tanggol, Sukarno D. (1990). 'Regional Authority and Social Development: Some Notes on the Case of Muslim Mindanao', *Philippine Journal of Public Administration*, 34 (January), 1–26.

——— (1994), 'Managing the Muslim Problem for Philippines 2000: Issues and Prospects', *Philippine Journal of Public Administration*, 38 (2), 108–22.

Vitug, Marites D. and Glenda Gloria (2000), *Under the Crescent Moon: Rebellion in Mindanao,* Quezon City, Philippines: Ateneo Center for Social Policy and Public Affairs and Institute for Popular Democracy.

PART VI

Postconflict

13. Fiscal Federalism in Bosnia and Herzegovina: Subsidiarity and Solidarity in a Three-Nation State

William Fox and Christine Wallich

This chapter begins with a comprehensive summary of the environment in Bosnia and Herzegovina prior to the war and of the intergovernmental system that was developed as an outgrowth of the war and prewar experiences and an evaluation of the issues created by the intergovernmental structure. The chapter concludes with some actions that could be taken to enhance efficiency in the existing government structure and an assessment of whether the system, which is characterized by a high degree of subsidiarity, is leading to a greater potential for solidarity.

HISTORICAL BACKGROUND AND THE DAYTON RULES

This section addresses the overall environment that existed prior to the war and why it resulted in the unique government structure that was adopted in Bosnia and Herzegovina.

The Yugoslav Legacy

The legacy of Yugoslavia has had significant relevance for the design of Bosnia and Herzegovina's intergovernmental fiscal system.[1] Indeed, some would say that it is the spectre that still hangs over the design of such policies. Yugoslavia was always the most decentralized of the socialist economies, both in terms of its economic and fiscal management and of its political structures. The system was characterized by political solidarity (under Tito), but by subsidiarity at a structural level.[2] Unlike in the rest of the socialist world, the Yugoslav republics had significant autonomy from the beginning, and their power was further increased by the 1963 constitution, which created the basis for the emergence of centrifugal forces. Tax reforms in 1971 gave greater revenue raising powers to the republics and local authorities, and the 1974 constitution transferred many functions to the republics, with areas of common interest remaining the responsibility of the federal budget, that is, the state's or centre's budget. These included military expenditures; administration; and economic interventions, which includes subsidies and support to state-owned or collectively-owned enterprises.

Yugoslavia's six republics—Bosnia and Herzegovina, Croatia, Macedonia, Montenegro, Serbia and Slovenia—were highly differentiated in income level and cultures. Slovenia was by far the most prosperous, with a per capita income in 1990 of US$6500, compared with US$1900 for Bosnia and Herzegovina and US$1430 for Macedonia. Furthermore, per capita budget expenditures in these republics reflected these large income differences. In the social sectors, for example, Slovenia's per capita social spending was twice the Yugoslav average, while social spending in Bosnia and Herzegovina and Macedonia was 70 per cent of the Yugoslav average (OECD 1992, p. 36). These spending differentials were in part the result of different initial endowments and incomes, but mostly they were the result of the strong reliance, peculiar to Yugoslavia and other countries of the socialist world, on so-called derivation-based systems of revenue sharing.

Under such systems of derivation-based revenue sharing, most fiscal revenues were notionally owned, and thus retained, by the areas in which they were collected. As a result, republics or regions with more robust tax bases collected and retained proportionately more revenues and therefore typically benefited from more taxes than other areas (Bird, Ebel and Wallich 1995).

Regional Redistribution Policies

Addressing the huge regional imbalances in income and expenditures was an objective of Yugoslav federal policy from early on. Yugoslav federal support to the republics came through two channels: a fiscal channel and a financial channel. The fiscal channel had several dimensions. The Fund for the Development of the Least Developed Regions, established in 1965, provided explicit support for Bosnia and Herzegovina, Montenegro, Macedonia and Kosovo. At its peak, this fund mobilized some 2 per cent of gross social product from the better off regions, which contributed a fixed proportion of their gross social product to fund its resources. Yugoslav federal budgetary resources were also directed towards raising the level of social outlays in the poorer republics. The financial channel operated through the republic-level commercial banking systems and the central bank, which rediscounted subsidized, directed credit and thereby contributed to both Yugoslavia's hyperinflation and external indebtedness. The system was thus characterized by asymmetry and differential treatment through fiscal and quasi-fiscal financial channels to achieve greater uniformity of outcomes.

Investigators have made attempts to estimate the overall magnitude and net effects of these fiscal and financial transfers between republics. Vodopivec's (1991) empirical estimate of the net redistribution of all the subsidies and taxes among the republics suggests that Slovenia, Croatia and Serbia, the three better off republics, were net taxpayers, and that Bosnia and Herzegovina, Macedonia and Montenegro, the three less developed republics, were significant net beneficiaries. However, such estimates can only be suggestive at best given that—as in much of the socialist world—the redistribution among republics through the fiscal and financial systems was, in the end, a series of ad hoc, bargained and completely nontransparent arrangements, whose effects and incentives were not well understood, and whose murkiness gave rise to much dissatisfaction among the republics.

Structural Vulnerabilities

The dissatisfaction of the better off republics with federal redistributive policies was compounded by another feature of Yugoslavia's intergovernmental fiscal system, namely, the bottom-up system of intergovernmental revenue flows, which Yugoslavia shared in common with most other socialist countries, and which still holds in Bosnia and Herzegovina (Bird, Ebel and Wallich 1995). This system conferred a special vulnerability on the Yugoslav federal budget, because all tax revenues were collected at the republic level (or below) and transferred upwards to the Yugoslav federal budget in agreed shares (the Yugoslav federal government received 100 per cent of the federal sales tax and all import duties, but the taxes were administered by the republics). In addition to the contributions that were made to the Federal Fund for Underdeveloped Regions, fiscal contributions from the republics were negotiated annually to balance the Yugoslav federal government budget.

Role of Fiscal Factors in the Break-Up of Yugoslavia

Yugoslavia broke up for many reasons, but suggesting that issues pertaining to fiscal and quasi-fiscal redistribution played no role would be misleading. Asymmetric redistribution policies appear to have nourished political separatism, as prosperous republics became increasingly reluctant to release resources for transfer to poorer republics. The lack of transparency in the system allowed each republic to argue that it bore the costs of the intergovernmental system while the benefits accrued to others, and thus each claimed that the other republics gained at its expense. Woodward (1995) argues, compellingly, that the centralizing budgetary and financial policies that attempted to force solidarity by reducing subsidiarity were not successful. Indeed, she argues that these policies, which were designed to give the central government more control over stabilization policy and were supported by the international community in the late 1980s, further exacerbated such tensions, because they reduced the budgetary autonomy of the better off republics, and by giving the central government greater command over resources, empowered it fiscally and financially. The vulnerability conferred by the design of the system finally surfaced in 1991, when Slovenia, Croatia and Serbia, the three most prosperous republics, withheld tax revenues owed to the federal budget. It was with this history—a strong desire for subsidiarity and arguments by the republics that subsidiarity was essential for solidarity—that the diplomats at Dayton began their work.

War, Independence and Emergence as a State

Prewar Bosnia and Herzegovina had a highly educated labour force and sold more than half its export products to Western markets for hard currency. The economy was fairly diversified, with a large industrial base and a highly capable entrepreneurial class that produced such complex goods as aircraft and machine tools. The industrial sector generated more than half of output and employment and was concentrated in the production of energy and raw materials (especially electricity generation, wood production, coal and bauxite mining and coke production), as well as textiles, leather, footwear, machinery and electrical equipment. Bosnia and Herzegovina also developed a strong capacity in civil engineering. Almost 500 engineering and construction companies operated out of Bosnia and Herzegovina before the war, generating roughly 7 per cent of gross domestic product (GDP).

Bosnia and Herzegovina was among the last republics of the former Socialist Federal Republic of Yugoslavia to declare its independence following the political manoeuvring that led to the secession and independence struggles of Slovenia, Croatia and Macedonia. The Bosnian Republic's leaders initially tried to piece together a compromise solution with Belgrade within a confederate structure for Yugoslavia. This failed, at least in part because of the active encouragement of the major Western countries and of the European Union (EU), which had suggested a referendum. Bosnia and Herzegovina became an independent country in March 1992, following the referendum vote in which 67 per cent of the population opted for independence (see Figure 13.1 for a map).

The United Nations and most countries officially recognized the Republic of Bosnia and Herzegovina in the months following the referendum; however, the Yugoslav National Army and local Serb militia challenged its independence almost immediately, resulting in the four-year war. Because of the war, about 250 000 people were killed or are missing and about 3 million left their homes, with about 1 million seeking refuge abroad. In 1993–94, hostilities

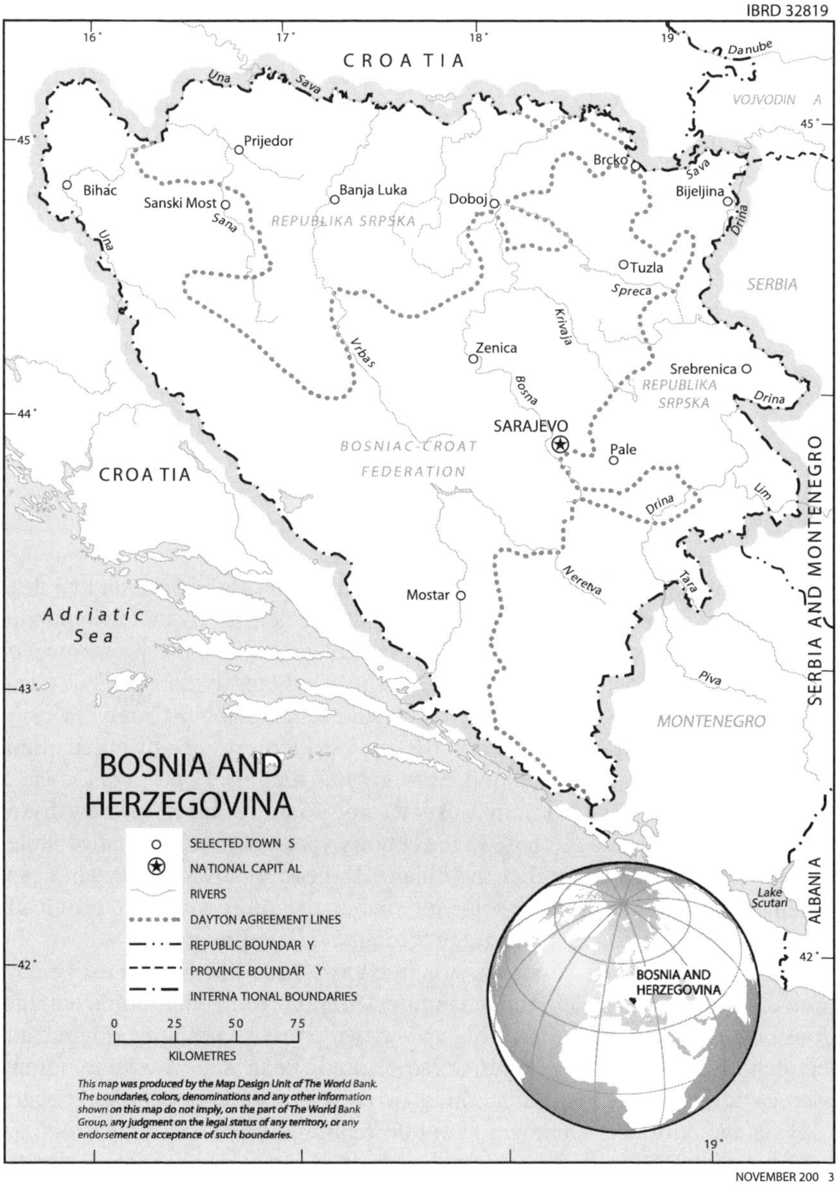

Figure 13.1 Bosnia and Herzegovnia

also broke out between secessionist Croats within Bosnia and the army of the Republic of Bosnia and Herzegovina led by Muslims and Bosniacs.[3] In November 1995, a comprehensive peace agreement among all parties was initialled in Dayton, Ohio, that established a framework for ending the conflict.

Under the Dayton-Paris Agreement, Bosnia and Herzegovina was set up as a single sovereign state composed of two entities: the Federation and the Serb Republic. Four tiers of government, including the state, were specified. The Federation comprised two major ethnic/national groups, and was split territorially between a relatively small Croat majority area concentrated near the coast and contiguous to Croatia proper, and a larger, interior, Bosniac majority area. The Serb Republic is a largely mono-ethnic entity as a result of the war, though some Croats and Bosniacs remain and about 10 per cent of the Serb Republic is non-Serb, as Bosniacs living in that area before the war were driven out and Serbs formerly living in what became the Federation fled and concentrated themselves in the Serb Republic following the war. These population movements could be partially reversed if successive elections increase security and make the right of return more feasible for refugees and those displaced.

Ethnically, the population of Bosnia and Herzegovina is Slav, and all three nationalities have the same ethnicity as would be defined by an ethnographer. All three groups promoted nationalist sentiments during the war, however, causing polarization, and have since come to see themselves as distinct ethnic groups aligned along lines of religious affiliation: Catholic (Croats), Muslim or Jewish (Bosniac) and Orthodox (Serb). Defined by self-attributed ethnic affiliation, the postwar population breakdown is roughly 11 per cent Croat, 20 per cent Serb and 69 per cent Bosniac, not counting refugees now living abroad. Linguistically, all those in the country speak Serbo-Croatian, although in the years since the conflict there has also been a move to call what each group speaks a dialect (and at some international conferences, each group will speak its own 'language' to the other through an 'interpreter').

Politically, the Federation was structured as a three-tier system: the Federation, cantons and municipalities (Figure 13.2). Of the Federation's ten cantons, eight are mono-ethnic, of which two are Croat (Herzegovina and Hercebosanska) and six are Bosniac (Bihac, Posavska, Sarajevo, Tuzla, Zenica and Gorazde). The remaining two are multi-ethnic cantons (Central Bosnia and Mostar). There are about 80 municipalities, many of which are multi-ethnic. The Serb Republic has a two-tier structure that consists of the Serb Republic government and about 60 municipalities. In 1999, the Serb Republic flirted with the idea of developing an intermediate level of government comparable to the cantons, but ultimately backed away. In addition, Brcko was permitted to remain as an independent city because agreement on its disposition was never reached. Brcko magnifies all of the problems of tax competition, because it seeks to undercut the entities, as would be expected from an extremely small government (Kanbur and Keen 1993).

In addition to this political structure and other features of the Dayton Accords, the constitution also spelled out a number of other elements. These reflect a high degree of subsidiarity intended at creating solidarity. These features include the following:

- An executive branch whose highest powers reside in a three-person presidency (one to be directly elected by the Serb Republic and two by the Federation, one from each ethnic group) and the Council of Ministers, which oversees the central government. The member of the presidency with the largest number of votes is the chair of the presidency.[4]
- A judiciary branch whose highest powers reside in a constitutional court that rules on constitutional disputes, including those on appeal from entity courts.
- A central bank, organized as a currency board and led by a governing board consisting of one governor and three other members, one from each ethnic group, that determines monetary policy. The constitution stipulates that the central bank governor shall be a foreigner, appointed by the International Monetary Fund for a six-year term, and that he or she shall not be a national of any neighbouring country or of Bosnia and Herzegovina.

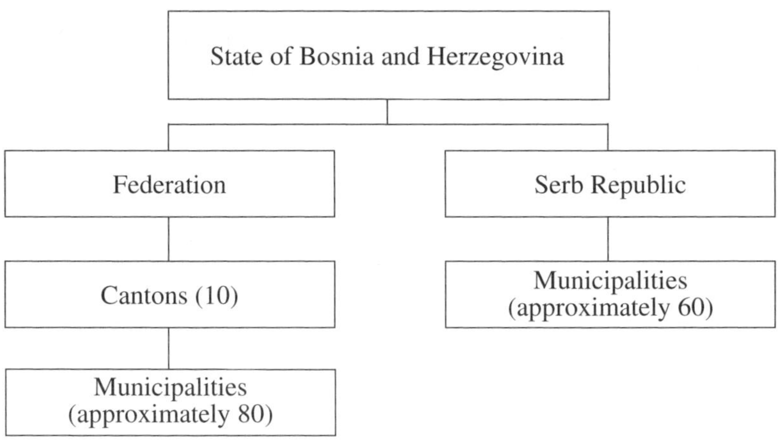

Source: Authors.

Figure 13.2 Post-Dayton structure of government

INTERGOVERNMENTAL SYSTEM

This and the following section describe the specific intergovernmental fiscal structure that has been adopted for Bosnia and Herzegovina.

Legacy of Yugoslavia

The legacy of Yugoslavia was clearly reflected in the new structure that emerged from Dayton, and also represented an important set of constraints. First, the legacy of suspicion of a strong central state and its perceived potential for abuse limited the role that could be given to national-level taxing powers or centralized spending. This led to the demand for a currency board with a foreign governor that could not extract seignorage for one group at the expense of another or use the institution of central banking to direct credit so as to favour nationalist agendas or ethnically owned state-owned enterprises. Second, the designers found that the notion of entitlement to revenue collected in a particular territory was hard to overcome, perhaps particularly in the ethnically concentrated regions of Bosnia and Herzegovina, where territorial claims to revenues were extremely strong, based as they were on the old socialist practices. As previously noted, local communities are increasingly accepting of the notion that the revenue on their territory is best interpreted on a destination rather than on an origination basis. Nonetheless, each entity is adamant that it must collect its own revenues, even if evasion could be limited through more cooperative administrative techniques. Third, and related, the designers had to contend with a *prima facie* need, but apparent virtual intolerance for, fiscal transfers such as the Federal Fund for Underdeveloped Regions or other cross-subsidies between national groups, and indeed, they even encountered resistance to cross-subsidies between groups within the same multi-ethnic municipality.

Of course, the notion of a *prima facie* need for cross-subsidies assumes the objective of the intergovernmental system is distributional equity or equal opportunity across ethnic groups. While this, together with the delivery of efficient public services and the preservation of national boundaries, was among the considerations the foreign framers and advisers at Dayton took into account, the objective of the actual parties involved was clearly the survival of identifiable ethnic groups and their economic protection from encroachment. No significant change has occurred in the unwillingness to engage in cross-subsidies, both between entities and within the Federation. Even in the more homogeneous Serb Republic, cities such as Banja Luka are concerned about ensuring that they receive their full complement of revenues without significant transfers to other places.

If no other fiscal lesson was learned from the demise of Yugoslavia, the federal treasury's vulnerability to transfers from below was clear to the foreign framers and the parties designing the new structure, yet the state that emerged had no revenue powers of its own. The federal treasury's vulnerability to a decentralized tax administration was similarly evident, yet the bottom-up system of revenue administration remained, a perspective that actual experience with the state's financial difficulties has not changed. This reflects the fact that the design of Bosnia and Herzegovina's new system was driven by the interests of the entities, which had to agree to the new structure. Their additional objective was revenue autonomy and continued segregation of systems. Anticipating the future departure of the foreign community and NATO, interdependence and integration would imply vulnerability and were therefore to be avoided. The system, from the parties' perspective, should also be easy to dismantle and re-establish independently.

Wartime Fiscal Setting

At independence, Bosnia and Herzegovina inherited the fiscal system of the former Yugoslavia, with many of the characteristics of a traditional socialist tax system (Bird, Ebel and Wallich 1995). However, because of the war, the unified fiscal system of the old Republic of Bosnia and Herzegovina was broken up, and until recently the country had three totally different fiscal systems: one in the Croat majority area of the Federation, one in the Bosniac majority area of the Federation and one in the Serb Republic. While all three systems bore the imprint of their Yugoslav origins, over the course of the four years following Bosnia and Herzegovina's declaration of independence, the system in the Croat majority area became harmonized and integrated with that of Croatia, while that of the Serb Republic became harmonized and integrated with that of the Federal Republic of Yugoslavia. The Bosniac system evolved to meet the needs of a war economy. In addition, both the Croat and Serb areas received significant resources and support from their patron states, Croatia and Yugoslavia, respectively, including military support, but also transfers to pension funds and social welfare funds and support for education and other outlays.

These wartime fiscal systems were designed to serve each nationality group's needs, providing defence services and social support, education services, health and pensions (to the extent they could be provided), as well as generating inputs and foreign exchange for the war economy in each region. The three budgets were entirely separate and focused on the needs of each ethnic group. No revenue transfers or cross-subsidies across nationalities within Bosnia and Herzegovina took place. Each had its own separate tax administration with offices located in every municipality.

Three separate currencies also came into operation: the kuna, Croatia's currency, served the Croat areas; the Bosnia and Herzegovina dinar; and the Yugoslav dinar, which was used in the Serb areas. None of these currencies could be used, legally or by convention, in any of the other areas; however, the German mark was used as general tender in all three areas, initially as a store of value because of hyperinflation during wartime, but also to facilitate trade as peace emerged.

With peace, and within the context of the Dayton arrangements, these separate fiscal systems and currency regimes were to be terminated, the Croat and Bosniac systems were to be merged with the new Federation structures, and the fiscal arrangements agreed at Dayton were to be put in their place. A single currency for the new nation was adopted to replace the two foreign currencies and the Bosnia and Herzegovina dinar.

FISCAL RULES ACCORDING TO THE DAYTON ACCORDS

Under the Bosnia and Herzegovina constitution, major government budgetary responsibilities are divided among the four levels of government: the state, the entities, the cantons and the municipalities (World Bank 1996).

Role of the State

Under the constitution, the state government has exclusive responsibility for foreign policy; foreign trade policy; customs policy; monetary policy; immigration, refugee and asylum policies; air traffic control; payment of Bosnia and Herzegovina's international financial obligations incurred with the consent of both entities; regulation of inter-entity transport; communications; and international and inter-entity law enforcement (but not the raising of an army, which is an entity-level responsibility). All government functions not explicitly assigned by the constitution to the state are assigned to the entities. The entities may agree to delegate some of their responsibilities upwards, but have strongly resisted doing so. Thus extreme subsidiarity characterizes the expenditure side. The notion is that solidarity would grow from the cooperation necessary in those areas where service delivery requires the entities and ethnic groups to work together.

The state government has no independent tax sources under the constitution, thus it is expected to finance its activities almost entirely with transfers from the two entities, with two-thirds of the state's revenues provided by the Federation and one-third by the Serb Republic to cover the budget approved by the state parliament. These shares were derived from the two entities approximate population proportion in the total population of Bosnia and Herzegovina. The state's responsibilities for international debt service are also to be met by transfers from the entities.[5]

The state collects some fees, including all revenues from consular and passport fees, and is entitled to use these to defray the costs of its embassies abroad. These fees totalled only KM 20.9 million in 2000 (about 20 per cent of state spending), out of total government revenue of nearly KM 2 billion. Furthermore, the state may control any new revenue sources that are specified by parliament. To date, parliament has been adamant that the state should not have revenue sources of its own. The Bosniacs, with support from fiscal analysts in the international donor community, have pushed strongly for such state revenues. Some have seen the development of a value added tax (VAT) as the natural means to leverage a state tax source. Current plans call for implementing a VAT by 2006, although the entities can be expected to continue resisting for the foreseeable future. Extreme subsidiarity thus also characterizes the revenue side of the budget, and as with expenditures, this degree of subsidiarity was thought necessary to achieve solidarity. At Dayton the parties claimed that full subsidiarity was necessary to get their agreement on their cohabitation as ethnic groups within the same state.

Role of the Entities

The constitution has set up an asymmetrical system between the entities. The asymmetry resulted because each entity demanded a different degree of subsidiarity. The presence of two ethnic groups in the Federation led to the need for more levels of government and less centralization. This asymmetry is evident not only in the structure of government (three tiers in the Federation and two tiers in the Serb Republic), but also in the expenditure and revenue systems within each of the entities.

Under the constitution, the entity governments have a wide range of expenditure responsibilities, reflecting the emphasis on subsidiarity, including exclusive responsibility in their territories over defence (there are currently three armies, one in the Serb Republic and two in the Federation, one Bosniac and one Croat), internal affairs, police, environmental policies, economic and social sector policies, agriculture, industry, refugees and displaced persons, public investment and justice. The Federation's constitution notes that some of these functions may be exercised separately, jointly with the cantons or by the cantons as coordinated by the Federation government. Thus the Federation and cantons exercise joint responsibility for health, environmental policy, infrastructure for communication and transport, social welfare, interior affairs and so on.

On the revenue side, tax and customs administration are also entity responsibilities, again reflecting the desire for subsidiarity. All taxes and customs duties accrue to the entity (or its constituent governments) on a derivation basis. Thus customs duties on goods imported into the Serb Republic accrue to the Serb Republic, while customs duties on goods imported into the Federation accrue to the Federation. The state controls customs policy and sets rates for customs duties, which is considered a policy issue, and rates in the two entities must be identical. Excise taxes are entity taxes and can differ between the two entities as long as they are not implicitly tariffs; however, the international institutions worked with the entities to harmonize excise taxes and allocate the revenues on a destination basis to limit tax competition and encourage free trade between the entities.

Thus the entity revenue and expenditure system can be characterized as asymmetric in the sense that the entities can have different tax systems and different methods of political and fiscal organization. Spending is likewise fully delegated and can be organized in any way that suits the entity. Symmetry is apparent only in the sense that both entities enjoy full subsidiarity. At Dayton, the parties successfully argued that this subsidiarity was a condition for nationhood, and it was negotiated into the constitution.

Role of the Cantons and Municipalities

The cantons are responsible for all matters not expressly granted to the Federation. These include education, culture, housing, public services, local land use and social transfer expenditures such as subsidies to finance utilities for low-income households or former soldiers. The federal constitution authorizes each canton to delegate its responsibilities to the municipalities in its territory. The 1996 Law on the Allocation of Public Revenues entitles the cantons to revenues from the sales tax, corporate and personal income taxes and property and other taxes collected in their areas (all of which accrue on the derivation principle), as well as the fees charged for public services they provide. The law was altered somewhat in 1998, when the Federation took over some profits taxes, but otherwise remains essentially intact. In 1999, the cantons and municipalities owned 64.8 per cent of the Federation's total tax revenues (canton and municipality tax revenues of KM 1246.3 million divided by total Federation tax revenues of KM 1924.3 million), excluding insurance and fee revenues (Table 13.1).

The municipal governments in the Federation are granted self-rule on local matters, including all responsibilities delegated to them by the cantons. In the case of municipalities with a majority population that is different from that of the canton as a whole, the canton must delegate all cantonal responsibilities to the municipal government. Each canton except Sarajevo has passed legislation allocating revenues between the cantonal and municipal governments. Municipalities receive most of their revenues through tax sharing (normally a 20 per cent share of taxes), but have some own source revenues in the form of so-called citizen taxes (about ten small taxes that municipalities can levy on a

Table 13.1 Revenues by level of government, 1999 (KM millions)

Source	Federation government	Cantons and municipalities	Total federation	Serb Republic government	Municipalities	Total Serb Republic	Total
Taxes	678.0	1246.3	1924.3	522.1	64.2	586.3	2510.6
Sales tax	0.0	758.3	758.3	106.3	37.6	143.9	902.2
Excise taxes	313.0	0.0	313.0	85.1	3.3	88.4	401.4
Customs duty	347.0	0.0	347.0	141.2	0.0	141.2	488.2
Income taxes	18.0	264.9	282.9	49.7	12.9	62.6	345.5
Property taxes	0.0	33.6	33.6	0.0	4.6	4.6	38.2
Death and gift taxes	0.0	0.5	0.5	0.0	0.3	0.3	0.8
Gambling taxes	0.0	0.3	0.3	0.0	0.5	0.5	0.8
Other	0.0	11.8	11.8	24.5	2.3	26.8	38.6
Fee revenues	0.0	96.7	96.7	24.7	0.0	24.7	121.4
Miscellaneous	0.0	80.2	80.2	90.6	2.7	93.3	173.5
Utilities	0.0	0.0	0.0	37.0	0.0	37.0	37.0
Water	0.0	0.0	0.0	10.8	0.0	10.8	10.8
Forest	0.0	0.0	0.0	0.0	0.0	0.0	0.0
Other	0.0	0.0	0.0	26.2	0.0	26.2	26.2
Insurance	924.0	0.0	924.0	305.4	0.0	305.4	1229.4
Pension fund	497.0	0.0	497.0	153.3	0.0	153.3	650.3
Employment fund	57.0	0.0	57.0	25.9	0.0	25.9	82.9
Health fund	370.0	0.0	370.0	126.2	0.0	126.2	496.2
Total	1602.0	1246.3	2848.3	864.5	64.2	928.7	3777.0

Sources: Federation Ministry of Finance data; Serb Republic Ministry of Finance data.

range of items) and utility fees. This delegation of authority and entitlement to revenue is one of the significant elements of asymmetry in the system. Thus the symmetrical part of the system, which provides for full subsidiarity of responsibilities for revenue and expenditures, has given rise to extremely asymmetrical outcomes across units.

Municipal governments in the Serb Republic are responsible for all matters not explicitly the responsibility of the entity and largely parallel the narrower responsibilities of Federation municipalities except in a few limited places such as the capital, Banja Luka, where devolution is more extensive. Municipalities owned only 11 per cent of the Serb Republic's tax revenue (KM 64.2 million in municipal tax revenues divided by KM 586.3 million in total Serb Republic revenues) in 1999 (Table 13.1).

COMMUNITY WELFARE

This section considers the widely disparate fiscal resources that have resulted from the highly subsidiary system and the system that has been evolving under the Dayton rules.

Income Differences Between Ethnic Groups

Significant income differences are apparent between ethnic groups, and these differences are reflected in income differentials between the different parts of the Federation and between the Federation and the Serb Republic. Postwar estimates (World Bank 1996) suggest that in 1996, per capita annual income was about US$500 in the Bosniac majority area of the Federation, some US$1800 in the Croat areas of the Federation and roughly US$1000 in the Serb Republic. This disparity in per capita incomes results in major differences across these areas in terms of tax bases, taxable capacities and, in the absence of equalization policies, levels of service provision.

Public Spending Differences Between Ethnic Groups

Even before the war, public service levels differed across the regions, but the war significantly exacerbated such spending differences. In the Bosniac majority area, for example, the average retirement pension was DM 11.4 per month in 1995, while the scheme operating in the Croat majority area paid pensions of about DM 65 per month. While the pension systems were formally unified in the Federation and the payments were equalized after several years of discussion and significant pressure from the international community, most other services are financed with derivation-based taxes, which results in widely varying service levels across the Federation. Destruction of the physical capital stock hit the Bosniac areas the hardest (the World Bank estimates that more than 70 per cent of the destruction took place in Bosniac areas), because industry and most core infrastructure facilities had been strategically located in central Bosnia and Herzegovina since the early days of Yugoslavia. The tax bases of the Bosniac majority areas and their ability to generate income were thus significantly impaired.[6] Since the war, the Bosniac areas have benefited from significant donor funds and have made a substantial recovery: some 70 per cent of donor resources have been channelled to the Bosniac areas because of the disproportionate damage there. At the same time, the institutions that would ensure that growth continues after donors fade from the scene, such as banking and trade institutions, have not been built.

By contrast, the Croat majority area's strategic location near the coast enabled this region to control trade into the interior of the country during much of the war and immediately thereafter, and, despite its own limited resource endowment, to generate substantial revenues from customs and other trade-related levies. The Croat part of the Federation continues to grow more rapidly, with its access to the coastal areas, proximity to Croatia proper and its border-state status. The Serb Republic's economy was badly damaged by the economic embargo of Yugoslavia and then by the meltdown of the Yugoslav economy, and is expected to recover only slowly. The Serb Republic collected only 23.4 per cent of total tax revenues (KM 586.3 million in Serb Republic tax revenues divided by KM 2510.6 million in total tax revenue) during 1999 (Table 13.1).[7]

Trends and Directions

While some economic convergence has occurred since the war, it is not yet such that the three ethnic groups might be bound together by a common level of well-being or sense of common economic community. As a result, a strong aversion to cross-subsidies and an unwillingness to discuss them persist, despite the significant differences in spending and presumably in welfare.

Limited convergence has taken place in other areas. An EU vision of the region as a whole imposes significant pressure for solidarity. The vision of Europe and the incentives created by the Balkan Stability Forum have encouraged each of the parties to harmonize some policies broadly in the direction of Europe, and therefore to some degree also with each other.[8] To date, the Balkan Stability Forum has stressed that the region should perceive itself as a region and that it will be treated as such by the EU, with economic support provided based on the performance of countries (and groups within countries) as good regional citizens. Both have been helpful building blocks for the creation of a common economic space within Bosnia and Herzegovina. Furthermore, the requirement that member countries have a VAT prior to EU accession will remain a powerful force encouraging adoption of this revenue source, but revenues currently accrue to the entities and their constituent governments, so a mechanism for allocating the revenues must be developed (see Bird and Gendron 1998 for a discussion of issues related to alternative mechanisms for sharing VAT revenues). Work on the VAT will force cooperation between the governments.

Government coordination and competition can be seen in the full harmonization of indirect taxes (Fox 2003). Achievement of harmonization required the entities to work closely together, but harmonization is unlikely to have been achieved in the absence of intervention by the international community. Excise tax rates and bases were harmonized in November 2000, and a mechanism for sharing the revenues on a destination basis went into effect in early 2003. The sales tax structures were harmonized in June 2001. Harmonization required agreeing on the collection point for the tax, the rates and the tax bases. Unfortunately, the incentives for tax competition remain in place, even though indirect taxes are identical at this point. The existence of Brcko, a small autonomous district that did not fully harmonize with the entities and remains a tax haven, and the subsidiary control over indirect taxes, could ultimately lead to harmful tax competition. Each parliament has political incentives to undercut the others and may be more likely to do so as the international community's presence fades. Thus the cooperation on taxation could ultimately fall apart, resulting in a tax war that could create strong negative rather than positive feelings.

Creation of a common economic space is facilitated by harmonized policies, but is at least as dependent on the demand-side pressure of businesses operating across entities seeking harmonized policies. Development of the economy is dependent on a relatively large domestic market, and will benefit from the broader scale afforded by the two entities being a common economic space. Thus businesses with an economic stake in both entities must continue to push for harmonized regulations, taxes and administration.

Finally, NATO's push, which began in 2000, to arrest accused war criminals who were still active in the national leadership of each of the entities and/or were active behind the scenes is also helping. These accused war criminals have been a major stumbling block in creating greater harmonization. There is a strong expectation, perhaps created by the international community, that accused war criminals will be brought to justice. Approaches to dealing with atrocities that have been used in other countries, such as the truth commission in South Africa, would not be acceptable to many people. As wartime memories and mistrust fade, cooperative efforts might improve further, but the dimensions of ethnicity and nationalist politics will likely continue to be important constraints on more 'technocratically-based' intergovernmental policies such as might be suggested by best practice. Thus true convergence remains a distant prospect.

The challenge of creating a viable fiscal structure in Bosnia and Herzegovina is essentially a nation-state issue, with the Dayton challenge being to combine three 'nations' into a single state. Of overwhelming importance to the international community in framing the Dayton Accords was the requirement that international boundaries be preserved. The Bosnia and Herzegovina that received international recognition in 1991, and whose continued existence was cemented by the peace agreements, was the former republic of Bosnia and Herzegovina. However, as Woodward (1995) points out, the proposition that internal boundaries of provinces and republics are also the appropriate international boundaries in the event of the break-up of a state is questionable. In the former Yugoslavia, the federal constitution (in theory at least) carefully protected the rights of minorities regardless of which republic they lived in. These protections were no longer in place when the republics' borders became state borders. To agree to maintain the state intact, the parties demanded full subsidiarity, even to the point of allowing each municipality to control service delivery. However, the subsidiarity does not carry down to the individual level. Considerable internal pressure may be placed on individuals to support nationalistic views within each ethnic group.

ISSUES AND PROBLEMS: CAN DAYTON WORK?

Essential issues are whether the Dayton structure can work, and if it can, is this the best option for Bosnia and Herzegovina? This, of course, depends on the nature of the goals and on who determines them. Not enough time has elapsed to permit an assessment of the Dayton-Paris Agreement, but some general problems are apparent.

Political Sustainability, Ethnicity and Government Structures

The complicated, multilevel government structure that arose from the peace arrangements reflects an ardent aversion to a strong state government that derives from experiences as part of Yugoslavia. Better off minority groups are particularly concerned that their rights will not be upheld, and as a result, they envision being economically disadvantaged. The fear is that a strong central government would continue the Yugoslav tradition of cross-subsidies that would provide greater benefits to the less well-off majority group. The war further diminished the willingness of some nationalist groups to view Bosnia and Herzegovina as a single country and to work for the good of the whole. Suspicion has reached such a high level that even the least well-off areas fear they would lose out from a system that collects resources for redistribution between the entities or the cantons.[9] Creating a government in which most expenditure responsibilities and revenue raising powers are at the subnational level was designed to limit the opportunity for transfers from the richer Croat minority to the majority. The Serbs were also concerned that they would be disadvantaged by the majority, and a system devolved into two entities was the only structure to which all parties involved could agree.

Ethnicity plays a huge role in almost all aspects of nationhood. Procedures for election to all offices aim to ensure balanced Bosniac, Croat and Serb representation. Ministerial, diplomatic and other major appointments are negotiated and distributed in a way consistent with the political balance of power. Most are also structured to ensure that the representatives of the ethnic group cannot use their positions on behalf of their group without veto or countervailing influence from another group. Thus the central bank has representatives from each nationality, and the voting structure is such that two nationalities cannot gang up against the third because of the presence of the foreign 'honest broker' to break the logjam. Similarly, when a minister is from one nationality, the two deputies will be from the others and have a 'watching brief'. State-owned enterprises are, by convention, if not by law, owned by one ethnic group, and one of the most contentious, if unstated, issues in privatization has been whether state-owned enterprises can be privatized to any group of buyers or only to buyers within that ethnic group.

Overall, the system's combination of subsidiarity and veto points has significantly hampered the ability to reach effective decisions. The costs, both economic and social, are enormous, because of the implied policy paralysis that is evidenced by the length of time needed to reach many decisions, particularly in the Federation, and the uncoordinated and often conflicting decisions resulting from fragmentation.

The paranoia is such that favouritism of the majority is seen behind every programme. For example, apprehension exists within the Federation that government-run economic development programmes will be designed to support industries that predominate in majority areas. Thus while most government structures appear to be potentially sustainable, if not efficient, the state's roles and its funding sources are extremely limited. The areas of cooperation have been small, and the institutions being developed could easily be replaced if the state were no longer in existence. As a result, the state's sustainability is in question, and, arguably, the continued existence of parallel structures in the Federation and the emphasis the Croat and Bosniac parties place on avoiding interdependencies suggest that the Federation may also be at risk.

The relationship between Bosniacs and Croats in the Federation demonstrates how such issues permeate every aspect of governance. Croat majority areas favour relatively strong cantonal governments (subsidiarity), while the Bosniacs favour a stronger Federation, which they may feel able to control. The Croats, the better off minority population, want to continue decentralizing responsibilities to lower levels of government, where ethnicity and incomes are relatively more homogeneous, and therefore opportunities for cross-subsidies are lessened. Meanwhile the Bosniacs argue for service delivery and revenue collection concentrated in the Federation, where they may be able to effect more cross-subsidies. Efficiency would seem to indicate that many functions would be better performed at the Federation level, given the relatively small geographic area and size of the cantons; however, the discussions are heavily driven by economic sovereignty and subsidiarity considerations, not efficiency, and arguably also by the ability to allow for an orderly unwinding of the Dayton system.

Ethnicity and Shadow Budgets

Nowhere is the attention to ethnicity more striking than in the fiscal arrangements that have emerged as a result of the war. The wartime arrangements have proven remarkably robust, with the assignment of revenues and expenditures to each tier conflicting with economic sovereignty. Maintenance of the vestiges of the wartime structure allows relatively easy dismantling of the government structure. Shadow arrangements are used behind the Dayton formalities to fund armies for each of the three nationalities and safety nets and other social services. On the surface at least, the three pension funds have been reduced to two, and while each of the cantons in the Federation formally budgets social spending and education, some would say that the concept of multicantonal Bosniac and Herzeg-Bosna shadow budgets might be a better description.[10] Indeed, some evidence indicates that in multi-ethnic cantons, social services for the minority group in that canton are not funded from the cantonal budget at all, but by the shadow budgets that are the continuation of the wartime funding mechanisms of the republic and Herzeg-Bosna areas that, in theory, no longer exist. Bosniac and Croat sections of municipalities often exist even in the more homogeneous cantons (and in some cases they have been formally split into two municipalities), and in these cases the sections appear to operate as separate municipalities. Health care is, in theory, also financed at the cantonal level through payroll taxes paid into a cantonal health fund; however, health care revenues in the Croat majority areas of the Federation continue to go into a single Croat fund. In either case, the result is that the risk pools are small. Foreign borrowing is also the responsibility of the ethnic group that incurred it, thus a careful accounting and apportionment of all past debt, including all debt incurred by the former Yugoslavia, has been made according to the territory that benefited from the loan, and debt service is the responsibility of that group's budget, although formally it is paid by the Federation and Serb Republic to the state budget for servicing abroad.

Fiscal federalism is often viewed in spatial terms, but some of the cases described are similar to what has been termed sociological federalism and have many dimensions applicable to the literature on club goods (though the clubs are imperfectly competitive and most of the literature deals with competitive clubs). The service delivery system is established for the ethnic group (the people in the club) rather than for people living inside certain territorial boundaries. Thus, where possible, the spatial dimensions inside Bosnia and Herzegovina have been or are being realigned to accommodate ethnicity through the creation of the government structure and the further subdivision of the entities into more municipalities. In some cases, where territorial-based fiscal federalism is not possible because of the intermixing of the ethnic groups, services are limited to the ethnic group, such as the Croat high school in Mostar and the Croat health fund. Two major concerns of sociological federalism are diseconomies brought about by the small scale of services and service delivery spillovers in such areas as education, police and fire protection. These disadvantages suggest that delivering some services, such as roads and most utility services, would be extremely expensive on any basis other than spatial. Other services can be delivered to individual groups, but the delivery is likely to come at higher cost and with efficiency losses because of the spillovers. Nonetheless, the higher costs of ethnically-based clubs may be accepted to make separation easier should Bosnia and Herzegovina fail as a single country and to limit the extent of interaction between the ethnic groups.

With respect to revenues, customs and excise taxes have now been formally harmonized between the entities, but considerable uneasiness remains about how effectively the customs and excise taxes are collected in each entity. At this point, modest efforts have been made through the auspices of the EU to bring the tax administrations into accord. Widespread evasion of taxes on certain commodities has been asserted in each entity, and varying administrative practices across the entities are said to benefit one relative to the other. In theory, the Federation Tax Administration (FTA) has been established in Sarajevo with a Bosniac director and a Croat deputy. In practice, the areas act independently (though there is centralized reporting) and combined efforts to collect taxes are rare. Indeed, considerable evidence indicates that either the former governments in the Bosniac and Croat majority areas or the cantons and municipalities are still performing most responsibilities. The Federation has been receiving customs and excise tax revenues from the 'joint' customs administration since May 1996, but some evidence suggests that compliance is less than full and that collections are biased in favour of the Croat side, which remains in control at many customs border sites.[11] The strongly held Bosniac belief that sales taxes on excisable commodities were not being collected fairly in the Croat areas led to the decision to collect these taxes at the retail level rather than at customs points, despite the significant revenue loss associated with retail-level collection of taxes at high rates (more than 20 per cent), though this decision was recently reversed.[12] Also the cantonal leaders believed that retail collection would be more consistent with the destination collection of sales taxes.

Possible Role for Equalizing Policies

The extreme reliance on subsidiarity combined with the differences in taxable capacities give rise to large differences in public service provision levels. This would suggest, other things being equal, that from both an equity and an efficiency perspective, inter-entity (and intra-entity in the case of the Federation) fiscal equalization policies could have a constructive role to play in the new fiscal system. Such policies would prevent the large differences in access to fiscal resources currently available to the subnational entities and the groups within them from being translated into large differentials in the supply of public services and infrastructure. From both perspectives, the main concern centres around those public services with major externalities to the nation as a whole, such as health and education, which under the Dayton constitution are the domain of the entities (or the cantons in the Federation). Even within the Federation, there has been an unwillingness to engage in equalization policies. Some services such as tertiary health care or universities could be financed or delivered at the Federation level, but decisions have consistently kept service delivery as a cantonal responsibility. The result has been a proliferation in the number of universities. In many cases, the unwillingness to change has been both within and across ethnic groups. At this point, recognition of geographic benefit spillovers has been slight. Indeed, the spillovers may be small because mobility between areas is so small, but the spillovers will grow with migration and inter-entity trade. The question is whether the willingness to engage in cross-subsidies will grow with the spillovers.

Implicit in this view of equity and efficiency is that the relevant domain of concern (McLure 1994) for efficiency- and equity-focused redistribution policies is the nation as a whole. Under such a view, the population of Bosnia and Herzegovina sees itself as Bosnian rather than as Croat, Bosniac or Serb and supports policies that address inter-regional disparities. The objectives would be equal opportunity and welfare of individuals. By contrast, if people's primary allegiance is to the national groups within the entities, the view of the domain of concern will be more limited, and differences in the average incomes of groups within an entity or between entities, or in the average level of public service provision, may not be these groups' predominant concern. In other words, the goal is group welfare or the cohesion of national groups. A case for cross-subsidies can still exist on efficiency grounds if the goal is the group's welfare, albeit at lower levels than if an equity argument can be made as well, because of the spillover benefits associated with health, education and other services.

Equalization and a Role for Grants

Countries around the world normally use a system of grants to exploit economies of scale in tax collection, enhance equity in revenue distribution or account for geographic externalities in consumption. A case can be made for grants on each basis, but no grants exist across entities or in the Federation. Limited formula-based distribution of revenues occurs in the Serb Republic, where distribution of revenues to municipalities is based to some extent on a measure of need. Vertical imbalances are a likely outcome for both the state and the Federation. Creation of the FTA was an attempt to take advantage of economies of scale in collection, while allowing ownership to continue at the canton level; however, no attempt is made to take advantage of collection at the state or combined entity level. Thus far, the level of trust is so limited that the entities would rather accept higher administrative costs or greater evasion than work closely together in collecting revenues. For example, the entities' tax administrations have negotiated an information sharing agreement, but have seldom used it.

Structural conditions in Bosnia and Herzegovina suggest that grants should be an important financing source for cantons and municipalities based on the practice in most other countries. Weak economies in some areas leave them unable to provide minimum service levels. Some mechanism, presumably operating through a grant system, needs to be in place to smooth financing problems during the interim as assignments are finalized and regional economies rebound. Some need for grants could remain even once the economy begins growing again, because fiscal capacity differences will remain. However, the limited tolerance for cross-subsidies between geographic areas suggests that grants must play a small role in overall finance in the near term. Efforts to introduce grant formulas or to distribute tax revenues on a formula basis to take advantage of economies of scale in collection have been rejected. Any grant system that is ultimately introduced must be transparent and rely on objective indicators, unlike transfers made during the Yugoslavian years. A system of grants based on negotiated formulas or ad hoc procedures would be particularly inappropriate for Bosnia and Herzegovina given the lingering distrust prevailing among different groups.

The sustainability issue is whether the dissatisfaction arising from service delivery differences between areas is large enough to cause the country to splinter. In the Bosnia and Herzegovina environment, the tolerance for service delivery differences appears greater than that for cross-subsidies. Both the better off and worse off areas appear to prefer controlling their own taxes to the possibility of having more revenues but less direct control. This attitude results both because each group believes that it will lose out from any redistribution and because it does not trust that revenues will be distributed in a transparent and equitable manner.

Role for the Central State

The vast challenge of recovering from the destruction of war suggests that a strong central government that is capable of maintaining macroeconomic stability (Prud'homme 1994; Tanzi 1995), creating a common economic area throughout Bosnia and Herzegovina and mobilizing resources for reconstruction through effective budgetary and foreign borrowing policies could bring substantial benefits. With the almost complete destruction of the productive sectors' capital stock and with a major portion of the country's infrastructure destroyed, effective use of scarce domestic budgetary resources and foreign flows could not be more critical.

However, as noted earlier, the legacy of war and of the former Yugoslavia's intergovernmental fiscal system make a strong central government difficult, because the state has no taxing powers and is therefore totally dependent on the entities for resources. As a result, the state's ability to manage a stabilization policy using fiscal instruments is highly constrained. Its discretionary macroeconomic management tools are further limited by the fact that the central bank is to be run as a currency board. In addition, the state may not borrow abroad or indebt itself without the consent of the entities. In a nutshell, Dayton set up a bottom-heavy system (subsidiarity) with most responsibilities and rights in the hands of the entities, thereby making many of the traditional roles of the state moot.

Weaknesses Inherent in Financing the State

The constitution indicates that the state is to adopt a budget for the expenditures necessary to finance its responsibilities, with most of the revenue coming from the entities. No limitation is placed on state spending, except that the expenditures are to be necessary to meet its responsibilities. The financing structure differs from a conventional grant system, because the recipient is telling the grantor how much to provide. Disagreement between the state and the entities regarding what are necessary expenditures should be expected, and the entities are likely to balk about paying their share at times. Considerable difficulties were encountered in getting the entities to begin transfers to the state, and they only started with the assistance of the international community, though the entities have often been late in making their contributions. Difficulties with funding the United Nations may be an appropriate parallel. Tax rates will need to be higher in the Serb Republic than in the Federation to generate their respective revenue contributions, because of the greater aggregate population and incomes in the Federation. For example, the Serb Republic collected only 23.2 per cent of total Bosnia and Herzegovina tax revenues in 1999. The Serb Republic collected 28.9 per cent of customs tax revenues, which were subject to nearly identical rates and bases for much of the year, and may be a better indicator of the relative fiscal capacities of the entities. As a result of these differences, pleas of unfairness can be expected, and transfers to the state budget could be one of the first places where cuts are made during times of exigency.

The state may be less accountable for spending revenues raised by the entities. Also variability in revenue flows will be borne solely by the entities, which, in principle, are unable to reduce their contributions to the state to help lessen the effects of unexpectedly low revenues. There are two sides to this coin, because the entities benefit if they achieve better than anticipated revenues. Nevertheless, the size of transfers to the state for operational purposes is small, meaning that the overall implications for government finance are small.

State Budget and Debt Service

The capacity to undertake sovereign borrowing is essential for most countries, and Bosnia and Herzegovina is no exception. As the successor republic to Yugoslavia, it has inherited substantial international debt. In addition, as a recipient of donor resources in the postconflict environment, it has found that most donors require that their lending has to be to an internationally recognized government, which is the state. However, no agreement has been reached on how external debt service is to be financed. The constitution says that '[e]ach entity shall provide all necessary assistance to the government of Bosnia and Herzegovina in order to enable it to honour the international obligations'. Like many Dayton rules, implementation of this statement is unclear. One possible interpretation is that each entity is to make contributions according to the two-thirds Federation, one-third Serb Republic rule, but blind adherence to this rule is likely to generate controversy that could lead to one entity refusing to pay its share. At this point, even getting agreement from the entities to borrow through the state has been difficult, and determining how to finance debt service is more complicated.

The Dayton-Paris Agreement allows little flexibility for macroeconomic policy, but the entities' governments may seek to operate at a deficit, both to ease financing problems and to stimulate the economy. Some examples have been apparent since the beginning. The original 1996 Serb Republic budget assumed a deficit equal to one-third of spending, and the 1996 state budget included authorization for borrowing and for letters of guarantee. Nonetheless, in practice, the ability to borrow is extremely limited. The Serb Republic budget did not pass in parliament when it was recognized that it had no way to finance the deficit. The budgets passed in each entity during the intervening years have not been out of balance to the same extent, but revenue shortfalls have been frequent in both the Federation and the Serb Republic. The primary approach has been to use cash balancing rather than borrowing to finance the shortfall. With the central bank operating as a currency board and a weak banking sector, concerns about large deficits may be unimportant in the near term.

Imprecision of Expenditure Rules

Despite apparently clear guidelines regarding which government is responsible for delivering which services, the Dayton rules are confused and create overlapping responsibilities. Not surprisingly, different perspectives exist on what the final outcome should be. Overlap occurs when the state is charged with one aspect of service delivery and the entities with another. For example, customs policy is assigned to the state and customs administration to the entities, which leaves in question which level is to set tariff rates, which is to determine exemptions, which gets control over the revenues and how to deal with a number of other practical issues. Similar overlap occurs at the Federation and canton levels, because they are assigned joint responsibilities for human rights, health, environmental policy, transportation and communication infrastructure, social welfare policy, immigration and asylum matters, tourism and natural resources.[13] Trade issues were solved by allowing policies, such as tariff rates, to be set at the state level and administration, such as collection of customs duties, to operate at the entity level. Achieving this outcome required considerable input and pressure from the international community. Establishing practices in other cases where expenditure rules are imprecise, and with less input from the international community, has been difficult, given the propensity of each group to view issues solely from the perspective of how it will be affected. Most jointly provided services, such as higher education and health care, continue to be delivered at the cantonal level with the Federation playing essentially no role.

The constitution and the Dayton Accords say little about municipal responsibilities. The likely outcome in the Serb Republic is that it will retain the relatively centralized structure that is already in place. In the Federation, the issue concerns cantonal versus municipal responsibilities. Municipalities are granted self-rule and are also permitted to perform functions delegated by the cantons. The probable outcome is a different relative set of duties in each canton given their geographic and demographic diversity. Differing patterns of responsibilities will reflect the cantons' varying sizes, ethnic compositions and political strengths. No problems should arise from assigning provision to different government levels as long as governments are creative in achieving efficiency in production.

A series of other specific problems with the expenditure rules can be identified. In some cases, clear assignment of functions is absent. Pensions are an example, though they might be categorized under one of the general social spending functions listed in the Dayton Accords. In other cases, assignments are politically difficult, such as having defence delivered by the Federation when it has two armies. In a third set of cases, the assignments may be economically inefficient, for instance, higher education being set as a cantonal rather than as a Federation responsibility. By contrast, in some cases the assignments appear completely reasonable. For example, the Federation is responsible for major highways, the canton of Sarajevo is responsible for large roads, and municipalities inside the canton deal with small local roads. The international community has been involved in proposing or facilitating (and in some cases insisting on) such cooperation in most cases. The hope is that in the long term the entities will voluntarily engage in cooperation because it has proven to be sufficiently beneficial.

Expenditure responsibilities are not necessarily inefficient, even if imprecise or inappropriately assigned, because the entities' or cantons' governments could negotiate more efficient arrangements, such as cooperative service delivery. However, recent history makes such negotiations particularly difficult, meaning that economic inefficiencies are likely to persist in the short to medium term. Inter-entity cooperation has begun to occur in a limited number of cases and has resulted in apparently appropriate delivery mechanisms. For example, because of large economies of scale, the entities' ministers of health have formed a committee to coordinate drug procurement. Interestingly, they have chosen to do so without involvement by the state, making the arrangement less formal.

Expenditure Policy

The war arrested the transition to a market economy and the corresponding relative reduction of the public sector. Furthermore, the war years led to ad hoc and distorted budgeting and expenditure practices in the Bosniac, Croat and Serb areas. Expenditures were heavily focused on military purposes, with about 45 per cent of each entity's budgeted expenditures going for military uses. Data on the total extent of military expenditures were unavailable, because large off-budget military purchases and spending financed by foreign governments occurred as well. Budgets for nonmilitary purposes were only provided as necessary and as resources were available. Actual expenditures were made essentially on a cash basis. The wartime governments made payments when resources were available and suspended payments when they were not. Pensions and wages for both military and nonmilitary workers often went unpaid. Actual factor payments bore little relationship to market value.

Expenditure rationalization is an important area for reform. The size of the public sector needs to be limited to make room for private sector development, and the structure of public expenditure programmes needs to be improved to facilitate growth while maintaining an acceptable level of social protection. Public expenditures currently represent more than 40 per cent of GDP, and may be even greater if the substantial public sector arrears in wages, pensions, military wages and soldiers' back pay and debt service were included. Reduction of overall public sector expenditures to sustainable levels will require major cuts in many areas of public expense, especially defence, subsidization of the economy and entitlement programmes. Pension payments should not be based on prewar earnings and expectations and must be scaled back to a level that is consistent with reasonable wage tax rates. Nevertheless, strong efforts to raise pension levels abound, and they have already been increased to at least KM 150 per month in each entity. A significant problem is that the pensions are financed with high social insurance tax rates, because the number of formal market employees is not very much higher than the number of pensioners. At about 80 per cent of net wages, pension tax rates remain extremely high, even though they have been reduced significantly. The high social insurance rate, combined with the wage and personal income taxes, potentially has many distorting effects, including reducing the extent of formal sector activity, reducing business employment of labour and discouraging labour force participation.

Public expenditure programmes will have to be rationalized to accompany the process of downsizing the government. The highest priority must be given to those public expenditures that provide a framework that allows the private sector to flourish, and in this context, appropriately selected infrastructure is essential. The subsidization of outdated and unproductive public enterprises must be given the lowest priority and should be terminated.

Tax Policy and Administration

Tax structures, which are based on the Yugoslav tradition, are similar in each of the ethnic areas. Establishment of the centralized FTA, with offices located in each canton and each municipality,[14] was, at least in appearance, a major step towards integration. However, the extent of unification remains a significant question, particularly between the Bosniac and Croat areas. Discussion of a greater role for cantonal tax collection, even to the point of devolving the function to the cantons, continues to take place. The Serb Republic has its own administration and system, also with offices in each municipality (62 in total). The municipal tax offices appear to operate with significant independence and limited control from the central tax office, but this independence in the Serb area is not a threat to nation building.

Entitlement to tax revenues, control over tax rates and bases and tax administration are to some extent separable. Division of these, with say the Federation administering taxes that are owned by both the Federation and cantons, is normally based on conditions that may not be fully in place at this time. A level of trust must exist, so that the government owning revenues is certain that the administering government will transfer the appropriate amounts in a timely fashion. In Russia, for example, local offices of the Russian State Tax Service have at times retained resources in the regions and municipalities and given the Russian Federation government the residual. A similar pattern could ultimately arise in Bosnia and Herzegovina. Both cantons and the Federation fear that collection by the other will be to their detriment. If the FTA were to have strong cantonal and municipal offices, that would provide local areas with confidence that they would be able to retain the appropriate level of revenues. In concept, the municipal offices are local offices of the FTA, but the emphasis placed on these offices by the cantons and municipalities suggests considerable local control over collection practices. At the same time, the cantons and municipalities have complained about their inability to influence local tax offices and about local offices' failure to respond to their collection concerns.

The owning government must also feel that the administering government will make a good faith effort to collect revenues. Pressures and incentives in the administering government may be to focus more of its limited resources on collecting revenues that it can keep than on taxes going to other governments. Allowing the administering government to retain part of the revenues as a collection fee can help, but it still gets more revenue benefits from collecting taxes that it retains in full. The Federation is currently financed almost entirely by customs duties and excise taxes, which are collected mostly by the Customs Administration, although the FTA collects the excise tax on domestically manufactured products. The FTA also collects the remaining taxes whose revenues accrue almost entirely to the cantons and municipalities (the subentity governments receive about 85 per cent of revenues collected by the FTA). Nonetheless, the FTA is financed by the Federation budget, with the cantons only providing in-kind services. Each ethnic group, and particularly the Croats, believes that independent municipal tax administrations do a better job of collecting revenues than the FTA or any administrative unit operating across a larger geographic area.

In such a small country, administrative and compliance efficiencies should result from Federation (or state) control over most tax bases, because uniform bases would presumably be more difficult to achieve with devolved control. Tax policy has been an entity function even in the Federation, where tax revenue is primarily owned by the cantons and municipalities. However, political incentives can cause Federation officials to make concessions on tax bases where the revenues are owned by the cantons. For one level of government to grant concessions against another level of government's tax bases offers all the same political gains as granting them against its own base, but fewer costs, because the level of government granting the concession does not have to face the budgetary consequences of its actions. For example, soon after the Federation began, the canton of Tuzla complained that concessions the Federation gave to reduce the electric company's wage taxes significantly reduced Tuzla's receipts. Since then, the Federation has also granted sales tax concessions in several cases, such as for certain purchases by the army and for automobiles manufactured in the Federation. The Federation also passed legislation transferring 45 per cent of the profits tax from certain large firms to the Federation's budget. In addition, the Federation has often changed tax rates or bases without consulting the cantons, and in most cases without even informing them ahead of time. It reduced the payroll tax from 15 to 10 per cent, eliminated the 10 per cent tax on retail services and moved the collection point for sales taxes on excisable commodities to the retail level. General sales tax rates were lowered as well. The Federation weighed several factors when making these policy changes, including harmonizing the tax structures between the two entities and lowering labour taxes, but the cantons view these actions as significantly reducing their resources without making any corresponding changes in their responsibilities.

Despite the clear administrative and compliance advantages of entity (or state) control over tax bases, the imperative for control over tax rates is much less clear, and some cantonal control over tax rates would not create significant problems. Having a single rate across different geographic areas has few, if any, advantages in terms of compliance or complexity; however, limiting the degree of tax competition that can develop between cantons and having a coordinated structure with the Serb Republic is appropriate. Establishing minimum tax rates can lessen the propensity for tax competition and setting maximum tax rates lessens the potential for excessive taxes across the Federation (Kanbur and Keen 1993). Cantonal and municipal ability to determine service levels is the main advantage of at least some independence in setting tax rates. At this point the cantons have little flexibility, because they only control a small group of levies termed the citizens' taxes, and this authority may be eliminated with direct tax reform.

Some countries require local government participation in decisions on changes to tax policy that would affect their revenues. For example, Papua New Guinea constitutes a committee composed of central government officials, local government officials and independent officials who do not represent one of the levels of government. to reach agreement on tax policy changes prior to their implementation. Other countries require local government agreement before tax base changes can be adopted, for instance, Canada requires such agreement for changes to the VAT. Development of a Federation intergovernmental commission would be a way to arbitrate tax structure decisions and other issues.

ENHANCING THE EFFICIENCY OF THE PUBLIC SECTOR

Being prescriptive about the best government structure for a country where so much transition is under way is difficult. The complexity of making such prescriptions is exacerbated by Bosnia and Herzegovina's recent history that includes being part of Yugoslavia, participating in the war and reaching the various agreements that have already been made. Nevertheless, a series of recommendations that would enhance the public sector's operational efficiency is possible.

Shifting Functions to the State

A number of functions could be managed much more effectively at the state than at the entity level. The entities would be well served to identify where efficiency gains are likely and to seek agreement to transfer the pertinent functions to the state. Examples are administration of the new single rate national VAT (effective in January 2006) and of enterprise profit taxes and customs. The entities could delegate the functions to the state, but both entities would need to agree. Three conditions need to be in place for delegation to occur: (a) significant efficiency gains must result, (b) transfer must be Pareto optimal and (c) reasonable assurances must be given that agreements will not be violated.

The distribution of revenues collected at the state level is a particularly vexing issue. The cantons and entities are completely unwilling to consider formula-based distribution and the revenues are owned by the entities, or by the cantons in the case of the Federation. Thus political discord, fears that agreements will not be adhered to and envy could lead the entities to reject efficient delegation even if an objective analysis indicates that gains would result. The entities would certainly reject delegation at this time. Furthermore, new state responsibilities must be matched with reduced activity at other government levels to ensure that the overall size of the government does not increase. This means that new state functions must be shifted from the entities and that employees and expenses must be concurrently reduced at the entity level.

Enhancing Coordination Between the Entities

Open borders that allow the free movement of goods and services and permit the economy to expand are a requirement of the Dayton Accords, but oblige the entities to coordinate in setting tax administration and policy. For example, a VAT cannot be easily imposed at a subnational level without internal borders, but borders would violate the Dayton Accords. Even a tax or boundary check between the Serb Republic and the Federation is inconsistent with rapid economic growth and creates ample opportunity for abuse. One form of abuse would be imposing a recording fee at the checkpoint that could quickly be escalated to become, in effect, a customs duty. In the absence of checkpoints, effective cooperation in tax administration would greatly enhance sales and excise tax administration and allocation on a destination basis, thereby generating more revenue and a more neutral tax system. Close coordination must substitute for borders to ease tax administration, unless administration is delegated to the state. A few anecdotal instances of cooperation between the tax administrations can be identified, but systematic cooperation beyond the signing of an agreement has yet to develop. At this point, neither entity's tax administration is willing to allow the other entity to undertake any of the tax collection functions. At the policy level, the cooperation could be informal, based simply on observing the other entity's tax policies, or explicit through negotiations. More efficient tax policy is likely to result from explicit cooperation, but currently no formal mechanism whereby such dialogue could occur is in place.

Given the open economy, even at the borders with Croatia and Yugoslavia, the broad tax policy of each entity must also be carefully coordinated.[15] Tax competition can be positive in some cases, but indirect taxes are likely to create undesirable retaliation given the Bosniac environment. The geographic area is small, and the existence of Brcko as a tax haven raises the risks of tax-related distortions. The best way to limit tax competition and the resulting resource migration is for the entities to set tax rates on mobile factors, consumption and customs within a small range of each other. Differentials in tax rates between areas could provide significant opportunities for tax avoidance and evasion and will result in a concentration of imports, production and sales in the least taxed areas. In all cases, harmonization cannot be achieved solely by legislating the same tax structures. Administrative practices must be comparable between the two entities as well. As noted earlier, indirect taxes have been harmonized, but labour and capital taxes have not. There is no need for significant concern about harmful tax competition with regard to the taxation of labour and capital at this time, because the mobility of both is currently extremely limited.

Bird and Gendron (1998) demonstrate that a subnational VAT can work in certain circumstances, for instance, in Canada, and the International Monetary Fund has recommended that one be introduced in Bosnia and Herzegovina; however, implementing one in the latter in the near term entails a number of unique problems. First, there is no overriding tax administration, and both entities continue to operate their tax administrations independently. At this point, the tax administrations have undertaken few cooperative efforts and are unlikely to have developed sufficient cooperation to enable auditing and other functions to operate effectively across the country. The problem is complicated by the absence of any unique taxpayer identifier either across or within entities. Second, the Serb Republic and the ten cantons own their sales tax revenues. Both the entities and the cantons are unwilling to allocate revenues using formulas, which means that either an origin-based VAT must be employed or complicated procedures must be followed to distribute revenues on a destination basis. Furthermore, the International Monetary Fund has proposed a much higher rate in the Federation than in the Serb Republic in order to have revenue neutral tax changes in each entity, which means that the distortionary effects of an origin-based VAT would be large.

POLICY IMPLICATIONS AND CONCLUSIONS

Progress in developing the governments in Bosnia and Herzegovina has been slower than envisioned when the Dayton Accords were penned. This is not surprising, because world experience with developing governments on the short time line presumed in the agreements is nonexistent. While the signals are positive, in that a number of government institutions have become operative and revenues are being passed to both the state and the Federation, the challenge of achieving fully operational governments remains.

Traditional economic models of federalism suggest a government structure that assumes that the intent is to maximize efficiency for the entire country, but current attitudes appear consistent with a view that many people in each ethnic group see themselves as members of their group rather than as Bosnians and are not broadly concerned about the welfare of the country as a whole or about access to public services for those outside the group. The motivation for the fiscal federalism structure proposed in the Dayton Accords is therefore better interpreted as an effort to manage conflict between the ethnic groups. Federalism in a conflict management sense does not require that each group be given its own state, but does lead to the conclusion that institutions of power should be brought closer to people so that decisionmaking can be more sensitive to the different ethnic groups (Tishkov 1993). Decentralization in this context is a way to reduce the number of points where disagreement exists rather than a structure for obtaining economic efficiency. Common institutions at the state, entity or canton levels can be maintained, but only for functions that must be undertaken across broader geographic spaces. Nevertheless, the hope is that the fiscal (and other) interdependencies of common institutions at the state, entity and canton levels provide opportunities to build relationships and trust over time.

The government structure built under the Dayton Accords is working, but the question remains whether it is sustainable or whether the country will ultimately splinter. A fairly extreme version of subsidiarity was created, and in the view of the drafters of the Dayton constitution, and certainly in the view of the parties, an extreme approach was needed to create solidarity; to reach agreement on keeping borders intact; and to maintain national cohesiveness, such as it was. If the agreements had not pursued subsidiarity, the parties might have viewed independence as the only other acceptable alternative, which they would have pursued by further war. Thus subsidiarity was the only short-term option for pursing solidarity, but the Dayton formula of extreme subsidiarity (some would say subsidiarity to the point of nearly extinguishing any role for the state), does not seem to foster solidarity and nationhood in the longer term. In addition, the arrangements suffer from a number of other shortcomings, namely, diseconomies of scale and inefficiencies in service provision, inequality in services across regions and continuing vulnerability of the state budget to the entities' willingness to support it.

Thus unless governments negotiate other arrangements, the likely outcome in the short to medium term is inefficient delivery of certain services as some that can be provided at lower unit costs at the state level are provided at the entity level and some with lower unit costs at the entity level are delivered at the cantonal or municipal level. Services with geographic spillovers will be underprovided because governments will fail to adequately account for the benefits received by members of other ethnic groups. Higher-level governments, such as the state or the Federation, do not have the revenue ownership to account for spillovers, requiring the affected governments to fully negotiate any revenue transfers, and few examples of such transfers can be identified at this point. Furthermore, little consideration will be afforded to equity between groups, resulting in widely different access to services across the country. Better service delivery mechanisms from a national perspective will not be selected given the strong distaste for cross-subsidies and the fear by minority groups that a larger group will dominate them. The hope is that more efficient arrangements will evolve over time as confidence in the government structures grows.

Horizontal imbalances will be large in the Federation, and grants will be used to a limited extent, if at all, to offset these imbalances. The resulting problems will be lessened in the next several years to the extent that the former Bosniac or Croat governments are able to provide some resources to the more financially strapped areas or that donors help fund infrastructure and other needs. However, donors will not finance operating expenditures, and the maintenance of new infrastructure investments will place greater demands on limited budgets, so financial problems in the places least able to pay could expand. Economic growth that increases revenue raising capacities across the country is one solution to offsetting imbalances, assuming that growth brings convergence in regional incomes. Also differences in access to services could be lessened with a grant system that allocates revenues to places based on a positive correlation with expenditure needs and a negative correlation with fiscal capacity.

Arguably, large and growing divergences within a nation are not good for nationhood, and the current degree of subsidiarity does not lead to solidarity. These centrifugal forces could well be enhanced as Croatia's economy recovers and becomes more integrated into Europe, creating a powerful magnet for the Croat parts of Bosnia and Herzegovina to further disassociate themselves from their compatriots and from the joint institutions. Indeed, Croatia's entry into Europe could be as much a flash point for the country's Croats as was Croatia's 1991 declaration of independence a start to the war.

In relation to other tools needed to address the issues posed by Bosnia and Herzegovina, the work of the Balkan Stability Forum and NATO's actions in removing accused war criminals from positions of political influence are helpful. The continued presence of and support from the Office of the High Representative (the internationally established civilian force) to build joint political and economic institutions is key. The incentives offered by the prospect of joining Europe may also help, but it must be a joint prospect or one that makes region-supporting behaviour a key condition of entry.

As to whether the issues have been addressed or resolved, at least for the time being, the answer is probably no. While a stable equilibrium is in effect with troops and the Office of the High Representative present, if the international presence departs, the joint institutions are unlikely to continue to function. The Dayton fiscal agreements are thus perhaps best seen as a good 'quick fix' needed to keep the three-nation state intact within its existing borders. Subsidiarity down to the cantonal and municipal level was needed as the basis for the state's sustainability. Fiscal policies have thus played a role by giving the parties 'independence', that is, subsidiarity, within a three-nation state, but to the extent that divergence and other centrifugal pulls remain, the situation remains fragile. Solidarity will have been created only if the fragile system is held together long enough to develop sufficiently strong economic ties so that, when combined with encouragement from the EU and the international community, staying united is in the three ethnic groups' best interests.

Within this framework, several other institutional factors have helped to provide the solution: international donor funds helped to fund spending and make up for the revenue failings of either or both entities, but could also be used as the carrot to elicit agreement between the parties in some cases; the Office of the High Representative was in some instances able to force political agreements; and political pressure on Croatia and Yugoslavia from the international community also helped to reduce the role these neighbouring countries played in Bosnia and Herzegovina's politics. In sum, there was an intergovernmental solution in the short run, but even so, other supports were necessary for the structure to survive even to this point.

NOTES

1. This chapter draws on Fox and Wallich (1998).
2. Kuklis (2001) summarizes the concept of subsidiarity as one where 'political powers should intervene only when the individual parts of society are not able to meet the requirements'. The concept is found implicitly in much of the theoretical work on decentralization (see, for

example, Oates 1972), but has not been explicitly developed as a theoretical concept. Nonetheless, it is particularly relevant to European countries, because it is explicitly included as the appropriate form of government in the European Council of Local Self Government.

3. Bosniacs are Muslims and Jews, that is, all those resident in Bosnia and Herzegovina who are non-Serbs and non-Croats.
4. The former Yugoslavia had a six-person presidency with a rotating president of the presidency.
5. The state's debt service burden is considerable. As a legacy of the break-up of Yugoslavia, the new nation inherited its share of all the debts of the former Yugoslavia through a complex apportionment exercise that allocated the debt of Yugoslavia across all the successor republics. In addition, Bosnia and Herzegovina is significantly indebted to the international financial institutions through the same process of apportionment. Initially, the apportionment of debt service between the entities was to be done in the same one-third–two-third proportions, but concerns emerged that one entity might be servicing more than its share of the debt. Subsequently, an allocation of liabilities was made, with debt service apportioned on the basis of the location of the beneficiary or enterprise that had borrowed.
6. One could argue that the concentration of industrial conglomerates made unviable because of transition shocks in Bosnian majority areas would have led to some decline in the tax bases of this area even without the war.
7. Economic differences alone do not explain the different capacities to generate revenues. Rates are lower for several taxes, particularly the sales and services taxes, and tax compliance varies, though making an accurate judgement of which entity is doing a more effective job of collecting the taxes that are due is impossible.
8. The Balkan Stability Forum is a European initiative to support peace in the Balkans with diplomacy, technical assistance and funding.
9. For example, even the lowest-income Bosniac cantons in the Federation were unwilling to participate in a formula-based sharing of sales tax revenues collected on excisable commodities that would almost certainly have increased the revenues available in every canton.
10. Herzeg-Bosna was the name of the wartime Croat community, which continues to exist within the Federation, albeit illegally. It has, and still has, its own budget, army, pension fund, social welfare mechanisms, and so on. It is the Croat part of the Federation, even though the Federation formally consists only of cantons that are not ethnically defined in any formal sense.
11. In principle, all customs posts are manned by two officials, one Bosniac and one Croat, but the control over customs revenue remains a serious issue between the two groups.
12. The international community was also an important force in the decision to collect sales taxes on excisable commodities at a retail level, based on the argument that it would assist in the implementation of a VAT.
13. Bosnia and Herzegovina and Switzerland make immigration policy a subnational responsibility. Canada gives the provinces more limited control over immigration.
14. There are 85 municipal tax offices, because some municipalities have separate offices for their Croat and Bosnian areas.
15. International borders have been established, but they are not effectively monitored, with more than 400 roads entering Bosnia and Herzegovina and customs and border police present at only a few of the roads.

REFERENCES

The word 'processed' describes informally reproduced works that may not be commonly available in libraries.

Bird, R. and P. Gendron (1998), 'Dual VATs and Cross-Border Trade: Two Problems, One Solution?' *International Tax and Public Finance*, 5, 429–42.

Bird, Richard M., Robert D. Ebel and Christine I. Wallich (eds) (1995), *Decentralization of the Socialist State: Intergovernmental Finance in Transition Economies,* Washington, DC: World Bank.
Fox, William F. (2003), 'Destination Based Indirect Taxation: The Case of Bosnia and Herzegovina', *European Journal of Law and Economics*, 16 (1), 5–22.
Fox, William F. and Christine Wallich (1998), 'Bosnia-Herzegovina: Fiscal Federalism—the Dayton Challenge', in Richard M. Bird and Françoise Vaillancourt (eds), *Fiscal Decentralization in Developing Countries*, Cambridge, UK: Cambridge University Press: pp. 271–300.
Kanbur, Ravi and Michael Keen (1993), 'Jeux Sans Frontieres: Tax Competition and Tax Coordination When Countries Differ in Size', *American Economic Review*, 83 (4), 877–92.
Kuklis, Peter (2001), 'The Principle of Subsidiarity', Federal Decentralization Initiative for Central and Eastern Europe, Publications Online, http://www.decentralization.org.
McLure, Charles E., Jr. (1994), 'The Sharing of Taxes on Natural Resources and the Future of the Russian Federation', in Christine I. Wallich (ed.), *Russia and the Challenge of Fiscal Federalism*, Washington, DC: World Bank, pp. 181–217.
Oates, Wallace E. (1972), *Fiscal Federalism*, New York: Harcourt Brace Jovanovich.
OECD (Organisation for Economic Co-operation and Development) (1992), 'Regional Developments and Developments in the Republics of Yugoslavia', Paris, processed.
Prud'homme, Remy (1994), 'On the Dangers of Decentralization', Policy Research Working Paper no. 1252, World Bank, Washington, DC.
Tanzi, Vito (1995), 'Fiscal Federalism and Decentralization: A Review of Some Efficiency and Macroeconomic Aspects', in Michael Bruno and Boris Pleskovic (eds), *Annual World Bank Conference on Development Economics*, Washington, DC: World Bank.
Tishkov, Valery A. (1993), 'Nationalities and Conflicting Ethnicity in Post Communist Russia', Working Paper series, Harvard Law School, Conflict Management Group, Cambridge, MA.
Vodopivec, Milan (1991), 'Redistribution Through the Soft Budget Constraint', World Bank, Washington, DC, processed.
Woodward, Susan (1995), *Balkan Tragedy,* Washington, DC: The Brookings Institution.
World Bank (1996), *Bosnia and Herzegovina: Toward Economic Recovery,* Country Study, Washington, DC.

Index